# ESSAYS ON LINGUISTIC
THEMES

# ESSAYS ON LINGUISTIC THEMES

## YAKOV MALKIEL

*Professor of Linguistics and Romance Philology*
*University of California, Berkeley*

UNIVERSITY OF CALIFORNIA PRESS
Berkeley and Los Angeles · 1968

University of California Press
Berkeley and Los Angeles, California


© in this collection
Basil Blackwell, Oxford, 1968


Library of Congress Catalog Card Number: 68-15588


Printed in Great Britain

# Preface

THE thirteen pieces here assembled between hard covers have been selected from a substantially larger number of items potentially qualifying for inclusion on the strength of a single, two-faceted feature which they, and they alone, share and which was suggested as a unifying thread by the editor of this series: the breadth of their scope and the limited attention accorded to documentation. (An additional bond, of merely incidental relevance, which ties them together, is the fact that they were all originally conceived and written in English.) To the extent that illustrations have been doled out parsimoniously and, to be specific, that exhaustiveness has been attempted neither in the inventorying of raw data nor in the critical survey of earlier pronouncements, these studies certainly fall short of deserving the label of authentic monographs. Insofar as most of them contain, in varying measure, ingredients of exploration and experimentation, it may be allowed that they approach, and in some instances attain, the rank of genuine essays.

Because the articles, notes, and reviews here collected have not been arranged in chronological sequence, it may be useful to stress the fact that they span a period of roughly fifteen years. The earliest item dates back to 1953 and, in fact, presupposes a fairly long spell of microscopic research conducted in a necessarily more austere key. Only a total of four pieces can be credited to the 'fifties; eight have appeared in the 'sixties and a ninth piece so classifiable — the only one written for a reference work rather than a periodical or a reader — is likely to make its appearance almost simultaneously here and in the medium for which it was originally planned. The actual reason for the strict exclusion of another fifteen-year span of continuous productivity is by no means the disavowal of the earlier tone, choice of topics and methods, or underlying philosophy, but — if an auto-biographic remark may be injected at this point — the author's rather delayed and initially quite hesitant response to the challenge of the essayistic form.

Beyond question the lighter approach to scholarship suggested by the very term essay is most readily defensible in those nooks and crannies of the linguistic landscape where the more cumbersome

v

spade-work has been conscientiously accomplished with the full apparatus required for this exacting operation. Upon occasion one can actually engage in a point-by-point reduction of a major monograph to the more modest proportions of an essay; this process of concentration may be painful or amusing, according to the circumstances involved. In only one context did I actually go, as early as 1962, through the experience of condensing, with appropriate modifications, a previous article copiously illustrated and almost anecdotally spiced, until it was cut down to its bare skeletal frame: the slim and sketchy "Typological Classification of Dictionaries on the Basis of Distinctive Features" (here reproduced) reflects a preceding study anything but slender and tilted in polar opposition to abstractness ("Distinctive Features in Lexicography . . . Exemplified with Spanish", 1959). Under less ideal conditions of work, the writing of the light-winged essay defined as a companion piece may temporally coincide with the execution of the laborious monograph which it is designed to flank or may even, in exceptional instances, precede that monograph by a varying margin; or else, even if it follows in its wake, as is customary, it need not represent a rigidly organized extract, but may well afford to focus the less specialized reader's curiosity on certain broader implications, originally understated or side-tracked.

The material brought together here could have been ordered according to several principles, to some extent overlapping if not conflicting. The organization finally adopted is the one flowing most smoothly from the topical selection made as a result of several consecutive distillations; it is less random than would have been the straight chronological chain. The opening group of six pieces deals with Romance scholarship viewed in its obligatory relation to general linguistics — a perspective, alas, seldom favored. The following group bears on two inextricably intertwined disciplines, lexicology and etymology; these two jointly form a nucleus of problems which, as a consequence of an academic caprice, the majority of professional linguists have appreciated grudgingly at best, and have, in practice, little cultivated throughout the last quarter century. The third group, comprising only two articles (with, it is hoped, certain compensations for this numerical meagerness), is best characterized, in slightly unconventional manner, as devoted to "Formulaic Sequences in Language".

Were it not a shade presumptuous to do so, I might have been tempted to arrange the papers in an alternative pattern of succession, using as my classificatory principle the specific set of circumstances surrounding each venture. The justification for such an approach would clearly have been the demonstrable dependence of the manner of presentation on such ensembles of circumstances. Thus, I find in retrospect, to my own surprise, that not a single one of the items here joined owes its original stimulus to my diversified teaching activities. No. 1 of the series is an encyclopedia article tailored to specifications and left unretouched. No. 4 grew out of a public lecture delivered for the first time (1959) at Oxford. No. 10 sprang from my participation in a symposium held at Indiana University; No. 2, also invitational, was expressly written for a supplement volume to a learned journal expanded and attuned to a chosen theme, without any concomitant expectation of oral delivery or immediate discussion. No. 3 has been lifted from a *Festschrift*, a detail accounting for its severely limited size. No. 7, prepared for the enlarged issue of a journal commemorating an international congress of linguists, marks the product of a dual filtering. It aims to offer the quintessence of several earlier essays, of which only the last, deemed most ambitious, has here been independently included as No. 9; these essays, in turn, rest squarely on a solid block of thirty to forty monographic inquiries pertaining to an earlier stage of my research. Nos. 6 and 11 constitute review articles, one spontaneous, the other solicited; I sincerely regret that considerations of space have counseled against the inclusion of some large-scale appraisals of writings of other fellow-scholars (A. Alonso, Corominas, Gorosch, Hubschmid, Martinet, Rodríguez-Castellano, Tilander, among others). This break-down leaves only a fairly modest residue of analyses planned, from the start, as free-wheeling investigations undertaken entirely for their own sake, with the initiative, for a change, stemming from the author alone (Nos. 9, 12, and 13).

The typological approach to the study of languages, known for its tested fruitfulness, represents nothing new in the mid-twentieth century. Conversely, the application of typology to given genres of linguistic inquiry rather than to slices of raw data seems not to have been tried out adequately before the initial publication of items 5, 8, and 10 (and of the lengthy narrow-meshed monograph underlying the last-mentioned piece). I have stated my reasons for resolutely championing this genre and was recently pleased to discover that similar typologies of analyses have been accepted in disciplines of comparable texture; witness, for one parallel, some of Raymond Aron's stimulating and deservedly acclaimed surveys of the methodologies of historical reconstruction.

The predominance of the diachronic over the synchronic perspective is evident throughout the volume and, though admittedly atypical of current tastes, demands, I hope, no excuse or explicit vindication. The most salient characteristic of some articles — possibly not the leanest —, however, is their panchronic slant. Thus, if my own judgment is valid, the dominant theme of my "Studies in Irreversible Binomials" and, by the same token, of the "Secondary Uses of Letters in Language" is a distinctly non-temporal array of situations each of which has, of course, been historically arrived at and doubtless lends itself to historical dissection. Understandably, in the three papers pointed in the direction of typology the basic considerations are also structural, while the historical stratification of scholarly opinions and the temporal concatenation of primary data inviting such assessments for once take the second and the third seats, respectively. A certain elasticity in overcoming Saussure's excessively rigid categorization of all linguistic research into either the descriptive or the genetic variety seems to me very much the order of the day. While there would be little point in blurring a neatly established cleavage, there is no need to become a slave to a distinction, however skilfully drawn.

At the friendly and perfectly justified request of Mr. H. L. Schollick as spokesman for the publishing firm to which this collection owes its existence I have tried to avert an impression of utter chaos as regards the externals of typographic presentation. We seem to be living in an age where every journal (or comparable medium of diffusion) imposes on contributors its own set of editorial preferences. This widespread policy may tend to lend each issue an appearance of tidiness and pleasing uniformity, but greatly — and perhaps gratuitously — complicates the author's task in salvaging his scattered writings from periodicals and assembling them in more easily manageable volumes. With respect to the content and phrasing of the papers, I was fortunate to persuade the publisher to make allowances for a modicum of additions, corrections, cross-references, and mutual adjustments. On the other hand, there has been no intention on my part to recast any piece in a new stylistic mould, still less to create, *ex post facto*, the specious impression that all essays here, almost accidentally, brought together have sprung from a single, immutable,

tightly closed circle of theoretical commitment. I shall not feel dis-
mayed if critics point out residual incompatibilities as between essay
and essay as long as each constituent item remains relatively free
from the taint of embarrassing inconsistencies. It is clear to myself
(as it will be, I trust, to most readers) that an author seeking to detect
"Some Diachronic Implications of Fluid Speech Communities" —
a semijocose rêverie revolving around an imaginary state of affairs —
is practically forced to cut loose from conventions of analysis and
stylistic orchestration far more radically than would be the same
writer in some of his papers purporting to summarize, on an appropriately high level of abstraction, such inquiries as have been successfully conducted by generations of experts from before 1900. On
balance, it would seem just as insincere to pretend that fifteen years
of sustained involvement with many lines of research have left my
own earlier tastes and ways of thinking intact as it might be un-
engagingly immodest to proffer a self-centered account of the changes
they are likely to have undergone.

In conclusion, I feel prompted to tender my gratitude to those
who, over the years, have tried so hard to gloss over the patent
inadequacies of my English. So far as these thirteen essays are concerned, the names of Bernard Bloch, Percival B. Fay, Dell H.
Hymes, Judith M. Treistman, and Marilyn May Vihman come most
readily to mind. To Stephen Ullmann I owe, among other attentions,
a strong dosage of helpful advice at the stage of initial selection.

*Paris, October 1966*

# Contents

# Abbreviations

| | |
|---|---|
| *AGI* | Archivio Glottologico Italiano |
| *AILC* | Anales del Instituto de Lingüística de Cuyo (Mendoza) |
| *AION* | Annali dell'Istituto Universitario Orientale di Napoli (new series) |
| *AIS* | *Atlante Linguistico-Etnografico dell'Italia e della Svizzera Meridionale* (= *Sprach- und Sachatlas Italiens und der Südschweiz*), 8 vols., eds. K. Jaberg and J. Jud |
| *AL* | Acta Linguistica (Copenhagen) |
| *ALLG* | Archiv für lateinische Lexikographie und Grammatik |
| *ALMA* | Archivum Latinitatis Medii Aevi (= Bulletin Du Cange) |
| *AR* | Archivum Romanicum |
| *ArL* | Archivum Linguisticum (Glasgow) |
| *AS* | American Speech |
| *ASNS* | Archiv für das Studium der neueren Sprachen und Literaturen |
| *AUCh.* | Anales de la Universidad de Chile |
| *BDC* | Butlletí de dialectologia catalana |
| *BF* | Boletim de Filologia (Lisbon) |
| *BH* | Bulletin hispanique |
| *BICC* | Boletín del Instituto Caro y Cuervo |
| *BRAE* | Boletín de la Real Academia Española |
| *BSLP* | Bulletin de la Société de Linguistique de Paris |
| *DCE* | *Diccionario crítico etimológico de la lengua castellana*, by J. Corominas, 4 vols. (Madrid, 1954–[57]) |
| *DCVB* | *Diccionari català-valencià-balear*, by A. Mª. Alcover and F. de B. Moll |
| *DEI* | *Dizionario etimologico italiano*, by C. Battisti and G. Alessio, 5 vols. (Florence, 1950–57) |
| *DW* | *Deutsches Wörterbuch*, launched by J. and W. Grimm |
| *EDMP* | *Estudios dedicados a Menéndez Pidal*, 7 vols. (Madrid, 1950–57) |
| *ES* | English Studies |
| *EWFS* | *Etymologisches Wörterbuch der französischen Sprache*, by E. Gamillscheg (Heidelberg, 1928) |
| *EWRS* | *Etymologisches Wörterbuch der romanischen Sprachen*, by F. Diez (Bonn, 1853); rev. 2d ed. (1861–62); rev. 3d ed. (1869–70) |
| *FEW* | *Französisches etymologisches Wörterbuch* by W. von Wartburg (1928– ) |

| | |
|---|---|
| *Fil.* | Filología |
| *GSLI* | Giornale Storico della Letteratura Italiana |
| *HMP* | *Homenaje a Menéndez Pidal*, 3 vols. (Madrid, 1925) |
| *HR* | Hispanic Review |
| *Ib.* | Ibérida (Rio de Janeiro) |
| *ID* | L'Italia Dialettale |
| *IF* | Indogermanische Forschungen |
| *IJAL* | International Journal of American Linguistics |
| *It.* | Italica |
| *JAOS* | Journal of the American Oriental Society |
| *JEGPh.* | Journal of English and Germanic Philology |
| *KJb.* | Kritischer Jahresbericht über die Fortschritte der romanischen Philologie, ed. K. Vollmöller |
| *KwN* | Kwartalnik Neofilologiczny |
| *LEW* | *Lateinisches Etymologisches Wörterbuch*, by A. Walde and J. B. Hofmann, 2 vols. (Heidelberg, 1938–54) |
| *Lg.* | Language |
| *LGRPh.* | Literaturblatt für germanische und romanische Philologie |
| *LN* | Lingua Nostra |
| *LRW* | *Lateinisch-romanisches Wörterbuch*, by G. Körting (Paderborn, 1891); rev. 2d ed. (1897); rev. 3d ed. (1907) |
| *MÆv.* | Medium Ævum |
| *MIL* | Memorie dell'Istituto Lombardo |
| *MLJ* | Modern Language Journal |
| *MLN* | Modern Language Notes |
| *MLQ* | Modern Language Quarterly |
| *MLR* | Modern Language Review |
| *NJKA* | Neue Jahrbücher für das klassische Altertum |
| *NM* | Neuphilologische Mitteilungen (Helsinki) |
| *NRFH* | Nueva revista de filología hispánica |
| *PhQ* | Philological Quarterly |
| *PMLA* | Publications of the Modern Language Association of America |
| *RBAM* | Revista de la Biblioteca, Archivo y Museo |
| *RBPhH* | Revue belge de philologie et d'histoire |
| *RDR* | Revue de dialectologie romane |
| *RePh.* | Revue de philologie, de littérature et d'histoire anciennes (3d series) |
| *REW*[1] | *Romanisches etymologisches Wörterbuch*, by W. Meyer-Lübke (Heidelberg, 1911–20) |
| *REW*[3] | Id., rev. 3d ed. (1930–35) |
| *RF* | Romanische Forschungen |
| *RFE* | Revista de filología española |
| *RFH* | Revista de filología hispánica |
| *RH* | Revue hispanique |
| *RJb.* | Romanistisches Jahrbuch |
| *RL* | Revista Lusitana |
| *RLR* | Revue des langues romanes |
| *RLiR* | Revue de linguistique romane |

| | |
|---|---|
| *RMPh.* | Rheinisches Museum für Philologie |
| *RO* | Revista de Occidente |
| *Rom.* | Romania |
| *RPF* | Revista Portuguesa de Filologia |
| *RPh.* | Romance Philology |
| *RR* | Romanic Review |
| *SAW* | Sächsische Akademie der Wissenschaften (Philosophisch-historische Klasse), Verhandlungen |
| *SEER* | The Slavonic and East European Review (London) |
| *SIL* | Studies in Linguistics |
| *SMV* | Studi Mediolatini e Volgari |
| *SN* | Studia Neophilologica |
| *Sp.* | Speculum |
| *SPh.* | Studies in Philology |
| *UCPL* | University of California Publications in Linguistics |
| *UUÅ* | Uppsala Universitets Årsskrift |
| *VR* | Vox Romanica |
| *WAW* | Wiener Akademie der Wissenschaften (Philosophisch-historische Klasse), Sitzungsberichte |
| *ZDA* | Zeitschrift für deutsches Altertum und deutsche Literatur |
| *ZFSL* | Zeitschrift für französische Sprache und Literatur |
| *ZPh.* | Zeitschrift für Phonetik und allgemeine Sprachwissenschaft (later: Zs. für Phonetik, Sprachwissenschaft und Kommunikationsforschung) |
| *ZRPh.* | Zeitschrift für romanische Philologie |

## B. Series

| | |
|---|---|
| BAR | Biblioteca dell' "Archivum Romanicum" |
| BBRPh. | Berliner Beiträge zur romanischen Philologie, dir. E. Gamillscheg |
| BÉHÉ | Bibliothèque de l'École des Hautes Études Pratiques |
| BFUL | Bibliothèque de la Faculté de Philosophie et Lettres de l'Université de Liège |
| BR | Bibliotheca Romanica, dir. W. von Wartburg |
| BRH | Bibliotheca Romanica Hispanica, dir. D. Alonso |
| CFMA | Classiques français du Moyen Age |
| FRPh. | Forschungen zur romanischen Philologie, dir. H. Lausberg |
| IB | Indogermanische Bibliothek |
| MH | Manuali Hoepli |
| PFLS | Publications de la Faculté des Lettres de Strasbourg |
| RH | Romanica Helvetica, dirs. J. Jud and A. Steiger |
| SG | Sammlung Göschen |
| SKL | Sammlung kurzer Lehrbücher der romanischen Sprachen und Literaturen |
| SRE | Sammlung romanischer Elementarbücher, dir. W. Meyer-Lübke |

B

## C. Languages and Dialects[1]

(For supplementary information see n. 2 to "Typology of Historical Grammars")

| | | | |
|---|---|---|---|
| Alent. | Alentejano (Southern Portugal) | Extr. | Extremeño (Southwestern Spain) |
| Alg. | Algarvian (Southern Portugal) | F. | French |
| | | Franc. | Francien (i.e., the dialect of Ile de France) |
| Am.-E. | American English | | |
| Am.-Sp. | American Spanish | Frk. | Frankish |
| And. | Andalusian | G. | German |
| A.-Norm. | Anglo-Norman | Gal. | Galician |
| Apul. | Apulian | Gal.-Ptg. | Galician-Portuguese |
| Ar. | Arabic | Gallo-Rom. | Gallo-Romance |
| Arag. | Aragonese | Gasc. | Gascon |
| Arch.-L. | Archaic Latin | Gen. | Genoese |
| Ard. | Ardennais | Gmc. | Germanic |
| Ast. | Asturian | Goth. | Gothic |
| Ast.-Leon. | Asturo-Leonese | Gr. | Greek |
| B.-Beir. | Baixo Beirão (Central Portugal) | Gr.-L. | Graeco-Latin |
| | | Hebr. | Hebrew |
| Béarn. | Béarnais (Southwestern France) | Hisp. | Hispanic |
| | | Hisp.-Rom. | Hispano-Romance |
| Braz.-Ptg. | Brazilian Portuguese | IE | Indo-European |
| Br.-E. | British English | It. | Italian |
| Burg. | Burgundian | Jud.-Sp. | Judeo-Spanish |
| Cal. | Calabrian | L. | Latin |
| Campid. | Campidanese (Southern Sardinia) | Langued. | Languedocien |
| | | Logud. | Logudorian (North-central Sardinian) |
| Carol. | Carolingian Latin | | |
| Cast. | Castilian (i.e., the dialect of Castile) | Loth. | Lotharingian (or Lorrain) |
| C.-Ast. | Central Asturian | Merov. | Merovingian Latin |
| Cat. | Catalan | Miñ. | Miñoto, or Minhoto (Northern Portugal) |
| Ch.-L. | Church Latin | | |
| Ch.-Sl. | Church Slavic | Mod. | Modern |
| Cl. | Classical | Moz. | Mozarabic |
| Cub. | Cuban Spanish | N.-Cal. | North-Calabrian |
| Drav. | Dravidian | Nuor. | Nuorese (Central Sardinia) |
| E. | English | | |
| Engad. | Engadinian (i.e., eastern branch of Western Raeto-Romance) | NW-Sp. | Northwestern Spain's cluster of dialects |

[1] Pre- refers to a speech (often unidentified) which was locally used before the introduction of a given language; proto- to the primitive (usually reconstructed) stage of that language. ROMANIA denotes the aggregate of Romance-speaking territories, particularly in the Old World; Rumania, a country in Eastern Europe.

| | | | |
|---|---|---|---|
| Occ. | Occitanian (aggregate of Southern France's modern dialects) | Ptg. | Portuguese |
| | | R. | Russian |
| | | Rom. | Romance |
| OE | Old English | Rum. | R(o)umanian |
| OF | Old French | Salm. | Salmantino (or Salamancan) |
| OGal. | Old Galician | | |
| OHG | Old High German | Sard. | Sardinian |
| OIt. | Old Italian | Sic. | Sicilian |
| OLeon. | Old Leonese | S.-It. | Southern Italian |
| ONav. | Old Navarrese | Sp. | Spanish |
| OProv. | Old Provençal | Trasm. | Trasmontano (Northeastern Portugal) |
| OPtg. | Old Portuguese | | |
| OSard. | Old Sardinian | Tusc. | Tuscan |
| OSp. | Old Spanish | Val. | Valencian |
| Pic. | Picard | VL | Vulgar Latin |
| Pol. | Polish | W.-F. | Western French dialects |
| Prim. | Primitive (= G. Ur-) | | |
| Prov. | Provençal | W.-Gal. | Western Galician |

## D. MISCELLANEOUS

| | | | |
|---|---|---|---|
| Acad. | Academy (Dictionary) | obs. | obsolete |
| adj. | adjective | orig. | original(ly) |
| anat. | anatomy | pers. | person |
| bot. | botany | pl. | plural |
| coll. | colloquial | P(P) | point(s) — on a linguistic map |
| CVC | consonant-vowel-consonant sequence | | |
| | | p(p). | page(s) |
| dial. | dialectal | Pt. | Part |
| esp. | especially | quatr. | quatrain |
| f. | feminine | sg. | singular |
| fut. | future (tense) | SLP | Société de Linguistique de Paris |
| instr. | instrumental | | |
| LSA | Linguistic Society of America | SLR | Société des Langues Romanes |
| | | | |
| m. | masculine | Suppl. | Supplement (Volume) |
| MLA | Modern Language Association of America | surg. | surgery |
| | | topon. | toponym (or place-name) |
| MS(S) | manuscript(s) | v. | verb |
| n. | noun | var(s). | variant(s) |
| neut. | neuter | | |

## E. FONTS AND SYMBOLS

| | |
|---|---|
| italics | linguistic forms adduced (esp. those culled from Romance sources) |
| small caps | (a) Latin etymological bases; (b) emphasis |
| boldface | word transliterated from some other ancient script |
| superscript | numeral marking the edition of a book |

| | | | |
|---|---|---|---|
| III: 2 | Volume III, Part 2 | > < | regular phonetic change (to or from) |
| 1*b* | page 1, column *b* | | |
| 20 | Map 20 | → ← | other than regular phonetic change (to or from) |
| × | cross, blend | | |
| ≠ | unequal to | | |
| ~ | alternating with | ′ | syncopated vowel |
| [ ] | phonetic transcription | ⌐ ¬ | generalized lexical type |
| / / | phonemic transcription | | |
| ' ' | meaning | ⌐ ¬ | standardized lexical type |

# I

# Genetic Linguistics

ALTHOUGH consecrated by a century and a half of constant use, the term "historical" linguistics, as a designation of a discipline and in its full spectrum of connotations, is something of a misnomer, because the most exciting and controversial operations of that discipline concern the reconstruction of languages, i.e. prehistory, rather than (documented) history. For this reason, perhaps, Saussure, in his search for a label that would neatly contrast with the newly discovered "synchronic" perspective, suggested the qualifier "diachronic", which, possibly as a result of its paleness, later proved less than successful. In the mid-twentieth century, it might, in all likelihood, be most apposite to speak of "genetic" linguistics in reference to the entire domain, reserving the alternative designation "glottodynamics" for the hard core of general doctrine governing the analyst's major operations.

"Historical" linguistics is very often equated with "comparative" linguistics; to the extent that the tracing of genetic relationships involves some confrontation of an earlier with a later stage of the same language (of Old English, say, with Middle or Modern English), a measure of overlap is indeed unavoidable. For practical purposes, however, it seems advisable to refer to comparative linguistics only where several cognate languages — ideally, if they can be observed at the same time level — are jointly analyzed in an effort to arrive at the parental tongue, as when proto-Central Algonquian is reconstructed from available records of Sauk and Fox, Cree, Menomini, and Ojibwa. Of course, it is equally legitimate to engage in the typological comparison of languages with no thought of reconstruction and regardless of the presence of any kinship ties; cf. Bally's classic juxtaposition of Modern German and Modern French (1932), and the currently fashionable "contrastive" grammars.

Historical and comparative linguistics reached their first peak of development in the nineteenth century (there were some rudimentary attempts in Western and Central Europe during the period of incubation, 1500–1800). "Language history", in contrast, represents a relatively new genre of research; its roots are in broad-gauged introductory chapters to technically worded historical grammars. In terms readily understandable to layman and beginner alike, language history interweaves austere linguistic analyses with discussions — rarely devoid of amenity — of social, economic, broadly cultural, demographic, and literary conditions prevailing at the successive time levels, allowing also for remarks on the philological state of transmission. At its best, as in Migliorini's masterpiece (1960), language history excels at tracing the vicissitudes of a single language viewed within the matrix of the corresponding highly literate national culture.

- The individual facts ascertainable through the various analyses devised by historical linguists lend themselves to two entirely unrelated kinds of synthesis. Certain forms can be lifted out of their original philological context (which alone, in most instances, made their secure identification possible) and can be arranged on a higher plateau of abstraction, so as to illustrate broad aspects of a specific linguistic transformation, e.g. the development of sounds, derivational moulds, lexical meanings, or syntactic structures from Stage A to Stage B of the given language. Climbing to a still higher level of generalization, the analyst is at liberty to abandon even the context of the specific language at issue and to cite the modifications observed, for the sake of their illustrative value, in a general methodology of linguistic change. On the other hand, the slivers and nuggets of information obtained through stringent linguistic (in particular, etymological) analysis may be deftly inserted, as highly prized items, in the grandiose mosaics pieced together by patient and versatile historians. These are similar to the fragmentary bits of knowledge collected by physical anthropologists, archeologists, folklorists, and others who attempt to recapture the elusive past.

Traditionally, from the days of such pioneers as the Germanist J. Grimm and the Romanist F. Diez to that towering Indo-Europeanist of the early twentieth century, A. Meillet, the two conspicuously parallel ingredients of research in diachronic linguistics have been the manual of historical grammar and the etymological dictionary — the one providing a tightly ordered macrocosm and the other a loose kaleidoscopic array of microcosms. The full-sized historical grammar

— not infrequently a multi-volume venture — embraced phonology (with excursuses into prosody or accentology), inflection, "word formation" (i.e., affixal derivation and composition or their counterparts in exotic languages), and syntax. The latter centered, in ever widening circles, around the word, the phrase, and the sentence. An abridged version was limited to phonology and inflection. Inflection and the "syntax of the word" are so closely adjacent that they tend to merge, and a few scholars have gone so far as to consolidate all of morphology and syntax into the single domain of "morphosyntax", which forms the hard, inalienable kernel of linguistics. Excursions into semantics, metrics (also, through the inclusion of tropes, rhetoric or poetics), and stylistics — the last-mentioned more loosely organized and defined in a variety of ways — have at all times been regarded as optional rather than obligatory. Only in recent decades have grammatical and lexical studies drifted apart so sharply in techniques and appeal as to render problematic any joint ventures in the immediate future.

The relative stabilization of historical linguistics in the period 1850–1925 had the advantage of producing a far-reaching standardization in its terminology; this in turn, by virtue of the comparability achieved, invited and furthered at every step the confrontation of older and more recent studies, a procedure which has become more difficult in the last quarter-century. The long unchallenged pre-eminence of Central European scholarship in this field is mirrored by the wide acceptance of such technical terms as "Umlaut" (metaphony) and "Ablaut" (apophony), while other German labels, potentially just as helpful (e.g. *Lehnwort* 'assimilated borrowing' vs. *Fremdwort* 'unassimilated borrowing'), have enjoyed no such popularity. Early standardization was particularly beneficial in certain special types of nonverbal symbolization, e.g. single quotation marks for meaning, italics for quoted forms, Bold Face for transliteration into another alphabet, small capitals for data credited to an ancestral language (e.g. Latin vs. Romance vernaculars), large capitals for epigraphic material, square brackets for phonetic transcription, asterisks for hypothetical forms, and, above all, the two directional signs: > 'changes into' alongside < 'descends from'.

Before long, the very success of these symbols led to a temporary staleness, except where the stagnation was relieved by the introduction of signs manufactured by the more aggressively imaginative structuralist school (e.g., slanted lines for "phonemicization"). Thus, few historically oriented scholars have bothered to discriminate typographically between two logically distinguishable hypothetic forms: (a) those undocumented, yet assumed to have existed (*) and (b) those expressly presented as non-existent (*). Again, though scarcely any experts would deny the sharp cleavage between phonology and morphology, historical linguists have failed to capitalize on the possibility of contrastive symbolization of phonological as against morphological shifts (say, normal sound-change vs. suffix-change); here one might put to separate use such symbols as > beside →, etc. Some Romance scholars have distinctively used (without finding imitators) raised half-brackets to set off lexical or syntactic patterns, as against specific forms.

To the extent that genetic linguists are concerned with historical situations, unique by definition, they can resort to the device of "model formation" only on a limited scale. In a way, any reconstruction of genetic relationship between languages or dialects involves a generous measure of schematization aimed at eliminating those details (reflecting secondary and tertiary complications) that would tend to blur the broad outline. One can visualize an entirely different kind of model: Instead of focusing attention on concrete territories (at historical stages) or avoiding any commitment to the speakers' habitat (at prehistoric stages), the analyst may decide to invent imaginary countries with a sharply profiled distribution of coastlines, wastelands, mountain chains, ports of entry, emporia, cultural shrines, etc. He can further posit a certain succession of political, socio-economic, and strictly linguistic events (say, invasions, retreats into the hilly inland, reconquest of coastal lowlands, split into dialects) and project them onto the imaginary area, excogitating, in abstract terms, the likeliest concatenations of linguistic reactions to these pressures. By sharpening the analyst's alertness to possible and probable intricacies under artificial conditions that are relatively simplified, such schemata can prepare him for successful inquiries into real-life situations, incomparably more complex.

It should be emphasized that the postulate of historical uniqueness is not easy to reconcile with the search for evolutionary universals in the realm of language. However, the prospect of discovering such universals has for many decades been a source of constant titillation. One classic example is the often observed correlation of word order (and comparable syntactic devices) with the available wealth of inflectional endings. Clarity and economy jointly demand that, if relationships between members of a clause can no longer be unequivocally expressed by means of the latter (e.g., as a result of phonetic erosion), a stiffening of the word order should provide an adequate substitute. Also, etymologists have discovered that of all form classes adjectives, on balance, tend to present lexical nuclei most resistant to identification. In addition, semanticists report that fluctuations and changes of meaning undergone by verbs exceed, as a rule, those to which a typical noun would be subject. The difficulty with trying to establish absolute universals is that each such attempt presupposes the testing of hundreds of languages. On the other hand, characteristic samples would suffice to identify tendential universals.

As in all evolutionary sciences, the question of purposeful, or oriented, change is at the heart of the philosophy underlying any genetic analysis of linguistic data. Linguists are sharply divided on this matter of teleology: The great Danish theorist O. Jespersen and the founders of the Prague School categorically affirm the teleological principle (a few visualize a trend toward general improvement achieved through refinement, simplification, and economy); others, particularly L. Bloomfield — ever after 1920 — and a whole generation of American linguists claiming allegiance to his doctrine, just as vehemently deny it. Discernibly different from the teleological approach, though occasionally confused with it, especially by opponents, is the idealistic slant (characteristic of Croce's school in Italy and of Vossler's in Germany), which stresses the primacy of the speakers' thinking over their speech habits and grants them in the process a much wider margin of initiative and of control over linguistic change than would be accepted by believers in the preeminence of "blind forces" or by those (such as B. L. Whorf) who view the configuration of a grammatical structure as a prime determinant of thinking and perception. The more literate the speaker and especially the writer, the stronger the case for the idealistic approach; in analyzing "graphically" the comportment of ancient and medieval scribes, one can hardly refuse to distinguish between what they aimed to achieve and what they actually accomplished.

Basic to all operations in historical linguistics is the view which the analyst holds of the configuration of the speech community under study and of speech communities in general. This was clearly sensed by L. Bloomfield who, in his influential book *Language* (1933), without disregarding the varying density of communication nor denying the complexity of certain speech communities, impressed upon his readers the need to reckon with a far-reaching uniformity of speech habits. Similarly, in presenting the comparative method, he leaned toward favoring those situations that exhibit clear-cut dialect splits, without denying occasional alternatives. The current trends of thought have veered in other directions. Many younger scholars have recognized that the link holding together language communities is frequently mere similarity rather than actual homogeneity of speech habits, a point fraught with major implications for the geneticist. It is further held that bilingualism and even trilingualism are more widely disseminated the world over than is strict monolingualism, an assumption that demands flexibility in dealing with a multitude of diversified and changing situations. Thus, two groups speaking Language X, one composed of members who have, from infancy, also mastered Language Y and the other containing persons who happen to be constantly using Language Z in certain social contexts, are unlikely to react identically to any incipient innovations spreading from a monolingual zone. (One also readily conceives of innovations arising at the intersection of languages.) One final argument in favor of fluidity in the object observed and elasticity in the method applied to its elucidation is the discovery that many areas commonly assigned *en bloc* to certain languages often lack such "natural boundaries" as might preserve a community of speakers in quasi-hermetic isolation. The emergence of such zones is due rather to conflation, i.e., to successive reapportionments of neighboring territories, each initially sheltering a different language or dialect. Therefore, unless perfect leveling subsequently ensues, one may detect, beneath the present-day "roof" bracketing the dialects, remnants and splinters of their original phonic, grammatical, and lexical systems in almost kaleidoscopic confusion.

In linguistics, the relation of the descriptive (or synchronic) to the historical (or diachronic) perspective has been the subject of considerable speculation and discussion, the consensus being that descriptive analysis bears preponderantly on simpler, less opaque situations. From this nearly unanimous opinion several discrepant conclusions may be drawn. Some experts maintain that new techniques, such as the application of the structural method, should be tried out first on horizontal, later on vertical, slices of linguistic material. There are those who visualize a historical structure as a succession of descriptive structures superimposed on one another. The main difficulty in architecturing such an edifice lies in the fact that certain features structurally less than significant at one evolutionary stage may suddenly acquire conspicuous importance during the transition to the next stage. Thus, the descriptivist is free to assert that in words like *danc-er*, *kill-er*, the ending *-er* as the carrier of an identifiably specific meaning ('agent') represents a derivational morpheme, while in *hamm-er*, *pinc-er*, *rudd-er* the same sequence of sounds plays no comparable rôle. But the historical linguist, while acknowledging this distinction on certain temporal plateaus, must at all times reckon with the strong possibility of joint actions, inextricably interwoven, by homonymous genuine suffixes (such as the *-er* of *kill-er*) and mere suffixoids (the *-er* of *rudd-er*). One consensus is worth mentioning: From the minute inspection of any given state of a single language the experienced analyst can tentatively extract almost as much information on its earlier stages ("internal reconstruction") as he can from comparing that language "externally" with its congeners.

One way of doing justice to both perspectives has been to engage in a "stairway projection"; among the practitioners of this novel approach one may count such seasoned experimenters as O. Jespersen (for English), A. Meillet (for Latin), and W. von Wartburg (for French). This particular method of intricate surgery affords glimpses of the consecutive periods of the chosen language, slanted alternately in the descriptive and in the historical direction. The implication of this design is clearly that one may distinguish between periods of relative rest and stability, and others marked by spells of stress and strain.

One salient difference between the descriptive and the historical approach in linguistics is that the former in most instances enables the researcher to operate with a finite corpus, an intentional selection over whose scope he retains a modicum of control, while the latter often bears on an irremediably fragmentary volume of data. The ability to work with lacunary material and a certain flair for filling in gaps thus become important prerequisites for success in linguistic reconstruction, much as they are for research in geology, paleontology, and paleobotany. Developments are contrastively symbolized by solid lines (documented) as against broken lines (hypothesized); yet the latter do not invariably represent initial, prehistoric segments of trajectories. An archaic Stage A may very well owe its transparency to the realistic, readily adjustable spelling habits of the scribes concerned; conversely, Stage B, though temporally closer to the beholder, may become nebulous, because the scribes of that period, plagued by conservatism or subject to an inferiority complex, may have stubbornly endeavored to cling to the orthographic norms of their predecessors ("etymological spelling"), while the actual speech processes ran their course with unabated speed. Then again, Stage C may mark a vigorous return to graphic realism, entailing the relative translucency of actual speech events. A vivid illustration of these three phases is provided by early Latin; late Latin; certain varieties of "low" and medieval Latin; and, on an overwhelming scale, the budding Romance vernaculars.

It also happens that some word of unmistakably Latin provenience which, judging from its "normal" transmutations, must have been in constant use over two millennia ("mouth-to-mouth transmission"), disappears from written records in the fifth century, say, only to reëmerge a thousand years later. In cases of this kind, the literary genres of the extant texts act as prisms or filters, often seemingly capricious. They may long repress a word, keeping it submerged until there arises some opportunity — socially or aesthetically controlled — for its definitive surfacing into the standard language.

Systematic inquiry into the configuration of trajectories has not yet outgrown the stage of trial and error. Where regular phonological change occurs, older notions of strictly gradual transitions do not apply. Between, say, the Latin $\bar{u}$, as in $p\bar{u}ru$, and the French $\ddot{u}$, as in $pur$, it is no longer admissible to posit an infinity of intermediate nuances of the stressed vowel without concurrently accepting some kind of cut-off point at which a vowel already markedly fronted, but still representing no more than an unusual variant within the scale of "realizations" of the phoneme /ū/, must have become a member, decreasingly erratic, of the sound-family constituting the phoneme /ü/. In other words, structural thinking forces us to recognize an interaction of slowly working phonetic rapprochements, and more or less sudden occasional jumps. This composite scheme guarantees the semblance of a close-knit system to a language at any moment of its growth. Thus, the graduality of development — not superseded, but only qualified and hierarchized — remains a vitally important assumption. Significantly, the hypothesis that the shift $\bar{u} > \ddot{u}$, eminently characteristic of the transmutation of provincial Latin into French, is traceable to the contributing agency of Gaulish cannot be refuted by the argument that the Celtic language in question lacked a fully developed /ü/ in its own system. It would have sufficed for the local substratum language, at the start, to have slightly deflected the Latin $\bar{u}$ from its original status of high back vowel in the direction of $\ddot{u}$, thus producing a kind of chain reaction or even an accelerated advance along a straight line.

In yet another context, the configuration of a trajectory of linguistic change, properly interpreted, may be revealing. If the changes due to associative interference were to be plotted on a chart, some of them might give the impression of a bizarre zigzagging curve. On such a chart a relatively level line may suddenly start climbing as a result of an outside pressure, a "disturbance", until it reaches a certain peak. Then the language's inner mechanism (e.g., the total weight of its inflectional paradigms) may begin to wipe out the irregularity, causing the line to drop until it reverts to its original direction. If in such an up-and-down movement, anteceding the advent of trustworthy written texts, the descending stage completely absorbs the effects of the ascending stage, it is quite impossible to detect the original disturbance. If the "down-movement" falls short of counterbalancing the aberrancy or overcorrects it, there is bound to remain in its wake a residue of startling "exceptions". In case the irregularity happens to erupt at the very start of the written tradition, it may appear baffling in retrospect that the ancestral language and its eventual modern product should be in perfect mutual agreement while at such sharp variance with the intermediate step, which then, in fact, fails to perform any "mediation". Thus, the Latin 3d pers. sg. imperfect ending *-ībat* (orig. *-iēbat*) cast off in early Romance speech *-ia(t)*, which to this day survives in Spanish as *-ía*, a safely predictable form, but paradoxically it produced instead, in early Old Spanish, *-ié*, a variant difficult to reconcile either with its antecedent or with its sequel. Investigation (1959, 1962) has disclosed that the rise of *-ié* simply marks a minor temporary deflection (of ascertainable origin), ultimately neutralized, while the later form *-ía* represents far more faithfully the continuation of a basic trend.

Closely allied to the concern with the convolution of trajectories is the attempt to reckon with a certain more or less steady rate of attrition in the core lexicon, and to draw from such analyses tentative conclusions as to the degree of kinship between congeneric languages and the approximate date of their split. This approach, which rode the crest of a temporary vogue in the 1950s, has become known, broadly as lexicostatistics and, with special application to dating, as glottochronology. Exaggerated claims, especially the attempt of some practitioners to place these techniques on the same pedestal as the rigorous study of sound correspondences, have led to quick disenchantment and virtual abandonment of the method.

For better or worse, the vicissitudes of historical linguistics have been intimately linked with the theories of sound change. The recognition of regularity in these transmutations has been hailed as a milestone along the road to progress (cf. the radical programmatic statements of the "Neogrammarians" or "Junggrammatiker" ca. 1870) or, more intransigently, as a touchstone of stringent scientific thinking. In compressed classroom presentation of historical linguistics, lecturers have traditionally inclined toward concentrating on "regular sound changes" as the discipline's irreducible hard core. In the separate quarters of humanists and anthropologists alike, this rigid attitude has for decades contributed toward producing the impression of linguistics as a highly abstract subject, almost forbiddingly abstruse and, above all, divorced in its style and tone from cultural history, to say nothing of its aloofness from the realm of arts and letters. Moreover, because most provisional rules or "laws" admitted of a few exceptions, and some of countless ones, there was for a while a widespread apprehension that the "regularists" were actually propounding some kind of mock science.

In reality, there exist several categories of sound change, each fairly autonomous — but not entirely so — and tied to diverse facets of human comportment and different levels of the speakers' consciousness. The immediate goal of linguists is to devise one workable formula for presenting their interconnections, however tenuous, and another for discovering the elusive ties of sound change categories to discrete mental processes.

The techniques of accurately circumscribing individual sound correspondences that are inherently limited in time and space can be traced to the past century. By contrasting French *mer* 'sea' and *père* 'father' with their Latin prototypes MARE and PATRE, the analyst learns that the Latin *a* tended, grosso modo, to yield *e* in French. Further refinement of this first approximation is within easy reach. The discrepant first vowels in *père* and *parrain* 'godfather' (originally *parrin*, from PATRĪNUS) alert the observer to the possibility that the shift *a* > *e* hinges on a crucial accentual condition, while comparison of *père* < PA-TRE with *part* < PAR-TE dramatizes the share that the configuration of the stressed syllable may have had in an obvious bifurcation, according to whether that syllable ended in a vowel or in a consonant. By examining with scrupulous care all seemingly aberrant developments — amenable to observation with optimal results in Old French — the analyst isolates, step by step, the specific phonological ("internal") factors that must have presided over the evolution, erratic at first glance, of (IL)LĀC 'there' > *là*; PAUPERE 'poor' > *povre* (mod. *pauvre*); CLĀUU 'nail' > *clou*; AQUA 'water' > *eaue* (mod. *eau*); PĀLUS 'pole' > *pieus*; CAPUT 'head' > *ch(i)ef*, etc. Comparably detailed break-downs can be established for all other Latin sounds viewed in their transmission into a chosen "daughter language", and, by way of effective control, the linguist is free to reverse the perspective and select as a given the basic sound unit of the daughter language, assigning to himself the task of individuating its sources.

But this classification marks only a first step, yielding at best a tidily subdivided inventory of raw facts. The preliminary classification is non-explicative, lacks statistical underpinning, fails to throw into bold relief parallels, convergences (including some that are partial or have been arrested), and, worse, concatenations of events, and does not begin to take into account other forms of sound shift. Such taxonomy disregards several broad or distinct categories of internal linguistic change. Moreover, it is not elastic enough to do justice to the various external pressures (demographic, social, educational) on evolutionary trends in speech and in the written word as well. It is in these directions — many of them affording fruitful contacts with a whole spectrum of other disciplines — that the chief advances of late-twentieth-century research are bound to lie.

The following are a few illustrations of research in progress and tempting prospects of investigation. Alongside regular phonetic change (akin to Sapir's "drift") scholars have placed "sporadic" shifts (also called "spontaneous" and "saltatory"), such as metathesis (the transposition of a sound, or intermutation of two sounds, in contact or at a distance), haplology (the elimination of one or two successive segments partially identical), and certain dissimilatory processes. None of these, it has been argued, is confined to a specific locus or span of time, i.e., they are all, at least latently or tendentially, pantopic and panchronic. Granted the fundamental validity of this distinction, there arise several questions and second thoughts. Does the sound system of a language at a given stage, or does, alternatively, its pattern of regular sound changes typically stimulate or block "sporadic" shifts, or else does it let them take their own course?

Could it be true that, for all their uniqueness, "regular" sound changes, in any random selection, display such strong proclivities in a few characteristic directions that one discerns in them certain universals? Is it legitimate to grade the regularity of sound change (not as an ideal postulate, but as a bit of reality) and to contrast "strong" expectation of outcome, most likely to occur in monolithic societies, with "weak" predictability, attributable to, say, loose conflations of dialects, regional or social? Does such a state of prevalent weakness tend to intensify sporadic shifts and even to invite an excess of lexical contamination? Should frequency of lexical occurrence, or at least of incidence in actual speech, rank as a factor contributing to the degree of regularity, especially where a particularly unusual sequence of sounds falls into no broader pattern of immediate appeal? Can the exigencies of inflectional patterning slow down the pace of a sound change or counteract it to the point of weakening a phonetic "law"? Do other demands of this kind carry sufficient weight to set in motion or to accelerate potential and especially incipient sound changes? If the answer to the last two questions is affirmative, can one uphold the view that phonology operates in practically hermetic isolation? Specifically, is it still permissible to resolve the phenomena of genetic phonology into a neat interplay of sound relationships, to be precise, into an alternation of states of equilibrium and states of unrest or tension, to the virtual exclusion of all rival forces? Does it make sense to arrange sound changes in their presumed chronological succession (E. Richter) without explicit forewarning that such sequences neither invariably presuppose nor necessarily imply the flow of one change from another, or from the sum of all others already completed? Can one, in such contexts, ignore with impunity certain extraneous factors such as pressure of morphological paradigms and deflections from the straight course through associative lexical interference, and the like?

From earlier incidental mention it is clear that there are other kinds of change affecting linguistic form and, consequently, reflected in the sounds as the obligatory carriers of that form but not here caused by purely phonetic conditions. The most important of these supervenient categories of change is analogical. Speakers make adjustments bearing either on the configuration of a grammatical paradigm or on the shape of a single word; in the latter eventuality, both the radical and the affix are open to modification. Typically such adjustments follow upon sound change; only by way of exception may one suspect them of impinging, as prime movers, upon sound development. Since analogical changes involve, by definition, associative interference, they seem to occur on a higher level of awareness than straight sound changes; thus they invite psycholinguistic analysis.

Sound symbolism constitutes yet another autonomous category, of slightly controversial status. To the extent that sounds, in symbolic context (and nowhere else), are credited with conveying messages of their own, this marginal category represents a tenuous bridge to semantic change, ordinarily removed from the realms of articulation, acoustics, and auditory perception. Sound symbolism may be absolute or relative. The former category prevails if the analyst attaches, cross-linguistically, an unvarying evocative value to, say, a high front vowel or to a hissing prepalatal consonant; the problem then is to ascertain whether speakers will allow words endowed with major connotative force, through such ingredients, to participate in normal sound shifts, at the cost of heavy loss in suggestiveness. The effects of relative sound symbolism are conditioned by the given phonological system; thus, in a language generally averse to long consonants an occasional geminate may boast "expressive" value (which it would otherwise lack). Again, the language historian is curious to learn how speakers can maintain a word enhanced by such a feature in this privileged status amid the welter of pervasive transformations. At this juncture one notes a welcome contact with information theory.

Entirely different from the classes of change are the categories of forces that are apt to produce changes of any kind. But the linguist's operational procedure in tackling this new problem remains essentially unaltered: Again his dual task is first to isolate the forces in question and then to discover the closest available approximation to the formula for their interplay.

It is customary to divorce the internal from the external forces, at the outset, notably because the separate inquiries into them seem to appeal to radically different minds. In the former group one can readily distinguish two drives, sometimes acting in polar opposition — one toward economy of effort, the other toward clarity. Economy, syntagmatically conceived, involves the very speech act; in paradigmatic perspective economy relates to the acquisition of, and sustained command over, neuromuscular skills. The former type determines the course of most assimilatory processes, contextual by definition (e.g., Latin *actu* > Italian *atto*) and governs the choice

c

of those glides and buffer consonants that serve to smooth away troublesome contiguity (in Old Spanish viewed in its relation to Latin: HONŌRĀRE > *onrar* > *on-d-rar* vs. FĒMINA > *femna* > *femb-ra*). The latter type precipitates mergers of phonemes in the system where continued distinction between them would produce only a meager yield (/ã/ and /ẽ/ in the older Parisian, /ɛ̃/ and /œ̃/ with increasing momentum in present-day Parisian); also, it dooms to extinction minute groups of words displaying an infrequent sound or combination of sounds.

A groping search for increased clarity may be behind most dissimilatory and haplologic processes. It accounts, as would no other supposition, for the speakers' readiness to augment their vocabulary (in an effort to reduce lexical polysemy) and to accept longer and more cumbersome syntactic structures (in a recoil from ambiguity). It is perhaps at this point that the newly achieved refinement of transformational grammar would most benefit the classic researches conducted by geneticists. The same urge ultimately justifies the sometimes successful flight from harmful homonymy or from its mere threat — the nearest escape routes being substitute words borrowed from neighboring dialects and reinterpreted within one's own cultural heritage, or words freely invented.

After one deducts the two-pronged quest for maximum economy and clarity it is the residue that threatens to cause serious difficulty; the wisdom of applying to it some such pleasing blanket term as "expressivism", remains to be demonstrated, especially since it is doubtful whether, in the last analysis, one can reduce the remaining forces to a single denominator. One nucleus that cannot by any stretch of the imagination be subsumed under either economy or clarity contains those formations associated with special moods — playful, tender, or festive. In contemporary English the colloquially flavored compositional types *hush-hush, ping-pong, riff-raff, wishy-washy, pribbles and prabbles, topsy-turvy, mumbo-jumbo* — sometimes originating in the nursery and displaying a strong admixture of onomatopoeia — admirably fit this description. In Slavic and Romance, formations involving strings of hypocoristic suffixes would qualify as a counterpart. The Hebrew spoken in modern Israel, the twentieth century's linguistic melting pot par excellence, allows speakers the jocose lapse into the Ashkenazic rather than the officially favored Sephardic pronunciation for proper names affectionately uttered, thus proliferating doublets. On the other hand, one runs across a phenomenon such as hypercharacterization (i.e., the sharper, more explicit, even uneconomically generous marking of a major grammatical category — say, gender, number, or person). For instance, Latin SOCRUS 'mother-in-law', hampered by its conspicuously uncharacteristic -us, is more neatly profiled with regard to gender (and sex) at the Romance stage through a new and far more appropriate ending (It. *suocera*, Sp. *suegra*, etc.); cf. also the change of Latin PUPPIS 'poop, stern', marred by an ending indeterminate as to gender, into the clear-cut Sp. *pop-a*. In such instances, the change is, of course, analogical; but the driving force behind it seems less easy to identify. It certainly can be neither economy nor any overflow of emotion, and one is hesitant, to say the least, to press into service a quest for heightened clarity. The propelling force, one suspects, is the speakers' endeavor to redesign selected portions of the language, to make the medium of transmission more pointed or so silhouetted as to be aesthetically more satisfying (Sapir's reference to the "cut" of a language here comes to mind — a fait accompli or a goal toward which speakers may strive).

The most familiar external forces whose impact will produce the various types of linguistic change are those resulting from contact between languages (occasionally one living and the other dead, but preserved in ritual or intensely studied) or regional and social dialects. Typically, a protracted transitional period of thoroughgoing bi- or plurilingualism is needed before the contact produces sizable results. In gauging any such impact on a specific language, the historian tries first to determine the principal layer of that language by inspecting the core structure of its grammar and those ingredients of its lexicon best known for their resistance, if not total immunity, to infiltration. Numerals, kinship terms, names of parts of the body, grammatically functional words are typical examples of such elements. Once this frame of reference has been established, it becomes clear which layers, in the course of further study, will be labeled substrata and which superstrata — eloquent metaphors borrowed from geology and permitting a graphic projection of anteriority. Thus, vis-à-vis Great Russian the numerous Finno-Ugric languages now extinct or pushed back to the periphery of Eastern Europe constituted substrata; so did Coptic and, farther down the Nile valley in Egypt, the Greek *koinē* vis-à-vis Arabic, Frisian vis-à-vis Dutch in Holland, and French plus Canary Island Spanish vis-à-vis English in Louisiana. In the absence of any genuine symbiosis, it is doubtful whether American

Indian languages may rank as substrata in relation to English in North America, as they indisputably must in relation to Spanish and Portuguese throughout Latin America. In the twilight hour between Late Antiquity and the Middle Ages, Arabic in Southern Spain and Frankish in Northern Gaul represented superstrata in relation to divergent varieties of provincial Latin. To the extent that the Greeks tended to form independent cultural nuclei under the aegis of the expanding Roman Republic and later Roman Empire, their settlements qualify as examples of linguistic adstrata vis-à-vis Latin as well as the circum-Mediterranean indigenous languages.

Aside from such "vertical" relations, linguistic pressures are bound to operate "horizontally" across political borders and even at long distances, through cultural diffusion. Thus, heavy clusters of Gallicisms are found not only in Spanish, Catalan, Italian, German, and Dutch, to say nothing of English, but also in languages occupying non-adjacent areas, such as Rumanian, Polish, Russian, and Swedish. Words are more easily borrowed than sounds, and affixes travel more rapidly than inflectional endings. A classic example of super-imposed syntactic, semantic, and (probably) intonational patterns is provided by the multifarious Germanisms observable in Eastern Switzerland's Romaunsh, a language descended from Raetian Latin.

Over against the fairly trivial instances of direct, positive influence one may place the sorely neglected gamut of indirect or catalytic interferences. Thus, two early medieval Germanic kingdoms carved out of the ruins of the crumbling Roman Empire — that of the Suebi in Galician–Portuguese territory and that of the Burgundians in the Lyon–Geneva area — moulded local Latin speech sparingly through loan words, but exerted a powerful restraining influence by politic-ally and culturally isolating their territories, at crucial junctures, from such centers of ceaseless linguistic innovation as Toledo and Paris.

An independent kind of outer force comprises all sorts of non-linguistic events potentially rich in linguistic reverberations. The invention of novel tools and machines may breathe new life into a moribund suffix serving to denote instruments. The emancipation of women the world over is likely to develop dormant schemata (affixal, compositional, or otherwise derivational) for the designation of female agentials. A global vogue of formality or familiarity (in clothing, dwelling, human relations, etc.) can hardly fail to revolu-tionize the system of forms of address and to affect even personal pronouns and possessive adjectives. The sections of the linguistic edifice most vulnerable to these influences are, then, the vocabulary, the derivational machinery (at the midway point between lexicon and grammar), plus a few pieces from the morphosyntactic tool kit.

Far beyond this boundary the "idealistic" school of thought, entrenched in Italy and Germany (K. Vossler) only a generation ago, tended to assess very liberally the impact of changing modes of thinking on linguistic forms, extending that impact to the foundations of sentence structure. While the consensus of most generations of scholars has ascribed the disappearance of case endings to attrition, recognizing the rise of prepositional paraphrases as a relatively smooth replacement, the "idealists" preferred to view as prime mover the emergence of a new way of thinking (such as analytic rather than synthetic), crediting it with the manufacture of appropriate substitutes which eventually eroded the older grammatical framework. The advent of Christianity figured in these interpretations (especially in H. F. Muller's) as another favorite determinant of linguistic evolution. The idealistic position is thus diametrically opposed to that of Whorf who, in the wake of Sapir (1921), mused that patterns of thinking may, in the first place, be moulded by preëxistent grammatical structures.

The complex interaction of all these isolable forces can be illustrated with the differing, if reconcilable, answers to the classic question: What dooms a word to extinction? Plausible explanations offered either separately or in any number of free combinations include an excess of paradigmatic intricacy or phonological oddity in the fated word; the peril besetting the weaker of two conflicting homonyms; an intolerable dosage of polysemy; a sudden general demand at all levels of the given society for lexical rejuvenation or large-scale overhaul; the obsolescence of a specific cultural element (say, some container or garment) heretofore designated by the word at issue; the ineluctable effect of some socially controlled restriction (taboos, etc.); acceptance, through borrowing from the local prestige language, of a more attractive equivalent, as when the imported *Cousine* dislodged the native *Base* in eighteenth-century German.

For the projection of major phases of linguistic growth, and especially for signaling the relationship between cognate languages, experts in reconstruction have resorted either to the somewhat older "family-tree theory" (*Stammbaumtheorie*) or to the wave hypothesis. The former is associated with the name of Schleicher, that contemporary and counterpart of the evolutionist Darwin who actually refined rather than launched the "family-tree" concept. It operates with a filiation chart reminiscent of those long favored in the life sciences. The latter, germane in its verbalization and, even more so, in its graphic suggestion to the physicists' and chemists' views of radiation, cannot be traced to any advocate earlier than Schuchardt (1866) and, in particular, Schmidt (1871). The inherently rigid family-tree diagram presupposes uniform speech-communities and their sudden and clear-cut bifurcation. The more elastic wave diagram tends to dissolve any system (or, less orderly, any arsenal) of communication tools into its constituents, granting to each change, whether phonetic, morphosyntactic, or lexical, its own scope and history. Neither the lapse of time it demands nor the area it covers need be exactly identical with those involved in any comparable change. The latest thinking sees in these divergent hypotheses two complementary projections, neither satisfactory if applied in isolation. Regrettably, no theory apt to reconcile them and no technique capable of smoothly integrating their separate findings have so far been devised.

The wave theory has intrinsically tended to give unusual prominence to the territorial expansion of linguistic features, providing the logical justification for linguistic (or dialect) geography. The interest in dialect geography is now past its crest; for many decades it fed on its sentimental motivation, local patriotism, and its partisans' delight in open-air field work. Practitioners of this approach developed special methods for interviews, oral or written questionnaires, and the cartographic recording of field-notes (linguistic atlases). Dialect geographers endowed with historical flair then proceeded to transform the geographic patterns laboriously established into bolder chronological sequences, calling themselves the geologists, paleontologists, or stratigraphers of human speech.

One extreme formulation of these assumptions, tastes, and techniques ("Age-and-Area Hypothesis") relies chiefly or even exclusively on territorial patterns in piecing together temporal successions. An attempt to schematize these procedures of "areal analysis" was undertaken by the small group of Italian "Neo-linguists", a school that produced but a short flurry from 1920 to 1950. A point that has hitherto not been satisfactorily investigated and yet clamors for imaginative inquiry is the wisdom of positing, alongside that "outer radiation" dear to dialect geographers and to diffusionists like Boas, some kind of "inner radiation" that might account in undulatory projections for the continuous re-structuring of systems.

BIBLIOGRAPHY

BENVENISTE, ÉMILE, *Problèmes de linguistique générale* (Paris, 1966).

HYMES, DELL, "Glottochronology so far", *Current Anthropology*, I (1960), 3–44.

KURYŁOWICZ, JERZY, *Esquisses linguistiques* (Wrocław, 1960).

LEROY, MAURICE, *Les grands courants de la linguistique moderne*, 3d ed. (Paris and Brussels, 1963). [Reliable only in his account of nineteenth-century research].

MALKIEL, YAKOV, (a) "Toward a reconsideration of the Old Spanish imperfect in *-ía/-ié*", *Hispanic Review*, XXVI (1959), 435–481; (b) "Initial points versus initial segments of linguistic trajectories", *Proceedings of the Ninth International Congress of Linguists* (The Hague, 1964), pp. 402–406.

MARTINET, ANDRÉ, *Économie des changements phonétiques* (Berne, 1955).

RICHTER, ELISE, *Beiträge zur Geschichte der Romanismen.* Supplement 82 (1934) to *Zeitschrift für romanische Philologie.*

SAPIR, EDWARD, *Language, an Introduction to the Study of Speech* (New York, 1921).

SAUSSURE, FERDINAND DE, *Cours de linguistique générale*, eds. C. Bally and A. Sechehaye (Paris, 1916); 2d ed. (1922); 3d ed. (1931); 5th ed. (1955). English version: *Course in General Linguistics*, tr. Wade Baskin (New York, 1959).

VOSSLER, KARL, *Geist und Kultur in der Sprache* (Heidelberg, 1925). English version: *The Spirit of Language in Civilization*, tr. Oscar Oeser (London and New York, 1932).

# 2

# Some Diachronic Implications of Fluid Speech Communities

### Historical Linguistics Versus Glottodynamics

As linguistics on the American scene is passing, at this very moment, through one of its most violent convulsions, there is every reason to expect that the long-endangered balance between the static and the dynamic approaches to language will in the end be restored. In their quest for a fairer hearing, students of evolutionary, especially of genetic, linguistics must remind themselves that, almost by definition, they have tended, to their own lasting detriment, to scatter their talents and energies on factual details devoid of broad implications. While the complexity of historical processes, by its nature, demands unremitting attention to minute intricacies, the recognition of major trends — mutually interwoven, hence, as a rule, difficult of strict isolation and direct inspection as they are — seems no less imperative. There may be some point in drawing a line between, on the one hand, free-wheeling and adventurous GLOTTODYNAMICS, if we agree so to label the study of constants or even universals abstracted from concrete speech developments, and, on the other, straight HISTORICAL LINGUISTICS, firmly tied to painstaking (if need be, downright pedestrian) philological inventories. Unavoidably, the former, if it is to be proffered in a persuasively realistic key, must feed on the accurate findings of the latter. The present considerations may seem and are, in fact, intended to be glottodynamic in essence and tone, but happen to rest on scrupulous sifting of diversified specimens of Romance material known for their comparative abundance and reliability.

### Rigid and Fluid Models of the Speech Community

Though on the theoretical plane no linguist would seriously question the agency of such processes as borrowing and diffusion, or of

Reprinted from *American Anthropologist*, LXVI, 6 (December 1964), 177–186.

such widespread situations as bilingualism and fluctuation, the practice of his day-to-day research has forced many an analyst to operate, wittingly or unconsciously, with the rigid concept of a virtually invariant society, in synchronic terms, or its frequent diachronic counterpart of an outwardly almost immobilized society developing from within. Even such sets of familiar labels as Old French → Middle French → Modern French, or Old High German → Middle High German → Early Modern High German → Contemporary High German conjure up the image of a fundamentally undivided speech community bequeathing, from one generation to another, a certain cultural heritage, subject to gradual modification only within narrow limits (cf. such characteristic terms as G. *Sprachgut*, Sp. *voces patrimoniales*). Though, beyond dispute, the areas assignable cross-temporally to a given language may vary considerably at successive stages of the development, through expansion (as with Old and Middle *vs.* Modern English), contraction (as with Old *vs.* Modern Basque), or radical displacement (as seems to be true, at least in part, of Rumanian), the average linguist, unless he specializes in piecing together territorial shifts of linguistic features, will in his actual operations tend to belittle the importance of these areal discrepancies.

While ideal instances of almost perfect territorial continuity, over centuries and millennia, may be on record, they have hardly been common. Cases of radical reapportionment of dialectally colored zones, on the other hand, have been by no means unusual. Consider the following propositions, outlined in terms of a hypothetical chain of events.

### A Hypothetical Case of Reapportioned Dialect Zones

### Stage I: An initial pattern of stable dialects

There existed — say, in some roughly square-shaped peninsula[1] at a moment identifiable as Phase I — four sharply profiled sectors, to be known as A, B, C, and D, whose administrative, cultural, and linguistic centers (*a*, *b*, *c*, and *d*) were located on opposite seashores, i.e., at a considerable distance from one another (see Fig. 1), a geographic configuration favoring a steadily rising degree of differentiation between the respective dialects α, β, γ, δ. These dialects, let us further assume, pertained to the same language (originally transplanted onto peninsular soil from some other territory not necessarily contiguous) and remained, to the end of Phase I, mutually intelligible.

## Stage II: The shift to a new center

Let us next suppose that centuries later, through some cataclysmic events, the political, socio-economic, and ecclesiastic quadripartition of the imaginary peninsula was eroded and eventually collapsed, and that there arose — marking the advent of Phase II — a new, vigorously thriving unit E, encompassing the "backwoods" districts of the four original sectors, and governed from a new capital city $e$, as roughly suggested by Fig. 2.

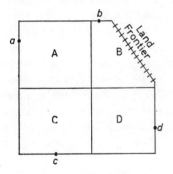

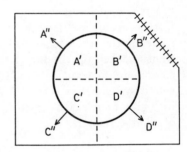

FIG. 1. Phase I                        FIG. 2. Phase II

The question is: What will the gradually emergent dialect ε, peculiar to the territory newly carved out from the shambles of Zones A, B, C, and D, probably look like?

*The determinants of dialectal leveling.* Much as a new society was bound to evolve, through conflation in those four mutually abutting corners of the original sectors A, B, C, D which came under the sway of the new political entity E, so the subdialects pertaining to them reversed, through the interplay of new pressures, the previous course of gradual differentiation and began to coalesce. (These corners shall be known as A′, B′, C′, D′, and their respective sub-dialects as α′, β′, γ′, δ′.) In many respects these subdialects, at the critical moment of reorientation, were still identical or, at least, very much alike; the analysis revolves far less around these features of identity than around the leveling of the relatively few discrepancies.

In this process, seldom brought to any successful, definitive conclusion, one can isolate several determining factors. First, granted the new capital city *e* lay in the territory C', the prestige value of that area's subdialect (γ') is likely to have risen commensurately, and its speakers may have imposed certain idiosyncrasies of their speech, especially those of the phonological and inflectional order, on their less highly regarded neighbors, by virtue not of linguistic supersiority, but of sheer external supremacy. Second, certain characteristic ingredients of the lexicon (e.g., such as relate to the configuration of the terrain, to agricultural products, to plants and animals restricted to sharply bounded habitats) may have been exclusively peculiar to, say, the underprivileged Zone B', while the inhabitants of the other zones at issue, familiar with the words and their referents only from hearsay, may have, without any inhibition, adopted those initially local forms for use on a larger scale. The less operative these factors rooted in the speakers' status and in the geographic spread of certain things spoken of, the better the chances for purely linguistic considerations to come into play. If subdialect δ' boasts the tightest sound system, then this dual advantage of economy and symmetry may give it a decisive edge over the remaining subdialects, regardless of all other factors.

*Retardatory factors in leveling.* On close inspection, dialectal leveling turns out to operate with varying speed and efficiency; under certain circumstances it even threatens to come to a complete standstill. The retardatory forces are in part narrowly linguistic, in part broadly societal (sparseness and superficiality of contacts, and the like).

To revert to our model, let us assume that within the incipient unit E, the inhabitants of Sector A' use consistently one phoneme (for instance, /ž/), where those of Sector B' favor another (say, the palatal lateral /ʎ/). Such a one-to-one correspondence is likely to ensue where all respective occurrences of /ž/ and /ʎ/ are traceable to a single source in the ancestral language. Under these sharply profiled circumstances, the chances for /ž/, as a result of dialect mixture, to yield to /ʎ/, or the reverse, are excellent. The specific direction of the shift may, in the last analysis, be subliminally determined by the phonological advantage of one phoneme over the other (thus, the preëxistence of /š/ all over the territory of E would invite the rapid spread, over the same expanse, of its voiced counterpart, /ž/; contrariwise, widespread coexistence of /n/ and /ɲ/ would favor the sweeping generalization of /λ/ alongside /l/). Or again, the direction may be conditioned by the social inequality of the groups of speakers involved, the rule being the adoption, by the lower classes, of the greatly admired middle-class or upper-class standard. Most intricate is the case of a decision resting on a hidden phonological foundation, but lending itself, at the same time, to a social rationalization on a higher level of awareness. But, whichever particular course the events may follow, the general prospects for the final attainment of complete uniformity remain excellent throughout. Here indeed it would be legitimate to expect a perfect display of *Ausnahmslosigkeit.*

By way of contrast, imagine, under the joint "roof" of E, the following relation between subdialects β' and γ' at the outset of Stage II: The former had by then lost its primary intervocalic /d/, whereas the latter had preserved it. At first contact between the two subdialects, deflected from their earlier course of reciprocal aloofness, a certain degree of intermingling of rival forms must have ensued, a process which in this case — quite unlike those just adduced — fell short of disclosing any clear-cut prevalence of one mode over another. The reason for this atypical behavior: Though subdialect β', as here visualized, lacked, I repeat, any trace of primary /d/, it nevertheless included — a new assumption on our part — numerous examples of secondary /d/ (derived from, say, the intervocalic /t/ of the parent language), so that all over the territory of B' indigenous /-d-/ (from /-t-/) and imported /-d-/ (acquired through infiltration from Zone C') became inextricably enmeshed. There occurred, then, no subsequent recoil from the initial confusion at first contact.

*Dialect mixture and weak phonetic change.* Any clashes between parallel sound developments left unresolved (for purely linguistic reasons) in the wake of some dialect mixture (itself essentially a demographic process) are bound to lead to a state of extra-low predictability for any specific development involving the feature left in abeyance. For this situation the label "WEAK PHONETIC CHANGE" — by no means incompatible with the assumption of regular phonological change in a stable, homogeneous society — has lately been proposed; the situation of insecurity may be aggravated by several concomitants. For it is highly probable, though the hypothesis has not yet been statistically underpinned, that in an area permeated by such currents of flux — set in motion by an unstable population — certain forces normally held in check are unleashed and thus tend to add to the confusion. Possibly as many as four discrete categories of such interferences with normal sound development can be set off:

(a) Morphological, especially inflectional, impingement on regular sound change. The interference can be either retardatory or accelerative, depending on whether the paradigm of a noun or of a verb produces a blocking effect on an impending sound change or, inversely, sets a precedent on which a sound shift (typically one of minor scope) can be modeled;

(b) So-called sporadic or saltatory sound shifts, whose character and status in the hierarchy of linguistic changes is notoriously controversial. Thus, it has been remarked that almost all instances of dissimilation lend themselves, on second thought, to some different diachronic interpretation, no less cogent. A slightly divergent way of describing this indisputably disturbing state of affairs is to affirm that dissimilation is most clearly observable where its agency coincides with some preëxistent disturbance, ordinarily traceable to phonic fluctuation;

(c) Lexical contamination (through folk etymology, blend, etc.). The flux helps speakers to overcome the restraint that ordinarily hampers the workings of their imagination;

(d) Such elusive processes as flight from homonymy, avoidance of polysemy, expressive orchestration, and the like. The stumbling-block here consists in the fact that certain languages, or certain phases in the evolution of a single language, are far more resistant to this search for increased effectiveness, or for escape from ineffectiveness, than are others. If one risks the contention that phonetic flux, attributable to demographic displacements, acts in such contexts as a catalyst and stimulates retreats from harmful homonymy, polysemy, or semantic voidness, then the hidden factor spelling the difference between the success of these efforts in some languages and their relative failure in others may very well have been identified.

Under the circumstances it should cause little surprise to discover that in the newly constituted Zone E, predictably rich in not-fully-reconciled "drifts", the incidence of morphological intrusion, saltatory sound shift, lexical merger, and therapeutic reaction to homonymy was much higher than in the original sectors A, B, C, and D.

## Stage III: Fanlike expansion of the new center

Pursuing further the imaginary course of events in our model peninsula, we can posit as the third evolutionary stage the fanning-out, in all directions, of the aggressive political entity confined originally to Zone E (see Fig. 3). Through this new explosion, the speech habits of that central zone, including the traits assignable to subdialects $\alpha'$, $\beta'$, $\gamma'$, $\delta'$, are now bound to filter through into those territories (to be tagged henceforth as A″, B″, C″, D″) — initially parts of A, B, C, and D — which have not meanwhile been absorbed into E. The subdialects corresponding to these residual zones shall be known as $\alpha''$, $\beta''$, $\gamma''$, and $\delta''$.

To reduce the development to a geometrically regular design, let us (unrealistically) assume that the speech forms of $\alpha'$, in flowing back from their redoubt in the mountainous center toward the

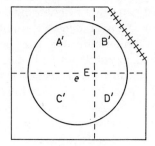

FIG. 3. Phase III.

coastal lowlands, will reach solely the territory of $\alpha''$, etc.; in other words, that $\alpha'$, despite the likelihood of powerful lateral pressures, will be prevented from establishing any direct contact with $\beta''$, and the like. During the gradual rise to hegemony of A′, as part of the nascent unit E, A″ may have politically or economically stagnated, or may have succumbed to military occupation by some invader from across the sea, or else may have fallen under the cultural spell of some foreign, extrapeninsular power. Accordingly, the so-far-neglected subdialect $\alpha''$ may have become shot through with lexical or even phonological and grammatical borrowings. But once the analyst has removed that misleading veneer, the dialect's kernel clearly recognizable under the motley surface may reveal the very same archaic features that were so characteristic of Stage I, whereas subdialect $\alpha'$, through the interplay of forces already isolated, may very well show an incomparably livelier, less predictable development. As α′ and α″, here chosen as mere representatives of the four matching pairs, relentlessly converge and blend through the dynamics of new events, the various innovating features of α′ (including secondary and tertiary reactions to them, such as dissimilation, escape from harmful homonymy, etc.) and the archaizing features of α″ jointly form a bizarre tapestry of incongruities. In much the same way the corresponding societies of the coastal strips included descendants of long-time local dwellers who had never bothered to move away, not even under catastrophic conditions, and the children of "re-migrants" ( = *Rückwanderer*)—undeniably an odd and highly explosive ethnic amalgam.

*Chains of internal upheavals* versus *successions of external interference*. This very schematic presentation of an, all told, single episode — the collapse of a rigidified pattern of neighboring cognate dialects and its subsequent replacement by a dynamic, multipronged movement spreading from a new center born in an area once underprivileged — may appear to abound in subtleties and otiose, artificial complications. Actually, the reconstructed sequence of events involves a CRUDE OVERSIMPLIFICATION of a typical chain reaction in real life.

In terms of linguistic processes, no mention at all has so far been made of the crucially important morphological adjustments, brought about in the wake of sound shifts, through the workings of analogy; and severe restraint has been exercised vis-à-vis certain processes recalcitrant to rigorous analysis or presumably marginal to the main stream of transformations (sound symbolism, hypercharacterization). In terms of social phenomena, one can readily imagine the motley societal and linguistic pattern of the hypothetic peninsula if its development were to be pictured as a long succession of such jolts and subsequent attempts at territorial reapportionment, with yesteryear's no-man's-lands emerging periodically as new centers. One fact would particularly add to the variegated effect of the cultural "surface": As the re-zoning would repeat itself over and over again, in cycles as it were, there would scarcely be any need for the peninsula to remain consistently quadripartite in its broad social architecture and for its rapidly changing centers either to dot monotonously the coast-lines or to be hidden away in the heartland of the interior. In both respects, all manner of intermediate solutions are possible and, indeed, likely, so that the succession of superimposed patterns would tend to produce the impression of rough-edgedness and irregularity.

But quite apart from this incessant variation upon the intrinsic geometric design one must reckon with altogether different categories of tremors and of subsequent attempts at reshuffling property and at gerrymandering boundaries. Our peninsula, by definition, is accessible to peaceful infiltrators and warlike conquerors alike, who may be expected to come by land or by sea; and the impact of their external infringements will of necessity differ vastly from any effects of purely domestic upheavals. We incline, in fact, to appeal to this category of concussion to justify the assumed initial differentiation — not yet accounted for — of the peninsula's four congener dialects α, β, γ, and δ.

Whether or not our peninsula had been inhabited from time immemorial (the presence of homogeneous and especially of heterogeneous groups of aborigines would only increase, but not necessarily create, the complexity of the situation), we are free to posit its conquest and settlement, before the dawn of history, by colonizers coming from some other country, to be operationally identified as $X$. If this is so, the quadripartite social structure of the peninsula at the earliest stage amenable to observation might be traced to several neatly isolable causes, or, far more plausibly, to one out of several conceivable combinations of such causes. The differences acting as determinants may have lain in (a) the varying occupation dates (the language of $X$, like any other, being itself steadily on the move); (b) the dissimilar length and safety of communication lanes between the metropolis and the colonies; (c) the divergent status of the peninsula's moribund or extinct indigenous languages and other social institutions; (d) the noncomparable social classes and degrees of literacy of the settlers attracted; (e) the irreconcilable characters of the several administrative machineries set up (military vs. civil; with or without the participation of the natives or of their descendants); (f) the spectrum of attitudes of those conquered and possibly enslaved toward their new masters, on the local scene and in the far-off metropolis of $X$; (g) the degrees of proximity (in terms of geographic distance and of cultural affinity) of some rival magnets, e.g., the insular outposts of a certain sea power then in the ascendant; (h) the extent of social and linguistic cohesion of the occupying forces, as distinct from their military amalgamation.

D

*Intricacies of social stratification.* We have so far been chiefly concerned with large-scale shifts of the population, of political frontiers, of administrative centers, and the like, without paying close attention to the internal stratification of the hypothetical society. Yet the patterns of such layers can play a decisive rôle, especially where a certain linguistic feature, or an ensemble of such features, spread without concurrent demographic displacements.

Let us assume that at some point postdating the events previously described, the peninsula, on one count of its linguistic behavior, splits into parts. Let the west favor word-initial /č/ where the east steadfastly maintains the /pl/ cluster (bequeathed by the ancestral language), while a corner of the extreme north stands alone in preferring /λ/. Let us next argue that, through a turn of the wheel of fortune, the /λ/ pronunciation, once deemed strictly provincial, pushes back the /pl/ zone and drives a deep wedge into the /č/ territory, with all upper and middle classes, from the ducal court down, succumbing one by one to the lure of the elegant /λ/ where it lends itself to easy substitution for the rejected /č/. Only the utterly illiterate groups of sheepherders, fisherfolk, and farmhands may be expected to show such a stubborn indifference to socio-linguistic self-improvement as not to heed the advantage of a speedy switch from /č-/ to /λ-/. Is it not likely, under these circumstances, that certain words known almost exclusively in these underprivileged milieus (for species of small fish used as bait, for unmarketable herbs, berries, and similar items of rural economy, for inconspicuous tools, especially if crude and self-made) should here survive for centuries with the indigenous /č/, originally restricted in their scope to low-class speakers? In some cases the words bearing this imprint of rusticity will eventually seep back into the surrounding standard language (especially if that language has a /č/ of its own, extracted from some different source), destined to confuse the future students of historical phonology. The temporary shelter of an isolated social dialect has exempted them from immediate participation in a linguistic fashion, but more often than not only the trained analyst, not the ordinary speakers, will recognize their quaintness in retrospect and will set them apart, at first blush, as "exceptions".

What complicates immeasurably the diachronic study of social dialects is the fact that of the most noteworthy among them we lack records and cannot expect to discover any, simply because the spontaneous utterances of those untutored speakers fell short of the long-obligatory standard of conventionality — the steep price that had to be paid for costly perpetuation of fluid speech through written records.

## Two Functions of Schematization

What is the advantage of the schematic, quasi-mathematical approach here advocated? To begin with, let me emphasize that this approach is not at all recommended as a substitute for the time-honored historical reconstruction, but as a mere adjunct or concomitant. By virtue of the abstractness inherent in it, it can perform two rôles for which the more circumstantial kind of full-fledged historical inquiry seems to qualify not nearly so well.

First, schematization can feed back the gist of methodological information obtained by dedicated language historians into the pool of ever mobile linguistic theory. Experience teaches us that, unless bold countermeasures are taken, historical research, left to itself, tends spontaneously to become ponderous and cumbersome, simply because there is no limit to the accumulation of factual details, directly or indirectly useful, short of the actual absence of requisite raw data; and, where fluctuation is studied, the observer's concern with every minute departure from the expected standard threatens to swell the material doubly and triply. Ironically, not to say pathetically, the small dosage of fresh information that students of general linguistics have of late absorbed in their slow advance along the line of diachronic inquiry has been from sources known for offering only fragmentary, sorely deficient documentation. Conversely, the storehouse of splendid Romance monographs has left a disappointingly weak impact on general linguistics, chiefly (one gathers) as a result of these studies' almost excessive specificness and of their authors' well-nigh irritating meticulosity — features which make it painfully difficult even for the highly trained outsider to extrapolate such nuggets of information as transcend the scope of the particular problem at issue and might be applied to other, utterly different collections of data. Controlled simplification, achieved by an expert, enables the sophisticated nonspecialist to recognize at a glance the configuration of the chosen problem and the bare contour of the novel solution proposed.

Second — and, on balance, probably more thought-provoking —, schematization may be heuristic. Acting as an eye-opener, it can help the analyst to identify, on the purely theoretical plane, evolutionary problems not yet recognized by the teams toiling in archives or laboratories, and may induce the *détailliste*, heavily armed with erudition, but notoriously exposed to the hazards of shortsightedness, to probe with a fresh supply of zest these issues, newly isolated and labeled.

The working with models temporarily relieves the explorer of certain onerous obligations (e.g., of the need to pay constant attention to distracting details characteristic of societies in flux or to engage in time-consuming bibliographic research); for a while it frees his mind and channels his cognition in the direction of, dynamically speaking, essentials. In this manner, hidden possibilities of interaction between discrete forces can sometimes be visualized for the first time. At a later date, the wisdom of such assumptions can be tested by application of the schema to ensembles of interlocking circumstances operative in actual linguistic change, i.e., to a set of situations necessarily far more complex than are the initial schemata.

## NOTE

[1] Though the imaginary peninsula — both in its static geographic configuration and in the dynamics of its demographic and linguistic evolution —unmistakably bears a measure of resemblance to the Iberian Peninsula, it can at best pass off as its idealized or stylized version. One of the salient differences between traditional historical grammar and glottodynamics, a discipline whose potentialities we have just begun to adumbrate, lies precisely in the fact that glottodynamics, as the more abstract and general variety, leaves ample room for imaginary trajectories. To this extent it resembles studies and exercises in descriptive linguistics that operate with nonexistent languages. As it grows in sophistication, it may also develop a certain affinity for the kind of models dramatized by the latest vogue of logico-mathematical linguistics.

The following bibliographic hints, referring to some of my own monographic studies, must consequently be taken with a grain of salt. On the problem examined in the section *The Determinants of Dialectal Leveling* see 1962; on the evidence of homonymy, 1952; on hypercharacterization, 1957 and 1958; on morphological interference with the regularity of sound change, associated with a situation of fluid speech communities, 1960, especially pp. 345 f. in relation to the present paper; on numerous other problems here touched upon, 1963 and 1964.

## REFERENCES CITED

1952 "Studies in Hispano-Latin Homonymics", *Lg.*, XXVIII, 299–338.

1957–58 "Diachronic Hypercharacterization in Romance", *ArL*, IX, 79–113; X, 1–30.

1960 "Paradigmatic Resistance to Sound Change", *Lg.*, XXXVI, 281–346.

1962 "Weak Phonetic Change, Spontaneous Sound Shift, Lexical Contamination", *Lingua*, XI, 263–275.

1963–64 "The Interlocking of Narrow Sound Change, Broad Phonological Pattern, Level of Transmission, Areal Configuration, Sound Symbolism", *ArL*, XV, 144–173; XVI, 1–33.

# 3

# Weak Phonetic Change,
# Spontaneous Sound Shift,
# Lexical Contamination

**1. Three phenomena chosen for joint analysis.** Linguists of
different persuasions, concerned with improving their methodologies,
have lately tended to establish the neatest possible distinctions between certain categories of change and certain levels of synchronic
arrangement. After an acceptable rule for discriminating between
these layers has been laid down, it remains to build connecting links
between them, so as to arrive at a tidily architectured total edifice.
In synchronic research, continued efforts in this direction have
lately been so numerous and, on the whole, so successful as to be
almost taken for granted. On the diachronic side, which offers
problems of far greater complexity, scholars, after much initial
confusion, have learned how to separate dissimilar processes, but are
just beginning to master the art of ultimate synthesis. We shall here
focus attention on three phenomena seldom subjected to joint
analysis: (a) a certain variety of "regular" phonetic change, (b) spontaneous or saltatory or panchronic sound shift, and (c) lexical
contamination, in an effort to determine possible connections between
them.

**2.1. Typical phonetic changes; qualification of their regularity.**
The phonetic change, which Sapir, in one of his most suggestive
metaphors, likened to a drift, is defined by its uniqueness, i.e., by
its spatial and temporal limitations. Failure of a word to show an
expected change of this kind commonly allows the linguist to declare
it non-indigenous and, by the same token, to assign it to a late
stratum of the lexicon. Most scholars have operated with two

Reprinted from *Lingua*, XI (1962) 263–275 (= *Studia Gratulatoria* A. W. de
Groot).

postulates, which indeed seem acceptable if properly qualified. First, phonetic changes tend to be "regular", to the extent that they occur in clearly delimited speech communities. Since, in reality, most such communities are markedly fluid, "irregularities" inevitably seep through. Second, phonetic changes tend to be mutually conditioned, a cluster of simultaneous (or nearly simultaneous) changes or else a chain reaction being the rule rather than the exception. Again, powerful counter-forces (asymmetry of speech organs, cultural conservatism) may block this interaction, loosening the threads between the phonemes or even completely cutting some of them. The result of the former hindrance may be designated as a "weak" sound change; the latter obstacle, which will not be further examined in this context, may produce an unintegrated sound shift.

**2.2. Varying degrees of predictability.** Possibly no point of linguistic theory has been discussed so passionately and dogmatically as the perplexing contrast between the ideal regularity and actual (or apparent) irregularity, i.e., unpredictability, of sound change. The question as to whether this long-drawn-out debate has been predominantly fruitful or sterile is here not at issue. The almost theological furor of the altercation has drowned out some less conspicuous, but surely not less promising, lines of discussion. Whichever reasons we care to adduce for this variation, a seemingly unobjectionable procedure enables us to measure the ACTUAL OUTCOMES of given sounds and sound groups on a scale of relative predictability. The change, in the core vocabulary of Old French, of L. ū to /ü/, under any conditions, and of L. A to a phoneme conceivably best marked /æ/, under restricted conditions, or the voicing — and ultimate spirantization — of Hispano-Latin voiceless stops in intervocalic position exemplify transformations of a very high degree of predictability. At the opposite extreme, the distribution of OSp. -ç- /-z-̦- as products of [tj] and related groups, the development of syllable-final L. L (Sp. *alto* 'high' vs. *ot-ero* 'elevation', Sp. *polvo* vs. OPtg. *poo* >*pó* 'dust', pl. 'powder'), the outcomes of initial clusters such as L. CL-, FL-, PL- (CLĀUE > Sp. *llave*, Ptg. *chave* 'key' vs. CLĀUU > Sp. *clavo*, Ptg. *cravo* 'nail'), and the partial preservation, in Ibero-Romance, of voiced intervocalic Latin stops, especially of -D- (NĪDU 'nest' > Sp. *nío* beside *nido*), all four display an exceedingly low degree of regularity. Microscopic inspection tends to reduce the area of uncertainty, showing, e.g., that the chances of preservation for -*d*- increase the

farther east one moves, short of the Catalan zone, and that the -ç-
may be as characteristic of medieval western dialects as was the
-z- of Old Aragonese (cor-açón 'heart', peçón or peçonha 'poison' vs.
corazón, pozón). Despite such slight advances, the results attained
seem unsatisfactory, and some investigations once deemed attractive
(e.g., the study of Old Spanish sibilants) have in recent years been
almost entirely abandoned. Occasionally, we succeed, by hindsight
(as it were), in offering plausible lexical reasons for the eventual
prevalence of one of two or three recorded or reconstructed variants.[1]
Yet such discoveries, however gratifying, explain mere details of
the ultimate apportionment of resources rather than their initial
generation. Neither does the familiar supposition of dialect mixture
serve as a suitable concluding argument, though it may represent a
stop gap. The statement that Tusc. *strada* 'road' — to select one from
among scores of similar words — is necessarily classifiable as an im-
portation from the north, just because its -*d*- < L. -T- shows erratic
development, involves a dangerous logical circularity unless one is
in a position to demonstrate, on the strength of independent cultural
evidence, that the Tuscans had overwhelmingly powerful reasons for
associating common roads with their northern neighbors' territory
rather than with their own. If decisive proof cannot be furnished —
and in most instances all endeavors to this effect have been of little
or no avail —, there remains the suspicion that some hidden internal
reason may have prompted Tuscans to strengthen the meager supply
of their own voiced stops via culturally unmotivated or weakly
motivated lexical borrowing. We dimly recognize the possibility of
such alternatives, but are still unprepared to tackle concrete problems
in these terms, just as the relation between frequency (both paradigmatic or lexical, and syntagmatic or contextual) and regularity of
phonetic change, with special reference to individual phonemes and
to broader patterns, has not yet been thoroughly explored.

---

[1] Thus, OSp. *plañir* 'to wail' < PLANGERE (instead of *\*llañir*) beside *llanto*
'wailing' < PLANCTU may illustrate the tendential avoidance of two syllable-
initial palatals in close succession. *Llave* as against *clavo* (and their similarly
polarized Portuguese counterparts) show a lexically advantageous padding of the
originally slight contrast between two distantly cognate words no longer semantically associated; the preference given to learned CL- in the word designating a 'nail'
may betray the latter concept's ecclesiastic implications. Sp. *flor* (beside topon.
*Llor-edo*) and Ptg. *flor*, orig. *fror* (beside *chor-ume* 'fat, abundance'), as generics,
tend to perpetuate the more learned variants, and Gallo-Rom. *flo(u)r* may, for
culturally transparent reasons (cf. Sp. *vergel* 'flower garden' < OF *vergier*; also
Sp. < F. *jardin*), have here acted as a concomitant.

**2.3. Operational advantages of the qualifier "weak".** The usefulness, then, of introducing a provisional term like "weak" phonetic change amounts to this: Without formally committing the analyst to any definitive stand on the exact reason(s) for the varying recurrence of expected phonetic changes — and without blocking his quest, or blunting his curiosity, for additional information on a matter so elusive —, this makeshift label for a frequent real-life situation allows him to start probing at once any possible interplay between, on the one hand, a fairly scant yield of regular sound correspondences and, on the other, miscellaneous sporadic sound shifts and lexical aberrancies. In simpler words, it prevents him from bogging down at a disadvantageous point of his inquiry and maintains the momentum of his advance, at the cost of saddling him with a term not fully explicated.

**3. Clashing measures of concern with spontaneous sound shifts.** Few points of linguistic change occupy a position as precarious within the total edifice of contemporary doctrine as do "spontaneous" sound shifts. The difficulty is threefold: Scholars are in sharp disagreement regarding (1) the label to be attached to the phenomenon, (2) the range of processes to be subsumed under an appropriate label, (3) the place to be assigned to the whole in formal presentation of historical grammar, i.e., its nature. Add the fact that some linguists have displayed very definite concern with, and others an equally discernible indifference toward, this set of problems. The extremes are exemplified, on the one hand, by M. Grammont, not only in his thesis on consonantal dissimilation (1895), but also in the core section, "Les grands phénomènes d'évolution phonétique" (183–373), of his masterly *Traité* (1933); and, on the other, that same year, by L. Bloomfield who, in less than two meager pages appended to Chap. XXI ("Types of phonetic change") of his manual, counter to his general nomenclatural leanings refused to propose a common denominator for a mere half-dozen isolated processes: phonetic change through other than gradual alteration of phonemic units, dissimilation (including dissimilatory loss), assimilation at a distance, metathesis, and haplology.

**3.1. Alternative labels.** Nothing characterizes more eloquently the protracted state of confusion than the fact that numerous scholars (G. Baist and J. Cornu in 1906; M. L. Wagner in 1941; and, I repeat, a theorist of Bloomfield's rank) discussed facets of the general problem without once bothering to identify it, unless it be the paradox that some experts speak of "fenómenos especiales" (Menéndez Pidal, 1904, 1908), "changements particuliers" (Grammont in his posthumous Greek phonology [1948]; note the contrast to the *Traité*), while others favor as their frame of reference some such irreconcilably opposed term as "allgemeine Gesetze der Behandlung der Laute" (P. Förster, 1880), "allgemeine Erscheinungen" (J. Huber, 1933), echoing G. I. Ascoli's classic "accidenti generali" (1873). A still older division of all sound changes into qualitative and quantitative (epenthesis obviously figures among the latter), championed by H. Schuchardt (1867), has apparently found no advocates. Two successful qualifiers, over the years, have been "spontaneous" (in E. Schwan as early as 1893; A. Kuhn, in 1935, showed a dialect geographer's greater explicitness: "phenomena lacking any focal point") and "sporadic" (F. Hanssen, 1910, who seemed to prefer "springend" in view of the lack of transition; cf. Bloomfield's Point 1; also E. B. Williams, 1938, who, despite his attention to details, failed to define the broad category). J. Ronjat, in his monumental Occitanian grammar, spoke of "Inductions au contact et à distance".

**3.2. Contrasting scopes and finer distinctions.** The insecurity just observed reflects only in part the linguists' general propensity to coin fresh terms or to assign new functions to those inherited from an earlier generation. A more important contributing factor has been the widely varying scope assigned to spontaneous sound changes. Ascoli subsumed under "accidenti generali" a fairly neat assortment of shifts, including displacement of accent, assimilation, dissimilation, apheresis, "eclipsis" (= syncope) and apocope, pro(s)thesis, epenthesis, "epithesis" (= paragoge), metathesis, and attraction. Other scholars have, for the most part, assembled fewer items, among them one or another excluded from Ascoli's list. Thus, Baist (1888, 1906) grouped (a) prosthesis, resolutions of the Latin and the Spanish hiatus, accent shift, beside attraction into the stressed syllable and (b) echoing of a word-initial nasal with all manner of epenthesis stimulated by a medial consonant, metathesis, haplology, beside shortening in formulaic address. In those same years, Cornu treated in separate chapters, though in close succession, (a) metathesis and (b) a variety of "euphonic phenomena" including antihiatic semivowels, svarabhakti (= anaptyxis), also miscellaneous epentheses classed by consonant $(v, b, g)$ and locus. The understanding of sporadic sound change was temporarily retarded by unwarranted association with other processes involving a measure of "unpredictability": lexical blend, confusion of prefixes, folk etymology, sandhi (syntactic phonology), even doublets and homonymy. One finds vestiges of these tentative rapprochements from P. Förster to E. B. Williams; Menéndez Pidal distinguishes between "influence of neighboring sounds" and "influence of one word on another", but discusses them consecutively in a single chapter. The involvement of free variation ("equivalencia acústica") is a characteristic of the Spanish school extended to the work of non-native Hispanists (Kuhn). The main stream of events, however, led to the growing realization that mere proximity at a certain distance and immediate contiguity constitute radically different situations; as regards assimilation, only the former involves sporadic change (Bloomfield). The neatest line of demarcation was drawn by Grammont (1933), who opposed one triad of "sounds in contact" (assimilation, differentiation, interversion) to another triad of non-contiguous sounds (dilation, dissimilation, metathesis).[2] Much of his precise thinking and novel terminology spilled over into Ronjat's exhaustive analysis. Further refinement prompted scholars to discriminate between change and total loss (in dissimilation), between the involvement of a mere sound and of a whole syllable (e.g., "syllabic superposition"), between simple transfer and dual exchange (in metathesis), between anticipation and echoing (in epenthesis), between preventive and *post-factum* reaction, between transposition and penetration (in Grammont's interversion), between dissimilatory loss of a syllable at a morphemic boundary and within a morpheme (hapaxepy).

### 3.3. The place assignable to spontaneous changes. Neither in traditional handbooks nor in more experimental monographic ventures does there exist any fixed place where one can confidently expect to find a survey of this kind of sound shifts. One ever-present possibility is to discover some hints of them preceding the treatment

[2] I cannot begin to enumerate, still less to discuss, here all the individual shades and variations of opinion, starting with Schuchardt's highly unorthodox *Vokalismus*. But the section "Isolated changes" in Chap. III of E. H. Sturtevant's *Linguistic Change* (Chicago, 1917) must be singled out for its ill-assorted documentation and the weakness of the argument, even by contemporary standards — a weakness more conspicuous than E. P. Hamp would lead the present-day reader to anticipate in his Introduction to the book's new printing in the Phoenix series (Chicago, 1961), p. ix.

of regular sound correspondences (Förster); another, distinctly more widespread, is to see them appended to phonology proper, overtly (Cornu, Huber, Kuhn, Williams) or tacitly (P. Delattre, *PMLA*, LXI [1946], 7–41), sometimes, we recall, in the close vicinity of sandhi alone (Cornu, §§ 253–298: "Kontraktion oder Zusammenziehung"; Ronjat, II, 418–449: "Le mot dans la phrase") or of sandhi plus other anomalies, such as infantile formations and partially assimilated foreignisms (Wagner, §§ 374–485). Within Menéndez Pidal's hierarchy, I repeat, they occupy a higher rank, in rather strange company, but again midway between phonology and morphology. It is not uncommon for an analyst to examine some of these erratic shifts in the wake of normal vocalic changes, and the rest under consonants; the dividing line is easy enough to trace (Baist, Hanssen). In his Greek phonology Grammont went one step further in this trend toward fragmentation: He focused on consonant dissimilation in a section of the subchapter on liquids, reserved for assimilation and "differentiation" a separate subchapter ("Changements particuliers") of the elaborate chapter on consonants, and grouped metathesis with nasal infix, syntactic phonology, and syllabic superposition (344–387) under an entirely unorthodox major division of his treatise ("Le mot", 327–415). Over against this maximum explicitness and assurance stands a mature Bloomfield's stirring doubt: "Changes like these are very different from those which are covered by the assumption of [regular] sound-change; it is possible that they are akin rather to the types of linguistic change which we have still to consider — analogic change and borrowing". True, the opposite view has also been voiced, particularly in the camp of antineogrammarians, to the effect that the two categories of change are separated by a difference of degree rather than of essence.

**3.4. Possibilities of improved integration.** On all these controversial matters, the actual diversity of opinions is many times greater than would follow from such random samplings. For our immediate purposes, however, the simplest procedure is to ignore the hidden roots and ultimate affinities of sporadic sound shift and to concentrate on its typical surface manifestations — by and large those which Ascoli's keen eye recognized ninety years ago. Is it possible to free these shifts from their apparent isolation and, at the same time, to qualify somewhat their disturbingly panchronic, omnipresent character? For decades, the joint operation of dissimilation, metathesis, etc., on the one hand, and of associative lexical interferences, on the other, has been observed with growing frequency; their simultaneous impact is particularly noticeable in the Romance nasal insert, quite different in its origin and agency from the IE nasal infix (cf. *NRFH*, IX, 240 f., 266–273). Tentative ways and means have been proposed for integrating "acoustic equivalence" in the total design of sound changes (*Lg.*, XXX, 142–146). In recent lectures (apparently left unpublished), the late A. Sommerfelt, using Celtic and Scandinavian illustrations, confirmed the expected close ties between the configuration of a specific sound system and the speakers' preferences for certain spontaneous shifts. On the other hand, woefully little attention has been paid to the possibility of a significant interplay between "weak" phonetic changes and spontaneous sound shifts:[3] Since weakness in the former, very plausibly, sets in motion fluctuations, which, in turn, give rise to numerous variants, the latter stand conspicuously good chances of thriving unopposed.

**4. Lexical associative processes.** Lexical associative processes are often examined in grammars against the distant background of phonic conditions, but the etymologist worth his salt is tempted to start from the lexical units, to the point of endowing them — metaphorically — with a measure of initiative ("the word penetrates a barrier, extends to a region, allies itself with a partner, dislodges a rival, splits into two, acquires a meaning, casts off a derivative", etc.). Except in homonymic conflicts, regular and, in particular, desultory sound shifts are supposed to intervene in "word biographies" as mere concomitants. Ordinarily, linguists assume that semantic polar opposites ('left' ~ 'right', 'black' ~ 'white'), or links of a close-knit chain ('four', 'five', 'six' . . . ; 'Monday', 'Tuesday', 'Wednesday' . . .), or near-synonyms, or else words unrelated in meaning but of strikingly similar outward configuration are most likely to influence one another. Less obvious conflations may be due to the exploitation of a humorous situation, to the abrupt avoidance of taboo and bothersome homonymy or polysemy, to pseudo-etymological titillation (G. Gougenheim's "fausse étymologie

---

[3] One reason for this lack of liaison has been the fact that scholars of very different training, temperament, and bent of intellectual curiosity have concerned themselves with these two types of transmutation. In the rare instances where the same scholar achieved distinction along both lines (M. Grammont, A. Alonso), he accomplished this, as a rule, at widely separated stages of his growth.

savante"), to the migration of a word from language to language or from a dialect into the standard, and the like. If the image of a word surrounded by its regional variants, or that of the head of a family circled by its direct and indirect derivatives can be projected with microscopic detail onto a plane, the outer periphery of the projection will, with but a few exceptions, be occupied by "contaminated" members marking the transition to a neighboring word or word-family.[4]

Now, it should be possible for the explorer to invert the perspective, at least on an experimental basis, to wrest the initiative from the words and to assign it, upon occasion, to "weak" phonetic changes or to sporadic sound shifts which, in some instances, may have acted as stimulants and have thus become primarily responsible for a reshuffling of linguistic elements. For a variety of reasons, L. -NS- > -s- and -NF-, -NV- > -f-, -v- (OSp. *mesa, yfante*) represented weak changes in the development from Latin to Western Romance, and the resulting fluctuation (Late L. OCCANSIO 'occasion, incident', THENSAURUS 'treasure') may have been the chief reason for the amalgam, in Spanish and Portuguese, of Gr.-L. CAMPSĀRE 'to dodge, eschew, circumnavigate' [kansˈare] and iterative QUASSĀRE 'to shake' (from QUATIŌ -ERE), which at a certain stage tended to be pronounced [kasˈare], cf. QUATT(U)-ORDECIM > Sp. *catorce*.

**5. Epenthesis and weak phonetic change.** Let me now provide a few sketchy examples of the assumed interactions. The derivation of Sp. *peldaño* 'step (of a staircase)', a synonym of *escalón* and *grada*, from L. PEDĀNEU 'pertaining to the foot', has caused serious difficulty, leading astray even expert etymologists, especially since *peaña* (beside lately more common *peana*) 'base, pedestal, stand', from the corresponding feminine PEDĀNEA, offers no comparable stumbling block. True, scholars have ferreted out a few isolated instances of epenthetic *l* before voiced dental stop, or near-stop, as in OSp. *cada(l)-día* 'every day', OPtg. *esco(l)drinhar* 'to scrutinize' (reflecting a verb cast off by SCRŪTINIUM, itself an offshoot of SCRŪTĀRĪ); but these random and more or less remote parallels afford not much of an explanation. However, if one remembers that the ideal Castilian products of PEDĀNEU, namely *\*peaño* beside *\*pedaño*, must have been

---

[4] Examples can be adduced from almost every far-flung lexical family viewed through a battery of microscopes, cf. *PMLA*, LXIV (1949), 578, 584; *RPh.*, I (1947–48), 218–220 and 228–234; *SPh.*, XLVI (1949), 500, etc. Exceptions are fairly rare; one Hispano-Latin family resistant to contamination has been that of PALATIUM, see *PMLA*, LXV (1950), 944–974.

locked in close rivalry throughout neighboring communities, *peldaño* appears in a new light, with *-ld-* acting as a reinforcement of jeopardized *-d-* [ð], in terms of hypercharacterization. In all likelihood, an analogous explanation applies to oscillating *cada(l)día*. The rôle of the *-ld-* cluster as an emphatic substitute for an endangered or unusual simple dental appears independently in the trajectories of Ar. *bayāḍ* > Sp. *albayalde* 'white lead', Ar. *qāḍī* > OSp. *alcalde* beside *al-calld(e)*, *-calle*, *-galde* 'judge' > 'mayor', and Ar. *rabaḍ* > Sp. *arrabal(de)* 'suburb'.[5] Desultory epenthesis of *l* before dental, as in *peldaño*, constitutes, then, a direct consequence of, or rather a reaction against, the locally unsettled legacy of Latin medial -D-.

**6. Dissimilatory loss of a nasal and simplification of consonant clusters.** Any attempt to examine in strict isolation the visibly convergent and interdependent Romance courses of L. -NS-, -NF-, and -NV- would mean an unwarranted relapse into "atomistic" phonology. Yet, despite the common tendency of the three medial clusters to shed the nasal component, the parallelism remains incomplete. While the loss of -N- in -NS- may here and there have been scotched by morphemic boundaries or erudite affectation, it visibly does not depend on the presence of another nasal in the word (MĒNSA > Sp. *mesa* echoes TĒNSU > *t(i)eso* 'taut, tight, stiff'), whereas in the cases of -(N)F- and -(N)V- this latter condition apparently represents one of the prime controlling factors: cf. CONVENTU 'assembly' > OProv. *coven*, F. *couvent* 'convent', INFANTE 'newborn baby' > OSp. *y(f)-* ~ *yn-fante* 'prince', INFERNU 'lower region' > Engad. *ifiern* 'hell'; note also OF *roncin* 'thick-set horse' (> OIt. *runzino*), later *roussin*, beside OProv. (> OSp.) *rocin*, of disputed parentage, in case the controversial base actually was RUNC-. Dissimilatory loss of the nasal, a desultory sound shift, and the simplification of certain dyadic consonant clusters, involving a set of standard correspondences, thus appear inextricably intertwined. The approach here advocated tends to tighten connections between seemingly isolated facts — not exactly along the line of diachronic phonemics — and to cut out a good many loose ends.

**7. Lexical restructuring and weak phonetic change.** Lexical reapportionment too lends itself to smoother integration when

---

[5] One striking parallel: Ind. *ṇ* was rendered in Sogdian (an Iranian language) by *rn*. See É. Benveniste's remarks in *BSLP*, L: 2 (1954), 62.

examined in conjunction with weak phonetic change. Take the case of the crumbled family of MEDEOR -ĒRĪ 'to heal', deprived of its head at the Romance phase and further impaired in Hispano-Romance through the disappearance of MEDICUS except in learned or foreign garb (*médico*; OSp. < OProv.-Cat. *metge, menge*). The two remaining fragments, MEDICĪNA and MEDICĀMINE, appear, at the medieval stage, in very startling disguise, as *melezina* (vars. *med-ezina, -e(s)cina, -icina*, each one step closer to the state of pure "cultismo"; OPtg. *me(e)zinha*) and *vedegambre* (vars. *me-, ve-, ven-, vi-gambre*; OLeon. *b-, v-edegame* [f.]; mod. dial. *verde-, verdi-gambre*), respectively; experts have argued, not inconclusively, that *melezina* presupposes contamination with *miel* 'honey', while *vedegambre* 'drug, poison, hellebore' involves a blend with OSp. *vedar* < VETĀRE or *venino*. Both explanations are attractive and, despite serious criticism aimed at the latter,[6] probably correct, but, presented in anecdotal fashion or as mere footnotes to "sound laws", they hardly tell the full story. While a medical lozenge sugarcoated or bathed in honey makes good sense and a 'forbidden drug' (poison), through a somewhat greater stretch of one's imagination, also can be fitted into a plausible cultural context, the semantic distances between the two partners in each instance of amalgamation are strikingly great. As a result, the posited association appears far-fetched, so long as mutual topical attraction, or intrinsic affinity of human experiences, is viewed as the prime mover. As a rule, lexical changes of this less than obvious sort occur only when there is a powerful indirect motivation for them; in particular this follows from the teachings of dialect geography, as when Gilliéron persuasively demonstrated that the use of 'pheasant' or, facetiously, 'vicar' for 'rooster' in certain sections of southwestern France, far from being attributable to imprecision and playfulness alone, marked the direct consequence of a homonymic clash (latent or temporarily consummated) between the local products of GALLUS 'rooster' and C-, G-ATTUS 'cat'. In the two cases here at issue, the discomfort was of an altogether different order. The

---

[6] For brief orientation see Menéndez Pidal, *Rom.*, XXIX (1900), 374 f.; G. Baist, *KJb.*, VI: 1 (1903–05), 397; W. Meyer-Lübke, *REW* § 5456; V. García de Diego, *Contribución* (Madrid, 1923), § 396; J. Corominas, *DCELC*, IV (1957), 684a–685a, 1089a. For a considerably more searching analysis of the MEDĒRĪ family see my contribution to the *Mélanges M. Bataillon*, a joint French-Brazilian venture, in *Ibérida*, VI (1961[-63]), 127–171. For a counterview in broader perspective, cf. Section 12.5 of my article "Etymology and General Linguistics", *Word*, XVIII (1962), 198–219, an item included in the present volume; see pp. 191f.

E

fluctuation characterizing the use of primary -*d*- (possibly [δ]) must
have led to protracted coexistence, in neighboring villages, if not
households, of *medezina*, \**me(e)zina* (cf. Ptg. *mèzinha*) and \**medegambre*, *me(e)gambre*, so that the seemingly far-fetched blend of the
former group with *miel* and of the latter group with *vedar*, *venino*
carried with it, as chief advantage, not an additional dosage of
conceptual or pictorial spicing, but the elimination of awkward
clusters of variants, neither regionally nor semantically differentiated.
The dual change achieved thus at long last conferred a measure of
stability on the remnants of the MEDĒRĪ family, since in the central
dialects -*l*- and secondary -*d*- (probably [d]), from L. -T-, were not
at all subject to wavering. The fact that *m*- and *v*- are both labials
and that [d] and [δ] are homorganic was certainly a helpful concomitant, but there would be little point in continuing to set up the permu-
tation of initial labials as an unintegrated, autonomous "general
accident". It rather acts as a lubricant facilitating, accelerating shifts
needed for the total economy of the given language.

**8. Three contributing forces at work.** Here is a case further
complicated by the addition of a third contributing force. On the
surface, Sp. *despedir* 'to dismiss, discharge' looks like a trivial compound of *pedir* 'to ask (a favor), request' < PETERE, but a minute
inspection of its core meanings, especially in the older texts ('to
throw, hurl, cast off, emit, exude') makes it highly probable that its
hard kernel is a descendant of EXPEDĪRE 'to disengage, disentangle,
set free, bring forth'; for details see *UCPL*, XI (1954), 40–54, 155–
169. In the west of the peninsula, where Latin intervocalic -D-
disappeared to the point of predictability, EXPEDĪRE produced
(*d*)*espir* 'to strip, bare' without encroaching in the least on the local
fields of PETERE. But in the central dialects characterized by an almost
erratic evolution of -*d*- (contrast *nido* with *caer* and *sabio*) a — morphologically advantageous — merger of EXPEDĪRE and PETERE was, from
the outset, very plausible. When it occurred, it entailed a shift of
emphasis in the semantic structure of *despedir*, the new center of
gravity becoming increasingly 'to give leave', (refl.) 'to take leave'.
At a much later date, the newly consolidated *despedir* spread to the
west, where its partial cognate (*d*)*espir*, semantically remote and
formally aloof, was not in its way. The conclusion to be drawn from
this concatenation of events is that, to account for a conflation, it
would be quite insufficient to measure merely the semantic distance

separating the two words in question — even if a precise assessment of this kind were possible for past linguistic stages. Important (in many instances decisive) supervenient factors include: (a) the readiness of the local dialect to sanction the blend, the trend being to overcome the consequences of weak, inconclusive phonetic change, say, obnoxious wavering between (d)espedir, *(d)espeír, (d)espir, through a helpful link to solidly entrenched pedir; (b) acceptance of the innovation on a larger scale by a bundle of dialects through an ensemble of favorable morphological circumstances, as one may call the fact that EXPEDĪRE, originally a parasynthetic verb, had cut loose from its moorings to PĒS PEDIS 'foot', while PETERE in colloquial Late Latin lacked an important compound in DIS- or EX-, so that pedir and (d)espedir could be most effectively paired off. The difference between melezina-vedegambre and (d)espedir lies, then, in the active intervention of a potent morphological factor in the latter case.[7]

## 9. Ensembles of interlocking causes.
We are thus more and more led to recognize ensembles of interlocking causes at work. Whereas the older historical grammar operated chiefly with alternatives (e.g., substratum influence vs. internal sound change), the explicative grammar of the future, after carefully isolating and defining each force that can possibly have been involved, will start from the assumption that in the overwhelming majority of observable situations there have been at work configurations of contributing forces. The highest attainable level of analysis will then be a systematic inquiry into the tendential complementarity, i.e., coefficiency, or mutual exclusion, of such isolable agencies.

[7] The full titles of several writings alluded to in this paper can be identified through the bibliographic supplement (pp. 148–164) to my article — included in the present volume — "A Tentative Typology of Romance Historical Grammars".

# 4

# Distinctive Traits of Romance Linguistics

### The Scope of the Problem

AT the critical borderline between physical sciences, social sciences, and humanities, general linguistics has become one of the rallying points for particularly ambitious mid-century scholars. Earlier systems of analysis are being appraised and mostly repudiated on the strength of their insufficient applicability to the widest possible range of differently structured languages. Under these conditions, is it feasible and advisable for workers in a neatly bounded subfield of linguistics to strive for limited autonomy, i.e., for their right to use a private scale of values, not incompatible with the broad principles and aims of the chosen science, but neither necessarily identical with such tastes and emotional preferences as have in actual life become inextricably tangled with those theoretical foundations? Many will hasten to deny this privilege without further hearing, for disciplinary reasons that can readily be anticipated, but the problem has too many ramifications to be summarily dismissed. Indeed, the chances are that the most effective answer that can be provided will be neither a flat denial nor an exuberant affirmation, but an unhurried tracing of the limits beyond which the autonomy of a part cannot be stretched without impairing the common weal.

Let Romance linguistics serve as a test case of a defensible share of "separatism", in a climate of debate free from apology and inculpation. Once a strong case for a partial autonomy of one meaningfully delimited subdiscipline has been established, spokesmen for any other comparable smaller unit may legitimately invoke this principle, adjusting its implications to varying circumstances.

This paper contends that most distinctive traits of Romance linguistics may be deduced from an inventory of its characteristic

Reprinted from *Language in Culture and Society*, ed. Dell Hymes (N.Y., Evanston, and London, 1964), 671–686.

resources. The chief advantage of this strategy is the reduction of subjectively colored choices to a reasonable modicum. This platform does not force one to disregard the agency of other powerful determining factors. At least three such additional ingredients seem worthy of mention: the specific evolutionary stage that the subdiscipline has reached, the matrix of the national (or continental) culture that gave it birth and initially sheltered it, and the impact of magnetic personalities among its leaders, past and present. The discussion of these supervenient influences will be relegated to the concluding section.

### Characteristics Traceable to the Material

**The available records.** The peculiar ambit and even the tone of Romance linguistics have to an astonishing extent been predetermined by the abundant material — either relatively well-preserved petrifacts or elements still in a state of flux and accessible to direct scrutiny — which generations of competent workers have become accustomed to handling. The bulk of these raw data, in its bare essentials, includes several standard languages, observable over periods of from four to ten centuries and known to have served as carriers of influential literatures; a wide variety of not too sharply differentiated clusters of dialects, a few of them lacking archival documentation, hence explorable through field work alone; scattered vestiges of ancestral lexical material in less closely related media, e.g., stray Latin words fossilized in Numidian (Berber), Germanic, or Celtic dialects; plus — a priceless possession — the thoroughly documented parent language itself, Latin. This language, used at widely discrepant social levels, counted among its speakers many who were in the process of gradual assimilation to Graeco-Roman culture; it occupied a far-flung expanse of territory fringed by ever fluctuating contours, an area subjugated in the course of four centuries of almost relentless warfare. An inwardly corroded Roman empire started falling apart at its seams in the third century; it is plausibly argued that as a result of its piecemeal dismemberment in the following two hundred years, colloquial Latin, except possibly among the highly literate, began to adopt several regionally colored forms in ever quickening tempo.

Scarcely any reliable records of the suspected varieties of spoken Latin have been directly transmitted, with the probable exception of the early comedy (Plautus), phrased in an idiom true to life, and of

Petronius' sensitive rendition of conversations held by a motley crowd at Trimalchio's Banquet. However, an impressive mass of circumstantial evidence enables the experienced "restorer" to piece together a few of the fleeting or (as we sometimes know from retrospect) lasting features of that submerged Latinity. Between the gradual extinction of a relatively unified, if finely graded, Latin and the emergence of the earliest, awkwardly styled texts in the major vernaculars (ninth to twelfth century), there lies a critical gap totaling, according to zone and language, from four to six hundred years, with Portuguese, Spanish (except in its archaic Mozarabic garb), and Italian trailing conspicuously behind French and Provençal. Texts (legal, historiographic, religious, didactic, and epistolary) dating from this transitional period (the tag "dim" rather than "dark" would most eloquently characterize such a twilight age) were often composed in some kind of semiconventional minimum Latin, affording occasional glimpses of the presumable actual speaking habits of writers, copyists, and notaries.

Eventually the vernaculars were recognized as fitting media for at least some literary genres and for charters; their coming-of-age was exceedingly slow in entailing the recession of medieval Latin as a favorite vehicle of writing, a vehicle subject, not unlike many other immobilized and slightly rusty prestige languages, to periodic attempts at "purification" imposed from above. This strained situation nourished a protracted osmosis between, on the one hand, an artificially maintained Latin seemingly almost arrested in its development but in fact never quite immune to steady erosive infiltration, and, on the other, a constellation of local dialects each almost free (but at no time entirely so) to follow its own natural bent or drift. In short, early Romance in all its protean manifestations is the very image of shackled spontaneity.

**Overlapping of philology and linguistics.** At this point a short terminological digression is in order. Whether one takes philology in its narrow, archaeological sense (bibliography, paleography, textual criticism, epigraphy, numismatics, toponymy) or in its broader meaning of cultural history moored to the meticulous examination of records, there are many temptations for moderns to establish valid contrasts, as regards definition and characterization, between this "antiquarian" branch of knowledge and a thoroughly refurbished linguistics.

The provinces of the two disciplines are not exactly coterminous, their respective degrees of abstractness are incongruous, their appeals to imagination are unequal in intensity and in direction, their affinities to other lines of learning could not, one is at intervals sharply reminded, be less germane. But granted this pervasive divergence between the two climates of research, it still remains true that a radical, unhealable break between the two approaches cannot be seriously advocated in a subfield as clearly predestined to yield a perfect testing ground for experiments in diachronic research as is the Romance domain.

In this privileged precinct ancient idiosyncrasies of spelling (suggestive, if deftly interpreted, of otherwise unobservable or elusive vocal habits) and present-day patterns of dialect speech, lending themselves to advanced techniques of recording and analysis, are at bottom mutually complementary and invite systematic comparison. One can, then, with a measure of justification set off philology from historical linguistics in formal presentation (much as in Ernout and Meillet's admirable etymological dictionary the unexciting inventory of recorded and readily inferrable Latin forms has been neatly segregated from the corpus of hazardous reconstructions relating to a nebulous past); but one cannot, in actual operations, expect to enforce this disentanglement without grave danger to the chosen inquiry.

**The changing hierarchy of approaches (arrangement vs. sequence).** In theory most linguists are likely to admit the perfect equality of status between synchronic and diachronic studies. Yet in practice powerful currents of fashions in scholarly thinking have tended to upset this equilibrium in favor of some kind of hierarchization. Fifty years ago, under the aegis of historicism refined by evolutionism, the dominant perspective in language study was diachronic. Today's heightened concern with exotic languages — many of them lacking a knowable past — and a general shift of focus in the direction of behavioral sciences, reinforced in some tone-setting milieus by an emotionally nurtured indifference to history, are jointly giving tremendous impetus to synchronic studies and concomitantly tend to discourage large-scale undertakings along the time axis. Romance linguistics can only profit from increased sophistication in structural analysis, but its stock of precious material is so distributed as to have inescapably predetermined the greatest potential services that its practitioners can hope to render to the advancement of knowledge. These services lie unequivocally along the path of diachronic inquiries. To put it differently: The patterns of arrangement in Romance languages and dialects seem less diversified, hence conceivably less thought-provoking, than those discovered in other not quite so prominent families. In contrast, the patterns of temporal sequences can here be recognized in all their complexity with such uniquely gratifying precision as to lead one to expect from the Romance quarters particularly weighty contributions to this phase of general linguistic theory.

**Some special implications of historicism.** Just as some perceptive theorists make it a point to discriminate between the labels "general", "synchronic", "descriptive", "functional", "structural", and "static" applied to closely allied perspectives in linguistics, so the three tags used in the opposite camp, "diachronic", "historical", and "dynamic", though practically interchangeable in informal scholarly discourse, deserve each to evolve a slightly distinctive connotation. Diachrony preëminently implies unilinear reconstruction of earlier stages by means of linguistic comparison alone, a procedure reminiscent in its rigor of logical and mathematical analyses. Historicism may well with equal force suggest a scholar's indebtedness to all sources of historical information (external and internal evidence alike) and presuppose on his part a special virtuosity in tapping these disparate sources as well as a liberal endowment of judiciousness in weighing them against one another. Dynamics, though inconclusive with regard to the selection of sources, seems closer to historicism, being chiefly attuned to the interplay of such forces as shape (or forcibly keep intact) a closely cohesive mobile mass of linguistic molecules.

Granted that much, one may thus elaborate upon the preference which most Romance linguists display for the time perspective. Theirs tends to be a truly historical approach with all the heavy implications of this qualifier rather than purely diachronic extrapolation; consequently the grasp of the dynamic formula presiding at each juncture over the combination of forces and counterforces locked in a ceaseless struggle is to them a goal worthy of earnest endeavor.

To be sure, it is hazardous to introduce non-linguistic assumptions into the reconstruction of most hypothetical parent languages, which the analyst is rarely in a position to assign, on independent grounds, to specific primeval habitats and itineraries, still less to definite ethnic stocks; few who have played with this avenue of approach have entirely eschewed the risk of circular thinking. On the other hand, the events surrounding the gestation of Romance languages were for a long time in the limelight of ancient and medieval historiography, hence merited rough dating and localization at the hands of articulate and literate contemporaries, including not a few eyewitnesses. Also, archaeology and physical anthropology, furnishing their evidence under so tightly controlled conditions, may act as fairly trustworthy handmaidens to "linguistic paleontology" (to use G. I. Ascoli's and W. Meyer-Lübke's favorite term). For these reasons numerous Romance linguists, to round out their training, have striven to acquire additional skills in ancillary disciplines and have cheerfully put these skills to good use in linguistic projection.

This proclivity toward an intricate argument, involving frequent and adroitly executed shifts from one discipline to another, in turn explains why most Romanists have tacitly avoided an austerely isolationist theoretical platform. Their policy, on the tactical and the strategic levels, has rather been interventionist (at times excessively so for their own good), that is, geared to the exploration, by free imaginative blends of all devices legitimate in identification, of the constant interaction between language and nonverbal culture. Hence a Romance linguist is more likely than not to deprecate any rash equation between linguistics and straight grammar, while acknowledging a flair for formulating grammatical relationships as a desirable part of one's professional equipment.

**Lexical emphasis.** Heightened alertness to concrete detail, viewed at close range in multidimensional projection, calls for sharpness of focus balanced by narrowness of scope. Applied to linguistic conditions and translated into the appropriate terminology, this kind of curiosity ordinarily signifies keener concern with the loosely split-up lexicon than with close-knit sound-systems or with fairly tight morphological scaffolding. In fact, Romance linguistics has lately perfected to an enviable degree lexicography (the art of cogently arraying lexical data in reference works of varying size), lexicology (stage-by-stage analysis of bundles of lexical trajectories), and etymology (inquiry into the inceptive phases of lexical evolutions), pouring out lavishly documented monographs on individual words of rich associative potentialities, striking cultural implications, or unusual areal configurations; on intricately ramified word families; on neatly delineated semantic clusters (including anatomic designations, kinship terms, and especially names of tools, containers, vehicles, buildings, and textiles examinable in the graphic *Wörter-und-Sachen* style). Other researches revolve around strings of secondary formations tied together by powerful morphological bonds, e.g., sharing a prefix, a suffix, or an "interfix", a compositional pattern, a characteristic distribution of sounds in "expressive" words. Regrettably, praiseworthy sustained excellence on the lexical side has sometimes been gratuitously achieved at the painful cost of relative indifference to equally thought-arresting grammatical patterning.

**Visual aspects of language.** Like all linguists, Romance scholars recognize a flexible pattern of auditory symbolism as the primeval origin and continued foundation of all speech. Yet their special preoccupation with the lexicon, in particular with semantic extensions and restrictions, has furthermore sharpened their awareness of visual problems in language. (Visual is here taken in the psychological or poetic sense of imagery, not in the pragmatic sense of written records or of any comparable artificial devices.)

At the present stage of scientific progress the student of imagery finds himself at a disadvantage, since he lacks apposite machinery or even an unassailable rule of thumb that would lend authority to his observations, whereas the auditory base of speech invites a dual set of precise descriptions: one on the articulatory and one on the acoustic level. But even impressionistic work, with its unavoidable margin of subjectivity, may be rewarding as long as its limitations (calling for further revision) are expressly recognized and as it is superadded to more rigorous dissections. Moreover, within the fabric of our culture this pictorial approach, for all its imprecision or even, paradoxically, on account of it, has acquired a certain inherent charm which attracts into the fold of linguistics not a few artistically sensitive and imaginative intellectuals who might feel discouraged by an accumulation of unmitigated severity.

Pictorial analysis can be of great usefulness for any investigation into the metaphoric extensions of a word's limited semantic ambit. Thus, in studying the names of the flail across language and dialect borders, one needs a statement that would set this tool apart from others displaying comparably sharp and suggestive contours, like the ax, the pickax, the shovel, the pitch fork, the saw, and the comb. The typical features of a European flail, reduced to its bare essentials, include a long slender bar (handle) at one end of which a stouter or shorter stick (swingle), occasionally curved or rounded, is so attached as to swing freely. Normally it serves to beat the grain out of the ear, but it may equally well qualify for separating beans from their pods, for handling flax, and for comparable subsidiary functions. There are many variables: The connection between the two sticks shows several degrees of elaborateness, the material out of which the sticks are carved is mostly, but not always, wood (for instance, in the medieval military weapon called flail the swingle was replaced by a metal ball or a piece set with spikes and the short handle was generally of metal). The irreducible elements that make up the pattern, then, are three: (1) difference in length between the two bars, ordinarily in favor of the handle; (2) irreversible distribution of functions between them; (3) provision for free swinging, yet solid attachment. This last-named condition explains such figurative uses in English as (obs.) *flail* 'swinging part, as a gate bar or the lever of a press'; (anat., surg.) *flail joint* 'joint showing abnormal mobility'; (coll.) *to flail about* (*one's arms*, etc.). One may similarly go about defining with utmost economy the basic design of a comb, to appreciate its use, in numerous languages, as a designation not only of certain toothed tools and adornments for separating, cleaning, and keeping human hair (primarily, the woman's hair) well-groomed, but also of a miscellany of characteristically shaped instruments adopted in traditional crafts and trades no less than in modern industry for the processing of wool, flax, oakum, etc., for weaving fabrics and mats, and for embroidering. Moreover, the local word for comb denotes a musical instrument (in classical Portuguese); parts of the human or animal body ('crest of a cock' in English; 'pubes' in Latin and Hispano-Romance); the top of a wave or a hill (in Germanic); an aggregation of cells for honey (in English); several plants, some of them expressly described as prickly (in Brazilian Portuguese), etc.

**The geographic dimension and the diffusionist doctrine.** The general propensity of Romance linguists toward concreteness, plus their prominent representation among the pioneer dialect cartographers and fieldworkers have sensitized most younger workers in their ranks to the crucially important geographic factor in every ensemble of causes-and-effects bearing on language. In their consciousness a given linguistic form and its neatly pinpointed locus belong as intimately together as do the numerator and the denominator of any vulgar fraction. Other teams of linguists may have displayed a more impressive degree of attention to such variables as oscillations on the social scale, the tempi of speech, the intonational curves, the controlling phrasal environment of words at issue; on the credit side of Romance scholarship one must place progressive alertness to localization.

This flair for static ordering of restricted or vast zones, in conjunction with a vivid grasp of the subtle interlocking of historical events, has made Romance dialect geographers experts in stratigraphy, centering their attention on patterns of successive layers, and, indirectly, the staunchest advocates — and most enthusiastic practitioners — (outside the Boasian school) of the diffusionist doctrine. The major risk that one runs in putting these ideas into practice lies in calculating on the scale of increasing abstractness the precise degree beyond which any appeal to them may become more of a liability than of an asset. The staking-out of minor self-contained linguistic zones (*Sprachlandschaften*) bounded by an approximate consensus of isoglosses is an unimpeachable procedure. The identification of recurrent specific areal patterns in the linguistic growth of a major territory (say, the pervasive aloofness of Gascony vis-à-vis the remainder of Gallo-Romance or the coincidences, too frequent and striking to be discounted as fortuitous, between Leonese and Aragonese on either flank of Old Castilian) also deserves unqualified endorsement. But Bàrtoli's attempt to advance one step further by extracting, from the comparison of some such concrete situations, a set of generally valid norms for the reconstruction of hidden sequences of events on the sole basis of resultant areal configurations ("Age-and-Area Hypothesis") has failed to outgrow the stage of a stimulating experiment.

**Literary languages as objects of study.** The earlier variety of anthropological linguistics, which crystallized at a moment when anthropologists were mainly engrossed by primitive, exotic societies lacking any sustained tradition of literacy, militantly emphasized not only the temporal priority of speech over script, but — less persuasively — also its supremacy in other respects, the chief argument being the customary omission from most conventional notations of such prosodic key features as pitch and stress (also of juncture).

In some quarters this attitude of diffidence toward any kind of records coalesced with cultivated indifference toward the study of fine literature, possibly as a recoil from the excessive subjectivism in aesthetic appreciation or in tacit protest against the glaring disparity in recognition which our society bestows on broadly literary as against stringently linguistic pursuits.

Romance linguists here stand apart almost en bloc: They cherish treating the spoken and the written on a par, delight in tracing their interactions (including the increasingly frequent surrender of speech habits to the pressure of spelling), and refuse to abjure their active interest in literary analysis, again along the axes of time and of arrangement. In fact, joint concern with spontaneous dialect speech and with stylized, sophisticated discourse, and purposefully developed deftness in examining their complicated interactions have become the hallmark of Romance scholarship at its most satisfying. Such specialists as choose to concentrate exclusively on the one or on the other unwittingly relegate their researches to some fringe of our domain.

There are numerous reasons for this idiosyncrasy. For one thing, the Romanist — unlike, say, the Latinist — witnesses no gradual spread of a single, fairly homogeneous city dialect over a widening expanse of territory, but rather protracted rivalry between clusters of cognate dialects vying for the privilege of serving the needs of a written standard, especially at the opening period of the vernacular literatures and with particular regard to the frequently conflicting preferences of authors, revisers, and copyists. With the possible exception of the Old Provençal troubadour lyric couched from the outset in a fairly undifferentiated idiom (a leveling of form that matches the exquisite conventionality of much of its content), the early Romance texts from France proper, Italy, and Spain all show a high incidence of regional features, and those transmitted through devious routes often display a confusingly erratic intermingling of such traits. Though medieval and modern dialect literature, despite its spontaneous ring, uses a vehicle not entirely immune to inroads of convention, the distance separating unpremeditated utterances from polished written statements is here conspicuously short.

For another thing, in such complexly structured and tradition-ridden societies as those of the northwestern and central Mediterranean it would be naïve to reckon with the consistent preservation of parochial speech habits, transmitted from mouth to mouth, except in a few almost hermetically isolated nooks. All over the plains, in hilly terrain, along the coasts, and especially down the valleys of navigable rivers it is perfectly normal for trends of local and regional drift to have been disturbed by the infiltration not only of patches of neighboring dialect speech, but also of chunks of the prestige language (which, in the last analysis, merely represents the sublimation, through deliberate sifting, of just another humble rural dialect); to this formula add, for the earlier periods, the ever-present unweakening grip of Latin, especially in the ecclesiastic domain. Symptomatic of this ceaseless bidirectional oozing is the presence, by the hundreds, of original dialect words in the most selective standard languages: Tuscan, for example, is replete with words drawn from Lombard and other northern dialects, Spanish and Galician-Portuguese are, at least lexically, a classic illustration of communicating vessels, and the French vocabulary teems with patois words, despite early political centralization and aloofness from rusticity. By way of compensation, as it were, rural and partially rural dialect speech has absorbed a vast amount of "semilearned" features, often not immediately recognizable in their new disguises: combinations of sounds — typically, jarring diphthongs or unfamiliar medial consonant clusters —, garbled pretentious affixes, half-understood sesquipedalian words, syntactic constructions clumsily imitative of classical Latin, even accentual schemes and pitch contours. These linguistic trading posts are ideal breeding places for folk etymology and hypercorrection.

Two final considerations. First, no coolheaded Romance linguist would deny the chronological priority and continued preëminence of the actual flow of speech, provided one makes due allowance for the fact that the written language, whether living or dead, may at any propitious moment have acted as a powerful force (a stimulant or a barrier) in the shaping of that speech and will in all likelihood continue to leave its impress on the colloquial medium at an accelerated rhythm. In not a few instances spelling has demonstrably deflected pronunciation from its predictable course (a fact gratuitously played down in some quarters), while the luxuriant growth of hyperurbanism reveals in what direction the pressure of social forces is most effectively at work. In modern western societies average speakers, for scientifically valid or indefensible reasons, are eager to attach to their pronunciation a cachet of respectability, i.e., of a certain conformity to recognized spelling habits, and correspondingly to mould their grammar and vocabulary, as best they can, by standards officially encouraged or enforced. If linguists are sincere in confining themselves to the rôle of detached observers and analysts rather than of active participants, they should refrain scrupulously from either abetting or obstructing this controversial trend.

Second, the fully grown literary language, whatever trickling or torrential sources and tributaries may have fed it, tends to fall into a system, or subsystem, of its own, laying itself open to analytical inspection no less than does any representative corpus of elicited utterances. In some respects (nonobligatory features of lexicon and clausal architecture) this stylized language may display a greater abundance of resources or more delicately graded patterning, bordering on the ornamental. As an intricate but ordered whole (if one discounts the rare occurrences of intentional obfuscation), it invites individuating study at the same levels — sounds, forms, constructions — as any adequate speech specimen and is available in various sizes, ranging from a single passage, stylistically uniform or split, via an extant text, fragmentary or complete, to the collected works of a given author, to a genre, or to the cross-section or even the sum total of writings attributable to a certain period.

**Romance scholarship and the structural approach.** Do these deeply rooted, in part immutable, traits of Romance linguistics create a barrier to the establishment of fruitful liaison with structuralism? Divorced from surrounding circumstances, the two approaches are not mutually exclusive; on the contrary, the injection into Romance researches of a reasonable dosage of structuralistic thinking — bent on the redefinition of basic concepts, relativistic, and intent on subordinating the irrelevant to the relevant — would act as a wholesome corrective to any measure of lopsidedness and staleness that might otherwise develop and would thus produce an effect at once remedial and rejuvenating. Under adverse conditions an overflow of primary data and a plethora of uncoördinated studies bearing on them may constitute two focuses of acute danger; the reintroduction of a compelling hierarchy would, at least temporarily, tend to restore the balance. Historical grammar, in particular, might profit from some degree of tightening through integration of myriads of disconnected details not into a congeries of gross facts, but, after meticulous distillation, into elegantly designed chain reactions, such as have been proposed by economy-minded phonologists. The scrupulous, but excessively detailed dialect studies bearing the hallmark of Romance workmanship may profit from streamlining through diminishing resistance to the phonemic principle, refined through increased attention to contrasts in the chain and in the system. Yet in those domains in which Romance materials happen to flow most copiously, e.g., the lexicon, one hesitates to apply structuralistic thinking except cautiously and, lest it cause more harm than good, without detriment to other viewpoints. Effects of analogy (associative interference), which, until after one learns how to handle with assurance raw statistical data, do not seem to fall into comparably clear-cut patterns, excite the Romance scholar not one whit less than does the establishment of schemas, while familiarity with geographic shifts doubles his awareness of temporarily unstable, oscillating systems. As a result of these cautioning experiences, he is not quite at ease in an environment where stringency and trenchancy of static classification alone are judged matters of overruling importance. It is not the essence of functional thinking traceable to Saussure that seems difficult to reconcile with the finest traditions of Romance research, but, on the one hand, strident demands for a new orthodoxy pressed by certain reformers, which clash with the ideal of elasticity and with the standards of tolerance cherished by most Romanists, and, on the other, the well-founded realization that structuralism at its most daring and successful has come to full fruition in descriptive inquiries into exotic languages, with whose unique conformation it seems impossible to cope intelligently in other terms, whereas in the Romance domain, given the peculiar slant of its data, structuralism is at best apt to play a powerful supporting rôle. The full implications of this briefly sketched suspicion would require a thorough discussion of the seldom admitted correlation and mutual conditioning between favored method and the material at hand.

**Modern alternatives to formal analysis.** It has been occasionally suggested that the inescapable alternative to standard structuralistic practice is utter chaos, a haphazard array of colorful odds and ends, a bric-à-brac shop. This description of the choices facing a beginner might be partially correct if it did not operate with a straw man. The conventional type of Romance linguist — a scholar versed in philology, old-style historical grammar, a conservative variety of dialect geography, and an etymology heavily mortgaged with conjectures — may have shied away from steeper altitudes of abstract reasoning

F

and stopped short in his phonological pursuits at the precise un-ambitious point where they served to localize a text, to circumscribe a dialect, or to identify a word-origin; measured by modern demands, his semantics and esthetics may appear homespun. Yet a program of studies conducive to this meaningful blend of diverse interests and techniques, with a perceptibly heavier emphasis on the unassuming establishment of sober facts, or approximations to facts, than on pretentious experiments with untried explicative or classificatory methods, has distinct virtues of its own, and future generations may some day declare our hasty retreat from this program to have had deleterious consequences.

Richer in potential repercussions is the fact that Romance scholars (and others in their company) have tried out significant patterns of ordering fairly removed from the prime concerns of organized structuralism. The most exacting and promising among such experi-mental groupings has been the attempt to present sound shifts of a particular language not in a routine enumeration based on articulatory conditions (or, worse, on the alphabetical order), but in their pre-sumable chronological succession. In broad outline, Meyer-Lübke essayed this tour de force for proto-French as early as 1908; a quarter of a century later, E. Richter embroidered on his master stroke. The elaboration of such relative chronologies may be extended to inflec-tion, derivation, syntax, etc., and seems perfectly compatible with research in diachronic phonology. Other scholars have endeavored to segregate certain sound shifts as particularly illustrative of a unique nonlinguistic sequence of events, so as to weave them into the fabric of specific demographic processes and cultural develop-ments. This Menéndez Pidal strove to accomplish for the period of the early *reconquista* (eighth to eleventh century) in the bulk of his masterly treatise *Orígenes del español* (1926); W. von Wartburg matched his effort for the prehistory of French, Provençal, and Italian, in a proliferation of books and monographs issuing from his famous programmatic article (1936) on the fragmentation of Late Latin. The theoretical justification for this preferential treat-ment of assorted features, to the neglect of others, rebellious to the favored pattern, a treatment without explicit vindication of the criteria of selection, remains to be provided.

A third cogent marshaling of disjointed facts, eminently charac-teristic of the historical method, would be to arrange them roughly in the order of decreasing transparency. Thus, an etymologist grappling with thousands of equations of varying complexity may proceed from relatively simple cases involving no (or just a few easily eliminable) unknowns to progressively intricate tangles, ending up with a residue of issues inextricably confused or wholly recalcitrant. (He may at least toy with this grading at the operational stage, if not in the definitive product which, like most dictionaries, should be alphabetical to satisfy the layman's need for maximum speed in casual consultation.) This rational arrangement presupposes, on the worker's part, the ability to denude each situation of its frills, reducing it to an algebraic formula, and a concurrent willingness to deëmphasize, without ruling them out entirely, the ingredients of intuition and of chance that have undeniably presided over some etymological discoveries.

Finally, to reconcile the various causes of linguistic change so far adduced (phonological drift, which may run afoul of inertia or of morphological obstacles; a state of bilingualism created by ethnic sub-, ad-, and superstrata, by intermarriages, by economic inducements, by religious habits, or by intellectual aspirations; diffusion; social upheavals; unconscious internal economy revolving around minimum effort, evenness of distribution, and a desirable degree of clarity; "expressivism", sensuous delight in certain well-developed features; deliberate search for reputed betterment), one may attempt to excogitate some system of possible alliances, concomitancies, mergers, or mutual hindrances and exclusions between these discrete forces.

These are just a few possibilities that can, at first glance, be successfully tried out within a limited subfield; a broader frame would invite other, more tempting experiments, such as the audacious survey of well-established categories across language families, a type of monograph launched by Humboldt, or the discovery, delimitation, and labeling of new categories, either static (witness É. Benveniste's newly identified "delocutive verbs") or dynamic (such as E. Schwyzer's overstated "hypercharacterization" or B. Migliorini's neatly delimited "synonymic radiation").

### Characteristics Traceable to the Stage of the Discipline

**Transition from learning to science.** The absolute age of a semiautonomous discipline and the stage that it has currently reached in its development are matters of great moment in any inventory of its salient features. There is no denying that Romance linguistics has irreversibly outgrown its adolescence. As a fully developed discipline, conscious of its topical independence and later also of its methodological originality, it is at least 130 years old. Even certain ingredients of markedly older Renaissance scholarship can hardly be brushed aside as prescientific, inasmuch as traditional linguistic "learning" and modern linguistic "science" have failed to drift apart from each other with anything like the same speed as, say, alchemy and chemistry. (Even some of the etymological lore of Antiquity and the Middle Ages, if adroitly winnowed by discriminating minds, continues to be grist to our mills, and for the external history of pronunciation we still rely heavily, if with reluctance, on the quaintly phrased statements of the old normative grammarians, foreign-language teachers, and missionaries.)

**Cycles of emphasis.** Even if one restricts his observation to the probings of indisputably solid science, certain recurrent cycles of emphasis become discernible. Thus rough grammatical sketches, diachronically slanted, became available for most Romance languages under the Neo-grammarians and their immediate followers in an atmosphere of austere isolationism and unquestioning dogmatism not very different from the atmosphere prevailing until all too recently among all too many straight descriptivists. After the richest yield of this method had become exhausted, the pendulum began swinging in the opposite direction, when the talented generation of Gauchat, Jaberg, and Jud, sated with schematization which at best had merely accounted for a privileged portion of the total stock of data, started exploring with great alacrity those attractive problems of erratic growth that had slipped through the wide meshes of the Neo-grammarians.

This new trend, at least among the level-headed, did not entail the abandonment of phonetic correspondences (though their magic glitter had become tarnished) or the neglect of the edifice of historical grammar built on this foundation. But it implied diversion of the focus of attention toward other goals: word biographies replete with cultural content, welters of dialectal cross-currents, fireworks set in motion by homonymic clashes, and lexical masquerades unleashed by folk etymology became the staple food of the most imaginative Romanists. Among the sound changes examined at rare intervals, most were of an abnormal nature; they included either broad, tendential, recurrent transmutations (metathesis, haplology, assimilation, dissimilation, echoing of nasal resonance; in short, Ascoli's "accidenti generali"), reaching athwart such basic shifts as are sharply limited, by definition, in space and time; or they were confined to the language of the educated and the gifted and spiced by some manner of cultural piquancy, i.e., again cutting across the major drift. The new watchword was the reconstruction of the unique set of circumstances, not a few of them extraneous to linguistics proper, that govern the trajectory of each separate word.

This vigorous reaction to schematization, aside from filling in countless factual gaps, tended to place linguistic research in another academic (and, marginally, even artistic) context; it made itself felt not in Romance quarters alone, but nowhere did its impact produce a more powerful jolt. Still later, abstractionism became again the irresistible fashion in general linguistics, geared by definition to ceaseless search for constants, even universals, and, in the New World, concerned primarily with skeletal sketches of unexplored indigenous languages. At this point the smaller pendulum in the restricted Romance field was temporarily delayed, failing to swing back into its initial position; the retardative force was, of course, the special commitment of this team of workers to the ideals of concreteness, plasticity, and individualism.

An inherent affinity between the Neo-grammatical and the (American-style) descriptive approach explains the curious paradox that to the Romance scholar, steeped exclusively in the tradition of his subdiscipline, some elements of the most advanced speech analysis (e.g., the schematization, the evasion or postponement of references to meaning, the emphatic divorce from other cultural analyses) may smack of reaction, insofar as they remind him of premature generalizations in Neo-grammatical practice, i.e., of errors which he was cautioned to avoid or trained to correct. Conversely the shortsighted avant-garde descriptivist is not unlikely to deride the present-day Romanist for being behind the times in clinging so tenaciously to minute concrete details. By the same token, half a century from now students of exotic languages (by then, let us hope, no longer in critical need of provisional sketches) may very well, in their predictable anxiety to cover each "skeleton" with flesh and skin, fall back, perhaps unknowingly, on many assumptions and techniques that now hold sway in the Romance camp.

Couched in more general terms: Aside from its pivotal theoretical postulate the unvarnished Neo-grammatical position (or some of its modern derivatives) need not be regarded as something absolutely right or wrong, but rather as a method which at fairly early stages of a typical inquiry is apt to yield optimal results. Beyond that stage, once the requisite sound correspondences have been set up, the usefulness of the method diminishes rapidly, since such painstaking operations, for instance, as must be brought to bear on the hard core of refractory etymologies demand a program of research at the opposite pole of isolationism, presupposing close integration with kindred disciplines, if attainable without loss of identity. Granted that this cyclic argument has any merit, then a tolerant (though by no means lax) attitude of relativism, which for decades has been the stock-in-trade of any enlightened anthropologist and linguist analyzing the raw data of a culture not his own, however aberrant, should at long last be extended to the serene appraisal of heterodox linguistic doctrines.

**Degree of specialization.** The age of a subdiscipline carries with it one peculiarity which some may deem an asset and others, a liability: the tendency, on the part of each successive generation, to examine under a more powerful microscope a commensurately smaller sliver of material. The reason for this temptation is obvious. As a rule, the pioneers have no qualms about surveying, as best they can, a vast slice of territory, at the risk of a high quota of errors. Their successors, on the average more scrupulous but less daring, set about to eradicate these flaws by allowing themselves more leisure to examine a smaller piece from all possible angles. An ambitious generation of workers will always succeed in weeding out a crop of inaccuracies, oversimplifications, and plain slips in the research of their immediate predecessors by concentrating on more narrowly staked-out assignments.

But such victories may turn Pyrrhic through the concurrent loss of perspective and of evenly spread competence in the broader field. By cutting up a language into countless subdialects and analyzing each to the limit of one's patience one merely succeeds in scratching a surface with ever greater effectiveness. Some of the truly important problems plaguing a historically-minded linguist do not even acquire shape except through reference to closely and even distantly related languages. And yet, pathetically, wide-ranging comparatism has been on the decline. The full magnitude of this danger of excessive shrinkage has begun to dawn upon us, but no infallible means has yet been devised for underpinning the entire discipline without disrupting the flow of useful small-scale operations.

**Analysis of facts and analysis of opinions.** Another peculiarity — which again may constitute an advantage or a drawback — flowing from the respectable age of Romance linguistics is the overgrowth of earlier pronouncements on many crucial issues. In extreme cases (for instance, to etymologize certain words that have exercised or merely titillated the imagination of generations of conjecturers, such as F. *aller*), up to twenty or even thirty irreconcilably different hypotheses have been advanced over the years. Points of syntax prominently represented in practical language teaching, such as the use of the subjunctive in French, have been mercilessly labored, for the most part by unqualified analysts.

To what extent should a modern scholar, before or after frontally attacking a chosen problem, attempt to disentangle this complicated skein of previous opinions? No entirely satisfactory answer to this ever-present question has been offered in the past or seems to be forthcoming. Some escapists from bibliography, infatuated with the idea of a clean slate, altogether disregard the toiling of their predecessors. Other scholars apologetically relegate the digest of earlier researches to some kind of supplement or annotated bibliography (which a last-minute decision may then prompt them to omit). Still others, in an effort to draw a line somewhere, confine their curiosity to a limited span of time, starting from, say, the threshold of the twentieth century or from the publication date of some revolutionary book. A minority may decide on the selective coverage of a long period, using as the prime criteria of choice the originality, accessibility, temporary influence, or continued relevance of pertinent statements. A very few are likely to aim at exhaustiveness, and among these an occasional virtuoso may present the expected meandrous account with such zest and incisiveness as to afford fresh insights into turning-points in the history of linguistic science. From case to case, considerations of expediency and economy may dictate the most opportune course of action. Generally speaking, a subfield like Romance is not a suitable maneuvering terrain for scholars emotionally reluctant to examine with patience, sympathy, and humility the gropings of their elders.

## The Matrix of National Cultures

The remaining determinants need not detain us long. A particular national culture fostering a line of inquiry on a grandiose scale inevitably leaves its impress on nomenclature, tone of phrasing, and even slant of analysis. During its critical growing years Romance linguistics was preponderantly under the tutelage of Central European scholarship, entrenched far beyond the boundaries of the German-speaking countries proper. This style of learning displays a peculiar cleavage of accumulated knowledge — especially at the standard-setting level of the Academies — into a "physical" and a "spiritual" realm, the latter roughly coincident with the Humanities (minus their concern with pedagogy and the arts), to the virtual exclusion, especially at the outset, of some such stretch of middle-ground as is suggested by the social sciences. Without hesitation linguistics, initially embedded in philology, was assigned to the domain of the flourishing *Geisteswissenschaften* and so tailored and weighted as to fit its surroundings with a minimum of rough edges.

For a while this classic design was indiscriminately imitated in other countries, from St. Petersburg to Chicago and Santiago de Chile, even though the academic edifice of some was quite differently designed, until it became clear that an immediate transfer of isolated pursuits of knowledge from one citadel of learning to another, reflecting divergent tastes and dissimilar aims, was impracticable, at least in fluid disciplines lending themselves to multiple classification. This discovery came as a shock and has ever since provoked considerable and, all told, unnecessary irritation, inasmuch as a few workers hypersensitive to differences in national taste and regional traditions have magnified out of all reasonable proportion the importance of clashing integuments, oblivious of the incomparably more significant common pith. The smoothest way of producing within a locally underdeveloped subfield a style of research that harmonizes with the broader trends of a self-conscious national culture, instead of violently impinging on them (and grating on some participants' nerves), is to channel unobtrusively as much talent as possible in that neglected direction. The prompt acquisition of apposite styling will then presumably take care of itself.

Outside Central Europe there crystallized some minor styles, in part ephemeral and hardly qualifying for exportation. In his memorable essay on "The Spaniards in History", Menéndez Pidal, musing on Spain's destiny, remarked that his country was apparently fore-doomed to regale the world with the late, exquisitely mellow fruits of cultural attitudes and endeavors elsewhere long extinct. It certainly is true that the recipe for this century's Spanish linguistics, a few drops of which spilled over into Latin America, represents a blend of studies in folklore, literature (down to Gongorism), straight history, and linguistics proper that calls to mind the Germany of Jakob and Wilhelm Grimm, propelled by philological curiosity. Peculiar to romantic Germany and to neo-romantic Spain alike is further the close and, on the whole, gratifying liaison between current creative literature and organized research in philology and linguistics, a spontaneous harmony comparable to that which exists between deep undercurrents of modern American civilization and the fine flowering of professional anthropological inquiries.

The Italian scene is quite different. The character of linguistics has there been cosmopolitan and polygot, its ambit encompassing with undiminished intensity Latin and Greek, but rarely extending beyond the ancient and modern Near East, in accord with Italy's severely limited commitments to, and investments in, overseas terri-tories (aside from immigration). Two facts give extra touches of authenticity to that country's native school of Romance linguistics. First, knowledge of Latin (as a member of the Indo-European family), of the "Mediterranean substratum", and of the neo-Latin, i.e., Romance, languages is typically imparted by the same chair of *glottologia*, a state of affairs maintaining a vital cross-connection severed or curtailed elsewhere. Second, dialectology, long fostered by political conditions and to no appreciable extent thwarted by the late unification, until very recently here enjoyed almost the same prestige as the study of the literary language.

The inclusion of a given language in a nation's collegiate curricu-lum may act as a stimulant or as a deterrent to its liberal utilization in advanced linguistic inquiry. The former possibility undoubtedly points to a healthy climate; the alternative, to some conflict of loyalties, some exaggerated fascination for the unknown, or some morbid revulsion against the known mistaken for the stale and banal. Many hope that the almost complete divorce of advanced linguistic investigation not only from Latin and French, less tho-roughly explored than the voice of rationalized indifference avers, but also from Spanish and Portuguese, which boast enormous stretches of uncharted territory, will not harden into an unremovable characteristic of progressive British and American scholarship, otherwise so elastic and versatile.

### The Impact of Powerful Personalities

As the final component, whether or not one inclines to consider it an imponderable, it is fitting to mention the impact of magnetic personalities. Diez, Schuchardt, Ascoli, Cuervo, Meyer-Lübke, Leite de Vasconcelos, Gilliéron, Menéndez Pidal, Bally, Jaberg, and Jud are some of the luminaries in the ranks of Romance linguists who have each opened up new vistas, set or raised standards, and for decades left the stamp of their private and public performance on a wealth of significant output. On the debit side of the ledger let us readily admit that among these splendid thinkers, writers, and teachers only very few have cultivated in more than casual fashion either languages not included in, or bordering upon, the Romance domain (Ascoli) or linguistic theory for its own sake (Bally); the incomparable Schuchardt, dynamically curious along both lines, represents the great exception. In this single respect of deplorable self-sufficiency the logbook of Romanists has lately been in less than satisfactory shape, particularly if one wistfully contrasts the glorious elasticity and ability for forceful synthesis of a Jespersen, a Troubetzkoy, or a Sapir; here alone they may do well to chart their future course with a livelier spark of imagination.

### The Contribution of Romance Scholarship to Linguistics

The distinctive features of Romance linguistics as here projected from four vantage points are by no means immutable. Very opportunely they contain, caught in an attractive balance, both variables and near-invariables, thus offering the dual guarantee of flexibility and continuity. Easily the most precious gifts that Romance scholarship has so far tendered to general linguistics include an almost oversubtle approach to dialect geography, a firm grasp of the osmosis between literary languages and the corresponding gamuts of vernaculars, and a vast reservoir of practice in etymology, with a record of meticulous, zestfully conducted monographic researches not yet welded into a single thoroughly integrated doctrine. At this critical point Romance linguistics happens to represent a highly atypical subdiscipline. But is typicality a measure of inherent value? And may not a closer rapprochement with general linguistics be smoothly achieved through mutual concessions? Thus far Romance linguists have handled with astonishing assurance slivers of concrete, unique, historically controllable material, at the crossroads of language and nonverbal culture and at the opposite pole from that of sweeping schematization. No general theory of language nor, indeed, any history of linguistic science is complete that fails to treat understandingly such a privileged store of experiences and experiments.

The recognition that one major subdiscipline may, under favorable conditions, quite legitimately develop certain unmistakable characteristics of its own carries with it the significant implication that linguistic research at its most engaging and rewarding need not, indeed should not, be conceived as monolithic. There must, of course, exist a hard core of agreement on essentials of purpose, assumptions, and techniques; it may be useful, in times of stress, to set limits to the margin of tolerable individual departures from the common standard. But the leeway left to individual taste and initiative and to the preferences of well-defined groups must be more than minimal and should take into account such factors as peculiarities of material, stage of research, academic traditions, and personal leanings. A community of linguists at its best calls to mind a fine symphony orchestra in which, enviably enough, each instrument and each group of instruments retains a perceptible measure of individuality while contributing its share to the tonal effect of the whole.

# 5

# A Tentative Typology
# of Romance Historical Grammars

THIS paper has been written with full knowledge of the relative eclipse, throughout the last decades, of historical grammar as a genre of scholarly inquiry. The author has also been keenly aware of the modest rôle played by Romance scholarship — so brilliantly represented in etymology, dialect geography, and stylistics — along this particular line, even at the height of the Neo-grammatical vogue, which truly marked the Golden Age of the genre.

The justification for the present experiment, despite these implied disclaimers, is dual. First, it represents a pilot study, another link in a so far very short chain of exploratory typological surveys and, if found worthy of attention, may at some future date lead to a more ambitious typology of diachronic grammars, cutting through all known language families (references to non-Romance languages have been here kept to the barest minimum). Clearly, a start had to be made somewhere, and every worker, I suppose, enjoys the privilege of conducting the initial, most hazardous experiments on his home-ground. Second, the project is based on the broad assumptions that the pendulum of taste and preference in linguistics may soon start swinging back toward dynamics; that in this connection a vigorous revival of diachronic grammar is a strong and pleasant possibility; that, to be effectively resuscitated, the genre must undergo a radical change; that a typological survey of distinctive features in the older output may very well alert us not only to past accomplishments, but to fruitful approaches thus far overlooked; and that in the rejuvenation of historicism Romance scholarship, by virtue of its unrivaled resources, may yet be called upon to play a leading part.

The typological classification of scholarly writings has been defined

Reprinted from *Lingua*, IX: 4 (1960), 321–416.

elsewhere.[1] Whereas even the most sophisticated bibliography inevitably treats each item as an indivisible unit, typology — taking its cue from Sapir's flexible classification of languages and from the separation of a speech sound into a number of distinctive features — operates on the theory that a monograph or a handbook is analyzable as a bundle of characteristic traits that can be reassembled, as it were, in miscellaneous arrangements. Undoubtedly, such arrangements can, if necessary, be expressed in a simple formula. The present article stops short of providing actual formulas (useful, at best, as a reference tool), but leads the reader to the point from which such succinct labeling can be freely envisaged. The reason for this restraint is that the theoretical discussion of the fission of grammar into constituent elements seems far more rewarding in its implications than do any immediately anticipated practical results.

## *Preliminaries*

**0.0. Definition.** A historical grammar may be defined as a formal arrangement of strictly linguistic data pertaining to structure rather than to the lexicon and viewed in diachronic perspective; that is to say, it presupposes at least two parallel sets of forms separated by a sufficiently extended period of time for sharply marked contrasts between corresponding forms to have crystallized, if not in every instance, at least on a considerable scale. A running commentary on a linguistically noteworthy text, even if it is as weighty as E. Löfstedt's classic annotations to the *Peregrinatio Aetheriae* (1911), is no substitute for a historical grammar because of its inherent looseness and selectivity; nor would any essentially historical account spiced with stray linguistic illustrations provide an acceptable replacement.

**0.1. Minimum scope.** Historical grammars further presuppose a modicum of quantitatively adequate coverage. A narrowly delimited monograph, however valuable as a piece of spadework or as the

---

[1] See my earlier articles "The uniqueness and complexity of etymological solutions", *Lingua*, V: 3 (1956), 225–252; "A tentative typology of etymological studies", *IJAL*, XXIII (1957), 1–17; "Distinctive features in lexicography: A typological approach to dictionaries exemplified with Spanish", *RPh.*, XII (1958–59), 366–399, and XIII (1959–60), 111–115, a condensed and revised version of which was offered at the Indiana University Conference on Lexicography in November, 1960, under the title "A typological classification of dictionaries on the basis of distinctive features" (included in this book, pp. 257–279), and a lecture, delivered in November, 1959, at the Universities of Oxford, Leiden, and Copenhagen: "Distinctive features of Romance linguistics" (see pp. 47–69 in this miscellany).

testing of a method, represents, at best, a potential contribution to historical grammar, but no full-blown specimen. Neither do loose groups of related studies in, say, phonology, such as Cuervo's trail-blazing *Disquisiciones* (1895) or its modern counterpart, A. Alonso's inquiries into the pronunciation of pre-Classical and Golden Age Spanish (1955–), constitute samples of a well-organized historical grammar; still less so does an anthology of previously published articles, a venture frequently planned by well-wishers as a tribute to an eminent scholar, even if each item included bears on diachronic linguistics.

**0.2. "Comparative" versus "historical".** Every historical grammar is, by definition, comparative, the minimum comparison residing, we recall, in a point-by-point confrontation of two successive, reasonably distant stages of the same language. (Conventionally, one speaks of "comparative historical grammar" only where more than one daughter-language is contrasted with the actual or putative ancestral tongue.) On the other hand, the reverse may not be true: A comparative grammar need not be historical, since two autonomous systems, whether or not cognate, may be legitimately opposed in terms of architectural design, without any concern for genetics; witness Bally's austerely synchronic dismounting, on a grandiose scale, of the mechanisms of contemporary German and French (1932).

**0.3. Prototypes.** It is customary to label historical grammar as, fundamentally, a genre of mid- and late-19th and early-20th-century scholarship. For practical purposes, this rather short-sighted chrono-logical attribution is defensible. Yet certain prototypes of the modern genre, traceable, in extreme cases, as far back as pre-Humanism, are not wholly unworthy of the present-day analyst's attention, not only because they may significantly anticipate later developments, but, more important, because, upon occasion, their peculiar slants, re-flecting an untutored attitude on the part of pioneers, may naïvely exploit certain worth-while possibilities later neglected or even de-liberately ignored.

## 1. Scope

**1.0. Definition and subdivision.** Under scope one advantageously subsumes not the number of linguistic disciplines (morphology, syntax, etc.) brought into play, but the breadth and depth of the material chosen for analysis and the general evolutionary perspective in which the observer elects to examine it.

We shall designate as BREADTH the number of families, languages, or dialects subjected, as independent entities, to systematic comparison. DEPTH will signal the length of time selected along the chronological axis, both in absolute terms and with special attention to the number of clearly discernible stages with which the analyst decides to operate. The DIRECTION is twofold: either prospective, when the starting point is the older of two, or the oldest of several, consecutive phases compared; or retrospective, if the reverse view is favored, as when the examination of a modern Romance language is punctuated with flashbacks to the Latin or medieval antecedents, or the entire distance is covered in converse direction.

**1.1. Breadth.** It is not unnatural that, as new languages come to light, through archeological excavations and anthropological canvassing, the breadth of coverage should tend to expand. This is true even of the Romance domain, where, on the whole, discoveries have lately been unsensational. Of the two classic treatments of Romance grammar as a unified field, Diez's pioneer work (1836–44) operated rather consistently with six languages: Portuguese, Spanish, French, Provençal, Italian, and "Valachian", i.e., Rumanian; his comparative dictionary, launched at a later date, afforded, in addition, occasional glimpses of "Churwelsch" (in modern taxonomy, Western Raeto-Romance). Meyer-Lübke's monumental comparative grammar — and, in its wake, Guarnerio's pan-Romanic phonology — shows a lesser degree of consistency, the number of languages and dialects contrasted depending entirely on the diversification achieved by each single feature (the typical range of possibilities varies from five to ten).[2] In his methodological primer — not, strictly speaking, a historical grammar — the same author allowed initially (1901) for

---

[2] Thus, to limit ourselves to those tabulations with which his *Lautlehre* is dotted, Meyer-Lübke sliced the sum total of the Romance progeny of a given Latin vowel, diphthong, or consonant (each confined to one peculiar position) into a varying number of units: five for stressed A (§ 223: Rum. Friul. It. Prov. Sp.), for the early syncope of the posttonic vowel (§ 325: Rum. Eng. Tusc. F. Sp.) and for pretonic AU (§ 354: same constellation); seven for stressed AU (§ 282: Rum. Eng. Tusc. Prov. F. Sp. Ptg.); eight for pretonic Ē, Ĕ (§ 352: Rum. Friul. Surs. Tusc. Mil. F. Sp. Cat.); nine for stressed Ŏ (§ 183: Rum. Friul. Eng. Tusc. Mil. Prov. OF. Sp. Ptg.) and for the late syncope of the posttonic vowel (§ 332: Rum. Eng. Friul. Tusc. Emil. Mil. F. Prov. Sp.); ten for Kᵉ·ⁱ (§ 403: Logud. Vegl. Alb. It. Rum. Eng. Ven. Gen. F. Sp.). Guarnerio's *Fonologia* offers a scope similarly varying from case to case: § 157 (eight), § 180 (five), § 198 (eleven), §§ 212 and 224 (eight).

eight languages (all subject to further subdivision), including Sardinian but omitting Catalan; to these, on second and third thought (1909, 1920), he added Dalmatian for good measure. Understandably, elementary treatments catering to the needs of beginners and of captive audiences may arbitrarily reduce the number of languages examined; thus, Zauner, in his contribution to the Göschen series, and Bourciez, in his *Éléments*, down to the latest revisions of both books, have each been satisfied with analyzing seven languages, including Raeto-Romance, but dispensing with Catalan, Sardinian, and Dalmatian. At present, the well-informed grammarian, even if his book is small-sized (as is true of Lausberg's), takes into account all ten sharply profiled languages. Though a good deal of advanced research has been carried out on the fragmentarily preserved Latinity of the upper and central Danube basin (the Roman provinces of Noricum and Pannonia) as well as of Northwest Africa and — quite recently — even of Egypt (R. Cavenaile, 1956–58), and though reports on current investigations, such as Kuhn's (1952), do make it a point to digest and to appraise these findings, a formal Romance grammar so organized as to do justice, at every level, to all twelve or thirteen Romance languages, living and extinct, is neither presently available nor expected in the foreseeable future.

Within a comparative arrangement, ONE LANGUAGE may be assigned a position of such preponderance as to make it outweigh any other in isolation, and, in extreme cases, all others taken jointly. Diez's pioneering dictionary (1854) reserved a favorite treatment for Italian. Among the grammarians, Darmesteter showed a measure of discrimination in his early treatise of Romance composition (1876), probing into French more than into all its cognates combined.[3] On a smaller

---

[3] This disproportion shows clearly in the exhaustive three-column index of quoted forms (257–316): French compounds occupy roughly two thirds of the space (257–296), even after the subtraction of proper names, while the space allotted to Provençal, Italian, Spanish, Portuguese, Rumanian, Ladin (i.e., Raeto-Romance), and "Vaudois" (310–313) is equal to the space reserved for classical Greek (307–310), a pathetic premonition of the French educational system grouping the national language with Latin and Greek to the lasting detriment of Romance comparatism.

---

Abbreviations used in this paper which may not be self-explanatory include Alb.: Albanian, Emil.: Emiliano (between North and Central Italian), Friul.: Friulano (Eastern Raeto-Romance), Gen.: Genoese (medieval and modern Ligurian), Mil.: Milanese (Central Lombard), Surs.: Surselvan or Obwaldisch (western branch of Western Raeto-Romance), Tusc.: Florentine Tuscan (underlying standard Italian), Vegl.: Vegliotic (last residue of Northern Dalmatian), Ven.: Venetian (language of Venice and/or the Veneto).

G

scale, Bourciez in his *Éléments* evinced the same bias, earmarking Old French and Modern French for separate treatment, while allowing congener languages, temporally flattened, to come up, at best, for a single discussion. This trend may lead to a "comparative" grammar, however paradoxical, of ostensibly a single language, as undertaken by Meillet for Armenian (1903) and by Sturtevant for Hittite (1933).

Two matters of signal importance, particularly for the expert in linguistic classification, are (a) the ORDER in which the members of a group are arrayed (note, in Meyer-Lübke's scheme as of 1909, the shift of Sardinian from the final position to the point midway between Italian and Provençal) and (b) the joint treatment of certain PAIRS AND TRIADS, implying the existence of SUBGROUPS within the family (as when Bourciez, bent on economy and concentration, subjoined Provençal to French and Portuguese to Spanish).

Systematic comparison of just TWO OR THREE out of several cognate languages has been far less assiduously practised in Romance than in Indo-Europeanist quarters, conceivably because there has been less stimulus or excuse for engaging in it. Thus, the age-old two-pronged study of classical philology created a background against which there arose a demand for comparative grammars of classical Greek and Latin — a demand which specialists of the stature of Buck and the Meillet-Vendryes team readily filled on either side of the Atlantic. No comparable large-scale ventures come to mind where the Romance offshoots of Latin are concerned, not even one of such obvious usefulness as might be the systematic confrontation of Spanish and Portuguese projected against their common source.[4] Among respectable minor projects of this kind, easily the best-known are Suchier's joint treatment of French and Provençal, echoed by Gamillscheg in 1921, and Meyer-Lübke's somewhat biased (hence, controversial) analysis of Catalan against the dual backdrop of Provençal and Castilian — inexplicably, to the near-exclusion of Aragonese. Add Delattre's ingenious, if modest, attempt to demonstrate that characteristic sound developments peculiar to fairly recent layers of Spanish closely parallel those plausibly reconstructed for the early history of French.

---

[4] One may disregard in this context P⁰ Martín Sarmiento's pioneer work on Galician vs. Castilian viewed in comparison to Latin and, on still better grounds, the sporadic attempts of certain patriotic Renaissance *dilettanti* to demonstrate that one Romance language, by virtue of its greater proximity to Latin, hence its superior "purity", carried more literary prestige than its closest rival; see the Bibliographic Supplement, under E. Buceta.

As a slightly anachronistic curiosity note further Deferrari's separate treatment, between two covers, of three related historical phonologies — those of French, Spanish, and Italian —, an experiment involving a measure of tacit, unintegrated comparison. This repetitious blueprint is inferior to the encyclopedia-like arrangement of grammatical sketches of cognate languages drawn by a skillfully coördinated group of specialists, with cross-linguistic methodological surveys underpinning the separate sections, as planned in Gröber's *Grundriß*; for strings of sketches executed by a single expert, cf. Monteverdi's *Avviamento* and Tagliavini's *Origini*.

Ordinarily, the diachronic dissection of a SINGLE fully documented language is deemed of sufficient latitude to justify a self-contained HISTORICAL grammar. Thus, to name at random a few middle-sized samples of this genre, scholars and especially students have at their disposal manuals so organized for Rumanian (Tiktin), Raeto-Romance (Gartner), Old Provençal (Schultz-Gora), Catalan (Moll), Spanish (Hanssen), and Portuguese (Nunes). In further subdividing this abundant output, one must determine whether the literary language occupies the focus of attention (except for the medieval period where, for transparent reasons, dialectal cleavage cannot be entirely ignored) or whether the author also takes into account regional speech, down to its present stage, frequently characterized by inner disintegration and loss of social prestige. An example of the former slant is Brunot's handbook, even after its thorough revision by Bruneau. The latter preference is best exemplified by Meyer-Lübke's original Italian grammar (not necessarily by its adaptations), also, more explicitly and on a grandiose scale, by Rohlfs' mid-20th-century counterpart. In Ronjat's lifework, the polyphony of the Occitanian dialects practically drowns out the thin voice of the vehicle of Provençal literature. In the case of marginal cultures lacking a universally recognized literary standard, a generous measure of dialectological coloring is unavoidable in any unilingual historical grammar; witness Wagner's many-faceted approach to Sardinian and Gartner's equal concern with all ramifications of Raeto-Romance. Inevitably, the typologist discovers multifarious transitions and compromises; thus, all Old French grammars of necessity dwell on dialectal peculiarities, but Schwan-Behrens' alone is advantageously known for its deliberate concentration on this feature, an interest marked by its geographically even spread; in contrast, Pope, without failing to do justice to the whole, designedly selected for preferential treatment a single dialect of favored cultural implications, Anglo-Norman.

Further narrowing the latitude, one arrives at those historical grammars which deal with DIALECTS and DIALECT GROUPS, that is, with mere fractions of a unilingual domain. The border-line between "language" and "dialect group" remains, of course, quite imprecise; an imaginative scholar, starting out with a modest, well-conducted dialect study, may be ultimately led to posit, on the strength of his own unanticipated findings, the existence of an independent language. Conceivably this, or some similar, experience underlies Ascoli's inquiries into Raeto-Romance and Franco-Provençal, both representing milestones in the annals of our discipline, though only the former has led to the indisputable establishment of an autonomous Romance language. Examples of less sensational, but equally solid historical grammars of major dialect groups include Staaff's analysis of medieval Leonese, on the basis of neatly dated and localized archival material (but note Menéndez Pidal's friendly strictures), and Kuhn's synoptic picture of modern Upper Aragonese, resting on a foundation of independent fieldwork, while Rohlfs' monograph on Gascon presupposes, on the part of writer and readers alike, an unusual degree of familiarity with Gilliéron's earlier linguistic atlas. Historically slanted dialect grammars, whether full-grown or sketchy, did not develop simultaneously for the various territories concerned. One finds them, as expected, at a relatively early date in Italy, amid an intellectual climate dominated by historicism and even antiquarianism at its liveliest (to say nothing of impressively widespread practical command of Latin), while Spain, as usual, has been lagging by a discernible margin: The earliest outlines, incidentally, were here prepared either by foreigners (Munthe, Leite de Vasconcelos) or by natives temporarily immersed in a foreign academic atmosphere (Múgica). The two manuals of peninsular Spanish dialectology presently available (García de Diego, Zamora Vicente) both embody rough sketches of historical grammar.

The logical minimum scope for a historical dialect grammar would be the speech of a SINGLE RURAL COMMUNITY, cf. Sánchez Sevilla's unsurpassed dissertation on the Eastern Leonese subdialect of Cespedosa de Tormes. A fitting philological counterpart, namely a full-fledged historical grammar attached to a SINGLE TEXT — i.e., in the last analysis, to a single idiolect or, at best, to the idiolects, frequently at variance, of author and copyist(s) — forms part of Menéndez Pidal's masterly *Cid* edition.

Generally speaking, the narrower the geographic spread, the greater the risk of a misapprehension, on the worker's part, of the true reshaping power of diffusion. Another controversial issue among the minority of historically oriented dialectologists has been the extent and authenticity of regional coloring detectable in the oldest texts. As Remacle and, after him, Gossen and others have amply demonstrated, an ancient provincial "scripta" is far from representing a faithful, unretouched record of local speech.

In discussing breadth, we have so far taken for granted that only languages conjoined by genetic kinship can be fruitfully discussed in a single context. This requires a qualifying correction: Territorial ties may act as a substitute for, or as an adjunct to, family relationship. In Romance the prime example was set by Gröber (1888), whose *Grundriß* gave equal attention to the Romance languages descended from Latin and to such prehistoric tongues (Iberian, Celtic, etc.) as were spoken in areas later converted to Romance culture. From here the path leads, outside the periphery of formal historical grammar, to K. Sandfeld's strictly regional concept of "Balkan linguistics" and to those surveys of linguistic conditions in the Iberian peninsula which have placed a premium on treating Basque on a par with the three local Romance languages (Entwistle, Šišmarëv, Kuen).

**1.2. Depth.** More difficult to measure (among other reasons, because it is seldom expressly stated in titles and subtitles)[5] is the dimension of TIME DEPTH. At this point one must rigorously distinguish between two problems: first, the total span involved; second and more intricate, the scheme of temporal subdivision within the inner structure of the book.

In the Romance field the typical historical grammar embraces the millennium and a half that separates a more or less unified Late Latin from the present stage of the given vernacular. A glaring exception to this tradition has been Provençal; since, at the formative stage of Romance scholarship, Old Provençal alone was in the focus of

---

[5] An exception is the clear-cut syntactic pattern "From . . . to", unequivocally marking off the starting and the finishing point. It has had a small vogue on both sides of the Atlantic, but only in English-speaking countries (cf. Grandgent, Pope, and Williams). Conceivably a faint echo of this fashion is perceptible in the title of A. Alonso's posthumous work *De la pronunciación medieval a la moderna en español*, on which he worked at Harvard during the declining stage of his career (1947–52). Cf. also fn. 49, below, and the Voretzsch-Rohlfs entry in the appended Bibliography.

enthusiastic attention, a Provençal historical grammar ordinarily concerns itself exclusively with the development from Latin to, say, the early 13th century (cf. Adams, Appel, Crescini, Grandgent, Schultz-Gora). Because of a certain parallelism, in academic offerings, requirements, and expectations, between the ancient languages and literatures of Northern and Southern France and, secondarily, as a result of the deep gap separating medieval from modern French, there has also arisen a sporadic need for special grammars of Old French (Schwan's, later revised by Behrens, Luquiens', L. Jordan's, Rheinfelder's, and many others). These must be carefully distinguished from those aiming to span the ENTIRE TRAJECTORY of French (Brachet, Nyrop, Meyer-Lübke, Pope, Alessio, Regula).

With regard to the other Romance languages, each less sharply differentiated along the chronological axis, the tradition of breaking off the account at the conclusion of the medieval stage has been confined to German and Austrian centers of learning. Contrast, in this respect, Zauner's Old Spanish grammar with those of Spanish — free from chronological shackles — prepared by natives (Menéndez Pidal, García de Diego) and foreigners (Förster, Baist, Hanssen, Pellegrini) alike; Huber's grammar of Old Portuguese with Reinhardstoettner's, D'Ovidio's, Leite's, Michaëlis', and Williams' broader-gauged ventures; Wiese's grammar of Old Italian with Meyer-Lübke's, Grandgent's, Pei's, and Rohlfs' unqualified concern with Italian at all its evolutionary stages.

It is unusual for time depth to measure less than two or three centuries; the torso of A. Alonso's *magnum opus* (see n. 5, above), though not strictly representative of historical grammar, would come close to this specification for a MINIMUM SPAN. Where the focus is on the speech conditions of a single century, even one linguistically as different at its inception from what it became toward its end as was the 16th century in France and Spain, the chances are that the internal treatment will become basically descriptive and synchronic, enlivened by, at best, flashes of evolutionary thought, though there may remain an ever-present tacit contrast to the usage of the modern period, familiar to readers either from introspection or from elementary training (Darmesteter and Hatzfeld, Gougenheim; Keniston). Also, where the late medieval stage is examined for its own sake, as it were, without constant reference to the parent language (cf. L. Foulet's introductory syntax of Old French), the author will almost unavoidably tend to indulge in a static approach and thus arrive at a flattened projection of near-contemporary facts. Conversely, the study of a single text, if it is accompanied by a grammar cast in bold relief, with each form shown echoing its distant prototype (as is true of the opening volume of Menéndez Pidal's *Cid* edition), may allow the element of dynamics to come to the fore.

The choice of a pattern of INTERNAL PERIODIZATION is one of the crucially important decisions the author of a historical grammar has to take. While the writer of a "language history" (as defined in Section 6.2, below) ordinarily receives his ideas on temporal segmentation from the straight historian or from the student of literature (cf. F. Brunot's monumental venture), unless he selects some such arbitrary unit as a century, the grammarian must rely on unadulterated linguistic data and remains answerable for his proposals only to fellow linguists. The segmentation may be very crude, as in the original blueprint of Keniston's unfinished *Syntax of Castilian Prose*;[6] it may be subtle and apply to a single slice of the total material, as when Meyer-Lübke, in his diachronic analysis of Old French vowels (*Hist. frz. Grammatik*, I, §§ 46 f., 82), distinguished between a pre-literary period favoring diphthongization, and an early literary period tending just as strongly toward monophtongization. A similarly sharp reversal of the dominant trend, coincident with a cultural event such as the rise of vernacular literature, need not recur in the evolution of consonants, suffixes, or clauses. The morphological section of Schwan-Behrens' grammar places, on the Vulgar Latin pedestal, a first Old French period, extending to 1100, and tops it with a second Old French period. There remains a lingering doubt: Is this division merely a matter of didactic expediency or does it correspond to an actual cleavage in the stratification? One can further operate with tripartition signaled by the labels Old, Middle, and New (or Modern); this scheme, familiar from English, German, Persian, Indic, etc., has occasionally been extended to French, see J. L. Grigsby, *RPh.*, XX (1966–67), 224–230.

The pattern of periodization adopted frequently reveals some of

---

[6] The jacket of the volume subtitled *The Sixteenth Century* identifies it as the second of a series of four. The others were to deal with the Middle Ages (1200–1500), the Modern Period (1600–1900), and the Contemporary Period (1900–). A distinctly more cogent division would have set off the scattered pre-Alfonsine writings (–1250) from the crest of the Old Spanish output (1250–1400); a new period of transition (1400–1525) was followed by another epoch of consolidation ("The Golden Age", 1525–1675). The most suitable dividing point for the Modern Period has not yet been determined, though, so far as the literary idiom is concerned, it may well be placed around 1825 (advent of Romanticism).

the author's basic assumptions. If he prefers to segregate, with Bourciez (*Éléments*), a "common Romance" or "Vulgar Latin" period, in which he jointly examines the prehistory of most shifts traceable to the individual vernaculars, the underlying supposition is that this period (stretching from, say, 300 to 800 A.D.) was one of relative territorial uniformity of usage. By the same token, the chief features of differentiation are tacitly or overtly attributed to later periods. A scholar espousing the opposite viewpoint, i.e., inclining to operate with the hypothesis of early provincial coloring of Latin speech, cannot with a clear conscience adopt this schema, at least not in comparative research.

**1.3. Direction.** Inherent in the evolutionary approach to history is the placing of the earlier ahead of the later stage, the obvious premise being that certain peculiarities of Phase A, often in conjunction with some supervenient factor, best explain the specific configuration of Phase B. In all likelihood, ninety-nine out of a hundred historical grammars chosen at random abide by this self-evident rule, so that it would be otiose to cite examples.

Nevertheless, one can ferret out a few exceptions. In the early years of this century, Meyer-Lübke urged contributors to a series of historically slanted textbooks (Winter's "Elementarbücher"), published under his supervision, to experiment, if only for pedagogical reasons, with the reverse perspective. At least two members of his team complied with this request; as a result, the original editions of B. Wiese's introduction to Old Italian (1904) and of A. Zauner's introduction to Old Spanish (1908) actually took as their point of departure the medieval stage — which in those instances represented the terminal limit — and led the inexperienced reader back to the assumed starting point.[7] Not improbably, this was a widely accepted academic classroom practice in Central Europe, here for once consecrated in formal presentation. The experiment must have soon been written off as a failure, since, in the initiator's lifetime, revised editions of these manuals, traceable to the 'twenties, reverted to the traditional sequence at the cost of a completely recast phonology, while later

[7] The following passage from B. Wiese's original Preface (1904) to his *Altitalienisches Elementarbuch* seems very quotable: "Einerseits war dafür der Wunsch des Herausgebers dieser Sammlung, ... Meyer-Lübke, maßgebend, andrerseits die pädagogische Erwägung, daß der Lernende, welcher die Texte liest, namentlich wenn er allein arbeitet, schneller vom Gewordenen zur Quelle emporsteigt, als von dieser, die er oft erst mühevoll suchen müßte, zu jenem hinab."

additions to the series, such as J. Huber's volume on Old Portuguese (1933), from the start adhered to the conventional pattern. It is, of course, theoretically conceivable to take two steps backward, by leading the reader, e.g., first from Modern to Old Italian, then from the latter to the parent language.

In adjoining provinces of linguistic endeavor (e.g., in such avowedly propaedeutic treatises as Voretzsch's introduction to Old French, Krüger's to Modern Spanish, and Gartner's to Rumanian), it was quite natural for the textbook writer to offer his student-readers a few specimens of the material they were most eager to assimilate, and to downgrade such ingredients of historical grammar as were at all deemed worthy of inclusion at the outset to incidental remarks, parenthetic statements, or, at best, intermittent flashbacks of slightly greater length. Significantly, these and similar books were expressly planned as emergency substitutes for normal classroom instruction at the university level.

A partial compromise between the two directions is not impossible, though in practice it is customary — and advisable — to subordinate the one to the other. Thus, in 1908 Zauner devoted two long chapters to the projection of Old Spanish sounds onto the plane of Latin (pp. 13–56), then, in lieu of an ordinary summary, offered a brief formulaic counterview (56–64).

## 2. Comprehensiveness

**2.0. Definition and subdivision.** If "scope" was used as a yardstick for measuring the number of languages involved and the distance between the linguistic stages compared as well as for determining their sequence, "comprehensiveness" here refers to the number of isolable disciplines included in a given piece of diachronic analysis. We shall designate as "unidisciplinary" a grammar concerned with, say, phonology or inflection alone; its "multidisciplinary" counterpart may comprise up to five separate dissections. In Romance scholarship, the traditional succession of core disciplines, which claim our immediate attention, has been this: phonology, inflection, word formation, and syntax. A very few extra-comprehensive books extend beyond this conventional limit, including in their purview such peripheral disciplines as semantics and poetics (or at least prosody). Occasional departures from the standard sequence are invariably noteworthy and will elicit some comments at a later juncture; what matters here primarily is the total width of the framework, not yet the pattern of distribution of pegs and notches.

Through a curious coincidence, some disciplines seem each to fall quite naturally into two roughly even parts; thus, phonology is concerned with vowels and consonants; inflection, with declension and conjugation; word formation, with derivation and composition; syntax, with the comportment of words viewed in their immediate context (phrases) and with the configuration of clauses and sentences. Whether this binary division, seductive at first sight, is in the long view defensible, even if one limits it to Romance, is a delicate question; the typologist will probably class studies centering about such "half-disciplines" (e.g., Schuchardt's inquiry into Vulgar Latin vowels or Lombard's researches in Rumanian conjugation) as occupying the mid-point between an authentic grammatical cross-section and a generously carved-out monograph. Investigations still narrower in scope will figure in this survey as straight monographs, capable of ceaselessly nourishing historical grammar and, conversely, at all times fed by it, but, for all this measure of affinity, constituting a separate genre.

The lexicon lies outside the legitimate jurisdiction of historical grammar, though the establishment of a workable liaison between these two poles has been for over a century an ever-present problem of first magnitude (see Section 6.6, below). It does happen, however, that for reasons of expediency publishers offer prospective buyers all kinds of "package-deals": combinations of historical grammar (or, at least, a sketch or prospectus of its nuclear disciplines), on the one hand, and a dictionary, a reader (anthology, chrestomathy), and the like, on the other. The result is either a hybrid book, in which the various ingredients appear amalgamated, or, less offensive, some kind of omnibus volume, in which they are distinguishable, despite the place that they forcibly share between two covers. The separation is more pronounced if the heterogeneous sections have been contributed by different authors.

**2.1. Unidisciplinary grammars: the core disciplines.** Where limitation to a single discipline prevails, PHONOLOGY traditionally leads by a wide margin, for two quite dissimilar reasons. First, ever since the elevation of sound correspondences to the rank of "laws", under the régime of Neo-grammarians, phonology has — rightly or wrongly — enjoyed the reputation of being the most rigorously organized, "scientifically" slanted discipline, allowing clear-cut distinctions and inviting a modest measure of prediction. Esteemed by many experts and most outsiders as the explorer's most reliable guide in the classification of languages and dialects and in the dating and localization of texts, and dreaded by chance acquaintances (such as the average modern-language student) as the most formidable, obtrusively technical approach to language, it has been recognized in university curricula the world over as the safest means of providing an irreducible minimum of linguistic training — a situation which has led to a steady demand for, and correspondingly lively flow of, textbooks of varying degrees of excellence and sophistication. The second and more trivial reason for the margin, in terms of representation, of phonology over its sister disciplines is its normal position as a first link in a chain: Not a few initially ambitious authors, after publishing a sketch or treatise on phonology as the opening volume, fascicle, or installment of a major undertaking, became so discouraged by the lack of response or the shrinkage of financial resources as to abandon or curtail their original plans. In this event, the phonological tract amounts not to a carefully thought-out terminal project, but, pathetically, to a mere torso — and a grim reminder of human frailty.[8]

Although the latest theoretical thinking recognizes MORPHOLOGY as the very kernel of linguistic analysis, books and articles devoted exclusively to a diachronic view of inflection and word formation have been fairly infrequent, at least, in the Romance domain. One possible contributing factor to this imbalance: Phonology, quite properly, ranks as a key opening up morphology, so that a discussion of the latter in isolation reminds one of the possession of a hopelessly

---

[8] There would be some danger of skirting the domain of the anecdotal in any attempt to discuss here projects left — or seemingly left — unfinished. Aside from the "torso" of Keniston's Spanish syntax and of Múgica's grammar of Old Spanish, one is reminded of Lerch's French syntax, the concluding volume of which (announced in III, xi) never appeared. Shall we live to see Vol. II of Rheinfelder's Old French grammar, which is to complement his phonology, carefully marked as Vol. I (1937; 2d ed., 1953–55)? As regards the chronological limits of works geared to periodization, Densusianu's history of Rumanian was meant to transcend the 16th century. Of some important undertakings only small fragments have so far become accessible. Thus, an aged Meyer-Lübke's ebbing energy fell short of revising his Romance phonology (1890) except for a few chapters of special appeal, published in the 'thirties as separate articles. Of Menéndez Pidal's monumental *Historia de la lengua española*, for which the *Orígenes* was to serve as an opening wedge, only a few short sections, mainly concerned with the substratum, have become available in print as independent publications.

locked treasure-chest. There has, of course, been no dearth of mono-graphic inquiries into minor points (in particular, those of conjuga-tion and derivation), possibly on account of the somewhat greater isolability of, say, a well-defined suffix than of a speech sound. A border-line case, involving a commendable practice, calls for the writing of a separate handbook of morphology based squarely on an earlier treatise on phonology — by the same or, still better, by a different author: Examples in point are the twin volumes of the Latinists Niedermann and Ernout, each a semi-independent piece of masterly, if conservative, research. It remained for P. Fouché to start out the evolutionary probing of French with a report on the verb (1931) and to conclude it with a circumstantial account of phonology (1952-61).

The climate of SYNTACTIC INQUIRY is so strongly at variance with those that prevail in the two preceding domains (starting with the techniques used in collecting evidence) that it is not unusual for an imaginative linguist to become specialized as a "syntactician" and to aim at a synthesis of his findings in this field alone.

Random illustrations of unidisciplinary treatises:

(a) PHONOLOGY: Guarnerio (pan-Romanic), Múgica (Spanish; also Ford in the Introduction to his *Readings*), Sanchis Guarner (West Catalan), Appel — if one separates his *Abriß* (1918) from the under-lying older chrestomathy (Old Provençal);

(b) INFLECTION:[9] Keller (Spanish) and Šišmarëv (French); studies concerned with the verb alone have here been barred from considera-tion;

---

[9] A point of terminology: Though, from the start, morphology (G. "Formen-lehre") was understood to include derivation and composition (cf. Munthe, Tiktin [1905], Nunes [1919], Sánchez Sevilla, Densusianu, Rohlfs [1935], and many others, in the wake of Diez and Meyer-Lübke), numerous authors have used it as coterminous with "inflection" (G. "Beugung, Flexionslehre"). This applies equally to separate books and to chapter or section headings in countless manuals, e.g., Gartner's (1883), Pope's, and Williams'. J. Wiggers (1884) examined word formation in a supplement to his morphology of Spanish. Ronjat conjoined the two disciplines without merging them. The norm has been to assign them separate chapters of equal rank, with little unanimity as to the headings: While García de Diego (1914) opposed "morfología" (i.e., inflection) to "temática o lexicogenesia" (i.e., derivation and composition), Pellegrini (1950) contrasted "morfologia" with "composizione", the latter, inexplicably, including suffixal derivation. On the "dispersion de certains sujets à plusieurs endroits de la grammaire" (with special reference to inflection, derivation, and syntax), see É. Benveniste's comments in *BSLP*, LIII: 2 (1957-58), 69, on G. Lazard, *Grammaire du persan contemporain*.

(c) WORD FORMATION: Adams (Provençal), Alemany Bolufer (Spanish);

(d) SYNTAX: Haas, Foulet, Lerch, and Gamillscheg (French).

In one important respect, syntactic treatises of the older school differed from researches bearing on phonology and morphology: Their orientation was intermittently rather than consistently diachronic, since the historical analysis was again and again diluted and distorted by "panchronic" logical or, worse, "ethnocentric" psychological considerations. Thus, Haas (1916) conscientiously followed the trajectory of each French construction from the peak of the Middle Ages to the threshold of our own century; to that extent his outlook was historical. But, inexplicably, he set up the incipient stage of Old French as some kind of (unacknowledged) *creatio ex nihilo*: The earliest known constructions issued forth — one gathers from his introductory remarks to each chapter — from certain general, immutable conditions of the human mind, rather than from the unique configuration of colloquial Late Latin syntax, itself the product of neatly identifiable, non-recurrent forces.

**2.2 Border-line disciplines.** Of the disciplines marginal to historical grammar we seldom possess separate accounts qualifying for unconditional consideration in this context. Thus, even if one agrees with Bally that STYLISTICS is convertible into an integral part of linguistic inquiry, his own pioneering *Traité de stylistique française* is deliberately synchronic, and none of his closer followers has bothered to tread the same ground in a different direction. Again, the status of SEMANTICS is dubious; if one interprets the kernel of this discipline, along with European-style onomasiology (a refined version of cross-linguistic synonymics; see Quadri), essentially as a subdivision of lexicology, there is little point in attaching it to historical grammar. Is it ever certain that the semantics of a particular language, let us say, of French (cf. the heterogeneous specimens furnished by Ullmann and Gamillscheg), amounts to more than an array of specific illustrations of universal phenomena for which the analyst prefers to draw on a particular source?[10] A negative answer to this question

---

[10] Not insignificant, in this context, is the descriptive subtitle of Hatzfeld's tract: "Versuch einer Zusammenstellung charakteristischen semasiologischen Beispielmaterials aus den bekanntesten Sprachen". It would have been far more difficult to do equal justice to Greek, Latin, French, Spanish, Italian, German, and English on the level of phonology, where each language has its own sharply profiled configuration, making common denominators, for the most part, unobtainable.

would imply that the writer aims at documenting a series of assumed semantic shifts with French examples, much as he is free to illustrate a set of "accidenti generali" with Italian or, for that matter, Spanish instances, but without any expectation of observing a clear-cut French pattern of changes in meaning comparable in the autonomy and uniqueness of its design to, say, the pattern of French vowel shifts. As regards POETICS, a unified discipline truly worthy of this label has not yet emerged, despite a rich and partly very old store of disconnected researches in, on the one hand, METRICS, and, on the other, METAPHORICS. Historically projected metric treatises for a given Romance language, contributed by foreigners (A. Tobler, W. Suchier for French) or by natives (T. Navarro for Spanish), have a venerable tradition of their own.

**2.3. Combinations of disciplines.** The rule has been since Diez's pioneer effort for a full-fledged historical grammar to embrace four disciplines (if inflection and word formation for once be counted as two), and for an abridged, inexpensive variety — typically, a textbook suiting the student's budget of time, effort, and money — to include at least two. A unidisciplinary grammar definitely gives the impression of inadequacy or lopsidedness. The grouping of disciplines into bundles is not entirely arbitrary. Two considerations seem to dictate the discernible patterns of arrangement: First, a hierarchy of ESSENTIALITY, which, rightly or wrongly, tends to assign the humblest position of all to word formation; and, second, a tacit recognition of certain INHERENT AFFINITIES between disciplines—degrees of kinship extending to material examined, method of investigation, and climate of discussion. Thus, since phonology and syntax occupy the two extremes of the spectrum, it would be unthinkable to pair them off to the exclusion of interjacent morphology. These two basic considerations are sometimes locked in unacknowledged CONFLICT. For instance, the scale of essentiality would favor assembling in a tripartite work phonology, inflection, and syntax (a structure which Hanssen, in fact, accepted in 1910), while on the scale of intrinsic affinity phonology, inflection, and word formation might form a more harmonious triad; witness P. Förster's ground-breaking grammar of Spanish and, as of this date at least, the aggregate of Wagner's grammatical researches in Sardinian, provided one agrees to regard each of his three relevant monographs, published independently (1941, 1938–39, 1952, in this unorthodox order), as forming part of an indivisible whole.

There probably exist upward of a hundred manuals in the Romance domain alone — some of them of very ephemeral distinction — that include a BARE OUTLINE of phonology and inflection. Perhaps this kind of manual, especially if unimaginative in approach, jejune of analytical incisiveness, and derivative in factual information, has contributed more than any other factor to the sad reputation of aridity which research in historical grammar is still widely accorded by impatient humanists. Most of these ventures have been planned, no less by aggressive publishers than by the scholars themselves, either as textbooks or as reference works; relatively few are bold and exploratory. Among the most meritorious, one may cite Cornu's treatise as well as Nunes' and Williams' handbooks, all three concerned with Portuguese. In the Spanish field, Baist's and Pellegrini's outlines are so organized; in the Italian and the Provençal, Grandgent's; in the Old French, Schwan's and Pope's.

The addition of a special chapter or, better still, section on word formation gives a welcome touch of elaboration to a nuclear historical grammar; still incomplete, it becomes MIDDLE-SIZED in topical coverage. A classic example, triadic in content if not in formal arrangement, is Menéndez Pidal's *Manual* (*elemental*). The alternative, we recall, is to expand the bipartite nucleus in the direction of syntax, on the basis of that discipline's priority in real-life situations, especially in practical language teaching.

The QUADRIPARTITE schema, consecrated by Diez's and Meyer-Lübke's monumental syntheses, underlies Rohlfs' Italian grammar and, on a miniature scale, not a few handy textbooks, e.g., Zauner's for Old Spanish and Huber's for Old Portuguese; Hanssen eventually chose it for a revision of his lifework (1913), and Menéndez Pidal adhered to it in his *Cid* grammar (1908). If the syntax receives more superficial examination than the other disciplines, this disparity may be expressly indicated by the chapter heading (e.g., "Syntaktisches" rather than "Syntax").[11] Cf. infra n. 42.

The QUINQUEPARTITE schema in formal historical grammar has seldom been adopted, though semantics (or SEMASIOLOGY) figures

---

[11] Even more eloquent than the choice of a non-committal chapter heading is the pathetically inadequate allotment of space to syntax. Gossen's grammar of Old Picard devotes 64 pages to phonology, 21 to inflection, 3 to syntax. Kuhn's monograph on modern Upper Aragonese, held by many to represent a model study, accords a picayunish 6 pages to syntax (for which the author has set aside no separate chapter) as against 106 for phonology, 36 for inflection, and 48 for word formation.

prominently in Zauner's revised pocket-book introduction to Romance linguistics and even occupies a separate volume in Nyrop's historical grammar of French, which visibly aims at completeness. In the 19th century scholars not infrequently toyed with the idea of granting a modest status to "POETICS" — usually by way of an excursus or of a supplement to the main corpus; thus, Vol. I (1870) of Diez's revised grammar contains a concluding section on prosody (486–514), a practice later discontinued.[12] A brief (as a rule, introductory) chapter on ORTHOGRAPHY is a very common, self-explanatory companion feature of a balanced historical phonology and contains the germ of GRAPHEMICS, a discipline at this date still in the process of crystallization. The inclusion of LEXICOGRAPHIC chapters, as in Bourciez's *Éléments*, has lately been abandoned in formal grammars, though, by the same token, such problems play a deservedly prominent part in less austerely conceived "language histories" (see Section 6.2, below).

**2.4. Transition to monographs.** From a full-fledged historical grammar to a monograph pinpointing an exceedingly narrow problem there exists a continuum of transitions, so that any border-line one elects to draw, including our own (see Section 2.0, above), is doomed to remain arbitrary. After having segregated the monographs as a genre, one may attempt to classify them in the order of decreasing breadth. By way of example, take word formation: After the deduction of full-sized treatises (regardless of the number of languages involved), the residue falls into such studies as attempt to cover the entire territory of derivational suffixation (Allen) or composition (Darmesteter, 1874); such as are concerned solely with productive patterns (Darmesteter, 1877; Pichon); also such as cut across a great variety of allied problems, formally or semantically analyzed (Cohn's inquiry into all manner of suffix change as against Kahane's investigation of the augmentative feminine), or are limited to particular issues rich in methodological implications (Gamillscheg, 1921). Farther down the scale one may place researches in smaller

---

[12] Diez's closest followers paid sustained attention to this side issue: Reinhard-stoettner (1878) included a stylistic and a metric Supplement ("Einzelne Abweichungen vom gewöhnlichen Stile", "Zur portugiesischen Metrik", 393–398), and Förster, two years later, contrived a long opening chapter (1–56) immersing his readers at once in niceties of pronunciation, prosody, and accentuation. The inclusion of an accentologic account ("Prosodia", 66–76) in García de Diego's grammar (1914) was almost an archaizing feature.

conglomerations of suffixes, e.g., on the formal side, investigations of items erratically stressed (Menéndez Pidal) or epicene (Spitzer); and, on the semantic side, studies in the derivation of mass-nouns (Baldinger) and diminutives (Hasselrot). From here one proceeds to still smaller units, mere molecules of suffixes strung together by a thin thread (say, a single consonant phoneme: cf. Horning, for French, and Menéndez Pidal and Tovar recently teamed up for Spanish). Examples of further progressive atomization would comprise microscopic inquiries into isolated variants (several such experiments have recently been staged in the Luso-Hispanic field, e.g., on -*azo*, -*iego*, -*uno*, and deverbal -*e*), and, still narrower, on fairly unusual "chains" or sequences of formatives (cf. Rohlfs' note on Sp. -*arrón*).

Understandably, most pioneers (a strikingly young Fuchs [1840], also Brachet [1866], Horning, Ulrich, and others) were far less reluctant to write monographs straddling several languages than were the cautious scholars of later generations, faced with the task of meeting steadily higher standards of rigor and of digesting ever-increasing amounts of primary and secondary sources. In the controversial field of Old Spanish sibilants, for instance, the break lies between Joret's and Horning's explicitly comparative approach (excitingly broad-gauged, but somewhat superficial) and, starting with 1894, Cuervo's, Ford's, Saroïhandy's, and Tallgren-Tuulio's concentration on a single language, conducive to distinctly more technical inquiries.

**2.5. Combinations with other genres.** Under special circumstances a historical grammar may be downgraded to a mere constituent of some broader book venture. If it is attached to a reader (chrestomathy, etc.),[13] as happens not infrequently in medievalistic and allied

[13] Note that the once fairly undifferentiated, multi-purpose type of "reader", of the kind familiar from Menéndez Pidal's excellent *Antología de prosistas castellanos* (1899), has started to split up into a variety of well-defined subtypes. The paleographic medievalistic chrestomathy, which has its unsurpassed model in W. Foerster and E. Koschwitz's *Altfranzösisches Übungsbuch* (3d ed., Leipzig, 1907; 7th ed., 1932), contains details so finicky as to be out of place in a strictly literary reader, planned as a companion piece to a history of literature (E. Werner, *Blütenlese der älteren spanischen Literatur*) or designed for esthetic enjoyment (as is true of various anthologies compiled by D. Alonso). The chrestomathy geared to the needs of historical grammar, as distinct from textual criticism and literary analysis, favors extracts from texts dialectally colored (many of them admittedly devoid of literary merit) and as little as possible tampered with by successive scribes. A prototype is the Supplement Volume to the revised Schwan-Behrens grammar; two

H

researches and especially teaching aids, the question arises as to whether the two sections are approximately on a par (Crescini, Gorra, Alemany Bolufer) and, if not, whether the grammar is a mere introductory prospectus echoed in all likelihood by an appended glossary (Ford; but Appel, content with an inconspicuous morphological sketch ancillary to his chrestomathy, subsequently developed the phonological counterpart into an independent companion piece of considerable weight) or, conversely, whether the reader merely represents a supplement or sampler (Wiese, Tiktin [1905], Zauner, Schultz-Gora, Huber;[14] Behrens' revision of Schwan). In Jordan's Old French grammar this frame of reference (extracts from the Munich *Brut* and the *Roman de la Rose*) ushers in the analysis.

A brief sketch of historical grammar may likewise precede or follow a dictionary, even one compiled for laymen, — a practice, to be sure, more in accord with late-19th-century historicism than with current trends of taste (*RPh.*, XII, 395 n. 38). In at least two instances, extensive and influential historical grammars, from the pen of experts, represent opening sections of major dictionaries, as if to whet the reader's appetite or to serve as a wedge for deeper penetration: Coelho's 240-page treatise shared with T. Braga's essay in literary history the honor of heralding Vieira's five-volume dictionary, and A. Darmesteter's authoritative *Traité de la formation de la langue française*, very stringently organized and expanded posthumously to even greater length by L. Sudre and A. Thomas, was from the start designed as an entrance gate to the *Dictionnaire général*. The combined grammar and dictionary of a text chosen for its difficulty represent a conventionally delimited piece of research (Fernández Llera).

There are on record subtler ways of subordinating a small historical

---

[14] Where grammatical series were sponsored by well-established publishing houses (such as Winter and Niemeyer in pre-war Germany), the scholar acting as counselor or supervisory editor was free to urge the adoption of this pattern which, incidentally, obviated the student's need for purchasing a separate reader. A "language history" is also apt to include a selection of sample texts (Ewert, Pei, Oliver Asín), but Lapesa was doubtless well advised in eliminating this too pedagogically flavored section from all revised editions of his *Historia*.

---

modern representatives: Šišmarëv's *Kniga dlja čten'ja po istorii francuzskogo jazyka* (for which a separate glossary has been issued) and D. J. Gifford and F. W. Hodcroft's *Textos lingüísticos del medioevo español* (Oxford, 1959; rev. ed., 1966). Menéndez Pidal's latest venture in this direction, the splendid *Crestomatía del español medieval* (1965–66), does equal justice to literary, philological, and linguistic needs, thus marking a return to an old model.

grammar to a distantly related project which, in exceptional instances, even exceeds the precinct of linguistics.[15] A parsimoniously worded outline of phonology, sometimes in conjunction with inflection, may more or less appropriately form part of a detailed, high-reaching "practical" (i.e. normative) grammar, to give it a certain cachet of distinction (Wiggers, Tagliavini). It may likewise find a place in a loosely structured "language history" — to be precise, may represent the solid backbone of that history —, a procedure adopted not only by a succession of pioneers (cf. the miniature phonologies — strictly speaking, lists of correspondences between Spanish and Latin "letters" — in Nebrixa, Sarmiento, etc.), but also by a dwindling rear-guard of moderns (Oliver Asín). Some such epitome may further function as a systematic, succinct recapitulation of remarks haphazardly injected into the introductory pages of a graded textbook, e.g., Voretzsch's *Einführung* (cf. Parts II and especially IV of its definitive edition). A similar service may be performed by the tight grammatical counterview of a slightly rambling lexicological monograph such as C. Michaëlis' once valuable, if whimsically mistitled, study of Spanish doublets (1876). There remains the case of a compact historical grammar (e.g., Morel-Fatio's of Catalan, later partially revised by Saroïhandy, or Gartner's of Raeto-Romance, or again Tiktin's of Rumanian) incorporated, from the outset, into a battery of precision instruments jointly trained on the distant past, as one may fittingly call Gröber's *Grundriß* in nostalgic retrospect.

## 3. Grand Strategy

**3.0. Definition and subdivision.** Under this heading one is tempted to subsume some major strategic arrangements affecting, as a rule, more than one section of a historical grammar and second in im-

[15] Except in specialized encyclopedias such as Gröber's, a straight historical grammar is unlikely to share the platform with an outline of literature, though some kind of linguistic survey including chosen features of historical analysis — if at all possible, pruned of burdensome technicalities — may be not unwelcome even to today's general cultured reader. The range of possibilities is best suggested by A. Darmesteter and A. Hatzfeld's parallel 16th-century *Tableaux*, by an exiled Auerbach's less than successful attempt to impart equal amenity, in his new Turkish homestead, to the teaching of Romance literature and linguistics, and by Meyer-Lübke's readiness to share the spotlight with Morf in a bold synthesis of Romance languages and literatures (1904–09). For unfamiliar cultures of limited scope, such as Raeto-Romance, it makes, of course, excellent sense to offer the few enticeable readers a joint treatment of language, literature, and even folklore; cf. Gartner's *Handbuch*.

portance only to those three discussed under "Scope" ("breadth", "depth", and "direction"). One strategic decision concerns the precise delimitation of the disciplines at issue. The treatment of word formation, for instance, — quite aside from the variable degree of detail which it invites — depends on the specific place assigned to it in the book's total architecture. Most Romance scholars would analyze all questions pertinent to affixation in a separate, unified section, but a minority (including an expert of Menéndez Pidal's caliber) pairs off, in Indo-Europeanist fashion, nominal derivation with nominal inflection, and verbal derivation with verbal inflection. Again, the border-line between morphology and syntax is quite fluid.

Another far-reaching decision centers around this problem, particularly acute in phonology: If the Romance scholar's chief responsibility is to establish accurate sound correspondences mediating between Latin and Romance, just what place — if any — in this schema should he assign to the substratal layers as well as to Greek, Oscan, Germanic, Arabic, Turkish, Hungarian, Basque, and Slavic strains of the local lexica?

Of even greater significance is the general array of all data within the chosen perspective. At this point, the "standard arrangement", tending to isolate the features and to enumerate them in almost indifferent fashion, may be effectively contrasted with some more imaginative procedures not yet enjoying wide recognition, but opening up distinctly more rewarding vistas. Most attractive and, at the same time, controversial among such experimental arrangements are these: (a) the ordering of events conformally to absolute or relative chronology; (b) their grouping on the basis of such broad categories of linguistic change as assimilation and dissimilation; (c) separate presentation of those changes in which cohesion and mutual conditioning are most clearly discernible, the analyst's ultimate goal being the reinterpretation in structuralistic terms of the aggregate of sound changes within a given system; (d) neat hierarchization of changes in the shape of words (division into [$\alpha$] genuine phonological drift, [$\beta$] "accidenti generali", [$\gamma$] associative processes, [$\delta$] effects of diffusion, [$\epsilon$] effects of expressivism and hypercharacterization, etc.); (e) choice of a pattern of selectivity justified by strictly dynamic considerations.

**3.1. Delimitation of disciplines.** In measuring the "comprehensiveness" of a treatise, i.e., the number of disciplines it purports to encompass (see Section 2.0, above), we took for granted the traditional delimitation of those disciplines and further tacitly assumed that each was self-contained to the point of steering clear of any overlap or tangle. At the initial stage, these were helpful assumptions which enabled us to gauge rapidly, by rule of thumb, the total breadth of a grammar. But, viewed at closer range, such sweeping presuppositions do not always hold water. One detects a good deal of interlocking between disciplines, a state of affairs calling at every step for subjective classificatory decisions.

Though phonology, in its prestructural definition, and syntax, however we may circumscribe it, seem far apart on the conventional scale of disciplines, they abut at one point which the Founding Fathers appositely called "Satzphonetik" — the conditioning of sound features by the word's position in a sentence. Meyer-Lübke, possibly sensitized to SANDHI by his early Indo-Europeanist training, was careful, in 1890, to assemble all relevant observations in a separate chapter ("Das Wort im Satze", pp. 502–522), which flanks another chapter on ACCENT. In his classificatory hierarchy he placed both on the same rung as the obligatory pillars of any conventional phonology: the chapters on vowels and consonants. Neither syntactic phonology nor accentology have later occupied positions of comparable prominence in Romance diachronic research, no doubt as a partial result of the relative stability of Latin stress and of the subordinate rôle of pitch, here consistently non-distinctive. If at all separately examined, syntactic phonology is relegated to an inconspicuous position toward the end of the phonological section (Menéndez Pidal, *Cid* grammar; Nunes, *Compêndio*).

GRAPHEMICS (less pretentiously, the study of spelling habits) is normally so lodged within the total framework as to herald the tabulation of sound changes, thus forming a natural bridge from paleography to linguistics proper. This optional excursus has been particularly dear to the medievalist steeped in archival research (cf. the routine treatment by Förster, Wiggers, Baist, Cornu, Grandgent [1905], Huber, Williams, and many others, typically in the opening section of the given book, as against Menéndez Pidal's masterly comments in the Introduction to his *Orígenes*).[16] Conversely, SYNTAX

---

[16] Occasionally, the chapter on orthography is transposed to a different part. Fuchs (1849) discusses "Lautbezeichnung und Lautverhältnisse" at a fairly advanced point of his treatise (296–310); Menéndez Pidal's *Cid* grammar (1908) assigns to the topic "Alfabeto y pronunciación" a secluded spot at the end of phono-

is ordinarily divested of references to the decipherment and presentation of manuscripts. This distribution of alliances and affinities flows mainly not from logical necessity, but from convention, which Foulet had the courage to defy in his *Petite syntaxe*, where he reserved a Supplement (3d ed., pp. 345–374) for the syntactic implications of a medievalist's analysis of manuscript transmission.

There is no predicting where references to the marginally recognized disciplines will be accommodated. While García de Diego (1914) reserves a separate chapter for SEMANTICS, Bourciez, in the opening section of his *Éléments*, and, much more fully, Ewert examine changes of meaning under Vocabulary, a privilege incident to the choice of language history in preference to historical grammar. In classical scholarship, old-fashioned stylistics, i.e., RHETORIC, normally follows upon syntax; cf. J. B. Hofmann's revision (1928) of Stolz-Schmalz. POETICS (metrics, versification) one expects to find in a Supplement (Wiggers) or in a concluding section (Nunes, *Crestomatia*; Brunot-Bruneau, *Précis*); in Crescini's *Manuale* (1926) the "Appunti ritmici" form a natural bridge from grammar to reader. Finally, some eccentric scholars operate with fancy disciplines; thus, García de Diego (1951) thought up a twenty-two page chapter on "ANALOGY" (phonological, morphological, and syntactic) which drives a most inopportune wedge between phonology and morphology.

**3.2. Subordination of disciplines.** In our initial schema the basic disciplines were introduced as peers, with equal claims on the linguist's attention, provided he cares at all to include them in his purview. The actual picture looks quite different: While Diez and Meyer-Lübke were careful to allocate approximately equal space to inflection and to word formation, many smaller grammars reduce the latter to a short catalogue of characteristic prefixes and suffixes, nonchalantly appended, by way of supplement, to a rather full discussion of declension and conjugation (one such offender is Huber;

---

logy (207–230); García de Diego's *Elementos* (1914) pigeonholes orthography between accentology and semantics (77–93). Numerous modern linguists, convinced that their science deals with sounds, not with script, go out of their way to omit or to screen references to letters; to whet the reader's historical curiosity, Deferrari's *Phonology of Italian* hastens to introduce him from the start to the sounds of that language (129–140), not to their symbolic representation. Some languages, famous as vehicles of literature, hence often visually absorbed, invite keener attention to their spelling than do others; French orthography is so erratic, hence exciting, as to have elicited separate medium-sized chapters in such relatively up-to-date manuals as Ewert's (1933) and Pope's (1934).

for similar treatment of syntax as a stepchild see n. 11, above). In Gartner's *Darstellung* a synopsis of "Wortbildung" (141–149) is bizarrely wedged in between phonology and morphology, i.e., inflection.[17]

In his major writings (*Manual*, *Cid* grammar, *Orígenes* — see 3d ed., § 329), Menéndez Pidal has split up the arsenal of affixes, attaching the nominal group to the discussion of declension and the verbal group to the analysis of conjugation — a legitimate practice, widely adopted by Indo-Europeanists,[18] but here conducive to loss of rank; cf. p. 94, above.

Unlikely as it seems at first glance that phonology and word formation should intersect, both editions (1888, 1906) of Cornu's Portuguese grammar contain a fairly detailed catalogue of suffixes, with appropriate illustrations, hidden away in, of all places, the chapter on stressed vowels.[19] The reason — no valid excuse — for

[17] Cf., however, the following footnote. Here are examples of further unusual niches carved out for derivation and composition. In "language histories", from Fuchs' (1849) to Bourciez's (*Éléments*, 1910: see Part I, Section 3) and Ewert's (1933), an independent lexical chapter which would have been inadmissible in a straight historical grammar, has most opportunely provided the requisite quarters. Rohlfs, inexplicably, placed syntax ahead of word formation (1954).

[18] Thus, M. Leumann, in his revision (1928) of Stolz-Schmalz's morphology, divides the section on the noun (199–300) into a chapter on "Stammbildung" largely, though not exclusively, concerned with derivational suffixes (199–254), and a shorter chapter on inflection (255–300). The Indo-Europeanist tradition (whose course, in turn, was by and large determined by the material available) calls for this peculiar sequence; witness also Chap. IV ("Nouns and adjectives") in Sturtevant's *Comparative Grammar of the Hittite Language* (1933), in which word formation clearly takes precedence over declension. This succession has been almost unparalleled in Romance scholarship except at its incipient stage. In the twilight period between Diez's and Meyer-Lübke's grammars some minor practitioners deviated from the established canon. Thus, C. von Reinhardstoettner (1878) wedged in a lengthy chapter on "Wortbildung" (111–156) between the sections on Portuguese phonology and inflection, and T. Gartner followed suit as late as 1904; P. Förster regaled the readers of his erudite Spanish grammar (1880) with a long hybrid section titled "Sprachschatz und Wortbildung" (159–239) similarly placed, or rather misplaced. In G. Meyer's account of Albano-Latin (1888), word formation, ranked as a constituent of morphology, anteceded declension and conjugation. It was the prestige of Meyer-Lübke's tone-setting Italian grammar (1890) and comparative grammar (1894) that swung the pendulum back to its initial position (Diez). Outside the Indo-European province, L. Bloomfield showed greater restraint in his concluding works than as a young experimenter. Thus, in the posthumous *Eastern Ojibwa* (which reflects his thinking as of the early 'forties), the chapters on Composition, Suffixation, and Roots form, conservatively enough, a bridge from Inflection to Syntax, while in his much earlier *Tagalog Texts* (1917) Syntax (146–205) was allowed to separate Phonetics (134–145) from Morphology (210–316).

[19] Thus, -*elo* (-*êlo*) < -ELLU is discussed under Ĕ (§§ 5 f.), -*ego* < -AECU under AE (§ 8), -*edo* < -ĒTU and -*ês* < -Ē(N)SE under Ē (§ 9), -*eza* < -ITIA, -*ez* < -ITIE,

this strange distribution is that, only if propelled by a stressed vowel, did Latin suffixes survive, as a rule, into Romance.

Given the importance of morphophonemics in several schools of modern descriptivism, it is wholesome to recall that some classic historical grammars acknowledged the existence of a "domain" (at that time "level" was not yet current) where phonological alternation coincided with morphological variation, the whole viewed in diachronic perspective. There remained the problem of discovering the proper niche for this elusive field. Cornu titled a supplement (§§ 41–65) to his chapter on stressed vowels in Portuguese "Comportment of stressed vowels in verbs and non-suffixal verbal nouns", adding, for good measure, such stray remarks on the strong preterite as should properly have fallen under apophony and metaphony. Conversely, Menéndez Pidal's *Cid* grammar opens its discussion of the verb with a statement (260–264) on the "Peculiarities of verbal vocalism".

**3.3. Reshuffling of disciplines.** Allowances for minor inter-disciplinary encroachments and for the unequal rating of disciplines, in terms of classification and of space allotment, blur our initially clear vision of several analyses, each neatly delineated, yet all harmoniously coördinated. Fundamentally, however, they imply continued recognition of the separate existence of the disciplines originally posited. One can visualize far more radical departures from the standard, leading to the reapportionment of the entire material or, at least, of a liberal share of it among a differently ordered set of basic disciplines.

Some schools of general linguistics insist on abolishing the borderline between morphology (or, at least, inflection) and syntax (or certain provinces of syntax). On the whole, this reform, despite its endorsement by Brunot-Bruneau, Ewert, and Rohlfs in the early 'thirties, has so far had limited effect on the main stream of Romance historical linguistics, conceivably because under the surrounding circumstances it is decidedly impractical.

Yet Romance scholarship has not been entirely immune to such trends. As early as the first revision (1905) of his pocket-sized Romance grammar, Zauner sliced his material into three pieces,

---

*-elho* < -IC(U)LU, *-ete* < -IUUU [sic], and, less convincingly, *-ivel* < -IBILE, *-ice* < -ITIE, *-iço* < -ICIU, *-ilho* < -IC(U)LU under Ĭ (§§ 12 f., 15; -ĪCLU, Cornu admits, is the alternative), *-inho* < -INU, *-il* < -ILE, *-io* < -ĪVU, *-iço* < -ĪTIU [but cf. above], and *-ijem* < -ĪGINE under Ī (§§ 16 f.), etc.; -IUUU is presumably a misprint for -ITTU.

inserting as a separate category of equal rank between (a) a succinct phonology and (c) a mere sketch ("Grundzüge") of syntax, his (b) "Wortlehre", an amalgam of (α) inflection, (β) old-style semantics, (γ) certain sections of syntax centered about the individual word, and (δ) word formation.[20] Zauner's enthusiasm for this mould spilled over, in slightly dampened form, into his introductory Old Spanish grammar, whose "Wortlehre" (65–123; 2d ed., 56–109) embraces traditional morphology plus a chapter-length digression slanted in the direction of function ("Verwendung der Wortformen").

**3.4. Merger or separation of different strains.** The task of the Romance grammarian is singularly complicated by the fact that, in addition to the prevalent Latin stratum, he has to deal intermittently with other ingredients or "strains". Whereas the lexicographer may, at will, comfortably segregate, say, the Italianisms in Spanish (Terlingen) or the Gallicisms in Dutch (Salverda de Grave) or else intermingle them with other words,[21] the tighter structure of grammar

[20] This unorthodox section, straddling the two tiny volumes, deserves an extra measure of attention. It falls into three main chapters, of which the first deals with inflection ("Die Lehre von den Wortformen", I, 120–169) and the last, with word formation ("Wortbildungslehre", II, 60–82). It is the central core (II, 9–59), titled "Die Lehre von der Bedeutung der Wörter", that was primarily meant to represent the innovation. This kernel falls, in turn, into three subchapters, of which the first (10–25), most infelicitously, bears the same title as the whole and boils down to a brief treatise of conventional semasiology dealing with the causes, "laws", and chief varieties of semantic shift. The second subchapter, "Bedeutung der Wortformen" (26–47), is concerned with syntactic implications of morphological change, such as the contrast between gender and sex, the pluralization of proper names, mass nouns, abstracts, etc.: "... die Bedeutung der Wortformen kommt hier nur insofern zur Sprache, als sie sich am alleinstehenden Wort zeigt; wenn es sich um die Bedeutung handelt, die eine Wortform im Verhältnis zu einer anderen hat, so haben wir ein Wortgefüge vor uns, das also in der Syntax zu behandeln ist" (26). The third (48–59), again badly mistitled ("Bedeutung der Wortarten"; a more appropriate heading, to use the author's own terminology, might have been "Verschiebungen zwischen den Wortarten"), deals with such extensions of form classes as the adjectival, pronominal, adverbial, and prepositional use of an erstwhile noun, and vice versa, — an elusive point of grammar which other scholars, dubbing it "dérivation impropre", incline to treat under word formation, and yet others, possibly the majority, under syntax. The original edition (1900), in a single volume of the Göschen series, displayed an even queerer structure, lamely placing, on the temporal level of Vulgar Latin, some unannounced random remarks on semantic change (37f.) which separate the sections on word formation and syntax, while on the plateau of Romance the topics were austerely confined to phonology and inflection, followed by a two-page excursus on word formation.

[21] Note, however, that W. von Wartburg, possibly for practical reasons, changed the structure of his *Französisches etymologisches Wörterbuch* in mid-stream, as it were: The concluding volumes strictly segregate lexical families of Latin, Germanic, and substratal provenience.

saddles its practitioner with entirely different responsibilities. A separate phonology of Arabic words absorbed into Hispano-Romance and South Italian, such as Steiger's, is an ever-present possibility; but what of the share of attention to be given to the pre-IE, Celtic, Greek, and Germanic lexical ingredients within the total fabric of pan-Romanic, or of a single Romance, phonology? Diez's initial answer to this question, in his original comparative grammar, rests squarely on a dichotomy — in retrospect, arbitrary — of Latin (116–269) and German[ic] (270–332) "letters", i.e., sounds, followed by a meager Supplement on Arabic sounds in Spanish (332–334). The definitive version of his grammar shows a thorough reorganization: A newly carved-out section, "The sounds of the source languages", forms the ground floor of the restructured edifice (120–270), and only here are Latin and Germanic consistently contrasted, while in the concluding section, an upper story devoted to the six languages chosen for separate consideration, a unified treatment prevails. Reinhardstoettner followed in the later Diez's footsteps, except that for him the "source languages" of Portuguese were Latin and Arabic, to the detriment of Germanic, while Förster reverted to a single chapter on the "Origin of Spanish sounds". Subsequent generations discarded both versions of Diez's approach; thus, Meyer-Lübke's French grammar makes almost casual mention of such significant imports from Old Frankish as the phonemes /h/ and /w/ (see Vol. I, §§ 154 f.).[22] This streamlining offers certain advantages; it also involves the drawback of deëmphasizing the — to the structuralist —

[22] It has proved virtually impossible to build the fragmentarily reconstructed substratum languages into the edifice of a formal historical grammar, though it is not at all difficult, in a straight language history, to reserve for their vestiges a separate chapter, even one of considerable length and elaboration; cf. Savj-Lopez's and Tagliavini's *Origini* and the almost overburdened opening chapter of Lapesa's *Historia*. Language histories are equally hospitable to superstrata, cf. Vol. I of Densusianu's lifework, with its detailed account of Bulgarian, Serbian, Polish, Albanian, Byzantine, Hungarian, and Cumanian infiltrations.

Makeshift solutions in grammars and near-grammars include (a) the phonologically evasive discussion of such strains in the Introduction (Pellegrini) and (b) the relegation of the topic to the equally non-committal chapter on vocabulary (Ewert: "Borrowed words", 282–305), while in Nunes' *Compêndio* the separate phonology of Germanic and Arabic words in Portuguese (161–184) marks a late echo of Diez's program.

The degree of close attention paid to Latin varies from author to author. Elcock has devoted one third of his synthesis to the "Latin foundation" (17–169) and has very wisely assigned a whole prominent section (300–333) to the afterglow of the parent language ("Medieval Latin and Romance vernacular"). In the nature of things, students of Romance have rarely been accomplished Latinists, with the all-important interplay between internal sound development, geared to trends of inner economy, and the enrichment of a phonic stock as a result of external pressure (ethnolinguistic contacts through peaceful diffusion or conquests). A truly satisfactory solution of this inherent dilemma has not yet been devised.[23]

Just as a scholar may concentrate on a collateral strain within Romance, so a minor Latin or Romance strain discernible within a language adjudged, on general grounds, to a different family may be made the object of special investigation. Take G. Meyer's grammatical analysis (the accent being, as expected, on phonology) of the Latin ingredients in Albanian, a "Mischsprache" par excellence; that monograph later acquired an added touch of authority through its revision by Meyer-Lübke. Ordinarily, in studies of this kind grammar takes second place behind lexicology; thus, one would look in vain for a grammatical presentation of colloquial Latin elements in Celtic and Germanic equal in finesse and cogency to Jud's lexical bird's-eye view in his classic "Altromanische Sprachgeographie".

**3.5. Novel arrangements.** While some scholars were busy refining the older approaches or reconciling certain discrepancies between them, real or apparent, others, more venturesome, have struck out

[23] The precise place assigned to the substratum depends on one important decision: Does the author primarily examine the linguistic layers of a fixed territory (say, Gaul or Iberia), or the gradual spread of Latin from its Roman fountainhead? If the former is true, Latin quite naturally falls into place between the succession of native substrata and any number of superstrata or "parastrata", cf. Entwistle's account of Hispano-Romance (1936), Pellegrini's of Old Spanish (1950), and Alessio's of French (1946). If the alternative is favored, the multifarious contacts of Latin with other languages invite discussion at a point, or at points, considerably removed from the Introduction. In this event, the writer retains his freedom of choice between (a) telescoping the accounts of all such interferences, as did P. Savj-Lopez in his composite Chap. v ("Tracce preromane e influssi estranei", 251–317), and (b) sharply segregating early from late non-Latin influences, as was Elcock's, all told, more judicious decision in 1960.

exception of the Italian group, notably G. Devoto. Through a startling division of labor, Romance linguists, while demonstrating, from Ascoli and Schuchardt via Bertoldi to Hubschmid, a touching readiness to delve into the study of recalcitrant archaic substrata, have for the most part been content to scratch the surface of Latin and have practically never ventured into Proto-IE, at least not in their manuals (a lone, probably well-meant, exception is the introductory chapter to the *History of the French Language* by Holmes and Schutz).

anew, with fresh criteria for assembling data. Of these experiments a few, at least in their embryonic stage, go back to the concluding years of the past century; nevertheless one is at liberty to call them all "modernistic". Since experimenters, as a rule, display notable perceptiveness, they — and such critics as were no less alert — have, on the whole, been aware of the margin of imbalance and often downright error that any untested arrangement is likely to involve. The feeling in these quarters has been that, since stagnation represents the worst enemy of scientific advance, any well-conducted experiment, even if it merely opens up an unsuspected alternative to the accepted order of things, constitutes a sound investment of intellectual power.

**3.5.1. Chronological sequence.** The importance of absolute and relative chronology must have dawned early on language historians, but the precise way of operating with these constructs, especially with the latter, which hinges on strict logical extrapolation rather than on philological "Einfühlung", must from the start have caused embarrassment; witness Otto Bremer's long hesitancy about publishing his "Relative Sprachchronologie", drafted in Leipzig as early as July 1885, until after he had thoroughly recast it in Halle more than eight years later (*IF*, IV [1894], 8–31). The early record of Romance scholarship along this line was impressive, ever since Meyer-Lübke's solid nineteen-page analysis, "Zur Chronologie des Lautwandels", found a niche as a separate chapter in his *Lautlehre* (1890). Unfortunately, the discussion picked up momentum quite slowly; a narrow path leads to the laconic, but admirably comprehensive "Historische Übersicht der Lautveränderungen", appended in 1908 as the Second Supplement (I, 261 f.; rev. ed., 266 f.) to the same author's revolutionary French grammar, where it acted as a foil to the equally helpful and incisive "Systematische Übersicht . . ." (252–260), more in the nature of a synopsis or restatement. The next step was E. Richter's programmatic paper (1910–11) — significantly dedicated to her teacher Meyer-Lübke — on the inner connection in the growth of Romance languages. After another quarter-century of unremitting research, she achieved the break-through in her book-length *Geschichte der Romanismen*, which modesty prompted her to qualify as mere *Beiträge*, incontrovertibly a brilliant contribution to Romance and, in an even truer sense, to general linguistics.[24]

[24] The following extracts from E. Richter's Preface (2 f.) to her *Beiträge* convey the flavor of deep dissatisfaction with past achievements which, of necessity, under-

Richter's ambition was to segment the entire phonic trajectory of proto-French, ranging from Latin at its all-time peak down to Gallo-Romance as spoken in the late 8th century, into approximately 170 successive shifts, arranged with little regard to the point and mode of articulation (through a twist of irony, she lavished on each shift meticulous physiologic comment). Since the one overriding consideration was temporal priority or posteriority, shifts closely allied when viewed in more familiar perspectives were torn asunder if relative chronology suggested the occurrence of other changes, whatever their locus, in the intervenient lapse of time. Take, for instance, the syncope of the posttonic vowel: Richter here distinguished six basic stages, not necessarily reached in close succession, and further split the second and the third into two almost consecutive phases. These assumptions led to the following schema (the bare paragraph numbers suffice to indicate the suggested distances, if not in absolute time depth, at least in evolutionary stage, since each paragraph was assigned to just one such step):

§ 10: First syncope (CALIDUS > *caldus*);
§ 60: Second syncope [I] (ALIQUID > *alqued*);
§ 69a: Second syncope [II] (VINCERE > *veɲtre*);
§ 109: Third syncope [I] (*LĪMETE > *limte*);
§ 111: Third syncope [II] (FĒMINA > *femna*);
§ 130: Fourth syncope (DUCTILE > *doitle*);
§ 144: Fifth syncope (GALBINU > *dʒalbne*);
§ 173: Last shortenings (*forˀdʒet* > *forge*).

Despite the rigor of this "Hilfskonstruktion für die Erfassung des sprachgeschichtlichen Vorganges" and the élan, even verve,[25] characterizing the entire venture, Richter's method and underlying

---

[25] A few passages may be adduced as evidence: "Daß die chronologische Darstellung von keinem der früheren Meister unternommen wurde, wirft ein Licht auf die Bedenken, die sie gegen die Ausführung hatten, wegen der nahezu unüberwindlichen Schwierigkeiten und der Aussichtslosigkeit, eine solche Aufgabe wissenschaftlich einwandfrei zu lösen. Doch reizt sie wie die Restaurierung eines alten Mosaiks, eines antiken, in tausend Scherben daliegenden Vasenbildes. Gewiß, es wird irgendeiner Gestalt der Kopf fehlen, der anderen ein Gewandzipfel usw. Aber durch die Zusammenfügung wird doch ein lebendiges Ganzes 'auf die Füße' gestellt, während bisher die Stücke nebeneinander lagen und von den wenig-

lies the restlessness of avant-garde workers: "Wir besitzen zahlreiche 'historische' Grammatiken . . . Aber eine Geschichte der sprachlichen Entwicklung geben sie nicht. Verfolgen sie doch den zumeist nach physiologischem Gesichtspunkt gegliederten Stoff in seinen Teilerscheinungen je über alle Jahrhunderte, ohne Rücksicht darauf, welche dieser Teilerscheinungen früher, welche später, welche erst infolge der anderen entstanden ist".

assumptions invite serious objections. Thus, to the extent that precedence and causation are interwoven, one phonetic shift seems to be
produced by a constellation of others — in splendid isolation, whereas
in reality the ensemble of contributing circumstances is discernibly
more complex. In principle, the author emphatically recognized the
collateral agency of psychic forces ("nur im Zusammenhang mit
anderen psychischen Vorgängen"), but, in practice, she failed to heed
the constant interplay of even phonology and morphology.[26] Then
again, though Richter's introductory remarks show an astonishingly
firm grasp of the regional and social (or educational) gradation of
Latin, she presupposed, in the course of her actual operations, an
almost complete lack of territorial differentiation throughout the
first six centuries. Making good her original promise (62) "das
unleugbar vorhandene alte Sprachmaterial im Lichte der experi-
mentellen physiologischen (resp. sprachpsychologischen) Forschung
zu zeigen" (62), a perfectly valid program in 1910, she relied too
heavily, for the experts' taste twenty-four years later, on the phonetic
laboratory, and too little, despite occasional flirting with "early-
Prague-style" phonology, on the new and fruitful concept of close-
knit sound-system and such ramifications of structuralistic thinking
as "phonetic yield". Finally, her inability to grapple with the problem
of other Romance developments, an inability of which she was painfully aware and which she candidly attributed not only to such trivial
causes as overexertion, but also to insoluble intrinsic complications
("weil die Gestaltung der verschiedenartigen nebeneinanderlau-
fenden Entwicklungen ein kaum zu lösendes Problem aufgibt"), explains why her *Beiträge*, despite their extraordinary sophistication,
not only remained a torso, but, worse, failed to inspire younger workers
with the desire to emulate and, if possible, surpass this venture of
a lone explorer.

[26] This limitation was not entirely due to neglect. Richter justified it by a theory,
sketched in Section VIII of her Introduction, to the effect that the genuinely "historical method", which makes ample allowances for lacunae, is acceptable in certain
linguistic disciplines such as word formation and syntax, whereas phonology, which
she defined as being essentially 'a phonetic history of unconscious imperfect trans-
missions', stands completely apart through its link to physiological processes open
to scientific inspection — and, in her opinion, to equally rigorous reconstruction and
prediction (18 f.). Note the lapidary pronouncement: "Die chronologische Phonetik
ist in erster Linie Phonetik".

---

sten als zusammengehöriges Eines erfaßt werden können. Die ungeheure Mehrzahl
der Betrachter sieht nur ein Nebeneinander ohne die Fähigkeit, das Gemälde
lebend vor sich erstehen zu lassen".

Among the few tillers of this field still alive and active it is only fair to mention G. Straka, chiefly on the strength of his early record (1953), before he allowed himself to become enticed by the search for such universals in sounds shifts as can be most readily supplied by observations made in the phonetic laboratory (1964).

**3.5.2. Transmutational categories.** Historical grammar has at all times, by definition, been concerned with change, but normally operates with material classified on the basis of static — or panchronic — categories, such as sounds arranged according to steady physiological conditions or to their positions in higher units (words, phrases), suffixes detached from the vocabulary at given evolutionary stages, and the like. One can imagine a radically different array, involving categories established on the basis not of what the items represent in a static cross-section, but of the type of change (assimilation, dissimilation, vocalization of a consonant and consonantization of a vowel, loss, restoration, confusion, etc.) which the analyst supposes these items to have undergone. Such an approach is apt to lead eventually to a typology of linguistic transmutation, of the broadgauged kind envisaged by general students of language from Paul and Saussure via Sturtevant to Hoenigswald.

A perspective so bold, opening up from the most abstract level of analysis, concerns us here only to the extent that the historical grammar of a single language (or, less likely, of a language family) may be rearranged to fit this schema. The choice of such a model would make the grammar difficult of casual consultation or even devoid of interest for, say, the philologian or etymologist, but may vastly enhance its value as a tool of straight linguistic research.

One may envisage either a complete or a partial adoption of this schema. A very notable example of the former, available only in fragmentary form and scarcely known even to Romance experts, is Chap. II ("Alteración fonética") in the distinguished Colombian R. J. Cuervo's treatise *Castellano popular y castellano literario* (unfinished; far advanced ca. 1905; published in 1944 after the author's death in 1911). His manner of presentation stems from the following synopsis:[27]

[27] I am the less hesitant to offer it in translation since Cuervo's *Obras inéditas*, as a book venture, represents a queer mixture of accomplishments and failures. The volume is fastidiously printed and equipped with an almost exhaustive bibliography (xiii), but it lacks so elementary a feature as a Table of Contents, doubly important in a congeries of fragments, — to say nothing of the absent word index.

I. Spontaneous shift (45–106)
   1. Vowels [in general]
   2. Consonants [in general]
   3. Special developments (A. Fronting; B. Vocalization [of consonants] and consonantization [of vowels]; C. Loss; D. Aspiration; E. [Interchange of consonants]; F. Confusion and false regression.

II. Combinatory shift (106–242)
   1. Consecutive phonemes (107–179)
      A. Vowels (a. Total assimilation; b. Partial assimilation; c. Dissimilation; d. Confusion and false regression)
      B. Consonants (a. Total assimilation; b. Learned reaction to ancient vernacular pronunciation; c. Partial assimilation; d. Dissimilation)
      C. Consonants and vowels (a. Total assimilation; b. Partial assimilation)
   2. Non-contiguous phonemes (180–242)
      A. Vowels (a. Total assimilation; b. Dissimilation; c. Partial assimilation; d. Assimilation through epenthesis and dissimilation through syncope)
      B. Consonants (a. Assimilation [α. Nasals; β. Liquids; γ. Other phonemes]; b. Dissimilation; c. Assimilation and dissimilation combined).[28]

If we may, for once, apply the labels "static" and "dynamic" to the contrast between array and development (rather than to anatomy vs. physiology of sound production), Cuervo clearly left the barest minimum of static categories, such as, on a pervasive scale, the age-old division into vowels and consonants and, at a single inconspicuous point (II2Ba), the further subdivision of the consonants on the

[28] In translating, I have gently retouched the headings; the one attached in the original to I3E makes little sense, and the replacement, inferred from the content, has the merit of echoing A. Alonso's label for the same phenomenon (*NRFH*, I [1947], 1–10), perhaps independently devised. One detects an occasional instance of overlapping, as when, in the face of Section I3F (101–106), the shorter Section II1Ad (126–128) seems redundant: In a final revision, that perfectionist Cuervo would no doubt have consolidated the two.

Cuervo's own desultory blueprint (ix) indicates that the fragment unearthed represents, at best, the initial quarter of the entire project, Parts II–IV having been reserved, respectively, for "Analogy" (including its impact on words [i.e., root morphemes], inflection, word formation, and contiguous areas of syntax and semantics), "semasiology" (with one of four chapters devoted to the study of metaphors), and "vocabulary" (segregation of archaic, provincial, and indigenous items, in this order). As regards the date of composition, in the Preface (xxiv) to the 5th ed. (1905) of his classic *Apuntaciones* Cuervo described himself as engrossed in the writing of this new treatise; the year of his death (1911) provides the *terminus ad quem*. Tantalizing is the question: Did Cuervo abandon this project on account of old-age infirmity, or, a dramatic alternative, because he ultimately despaired of its feasibility?

basis of locus of articulation. In every other respect, purely dynamic categories, suggestive of evolution, prevail in his pattern. One visualizes further progress along this line through complete elimination of residual static features and through simultaneous extension of the transmutational model to, at least, morphology and syntax.[29]

Significantly, almost every small, even smallest, division in Cuervo's schema, as here reported in crudely simplified form, is actually split into even shorter units, of paragraph length.

> A case in point is the dissimilation of non-contiguous consonants (for which the author could afford to rely on Grammont's spadework), here marked as Section II2Bb; it falls into numerous units more narrowly circumscribed, typified by (α) *árbol* 'tree', (β) *(co)frade* 'fellow member', (γ) *palafrén* 'palfrey', (δ) obs. *acipreste* 'archpriest', (ε) *alambre* 'wire', (ζ) *fiambre* 'cold meat', (η) *medrar* 'to thrive', etc.

An average historical grammar would tend to separate points here forcefully brought together, such as *-mb-* ( = *-nv-*) > *-m-*, *-rl-* > *-l-* or *-ll-* [λ], *-nm-* > *-m-*, *-sr-* > *-rr-* [r̄], whose common denominator happens to be "Total assimilation of contiguous consonants" (Section II1Ba).

One finds partial rather than integral adoption of this approach by way of compromise with more conventional groupings. Twenty years before Cuervo, Cornu introduced into his Portuguese grammar such sections as (α) "Assimilation of vowels to vowels" (§§ 81–88) and (β) "Assimilation of vowels to consonants" (§§ 89–97; repeated in 2d ed.). The difference between the two treatises consists in this: In Cuervo's schema, these broad headings, cutting across the vicissitudes of individual sounds in all positions or of certain sounds in restricted positions, constitute the major divisions; in Cornu's, they occupy a distinctly lower classificatory rank: The two quoted items jointly form Subsection (b) of Section (B), on unstressed vowels, which, in turn, enters into Chap. II ("Sound development")

---

[29] By way of background, note that the long chapter here examined is preceded by a full-blown treatment of "General phonetics" (7–41) — based on the writings of Sweet, Sievers, Passy, and Storm —, at that time far and away the safest available guide to Spanish. It is followed by three shorter chapters whose ultimate status and destination remain dubious — they almost give the impression of unintegrated articles or monographs: III. Accentuation (divided into two untitled subchapters); IV. Diphthongization; V. Syllabic count of successive vowels. Cuervo's principal authorities for the chapter on sound shift were, by his own admission (p. 43 n.), Baist, Brugmann, Meyer-Lübke, Passy, Paul, Schuchardt, and Sievers, a range constituting a splendid testimonial to his versatility.

of Phonology, the opening part of the entire grammar. See further our Section 3.5.9.

**3.5.3. Geographic focus: sharp, diffuse, or scattered.** An explorer concerned, in Munthe's and Sánchez Sevilla's footsteps, with the risky task of preparing the historical grammar of a single village patois operates, by definition, with a sharp geographic focus, especially if the field-work interviews are restricted to natives. Conversely, any historical grammar of a widespread language (say, French or Spanish) ordinarily carries with it deëmphasis of locale, i.e., a diffuse geographic focus; the great novelty of Menéndez Pidal's *Orígenes* (if, for the sake of the argument, we take this multi-faceted work to represent a grammar) was the author's constant attention to locus, despite the immense territorial sweep.

One can speak of a scattered focus only where each ancestral form contrasts with a profusion of neatly pinpointed reflexes, of which none occupies any position of cultural or territorial preëminence with regard to the others. The classic instance is Gartner's oft-repeated treatment of Raeto-Romance, as shown particularly in the Supplement (166–200) to his *Grammatik* (1883), throughout both editions of his contribution — characteristically entitled "Die rätoromanischen Mundarten" — to Gröber's *Grundriß*, and in his crowning achievement, the *Handbuch* (1910), where a typographic device in the list of etyma (xvii–xx) immediately draws the reader's attention to those passages in which a single Latin base was surrounded by from fifty to seventy Raeto-Romance, Lombard, and Venetian offshoots. Formal grammars in which the scattered focus is used on a wide scale, though less ostentatiously, include Ronjat's for Occitanian, Rohlfs' for Italian, and whatever Wagner contributed toward one for Sardinian.

**3.5.4. The structural approach.** Any structural approach to historical grammar involves — ideally, at least — the thorough integration of all individual shifts into a single complex pattern of interdependent moves, in chessboard fashion. Large-scale structural grammars so conceived are not yet available in Romance and may never come into existence. Even on a descriptive plane, structure, as L. Hjelmslev specifically admitted (*AL*, IV: 3, p. v), is little more than a seductive hypothesis; the chances of its fruitful application to language history are severely limited by the fact that the ubiquitous extralinguistic influences (which lend themselves with difficulty, if at all, to stringent patterning) seem inextricably interwoven with purely linguistic developments. Additional complications stem from the circumstance that, when structuralism put forth its first blossoms, Romance linguistic scholarship was veering at full speed in the opposite direction. The result of this disharmony is that major monographs impregnated with experimental structuralistic thinking, yet, at the same time, written by authors in full command of solid traditional learning, such as Kuryłowicz's researches in Indo-European accent and apophony, lack any worthy counterparts on the Romance side. Demonstrably, even scholars familiar at first hand with structuralistic tenets and terminology, such as Lausberg, exhibit studied restraint, not to say conservatism, in their attempts at broader syntheses. Since the few available inquiries diachronically oriented hark back to the Prague School, an expected emphasis on phonology, to the point of imbalance, is clearly in evidence; cf. Haudricourt and Juilland's reinterpretation of French, which critics call rashly conceived and no less rashly executed; Alarcos Llorach's researches in Spanish, flanking a full-length synchronic treatment; and, quite recently, H. Weinrich's ambitious venture into general Romance, with heightened attention to Italian dialects. Despite its rather immodest claims, structuralism has in fact scored its finest successes in neatly bounded fields, cf. Martinet's model studies in, on the one hand, Romance occlusives and homorganic spirants and, on the other, the early modern Spanish sibilants. Such "privileged areas" in the diachronic projection of phonological structure remind one of those equally privileged sectors of the lexicon, viewed either descriptively or historically, which display particularly clear-cut patterning, such as numerals beside anatomic and kinship terms.

**3.5.5. Hierarchization of sound shifts.** Whether or not one elects to adopt the structuralistic platform, it seems possible, in theory, to hierarchize linguistic change, especially in the realm of phonology. The grammars in which our analyses are encoded have lagged appreciably behind the new theoretical insights. Possibly as far-reaching in its reverberations as the Neo-grammarians' celebrated dictum denying that "sound-laws" tolerate any unaccountable exceptions has been the modern discovery — carried to its logical conclusion by L. Bloomfield (1933) — that in the section on phonology only straight phonological change, i.e., the smooth, undeflected workings of standard sound correspondences, should be subjected to close scrutiny. A phonology so constructed would be relieved of constant reference to the numerous "exceptions" which, in reality, represent so many results of heterogeneous conflicts between, on the one hand, the interplay of basic sound shifts and, on the other, totally different forces operative in language history.

If phonology is to be restricted to the analysis of genuine phonological sound shift (Sapir's "drift") rather than of any change whatsoever reflected in the fabric of words, the corollary is that an appropriate place must be found to discuss or, at least, briefly record other types of transmutation. This slightly amorphous residue includes:

(a) The agency of omnipresent, panchronic sound changes (Ascoli's "accidenti generali"), as against those specific sound shifts, limited in space and time, that are peculiar to individual languages at certain stages of their growth;

(b) Effects of analogy, whether due to (α) paradigmatic leveling or (β) lexical blend;

(c) Results of diffusion, conceivably caused by the fluidity of the speech community, some mixture of regional or social dialects (including "learned words"), the migration of an isolated linguistic feature across its original borders, or the simultaneous spread of label and referent;

(d) Extraordinary situations: evasion of homonymy, observance of taboo, abnormal rate of attrition through formulaic use, crystallization of an "expressive" (e.g., reduplicative) form, and the like.

A scientifically elegant solution of the problem of space budgeting remains, I repeat, to be found. It has become customary to reserve a special chapter or subchapter for assimilation, dissimilation, metathesis, and kindred phenomena, invariably in closest vicinity to the basic sound shifts, though discreet relegation to a supplement, safe from any possible tangle with "drift", would, all told, represent a more advisable course of action.[30] One may further argue that (bα),

---

[30] Among the familiar handbooks Menéndez Pidal's *Manual*, revised as of 1941, assigns to a separate, fairly long chapter on "Sporadic phonetic changes", wedged in between phonology proper and morphology, such obligatory topics as assimilation and dissimilation (including dissimilatory loss) of vowels and consonants, and simple beside reciprocal metathesis. To this irreducible core the author adds a motley assemblage of fringe phenomena: lexical blend, involving words allocated to a single series (= "serialization", as defined in *ArL*, IX, 106–113) and others, less exposed to group pressure; epenthesis, triply operative in antihiatic consonant, nasal insert, attachment of *-r* to well-defined consonants and consonant clusters; folk etymology, hyperurbanism, and "acoustic equivalence" (for a critique of this last-mentioned concept see *Lg.*, XXX, 142–146), i.e., certain forms of free variation.

strictly speaking, belongs in the section on morphology, while the
cases subsumed under (bβ) are best examined atomistically, i.e., in
an etymological dictionary. In practice, the compromise most frequently reached is to set off the "exception" from the "rule" by
examining it at the end rather than at the start of a given paragraph,
or by signaling the subordination in some self-explanatory typographic fashion (smaller print, downgrading to a footnote).[31] This

[31] A few random examples of the current inadequacy. It is not uncommon to
subdivide the affixes on the basis of transmission; the triadic arrangement "vernacular : learned : imported" appears embryonically in Darmesteter's treatise as
early as 1877 and dominates Nyrop's standard-setting volume (1908). But, with
regard to syntax, not even a scholar so alert to learned influence as was, almost to
the point of morbidness, Lerch (consistently so on the monographic level) would
consider the possibility of exploiting such an opposition on a grand scale, though
the indexes to the individual volumes of his diachronic *Französische Syntax* furnish
a few clues. Again, even a phonology as artfully constructed as is Meyer-Lübke's
(for French) abounds in allusions to strange side-lines, unexplained exceptions,
conspicuous words of presumably ecclesiastic or non-indigenous parentage, suspected analogical departures (e.g., §§ 109, 114, 118, 122) — in short, all manner of
qualifications and retractions which occasionally hedge in the main statements and

Why do antihiatic consonants belong here, while buffer consonants, such as the
intrusive stops in *-mbr-*, *-ndr-*, qualify for inclusion among regular consonant shifts?
    Grandgent (1927), after preacquainting his readers with the "more or less erratic"
doubling of consonants and the "occasional interchange" of *v* and *g*, subsumes under
"Irregular changes" (§§ 134–148), the concluding link in a chain of phonological
chapters, such miscellaneous items as "limitation" ( = consonant assimilation at a
distance), "diversification" ( = dissimilation), "transfer" ( = metathesis), "inser-
tion", [hypocoristic] abbreviation (nursery language, nicknames). He apparently
fails to distinguish with any degree of sharpness between (a) thwarted, arrested, or
partially concluded sound shifts of the ordinary kind, and (b) sporadic changes quite
unrelated to the general "drift".
    Williams (1938) subordinates to the broad section on phonology two chapters,
of which the first, "General phonological phenomena" (§§ 99–102), is concerned
with assimilation, dissimilation, and vowel contraction in hiatus, also with metaphony, nasalization, and assibilation, while the second, slightly tinged by classicist
terminology ("Sporadic changes", §§ 103–119), centers attention about [hypoco-
ristic] abbreviation, analogy (gingerly defined as proportional relation, yet left
undocumented), anaptyxis, apheresis, apocope, assimilation and dissimilation,
confusion of prefixes and of initial syllables (or rather segments), contamination
(including folk etymology and false regression), epenthesis (embracing, counter to
Menéndez Pidal's aforementioned practice, both antihiatic and buffer consonants),
metathesis, paragoge, prosthetic *a*, sandhi, false division. Again, one is prompted to
question the wisdom of classing apocope (or, as in Portuguese, of resistance to it) at
such a remove from ordinary sound shifts; of meting out unequal treatment to
prefixes and suffixes; of failing to group so common a process as the sonantization
of surds with other "general phenomena".
    In conclusion: Each author, in this secluded wing of his edifice, seems to obey
with greater freedom than elsewhere the dictates of his personal taste and occasionally even to indulge in gentle whims.

lame arrangement, distracting one's attention from the relevant, may facilitate the casual consultation of a manual by textual critics and other semi-outsiders, but betrays the best interests of the full-fledged linguist by failing to cast into bold relief the actual forces locked in constant struggle.

**3.5.6. Selectivity.** It has always been the prerogative of beginners' guides to offer a mere selection of salient points, rather than an exhaustive treatment, of historical grammar, and authors (if they were at all explicit about such matters) have not, as a rule, been held strictly responsible either for methods used in setting up criteria of selection or for their skill in adhering to such criteria. In the second quarter of this century, however, there developed a new type of high-level study practicing — sometimes unavowedly — a measure of discrimination, either by dealing overtly with select problems or by paying strikingly unequal attention to the ostensibly full array of problems included. The books here hinted at are neither loose collections of one scholar's articles assembled under a title which conceals a publisher's overstatement, such as Lerch's *Hauptprobleme*, nor learned testimonial volumes that serve as clearing-houses for *Prinzipienfragen*, but rather polished monographs conceived from the outset on the basis of a not fully explicated selection of features. The classic example of the genre is Menéndez Pidal's unsurpassed *Orígenes del español* (1926; 3d ed., 1950), a book of many appeals whose kernel — preceded by a masterly paleographic edition of some archaic texts, for the most part difficult of access, and followed by a broad historical synthesis, sparklingly phrased, — is a historical grammar, appearing at first glance almost complete. While this grammar outranks in freshness of design, precision of dating and localization, and volume and variety of documentation, the author's own earlier *Manual* (orig. ed., 1904) and *Cid* grammar (1908), it is, in important respects, less comprehensive and, above all, less evenly distributed than those not quite so personal contributions.

---

slightly obscure the view. In handbooks prepared by the lesser luminaries of that school (Schultz-Gora, Wiese, Zauner, etc.) the exceptions are allowed to pile up disproportionately at every step. Similarly, in the analysis of inflection the constant interlocking of sound law and analogy has traditionally been recognized as self-understood, but an attempt to compute separate balance sheets for the cumulative effects of each force would have appeared either impracticable or, worse, unorthodox, on the doctrinaire side.

The writer deals in astonishing detail with chosen points (such as monophthongization of Lat. AI and AU as against the diphthongization of Ĕ and ŏ, the voicing of the surds, the shift of F- to *h*- and eventually to zero), while offering perceptibly sketchier surveys of other domains (e.g., the medial consonant clusters, the conjugation) and remaining embarrassingly reticent on certain points of, one should think, equal importance, such as the development of primary -D- (for a few, almost casual, hints see § 47.2, 5). The norm for including a shift and for the specific degree of detail assigned to its elucidation seems to be primarily its relevance to Menéndez Pidal's magnificently reconstructed historical panorama ("Regiones y épocas", §§ 86–106).

One is left wondering why certain traits fraught with dialectal implications, such as, I repeat, the varying preservation of -*d*- or the regionally conditioned distribution of the verb classes -*er* and -*ir*[32] have been practically excluded, the upshot of the experienced reader's uneasiness being his ever-present doubt: Would the underlying historical schema require drastic revision in the light of supervenient evidence?

The extreme of selectivity is represented by Wartburg's *Ausgliederung*, where relatively minor features, such as the evolution of -CT-, are magnified out of all proportion, and others, of capital importance, such as the continued distinction of Ŭ Ō, Ĭ Ĕ, or the resistance of polysyllables to syncope in disconnected conservative territories, are almost neglected. True, this pamphlet no longer pretends to be a historical grammar, not even one in disguise.

In sober fact, both books represent valuable strings of miniature monographs integrated — the future will show whether or not prematurely — with significant slivers of non-linguistic archeological material.

### 3.5.7. The grouping by coöccurrence. Under special circumstances, particularly the demands of genetic classification, it is advisable to group the salient features of a language not on the strength of internal criteria, but on that of their reappearance in, or exclusion from, some other, usually neighboring or at least kindred, language(s) or dialect(s). What matters in such instances is no longer plain occurrence, but coöccurrence, whether due to mere coincidence or to (assumed) diffusion. Thus, Kuhn's monograph on Upper

[32] For details, see the concluding statement of my review of M. Gorosch's dissertation in *Lg.*, XXXI (1955), 261–291, as well as the opening section of my article "Paradigmatic resistance to sound change" in the same journal, XXXVI (1960), 281–346.

Aragonese breaks down all phonological changes observed (12–177) into three major types: (a) those displaying the familiar contrast between Castilian and general Hispano-Romance; (b) those traceable to a focal point in the northeast of the Peninsula or in some adjoining region, and (c) those lacking a specific focus, hence attributable to spontaneous polygenesis. Though Kuhn, regrettably, refrained from extending this laudable technique to other disciplines, it does lend itself to application in allied domains, including lexicology (cf. the sifting-out of Visigothic words in Romance by E. Gamillscheg in *RFE*, XIX [1932], esp. 229–243).

**3.5.8. The graded approach.** For the convenience (properly or improperly interpreted) of university students there have arisen two didactic genres, as it were: all kinds of charts of sound correspondences, paradigmatic tables, and the like, apparently for quick reference or, worse, for memorization (Boyd-Bowman); and graded textbooks, primarily for the autodidact. The graded approach is, of course, common practice in the teaching of normative grammar, sometimes so objectively presented as to border on the truly descriptive. It ultimately underlies all elementary language instruction, and not a few textbooks of this kind, compiled by recognized experts, show a touch of genuine linguistic sophistication.[33] In historical grammar this approach, already hinted at, has been infrequent, with Voretzsch (in the footsteps of the Anglist Zupitza) and Gartner, in the initial piece (1–61) of his Rumanian omnibus volume (1904),

[33] Distinguished philologists and linguists have at all times been available for the writing of elementary grammars (and have usually done a more workmanlike job than literary scholars, however eminent in their own field, cf. E. Faral's ill-fated grammar of Old French). A. Mussafia's guide to Italian had a considerable commercial vogue in Central Europe; K. Nyrop's, to Spanish, proved a boon at least to Scandinavians; E. Herzog and S. Puşcariu's, cut to the needs of German postwar learners of Rumanian, impresses one by its incisiveness and economy (while C. Tagliavini's parallel venture, vastly more erudite, shows traces of juvenile injudiciousness); F. Krüger's introduction to Modern Spanish fits into the cultural climate of *inter bella*; with an attractively light touch, F. Sommer stooped to preparing a comparative grammar of "collegiate" languages, dead and living, for his native Germany, while L. Bloomfield had to his credit an elementary grammar of German, for American high-school or college students, as well as a more recent grammar of Dutch, for army use; he also had his share in a parallel war-time project for Russian. If an introductory practical grammar, under auspicious circumstances, may boast authentic scientific value, it is equally true that a "comparative" grammar, holding out greater promise, may be distressingly mediocre; O. W. Heatwole's, devoted to modern French, Spanish, and Italian, yet interspersed with historical "flashbacks", is, regrettably enough, a case in point.

ranking as the best-known specialists. Rohlfs' *Vom Vulgärlatein zum Altfranzösischen*, whose title alone marks a concession to Anglo-American taste (otherwise the book embodies a routine revision of Voretzsch's classic), represents the latest venture in this direction. The graded approach, often geared to the line-by-line interpretation of model texts, must by all means be distinguished from printed lecture courses, such as J. Leite de Vasconcelos' on Portuguese and J. Wackernagel's on Indo-European syntax, designed to serve a select world-wide audience; from mimeographed lecture courses (a type of *aide-mémoire* lately very fashionable in France and in Italy) and textbooks recognizably based on them, such as Monteverdi's and even Tagliavini's, and from posthumously published lectures — an act of piety — e.g., C. Michaëlis'. All these tend to preserve the original climate of informality and a measure of redundancy, but are quite unlikely to arrange the material in the order of mounting difficulty.

Refreshingly, one finds certain elements of the graded approach — a consistent effort to capture, from the outset, the attention of the half-converted layman and to keep him enthralled — in R. Posner's paper-backed pocket book *The Romance Languages* (1966), avowedly an unconventional experiment in "haute vulgarisation". The author achieves her aim through the introduction of vigorous, occasionally flashy similes, through sparing use of technical terms, and a deliberate start in low gear; but she does not compromise on the quality of the analysis, refuses to stoop to a tasteless style, and, above all, offers original ideas and reactions.

### 3.5.9. Prospects of dynamic categories of classification.

Though historical grammar, along with etymology, is the diachronic discipline par excellence, designed to cut across time rather than to survey a single temporal plane, it is nevertheless true that most of the classificatory categories ordinarily introduced: Accentual conditions, configuration of the stressed syllable, the given sound's position vis-à-vis the word as a whole and vis-à-vis its immediate environment, and so forth (see the following Section), are strictly static, flowing in most instances from a descriptive analysis — however rudimentary — of the older stage. There are few exceptions to this tendency, aside from those examined under 3.5.2: First, any attempt at periodization, even if the division, as sometimes happens, is made by intuition, presupposes a minimum or modicum of deliberate segmentation of the time axis; second, the occasional progression, in the biography of a single sound, from retention through modification to total loss (Meyer-Lübke), reckons with evolutionary stages; i.e., indirectly, with the passage of time. One may considerably refine this latter analysis by distinguishing between various degrees of deflection from the original state of balance and, once such a scale has been established, by making the measure of remoteness the prime classifier, even beyond the limits of phonology. This approach via latitude of departure could lead to systematic inventories, for certain languages, of absolute retention, comparatively high degree of retention, etc. and ultimately to a forceful analysis of extents of conservatism vs. innovation.

There comes to mind the untested possibility of yet another dynamic approach, this time one confined to phonology. Practitioners of historical grammar are agreed that not all sound shifts have taken effect with equal consistency; contrast the pervasive change of L. A to F. *e* in stressed, open syllable with, say, the sporadic inconclusive developments of syllable-final L. L in Spanish (*alto* v. *ot-ero*). One finds no unanimity of opinion on the cause of such divergences: Some scholars think of different degrees of "blocking" by counterforces (e.g., analogical leveling, borrowing from adjacent dialects), while others operate with the bolder concept of sound laws inherently endowed with different measures of vitality, as a result of variable concomitants (interplay of sound pattern and "yield", the latter controlled by lexical frequency and frequency of actual occurrence). Whichever each expert's preference, one might, at least in theory, group all sound changes under consideration on the basis of (to use a controversial term) their relative degree of "regularity". Such an inventory, more than any other familiar arrangement of data, could lead to the detection of interferential and differentiating factors.

## 4. Tactical Arrangements

**4.0. Definition.** Over against the major divisions of material which stamp each historical grammar with an immediately recognizable character one may place that multitude of minor tactical decisions for ordering data which become visible only upon closer inspection. The oldest arrangements of this kind were based on either crude externals (e.g., the alphabetical sequence of letters) or traditions taken for granted without critical examination (e.g., the systems of "parts of speech" inherited from Graeco-Latin grammar). The main evolutionary trend has been in the direction of increasing stress on the functionally significant. Not only did the pressure of the classical models gradually weaken, but even among the Romance languages scholars eventually learned not to take one as an obligatory model for the others.

Since diversification, from school to school and from author to author, at this point reaches its maximum, we can offer only a few stray illustrations suggestive of the actual spectrum of possibilities.

**4.1. The ordering of vowels.** In Diez's original comparative phonology (1836) the analysis of vowels already shows undeniable sophistication.

> The specific and formal treatment of the Latin material (arranged in conventional succession: A, E, I, O, U, AE, OE, AU) is less noteworthy than some generalities relegated to an unobtrusive Supplement (164–175). In the formal section, Diez separates stressed from unstressed vowels, subdividing the latter into those so labeled *stricto sensu* (initial, medial, or final), and those involving hiatus (primary, secondary, etc.). The Supplement reëstablishes the cross-connections of which the reader may have lost sight in attending to details. Here the author posits such broad categories as quantity, contraction, metaphony, apophony, syncope, diphthongization (five genetic varieties), and, more important in retrospect, the inner configuration of the immanent vowel system (166). He deals with the special status of proparoxytones, against the background of learned vs. vernacular transmission (169), also briefly characterizes six concrete vowel systems (169–171), and in conclusion affords a cross-linguistic inventory of all diphthongs encountered (174 f.). The revised edition (1870) compresses some passages of the Supplement, but expatiates, as if by compensation, on the influence of surrounding consonants (196) and, without using these terms, points up contrasts between allegro and lento rhythm, the latter equated with poetic diction (202).

Without exaggeration, all subsequent refinements, to the extent that they signaled genuine progress, aimed at a closer integration of Diez's inventory of specific facts and of his methodologic afterthoughts.

The possibilities for rearrangement were numerous, though not unlimited; the more complex the facts, the greater the potential diversification of classificatory schemas. Thus, French shows a more intricate development than Spanish, for three independent reasons. First, the number of intermediate stages between the stressed vowels of, say, BOUE and *bœuf*, or of RĒGE and *roi*, is higher than is observable or inferrable in corresponding Latin-Spanish equations. Second, the configuration of the syllable exercises a controlling influence in the *langue d'oïl*, as against Spanish; this calls for a new category, checked vs. free syllable (contrast *mère* with *barbe*). Third, a following nasal consonant arrests the evolution of a vowel (*veine* vs. *roi*). The interplay of so many discrete factors opens up an unusual latitude of prospects, allowing the analyst either to examine each vowel separately, subdividing the different outcomes according to the changing concomitants, or else, in a more abstract vein, to distribute the entire material on the prime basis of the different representation of these forces (stress, nasality, contour of the syllable; also locale and evolutionary stage at issue).

A specialist such as SUCHIER leaned toward emphasis on external criteria (1888), minimizing the importance (recognized by Diez) of initial, medial, and final position for unstressed vowels, but tightening his outline by rigorous territorial distinctions: Standard French (572–592) sharply separated from five regional varieties, or alliances of varieties, of Gallo-Romance (592–605) and, within the former section, neat periodization: (a) before the 12th century, (b) during that century, (c) after that century, (d) present-day situation, in the manner here suggested in Section 1.2, and with occasional interposition of synchronic views. The resulting mixed perspective was later to develop much more fully (see Section 6.1.2, below).

The rash projection of categories from one language into another vitiates CORNU's otherwise elaborate treatment of Portuguese (1888, 1906). The author, whose contact with Old French grammar had made him hypersensitive to the distinctive evolution of certain vowels in free and checked syllables, examined the outcome in Portuguese of each Latin vowel under these two headings, apparently unaware of the fact that in Western Hispano-Romance the syllabic contour is diachronically irrelevant.

MEYER-LÜBKE's treatment of vowels (1890) shows noteworthy innovations. The fundamental distinction between stressed and unstressed has been maintained, but the vowels are no longer paraded in alphabetic order. The basic comportment of each stressed vowel is examined under three rubrics: (a) preservation, (b) spontaneous change, (c) conditioned change; the last-mentioned invites further subdivision, through localization and narrower categorization of the conditioning factor: (α) the following sound (nasal, palatal, labial, velar consonant; the back semivowel; a consonant cluster) or (β) the preceding sound (similarly classified in articulatory terms). These subdivisions are so skillfully executed that the various non-contiguous sections on, say, "preservation" permit immediate confrontation.[34]

The 20th century introduced few tactical innovations, though it brought several strategic maneuvers (and untold corrections of etymological details). Meyer-Lübke's oft-revised French grammar (orig. 1908), famous for its pronounced chronological orientation (see Section 3.5.1, above), exhibits a discernibly more flexible organization than his earlier Romance grammar, a concession to new tastes making it a less handy reference tool but a more effective interpreter of unique historical trends.

The writer takes as his cornerstone the discovery of a formula, pervasive, though historically and territorially specific (§ 47: in proto-Northern French, only lengthened stressed vowels are subject to conspicuous change), and builds his edifice around this one broad observation, first removing stray obstacles (§§ 48–52) from the beautifully landscaped terrain, then arranging the pertinent shifts in the logically most cogent, i.e., historically most plausible, succession. Characteristic of his broadened vision is the deliberate rapprochement of cognate changes, which an indifferent cataloguer would tend to keep apart, such as the parallel contrasts between *chier*: *mer* and *cire*: *voire* (§ 63). Similarly, nasalization, recognized as a single broad tendency, is examined in a close-knit sequence of discussions (§§ 67–72). Nevertheless, there remain some loose ends, through sporadic, unintegrated references to learned words and borrowings (§ 66) and to dialectal developments (§ 79); quite apart from the fact that whole categories of words forcibly excluded from consideration are set aside in an introductory section (§§ 32–45).

Meyer-Lübke's experimental book remains within the bounds of a standard historical grammar, but contains the germs of radical deviations from tradition: From here one path leads to the array in which straight chronology overrides all other considerations, as in Richter's *Romanismen* (1934); another to almost exclusive

---

[34] Even so, there remains a disquieting residue of exceptional arrangements. Under Ī, an unintegrated paragraph deals with conditions which prevail in oxytones, though neither the number of syllables nor the absolute position of the stress in given words are otherwise emphasized (§ 43); there further remains a dangling section (§ 44) on peculiarities unclassifiable within the chosen pattern, and a counterpart of this section later mars the discussion of Ū (§ 67). The neatness of the design is further jeopardized by an excursus on certain spontaneous developments of *ei* < Ē (§§ 71–78) and another on the sporadic transformations of Ē into [ẹ] and [i] (§§ 115 f.), both with exact parallels under Ō (§§ 120–126, 145–149). Additional complications arising from the slightly deviant treatment of Ĕ and Ŏ are redeemed by their perfect symmetry.

concentration on traits uniquely characteristic of the chosen language, as in Menéndez Pidal's *Orígenes* (1926, 1950).

It would be otiose to review here the countless minor variations embodied in the various outlines of Romance phonology.[35] Looking to the future, one may argue: Major improvements, within the framework of the traditional genre, are achievable by overcoming several recurrent (not to say endemic) deficiencies:

(a) The structural grasp of CONCATENATIONS may be introduced on a more liberal scale. The concept of the "empty case", applying particularly to French vocalism, allows one to set off a primary [u], at the Latin stage (with the usual cleavage into a long and a short variety); a secondary medieval [u], originally in free syllable, as in *-ous* < -ōsu; a tertiary modern [u], as in *court* < OF *cort* < CURTU, all changes occurring uninterruptedly in checked syllable, an innovation facilitated by the simultaneous shift of *-ous* to *-eux*, etc.;

(b) In dialect study, heightened concern with CONVERGENCE must balance sustained attention to divergence;

(c) A formal system is needed for measuring the dimension of LEARNED DEPARTURE from the vernacular norm (approximations such as "semilearned" inopportunely suggesting a fixed half-and-half ratio, are inadequate); the next desideratum is a technique for building the results of such measurement into the general edifice of historical phonology,

---

[35] A few random illustrations. Grandgent's rough classification (1927) is based on the character of the syllable (accented, "secondary tonic", unaccented, the last-mentioned with the expected subdivision); within each category the vowels of "Vulgar Latin" (i.e., proto-Italian) are individually reviewed in alphabetic order. The bulk of his material, which fails to fit into this straitjacket, the author presents, in small print, at the conclusion of each paragraph. While the remarks are for the most part neatly circumscribed, atomization reigns supreme, since no guiding principle is further perceptible at the lower echelons: One discovers a maze of lexical and onomastic problems, illustrations of analogical shifts, disquieting references to "puzzling words", "obscure associations", "peculiar developments"; examples of imitation of Provençal and French usage, of special dialectal developments, of contrasts between words poetic and colloquial (or learned and popular), and of separate norms for proclitics and enclitics; also, hints of apheresis, prefix change, and the like. Since the "exceptions", even if measured by so trivial a yardstick as the space allotted to them, far outweigh the rules and fall into no clear-cut pattern of their own, the reader despairs of recognizing in each actual form a compromise between a few independent forces, of which the phonological drift is only one.

Williams' chief improvements (1938) over his immediate model lie in providing multipronged rather than deceptively simple sound correspondences; in subordinating each of the dwindling number of exceptions to a particular, sharply delineated prong; in separating, even on the typographic level, plainly observable facts from explicative conjectures, however ingenious; and in altogether removing from the phonological field of observation purely lexical intricacies. As a result, his book is leaner, but tidier and tighter than Grandgent's.

much as scholars have engineered a schema, or rather rival schemas, for highlighting rural dialectal idiosyncrasies;

(d) The UNSTRESSED vowels have been the phonologist's stepchildren (textual critics, to be sure, have excellent excuses for concentrating on assonances and rhymes; also, for some less obvious reason, Guerlin de Guer translated only that part of Gröber's treatise which dealt with stressed vowels). The conventional analysis of atonic vowels demands overhauling. It is customary to start out with the syllables carrying the primary and the secondary stress, irrespective of their position in the word, while the unstressed syllables are classed, in part, on the basis of their position relative to the stress (e.g., "intertonic"), in part, on the strength of their absolute position within the word (e.g., "word-initial", "word-final"). This arrangement leaves some loose ends: the importance of oxytonic stress for the French development of A (*dé-jà*), the contrast in the Old Spanish outcome of -E between paroxytones and proparoxytones: *fe(e)*, *lueñ(e)*, *mill*, *noch(e)*, *sol* beside *ánade* (a contrast leveled where medial consonant clusters, primary or secondary, are at work: *madre* matches *conde*, *ombre*, *verde*), and similar points, too important to be hidden away in footnotes. A cogent classificatory system devised consistently, without redundancy, to heed a given syllable's relative and absolute position could throw the evolution of vowels, especially those unstressed, into impressively bold relief.

## 4.2. The ordering of consonants.

**4.2. The ordering of consonants.** No other section of this survey presents so complicated a pattern of rival possibilities, latent or tested. This extra margin of complexity is due to the concurrence of several independent factors:

(a) The NUMERICAL SUPERIORITY of consonants over vowels, at least in a typical Romance language, against the need for apportioning an equal share of attention to each phoneme;

(b) The tradition of identifying consonants by both LOCUS AND MODE OF ARTICULATION;

(c) The abundance, particularly in Spanish and in Old French, of consonant CLUSTERS, as compared with the relative paucity of straight vowel sequences and of diphthongs combined;

(d) The virtually OBLIGATORY inclusion of phonology in any historical grammar, vs. the optional status of disciplines equally intricate, such as derivation and syntax;

(e) The almost mandatory attention, in phonology, to discrepant DIALECTAL conditions (seldom, if ever, taken into account by syntacticians).

Though some characteristic classifications will figure here in chronological succession, such sequence implies no intention to trace the evolution of the schema. The task at hand is rather to contrast, for the sake of their clashing configurations, a few basic arrays whose authors, with the sole exception of Diez, had before them ingenious models which they were at liberty to adopt, to modify, or to reject.

Diez's method shows astonishing adroitness for its early date (1836).

> From the outset, he distinguishes between locus and mode of articulation, elevating the former above the latter, so that all labials are presented jointly, in this sequence: P, B, F, V, M. Each Latin consonant phoneme constitutes a unit, and all its outcomes are ideally included in a single section (I mention below, in n. 37, some compromises with common sense and economy). The further splitting of such a unit fundamentally reflects its position within the word and vis-à-vis its neighbors, the standard sequence being: word-initial, intervocalic, word-final; lengthened (geminate); constituting the first or the second ingredient of a bipartite consonant cluster, so that P-, -P-, -P, -PP- precede PT-, PS-, PN-, -PT- and -PT, -PD-, -PS- and -PS, while these lead to SP. (This arrangement entails the difficulty of requiring the discussion of each dyadic cluster in two disconnected passages.) Significantly, the individual results in each language represent the smallest classificatory unit, a tribute to Diez's superb grasp of Romance linguistics as a whole. This bold cross-linguistic perspective dominates, e.g., the analysis of -B- (180-182): The writer first breaks down the results into four basic possibilities: (a) change to -v-, (b) maintenance of -b-, (c) transmutation into some other labial, (d) loss,[36] and only then adduces specific illustrations.[37]

By the late 19th century, numerous other classifications, not always marked by improvement over Diez's, became available. Suchier's

---

[36] At this point a modern worker would have inverted the sequence of (a) and (b), so as to allow for a gradual rise from preservation through transmutation to total disappearance. After subsuming the new (b) and (c) under a common denominator, one arrives — granted the correctness of Diez's raw facts — at the following, less coarse-grained scheme: (a) preservation; (b) change into a labial ($\alpha$: $v$; $\beta$: some other labial); (c) loss.

[37] The succession of divisions is not rigid, allowing occasional reversal for the sake of increased economy or effectiveness. Thus, where the outcomes are similar for initial and medial position, as with F > $h$ and V > $b$ or $g(u)$, or for all three positions, as is true of M > $n$, Diez subordinates the (uncharacteristic) position to the (characteristic) development; where a given cluster is genetically restricted to a single lexical strain, as in typically Hellenic PT-, PS-, PN-, he introduces a parenthetic reference, strictly speaking irrelevant, to this strain; where striking convergence is at once apparent, as with CL-, FL-, PL-, he jointly discusses these shifts, with all requisite cross-references, in splendid anticipation of modern trends. The attention to word-stress is kept at a minimum, all channels of transmission are relegated to the background, and the profound difference between the comportment of primary and secondary clusters, though clearly apprehended in the case of MN ("ursprünglich" vs. "[durch] Ausfall eines Vokals"), remains hazy in the total design.

prime division (1888), for French and Provençal, was not into broad
categories of sound (vowels vs. consonants) nor into large geographic
chunks, but into chronological layers. In his weightiest chapter,
examining such changes as antedated the 12th century, he singled
out (§ 11) those common to both languages (DI = $j$ = G $^{e,i}$ , prosthetic *e*-, etc.), unfortunately remaining undecided as to whether the
wider regional spread, as a matter of principle, implied temporal
priority.[38] The following paragraph, arranged and phrased with
equal cursoriness, he reserved for consonantal changes showing Old
French opposed to Old Provençal (e.g., -TR-, -DR-; K$^a$-).

BAIST'S analysis of Spanish, also dating from 1888, passes in
review, first, simple consonant phonemes and, later, corresponding
clusters, each examined from several angles (the exact procedure is
nowhere clarified). It differs from Diez's in that the mode of articulation occupies a higher rank than the locus, so that P, T, and C (i.e., K)
jointly precede B (V), D, and G, while M and N, like R and L, are all
four grouped together as sonants. Despite Baist's noted philological
prowess and special concern with thorny etymologies, his treatment
suffers from serious weaknesses. One drawback is his inability to
recognize unifying tendencies behind the myriads of colorful details
(even § 38 is a mere tabulation of individual shifts); another, of a
more technical order, is his failure to draw the all-important distinction between primary and secondary clusters (an idiosyncrasy which,
e.g., utterly distorts § 50).

MEYER-LÜBKE'S grand classification of Romance consonant shifts
(1890) represents the sharpest conceivable break with all earlier
practice and, simultaneously, marks one of the all-time summits of
linguistic craftsmanship. If Diez's basic operational unit was the
single phoneme, however deftly placed in its proper niche, Meyer-
Lübke's far more "algebraic" division rested squarely on positions
abstractly defined. The three main divisions in the new schema
(A, B, C) involved the position of the consonant within the word:
initial (§§ 404–431), medial (§§ 432–548), or final (§§ 549–569),
followed by an anticlimactic fourth (§§ 570–591), which amounted
to little more than an appended catalogue of "accidenti generali"
(somewhat lamely labeled "Lautvertauschungen"); since this

---

[38] "... diejenigen, die sich über ganz Gallien und darüber hinaus erstreckt haben,
womit freilich nicht gesagt sein soll, daß die Veränderungen, welche nur einen Teil
des galloromanischen Gebietes umfaßt haben, zu einer späteren Zeit eingetreten
sein müßten." For subsequent periods Suchier took into account French alone,
except in a string of special chapters on dialect speech (§§ 26–39).

K

Supplement, judged by modern standards, only obstructs the free flow of genuine phonology, it will be advisedly disregarded.

The long section on consonants in medial position stimulated the author's climb to the highest peak of sophistication. Starting from the dual premise (§ 432) that the dominant factors here were the consonant's position vis-à-vis the stressed vowel (a circumstance practically irrelevant as regards initials; here most influential with respect to stops) and its occurrence in fixed syllabic-accentual types (paroxytones, etc.), Meyer-Lübke propounded the following schema for his next division (I, II, III, IV): "Simple consonants in paroxytones" (§§ 433–457), "Consonant groups in paroxytones" (§§ 458–522), "Consonants in proparoxytones" (§§ 523–540), and "Geminate consonants" (§§ 541–548); that is to say, at this classificatory rung the syllabic-accentual structure of the word and the degree of "involvement" of the consonant phoneme were granted equal consideration. Not all the groups thus sifted out were further subdivided with comparable elaborateness; Group I lent itself to the most cogent analysis. The next step was subdivision in terms of mode of articulation (a, b) opposing stops and spirants (§§ 433–447) to sonants, i.e., to N, M, R, L (§§ 448–457). Before itemizing the members of these small groups, Meyer-Lübke drew another dividing line, at least, through the first group, contrasting the posttonic (§§ 433–442) with the pretonic position (§§ 443–447), at a time when Verner's Law was in the focus of interest. Even at that stage the individual facts were not yet allowed to come to the fore. The posttonic group fell implicitly into three subgroups: voiceless stops (§§ 433–435), voiced stops (§§ 436–439), and spirants (§§ 440–442), and the pretonic into just two subgroups: stops (§ 443) and spirants (§§ 444–447).

In dramatic contrast, then, to Diez, Meyer-Lübke leads his reader to the specific consonant phoneme as the smallest unit, or one of the smallest, of his construct, and he sides with Baist rather than with Diez in his choice of mode rather than locus of articulation for any classificatory purpose, explicit or implied (§ 405), while periodization is deëmphasized throughout. Only at the lowest hierarchic level do some timid resemblances to Diez appear; cf. the studiedly subordinate importance accorded to individual "daughter languages".

Thus, in discussing word-initial [g] or [j] before front vowel (§ 407), Meyer-Lübke first establishes a chain of four evolutionary stages, of which the third presupposes the second: (α) preservation of the VL state, (β) shift to the voiced affricate [ǧ], (γ) de-affrication to [ž], (δ) complete loss, and finally illustrates each possibility that has materialized with examples drawn from one or several languages. Similarly, unconditional change of [l-] to [ʎ]- (§ 418) paves the way for all kinds of conditional fronting of the lateral, which the author characteristically tags as "sekundäre Palatalisierung" (§§ 419 f.: before front vowel in Rumanian and in Raeto-Romance; §§ 421–425: in the cognate groups

CL-, GL-, PL, BL-, FL-, examined in a progression from language to language).

In other words, the lower rungs of Meyer-Lübke's ladder are formed, somewhat haphazardly, by (a) concrete sound units of the parent language (consonant phonemes), (b) territorial units or specific linguistic systems of the "daughter generation", (c) evolutionary stages, whose range stretches from extreme conservatism to maximum departure from the assumed starting point.

The artfulness of Meyer-Lübke's approach shines forth in numerous details. Since the broad view is consistently in the direction of the daughter languages, from the immovable vantage point of the ancestral tongue, only primary consonant clusters in medial position qualify for representing a formal subdivision; the all-important secondary clusters, however, are somewhat surreptitiously brought in under proparoxytones (§§ 525–538). Despite many such felicities, the treatise, measured by present-day standards of rigor and explicitness, shows serious architectural flaws.

> Thus, the consonant clusters in paroxytones are discussed in impressive detail, but one misses a preliminary guide to their classification and is left wondering why some binary groups are defined by the mere point of articulation of both ingredients (e.g., "labial plus dental", § 458), others by specific mention of only the first phoneme (e.g., combinations with s-, §§ 468–473, and with r-, §§ 474 f.), yet others by equally specific identification of the concluding phoneme alone (e.g., consonants preceding l and r, §§ 487–495, and, of course, those preceding [w] and [j], §§ 501–522), while one restricted group of shifts is incongruously tagged not at all by any static characteristics of the elements, or of one element, involved, but by a dynamic trait: the stubborner resistance to erosion shown, counter to expectation, by the second element (§§496–500).

Meyer-Lübke's grandiose synthesis, then, marks a decisive step toward increased abstractness, but leaves ample room, if not for further tightening, at least for more rational apportionment.[39]

[39] Minor organizational flaws in the *Lautlehre* are quite numerous. The Table of Contents was hastily prepared; so were the headings for some sections. Thus, § 426 (on labialization: QU-), § 427 (on voicing of initial consonants), §§ 428–430 (on loss or addition of initial consonants), § 431 (on secondary initial clusters) inexplicably all appear subordinated to the section on secondary palatalization. Admittedly, lexical detail still obstructs the view (§ 427: "Es handelt sich dabei nicht um eine bestimmte Regel, sondern jedesmal um besondere Einflüsse, es ist daher jeder einzelne Fall für sich zu betrachten"). The division of final consonants into primary (§§ 549–553) and secondary (§§ 554–569) breaks the basic design. The phrasing of some sections is weak (§§ 450–454: -N-); stray references to the socio-educational dimension were built in haphazardly (§ 540); the French contrast pretonic : posttonic proparoxytones was introduced at too low a hierarchical level.

From the high-water mark of sophistication in formal array (1890) which Meyer-Lübke's position, despite vestigial flaws, undoubtedly signaled, there was only a succession of retreats and compromises throughout the following decades — to the extent that this kind of diachronic arrangement of consonants further occupied the focus of attention. A dubious excuse for this spell of fatigue or surfeit is the fact that for casual reference and for elementary didactic purposes, the degree of abstractness aimed at proved disquietingly high. In an effort to grapple with the concrete, isolated facts of language growth on a lower plane of analysis, as it were, some authors reverted to Diez's starting point (1836), presenting jointly or in close succession all outcomes of a given consonant. Typical of this attitude are Nunes' *Fonética histórica* (1895) — slightly more advanced in its treatment of vowels — and, above all, Bourciez's *Précis* which, as a result of its immense circulation, must have been instrumental in dulling its many young readers' acumen and imagination (the three introductory chapters on generalities offer scant compensation for such dry cataloguing of facts). The alternative for a textbook writer (and historical grammar at that stage tended to degenerate into a textbook industry) was to accept only part of the newly suggested hierarchization, e.g., the gross separation into initial, medial, and final position. This possibility was grasped by Ford in the introductory prospectus to his *Old Spanish Readings* (somewhat incongruously, he set up a fourth group for medial clusters and, within each group, proceeded — roughly and inexplicitly — from straight retention through modification to loss); throughout the grammatical sketch included in Crescini's tripartite *Manuale*, conservatism was enhanced by the supremacy accorded, as in Diez, to the point over the mode of articulation. Only in a single respect did the simplification of Meyer-Lübke's convolute schema harmonize with actual progress of knowledge: Younger scholars inclined to assess the importance of word-stress for consonant development more cautiously than was the order of the day two generations before; even downright denials of its rôle were no longer uncommon.[40]

[40] Remember that in his French grammar (1908) — at the midway point of his career — Meyer-Lübke resolutely swerved from this self-imposed line in favor of a near-chronological arrangement (see Section 3.5.1, above). His old-age monographs, such as *Die Schicksale des lateinischen L im Romanischen* (1934), afford a glimpse of how, strength permitting, the author might have organized a new phonology half a century later. The only formal subdivision is into *l-*, *-l-*, *l'-*, *-ll-*, $C+l$ [mostly word-initial], and $l+C$ [mostly word-medial]; no signposts mark

**4.3. Other domains.** In inflection, it is as common to see declension placed ahead of conjugation — for no more valid reason than convention — as it is in phonology to find the vowels preceding the consonants.[41] Possibly the most exciting cleavage that one observes in accounts of Romance inflection is between those grammars which, in plodding fashion, include all "particles" (prepositions, interjections, etc.), and others which take the definition of "inflection" quite literally, limiting its territory to declension, conjugation, and, at most, grading and the formation of adjectival adverbs. The former trend is exemplified — among countless conservatives — by P. Förster (1880) and A. Keller (1894); the latter, by Darmesteter's posthumous *Traité de la formation de la langue française* and, more recently, by Šišmarëv's Morphology. (In contributions, including Baist's and Cornu's, to Gröber's *Grundriß*, this restraint may have been imposed by scarceness of space rather than by doctrinaire considerations.) The barest minimum of the prestructuralist morphology is the paradigmatic table, cf. the "Abriß" prefacing Appel's *Chrestomathie*. By consolidating syntax and inflection, a writer automatically eliminates the problem of the invariable particles: Thus, the unified section "Formes et syntaxe" (241–698) in Brunot-Bruneau's *Précis* treats on a par verbs, nouns, interjections, and negative "mots-outils".[42]

---

[41] By way of exception, in several sections of Bourciez's *Éléments* the verb precedes the noun.

[42] Concerning the arrangement of chapters on Romance derivation and composition one finds many useful bits of information in Chap. 1 ("The theory of Romance word formation") of P. M. Lloyd's unpublished doctoral dissertation (California at Berkeley, 1960), *A Linguistic Analysis of Old Spanish Occupational Terms* (pp. 15–76 and 161–173 of the typescript); there is now available in print an enlarged and improved version of that chapter (see *RPh.*, XVII, 736–770). A rare example of extreme conservatism in the maintenance of a purely alphabetic ordering of Sanskrit suffixes is offered by A. Debrunner's otherwise meritorious revision (1954) of the monumental treatise *Nominale Suffixe* (= *Altindische Grammatik*, II: 2) by J. Wackernagel († 1938), a weakness excoriated by a generally appreciative É. Benveniste, *BSLP*, LI: 2 (1955), 27–29.

---

further subdivisions, but Chap. 1, not uncharacteristically, leads the reader from preservation of *l*- via transmutations into [ð] and [ð-] > [w-] (Calabria), into [d] (North Italian colonies in Sicily), into [λ-] beside [λ-] > [j-] (Catalonia and Leon) to sporadic total loss as the logical concluding point.

Syntax has likewise been disregarded, for a variety of reasons. Relatively few all-purpose historical grammars grant it adequate space (two such exceptions are García de Diego's [1951] and Hanssen's [1910, 1913] manuals of Spanish). Among

## 5. Presentation

**5.0 Delimitation.** In a book-length typological essay the presentation of historical grammar, to the extent that it involves certain minor preferences, the inclusion of several features of subordinate importance, and miscellaneous peculiarities relevant to the history of each project, to book trade, and to cataloguing techniques, would require special consideration. All such peripheral matters can here receive only the barest passing mention.

**5.1. Levels of style.** As regards sharply pronounced style, one finds the expected spectrum of possibilities, ranging from terseness bordering on the cryptic (Meyer-Lübke), to smoothness (Meillet), elegance (Benveniste), discursiveness, and even garrulity (Spitzer). Some scholars favor a long succession of brief paragraphs, an arrangement giving their grammars the appearance of a check-list (Deferrari; I. Gershevitch's *Grammar of Manichean Sogdian* [1954] would in this context represent a descriptive counterpart); others emphasize the essentials and subordinate the details; a minority dispense completely with "iron-clad" paragraphing.

**5.2. Volume of documentation.** With respect to illustration, some grammars are known for an excessive accumulation of examples, making their perusal uncomfortable (Cornu); this flaw may stem from a long-prevalent confusion of manual and reference work, a blemish from which even Meyer-Lübke's splendid *Einführung* cannot be pronounced entirely free. Other grammarians are renowned for their judicious restraint from such overindulgence (Williams). The documentation ordinarily cites bare forms, preceded by a brief qualifier marking period and dialect and sometimes followed by a succinct parenthetic identification of the source (e.g., medieval text or atlas map); that is, the availability of a standard dictionary offering further

---

those which do, some split it up according to the dictates of morphology; thus, Ewert's *French Language* (1933) examines syntax intermittently under infinitive, present participle, and gerund (183–186), imperative (203 f.), past participle (229–231), and so forth. Also, probably the majority of short and even middle-sized compendia are satisfied with desultory comments, appositely titled "Notes de syntaxe" (Darmesteter's posthumous *Traité*) or "Syntaktisches" (Gartner's *Darstellung*, Wiese's *Elementarbuch* [1904, 1928], Kuhn's *Der hocharagonesische Dialekt* [1935], and many others); cf. also L. Jordan's "Ausgewählte Abschnitte der Satzlehre". See further, Section 2.3, above.

clues is taken for granted. But there is no dearth of exceptions: Ascoli's monographs, for instance, and Menéndez Pidal's *Orígenes* — as against his more conventional *Manual* — are replete with facts either newly unearthed or up to that point not readily accessible.

**5.3. Special typographic devices.** Some books resort to all sorts of devices helpful to the beginner (tables, boxes, charts, diagrams, arrows, etc.); others provide emphasis through striking fonts (Meyer-Lübke guides the reader of his French grammar by the use of bold-face, to give prominence to key-concepts even in the middle of a sentence); still others contrast base and product by small capitals and italics respectively—with or without directional signs; Rheinfelder uses German type for glosses, etc.

**5.4. Optional features.** A wealth of optional features provide further variation. These include maps (as early as Fuchs, 1849, and Ascoli, 1873), all sorts of figures, charts, and tables (e.g., to illustrate sound production), miscellaneously arranged bibliographies (alphabetic or, as in the case of Gartner's *Handbuch*, chronological), tables of contents (*tables analytiques*), and word-indexes (some of them, e.g., Alessio's [1955], Behrens', Brunot's [1922, 1935], and Elcock's [1960], by dint of their elaborate subdivision represent miniature masterpieces in their own right),[43] synopses (note the two appended to Vol. I of Meyer-Lübke's French grammar), isolable etymological problems (in Vol. I, 563 f. of his Romance grammar, the same scholar

---

[43] The variety of indexes, and of techniques used in compiling them, is such as to justify a separate typological study. Some authors merge the Indices Rerum, Verborum, Nominum; others keep them apart. In the Index Verborum one finds up to thirty subdivisions on the basis of language; authors favoring a single alphabetic sequence have recourse to abbreviated qualifiers. As early as 1873, Ascoli set off Latin etyma by spacing (*Sperrdruck*); Baldinger (1950) reserved italics for such dialect forms as lack counterparts in the standard. Aside from words, scholars index prefixes and derivational (rarely also inflectional) suffixes, cf. Alessio (1955), pp. 496–513; toponyms and tribal names (id., 1946, pp. 211–213); "Flurnamen", i.e., microtoponyms (Kuhn, 1935); matters of potential ethnographic interest (my only example is from Bloomfield's *Eastern Ojibwa*, a descriptive monograph); meanings (*UCPL*, Vol. XI) and identificational terms (Bally, *Traité de stylistique*), etc. The older indexes (e.g., Cohn's) aimed frequently at selective, rather than exhaustive, listing. On account of the drudgery involved, the indexes have sometimes been prepared by persons other than the authors; F. Apfelstedt and E. Seelman took care of the "Register" to the last, posthumous ed. (1882) of Diez's grammar, while Giuseppina Da Re and Clara Messi compiled the long "Wörterverzeichnisse" (299–341) to Wagner's Sardinian phonology.

offered a roster of advocates of the various solutions; Lerch's *Hauptprobleme*, syntactically oriented, also contains an Index Nominum, not to be confused with a glossary of proper names, i.e., anthroponyms and toponyms, such as offered by Darmesteter as early as 1874, also by Appel and Alessio [1946]), Addenda and Corrigenda (in Schuchardt's *Vokalismus* these, together with the Index, form a separate volume), prefatory notes by the authors and supporting prefaces by their sponsors or executors (note É. Littré's to Brachet's French grammar, and Meillet's to Ernout's Latin morphology), lists of abbreviations, keys to transcription, glossaries of technical terms (Bourciez in his *Précis* and Deferrari), Supplements (Gartner's Raeto-Romance grammar [1883] includes a separately paged "Nachtrag" to his *Gredner Mundart* [Linz, 1879]; Holmes and Schutz fill a quarter of the total space with extracts from Vaugelas' *Remarques* [1647] and from a governmental "Arrêté" [1900]), and the like.

A didactic peculiarity of the earlier American product (Holmes-Schutz, Pei), almost invariably frowned upon by anti-pragmatic Continental reviewers, was the inclusion of exercises; so also (in England) D. Paton's *Manuel d'ancien français*. The current vogue of general and descriptive grammars in the United States gives a writer — or rather a publisher — intent on providing drill the option between the preparation of a separate "work book" (H. A. Gleason, Jr., 1955) and the marginal inclusion, in the textbook itself, of practice material (C. F. Hockett, 1958). Conceivably, the beginner's historical grammar of the future will likewise be accompanied by some kind of work book; W. P. Lehmann's *Introduction* points in this direction. On the European book market, dominated by Germany, practice exercises and diachronic projection are found side by side only in a modern layman's grammar ("Konversationsgrammatik") or a school grammar impregnated, to the point of obtrusiveness, with historical reminiscences, such as Tagliavini's for Rumanian. Because such hybrid grammars and others, candidly practical, cater to the autodidact, they are often supplemented by a "Key", which may also contain a bidirectional vocabulary (as is true of Tagliavini's textbook). Vol. II of Bally's *Traité de stylistique* stands apart.

**5.5. Publication data.** One final sheaf of relevant details is provided by the book's status in the publishing world. Is it an original or a translation? (Brachet, Morel-Fatio, and G. Paris teamed up to translate Diez's grammar, while Hanssen, in 1913, simultaneously revised, amplified, and himself translated his earlier handbook). Does the new venture amount to an abridgment, as is true of J. Haas' *Abriß* and of Bàrtoli and Braun's adaptation of Meyer-Lübke's book-length Italian grammar, or to a recasting by a fellow scholar (cf. E. Schwan and D. Behrens, K. Voretzsch and G. Rohlfs)? Is there close imitation of a model, as when F. B. Luquiens avowedly followed Schwan-Behrens' pattern? Is the monograph classifiable as a mere fragment, as is true of Ascoli's "Schizzi"? Has the text, left incomplete at the author's death, been brought to a formal conclusion by some obliging fellow worker(s) — an emergency which arose, and was met with varying success, in the case of A. Darmesteter (L. Sudre and A. Thomas) and P. Savj-Lopez (P. E. Guarnerio)? Assuming that two scholars collaborated from the start, were they tempted to draw some dividing line between their respective shares and, if the answer is yes, was this line meant to separate chronological layers (U. T. Holmes, Jr. *vs.* A. H. Schutz) or neighboring disciplines (M. Leumann and J. B. Hofmann's joint revision of the Stolz-Schmalz Latin grammar)?

### 6. *Relation to Other Genres of Linguistic Inquiry*

**6.0. Definition of the problem.** No matter how neatly a theorist succeeds in circumscribing, by elimination, the domain of historical grammar, this domain, in actual practice, is not hermetically closed. Aside from being sometimes confused with other genres, only superficially related, it overlaps with a few to which it is actually akin, to the extent that a worker in search of some specific bit of information must often consult these allied writings which, on theoretical grounds, one is inclined to separate from historical grammar. These sporadic contacts, at the periphery of our typological survey, deserve only a few brief comments.

**6.1. Relation to synchronic inquiries.** Though no linguistic dichotomy is more familiar than that — traceable to Saussure — which assigns synchronism and diachronism to two different axes, the connection between them involves more than just occasional points of intersection. In some instances, the overlap, dictated by practical considerations, is of a casual nature; in others, it rests on deeper theoretical insights.

**6.1.1. Casual references to synchronism.** In historical grammars serving primarily as introductory textbooks (for better or worse, a solid majority, we recall, in the Romance field), authors have often deemed it expedient to include a plainly worded phonetic sketch, with more or less specific reference to the language at issue; this sketch necessarily moves on a descriptive plane. Thus, the earlier editions of Menéndez Pidal's *Manual* were consistently diachronic; however, soon after the appearance (1918) of T. Navarro's descriptive *Manual de pronunciación* there was added to the successive revisions of his master's historical grammar a lengthy section on articulatory phonetics inevitably phrased in non-historical terms (§§ 5, 32 f.). No such expanded cross-reference to fruits of laboratory research was necessary in the *Orígenes*, a monograph addressed to thoroughly experienced readers, steeped in the study of history. Similarly, Bourciez's *Précis* contains a section on some "notions of general phonetics" (while his *Éléments* familiarizes the reader instead with the gist of "linguistic analysis" and with the essentials of "language growth"), and Nunes' *Compêndio* affords old-fashioned guidance to "physiological phonetics".

Instead of the final outcome a scholar may choose the inchoate stage of a given development for a bird's-eye view of synchronic structure. Historical grammars cut to Romance needs, from Schwan through Zauner's comparative manual to Williams, frequently contain an introductory chapter on Vulgar Latin, a reconstructed or fragmentarily recorded entity taken as the actual starting point for the journey through time. Such chapters tend to show a perspective chronologically "flattened" and regionally leveled; similar disregard of time depth with respect to the hypothetical parent language permeates the reconstructions of pioneer Indo-Europeanists.

**6.1.2. The "growth-and-structure" (or "staircase") projection.** Of discernibly greater merit is the systematic projection of language change through skillful alternate use of diachronic and synchronic analyses. Here synchronism is no mere adjunct, but forms an integral part of the design, based on the premise that no change in details, however conspicuous, lends itself to meaningful explanation except through reference to changes as between systems. Though such dramatic shifts of perspective, on a modest scale, were not unknown to the late 19th century (witness Suchier's contribution to the original *Grundriß*, 1888), the vogue of the genre and its explicit vindication and recognition coincide with the first half, or, to be precise, third, of the 20th. An apposite label, giving credit to Jespersen for his leadership, would be "growth-and-structure" projection; as a graphic alternative, coined in a lighter vein, one may propose "staircase" perspective. A firm theoretical foundation for the approach and an adequate technique (e.g., for establishing an unassailable pattern of periodization) remain to be provided. The most elusive among its chief problems is this: Should the synchronic cuts mark periods of relative stability (balance, lull), separated by spells of turmoil (groping, insecurity), i.e., of quickened development; or should they set off stages at which, with the means at the analyst's disposal, a coherent description can be most smoothly provided? In other words: Does an actual state of temporary repose in the object studied invite specific adjustments in the angle from which the linguist aims his camera lens at that object? In unadulterated form, Jespersen's schema, supported by Meillet's authoritative experiments (*Aperçu, Esquisse*), was tried out on Romance ground by Wartburg (*Évolution et structure*), who at the time was possibly unaware of having had predecessors. But indirectly the new idea also influenced several "language histories", perhaps most visibly Lapesa's (see Section 6.2.3, below); for Rumanian, cf. G. Nandriş.

**6.2. Relation to language history.** Under "language history", sometimes qualified "external", one understands either, in a narrow sense, the thread of major and minor historical events causally interwoven with the development of a given language (e.g., the dates for the foundation of academies, influential university chairs, and learned societies, for the promulgation of laws affecting language instruction, for the publication of tone-setting books such as certain normative dictionaries, prescriptive grammars, and widely imitated translations), an approach admirably exemplified by Brunot's "Sommaire chronologique . . .", left unchanged even in Bruneau's sweeping revision of his teacher's *Précis*; or, in a broader sense, the general historical matrix within which any specific development of a spoken or a written language can be significantly embedded, cf. the "Histoire et formation de la langue française" (12–86) preceding the kernel of Brachet's grammar (1867) and Leite de Vasconcelos' circumstantial account of Miranda [del Duero] and its environs (I, 3–165). Whichever way one cares to define it, language history, not least by virtue of its discursive presentation, seems distinctly closer to both general history and other specialized histories (e.g., those of law, literature, science, fine arts, etc.) than are historical linguistics, as a whole, and, in particular, diachronic grammar as its hard core. The latter, because of its high degree of formalization, invites an expository style reminiscent of the formulaic arrangements of logic and mathematics. That is why language history, as the looser of the two analyses, has traditionally had vastly greater appeal for cultured laymen of undifferentiated tastes, for weakly motivated language-and-literature students, and for esthetically hypersensitive humanists than has unsentimental historical grammar, hostile to all manner of vagueness and to merely verbal virtuosity. This peculiar relationship has led to multiple interlocking between the two disciplines.

A transitional form, differing from an orthodox grammar solely by the inclusion of a brief external history, a section on the lexicon, and, conceivably, a few appended sample texts, represents a "near-grammar"; fitting examples are Ewert's *The French Language* and Darmesteter's posthumous *Traité* which, through a noteworthy piquancy, contrasts with the same scholar's voluminous formal course in French historical grammar.

**6.2.1. Background information in formal grammars.** Semi-naïve curiosity about certain historical facts surrounding language — in particular, about the infiltration of exotic lexical strains indicative of ethnic contacts — arose at an early date and was partially satisfied in a country like Spain by such Renaissance scholars as B. Aldrete and later, long before the advent of organized linguistics, by G. Mayáns y Siscar. From these and other pioneers, on whom he leaned heavily, Diez doubtless adopted the idea of a separate, lexically slanted section on the general historical background, at the start of his comparative grammar. The intrinsic autonomy of this pre-liminary sketch is eloquently demonstrated by the fact that the revised text heralding the 2d ed. (1856) of the Phonology: "Bestand-teile und Gebiete der romanischen Sprachen" (I, 3–132), appeared in G. Paris' translation (1863) as an independent booklet. That same year also saw the publication of an English pamphlet embodying a parallel translation of this section alone.[44]

---

[44] Such introductory material was sometimes extended to include a brief state-ment on the primary sources of information (which only Görber's "Einführung" examined in adequate detail, for their own sake) and to review the earlier analyses ("l'historique du problème"), the alternative being to relegate this critical recapitu-lation to a Supplement, as did Brachet in his *Dictionnaire des doublets*.

This tradition, a harmless concession to the average reader's essentially non-linguistic curiosity, hardened with the passage of time. By 1866 so versatile an explorer as was Schuchardt even at that beginning stage of his meteoric career retained the distinction between, to use his own terms, an external and an internal history of the Roman vernacular (*Vokalismus*, I, 44–75 and 76–166). Coelho (1871) carried Diez's tradition into the Iberian peninsula. A succinct preliminary survey (§§ 3–8) of tell-tale features of the lexicon marks not only the original (1888) but, more noteworthy, also the revision (1906) of Baist's Spanish grammar; independently it left stray vestiges in Múgica's introduction to his muddled grammar of Old Spanish (1891). By 1900, a widely observed rule linked at least the introductory chapter of a full-fledged historical grammar to some relevant survey of "historical conditions" (Bourciez, *Éléments*: characteristically, in small print); cf. Grandgent (1905), Zauner (1908), Huber (1933), and Williams (1938), four spokesmen here chosen almost at random. M. K. Pope's detailed "External history" of French stands apart: It fills almost as many highly concentrated pages (1–48) as does Meyer-Lübke's Introduction to his multi-volume magnum opus.

### 6.2.2. Relation to the history of settlements and migrations.

This branch of learning ("Siedlungsgeschichte") has at all times been heavily indebted to toponymy; before long, there were established additional bridges to lexicology. The idea of connecting chosen features of historical grammar (almost exclusively phonological traits) with elements of political history stems from a liberal assessment of the agency of protracted bilingualism. Certain contacts activated or strengthened by this agency are dubbed substratum, adstratum, and superstratum influences, depending on one's — frequently arbitrary — choice of the main layer. There has been in the past no lack of enthusiasts eager to ascribe every possible feature of lexicon and even of grammar to a favored ethno-linguistic stock; substratum studies have acquired a reputation as potential storehouses of manias and phobias. Balanced scholars, avoiding such extremes, have attributed only single features or close-knit sets of such features to specific ethnic or social ingredients of the total population. Ironically, as a consequence of this restraint, they have seldom paused to integrate such individual findings with the currently preponderant view of language as a tightly coherent system, in which every change of relevant detail is likely to provoke a chain reaction of potentially significant repercussions. The weakness of this method, then, is patently rooted in its very selectivity (see Section 3.5.6, above); once that much has been granted, the abundance of factual information which this historical orientation, abetted by the phenomenal success of dialect geography, has poured forth deserves unstinting recognition. Classic examples of meticulous reconstruction of "isoglosses on the move" include Menéndez Pidal's persuasive revindication of the "F- > h- > zero" line for the Ibero-Basque substratum of Old Spanish (*Orígenes*, § 41) and Wartburg's oft-revised report, stretching between the two versions of his *Ausgliederung*, on the gradual withering of -*s* in North Italian dialects. The reconciliation of this ethno-historical method, only recently adopted by H. Kuen and, on a more ambitious scale, by K. Baldinger in regard to the Iberian peninsula, with the rival procedures of explicative phonology represents the most urgent problem in present-day Romance linguistics; for some stimulating, if cautious, hints of immediate prospects, see Togeby's incisive review of Weinrich's fairly recent monograph (*RPh.*, XIII, 401–413). Baldinger himself and D. Catalán (*Estructuralismo e historia*, III [1962], 69–80) have also engaged in anguished soul-searching.

**6.2.3. Integration with literary and intellectual history.** The interweaving of linguistic and literary history is of such striking importance and intensity in Romance culture — one of the most erudite, literate, and esthetically appealing in the annals of all time — that at first glance the wisdom of leaving the tangled skein intact seems quite obvious.[45] Accordingly, systematic inquiry into those languages that have served as vehicles of Romance literature, or at least of written communication, has for decades been considered a legitimate academic pursuit; the pendulum has swung between the identification of a separate "standard" ("Schriftsprache", Remacle's *scripta*), as distinct from the many colloquial media, and genuine concern with an artistic vehicle. As regards sheer monumentality, these endeavors have culminated in the set (still incomplete) of Brunot's and Bruneau's learned volumes. Concentration on Italian has produced in fairly rapid succession the less ponderous books by Devoto and, at a later date, by Migliorini, while on the Spanish side

---

[45] Significantly, Diez's earliest essay (ca. 1821), unpublished but obliquely known from mention in an application form, bore the title *Geschichte der Sprache und Poesie der Provenzalen*.

the genre has left an imprint on Lapesa's highly readable *Historia* which, incidentally, no less than Meillet's *Aperçu d'une histoire de la langue grecque* (with its triple emphasis on period, area, and genre), drives home the impossibility of drawing any razor-sharp line between this particular projection and the "staircase" perspective, previously defined in purely temporal terms (Section 6.1.2).

Upon closer inspection, however, serious — if not insuperable — difficulties begin to loom in the fusion of the two cognate historical disciplines. For transparent reasons, historical linguistics is at its most impressive in dealing with preliterary periods; in an expert's deft hands, it serves to drive a wedge into partially uncharted territory, a term which in Romance, broadly speaking, connotes the first millennium. The literary material inescapably calls for the reverse stress on later time segments. As a result of this split interest, each successive volume of the Brunot-Bruneau venture, through no fault of its authors, has been progressively skewed in the direction of literature and of its immediate ramifications: In a project so conceived, the farther the best-intentioned scholar advances along this path, the more generous the share of attention he is bound to bestow on stylistics (here taken to mean the study of individual styles), to the lasting detriment of meatier, if less palatable, disciplines. Between inflated accounts of nostalgic and exotic Romanticism and mordant and earthy Realism, as reflected in a language like French, it becomes embarrassingly awkward to insert even a slim matter-of-fact chapter on, say, the phonology of mid-19th-century patois.[46] After a long promenade through the gardens of poetry, a tasteful Lapesa has recourse to a string of appendages to do belated justice to dialect speech (peninsular, American, Sephardic) which, in a more auspicious context, might have been attached directly to late Old Spanish: a noteworthy illustration of how a slice of literary analysis may positively obstruct a natural concatenation of linguistic events. On the other hand, the tone of Lapesa's lengthy Introduction, dealing in exuberant detail with prehistory's lexical flint-stones, clashes unavoidably with the preëminently stylistic and syntactic facets of his exquisite "Siglo de Oro" chapters. In short, even distinguished works of this kind are bound to suffer from a lack of topical homogeneity and from the absence of a firm geometric design.

---

[46] Paradoxically, though literature usurps increasing amounts of space in works so planned, the "climate" of its discussion may fail to satisfy the fastidious connoisseur of letters. Cf. *RPh.*, VII, 83–86, and VIII, 230–235.

Yet even these are not the most formidable drawbacks of the attempted compromise. The core disciplines of linguistics, as represented in historical grammar, pertain to social-science researches; the analyst operates with averages, allowing the individual speaker for once to recede into the background. Conversely, in the study of literary styles powerful personalities come to the fore, bringing to bear their "culturally filtered" private preferences on the tradition of a speech community. Paradoxically, despite the topical remoteness of economic history, that science, which likewise operates with the law of averages, methodologically harmonizes better with diachronic grammar than does the topically contiguous province of literary history. To conclude: On account of inherent complications studies of this mixed type, if at all maintaining a high level of refinement, are likely to remain occasional tidbits rather than the scholar's staple fare.

**6.3. Relation to historical dialectology.** At this point, some statement on the relation of historical grammar to dialectology (understood as the polar opposite of esthetically slanted stylistics) seems overdue. Yet in groping for the proper words one stumbles over two serious difficulties. First, the key word "dialect" is imprecise, even equivocal, since its range varies from language to language, and from decade to decade (thus, in current Continental usage its connotation is strictly regional rather than both territorial and social, and rural rather than urban). Second, with Romance dialects, especially those of older vintage, the contrast to the preceding section is insufficiently neat, since not a few have served as vehicles for literary production (in fact, initially all vernacular literatures were dialectally tinged).

From the vantage point of linguistics the situation seems to be as follows: A standard historical grammar of a major Romance language may, at will, be richly nuanced through constant references to peculiar developments in surrounding dialect speech. This has been particularly true of leading Italian grammars, from Meyer-Lübke's to Rohlfs'; less so, except for the medieval period (Suchier, Schwan-Behrens), of those available for French. For peninsular Spanish, we have numerous historically slanted descriptions of exiguous dialect zones, old (Staaff) and new (Sánchez Sevilla), and a few attempts at a small portfolio of dialect sketches (Múgica, García de Diego, Zamora Vicente), but no major work comparable in weight and craftsmanship to, say, Thumb's on ancient Greek dialects.

A different situation prevails in a zone which lacks a major literary language. Under such conditions dialect study alone feeds historical grammar. The first large-scale inquiries so oriented were conducted by Ascoli; in this century, Ronjat's investigations of Occitanian and Wagner's of Sardinian may serve as models. Common to Ronjat, Rohlfs, and Wagner is their welcome comparatist bias: They provide no mere succession of isolated miniature sketches, but examine, point by point, the various reactions of the different dialects to essentially the same set of challenges of attrition.

Viewing the situation from the opposite angle of dialect research, one many argue that to start from Latin (as did Krüger in 1914 and later some students of his with regard to Western Spanish) is, all told, a wiser procedure than to catalogue deviations from the closest modern standard (a semi-naïve technique cherished by many native Hispanists; cf. the strictures of D. Catalán Menéndez-Pidal in *RPh.*, X: 2 [1956], 71–92). Nevertheless, this more praiseworthy procedure entails one drawback: It fails to take cognizance of the effects of diffusion. Structural analysis, not necessarily hostile to diachronism, though at this juncture still predominantly synchronic (Bjerrome), offers additional clues for setting-off dialect zones; as a yardstick for gauging the change in scholarly tastes, compare Leite de Vasconcelos' sixty-year-old "classic" treatment of Mirandese with Herculano de Carvalho's recent front-line study.

**6.4. Relation to layman's guides and student's manuals.** On the periphery of professional linguistic studies one discovers diversified semi-scholarly genres, designed partly to whet the layman's palate, partly to capsulize knowledge for the hurried student's consumption. The importance to the expert of this marginal output varies from book to book, depending on the general and the specific authority of the scholar involved and on several concomitants. Some writings of this kind, such as Wagner's *Lingua sarda*, possess genuine value, affording upon occasion more mature, if less technically phrased, appraisals of a controversial problem than earlier monographs by the same author; others, like Trend's superficially glittering *History and Language of Spain*, or Faral's ill-fated grammatical outline of Old French, have been rashly prepared by scholars indisputably prestigious, but not in the field at issue; still others, though written by specialists in the subject concerned, show so many patent traces of production in "assembly-line tempo" as to discourage

L

sustained interest: This is, unfortunately, true of Dauzat's last synoptic pictures of French. In such works of unashamedly broad appeal, historical grammar may either be concentrated — undiluted — in separate chapters (Oliver Asín), or may be dissolved and doled out in small, innocuous doses all over the book, as is true, to remain within the province of popularized Spanish philology, of the familiar syntheses by Entwistle, Spaulding, and Šišmarëv.

**6.5. Relation to normative grammar.** While the relation between descriptive and preceptive (normative) grammar is in dispute — some theorists insist that a mere observer and interpreter of linguistic facts, like any other social scientist, should keep aloof from involvement in decisions on "right" vs. "wrong", while others counter that no persons are better qualified than trained linguists to intervene in precisely such decisions,[47] — any connection between the historical and the normative approach is, incontrovertibly, tenuous, not to say problematic. Yet it can happen that historical curiosity — leading, in turn, to professional competence — matures as an unexpected by-product of a particularly enlightened and refined manner of initial didacticism. Sometimes, conversion to the new ideal of objective inquiry marks a complete, even dramatic, break with the past (much as our generation has seen descriptivists passionately abjuring their previous apprenticeship in traditional philology). Occasionally, there crystallizes a transitional stage, in which assorted features of the two approaches, for once, appear reconciled in a peculiar amalgam. Cuervo's explanatory notes to Bello's "Castilian" grammar and the successive scrupulous revisions of his *Apuntaciones* on the speech of Bogotá are two prime examples — so too the torso of his "syntactic" dictionary exhibits the transformation of normatively tinted descriptive lexicography (Golden Age and modern section under each entry) into the baldly phrased historical projection of linguistic facts (medieval substructures, appended by way of flashbacks). Theoretically, the only defensible bridge between diachronism and prescription would be the assumption — seldom, if ever, validated — that the ideal, enforceably correct state of a language was the one

---

[47] Not infrequently professional linguists have been called in to preside over discussions of spelling reforms. One is also reminded of T. Navarro's rôle in suggesting a universally valid standard for dialogues in Spanish-language motion pictures; of B. Migliorini's arbitration of Roman and Florentine rival claims to standards of diction on the Italian radio; of Brunot's official collaboration with P. Valéry in the "Office de la langue française".

flowing from the configuration of its historical curve rather than from any rival consideration, such as a collective or an individual standard of taste, easily rationalizable. Moreover, at the peak of historicism acquaintance with the rudiments of historical method was temporarily held to represent no mean asset in the practical acquisition of grammar, whether one's own or a foreign (especially a dead) language was involved. As a result of this widespread belief, some drops of diachronism spilled over into advanced collegiate grammars by tone-setting specialists like Brachet and Egger.

**6.6. Relation to etymology, lexicology, and onomastics.** There has developed an intricate and elusive set of relationships between the grammatical and the lexical disciplines. That these tend to congeal into polar opposites has been eloquently shown in Romance scholarship by the two crowning achievements of both Diez and Meyer-Lübke: With either scholar, a comparative grammar on historical principles preceded a comparative etymological dictionary by a margin of roughly one decade. On a more modest scale, Brachet's French pioneering studies showed the same characteristic cleavage in the 'sixties (*Grammaire historique* . . ., *Dictionnaire étymologique* . . .); so did Darmesteter's investigations. In languages boasting only a finite corpus of texts, or so far known through a limited selection of material elicited through dictation, ambitious scholars generally aim at a three-pronged attack on their objective: a reader (chrestomathy, anthology, collection of folk-tales) ordinarily flanking either a full-sized grammar or a mere grammatical sketch, and a vocabulary, which may or may not be etymologically slanted; witness, for an extinct language, Sturtevant's approach to Hittite and, for modern exotic languages, L. Bloomfield's researches, ranging from Tagalog to Eastern Ojibwa (the latter monograph contains an additional list of model sentences). In Romance, except where a language recorded from the lips of its last speaker, such as Dalmatian, invites multi-faceted analysis (M. Bàrtoli), the texts are ordinarily so abundant as to militate against their treatment on a par with lexicon and grammar, save in handy "omnibus volumes" designed for classroom use. For trail-blazers, of course, the borders between the contiguous disciplines were still quite fluid. Eighty-five years ago, it was less startling than it would be now for a scholar of Ascoli's stature to select, for his commentary on the Surselvan *Barlaam and Josaphat* version, morphology (including, in great detail, derivation and, more spottily, the "syntax of the word") and chosen problems of lexicology (with special attention to loan words and loan translations), to the rigorous exclusion of phonology — in retrospect, an odd mating of topics.

Attention may first center around theoretical problems, then be allowed to stray to practical implications. The contacts between grammar and lexicon in diachronic projections are at their most intense in phonology and word formation; they remain perceptibly strong in inflection, but grow weaker in syntax.

A phonological treatise, in particular, rests squarely on lexical equations, involving a latent scattered etymological dictionary, as it were. On a modest level of accomplishment Hauschild exemplified this situation by actually compiling (1843) an etymological vocabulary of French based almost in its entirety on Diez's venerable grammar (this cross-section must not be confused with Jarník's two indexes to successive editions of Diez-Scheler's labyrinthine dictionary). If some worker should command adequate skill and enjoy sufficient leisure to prepare a pan-Romanic word-index to Diez's original grammar or, at least, to its phonological component (1836), such inestimable counterview would represent the embryonic stage of that scholar's subsequent dictionary (1853). Conceivably, the impact of grammar on lexicology is most perceptible in a word list containing exclusively reconstructed bases, arrived at preëminently through phonological analysis; witness Gröber's deservedly celebrated *Substrate*. Another narrow bridge between lexicon and phonology is systematic inquiry into doublets (*Scheidewörter*) — whether or not semantically differentiated — as practiced from Brachet and Coelho via Michaëlis down to Schuchardt (1936), since here the prime criterion for discriminating between lexical items has been their different degree of exposure to the agency of relevant sound shifts.

The peculiarities of Romance inflection are such as to make the section or separate monograph (Gassner, Fouché, Lombard) dealing with conjugation a repository of valuable lexical information. The corresponding section on declension is ordinarily too meager — except possibly for Rumanian — to invite systematic consultation by those curious on the lexical side. A differently tilted grammatical structure may, of course, reverse this situation: The "broken plurals" of classical Arabic affect such a heavy proportion of all nouns as to make any thorough investigation of them a foreseeably handy clue to lexical problems as well.

In word formation, the connubium of the two disciplines reaches its maximum intimacy. The more microscopic the inquiry into a set of suffixes, the greater the share of individual attention accorded to each word. H. Lewicka's copiously documented report on Middle French derivation, as viewed through the prism of comic plays (an approach obliquely echoing Spitzer's earlier Rabelais monograph) so lavishly showers philological attention on each coinage as almost to force the broader outline of patterns into the background.

In practice the uneasy feeling that grammar and lexicon are, in essence, distinct, yet inextricably interwoven, accounts for a number of compromises. Characteristically, Diez's concluding treatise, *Romanische Wortschöpfung* (1875), an unassuming essay in lexical — to be precise, nominal — segmentation of the universe into twenty-seven slices (a few further subdivided), each chapter bracketing several etymological vignettes, was issued as a formal supplement not, as one might have expected, to his dictionary, but to his revised grammar. A few stringently organized historical grammars contain neatly delimited sections on the vocabulary (cf. Gartner's original *Raetoromanische Grammatik*, pp. 1–32, and Part II of Brunot-Bruneau's *Précis*). Such separate chapters, or recurrent subdivisions in consecutive chapters, are even more typical of semiformal or experimental grammars such as Bourciez's *Éléments* and Meillet's *Aperçu* and *Esquisse*, to say nothing of diluted language histories. Introductory chapters concerned with external growth (Diez, Baist) offer additional opportunities for lexical encroachment (see Section 6.2.1, above). Where the same author has a grammar and a dictionary to his credit (Diez, Meyer-Lübke), cross-references are conspicuously frequent. Finally, certain special devices facilitate the use of a grammatical treatise for lexicological research; typically, indexes — selective (Diez) or, better still, exhaustive (Darmesteter, 1874 and 1877; Hanssen, 1910 and 1913) of formations adduced, with complete words and mere affixes interfiled or kept apart. One finds numerous variations, some very ingenious: A few authors, for economy's sake, are satisfied with including items difficult to locate (Meyer-Lübke, 1925), or hidden away in footnotes (E. L. Adams); others restrict themselves either to modern formations (Bourciez, *Précis*) or, conversely, to etyma (Gartner and Horning, 1883). Normally, the entries of an index appear unaccompanied by comments, but Meyer-Lübke's contains corrections to his comparative grammar, while Gartner's (1904), adapted to his multi-purpose work on Rumanian, includes etymologies beside glosses and, moreover, flanks a Supplement on neologisms ("Kunstwörter").[48]

Of all lexical disciplines, onomastics is probably most remote from grammar, though certain points not only of phonology, but of morphology and syntax as well, can be strikingly illustrated with toponymic material, e.g., the marking of "possession" in proto-French and Old French. The establishment of effective liaison at this point, beyond casual inclusion of proper names in the supporting evidence and their occasional listing in a separate index, is a vital desideratum.

**6.7. Relation to genetic and classificatory studies.** A peculiar genre, bordering on historical grammar, especially of the comparative kind (see Section 0.2, above), without quite coinciding with it in scope and spirit of inquiry, is the study in genetic classification. The terminal problem here is to identify a family relationship: either to settle the inclusion of a given language within a family (a matter of gross classification, unless a "mixed" or transitional language is involved) or, a commoner situation in Romance, to pinpoint its specific place inside the larger unit. The position of Venetic vis-à-vis Italic (M. S. Beeler, as against M. Lejeune and H. Krahe) and such constructs, of dubious legitimacy, as Balto-Slavic and Celto-Italic are relevant issues, within the purview of an Indo-Europeanist. In Romance, the pioneering studies of this nature (e.g., A. Fuchs' posthumous *Die romanischen Sprachen in ihrem Verhältnisse zum Lateinischen*, 1849) are barely distinguishable from "language history"; later the separate development of the genre picked up

---

[48] Cf. n. 43, above. From these "grammatical" indexes one must distinguish such glossaries — bilingual, by definition, except when contrastable stages of the same language are involved — as facilitate the reading of appended illustrative texts (Alemany Bolufer's *Estudio elemental*, Gorra's *Lingua e letteratura*, and Zauner's *Elementarbuch*; Appel's, Crescini's, and Ford's chrestomathies, the first-mentioned equipped with a separate roster of proper names). It happens that Index and Glossary merge into a single reference list (Huber, 1933), or that one book includes both, keeping them tidily apart (B. Wiese's two-column "Wörterverzeichnis zu den Texten" as against his three-column "Wortverzeichnis"; similar arrangement in Schultz-Gora). Recall that a topical and a lexical index may be amalgamated (as in Brunot's *La pensée et la langue* — this index, later polished by Bruneau, is a gem of reference service; cf. also Grandgent, 1905) or be offered separately (3d ed. of Diez's grammar; Grandgent, 1927: "Index Rerum" vs. "Index Verborum"). Gartner's *Handbuch* (1910) is almost overelaborate, containing as it does a German-Raetian "Wörterbüchlein", matching sample texts (ix–xvi), beside two "Wörterverzeichnisse", one a list of etyma (xvii–xx) and the other a list of dialect forms qualifying for written use (xxi–lxi).

momentum. A case in point is the controversial status of Catalan vis-à-vis Gallo- and Hispano-Romance (with the phantom of Afro-Romance looming in the distance), a tangle conducive to the debate which culminated in A. Griera's and A. Alonso's independent rebuttals of Meyer-Lübke's vulnerable tract (1925), and Alonso's criticism of Griera's position. The genetic — or typological — status of a border-line dialect invites similar analysis; cf. Sanchis Guarner's cogent plea (1949) for assigning the speech of Aguaviva de Aragón to Western Catalan. The adjudication of a text, especially one of complex transmission, to certain linguistic strains poses comparable problems; note Lapesa's stimulating discussion of the Old Asturian *Fuero de Avilés*, shot through with Provençalisms. In all these researches historical grammar supplies the bulk of the requisite ammunition, but represents no aim in itself. Not infrequently, bits of extraneous evidence (areal configuration, archeology, physical anthropology, demography, etc.) are injected into such debates. Linguistic explorers of specific diachronic problems must at all times take into account pertinent literature of this sort, some of it very meritorious, though it hardly typifies historical grammar at its freest and most imaginative.

**6.8. Relation to studies in linguistic methodology.** Any handbook of general linguistics, like Vendryes', Sapir's, and Bloomfield's, or of historical linguistics, like Paul's, or of Romance linguistics, like Gröber's — included in his own *Grundriß* — and Meyer-Lübke's (also, on an introductory level, Ettmayer's), is bound to contain, in its illustrations, a good many examples of linguistic change, of direct concern to the linguistic grammarian. The same remark applies to initiations into special methods of diachronic analysis, such as Martinet's and, more recently, Hoenigswald's. The difficulty for the monographist is best described as mnemonic: It consists in remembering those books and specific passages in which certain facts relevant to his particular project are discussed —, topically, out of context — by way of exemplifying some point of a vast cross-linguistic methodology.[49]

[49] Some day, a more leisurely typological survey may give closer attention to the morphology of titles. The delimiting pattern *From ... to ...*, last favored by Boyd-Bowman (and Rohlfs), has been mentioned in n. 5. Distinctly older — in fact, rooted in Renaissance scholarship — is the schema *Origins of ...* : in Spain, its vogue stretches from B. Aldrete (1606) via G. Mayáns y Siscar (1737) to Menéndez Pidal (1926, 1950). Modern Italian counterparts are G. Alessio's *Le origini del*

It is painful to report that, aside from earning a questionable reputation as popularizers of linguistic science (Dauzat, Hall, Pei), Romance scholars have contributed few books on general linguistics; that, of these few, some, outside a narrow circle, have been less than influential (Migliorini, Sandfeld-Jensen), while others have been received with studied coldness (Entwistle's *Aspects*). It is no mere coincidence that explicit joint introductions into general and into Romance linguistics are so rare (for one example, see Coelho's *A língua portuguesa*; cf. also Brunot's *La pensée et la langue*): Their infrequency, no less than the scant attention paid by numerous "general linguists" to the theoretical implications of Romance material, points up a critical gap in the edifice of organized learning.

## 7. Conclusion

A tentative study such as this hardly calls for more than a tentative set of conclusions, subject to revision in the light of additional material and new reflections.

Can one establish a network of significant relations between the individual distinctive features here isolated? Some connections seem to recur too frequently to be casual. Thus, within the category of scope one notes an interrelation between breadth and depth: A comparative historical grammar involving numerous languages is unlikely to limit itself to a short span of time. Another interrelation is that between breadth and direction: The choice of the reverse temporal sequence makes it almost mandatory to operate within a unilinguistic framework. A certain temporal sweep also goes hand in hand with the choice of language history, of the "growth-and-structure" projection, and of the chronological sequence as the prime classifier.

The typologist soon detects a certain conflict between the ideals of maximum latitude and subtlest sophistication. Except in Diez's

---

*francese*, as well as the books by E. Gorra, P. Savj-Lopez, and C. Tagliavini. Most titles are matter-of-fact, unembellished, and one notes a healthy refusal to eschew the word "grammar", despite its potentially less than pleasant connotation in many influential quarters. Some authors stress the introductory, cursory, or didactic character of their treatment: *Éléments* (Bourciez), *Précis* (Brunot, Bourciez), *Tableau* (Dauzat), *Elementarbuch* (Huber, Schultz-Gora, Tiktin, Wiese, Zauner), *Estudio elemental* (Alemany Bolufer), *Manual elemental* (Menéndez Pidal; the qualifier was later omitted), *Profilo* (Devoto), *Lições* (Leite de Vasconcelos), *Vorlesungen* (Wackernagel).

pioneer effort and possibly in the opening volume of Meyer-Lübke's comparative grammar, the quest for maximum breadth, maximum depth, and especially, maximum comprehensiveness usually coincides with pronounced methodological conservatism: For all their usefulness, monumental undertakings such as Nyrop's six-volume grammar of French and the even bulkier language history by Brunot and Bruneau have not been advantageously known for methodological originality. The keenest minds among the structuralists, while eager to proffer complete or nearly complete descriptions of a given language, have shown marked caution, not to say hesitancy, about extending their new methods to more than relatively small slices, only in a few instances cross-linguistic, of historical material. The chronological and the "growth-and-structure" projections have likewise been applied with impressive consistency to single languages, even where their practitioners were demonstrably versatile comparatists (Meillet, Richter).

The temporary decline of historical grammar is attributable to an ensemble of unfavorable circumstances: a vast accumulation of raw materials and unintegrated monographs, without commensurate progress in analytical ordering or even in mere indexing; an infelicitous status — conducive to meager response — of academic courses devoted to it, within the total configuration of study programs, the world over, in classical and, particularly, in "modern" languages; the unremitting pressure exerted by lay readers — and by publishers who must cater to their tastes — in the direction of heightened amenity, a quality one can rightly expect to find in certain language histories (specifically those attentive to the contacts between literature and its linguistic medium), but scarcely in historical grammar, quasi-mathematical in its desirable austerity; finally, the dual demands for novelty and for greater earthiness which, for three long decades after 1910, gave such powerful impetus to lexicology and dialect geography, unfortunately at the exorbitant cost of suspended concern with the linguistic core disciplines.

The prospects of revival are today less bleak than they were thirty years ago. Now that the novelty of straight descriptivism has begun to wear off, now that lexicocentric linguistic geography certainly is past its peak, a golden opportunity for a new attack on diachronic structure is rapidly approaching. This opportunity cannot be made good through an unimaginative return to past practice. To be reactivated, historical grammar must move in the direction of general glottodynamics, not only away from the cloggy detail and toward a more coherent integration of the whole, but at the same time ever closer to the establishment of truly evolutionary — beside essentially static — categories of transmutation.[50]

### Bibliographic Supplement

[Most of the items mentioned, or alluded to, in the article, have been included in this Bibliography; no need was felt to list standard textbooks of general linguistics or certain easily identifiable studies briefly contrasted with historical grammars. The writer has personally examined, with widely varying degrees of attention, practically all books here recorded, but not all editions of those that were published more than once; on a few such editions even indirect information was sorely deficient. Authors' names are listed in alphabetical order, but, under each entry, the publications — regardless whether books or articles — follow a roughly chronological sequence. Ordinarily, biographical data accompany only posthumous items, except for random clues to separately dated prefaces and the like. Initials appear consistently in lieu of first and middle names, but titles and subtitles have, for the most part, been left unshortened, on account of their preponderant descriptiveness. Unless otherwise indicated, publisher and place of publication have remained unchanged throughout successive editions. Mention has been made of translations to the extent that they may indicate the reading public's demand and response. References to significant book reviews (and, occasionally, to authors' rebuttals) are fairly unsystematic; so are other subsidiary bibliographic signposts. In German and Portuguese 19th-century titles the spelling has been slightly modernized; the few Russian titles appear transliterated; there has been no tampering with the original names of publication places. Abbreviations of learned journals, monograph series, and the like are standard.]

ADAMS, E. L., *Word-Formation in Provençal*. Univ. Mich. Studies, Human. Ser., II (New York–London: Macmillan, 1913).

ALARCOS LLORACH, E., *Fonología española (según el método de la escuela de Praga)*. BRH (Madrid: Gredos, 1950); rev. 2d ed. (1954). Cf. W. H. Jacobsen, Jr. in *RPh.*, X (1956–57), 258–266. On the 3d ed., revised and expanded (1961), see D. Catalán, "Nuevos enfoques de la fonología española", *RPh.*, XVIII (1964–65), 178–191. The 4th ed. is in press.

ALDRETE, B. J. († 1645), *Del origen y principio de la lengua castellana ò romance que oi se usa en España* (Roma: Vulliet, 1606); 2d ed. (Madrid: de León, 1674).

ALEMANY Y BOLUFER, J., *Estudio elemental de gramática histórica de la lengua castellana*, 3d ed. (Madrid, 1911); 5th ed. (1919), 6th ed. (1928).

---

[50] Of the critical reactions produced by this paper two seem particularly worthy of mention: W. P. Lehmann's in *Lg.*, XXXIX (1963), 286–290, and K. Togeby's in *SN*, XXIV: 2 (1962), 315–320.

Id., "Tratado de la formación de palabras en la lengua castellana, la derivación y la composición, estudio de los sufijos y prefijos empleados en una y otra", *BRAE*, IV (1917), 564–597; V (1918), 70–88, 169–191, 333–349, 469–491, 648–667; reprint (Madrid: Suárez, 1920).

ALESSIO, G., *Le origini del francese; introduzione alla grammatica storica* (Firenze: Sansoni, 1946). Id., *Grammatica storica francese*, 2 vols. [I: Introduzione-Fonetica; II: Morfologia] (Bari: "Leonardo da Vinci" [1951–55]).

ALLEN, J. H. D., JR., *Portuguese Word-Formation with Suffixes.* "Language" Dissertation, No. 33 (Baltimore, Md.: LSA, 1941). Cf. Y. Malkiel in *Lg.*, XVIII (1942), 51–62.

ALONSO, A. (†1952), [with R. Menéndez Pidal], "La subagrupación románica del catalán", *RFE*, XIII (1926), 1–38, 225–261, reprinted in *Estudios lingüísticos: temas españoles*, BRH (Madrid: Gredos [1951]), pp. 11–100. Id., "Partición de las lenguas romances de Occidente", *Miscel·lània [Pompeu] Fabra* (Buenos Aires, 1943), pp. 81–101; reprinted in *Estudios lingüísticos . . .*, pp. 101–127. Id., *De la pronunciación medieval a la moderna en español*, I, BRH (Madrid: Gredos [1955]), cf. Y. Malkiel in *RPh.*, IX (1955–56), 237–252.

APPEL, C., *Provenzalische Chrestomathie mit Abriß der Formenlehre und Glossar* (Leipzig: Reisland, 1895); rev. 2d ed. (1902); rev. 3d ed. (1907); 4th ed. (1912); 5th ed. (1920); 6th ed. (1930). Supplementary fascicle: *Abriß der Lautlehre* (1918).

ASCOLI, G. I., "Saggi ladini", *AGI*, I (1873), 1–537. Id., "Schizzi franco-provenzali", ibid., III (1878), 61–120. Id., "Annotazioni sistematiche al *Barlaam e Giosafat* soprasilvano; saggio di morfologia e lessicologia soprasilvana", ibid., VII (1880–83), 406–602.

AUERBACH, E., *Introduction aux études de philologie romane* (Frankfurt a.M.: Klostermann [1949]; written in Istambul, 1943).

BAIST, G., "Die spanische Sprache", in G. Gröber, *Grundriß . . .*, I (1888), 689–714; rev. 2d ed. (1904–06), 878–915.

BALDINGER, K., *Kollektivsuffixe und Kollektivbegriff. Ein Beitrag zur Bedeutungslehre im Französischen mit Berücksichtigung der Mundarten.* Deutsche Akademie der Wissenschaften: Veröff. des Inst. f. Rom. Sprachw., I (Berlin: Akademie Verlag, 1950). Id., *Die Herausbildung der Sprachräume auf der Pyrenäenhalbinsel; Querschnitt durch die neueste Forschung und Versuch einer Synthese* (Berlin: Akademie Verlag, 1958); tr. E. Lledó y Montserrat Macau [*La formación de los dominios lingüísticos en la Península Ibérica*], BRH (Madrid: Gredos [1963]).

BALLY, CH. (†1947), *Traité de stylistique française.* 2 vols. (Heidelberg: Winter, 1909). Id., *Linguistique générale et linguistique française* (Paris: Leroux, 1932); rev. 2d ed. (Berne: Francke [1944]); 3d ed. [reprint] (1950). tr. G. Caravaggi [*Linguistica generale e linguistica francese*], with an Introduction and a Supplement by C. Segre (Milano: Il Saggiatore, 1963), cf. Fred M. Jenkins, *RPh.*, XIX (1965-66), 58-68.

BARTOLI, M. G., *Das Dalmatische; altromanische Sprachreste von Veglia bis Ragusa und ihre Stellung in der apennino-balkanischen Romania.* Kais. Akad. Wiss., II: Romanische Dialektstudien, I–II (Wien: Hölder, 1906).

BEELER, M. S., *The Venetic Language.* UCPL, IV: 1 (Berkeley and Los Angeles: University of California Press, 1949).

BEHRENS, D., *Beiträge zur französischen Wortgeschichte und Grammatik. Studien und Kritiken* (Halle a.S.: Niemeyer, 1910).

BJERROME, G., *Le patois de Bagnes (Valais).* Romanica Gothoburgensia, VI (Stockholm: Almqvist & Wiksell, 1957).

BLOOMFIELD, L. (†1949), *Tagalog Texts with Grammatical Analysis.* Univ. of Illinois St. in Lang. & Lit., III: 2–4 (Urbana, 1917). Id., *Eastern Ojibwa; Grammatical Sketch, Texts, and Word List* [ed. C. F. Hockett] (Ann Arbor: University of Michigan Press, 1957; field work completed in 1938).

BOURCIEZ, É. (†1946), *Précis historique de phonétique française*, rev. 2d ed. (Paris: Klincksieck, 1900); 3d ed. (1907); 4th ed. (1914); 5th ed. (1921); 6th ed. (1926); 7th ed. (1930); 8th ed. (1937; "plusieurs tirages auxiliaires"); 9th ed., rev. by J. Bourciez (1958); the original edition (1889) was entitled: *Précis de phonétique française; ou, Exposé des lois qui régissent la transformation des mots latins en français.* Id., *Éléments de linguistique romane* (Paris: Klincksieck, 1910); rev. 2d ed. (1923); rev. 3d ed. (1930); 4th ed., rev. by J. Bourciez (1946); tr. T. V. and E. V. Vencel (ed. D. E. Mihalči): *Osnóvy románskogo jazykoznánija* (Moskvá: Izd. Inostránnoj literatúry, 1952).

BOYD-BOWMAN, P., *From Latin to Romance in Sound Charts* (n. p., 1954).

BRACHET, A. (†1898), *Du rôle des voyelles latines atones dans les langues romanes* (Leipzig: Brockhaus, 1866). Id., *Grammaire historique de la langue française* (Paris: Hetzel, 1867); 2d ed. (ca. 1868); 7th ed. (ca. 1873); 27th ed. (after 1886); 37th ed. (after 1900); tr. G. W. Kitchin [with M. Müller's assistance]: *A Historical Grammar of the French Tongue* (Oxford: Clarendon, 1869, 1872); 7th ed., corrected from the 20th French ed. (1888); rewritten and enlarged by P. Toynbee (1896). Id., *Dictionnaire des doublets ou doubles formes de la langue française* (Paris: Franck, 1868); Supplément (1871). Id., *Morceaux choisis des grands écrivains français du XVIe siècle, accompagnés d'une grammaire et d'un dictionnaire . . .*, 4th ed. (Paris: Hachette, 1876). Id., *Nouvelle grammaire française fondée sur l'histoire de la langue à l'usage des établissements secondaires*, 4th ed. (Paris, 1876). Id., *Cours de grammaire française, fondé sur l'histoire de la langue; théorie et exercices. Cours supérieur*, rev. ed. (Paris, 1899).

BRUNEAU, CH., *Petite histoire de la langue française.* 2 vols. [I: Des origines à la Révolution; II: De la Révolution à nos jours] (Paris: Colin, 1955–58).

BRUNOT, F. (†1938), *Précis de grammaire historique de la langue française, avec une introduction sur les origines et le développement de cette langue* (Paris: Masson, 1887 [written: 1884–86]); 2d ed. (1889); 3d ed. (1894); 4th ed. (1899). New ed., completely revised by C. Bruneau (Paris: Masson et Cie., 1933); rev. 2d ed. (1937); 3d ed., completely revised (1949), cf. E. Gamillscheg in *ZRPh.*, LXVIII (1952), 424–449. Id., *Histoire de la langue française des origines à 1900* [in Vols. XII–XIII: . . . à nos jours]. Vols. I–XII [several divided into sub-volumes] (Paris: Colin, 1905–53; continued). There exist a rev. 2d and a 3d ed. of Vol. I and a rev. 2d ed. of Vols. II–III and VII. Id., *La pensée et la langue: méthode, principes et plan d'une théorie nouvelle du langage appliquées au français* (Paris: Masson, 1922); 3d ed. [with the assistance of C. Bruneau] (1935).

BUCETA, E., "La tendencia a identificar el español con el latín; un episodio cuatrocentista" [1498, Garcilaso de la Vega], in *HMP*, I, 85–108.

BUCK, C. D., *Comparative Grammar of Greek and Latin* (Chicago: The University of Chicago Press, 1933; reprinted, 1955).

COELHO, F. A., "Sobre a língua portuguesa", in Frei Domingos Vieira, *Tesouro da língua portuguesa*, I (Porto, 1871), pp. ix–ccxlviii; reproduced in *Questões da língua portuguesa*, I. Id., "Formes divergentes de mots portugais", *Rom.*, II (1873), 281–294. Id., *A língua portuguesa; noções de glotologia geral e especial portuguesa* (Lisboa: Magalhães & Moniz, 1881); rev. 2d ed. (1887).

COHN, G., *Die Suffixwandlungen im Vulgärlatein und im vorliterarischen Französisch nach ihren Spuren im Neufranzösischen* (Halle a.S.: Niemeyer, 1891).

CORNU, J., "Die portugiesische Sprache", in G. Gröber, *Grundriß . . .*, I (1888), 715–803; rev. 2d ed. (1904–06), 916–1037.

CRESCINI, V., *Manualetto provenzale per uso degli alunni delle facoltà di lettere; introduzione grammaticale, crestomazia, glossario* (Verona-Padova: Drucker, 1892–94); 2d ed. ["accresciuta"] (1905); 3d ed. [*Manuale per l'avviamento agli studi provenzali*] (Milano: Hoepli, 1926).

CUERVO, R. J. (†1911), *Apuntaciones críticas sobre el lenguaje bogotano* (Bogotá: Guarín, 1867–72); rev. 2d ed. (Bogotá: Echeverría Hnos., 1876); rev. 3d ed. (Bogotá, 1881); rev. 4th ed. (Chartres, 1885); rev. 5th ed. [. . . *con frecuente referencia al de los países de Hispano-América*] (Paris: Roger & Chernoviz, 1907); 6th ed. (Paris, 1914); 7th ed. (Bogotá: "El Gráfico", 1939); 9th ed. (Bogotá: Instituto Caro y Cuervo, 1955). Id., *Notas a la Gramática de la lengua castellana destinada al uso de los americanos de Andrés Bello* (included in numerous editions of Bello's grammar, e.g., 11th ed. [Paris, 1908]). Id., "Disquisiciones sobre antigua ortografía y pronunciación castellanas", *RH*, II (1894), 1–69; rev. ed. in *Obras inéditas*, eds. F. Restrepo [and P. U. González de la Calle] (Bogotá, 1944), pp. 351–492. Id., "Castellano popular y castellano literario", in *Obras inéditas*, pp. 1–318.

DARMESTETER, A. (†1888), *Traité de la formation des mots composés dans la langue française comparée aux autres langues romanes et au latin.* BÉHÉ, XIX (Paris: Franck-Vieweg, 1875); 2d ed., Preface by G. Paris. Id., *De la création actuelle de mots nouveaux dans la langue française, et des lois qui la régissent* (Paris: Vieweg, 1877). Id. (with A. Hatzfeld), "Tableau de la langue française au XVIᵉ siècle", in *Le seizième siècle en France* (Paris: Delagrave, 1878); 2d ed. (1883); 3d ed. (1886); 7th ed. (n.d.); 12th ed. (1919); 13th ed. (1920); 25th ed. (1928), frequently bound with *Morceaux en prose et en vers choisis . . .* Id., "Traité de la formation de la langue française", rev. by L. Sudre and A. Thomas, in Darmesteter, Hatzfeld, and Thomas, *Dictionnaire général de la langue française* (Paris: Delagrave [1890–1893]), pp. 1–300; 6th ed. (1920); originally issued in

3 vols. Id., *Cours de grammaire historique de la langue française*, 4 vols., eds. E. Muret [only 1st ed.] and L. Sudre [later also P. Laurent] (Paris: Delagrave, 1891–97); 8th ed. (ca. 1913); 9th ed. (ca. 1914); 12th ed. (ca. 1931); 14th ed. (ca. 1934; sets frequently include volumes of different editions); tr. A. Hartog: *A Historical French Grammar* (London-New York: Macmillan, 1899); reprinted 1907, 1922, 1934.

DAUZAT, A., *La langue française; sa vie, son évolution* (Paris: Stock, 1926). Id., *Histoire de la langue française* (Paris: Payot, 1930). Id., *Tableau de la langue française: origines, évolution, structure actuelle* (Paris: Payot, 1939). Id., *Le génie de la langue française* (Paris: Payot, 1943). Id., *Les étapes de la langue française* (Paris: Presses Universitaires de France, 1944); 2d ed. (1948); 3d ed. (1953). Id., *Précis d'histoire de la langue et du vocabulaire français* (Paris: Larousse, 1949). Id., *Phonétique et grammaire historique de la langue française* (Paris: Larousse [1950]).

DEFERRARI, H. A. (†1950), *The Phonology of Italian, Spanish, and French* (Washington, D.C.: [Roy J. Deferrari, Publ.] 1954).

DELATTRE, P., "Stages of Old French phonetic changes observed in Modern Spanish", *PMLA*, LXI (1946), 7–41.

DENSUSIANU, O., *Histoire de la langue roumaine* [I: Les origines; II: Le seizième siècle] (Paris: Leroux, 1901, 19 [14–26–]38).

DEVOTO, G., *Profilo di storia linguistica italiana* (Firenze: La Nuova Italia, 1953).

DIEZ, F. (†1876), *Grammatik der romanischen Sprachen*, 3 vols. (Bonn: Weber, 1836–44) [orig. Preface reprinted in *Diez-Reliquien* ..., ed. E. Stengel (Marburg: Elwert, 1894), pp. 15–17]; 2d ed. ["neu verfaßt"] (Bonn, 1856–60), cf. *Introduction à la Grammaire des langues romanes*, tr. G. Paris (Paris: Franck, 1863), and *Introduction to the Grammar of the Romance Languages: Elements and Jurisdiction of the Romance Languages*, tr. C. B. Cayley (London-Edinburgh: Williams & Norgate, 1863); 3d ed. ["neu bearbeitet und vermehrt"] (Bonn, 1870–72); tr. A. Brachet, A. Morel-Fatio, and G. Paris (Paris: Franck [Vieweg], 1874–76); 4th ed. (Bonn, 1876–77); 5th ed. [eds. F. Apfelstedt and E. Seelmann] (Bonn: Weber [Flittner], 1882), consecutively paged; "Handschriftliche Kollektaneen zur *Romanischen Grammatik* [2d and 3d eds.] aus den letzten 6oer und den ersten 7oer Jahren", in *Diez-Reliquien*, pp. 4–14. Id., *Grammatik* ... *Anhang: Romanische Wortschöpfung* (Bonn: Weber, 1875 [Preface dated 1874]), as against *Kritischer Anhang zum Etymologischen Wörterbuch der romanischen Sprachen* (Bonn: Marcus, 1859), a polemically slanted pamphlet. One example of early appreciation: H. Breymann, *Friedrich Diez, seine Werke und deren Bedeutung für die Wissenschaft* (München: Ackermann, 1878).

EGGER, É., *Notions élémentaires de grammaire comparée pour servir à l'étude des trois langues classiques* ... (Paris: Durand, 1852); 8th ed. (1880).

ELCOCK, W. D., *The Romance Languages* (London: Faber & Faber, New York: Macmillan [1960]).

ENTWISTLE, W. J., *The Spanish Language, Together with Portuguese, Catalan, and Basque* (London: Faber & Faber [1936]; New York: Macmillan, 1938). Id., *Aspects of Language* (London: Faber & Faber, 1953).

ERNOUT, A., *Morphologie historique du latin* (Paris: Klincksieck, 1914); rev. 2d ed. (1927); rev. 3d ed. (1953); tr. H. Meltzner [*Historische Formenlehre des Lateinischen*], IB, II: 5 (Heidelberg: Winter, 1913); 2d and 3d ed. (1920).

ETTMAYER, K. VON, *Vademekum für Studierende der romanischen Philologie* (Heidelberg: Winter, 1919).

EWERT, A., *The French Language* (London: Faber & Faber, 1933); 2d ed. (1943); reprinted 1947, 1949.

FARAL, E., *Petite grammaire de l'ancien français: XII<sup>e</sup>–XIII<sup>e</sup> siècles* (Paris: Hachette [1941]).

FERNÁNDEZ LLERA, V., *Gramática y vocabulario del Fuero Juzgo* [1900] (Madrid: R. Academia Española, 1929).

FÖRSTER, P., *Spanische Sprachlehre* (Berlin: Weidmannsche Buchhandlung, 1880).

FORD, J. D. M., "The Old Spanish sibilants" [Harvard dissertation, 1897], [*Harvard*] *Studies and Notes in Philology and Literature*, VII (1900), 1–182. Id., *Old Spanish Readings Selected on the Basis of Critically Edited Texts; Edited, with Introduction, Notes, and Vocabulary, by...* (Boston, New York, etc.: Ginn [1911]; frequently reprinted; orig. ed. [1906] lacked these three sections).

FOUCHÉ, P., *Le verbe français; étude morphologique*. PFLS, LVI (Paris: Les Belles Lettres, 1931). Id., *Phonétique historique du français*, 3 vols. (Paris: Klincksieck, 1952–61).

FOULET, L., *Petite syntaxe de l'ancien français*. CFMA, II:2 (Paris: Champion, 1919); rev. 2d ed. (1923); rev. 3d ed. (1930; Preface dated 1928).

FUCHS, A. (†1847), *Über die sogenannten unregelmäßigen Zeitwörter in den romanischen Sprachen; nebst Andeutungen über die wichtigsten romanischen Mundarten* (Berlin: Asher, 1840). Id., *Die romanischen Sprachen in ihrem Verhältnisse zum Lateinischen; nebst einer Karte des romanischen Sprachgebiets in Europa*, ed. [L. G.] Blanc (Halle: Schmidt, 1849).

GAMILLSCHEG, E., "Grundzüge der galloromanischen Wortbildung", in Gamillscheg and Spitzer, *Beiträge zur romanischen Wortbildungslehre*. BAR, II:2 (Genève: Olschki, 1921), pp. 1–80. Id., *Französische Bedeutungslehre* (Tübingen: Niemeyer, 1951; Preface dated 1949). Id., *Historische französische Syntax* (Tübingen: Niemeyer, 1957–58).

GARCÍA DE DIEGO, V., *Elementos de gramática histórica castellana* (Burgos: "El monte Carmelo", 1914). Id., *Manual de dialectología española* (Madrid: Instituto de Cultura Hispánica, 1946). Id., *Gramática histórica española* (Madrid: Gredos, 1951).

GARTNER, T., *Rätoromanische Grammatik* (Heilbronn: Henninger, 1883). Id., "Die rätoromanischen Mundarten", in G. Gröber, *Grundriß* ... I (1888), 461–488; 2d ed. (1904–06), 608–636. Id., *Darstellung der rumänischen Sprache*. SKL, V (Halle: Niemeyer, 1910).

GASSNER, A., *Das altspanische Verbum* (Halle: Niemeyer, 1897).

GORRA, E., *Lingue neolatine*. "Manuali Hoepli" (Milano: Hoepli, 1894). Id., *Morfologia italiana* (Milano: Hoepli, 1895). Id., *Lingua e letteratura spagnuola delle origini* (Milano: Hoepli, 1898).

GOSSEN, C.-Th., *Petite grammaire de l'ancien picard; phonétique — morphologie — syntaxe; anthologie et glossaire* (Paris: Klincksieck, 1951). Cf. C. Régnier's rev. in *RPh.*, XIV: 3 (1961), 255–272.

GOUGENHEIM, G., *Grammaire de la langue française du seizième siècle.* "Les langues du monde" (Lyon-Paris: IAC [1951]).

GRANDGENT, C. H., *An Outline of the Phonology and Morphology of Old Provençal* (Boston: Heath, 1905). Id., *From Latin to Italian; an Historical Outline of the Phonology and Morphology of the Italian Language* (Cambridge, Mass.: Harvard University Press, 1927).

GRIERA, A., "Afro-romànic o ibero-romànic?", *BDC*, X (1922), 35–43; "Castellà-català-provençal" [Rev. of Meyer-Lübke, *Das Katalanische*], *ZRPh.*, XLV (1925), 198–251, cf. M.-L.'s rejoinder, ibid., XLVI, 116–128.

GRÖBER, G., "Vulgärlateinische Substrate romanischer Wörter", *ALLG*, I (1884), 204–254 (A–B), 539–557 (C); II (1885), 100–107 (D), 276–288 (E–Fi), 424–443 (Fl-G); III (1886), 138–143 (H–Il), 264–275 (Il–La), 507–531 (La–Mi); IV (1887), 116–136 (Mi–N), 422–454 (O–P); V (1888), 125–132 (Q–Ra), 234–242 (Re–Ru), 453–486 (S); VI (1889), 117–149 (T–Z), 377–397 (Supplement). Id., ed. *Grundriß der romanischen Philologie*, I (Straßburg: Trübner, 1888 [project launched: 1883; Preface dated: 1887]); rev. 2d ed. (1904–06). Id., "Methodik und Aufgaben der sprachwissenschaftlichen Forschung", in *Grundriß . . .*, I (1888), 209–250. To the 2d ed. (1904) G. contributed "Einführung in die romanische Philologie" [A. Geschichte . . . ; B. Aufgabe und Gliederung], pp. 1–202, and "Anleitung zur philologischen Forschung" [A. Quellen . . .; B. Behandlung der Quellen], pp. 203–368.

GUARNERIO, P. E., *Fonologia romanza.* "Manuali Hoepli" (Milano: Hoepli, 1918).

HAAS, J., *Neufranzösische Syntax.* SKL, IV (Halle: Niemeyer, 1909). Id., *Französische Syntax* (Halle: Niemeyer, 1916). Id., *Abriß der französischen Syntax.* SKL, VIII (Halle: Niemeyer, 1922).

HANSSEN, F., *Spanische Grammatik auf historischer Grundlage.* SKL, VI (Halle: Niemeyer, 1910). Id., *Gramática histórica de la lengua castellana* (Halle: Niemeyer, 1913), cf. A. Castro in *RFE*, I (1914), 97–103, 181–183, also O. J. Tallgren in *NM*, XVIII (1917), 138–158, and F. Krüger in *RFE*, VIII (1921), 311–318; reprinted, with new Preface by L. Alfonso (Buenos Aires: El Ateneo, 1945).

HASSELROT, B., *Études sur la formation diminutive dans les langues romanes.* UUÅ, 1957, No. XI. Cf. Jerry R. Craddock's "Critique of recent studies in Romance diminutives", *RPh.*, XIX: 2 (1965), 286–325.

HATZFELD, H., *Leitfaden der vergleichenden Bedeutungslehre. Versuch einer Zusammenstellung charakteristischen semasiologischen Beispielmaterials aus den bekanntesten Sprachen* (München: Hueber, 1924).

HAUDRICOURT, A. G., and A. G. JUILLAND, *Essai pour une histoire structurale du phonétisme français* (Paris: Klincksieck, 1949).

HAUSCHILD, E. J., *Etymologisches Wörterbuch der französischen Sprache nach Friedrich Diez sowie Frisch . . ., mit durchgängiger Verweisung auf Diez's "Grammatik der romanischen Sprachen"* (Leipzig: Hinrich, 1843).

HEATWOLE, O. W., *Comparative Practical Grammar of French, Spanish, and Italian*; Foreword by M. A. Pei (New York: Vanni [1949]).

HOFMANN, J. B., "Syntax und Stilistik", in F. Stolz and J. H. Schmalz, *Lateinische Grammatik; Laut- und Formenlehre; Syntax und Stilistik*, rev. 5th ed. (München: Beck, 1938).

HOLMES, U. T., JR., and A. H. SCHUTZ, *A History of the French Language* (New York: Farrar & Rinehart [1938]; issued in three mimeographed editions since 1933).

HORNING, A., *Zur Geschichte des lateinischen C vor E und I im Romanischen* (Halle: Niemeyer, 1883). Id., "Grammaire de l'ancien français", included (3–61) in A. Horning and K. Bartsch, *La langue et la littérature françaises depuis le VIII<sup>e</sup> jusqu'au XV<sup>e</sup> siècle* (Paris: Maisonneuve, 1887). Id., "Die Suffixe -*iccus*, -*occus*, -*uccus* im Französischen", *ZRPh.*, XIX (1895), 170–188. Id., "Die Suffixe -*accus*, -*iccus*, -*occus*, -*ucus* (-*uccus*) im Romanischen", ibid., XX (1896), 335–353.

HUBER, J., *Altportugiesisches Elementarbuch*. SRE, I: 8 (Heidelberg: Winter, 1933).

JESPERSEN, O. (†1943), *Growth and Structure of the English Language* (Leipzig: Teubner, etc., 1905); rev. 2d ed. (1912); rev. 3d ed. (1919); 4th ed. (Oxford: Blackwell, and New York: Appleton, 1923); 5th ed. (Teubner and Blackwell, 1926); 6th ed. (1930); 9th ed. (Blackwell, 1948; also New York: Doubleday ["Anchor Book" A46], 1955).

JORDAN, L., *Altfranzösisches Elementarbuch; Einführung in das historische Studium der französischen Sprache und ihrer Mundarten* (Bielefeld-Leipzig: Velhagen & Klasing, 1923).

JORET, C., *Du C [latin] dans les langues romanes*. BÉHÉ, XVI (Paris: Franck, 1874; Preface dated 1873).

JUD, J., "Probleme der altromanischen Wortgeographie" [1913], *ZRPh.*, XXXVIII (1914–17), 1–75 and five folding maps.

KAHANE, H. and R., "The augmentative feminine in the Romance languages", *RPh.*, II: 2–3 (1948–49), 135–175.

KELLER, A., ed., *Altspanisches Lesebuch mit Grammatik und Glossar* (Leipzig: Brockhaus, 1890). Id., *Historische Formenlehre der spanischen Sprache* (Murrhardt, Wtb.: Lang, 1894).

KENISTON, H., *The System of Castilian Prose*, [II:] *The Sixteenth Century* (Chicago: The University of Chicago Press, 1937).

KRAHE, H., *Das Venetische; seine Stellung im Kreise der verwandten Sprachen* (Heidelberg, 1950). Id., *Indogermanische Sprachwissenschaft*, rev. 3d ed., I: *Einleitung und Lautlehre*. Göschen Sammlung, No. 59 (Berlin: de Gruyter, 1958).

KRÜGER, F., *Studien zur Lautgeschichte westspanischer Mundarten auf Grund von Untersuchungen an Ort und Stelle; mit Notizen zur Verbalflexion* (Hamburg, 1914; orig. in *Jb. Hamb. Wiss. Anst.*, XXXI [1913]). Id., *Einführung in das Neuspanische* (Leipzig-Berlin: Teubner, 1924).

KUEN, H., "Die sprachlichen Verhältnisse auf der Pyrenäenhalbinsel", *ZRPh.*, LXVI (1950), 95–125 ["Vortrag, überarbeitet und mit Anmerkungen versehen"].

KUHN, A., "Der hocharagonesische Dialekt" [Habilitationsschrift, Leipzig],

M

*RLiR*, XI (1935), 1–312. Id., *Romanische Philologie*, I: *Die romanischen Sprachen*. Wissenschaftliche Forschungsberichte, Geisteswiss. Reihe, VIII (Bern: Francke, 1951); cf. Y. Malkiel in *Lg.*, XXVIII (1952), 509–524.

KURYŁOWICZ, J., *L'accentuation des langues indo-européennes*, Prace Komisji Językowej, XXXVII (Kraków: Polska Akademia Umiejętności, 1952); 2d ed., Prace Językoznawcze, XVII (Wrocław-Kraków: Polska Akademia Nauk, 1958). Id., *L'apophonie en indo-européen*. Prace Językoznawcze, IX (Wrocław: Polska Ak. Nauk, 1956).

LAPESA, R., *Historia de la lengua española* (Madrid: Escelicer [1942]); rev. 2d ed. [1951], cf. Y. Malkiel in *RPh.*, VI: 1 (1952), 52–63; rev. 3d ed. [1955]; rev. 4th ed. [1959]; rev. 5th ed. (1962). Id., *Asturiano y provenzal en el Fuero de Avilés*, Acta Salmanticensia: Filosofía y Letras, II: 4 (1948).

LAUSBERG, H., *Romanische Sprachwissenschaft*, 2 vols. [I: Einleitung und Vokalismus; II: Konsonantismus; III: Formenlehre]. Sammlung Göschen, Nos. 128–128a, 250 (Berlin: de Gruyter, 1956–58).

LEITE DE VASCONCELOS, J. († 1941), *Estudos de filologia mirandesa*, 2 vols. (Lisboa: Imprensa Nacional, 1900–01). Id., *Lições de filologia portuguesa* (Lisboa, 1911); rev. 2d ed. (Lisboa: Biblioteca Nacional, 1926); 3d ed. (ed. S. da Silva Neto), Colecção Brasileira de Filologia Portuguesa (Rio de Janeiro: Livros de Portugal, 1959).

LEJEUNE, M., [Miscellaneous articles, some of them collected into a single volume: *Mémoires de philologie mycénienne*, 1 (Paris: C.N.R.S., 1958).]

LERCH, E., *Historische französische Syntax*, 3 vols. (Leipzig: Reisland, 1925–34). Id., *Hauptprobleme der französischen Sprache*, 2 vols. (Braunschweig, etc.: Westermann, 1930).

LEUMANN, M., "Laut- und Formenlehre", in F. Stolz and J. H. Schmalz, *Lateinische Grammatik*, rev. 5th ed. (München: Beck, 1928).

LEWICKA, H., *La langue et le style du théâtre comique français des XIV^e et XV^e siècles*, I: *La dérivation* (Warszawa: Państwowe Wydawnictwo Naukowe, and Paris: Klincksieck [1960]). Cf. M. Hoffmann [Langdon], *RPh.*, XVIII: 1 (1964), 54–63, and H. L.'s elaboration and self-criticism in *KwN*, X (1963), 131–142 ("Réflexions théoriques sur la composition des mots en ancien et moyen français").

LÖFSTEDT, E., *Philologischer Kommentar zur "Peregrinatio Aetheriae"; Untersuchungen zur Geschichte der lateinischen Sprache* (Uppsala: Almqvist & Wiksell, 1911).

LUQUIENS, F. B., *An Introduction to Old French Phonology and Morphology* (New Haven, Conn.: Yale University Press, 1909); rev. 2d ed. (1919); 3d ed. (1926); 4th ed. (Yale and Oxford University Press, 1934).

MARTINET, A., "The unvoicing of Old Spanish sibilants", *RPh.*, V: 2–3 (1951–52), 133–156. Id., "Celtic lenition and Western Romance consonants", *Lg.*, XXVIII (1952), 192–217. [A condensed translation of both articles is included in *Économie des changements phonétiques; traité de phonologie diachronique*. Bibl. Rom., I: 10 (Berne: Francke, 1955)].

MAYÁNS Y SISCAR, G. († 1781), *Orígenes de la lengua española, compuestos por varios autores, recogidos por . . .*, 2 vols. (Madrid: de Zúñiga, 1737); eds.

J. E. Hartzenbusch and E. de Mier, "La amistad librera" ([Madrid] Suárez, 1873).

MEILLET, A. (†1936), *Esquisse d'une grammaire comparée de l'arménien classique* (Vienne: PP. Mékhitharistes, 1903); rev. 2d ed. (1936); cf. *Altarmenisches Elementarbuch* (Heidelberg: Winter, 1913). Id., *Aperçu d'une histoire de la langue grecque* (Paris: Hachette, 1913); rev. 2d ed. (1920); rev. 3d ed. (1930); 5th ed. [ca. 1938]. Id., *Esquisse d'une histoire de la langue latine* (Paris: Hachette, 1928); rev. 2d ed. (1931); rev. 3d ed. (1933); 6th ed. [1952]. Id., with J. Vendryes, *Traité de grammaire comparée des langues classiques* (Paris: Champion, 1924); 2d printing (1927); 2d ed., rev. by Vendryes (1948).

MENÉNDEZ PIDAL, R., *Manual (elemental) de gramática histórica española* (Madrid: Suárez, 1904); rev. 2d ed. (1905); 3d ed. ["con muy escasas reformas"] (1914); rev. 4th ed. (1918); rev. 5th ed. (1925; new printing, 1929); rev. 6th ed. (Madrid: Espasa-Calpe, 1941); all subsequent editions (10th, 1958) are merely new printings. Id., "Sufijos átonos en español" [1903], in *Bausteine zur romanischen Philologie; Festgabe für Adolfo Mussafia* (Halle: Niemeyer, 1905), pp. 386–400. Id., ed. "*Cantar de Mio Cid*": texto, gramática [137–420] y vocabulario, 3 vols., with consecutive page numbering (Madrid: Bailly-Bailliere [printer], 1908–11); rev. 2d ed., included in *Obras completas*, III–V (Madrid: Espasa-Calpe, 1944–46; cf. Supplement, pp. 1165–1209). Id., *Orígenes del español; estado lingüístico de la Península Ibérica hasta el siglo XI*, Suppl. I to *RFE* (Madrid: Hernando, 1926); rev. 2d ed. (1929); 3d ed., completely recast (Madrid: Espasa-Calpe, 1950; *Obras completas*, VIII); 4th ed. (reprint).

MEYER, G., "Die lateinischen Elemente im Albanesischen", in G. Gröber, *Grundriß* . . ., I (1888), 804–821; 2d ed. (1906), rev. by W. Meyer-Lübke, pp. 1038–1057.

MEYER-LÜBKE, W. (†1936), *Italienische Grammatik* (Leipzig: Reisland, 1890); tr. M. Bartoli and G. Braun [*Grammatica storico-comparata della lingua italiana e dei dialetti toscani; riduzione ad uso degli studenti di lettere* . . . (Torino: Loescher, 1901)]; new ed. ["con aggiunte dell'autore e di E. G. Parodi"], ed. M. Bartoli (Torino: Chiantore, 1931). Id., *Grammatik der romanischen Sprachen*, 4 vols. [I: Lautlehre, II: Formen-lehre, III: Syntax, IV: Register] (Leipzig: Fues [Reisland], 1890–1902); tr. E. Rabiet (I), A. and G. Doutrepont (II–III), id., with A. Counson (IV) [*Grammaire des langues romanes*] (Paris: Welter, 1890–1906); reprint (New York, etc.: Stechert, 1923). Id., *Einführung in das Studium der romanischen Sprachwissenschaft*. SRE, I: 1 (Heidelberg: Winter, 1901); rev. 2d ed. (1909) and tr. A. Castro [*Introducción al estudio de la lingüística romance*] (Madrid: Centro de Estudios Históricos, 1914), also [unauthorized] A. da Guerra Júdice [*Introdução ao estudo da glotologia românica*] (Lisboa: Teixeira, 1916); rev. 3d ed. (1920) and expanded tr. A. Castro (1926). Id., *Historische Grammatik der französischen Sprache*. SRE, 1: 2; I: *Laut- und Flexionslehre* (Heidelberg: Winter, 1908); rev. 2d and 3d ed. (1913); rev. 4th and 5th ed. (1934), cf. E. Gamillscheg in *ZFSL*, LX (1935), 484–490; II: *Wortbildungslehre* (1921), cf. L. Spitzer in *AR*, VII (1923), 194–210. Id., "Die romanischen Sprachen" [1904], in H. Zimmer, H. Morf, et al., *Die romanischen Literaturen und Sprachen, mit Einschluß des Keltischen* (Berlin-Leipzig: Teubner, 1909; a volume forming part of *Die Kultur der Gegenwart*..., ed. P. Hinneberg), pp. 447–470. Id., *Das Katalanische; seine Stellung zum Spanischen und Provenzalischen sprachwissenschaftlich und historisch dargestellt.* SRE, V: 7 (Heidelberg: Winter, 1925); for reactions cf. A. Alonso and A. Griera, above. Id., "Die Schicksale des lateinischen *L* im Romanischen", *SAW*, LXXXVI: 2 (Leipzig: Hirzel, 1934). For instances of editorial collaboration see under G. Meyer, above, and F. d'Ovidio, below. At proof, I record the recent publication of the 2d ed. of M.-L.'s *Wortbildungslehre*, revised and expanded by J. M. Piel.

MICHAËLIS (DE VASCONCELOS), C., *Studien zur romanischen Wortschöpfung* (Leipzig: Brockhaus, 1876). Ead., *Lições de filologia portuguesa* (Lisboa: Ed. da "Revista de Portugal" [1946]).

MIGLIORINI, B., *Pronunzia fiorentina o pronunzia romana?* Bibl. di *LN*, V (Firenze: Sansoni, 1945). Id., *Linguistica* (Firenze: Le Monnier, 1946). Id., *Storia della lingua italiana*, 1st and 2d ed. (Firenze: Sansoni [1960]); 3d ed. (1961). There exist two abridged editions, one in English (tr. and ed. T. Gwynfor Griffith [*The Italian Language*], Glasgow and New York, 1966), the other in Italian (in collaboration with I. Baldelli (*Breve storia* ... [Firenze: Sansoni, 1964]) ); also a paper-backed unabridged edition (1966).

MOLL, F. DE B., *Gramática histórica catalana.* BRH, III: 5 (Madrid: Gredos, 1952).

MONTEVERDI, A., *Manuale di avviamento agli studi romanzi: Le lingue romanze* (Milano: Francesco [1952]); outgrowth of the "dispense" *Introduzione allo studio della filologia romanza* (Roma, 1943).

MOREL-FATIO, A., "Das Catalanische", tr. A. Horning, in Gröber, *Grundriß* ..., I (1888), 669–688; 2d ed. (1904–06), rev. by J. Saroïhandy, tr. G. Gröber and A. Horning, pp. 841–877.

MÚGICA, P. DE [with numerous footnotes by M. de Unamuno], *Gramática del castellano antiguo*, I: *Fonética* (Leipzig: Reisland, or Berlin: Heinrich & Kemke, 1891). Id., *Dialectos castellanos [sic]: montañés, vizcaíno, aragonés*; I: *Fonética* (Berlin: Heinrich & Kemke, 1892).

MUNTHE, Å. W., *Anteckningar om folkmålet i en trakt af Vestra Asturien* (Diss. Uppsala, 1887).

MUSSAFIA, A. (†1905), *Italienische Sprachlehre in Regeln und Beispielen, für den ersten Unterricht bearbeitet*, 5th ed. (Wien, later also Leipzig: Braumüller, 1872); 27th ed., rev. by E. Maddalena (1904); 29th ed. (1912).

NANDRIŞ, G., "The development and structure of Rumanian", *The Slavonic and East European Review*, XXX (1951), 7–39.

NAVARRO, T., *Métrica española; reseña histórica y descriptiva.* Syracuse University: Centro de Estudios Hispánicos (Syracuse University Press), 1956; cf. P. Le Gentil in *RPh.*, XII: 4 (1959), 1–32.

NEBRIXA, E. A. DE (†1522), *Gramática de la lengua castellana* (Salamanca, 1492); ed. ("reproduction phototypique") E. Walberg (Halle: Niemeyer, 1909); ed. I. González-Llubera (London, etc.: H. Milford

[Oxford University Press], 1926); eds. L. Galindo Romeo and L. Ortiz Muñoz (Madrid: Ed. de la Junta del Centenario, 1946).

NIEDERMANN, M., *Précis de phonétique historique du latin*. Foreword by A. Meillet (Paris: Klincksieck, 1906); rev. 2d ed. (1931; reprinted in 1945); rev. 3d ed. (1953); tr. E. Hermann [*Historische Lautlehre des Lateinischen*], with Foreword by J. Wackernagel (Heidelberg: Winter, 1907); 2d ed. (1911), reprinted in 1931; rev. 3d ed. (1953); tr. H. A. Strong and H. Stewart [*Outlines of Latin Phonetics*] (London: Routledge, 1910); tr. A. Gručko [*Istoričeskaja fonètika latinskogo jazyká*] (Moskva, 1910).

NUNES, J. J. (†1932), *Crestomatia arcaica; excerptos da literatura portuguesa . . . acompanhados de introdução gramatical, notas e glossário* (Lisboa: Ferreira e Oliveira, 1906); 2d ed., completely revised (Lisboa: Portugal-Brasil Ltda. [1921]). Id., *Compêndio de gramática histórica portuguesa; fonética — morfologia* (Lisboa: Teixeira, 1919); rev. 2d ed. (1930); 3d ed. (1945); this book goes back to the author's "Fonética histórica portuguesa" [with editorial notes by J. Leite de Vasconcelos], *RL*, III (1895), 251–307.

NYROP, K., *Grammaire historique de la langue française*, 6 vols. (Copenhague, etc.: Nordisk Forlag, later in partnership with Gyldendalske Boghandel, 1899–1930). Vols. III–VI appeared in 1908 (*Formation des mots*), 1913 (*Sémantique*), 1925 and 1930 (*Syntaxe*), respectively; of Vol. I (*Histoire générale . . ., Phonétique*) there appeared a 2d (1904) and a 3d (1914) ed.; of Vols. II (*Morphologie*, 1903) and III, a rev. 2d ed. (1924 and 1936). Vol. I was reprinted in 1935; Vol. II, in 1965.

OLIVER ASÍN, J., (*Iniciación al estudio de la*) *historia de la lengua española* (Pamplona, 1938 [Preface dated 1937]); 2d ed. (Zaragoza, 1938); rev. 3d ed. ("Heraldo de Aragón", 1939); 4th ed. (Madrid: Diana, 1940); 5th ed. and 6th ed. (1941).

OVIDIO, F. D' [in charge of linguistics], and E. MONACI [in charge of literature], *Manualetti d'introduzione agli studi neolatini*, 2 vols.: I. *Spagnuolo* (Napoli, 1879); II. *Portoghese* (*e gallego*) (Imola, 1881). D'Ovidio (tr. A. Horning) and W. Meyer[-Lübke], "Die italienische Sprache", in G. Gröber, *Grundriß . . .*, I (1888), 489–560 (D'Ovidio's share: Section I ["bis einschließlich der Tonvokale"]; 2d ed., rev. by Meyer-Lübke (1904–06), 637–711; tr. E. Polcari [*Grammatica storica della lingua e dei dialetti italiani*], "Manuali Hoepli" (Milano: Hoepli, 1906); 2d ed. (1919).

PATON, D. A., *Manuel d'ancien français* (*début du XII<sup>e</sup> siècle*). Nelson's "Modern Studies", II (London, etc.: Nelson, 1933).

PAUL, H., *Prinzipien der Sprachgeschichte* (Halle: Niemeyer, 1880); 2d ed. (1886); 3d ed. (1898); 4th ed. (1909); 5th ed. (1920); tr. H. A. Strong (rev. C. H. Herford) [*Principles of the History of Language*], 2d ed. (London: Sonnenschein, Lowrey & Co., 1888; New York: Macmillan, 1889); rev. ed. (1890–91); adapt. H. A. Strong, W. S. Logemann, and B. I. Wheeler [*Introduction to the Study of the History of Language*] (London-New York: Longmans, Green & Co., 1891).

PEI, M. A., *The Italian Language* (New York: Columbia University Press, 1941); rev. by R. A. Hall, Jr. in *Lg.*, XVII (1941), 263–269; author's

*Reply* privately published, distributed in 1946 (copy in New York Public Library); cf. also B. Terracini in *RFH*, V (1943), 276–287.

PELLEGRINI, G. B., *Grammatica storica spagnuola*. Collana di grammatiche storiche neolatine, ed. C. Battisti, II (Bari: "Leonardo da Vinci", 1950).

PICHON, É., *L'enrichissement lexical dans le français d'aujourd'hui; les principes de la suffixation en français*. Bibliothèque du "Français Moderne" (Paris: d'Artrey, 1942).

POPE, M. K., *From Latin to Modern French with Especial Consideration of Anglo-Norman; Phonology and Morphology* (Manchester: University Press, 1934); 2d ed., rev. by T. B. W. Reid and R. C. Johnston (1952).

POTTIER, B., *Introduction à l'étude de la philologie hispanique*, 2 vols. [I: Généralités et phonétique espagnole; II: Morphosyntaxe espagnole — étude structurale] ([Bordeaux] 1957–58); 2d ed. (Paris, 1960).

PUŞCARIU, S., and E. HERZOG, *Lehrbuch der rumänischen Sprache*, I: *Anfangsgründe* (Czernowitz, 1919); rev. 2d ed. (1920).

QUADRI, B., *Aufgaben und Methoden der onomasiologischen Forschung; eine entwicklungsgeschichtliche Darstellung*. RH, XXXVI (Bern: Francke, 1952).

REGULA, M., *Historische Grammatik des Französischen*, 3 vols. [I: Lautlehre; II: Formenlehre; III: Syntax] (Heidelberg: Winter, 1955[-56], 1966).

REINHARDSTOETTNER, C. VON, *Grammatik der portugiesischen Sprache auf Grundlage des Lateinischen und der romanischen Sprachvergleichung bearbeitet* (Straßburg-London: Trübner, 1878).

REMACLE, L., *Le problème de l'ancien wallon*. BFUL, CIX (Liège,1948).

RHEINFELDER, H., *Altfranzösische Grammatik*, I: *Lautlehre* (München: Hueber, 1937); rev. 2d ed. (1953–55).

RICHTER, E., "Der innere Zusammenhang in der Entwicklung der romanischen Sprachen" [completed in March, 1910], in *Prinzipienfragen der romanischen Sprachwissenschaft (Festschrift Meyer-Lübke)*, II, ZRPh., Suppl. XXVII (Halle a.S.: Niemeyer, 1911), pp. 57–143. Ead., *Beiträge zur Geschichte der Romanismen*, I: *Chronologische Phonetik des Französischen bis zum Ende des 8. Jahrhunderts*, ZRPh., Suppl. LXXXII (Halle, 1934); cf. E. Gamillscheg in *ZFSL*, LXI (1937), 89–106 (included in the reviewer's *Ausgewählte Aufsätze . . .*, ZFSL, Suppl. XV [Jena-Leipzig: Gronau, 1937], pp. 25–42).

ROHLFS, G., *Le gascon; études de philologie pyrénéenne*, ZRPh., Suppl. LXXXV (Halle: Niemeyer, 1935). Id., *Historische Grammatik der italienischen Sprache und ihrer Mundarten*, 3 vols. [I: Lautlehre; II: Formenlehre und Syntax, erster Teil; III: Syntax [zweiter Teil] und Wortbildung; Register]. Bibl. Rom., I: 5–7 (Bern: Francke, 1949 [-54]; entire text written 1943–46). Id., "Das spanische Suffix *-arrón* und Verwandtes", *ASNS*, CLXXXII (1943), 118–122. Cf. under C. Voretzsch.

RONJAT, J. (†1925), *Essai de syntaxe des parlers provençaux modernes* (Mâcon, 1913; thèse de Paris). Id., *Grammaire [h]istorique des parlers provençaux modernes*, 4 vols. [I: Introduction, phonétique: voyelles et diphtongues; II: Phonétique: consonnes et phénomènes généraux; III: Morphologie et formation des mots; notes de syntaxe; IV: Appendice: Les dialectes. Index], ed. W. von Wartburg (Montpellier: Société des langues romanes, 1930–41).

SÁNCHEZ SEVILLA, P. (†), "El habla de Cespedosa de Tormes (en el límite de Salamanca y Ávila)", *RFE*, XV (1928), 131–172, 244–282.

SANCHIS GUARNER, M., "Noticia del habla de Aguaviva de Aragón", *RFE*, XXXIII (1949), 15–65.

SANDFELD(-JENSEN), K., *Sprogvidenskaben; en kortfattet fremstilling af dens metoder og resultater* (København & Kristiania: Gyldendal, 1913–14); 2d ed. (1923); tr. and abridgment [*Die Sprachwissenschaft*], "Aus Natur und Geisteswelt", CDLXXII (Leipzig-Berlin: Teubner, 1915); new printing (1923). Id., *Balkanfilologien; en oversigt over dens resultater og problemer* (København: Lunos, 1926); tr. [*Linguistique balkanique; problèmes et résultats*], Soc. de Ling. de Paris, Collection linguistique, XXXI (Paris: Champion, 1930). Cf. L. Hjelmslev in *AL*, IV (1944), 136–139.

SARMIENTO, Pe M., "Elementos etimológicos según el método de Euclides" [1758–66], in "Escritos filológicos", ed. J. P., *BRAE*, XV (1928), 670–684; XVI (1929), 244–255, 366–382; XVII (1930), 275–290, 571–592, 721–742; XVIII (1931), 118–135.

SAROÏHANDY, J., "Remarques sur la phonétique du ç et du z en ancien espagnol", *BH*, IV (1902), 198–214.

SAVJ-LOPEZ, P. (†1919), *Le origini neolatine*, ed. [and final chapter] P. E. Guarnerio. "Manuali Hoepli" (Milano: Hoepli, 1920); tr. P. Sánchez Sarto [*Orígenes neolatinos*] (Barcelona, etc.: Labor, 1935).

SCHUCHARDT, H., *Der Vokalismus des Vulgärlateins*, 3 vols. (I: Einleitung, Qualitative Vokalveränderung [A]; II: Qualitative [B], Quantitative Vokalveränderung; III: Nachträge und Register) (Leipzig: Teubner, 1866–68).

SCHUCHHARDT, H., *Beiträge zur Geschichte der italienischen Scheidewörter*. BBRPh., VI: 3 (Jena-Leipzig: Gronau [Agricola], 1936).

SCHULTZ-GORA, O., *Altprovenzalisches Elementarbuch*. SRE, I: 3 (Heidelberg: Winter, 1906); rev. 2d ed. (1911); rev. 3d ed. (1915); rev. 4th ed. (1924).

SCHWAN, E. (†1893), *Grammatik des Altfranzösischen; Laut- und Formenlehre* (Leipzig: Reisland, 1888); rev. 2d ed. (1893). All subsequent editions were revised by D. Behrens (†1929): 3d (1898), 4th (1899), 5th (1901), 6th (1903), 7th (1907), 8th (1909), 9th (1911), 10th (1913–14), 11th (1919), 12th ed. (1925). Tr. O. Bloch, with Preface by F. Brunot [*Grammaire de l'ancien français*] (Leipzig: Reisland, 1900; after German 4th); 2d ed., 2 vols. in 1 (1913, after German 9th); 3d ed. (1923, after German 11th); 4th ed. (1932, after German 12th). The "Materialien zur Einführung in das Studium der altfranzösischen Mundarten" appeared first in the 8th ed., became a section separately paged — and sometimes even bound — in 1913 at the latest (3d ed., 1921, frequently bound with the 11th ed. of *Grammatik*).

ŠIŠMARËV, V., *Óčerki po istórii jazykóv Ispánii*. Romano-Germanica, V, Institút jazyká i mýšlenija ... (Moskvá-Leningrád: Izdátel'stvo Akadémii Naúk, 1941), cf. Y. Malkiel in *Lg.*, XX (1944), 155–160. Id., *Istoríče-*

*skaja morfológija francúzskogo jazyká* (Moskvá: Akadémija Naúk
[Institút Jazykoznánija], 1952). Id., *Kníga dlja čténija po istórii francúzskogo jazyká* and, with M. A. Borodiná and M. V. Górdina, *Slovár'
starofrancúzskogo jazyká, k Kníge* . . . (Moskvá: Akadémija Naúk
[Institút Jazykoznánija], 1955).

SOMMER, F., *Lateinische Schulgrammatik mit sprachwissenschaftlichen
Anmerkungen* (Frankfurt a.M.: Diesterweg, 1920). Id., *Vergleichende
Syntax der Schulsprachen (Deutsch, Englisch, Französisch, Griechisch,
Lateinisch)* (Leipzig-Berlin: Teubner, 1921).

SPAULDING, R. K., *How Spanish Grew* (Berkeley and Los Angeles: University of California Press, 1943).

SPITZER, L., *Die Wortbildung als stilistisches Mittel exemplifiziert an
Rabelais* . . ., *ZRPh.*, Suppl. XXIX (Halle a.S.: Niemeyer, 1910). Id.,
"Die epizönen Nomina auf -*a(s)* in den iberischen Sprachen" (82–182),
in "Über Ausbildung von Gegensinn in der Wortbildung" (81–230),
see Gamillscheg and Spitzer, *Beiträge zur romanischen Wortbildungslehre*, BAR, II: 2 (Genève: Olschki, 1921).

STAAFF, E., *Étude sur l'ancien dialecte léonais d'après des chartes du XIIIᵉ
siècle* (Uppsala: Almqvist & Wiksell, and Leipzig: Haupt, 1907 ["Étude
grammaticale": 171–347]); cf. R. Menéndez Pidal in *RDR*, II (1910),
119–130.

STEIGER, A., *Contribución a la fonética del hispano-árabe y de los arabismos
en el ibero-románico y el siciliano*, RFE, Suppl. XVII (Madrid, 1932).

STOLZ, F. (†1915), and J. H. Schmalz, *Lateinische Grammatik*, 5th ed.,
rev. by M. Leumann and J. B. Hofmann, in *Handbuch der Altertums-
wissenschaft*, ed. W. Otto, II: 2 (München: Beck, 1928 [orig. ed.:
1885; 3d ed.: 1900; 4th ed.: 1910]). Stolz is the sole author of: *Historische
Grammatik der lateinischen Sprache*: I. Einleitung, Lautlehre, Stamm-
bildungslehre (Leipzig: Teubner, 1894).

STURTEVANT, E. H., *Linguistic Change; an Introduction to the Historical
Study of Language* (Chicago: The University of Chicago Press, 1917).
Id., *Hittite Glossary; Words of Known or Conjectured Meaning, with
Sumerian Ideograms and Accadian Words Common in Hittite Texts*,
"Language" Monograph, IX (1931); 2d ed. [*A Hittite . . . Akkadian . . .
Occurring in* . . .] (Philadelphia: LSA, Spec. Publ. for Yale University,
1936). Id., *A Comparative Grammar of the Hittite Language*, W. D.
Whitney Linguistic Series (Philadelphia: LSA [for Yale University]
and University of Pennsylvania, 1933); [2d] rev. ed., with E. A. Hahn
(New Haven: Yale University Press, 1951). Id., with G. Bechtel,
*A Hittite Chrestomathy* (Philadelphia: LSA for Yale University, 1935);
"Index", by B. Schwartz (New York, 1937). Id., *An Introduction to
Linguistic Science* (New Haven: Yale University Press, 1947).

SUCHIER, H., "Die französische und provenzalische Sprache und ihre
Mundarten", in G. Gröber, *Grundriß* . . ., I (1888), 561–668 and 12
small maps; rev. 2d ed. (1904–06), 712–840, tr. P. Monet ["sur le
conseil de G. Paris": *Le français et le provençal*] (Paris: Bouillon, 1891
["M. Suchier . . . a modifié et amélioré nombre de passages du texte
primitif: en sorte que c'est, à vrai dire, une nouvelle édition"]). Id.,

*Altfranzösische Grammatik*, I: *Die Schriftsprache*; fasc. 1: "Die betonten Vokale" (Halle a.S.: Niemeyer, 1893); tr. and adapt. C. Guerlin de Guer [*Les voyelles toniques du vieux français, langue littéraire* (*Normandie et Ile-de-France*)] (Paris: Champion, 1906).

SUCHIER, W., *Französische Verslehre auf historischer Grundlage*. SKL, XIV (Tübingen: Niemeyer, 1952).

TAGLIAVINI, C., *Grammatica rumena* (Heidelberg: Groos, 1923). Id., *Rumänische Konversationsgrammatik*, Methode Gaspey-Otto-Sauer, 5th ed. ["vollständig neu bearbeitet"; actually replaces earlier Rumanian grammars in this series by R. Lovera and A. Jacob (1912; 2d ed., rev. by J. Slavici, 1919) and A. Storch (1921, 1923)] (Heidelberg: Groos, 1938). Id., *Le origini delle lingue neolatine* (lithoprinted "dispense", 1949 [outgrowth of a lecture course originally offered at Bologna, 1926–27, later at Nijmwegen and Budapest]); rev. 2d ed. (Bologna: Pàtron [1952]); rev. 3d ed. [new subtitle: *Introduzione alla filologia romanza*] (1959).

TALLGREN[-TUULIO], O. J., "Las *z* y *ç* del antiguo castellano iniciales de sílaba, estudiadas en la inédita *Gaya* de [Pero Guillén de] Segovia", *Mém. Soc. Néophil. de Helsingfors*, IV (1906), 3–50, 397–401. Id., *Estudios sobre la "Gaya" de [Pero Guillén de] Segovia; capítulos de introducción a una edición crítica* (Helsinki: Kirjapaino-Osakeyhtiö Sana, 1907), esp. Chap. VI: "Monografía fonética: *Ç, Z*" (78–91).

THUMB, A. (†1915), *Handbuch der griechischen Dialekte*. Indog. Bibl., I: 1: 8 (Heidelberg: Winter, 1909); 2d ed., completely revised by E. Kieckers (Part I, 1932) and by A. Scherer (Part II, 1959).

TIKTIN, H., "Die rumänische Sprache", in G. Gröber, *Grundriß* ..., I (1888), 438–460; rev. ed. (1904–06), 564–607. Id., *Rumänisches Elementarbuch*. SRE, I: 6 (Heidelberg: Winter, 1905).

TOBLER, A. (†1910), *Vom französischen Versbau alter und neuer Zeit; Zusammenstellung der Anfangsgründe* (Leipzig: Hirzel, 1880); 2d ed. (1883); 3d ed. (1894); 4th ed. (1903); 6th ed. [new printing] (1921); tr. K. Breul and L. Sudre, based on 2d German ed., with Preface by G. Paris [*Le vers français ancien et moderne*] (Paris: Vieweg, 1885); tr. and ed. E. W. May (typescript, Univ. of Chicago M.A. thesis, 1923).

TREND, J. B., *The Languages and History of Spain*. Hutchinson's University Library, Modern Languages, ed. N. B. Jopson (London: Hutchinson House, 1953).

ULLMANN, S., *Précis de sémantique française*. Bibl. Roman., I: 9 (Paris: Presses Universitaires de France, and Berne: Francke [1952]); rev. 2d ed. (1959). Id., *Semantics. An Introduction to the Science of Meaning* (Oxford: Blackwell, 1962).

ULRICH, J., *Die formelle Entwicklung des Partizipiums Präteriti in den romanischen Sprachen*, Diss. Zürich (Winterthur, 1879).

VORETZSCH, C. [later K.], *Einführung in das Studium der altfranzösischen Sprache zum Selbstunterricht für den Anfänger*. SKL, I (Halle: Niemeyer, 1901); 2d ed. (1903); 3d ed. (1907); 4th ed. (1911); 5th ed. (1918); 6th ed. (1932). Replaced by G. Rohlfs, *Vom Vulgärlatein zum Alt-*

*französischen; Einführung in das Studium der altfranzösischen Sprache.*
SKL, XV (Tübingen: Niemeyer, 1960).
WACKERNAGEL, J. (†1938), *Altindische Grammatik* : I, Lautlehre (Göttingen: 1896, Vandenhoeck & Ruprecht); II: 1, Einleitung zur Wortlehre; Nominalkomposition (1905); II: 2, Die Nominalsuffixe, ed. A. Debrunner (1954); III: 1-2, Nominalflexion, Zahlwort, Pronomen (1929-30); IV, Register, by R. Hauschild (1964). Id., *Vorlesungen über Syntax mit besonderer Berücksichtigung von Griechisch, Lateinisch und Deutsch*, ed. Philologisches Seminar Universität Basel (Basel: Burkhäuser, 1920); 2d ed., 2 vols. (1926-28).
WAGNER, M. L., "Flessione nominale e verbale del sardo antico e moderno", *ID*, XIV (1938), 93-170; XV (1939), 1-29. Id., *Historische Lautlehre des Sardischen, ZRPh.*, Suppl. XCIII (Halle a.S.: Niemeyer, 1941). Id., *Historische Wortbildungslehre des Sardischen.* RH, XXXIX (Bern: Francke, 1952). Id., *La lingua sarda; storia, spirito e forma* [ed. G. Nencioni]. Bibl. Rom., I: 3 (Berna: Francke [1951]).
WEINRICH, H., *Phonologische Studien zur romanischen Sprachgeschichte.* FRPh. (ed. H. Lausberg), VI (Münster i.W. [1958]); cf. K. Togeby in *RPh.*, XIII: 4 (1960), 401-413.
WIESE, B., *Altitalienisches Elementarbuch.* SRE, I: 4 (Heidelberg: Winter, 1904); rev. 2d ed. ["völlige Neuordnung des Stoffes"] (1928).
WIGGERS, J., *Grammatik der spanischen Sprache*, 2d ed. (Leipzig: Brockhaus, 1884). [This seems to be the earliest ascertainable edition.]
WILLIAMS, E. B., *From Latin to Portuguese; Historical Phonology and Morphology of the Portuguese Language* (Philadelphia: University of Pennsylvania Press, 1938); rev. 2d ed. (1962).
ZAMORA VICENTE, A., *Dialectología española.* BRH, III: 8 (Madrid: Gredos [1960]).
ZAUNER, A. (†1940), *Romanische Sprachwissenschaft.* Sammlung Göschen, No. 128 (Leipzig: Göschen, 1900); 2d ed., entirely revised, 2 vols., SG, Nos. 128, 250 (1905); rev. 3d ed. (Berlin-Leipzig: Göschen, 1914); 4th ed., mere reprint ["Neudruck"] (Berlin: de Gruyter, 1944-45). Cf. under H. Lausberg, above. Id., *Altspanisches Elementarbuch.* SRE, I: 5 (Heidelberg: Winter, 1908); cf. review by F. Hanssen, "Sobre un compendio de gramática castellana anteclásica", *AUCh.*, CXXII (1908), 671-695; 2d ed., completely revised (1921).

# 6

# Leonard Bloomfield in Retrospect*

It has long been known, through statements from Bloomfield's inner circle (cf. B. Bloch, *Lg.*, XXV [1949], 89; R. A. Hall, Jr., *Collier's Encycl.*, ed. 1960, III, 412a), that among the major projects left unpublished at the time of that pioneer's incapacitation (1946) or untimely death (1949), there figured beside two descriptive monographs in his favorite domain of Central Algonquian, a primer and reader involving a novel method for teaching American grade-school children the art of reading. The first two items (*Eastern Ojibwa; Grammatical Sketch, Texts, and Word List*, Ann Arbor, 1957; and *The Menomini Language*, New Haven, 1962) have since appeared, thanks mainly to the efforts of C. F. Hockett. From the start, the chances for the third venture — almost doomed to oblivion by the unorthodoxy of its approach — to become widely available, which was its *raison d'être*, were conspicuously slim. It took the energy and dedication of that enlightened lexicographer and commercial publisher, C. L. Barnhart — initially, through direct coöperation with Bloomfield in the concluding years of the latter's appointment at Chicago, later almost entirely on his own — to produce at long last a beautifully printed book embodying, in slightly revised shape, the second, elaborate version of the experimental reader.[1]

This journal's Review Section seldom examines educational literature, the lone exception being books noted for their theoretical implications or written by theorists as by-products of their broader activities (cf. *RPh.*, XIII, 454–457: W. G. Moulton's rev. of Gougenheim-Mauger, *Le Français élémentaire*). Readers unacquainted at first hand with the American pedagogical scene will benefit by

Reprinted from *Romance Philology*, XVI (1962-63), 83-91, by permission of The Regents of the University of California.

*Bloomfield, Leonard, and Clarence L. Barnhart, *Let's Read; a Linguistic Approach*. Detroit: Wayne State University Press, 1961. Pp. 465 (Index in four columns: 431–465).
[1] Interestingly, the open-mindedness of Wayne University Press was due, at least in part, to an earlier classroom association of Bloomfield's with its current director.

perusing here, in the Forematter (3–44), R. C. Pooley's deftly
phrased "Introduction for Teachers" (5–8), which contrasts the
Bloomfield System with (a) the older method of imparting elementary
reading skill through "phonics" (a straight return to this method,
which professionals now dismiss as outmoded, was last advocated in
R. Flesch's sensational exposé *Why Johnny Can't Read* [1955]) and
(b) its currently accepted word-centered substitute, which trains the
tyro to associate at once the graphic configuration of an entire
printed word, barely analyzed into its constituents, with the corresponding semantic nucleus, at the cost of sharply curtailed attention
to such smaller units as speech sounds (or letters, their visual symbols). Not unexpectedly, Bloomfield's central thesis was: An "inseparable relationship exists between the words as printed and the
sounds for which the letters are conventional signs", requiring from
the outset a "concentration upon letter and sound to bring about as
rapidly as possible an automatic association between them" (6). In
thus restricting the function of meaning and in laying down other
norms, Bloomfield wisely exercised restraint. As a frame of reference,
he emphatically recommended the speech of educated persons in
the given student-group's environment; like Sapir (1921), he granted
lexical units a certain autonomous status within his hierarchy, but
subordinated them in rank to sounds. He avoided any appeal to
phonetic script — its use might have later entailed the need for a
painfully disturbing readjustment to the standard notation — by
introducing for a long stretch only such "regular" material as
enables the groping learner safely to equate sounds and letters and
thus to build up, step by step, his confidence in the guide and a
zest for continued learning.[2] Here are a few sample sentences:
*Sam tramps mud on the rug; the tents at Pat's camp had ten cots;
Dad had a box three feet in width and six feet in length.* This approach
presupposes, then, a pattern of grading on the basis not of either
incidence or lexical frequency, but of varying predictability of a
given letter's actual sound value. It is applicable to any language —
such as modern French — that suffers from an unbridgeable gap
between solidly entrenched norms of speaking and of spelling. (One
is reminded of Arabic textbooks — in my own student days I profited
from using an edition of the Sindbad story so arranged — which

---

[2] Theoretically noteworthy is the statement on nonsense words: "All readers will
agree as to the sounds they utter when they see unconventional combinations, such
as *pid, nin, pins* . . ." (25 f.).

gradually omit vowel signs in the approximate order of their decreasing predictability from grammatical and topical context, lexical commonness, and the supporting *matres lectionis*.) The crux of the method is this: The learner — as yet unmotivated, hence easily discouraged — is spared the premature discovery of the large share of unremovable irregularities; with these he will become acquainted in the three concluding parts.[3] The specific ingredient of rationalism consists in the deliberate postponement effected through this "shunting", much as Bloomfield's (and some of his fellow *Jüngstgrammatiker's*) rigidly regularist position in matters of sound change, in the last analysis, neither eliminates ineradicable, nor solves at higher speed slowly yielding, difficulties, but simply seeks — for tidiness' or effective pedagogy's sake — to transfer their analysis from an earlier to a later phase of the operation.

Highly readable, through the profuse inclusion of "exhibits", is the second of Barnhart's introductory statements, "The Story of the Bloomfield System" (9–17). Devotees will find here the complete chronicle of their favorite linguist's frustrations, over twelve long years (1937–49), in his attempts to have the present book launched, be it only by a subsidized university press. They will also learn about a few parent-enthusiasts who in those dreary years volunteered to put it to private use, about the first stamp of approval (1945) which the educationist E. L. Thorndike placed on this plan for SEE-SAY connections, about its temporary trial adoption in the Chicago Archdiocesan Schools, and about the earliest professional assessment of this modest experiment, under controlled conditions, in Sister Mary Fidelia's unpublished Ottawa Ph.D. thesis, *Bloomfield's Linguistic Approach to Word Attack*. Though Bloomfield's dissatisfaction with accepted teaching practices on all levels — up to the Graduate School — antedates this particular series of disappointments (one finds unmistakable traces of acrimony as early as his first synthesis [*Introduction* . . . 1914]), one gathers that the humiliating setbacks experienced at this advanced stage of his career must have raised his long-simmering anger to the boiling point. Defeats and vexations of this kind account, in large measure, for that querulous tone, that almost complete lack of humor (though not of acid

[3] IV: "The Commonest Irregular Words" (203–280); V: "The Commonest Irregular Spellings of Vowel Sounds" (281–353); VI: "The Commonest Irregular Spellings of Consonant Sounds" (355–430). The whole book is divided into 245 lessons, of which the first 97 pertain to Parts I–III ("First Reading", "Easy Reading". "More Easy Reading").

sarcasm), and that readiness to act as a social critic which pervade and, in many readers' opinion, adversely affect some of the later Bloomfield's most celebrated polemic writings.

Beyond question the book's *pièce de résistance* is Bloomfield's essay "Teaching Children to Read" (19–42), heretofore available only in a severely abridged version.[4] It afforded the author one of his last occasions to take stock, in bird's-eye perspective, of almost the entire body of applied linguistics. Without quite reaching Sapir's virtuoso performance, Bloomfield was, ever since his fledgling years, a meticulous, accomplished stylist. In fact, he elaborated three styles, each typical of a different period of his life. His early reviews (e.g. those contributed to *JEGPh.*) were worded in an artful, almost precious vein, though never with baroque exuberance. The middle stretch of his career, familiar from his book *Language* (1933), was characterized by a style less caustic and allusive, indeed, studiedly plain, at intervals even plodding — emulating that of solid textbooks. In some of his latest writings, undertaken to convey his insights to a wider circle of laymen and novices, Bloomfield developed a powerful, monumental style of chiseled simplicity, nay austerity, rich in lapidary statements, free from distracting casual metaphoric embellishments, but inlaid with a very few passages of sustained, almost haunting beauty. Of this third style, remembered from a few parting contributions to the journal *Language* (whose foundation he inspired) and from his unassuming *Outline Guide for the Practical Study of Foreign Languages* (1942), the essay now unearthed will doubtless be henceforth known as the most exquisite example (cf. 27: "In its basic character, in its bones, blood, and marrow, our system of writing is alphabetic"). Yet the simplicity — which never turns into triviality — is deceptive: While a bright high-school student may painlessly assimilate many pages, there is no dearth of exacting passages bordering on the hermetic, as where the "main outline" of scientific progress is contrasted with lesser variables (34).

On balance, the essay, neatly subdivided into fourteen subchapters, falls into three major sections left unmarked: (a) a highly concentrated history of the three prevalent styles of writing (picture writing, word writing, alphabetic writing), which at once invites comparison with Chap. 17 of *Language* ("Written Records"); (b) a polemic, hard-hitting but always in good taste, with the champions of the three rival teaching methods which Bloomfield repudiates with equal vigor: (α) phonic,

[4] "Linguistics and Reading", *The Elementary English Review*, XIX (1942), 125–130, 183–186.

which trains the first-grader to utter speech sounds, as if at that stage such training, for the overwhelming majority of children, were not superfluous, especially if carried out in unnatural articulatory contexts; (β) lexical, which tends to conceal the alphabetic principle, crucially important for English; and (γ) ideational, which, in its excessive stress on content ("sentence method", "non-oral method"), wrongly equates the child's and the experienced adult's powers of mental absorption. Finally (c), Bloomfield the pragmatist offers a set of specific instructions, presented in a purposefully matter-of-fact tone, on preparatory training (recognition of letters, facility in stringing them from left to right) and on the organization of first materials.

Those previously exposed to Bloomfield's theoretical tracts will be struck by the recurrence of familiar themes and emphases which he rather deliberately used like so many *Leitmotivs*: the rigidly pre-scribed sequence of operations (let the child first learn to identify all letters, only then start him on reading: 35), the barely controlled impatience with conventional writing, and especially with the in-competent educationists' prescription for tackling it, the demand for naturalness and the unshaken belief in *laissez-faire* (as when the author inveighs against any prissy, priggish, or affected speech habits imposed by misled teachers: 37 f.), the strict separation of pattern from residue, the pervasive subordination of meaning to form (as regards the denotation of individual words and, independently, the topical content of whole passages) both in the array of teaching material and in the expected degrees of a learner's proficiency, the downgrading of the word in favor of the speech sound, the anticipa-tion of a child's delight in the mechanics of speech production. Barring a few pathological cases, Bloomfield tacitly assumes that all learners react alike (the concepts of the gifted and the retarded child are markedly alien to his scheme), just as his view, in 1933, of a smoothly functioning speech community presupposed almost com-plete homogeneity rather than mere similarity of significant habits — easily the most vulnerable spot in his entire doctrine. One irksome infelicity: The author harps decidedly too often on his theme of the inferior prestige of linguistics in our society — as compared to, say, chemistry (19, 30, 32). Are there not certain advantages in esoterism, provided its practitioners refuse to feel the sting of self-pity, and is it not true that excessive popularity of linguistics, such as the post-romantic vogue of "Indo-Germanic" studies in nineteenth-century Germany, may later lead not only to dilution but, worse, to distortion? Again, Bloomfield's notoriously puristic, not to say puritanistic, and isolationist leanings show in that the primer and first reader, though full of charming verbal messages, is practically bare of any pictorial adornment, as if the child's immersion in speech and script might be thwarted by the slightest distraction at the sight of some non-verbal amenity.

Despite Bloomfield's calmly cogent persuasiveness, a dissenter will discover, on second or third reading, a surprisingly large number of loose ends. The solemn initial statement on literacy as the "most important factor in keeping up our civilization" (19) and the subsequent almost grotesquely exaggerated insistence on the sparsity of literacy until the threshold of our own time (20) somehow fail to dovetail;[5] there is, in fact, more grim consistency in a reported semijocose remark by another American linguist of Bloomfield's generation, to the effect that, being an incurable evil, conventional spelling of a language like English should not at all be taught in grade schools and should thus become extinct. The category of word writing is not very tidily circumscribed: Surely a system enabling readers to distinguish between *horse, nag,* and *steed,* i.e., geared to the specific needs and lexical idiosyncrasies of a single language, cannot even roughly be equated with the cross-linguistic use of numerals and comparable mathematical signs, which rather seem ideogrammatic; thus, × is read by a German as *mal* (one word), yet by a Russian as *pomnožennoe na* (two words). One feels hopelessly lost upon learning, first, that "the existence of speech unit sounds, or phonemes, is one of the discoveries of the language study of the last hundred years", then, in abruptly close succession, that "it is remarkable that long before scientific students had made this discovery, there had arisen a system of alphabetic writing — a system in which each character represented a phoneme" (24). If the facts reported are correct — and not a few may feel that the statement clamors for qualification — , then a reputed major accomplishment of linguistic science emerges as a mere restatement of truth long ago intuitively grasped, thus severely reducing our discipline's title to

[5] The picture might have looked different had Bloomfield bothered to take into account a miscellany of relevant factors, e.g. the age-old literacy of entire minority groups (such as the Jews) within the traditional European society; the large-scale coincidence of literacy and socio-economic prestige, a state of affairs which made one literate person far more influential, in his speech habits and in other respects, than any of his illiterate counterparts; and the existence of a transitional group, by no means inactive or unimaginative, namely that of the partially or vestigially literate, who acted as the main channel of transmission.

recognition. The gaps here are as wide as those left in Bloomfield's earlier *magnum opus* between the stress on the regularity of sound change and the free admission (traceable, of all authorities, to Schuchardt) that each word has a history of its own; between loyalty — despite disclaimers — to family-tree projection and partial acceptance of the wave theory of propagation; between the flat rejection of any teleological principle and the simultaneous espousal of Gilliéron's explicative conjectures, resting squarely on that same principle. Nor is the essay free from palpable exaggerations, as when the same child credited with usually outwitting, in the end, any misleading teacher is expected to be seriously harmed by early exposure to such mild discrepancies as *get* vs. *gem*, or as when the author's own method is pictured, by unmistakable implication, as almost thaumaturgical: "Even at the end of eight years many of our pupils cannot be said to read; yet eight months ought to suffice" (19).

These, however, are mere frills in comparison with two problems of great magnitude which the essay merely skirts, but which are central to Bloomfieldian linguistics in all its ramifications and repercussions. One of them comes up in Subchap. 11 ("The Content"). In general, the author, chivalrous in championing his cause, not only recognizes that his opponents' errors for the most part stem from excellent intentions gone awry through some inadvertent miscalculation of effects, but also anticipates, and tries to parry, serious objections to his own advocacy. Specifically, in his plea (34 f.) for generous use of disconnected sentences and even of nonsense syllables like *nin* apt to convince the child that he is "gaining in power", in preference to "silly" stories studded with words of forbiddingly irregular spelling such as *gem*, the author remarks:

> There is always something artificial about reducing a problem to simple mechanical terms, but the whole history of science shows that simple mechanical terms are the only terms in which our limited human capacity can solve a problem. The lesser variables have to wait until the main outline has been ascertained, and this is true even when these lesser variables are the very thing that makes our problem worth solving. The authors of books on reading methods devote much space to telling why reading is worth while. They would have done far better to stress the fact that the practical and cultural values of reading can play no part in the elementary stages.

This passage is not only another profession of faith in gradualism, it also shows Bloomfield's awareness of the fact that the linguist

N

taking up the cudgels for pure or predominant formalism lays himself open to severe criticism for providing a technique with possibly little worth while behind it, a set of superb tools ready to be set in motion in an empty space. Bloomfield regales the reader with a memorable simile:

> If you want to play the piano with feeling and expression, you must master the keyboard and learn to use your fingers on it. When you have mastered the keyboard and the fingering, you may still fail for other reasons, but certain it is that if you have not the mechanical control, you will not be able to play.

An unimpeachably honest statement indeed; except that not every child is motivated preëminently by seeing himself gain in power along the straight line of a single accomplishment. More important: Once applied to the training of young adults in foreign language learning and in linguistics, this philosophy of drill, discipline, and overpractice at the cost of contentual emptiness, if doled out in isolation, is bound to produce little more than good short-range results (Bloomfield himself, a person of great refinement, needless to say, did not represent a product of this education). Unless counterbalanced by morsels of a very different intellectual and artistic diet, this program of study will produce superb craftsmen, but hardly inspired master architects, just as the piano player held up as a model is, characteristically, a splendid performer, not a powerful creator.

Of course, a Bloomfieldian may try to overrule this objection by arguing that "feeling and expression" in music or "cultural values" in verbal arts may be acquired through courses other than straight piano or reading classes. But since, in practice, such collateral exposures are virtually nonexistent in our curricula, delegating the responsibility for this separate dimension of progress to someone else amounts to sweeping the problem under the rug, handling it as a kind of educational "residue", postponing its discussion until some undefined propitious moment. This lack of total responsibility for the transmission of unified knowledge, as a result of almost morbid infatuation with just one facet of an indivisible whole — a facet, Bloomfield never tired of repeating, sorely misunderstood or even deliberately endangered —, surely marks one of the greatest limitations of his approach.

The other passage, of special concern to the Romance linguist, appears under the rubric "Speech and Writing" (20). Its compelling

persuasiveness may cause such serious confusion as to prompt me
to quote it in full:

> What happens to a language if the people who speak it have no books —
> no dictionaries, grammars, spelling books, and so on? The answer to
> this question was one of the first and most surprising results of lin-
> guistic study: unwritten languages function and *develop* [emphasis
> mine] in the same way as languages that have been reduced to writing.
> In fact, taking the great mass of human history, the non-use of writing
> is the normal state of affairs, and the use of writing is a special case
> and, until very recent times, a most unusual case. The effect of writing
> on language, where there is no popular literacy [i.e., according to B.,
> prior to the last hundred years], is practically nothing, and where
> there is popular literacy, as among us, the effect of writing is merely
> to introduce a few small *irregularities* into the process of linguistic
> development. This, of course, is the opposite of the popular view, but
> it is the result of every investigation that has been undertaken and is
> today firmly accepted by every student of language.
>
> Writing is merely a device for recording speech. A person is much the
> same and looks the same, whether he has ever had his picture taken or
> not. Only a vain beauty who sits for many photographs and carefully
> studies them may end by slightly changing her pose and expressions.
> It is much the same with languages and their written recording.

The statement is less unequivocal than it seems at first reading. If
the author means that it did not greatly matter, on the level of actual
evolution, whether medieval scribes favored *ç* or *z*, *k* or *q*, *nh* or
*nn* or *gn* for recording certain sounds, especially those for which
Antiquity had set no precedents, his statement will cause few raised
eyebrows. That, in other instances, reverent attention to spelling
has altered pronunciation, incidentally far more among the semiliterate and the vestigially literate than among genuine intellectuals,
is a fact very well known, still observable, monographically investigated (e.g., by V. Buben for French), and surely exceeding one
century in depth. That the existence of a revered written tradition
has measurably slowed down attrition, in other words, that the
literacy of a tone-setting élite has had a scotching effect on the tempo
of linguistic change within the most influential of all social dialects,
is a fact which I have never heard a qualified Romance linguist seriously deny, though the specific assessments may have varied considerably and the experts' accompanying reactions may have run the
full gamut from glee to sadness. All such emotional orchestration in
scholarly quarters has been unnecessary and harmful; some voices,
by coinciding with the popular view, would understandably irk any

linguist convinced, as was Bloomfield from an early date, of the basic fallacy of most "secondary reactions to language". But that some languages, including those of the Romance family, are in far higher degree conscious of their heritage — of which conventional spelling is an isolable ingredient — than are others, is a circumstance which objective research must learn to accept in a dispassionate mood. This attitude, retrospective if you wish, of influential speakers, disturbs the "blind" working of sound correspondences in much the same way as do analogy and dialect mixture, regional and social; it immeasurably complicates the task of the analyst, who may elect to free himself from this kind of mortgage by studying the speech of tribes unencumbered by such heritage. This is essentially what Bloomfieldian linguistics accomplishes: It is not good or bad in any absolute sense, but seems rather at its most effective in dealing with relatively uncomplicated cultures, and at its least satisfactory in coming to grips with cultures of extraordinary sophistication. In most Romance languages (down to rural dialects, if only on a minor scale), spontaneous developments and artificial developments have been locked in an unending struggle, creating the stage for a drama that it is precisely the business of the Romance scholar to reconstruct in all its vividness.

To sum up: Bloomfield's linguistics has its distinct merit for the classification of field flowers. But in the Romance household one must take care of field flowers and hothouse flowers alike, with equal devotion or, at least, equal serenity. Bloomfield's lack of equanimity, understandable as the reaction of a hypersensitive person of anthropological leanings to a radically different scale of values enforced by his own society, makes it very difficult to adopt his system, without proper antitoxins, for Romance scholarship. A trained and sophisticated Romance linguist can reap immense benefit from assimilating the sounder ingredients of Bloomfield's thinking; but a still uncommitted person suddenly aroused to enthusiasm about linguistics through the Bloomfieldian approach is most unlikely to specialize in Romance or, after making such an improbable choice, to attain in this field a truly high degree of originality.

# 7
# Etymology and General Linguistics

**1. The anomalous status of etymology.** Within the bundle of linguistic disciplines etymology occupies a position difficult to define. It does not, strictly speaking, mark a transition between the domains of language viewed chiefly as a means of communication (linguistics) and language considered as a vehicle of art (literature), in the way poetics, stylistics, and folklore may be interpreted; neither does it bear any resemblance to semantics. Of every other discipline (say, phonology and syntax) one can imagine a synchronic and a diachronic projection. But synchronic etymology — despite the authority of an aging Vendryes (*BSLP*, XLIX: 1 [1953], 1-19: "Pour une étymologie statique") — amounts to scarcely more than a paradox. For approximately a century scholars have been operating with the term and concept of folk etymology, which again lacks any counterpart in other disciplines.

**2. Conflicting views.** An appeal to leading authorities to clarify the situation is of little avail, since their verdicts have been either evasive or contradictory. In some slimmer introductory treatises, from the eleven loosely strung essays forming Sapir's *Language* (1921) to the six stimulating, if uneven, chapters which Martinet has combined into his *Éléments de linguistique générale* (1960), etymology barely, if at all, receives incidental mention. The situation is somewhat different, but hardly less disappointing, with the broader outlines. Even that most lucid of theorists, Saussure, who relegates — surely not by chance — his brief discussion to an Appendix, presents a picture not wholly convincing. For him etymology is neither an autonomous discipline nor a smoothly integrated part of evolutionary linguistics: It amounts to a special application, to early stages of word history, of principles generally valid in linguistic research. Saussure's prime examples are four pairs of words — all perfectly transparent — illustrating, in this order, sound change, semantic change, simul-

Reprinted from *Word*, Vol. XVIII, Nos. 1-2, April-August, 1962, pp. 198-219.

taneous change of sound and meaning, and derivation. Later, more complex relationships come up for mention, e.g., the link of F. *oiseau* to L. AVI(CELLU)S; the (historical) study of suffixes and prefixes is likewise included. After a somewhat lukewarm remark to the effect that explaining one word means tracing it to other words, Saussure recognizes certain ties between etymology, on the one hand, and such better established disciplines as phonology, morphology, semantics, on the other, but doubts that any strict methodology can be prescribed and expressly discards the possibility of rigorous operational arrangement.[1]

Bloomfield's approach (1933) is equally unpromising. His book contains no single section, let alone chapter, on etymology pure and simple, but the Index leads one to some relevant passages, as when etymology is identified as a special concern of ancient Greek scholars (4) and, later, as a butt of Voltaire's sarcasm (6). More important is the modern "precise" definition of the etymology (15) of a speech-form as "simply its history . . . obtained by finding the older forms in the same language and the forms in related languages which are divergent variants of the same parent form" (15); the tracing of E. *mother* via OE *mōdor* and its congeners to Prim. Gmc. *\*mōder*, hence to Prim. IE *\*mātēr* serves as a prime example. In accordance with this definition, the technique of etymology is obliquely mentioned first under Phonetic Change (346 f., 351–355), later under Semantic Change (427–430).

The dual disadvantage of such a position consists in this: (a) etymology is reduced, as it were, to a small-scale — indeed, the smallest — operation within diachronic phonology, a rôle which

---

[1] "Comme la linguistique statique et évolutive, elle décrit des faits, mais cette description n'est pas méthodique, puisqu'elle ne se fait dans aucune direction déterminée. . . . Pour arriver à ses fins, elle se sert de tous les moyens que la linguistique met à sa disposition, mais elle n'arrête pas son attention sur la nature des opérations qu'elle est obligée de faire" (2d ed. [Paris, 1922], p. 260; Supplement C to Parts III–IV). Between 1893 and 1912 Saussure taught several formal courses on etymology, with emphasis on Greek and Latin, and his ideas on the scope of the discipline must have wavered considerably; see R. Godel, *Les sources manuscrites du "Cours de linguistique générale"* (Geneva and Paris, 1957), pp. 24 f. and 134. In his earlier synthesis *Le langage* (1921; completed in 1914), p. 206, Vendryes equated etymology with diachronic lexicology; what he accomplished in 1953, under the avowed influence of Saussure and some ancient Indian grammarians as interpreted by F. Edgerton, was to substitute "static etymology" for synchronic lexicology, a less than felicitous decision. Meillet's etymological testament (1932) will be found in his prefaces to the *Dictionnaire étymologique de la langue latine* and to O. Bloch's *Dictionnaire étymologique de la langue française*.

deprives it (to make things worse, inexplicitly) of any independent status; (b) the reader remains unaware of the fact that professional etymologists will rebel against examining problems as transparent as the provenience of *mother*. Surely, it is no mere coincidence that a handbook as influential in the English-speaking countries (and later the world over) as Bloomfield's has singularly failed to stimulate the slightest curiosity about genuine etymological research, at its most exciting.

**3. Four claims to autonomy.** The correct place of etymology, if one agrees to define it as the search for word origins, must be sought elsewhere. If it is true that word biographies lend themselves to graphic projection, then the etymologist's task is the elucidation of the starting point, better still, of the initial segment of chosen lexical trajectories. Etymology is thus a mere subdivision of lexicology (here taken to mean 'theoretical, preëminently historical, study of the lexicon', in contrast to lexicography, viewed as an applied science),[2] but a subdivision endowed with several peculiarities which tend to give it special rank. One can single out at least four such claims to autonomous high status:

(1) Though classifiable by present standards as a mere subdivision, etymology boasts a venerable history of its own, throughout Antiquity and the Middle Ages, a history involving significant contacts with areas of human endeavor unrelated to lexicology and even to linguistics, as that science is currently understood. Compressed into a formula, the paradoxical situation may be described thus: The part is older than the whole.

(2) Because creative etymology presupposes, on the part of its practitioner, a desire to transcend the domains of the obvious and of the highly probable in the matter of lexical equations and to operate

---

[2] Not all lexical monographs exhibit an etymological slant. H. and R. Kahane's article on the (predominantly nautical) progeny of SURGERE (*RPh.*, IV [1950–51], 195–215) embodies an experiment in spatio-temporal semantics. The prime purpose of my reconstruction of the Hispanic branch of PER-, RE-, SUC-CUTERE (*HR*, XIV [1946], 104–159) was to demonstrate that Cl. and Mod. *acudir* — semantically many-faceted, hence genetically elusive — perpetuates OSp. *recudir*. In special instances, as where a blend is involved, heavy documentation seems indispensable; cf. OSp. Gal.-Ptg. *desmazelado* 'wretched' (from MAC-ULA, -ELLA 'spot') × Hebr. *maz·āl* 'star, destiny' > (Jud.-) Sp. *desmazalado* 'weak, destitute' (*HR*, XV [1947], 272–301); but consistent use of massive illustration, as advocated and very effectively practiced by W. von Wartburg (on his technique see *Word*, X [1957], 288–305; also, in his Bibliography [1956], items A 138, 209, 350; B 19, 21), tends to smother the nuclear problems of etymology.

in the hazardous realm of the increasingly conjectural, it often attracts a totally different type of personality than does grammar, even in its modern garb of "structure".

(3) Like all lexical subdisciplines, etymology is equally concerned with form and with meaning and, through the latter, also with the outer world of realities. But in a more intimate sense than the others, this subdiscipline is tied up with certain facets of historical grammar, chiefly phonology and derivation — a point duly recognized, but magnified out of all proportion, by Saussure and Bloomfield.

(4) The main idiosyncrasy of etymology stems from the fact that, unlike most cognate subdisciplines, it operates consistently with fragmentary evidence, with dotted evolutionary lines. Every etymologist protests that he would prefer to rely, in his reconstructions, on a vastly increased stock of recorded forms; few would be candid enough to admit that truly complete records would deprive the etymologist's endeavors of their real charm, even of their *raison d'être*. The sparseness or even unavailability of critically needed material has fascinated some workers (moulding, in the process, their personalities) and has, with equal power, repelled others.

Were it not for these four considerations, particularly the last three, etymology could be safely eliminated from the roster of legitimate linguistic pursuits and stored away as a curious relic of prescientific concern with language.

**4. A science or an art?** Some observers argue that the place of etymology within the alliance of linguistic disciplines has been jeopardized through the linguists' growing endeavor to attain the status of exact scientists. The two main obstacles confronting etymologists who strive to keep pace with fellow-linguists so oriented,[3] these critics contend, are, first, the element of haphazardness inherent in their discoveries; second, the fact that their researches and working habits suggest an art rather than a science.

Either objection has merit, but loses something of its weight if carefully qualified. In apprising both, it is helpful to delimit, more sharply than has been done in the past, three phases of etymological

---

[3] For the sake of the argument, etymologists are portrayed as forming, so to speak, a separate task force. In reality, the same scholar often acts now as etymologist, now as grammarian, now as textual critic; the greater his elasticity — if balanced by seriousness of purpose —, the more significant and the less lopsided his total contribution.

inquiry: (a) the preparation or training; (b) the actual discovery; (c) the presentation of results.

**5. The "accidental" ingredient.** Undeniably, there is an ineradicable element of casualness at the actual stage of discovery; it follows from the invariably fragmentary character of the material available. The etymologist (like every other archeologist) may literally stumble upon the missing link: An intermediate form deemed hypothetical may appear in a text recently discovered or freshly re-read, a trace of the uncontaminated product justifying a hazardous conjecture emerges in a newly surveyed dialect, etc. Possibly more arresting and conducive to the injection of some such term as "intuition" are etymological identifications involving an abrupt semantic change or a bold metaphor. These are sometimes made through direct contact with nature (in a museum or in the open air), through increased familiarity with the trades and with rural living, through immersion in past ideas, beliefs, and sentiments, or through felicitous associations with neighboring cultural climates and linguistic areas.

But Spitzer's familiar bon mot: "Suche keine Etymologien; finde sie!" must not be taken at its face value. Though the actual *Einfall* may be an instantaneous, unforeseeable event (does not a similar situation — a sudden flash of imagination — prevail in the physical sciences?) and though in etymology certain mental qualities associated with creativeness, memory, vividness of association, and even visual impressionability play a part at least as crucial as that of straight indoctrination (and conceivably more appealing to the sensitive layman), it is nonetheless true that important phases of etymological inquiry may and should be placed under rational control. Significant conjectures are not known to occur to the uninitiated; it takes a mind not only plastic and versatile, but thoroughly attuned to pending etymological problems (as a rule, through long, systematic exposure to specialized teaching or to technical literature) to respond at once to the challenge of a "hunch". No less important is the slow, predominantly rational filtering of one's instantaneous insights, and in such final decisions as whether to publish the new solution as a separate venture or to make it part of an intricate strategy of long-term research, analytical thinking becomes the determining factor. Of the three phases of inquiry established in the preceding Section, only Phase (b) shows a strong, apparently irreducible admixture of the accidental.

**6. The artistic element.** Far more elusive, hence difficult to circumscribe, is the artistic constituent of etymology, partly referring to the conduct of the inquiry and to the comportment of its practitioner, partly crystallizing from the analysis of the finished product. Yet its existence is no mere figment of unbridled imagination; dedicated and seasoned workers have repeatedly asserted its reality, as when a mature V. Bertoldi titled his introductory treatise *L'arte dell'etimologia*.[4] Those who designate etymology as an art seem to hint at four isolable qualities, or at any conceivable number of their free combinations: (a) the inventive strain in the worker's mind, which prompts him to engage in felicitous, unexpected associations of isolated facts or to fill successfully a gaping lacuna in the available information; (b) a certain finesse and elasticity in bringing to bear on an etymological problem — successively or conjointly — very disparate analyses (phonological, grammatical, semantic), all of them within the realm of linguistics, though at varying distances from its core; (c) the readiness, of late increasingly rare among tone-setting linguists, to balance linguistic evidence against an extraordinarily wide range of complementary material — so wide as to require an encyclopedic range of curiosity and even of expertise. This operation demands not only erudition, but also delicacy of touch, since the number and the proportion of differently labeled exhibits vary from case to case; (d) a flair for selecting the ideal moment to halt the accumulation of raw data and the proliferation of digressions, also for the calculated risk in announcing, at a chosen turn, the preliminary or final results of the inquiry — a flair reminiscent of the talented writer's ability to stop elaboration at the right juncture, or the experienced visual artist's knack for refraining from, say, obtrusive overpainting. (Note that, while there may be some affinity between musicianship and alertness to the phonic, especially melodic, features of speech, imagery impinges on language nowhere with nearly the same force as in those strata laid bare by etymology and by metaphorics.)

---

[4] This situation clashes with the Renaissance use of *arte* for 'practical grammar' of a foreign tongue (P. de Alcalá), including those of the New World; there *arte* connotes 'skill', 'training', i.e., a body of knowledge and a measure of thoroughly communicable deftness — in contrast to the nimbus of uniqueness surrounding the preponderantly modern concept of art. Artistry and artfulness in etymology are distinct from the artistic pose, which may serve as an excuse for pyrotechnics or licentiousness; cf. E. Gamillscheg, "Zur Methodik der etymologischen Forschung", *ZFSL*, L (1927), 216–298.

## 7. Etymology and the changing climates of linguistic research.

The intensity with which etymology is cultivated may, then, be expected to depend on the general climate of linguistic research in a given environment. It seems almost platitudinous to state that a broad proclivity to historicism (whether romantically tinged, as in the early nineteenth century, or adorned with the trappings of evolutionary theory, as after Darwin) fundamentally favors etymology, whereas a heightened concern with description, specifically with distribution, at the expense of diachronic probings, tends to retard it. The reality is far more complicated, since the peaks of historical grammar and those of etymological exploration rarely coincide.

Granted the impact of *Zeitgeist*, one ventures to predict, for our own time, a dual effect on etymology of that mathematical styling which has in recent years become a hallmark of the social sciences at their most ambitious: Attempts to press etymological research into the mould of mathematical formulae (the positive reaction to the new current) are periodically balanced by spells of completely reckless impressionism playing havoc with those ingredients of rationalism which have so far given etymology a semblance of scientific respectability. For a telling instance of such statistical and mathematical inroads cf. A. S. C. Ross's booklet *Etymology, with Especial Reference to English*, and its rather trenchant appraisal by W. P. Lehmann (*Lg.*, XXXV [1960], 351–353); É. Benveniste's parallel assessment (*BSLP*, LIV: 2 [1959], 40 f.) was couched in ironic terms. Some Continental journals still abound with examples of the countertendency, the playful attitude toward the study of lexical origins, almost on the level of genteel entertainment.

Structural linguistics and etymology are not incompatible in their logical foundations; but the emotional subsoils that have, at different periods and in different places, nourished the growth of each seem indeed to have tended to make them mutually exclusive. One thinks of several linguists who have distinguished themselves in structural analysis (brought to bear, e.g., on comparative Indo-European, on Slavic, on Romance, on Dravidian, on American Indian) and who have, at the same time, refused to turn their backs on etymology. Their data have been very neatly filtered through stringent phonemic analysis.[5] But there has, to my knowledge, never occurred a true

---

[5] Some notable examples of continued etymological curiosity on the part of scholars committed to structuralism: R. Jakobson's substantial review, in several instalments, of M. Vasmer's *Russisches Etymologisches Wörterbuch* and his earlier

fusion, a complete integration of the two disparate skills, or, by way of alternative, any clear delimitation. In extreme cases one is reminded of those by no means uncommon scientists who in their spare time are virtuoso violinists or almost professional portrait-painters.

**8. Etymological universals?** Can one legitimately speak of universals in etymology? In such a context, this term would not, of course, mean 'recurrent patterns of changes in meaning', a problem which has its place in diachronic semantics; still less 'patterns of change in form'. More defensible would be the use of "universal" in reference to high predictability of lexical contamination, or of deflection from regular phonetic change in response to sound symbolism, playfulness, "expressivism", and the like — designations which directly affect the very kernel of etymological research; still, one might be in doubt whether such matters do not come more appropriately under the heading "linguistic change". An irreducibly etymological universal, on the other hand, would be a recurrent degree of genetic transparency.

Thus, in numerous languages the — parallel or discrepant — words for 'boy' and 'girl' show not only an unusual rate of attrition (incidentally, for slightly different reasons), but also an alarming degree of etymological intricacy: E. *boy*, F. *garçon*, Sp. *muchacho*, OSp. *mancebo*, Ptg. *moço* and *menino*, to adduce a few examples out of hundreds,[6] have all long baffled seasoned etymologists and involve,

---

[6] Aside from A. Sperber's pilot study (1911), the key monograph, especially for Gallo-Romance and Italian, remains I. Pauli, *'Enfant', 'garçon', 'fille' dans les langues romanes* (Lund, 1919). Though essentially a "travail de patience", it provoked weighty reviews, identifiable through Hall's bibliography, by experts (A. Wallensköld and O. J. Tallgren [-Tuulio], E. Tappolet, L. Spitzer, A. Castro, G. Rohlfs, W. von Wartburg, L. Jordan); cf. Rohlfs, *AR*, VIII (1924), 161–166. On *boy* see E. J. Dobson, *MÆv.*, IX (1940), 121–154. There has recently been no uncertainty about the Frankish provenience of *garçon*, but authorities disagree as to the specific base. OSp. Ptg. *moço* has been another apple of discord; note that J. Corominas, *DCE*, III [1956], 463b–465b, seriously questions the widely accepted etymon MUSTEU 'musty, fresh' and toys with reverting to Schuchardt, Baist, and García de

lexical studies buttressing his dating of the *Igor' Song*; M. B. Emeneau's *Dravidian Etymological Dictionary* (1961, in coöperation with T. Burrow), as a sequel to his descriptive research in Kota and Kolami; M. R. Haas's articles on the Proto-Gulf and Proto-Hokan-Coahuiltecan words for 'water', *IJAL*, XVII (1951), 71–79 (cf. the comment ibid., XXIII, 7) and *UCPL*, X (1954), 57–62; W. Bright's incisive Indianistic study in Californian animals of acculturation (ibid, IV: 4), cf. *RPh.*, XIV (1960–61), 360 f.; and the astonishing diapason of É. Benveniste's inquiries, reminiscent of Sapir's.

at least in some recalcitrant details, problems still unsolved. Another scaling of this kind may be carried out with the names of domestic animals: In the Romance domain those of the females ('nanny goat', 'cow', 'mare', etc.) display an incomparably higher rate of preservation and concurrent etymological translucency than those of the corresponding males (both reproductive and castrated) and of the young.[7] In either case the socio-cultural matrix is to a higher degree responsible for this special lack of transparency than are purely linguistic conditions. Any parallel appeal to interjections may be summarily dismissed with the remark that these take us to the very periphery of grammar and lexicon. A distinctly more promising avenue of approach is Meillet's observation — based on inspection of paleo-IE material — to the effect that adjectives offer a far greater proportion of etymological complications than, say, equally abstract verbs. The Romance languages confirm this suspicion, and if it receives substantial support from other sources, we may come close to identifying, at least, one tendential etymological universal.

**9. Typology of etymological studies.** A not unwelcome touch of stringency can be added to etymological research through use of the typological approach. Thus, by resorting to a technique of analysis known as "typology of the genre" one can resolve the overwhelming majority of etymological studies, kaleidoscopic as they appear at first glance, into certain more or less fixed categories. One such experiment (*IJAL*, XXIII [1957], 1–17; reprinted in this book, 199–227) was conducted as follows: The multitude of possible fruitful approaches were broken down according to three major criteria: (a) the varying scope of the inquiries; (b) the kind and amount of material adduced as evidence; (c) the inherent degree of simplicity of each problem at issue (cf., in the present article, the statement on transparency in the preceding section). The order of these three criteria may be freely inverted, and the possibility of introducing others of equal rank remains open. Application of the first criterion allows one to set off: (a) the entry in an etymological

---

[7] One thinks of Sp. *chivo* 'kid', *garañón* 'stud jackass' (Am.-Sp. 'stallion'), *jato* 'calf'; It. *becco*, and the like.

---

Diego's minority view. Possibly the latest statement on the suffix of *much-*, orig. *moch-acho* is found in *Lg.*, XXXV (1959), 215–224, esp. n. 75. *Sp. niño* and Ptg. *menino* may be congeners, but what of *me-*? It. *ragazzo* need not be onomatopœic, but certainly resists analysis.

dictionary (of variable size, specificity, styling, etc.); (b) the short etymological note (a bit of independent gleaning, a shred of supplementary information, a trial balloon), (c) an item culled from a historical grammar's mosaic of etymological equations; (d) the by-product of some such philological venture as the edition of a text studded with lexical difficulties; (e) a middle-sized self-contained etymological study; (f) a major article or full-blown monograph, which in turn may alternatively stress (α) the origin and early development of a single word, with emphasis on the fluctuating semantic ambit; (β) the specific evolutionary anomaly identified as the crux of a unique difficulty; (γ) the clustering of several etymological problems, typically around a noteworthy historical situation; (δ) the dyadic or triadic arrangement of etymological problems as a result of such purely linguistic situations as lexical polarization and serialization (for additional data see *ArL*, IX [1957], 79–113, esp. 103 ff., and X [1958], 1–36); (ε) the impact of homonymy; (ʒ) the array of (near-)synonyms, especially that kind of cross-dialectal synonymics which reached its crest in the *inter bella* variety of "onomasiology" (cf. B. Quadri's survey of 1952), entirely unrelated to onomastics as currently understood.

One can establish, in comparable detail, some kind of scale or gradient of etymological researches on the basis of the two remaining criteria. The conceivable crowning achievement of this approach — unfortunately, omitted from the tentative survey ten years ago — might be a complete integration of the three analyses: Does there (or, at least, should there ideally) exist a close correlation, describable in specific terms, between scope, material, and degree of intricacy? Such a final balance-sheet would not only cut a path through the maze of the etymological output, but serve as a frame of reference (by way of encouragement and of deterrent) for future planning.

**10. Typology of problems and of solutions.** Distinctly richer in prospects is a typology of etymological problems and of their successive analyses; the sketchy presentation in *Lingua* V: 3 (1956), 224–252 (reprinted in this book: pp. 229–256), with its emphasis on a single intrinsic discrepancy ("uniqueness vs. complexity"), provides little more than a foretaste of this classification. Any protracted etymological debate can be epitomized in, at least, two fashions:

(a) In straight annalistic manner, as a zigzagging narrative, with full attention to each new conjecture and to each fresh facet of an old conjecture newly championed as well as to the miscellaneous reactions such proposals elicit, until the problem has either been solved through a consensus, or, if the discussion grows sterile, been shelved pending the discovery of some new decisive piece of evidence. This approach ordinarily takes notice of the "human element", the drama pervading the debate, and is thus at the farthest conceivable remove from austere scientific styling;[8]

(b) With the material and the matching ideas grouped in more abstract, analytical fashion around the major solutions — provided one rigorously subordinates all interludes. The bases advocated may, but need not, follow a strictly chronological line; if they do, that line is either a string of the exact dates of formal scholarly identifications, or a sequence of the approximate dates when assumed bases emerged in actual speech. As an alternative to historicism in either garb, the hypotheses could be arrayed on the basis of source language, word family, derivational structure, semantic background, or degree of plausibility.[9]

From this less narrative, more interpretive treatment one arrives (as the 1956 article failed to make sufficiently clear), by deliberate trimming — omission of such conjectures as are of merely antiquarian interest or mark a step backward —, at the actual "nucleus of the problem", frequently a restatement of some irreducible dilemma.[10] Essentially, this sifting of opinions and narrowing-down of choices represents a preliminary analysis, through injection of value judgments. Further gradual schematization allows the analyst so to simplify a highly complex state of affairs as to have on hand a mere residual formula symbolizing the farthest advance short of the so far unachievable break-through. He can then proceed to categorize the various types of impasses: genuine alternatives, specious alternatives, instances of admittedly complete ignorance, examples of a single preference still insufficiently substantiated and of hesitation between three or more partially acceptable solutions.

It seems equally rewarding to build up a separate typology of

---

[8] Cf. my Luso-Hispanic studies of *albricias* '(reward for) good news', *SPh.*, XLIII (1946), 498–521, esp. 499–504; *asperiega*, Carol. *sperauca* 'species of apple', *PhQ*, XXVIII (1949), 294–311, esp. 295–298, 308–310; *despedir* 'to dismiss', refl. 'ask leave', *UCPL*, XI (1954), 40–42, 155–157; *lozano* 'proud, exuberant, verdant' and Ptg. *trigar-se* 'to hasten', ibid., I: 7, 244–267, 283–288.

[9] Cf. my studies of Sp. *lerdo* 'dull, slow', *PhQ*, XXV (1946), 289–302, esp. 289–292, and OSp. *maznar* 'to knead', *MLR*, XLIX (1954), 322–330, esp. 323–325.

[10] Cf. my study of OSp. *cuer* ~ *coraçón* 'heart' (the latter orig. *'heartburn') in *BH*, LX (1958), 180–207, 327–363, esp. 195–197.

ultimately successful solutions, distinguishing between (a) clarifications achieved through outside help (e.g., through discovery of unsuspected raw facts), (b) satisfactory compromises between earlier not quite acceptable proposals, and (c) fruitful mergers of two different techniques of analysis, each inadequate if used in isolation.

**11. The graded approach.** Haphazard as may be the sequence of the actual flashes of etymological thought, one need not report them in such capricious succession; nor is it customary to proceed quite so impatiently. However, the currently favored alternative to haphazardness, namely assembling etymologies in alphabetical order, has equally limited usefulness: Though it facilitates casual consultation, it fails to highlight the actual drama of etymological probings and, in particular, to identify the fluctuating front-line. For all its unquestioned practicality as a reference tool, the etymological dictionary, viewed as a scholarly enterprise, reminds one of the phonological section of an old-style historical grammar, in which the individual sound correspondences were established tidily enough to enable the philological reader to classify cogently any manuscript at issue along the two axes of time and space, but which consistently neglected the interaction of the shifts expertly identified. One way of presenting etymologies in a significant sequence likely to stimulate further research is to arrange them roughly in a line of increasing complexity — on the basis, as it were, of the presumable number of unknowns; an appended alphabetic index may then provide the necessary references. Such an experimental array, suggested in *Word*, VI (1950), 42–69, was not meant to be binding on anyone, not even on its proponent, so that its acrimonious rejection by the ranking advocate of free-wheeling practice (L. Spitzer in *RF*, LXXII [1950], 227–234) was quite unjustified. In reality, the opposite pole to the policy of gradualism is represented by a deliberate concentration on the most rebellious, hence titillating problems, as when J. Hubschmid tends to by-pass the Latin layer of Romance in favor of the vastly less accessible substratal bases; for criticism, see my review of two monographs of his in *Lg.*, XXXVIII (1962), 149–185.

**12. Etymology and diachronic structure.** The cornerstone of the entire edifice of etymological theory is the paradox that this area of knowledge, though an inalienable part of lexicology, owes its prime distinction to its conspicuously close ties with diachronic grammar. While in the descriptive perspective structure and lexicon, despite certain points of contact and even an occasional overlap, lend themselves to neat separation, the language historian in his daily work finds them inextricably interwoven. This intimate relation is not the least striking peculiarity of all manner of glottodynamics, as against all, or nearly all, static approaches to language. Numerous specific problems of theory and practice flow from this general situation.

**12.1. Estrangement between etymology and grammar.** No historical grammar can boast any measure of usefulness unless its smallest constituent elements — the etymological equations — have been painstakingly refurbished. In the classical age of historical linguistics this truism posed no serious problem, since the same experts worked — often almost simultaneously — on grammatical and on lexical projects; witness Grimm, Meillet, Ernout; or, for that matter, Diez and Meyer-Lübke. In recent decades, however, the liaison has slackened, with the result that the grammarian may deem himself exempt from the obligation of keeping abreast of etymological advances. Among the preponderantly severe reviews of Vols. I–II of M. Regula's ill-fated historical grammar of French (1955–56) K. Baldinger's was even more enlightening than those emanating from structuralistic quarters, disclosing as it did that the book's author, not only conservative but, for good measure, slipshod, was sorely vulnerable on his own ground (see *ZPh.*, XI [1958], 282–288; cf. *RPh.*, XIV [1960–61], 361 f.).

The harmful gap between etymology and grammar began to widen thirty to forty years ago through a fatal coincidence: While leading lexicologists apparently felt that old-style grammar, especially if applied to the more familiar languages, had nearly exhausted its possibilities (which was almost true), that there was little point in further experimenting with grammatical material except possibly in derivation and syntax (which was patently untrue), and that new factual (i.e., in this context, etymological) insights alone could lead to eventual progress (at best, a one-sided decision), the die-hard grammarians, attacking preferably languages hitherto unsurveyed, were quick to establish the reverse scale of values and priorities.

**12.2. The varying impact of etymology on branches of grammar.** The diachronic interpenetration of etymology and grammar is

o

not evenly distributed over the entire expanse of the latter. It reaches its maximum intensity in certain divisions of phonology and in that broad province of morphology which has been variously labeled as derivation or word-formation, embracing both affixation and composition. It is less apparent throughout inflection — though it clearly matters to the student of Spanish conjugation whether OSp. *troçir* 'to pass' reflects TRĀDŪCERE (*NRFH*, X [1956], 385–393), how reliable is the connection with OSp. *deçir*, Ptg. *de(s)cer* 'to descend' claimed variously for DĒSIDERE, DĒCIDERE, DĒICERE, DISCIDERE, and DISCĒDERE (cf. *Lingua*, V, 229 f.), or just what is the prototype of *asir* 'to grasp' and *(de)rretir* (Ptg. *-er*) 'to thaw, melt' — given the severely limited vitality of the local *-er* and *-ir* classes. Syntax and etymology share fewer interests, though one can point out an occasional encroachment. Thus, J. Jud's brilliant demonstration, with the aid of a Raeto-Romance congener, that OF *estovoir* 'to be necessary' derives, in the last analysis, from EST OPUS (*VR*, IX [1946–47], 29–56), the cleavage of L. FALLERE 'to deceive' into F. *falloir* 'to be necessary' and *faillir* 'to err, be on the point of' (beside Sp. *fall-ecer*, orig. *-ir* 'to run out, decease') and the transmutation of CAPERE 'to seize, catch' into Sp. Ptg. *caber* 'to be contained in', cf. LACERĀRE 'to tear' > OSp. *laz(d)rar* 'to suffer hardships', CONDĪRE 'to season' > Sp. *cundir* 'to spread, swell, multiply' (intr.), all five bear on such fundamentally syntactic problems as personal vs. impersonal or transitive vs. intransitive construction in provincial Latin and Romance.

The link with historical semantics is so self-explanatory as to require no documentation — a decision possibly the more welcome as the field rules for the formulation of semantic change are in process of reorganization; cf. in particular É. Benveniste, *Word*, X (1954), 251–264. This link must be scrupulously distinguished from etymology's miscellaneous intrusions upon the territory of synchronic semantics — via either folk etymology or, less familiar, the artistic reinforcement of fading etymological connections (S. Ullmann, *Précis de sémantique française* [Berne, 1952], pp. 115–120). An additional line of inquiry, dear to E. Lerch and programmatically stated by G. Gougenheim,[11] would be the systematic search for erroneous learned adjudication in matters etymological, a search presupposing an antiquarian curiosity akin to that which presides over mosaic reconstructions of etymological debates (see Section 10, above). At the intersection of the semanticist's and the antiquarian's lines of

---

[11] "La fausse étymologie savante", *RPh.*, I (1947–48), 277–286.

thought one might place the procedure of a poet so learned as to have tendentially included, in his quest for elegant ambivalence, the favored key-words' etymological meaning as one of their many splendors, but neither so well-informed as to have selected a truly up-to-date guide to word origins, nor technically expert enough to have made forceful decisions of his own in the face of erudite controversy. Paul Valéry is rumored to have been one such poet, ever in the throes of etymological anguish;[12] if this report is correct, his hidden etymologizing would be on a par with Flaubert's Carthaginian archeology, Rimbaud's evocation of tropical South America (known to him solely from hearsay and readings), and Tolstoy's logistics.

**12.3. Need for continued momentum of etymological research.** Those linguists who view etymology with a jaundiced eye sometimes question its usefulness beyond the collection of a small sampling of equations needed to establish the all-important phonetic correspondences. This indifference may be countered with two arguments. First, the edifice of phonology can be improved both through refinement of method (the currently fashionable approach) and through continued expansion of factual knowledge (here etymology acts as a powerful cutting wedge which the trained linguist deftly drives into layers of unknown material). Second and more important, even the staunchest "regularists" admit that an original phonetic correspondence — inferrable, e.g., from the total sound pattern — may have been locally overlaid on a considerable scale, sometimes to the point of shrinkage.[13] If such an abnormal situation — by no means infrequent — has crystallized, then the last haul of painstakingly established etymologies may constitute, not some unexciting aftermath merely confirming or further specifying earlier findings, but the first direct clue to an earlier radically deviant stage so far adumbrated only through circumstantial evidence.

---

[12] He was ill-advised enough, I understand, to select Clédat as his etymological mentor. For an appraisal, in critical retrospect, of A. Henry's *Langage et poésie chez Paul Valéry* (1952) and of scholarly reactions to that book see Fred M. Jenkins' forthcoming contribution to the review section of *RPh*. Rilke, in his correspondence, admitted consulting Grimm's *DW* for translation purposes, but his lexicon (unlike George's and particularly unlike Borchardt's) remained consistently free from deliberate archaisms of form, let alone allusions to obsolete meanings.

[13] One relentless champion, for almost twenty years, has been R. A. Hall, Jr.; see, in particular, *It.*, XXIII (1946), 31 f. (n. 5) and *RPh.*, XV (1961–62), 234–244.

**12.4. Overlap between grammar and etymology.** Between the domains of historical grammar and of etymology there exists a sizable, possibly ineradicable overlap. Decisions as to whether a set of problems merits discussion under the one or the other head affect the economy of research and thus become an essential part of long-range planning (cf. *RPh.*, VIII [1954–55], 187–208). There are two reasons for this tangle.

On the one hand, to the extent that interpretive historical grammar moves away from mere cataloguing and that numerous minute facts refuse to fall into the vitally important broad patterns, the residue created by this hierarchization tends to form a kind of no-man's land. Countless phonological details thus dislodged from their former niches in footnotes and small-print sections (as still predominant in Grandgent's *From Latin to Italian* [1927]) are of potentially greatest interest to the etymologist. Thus, the progressive author of a historical Romance grammar, to avoid miring in irrelevant details, may fully list the sharply silhouetted development of stressed Latin vowels — few and each copiously represented — but merely exemplify prevalent trends where the extraordinary variety of secondary consonant clusters is involved. True, of those newly learned by speakers some were neatly predictable from the total pattern (e.g., -*xtr*- [*štr*] as in OSp. *yxtré* 'I shall go out', from *exir*, cf. -*mbr*-, -*ndr*-, etc.). But other examples of secondary contiguity (say, OSp. -*zd*-, -*zl*-, -*zr*-, -*zt*-) display both an unusual configuration and an extremely low incidence; speakers, apparently reluctant to acquire a neuro-muscular skill of such scant usefulness, resorted to an astounding range of devices to lighten their burden,[14] with the result that regularity of sound change reached its nadir.

On the other hand, the etymologist again and again encounters minor but obnoxious stumbling blocks — e.g., puzzling developments of sounds or affixes — for which he cannot, with a clear conscience, refer his reader to any standard historical grammar. What is he to do? He may limit himself to hinting briefly at a similar

---

[14] For a detailed discussion of L. -CER- > OSp. -*zr*-, apropos of LACERĀRE 'to tear to pieces' and MĀCERĀRE 'to soak', see *NRFH*, VI (1952), 209–276, and *MLR*, XLIX (1954), 322–330. On the importance of relative yield I find myself in agreement with Martinet. There exists, of course, no direct ratio between yield and regularity, since the total sound pattern exercises its share of controlling influence, occasionally making an infrequent sound shift astonishingly firm. But given equality of all conditions (including qualitative suitability), a sound shift common in terms of lexical representation and of incidence stands a good chance of scoring a high degree of regularity.

difficulty identified in another word — a lightness of touch which leaves the problem slightly widened, but still unsolved (this practice seriously vitiates Spitzer's conjectures); or he may inflate his dictionary, if such is the form of his project, with long-winded phonological discussions under the one favored entry and later provide a few cross-references, a solution adopted by Corominas (1954–57) and amounting to a scattered grammar concealed within a dictionary. Gilliéron's idea of supplying a string of supplements or excursuses, as he did in his "genealogical" monograph on the Gallo-Romance names of the bee (1918), may, on balance, be more felicitous, except that such discussions need not be relegated to the very end: All that matters is to set them off with maximum tidiness, to ease the reader's strain and to catch the eye of some future grammarian.[15] This preference implies that the proper place for microscopic etymological inspection should be the article or the monograph rather than the dictionary, which ought to be returned to its proper size and rôle of a mere inventory of succinctly classified and documented forms, and an accurate guide to pertinent discussions.

**12.5. "Weak" phonetic change, sporadic sound shift, lexical contamination.** The relation between etymology and phonology may be expressed in terms far more intimate than those suggested by tactical or strategic considerations. There is a strong possibility that the very frequency or degree of etymological opaqueness may to some extent depend on internal phonological conditions. Suppose some sound disappears consistently in the west, survives almost invariably in the east, and exhibits an erratic record of persistence in the center of a given territory, as is, e.g., true — except for one detail — of Latin primary intervocalic -D- in the Iberian peninsula (short of the Catalan zone; see *Lg.*, XXXVI [1960], 284–290). Presumably old dialect mixture (due to successive political reapportionments of the area?) accounts for the instability in the center.

---

[15] In retrospect I find my own earlier performance heavy-handed, cf. the long paragraphs (a) on patterns of vowel dissimilation in the study of OSp. *re-*, *sa-codir* (*HR*, XIV [1946], 133–135) and (b) on the alternation of OSp. [dz] ~ [ž] apropos of *cosecha* (*Lg.*, XXIII [1947], 389–398, esp. 393–397). For later examples of chapters or sections so clearly marked off as to make them easily transferrable to grammatical terrain, see the discussion of *s(s)* ~ *ç* (210–222) in the paper on OSp. *assechar* 'to stalk' (*HR*, XVII [1949], 183–232) and comparably placed statements on the wavering between *per-*, *por-*, *pro-*, and *pre-* (*RPh.*, III [1949], 27–72, esp. 61–67) and on the sources of the cluster *-ld-* (*EDMP*, I [1950], 91–124, esp. 102–121).

Be that as it may, predictability is so low in the transitional territory as to entitle us, irrespective of the historical explanations advanced, to posit a "weak" phonetic law. One may now plausibly make this surmise: (a) Such a state of low predictability of regular phonetic change, aside from actually entailing specific vacillation (*crúo* ~ *crudo*, *nío* ~ *nido*, etc.), creates, in regard to this feature, a general climate of insecurity which (b) invites an extra-heavy proportion of lexical blends (associative interference), and (c) concurrently stimulates, outside the pale of regular phonetic change, those more or less latent sound shifts which have long been known as "sporadic" or "spontaneous" (haplology, metathesis, dissimilation other than in contact, etc.).[16] Clearly, each of these three discrete forces viewed in isolation would of itself tend to obscure a word's provenience. If a statistical demonstration can some day actually gauge the mutual attraction and consequent reinforcement between the three, the integration of etymology with the core disciplines of historical grammar will have taken a major step forward.

What increases the plausibility of such interaction is the fact that it provides the missing link which at once straightens out numerous, at first glance disconnected, difficulties. One is predisposed to link Sp. *peldaño* 'step (of a staircase)' to PEDĀNEU 'pertaining to the foot', but the epenthesis of -*l*-, viewed out of context, is baffling (this circumstance makes the analysis in *AGI*, XXXVI [1951], 49–74, seem incomplete, despite the profusion of details). The link between OSp. *vedegambre* 'poison' and MEDICĀMINE appears at first glance self-evident, but why has *\*medegambre* left no easily detectable traces, while among the syncopated variants *megambre* visibly flanked *vegambre* 'id.' (free alternation of initial labials)? The closer one inspects Sp. *calavera* 'skull', fig. 'madcap', the more one is perplexed as to which of its two obvious ingredients, CADĀVER 'carcass' or CALVĀRIA 'scalp', constitutes the irreducible base, and which merely the contaminator. A dozen or more such convergent ramifications of problems arouse one's suspicion that the weak comportment of the -*d*- was a prime factor in activating the two other categories of shifts.

---

[16] For a more fully developed preliminary statement see my contributions to (a) the *A. W. de Groot Testimonial* ("Weak Phonetic Change, Spontaneous Sound Shift, Lexical Contamination"), reprinted in this book (pp. 33–75), and (b) the *Mélanges M. Bataillon*, a Franco-Brazilian venture ("Etimología y cambio fonético débil: la trayectoria iberorrománica de MEDICUS, MEDICĪNA, MEDICĀMEN"), in *Ibérida*, VI (1961 [–63]), 127–171. See also the second essay in the present volume.

## 12.6. Non-cultural concomitants to learned transmission.

Whether or not the application of this principle may lead to sensational discoveries, its chief merit so far lies in strengthening our grasp of fundamentals. It takes only a modest training to discern the "learned" character of Sp. *dulce* 'sweet' as against Ptg. *doce*, It. *dolce*, F. *doux*, etc., all of them outgrowths of L. DULCE; but a cogent account of this regional departure requires sophistication. To be sure, DULCIS, -E, with its rich spectrum of connotations, occupied a place of honor in Church Latin, but why should that common matrix of Western medieval culture have at this point unequally influenced Romance vernaculars so closely akin? The discovery of inconspicuous Old Spanish by-forms (*doz, duz, dulz*, etc.) and the realization that the development of Latin syllable-final L precisely in Proto-Spanish was erratically tripartite (loss ~ shift to semi-vowel ~ preservation), thus entailing a very weak phonetic change, jointly alert us to the possibility of a speech community's escape from protracted wavering through adoption of a fixed prestige form. This therapeutic explanation echoes Gilliéron's earlier contention that French occasionally appealed to Latinisms to solve homonymic conflicts, or that, under analogous conditions, standard French words evicted patois formations in rural speech.

## 12.7. Etymology and derivation.

There exists a comparably intricate set of relationships between etymology and derivation. An unusual affix, especially if known to have long been unproductive, may be the safest clue to an etymological crux, cf. Sp. *pendencia* 'quarrel' < POENIT-ENTIA '[loud] repentance' (*RR*, XXXV [1944], 307–323), OSp. *cans-a(n)cio*, Ptg. *cans-aço* 'fatigue' < QUASS-ĀTIŌ 'break-down' (× CAMPSĀRE 'to dodge') and OSp. *posfaçar* 'to mock', OGal. *pos-faz* 'mockery' < POST FACIEM (RĪDĒRE) '(to laugh) behind one's face' (*RPh.*, III [1949–50], 27–72). Conversely, a paucity of tell-tale derivatives isolates the word etymologically and may critically retard its classification; in Indo-European this liability affects most primary conjunctions and prepositions and many pronouns (cf. *Word*, X [1954], 265–274).[17]

[17] The coexistence of significant variant forms ordinarily favors the etymologist, while their lack impedes him (cf. Sp. Ptg. *tomar* 'to take' < ?; F. *tirer*, It. *tirare* 'to draw', Sp. Ptg. *tirar* 'to throw, fling, draw' < ?), though there is no dearth of richly diversified lexemes awaiting etymological clarification (e.g. OSp. *combr-*, *combl-ueça*, Ptg. *comborça*, etc. 'concubine'). Can one draw chronological conclusions from the protracted coexistence of variants neither regionally nor semantically diversified?

To serve as a guidepost, the affix need not be exceptional per se; what matters most is the aberrancy of its relation to the root morpheme. Thus, the -*a* of Sp. *burr-a* 'she-ass', fig. 'drudge', *perr-a* 'bitch' neither poses a genetic problem nor sheds any light on the disputed ancestry of *burr-o*, *perr-o*; but *mentir-a* 'lie', involving the same desinence uniquely joined to an infinitive, displays a potentially revealing pattern (*RPh.*, VI [1952–53], 121–172; for additional examples, see *Word*, X, 269 ff.).

**12.8. Summits of grammatical and of etymological research.** Since progressively less gross phonetic correspondences are established by increasingly microscopic inspection of "residues", it is natural that the most refractory items, which invite the closest etymological examination, should mainly claim the attention of that generation of scholars which follows upon the creators of monumental grammatical syntheses. It is equally understandable that such a generation, not necessarily of epigones, should tend to develop radically different study habits and gamuts of taste. In Romance scholarship, the leading dialect geographers, through a noteworthy twist of events half a century ago, assumed the collateral responsibility for the etymological aftermath. This activity, of which they brilliantly acquitted themselves, sensitized them to the multiple cross-connections between (to quote Bally) language and life, but, psychologically, blunted their curiosity about structure — since their task was to react against extremes of neogrammatical schematization and isolationism — and, as a result, thwarted any possibility of their fruitful coöperation with the new schools of structuralists.

**13. Logical implications of etymology.** Despite one's misgivings about the approach to word origins via mathematics, one discerns some undeniable contacts between logic and etymology. Here are a few random illustrations.

---

Some cautious inferences as to fairly recent coinage or, at least, reshaping are perhaps admissible, especially if one part of a given paradigm clashes with the remainder, relatively free from such oscillations; cf. such ill-delimited syncopated futures as OSp. *porré*, *porné*, *pon(d)ré*, beside root morphemes of other tenses of *poner* leveled to the point of monotony. It behooves, then, the student of inflection rather than the etymologist to conduct the initial experiments along this not unpromising line.

**13.1. Ambiguities hidden in uniquely correct equations.** Not only is an etymological solution unique whatever its complexity, but it may be definitively correct despite our temporary or permanent inability to give unequivocal account of one or more evolutionary stage(s). Thus, the genetic link between, on the one hand, PECTORĀLE 'pertaining to the chest' and, on the other, archaic Sp. *peitral* > Old, Cl., dial. *petral* > Mod. *pretal* '(horse's) breastband' is unassailably certain — the eventual metathesis being due to the influence of descendants of the PREMERE family (*BICC*, IX [1953–55], 1–135) — though it remains arguable whether the latest Latin and the earliest recorded Central Hispanic form can be most effectively bridged by *\*peitoral* (which was actually used in Portuguese) or by *\*peitrale*, or by both, according to the area at issue. If the last-mentioned possibility holds water, then a single word would have split into two which ultimately coalesced.

**13.2. Diverse categories of hypothetical bases and intermediate forms.** In operating with hypothetical bases, scholars have been traditionally satisfied with the rough distinction between recorded and unrecorded forms. Under a single undifferentiated symbol, the asterisk, we tend to subsume (a) items of whose existence we are so firmly convinced as to deem their absence from the record purely accidental (e.g., L. *\*CRĒDENTIA* 'belief', judging from Ptg. *crença*, Sp. *creencia*, F. *croyance*, Rum. *credință*, etc. and against the background of fervent faith characteristic of early Christianity; starred intermediate forms are very frequent in reconstruction) and (b) items whose existence we expressly deny. The latter comprise, inter alia, (α) ideal outcomes of phonological drift — results which some such interference as devious channeling (e.g., learned transmission), morphological leveling, internal lexical association, or diffusion prevented from materializing (NŪRU 'daughter-in-law' > It. *nuora*, not *\*nuro*); and (β) deliberately misleading forms used as a pedagogical foil against which the true development stands out the more sharply (MANU > F. *main*, not *\*men*). A logically preciser notation may distinguish between these two, or even three, possibilities (cf. *Word*, VI, 49–57).[18]

[18] E.g., one asterisk placed at different levels (a subscript star was widely favored in the mid-nineteenth century), or varying constellations of asterisks (\*, \*\*, etc.). While descriptivists have gone overboard in their enthusiasm for newly devised signs and unusual fonts, language historians have displayed undue restraint. True, large capitals are used to set off epigraphic material, small capitals may signal Latin (and

**13.3. New auxiliary constructs: generalizers and standardizers.** To relieve the pressure on the asterisk, and to establish a rapport with the symbolic logicians' uninterpreted forms,[19] one may introduce other constructs. J. Jud, a superb practitioner but, unfortunately, no theorist, launched half-bracketed forms to mark, if one may revert to his own and his peers' terminology, lexical types. Upon closer inspection such forms turn out to function (a) as generalizers, bracketing in non-committal fashion several closely related forms; and (b) as standardizers, replacing one highly special form, not immediately transparent to the outsider, by a variant more readily assimilable, though, strictly, non-existent.

Generalization may be an advantage in dealing (α) with cruxes, as when one subsumes under common denominators like ⌈al(l)are⌉, ⌈tirare⌉, ⌈tomare⌉, ⌈tropare⌉ scattered dialect forms without committing oneself as to specific source language, exact primary meaning, any minor detail of form (⌈tōmāre⌉ or ⌈tŭmāre⌉?), or combinations of these three features.[20] It is further justified as (β) a makeshift designation of a lexical nucleus still unanalyzed but provisionally classed as unified, if one leaves open the possibility of a homonymic tangle (Sp. ⌈cach-⌉: Corominas, *RFH*, VI [1944], 33 f.; ⌈pech-⌉: *Lg.*, XXVIII [1952], 299–338; cf. also *HR*, XXI [1953], 20–36, 120–134). Operating with such uninterpreted bases, the analyst voluntarily suspends judgment on points he deems inessential in this particular context, and thus, besides saving time and effort, avoids the risk of bogging down; he also contracts a debt, because after isolating and quickly by-passing an area of indeterminacy he places himself under the obligation of later redeeming the mortgage.

As a standardizer, the half-bracketed form provides the ideal

[19] See I. M. Copi, "Artificial Languages", in P. Henle, ed., *Language, Thought, and Culture* (Ann Arbor, 1958), pp. 96–120, esp. 102 f.; cf. *IJAL*, XXV (1959), 131.

[20] This use simplifies operations with regional lexical types found in areas of highly diversified dialect speech, such as Franco-Provençal and Raeto-Romance. In all likelihood the divergent minor features mark a recent overgrowth of narrowly local innovations, through which the reconstructionist must blaze a trail. To the historian, then, the half-bracketed form symbolizes a provincial prototype; but synchronically it lends service as some kind of master-key.

---

other ancestral) bases of Romance words, roman boldface marks transliteration, as with Mozarabic. Why not use italic boldface for lexical items culled from glosses, and italic small capitals for numismatic data? We should further restrict the signs > < to strictly phonetic change, introduce → ← for derivation, also devise a set of differently shaped arrows for diffusion, and select symbols less crude and more nuanced than + or × for associative interference. Cf. *RPh.*, XX (1966–67), 190 f.

counterpart, in the standard language, of obscure dialect forms, even if the word at issue happens to have become extinct in the standard or to have at all times been alien to it. Thus, though *dévidoir* ( <OF *des-vuid-oir*, *-eour*) 'skein-winding reel' survives only on the patois level, we may use a legitimate shortcut by contending that at pp. 459 and 478 of Gilliéron's atlas map ∟*dévidoir*˩ and ∟*travouil*˩ overlap.[21] If a tool known in French as *tourn-ette* corresponds to Béarn. ∟*tourn-et*˩ and, in Aveyron, Lozère, Haute-Loire, Ardèche, to ∟*tour*˩, the use of "idealized" rather than actual forms involves an abstraction helping writer and reader to jot down just the one distinctive feature of immediate interest in, say, a suffix study and to disregard all irrelevancies.

**14. Sound symbolism, onomatopœia, expressivism.** These three key terms presumably mark that aspect of etymological research which is fraught with the greatest number of intrinsic difficulties (sometimes called "intangibles"), increased by a heavy accumulation of haziness on the part of generations of analysts. Stringent scholars, thoroughly aware of these forces (Sapir hinted at playfulness in language [1921], Bloomfield's manual dissects symbolic words: § 14.9), have tended to shirk, sidetrack, or postpone their discussion, while imaginative etymologists, from Schuchardt on, may conversely have sinned on the side of overindulgence. This entire range of problems clamors for cool-headed reëxamination, with sharp distinction between absolute and relative sound symbolism (the former based on physiological realities, hence cross-linguistic, as in Jespersen's famous treatment of [i] [1922; cf. Nos. 312 and 316 of his Bibliography]; the latter flexibly geared to specific sound systems), also between primary and secondary expressivism, i.e., a recognizable design which a word may acquire at different stages of its growth.[22] If impressionism and circular reasoning are to be avoided, "expressivism" had best be independently attacked from two angles: (a) the psycholinguistic analysis — possibly with laboratory apparatus — of such sensations as provoke measurably strong reactions (gaudy

---

[21] For details see C. H. Livingston's well-known monograph (1957) and its discussion in *RPh.*, XII (1958–59), 262–282. (It is tempting to go beyond Jud and use the complementary symbols ∟ ˩ for this standardizing function.)

[22] Cf. the contrasting semantic ambits of Sp. *duende* and Ptg. *dondo*, both regularly developed from L. DOMITU 'tamed' (*Homen. A. M. Huntington* [Wellesley, 1952], pp. 361–392). On certain theoretical implications see also the first essay in the present volume.

colors, shrill, loud, or intermittent sounds, circular or zigzagging lines, exceedingly thin or thick bodies), in conjunction with their lexical correlates, such as those surveyed in Jaberg's masterly study of the Portuguese designations of the 'swing' (*RPF*, I [1947], 1–44); (b) a purely linguistic analysis of varying partial deviations from completely non-committal forms (the Geneva School's "arbitraire du signe") via suggestive vocalic gamuts, reduplication of a word's core segments, and the like — provided such geometric configuration fulfills no grammatical requirement (cf. *RLiR*, XXIV [1960], 201–253, esp. 221–233). Psycholinguistics may some day also buttress the unduly discredited domains of onomatopœia (as in evocations of animal cries) and interjection.

**15. Concluding remarks.** Aside from its temporarily forfeited controlling position within linguistics, etymology, deftly handled, is of potentially unlimited appeal to the cultural historian and may thus help liberate the study of language from excessive isolation. A multi-level etymological essay, elegantly phrased and saturated with literary implications (Baroque), such as Jaberg's on the 'birthmark' (*RPh.*, X [1956–57], 307–342), converts even the most militantly indifferent "humanist" to an appreciation of linguistics.

In our curricula formal seminars on etymology, properly organized, could raise a dormant interest to a high pitch of active curiosity. But only at rare intervals do etymological cruxes qualify as thesis subjects, since they present an uncomfortably high concentration of difficulties and presuppose such balanced perspective as can be slowly gained from experience alone.

Will the refinement of etymological theory improve etymological practice? Such a corpus of theory is already in existence, but in disappointingly diffuse, inexplicit form.[23] Rejection of theory as something essentially sterile is not new (a mouthpiece of Goethe's advanced it in his *Faust*, even more articulately in the *Urfaust*). Just as a keen esthetician is not necessarily an overpowering artist, so an etymological theorist need not be the most inspired elucidator of word origins. But at this critical stage in the reorganization of human knowledge, etymology cannot be redeemed without solid theoretical underpinning.

---

[23] Cf. *Etymologica: Festschrift für Walther von Wartburg* (Tübingen, 1958), passim.

# 8

# A Tentative Typology of
# Etymological Studies

## 1. Introduction

NOT only is etymology one of the oldest linguistic disciplines, but some kind of lay curiosity about word origins seems to have everywhere preceded organized research by a margin of millennia. Even if one disregards as scientifically irrelevant the magic, mythical, and allegoric preoccupations with etyma, the remaining corpus of researches is forbiddingly vast. A typology of these studies that would attempt to do equal justice to all such legitimate genres, fashionable slants, and personal styles as are on record can hardly be undertaken without years of preliminary canvassing. The unpretentious sketch here presented, which embodies the outgrowth of a few weeks' thinking and searching, at best aspires to provide a MINIMUM OF TENTATIVE ORIENTATION. It bears thorough revision, with an aim, above all, at more widely spread and more evenly distributed documentation.

The multitude of possible fruitful approaches (only these have I thought worth-while taking here into account) has been broken down, by way of an experiment, according to THREE MAJOR CRITERIA: First, the varying scope of the chosen inquiries; second, the kind and amount of material adduced as evidence; third, the inherent degree of transparency of each problem at issue. The order of these three criteria may be freely inverted. Overlapping, I hope, has been if not entirely eliminated, at least severely reduced. Whether still other systems of typological classification may be successfully introduced into etymology (and, if so, how many and which), I do not undertake to determine at this point. For a while I toyed with the idea of arranging typologically the varying conditions of actual etymological discoveries (chance findings, results of systematic surveys, testing of combinations of sounds, etc.), but abandoned it upon realizing that

Reprinted from *International Journal of American Linguistics*, XXIII (1957), 1–17.

the majority of meritorious workers, for the sake of decorum, have been satisfied with presenting carefully retouched versions of their original drafts, without expatiating on the intuitional or anecdotal side of their labors.

The classification here essayed refers strictly to APPROACHES, not to solutions. Etyma that come up for mention are quoted exclusively for the sake of the technique involved in formally identifying them. Unless the opposite is stated, the bases do not bear any stamp of approval or acceptance, beyond a tacit acknowledgment of respectability. In important respects, then, this essay is the polar opposite of another paper included in the present miscellany, "The Uniqueness and Complexity of Etymological Solutions" (see pp. 229–256, below).

For clarity's sake, a border-line, however thin, must be traced between the domains of etymology proper and of LEXICOLOGY (most scholars make it a point to distinguish the latter, in turn, from LEXICOGRAPHY, the art of compiling dictionaries). Etymology has been traditionally defined as the elucidation of word origins, by means (its modern practitioners would add) of several increasingly rigorous, mutually complementary controls. By virtue of its dependence on phonemic and morphemic transmutations, etymological analysis partakes of historical grammar. To the extent that it heeds the evidence of word histories ("lexical biographies, trajectories"), etymology partially coincides with diachronic lexicology. More specifically, etymological research is coterminous with the inquiry into the incipient phase of a given word history, a phase ordinarily shielded from direct observation ("lexical embryology"). On this assumption, a lexical study (including one historically slanted) that fails to concern itself explicitly with the crystallization of a lexical unit or with its initial penetration into a new speech medium would fall outside the scope of etymology. In contrast, an etymological study is invariably a contribution to lexicology, except that occasionally the full examination of the record may be dispensed with or curtailed (e.g., if the complete material has already been assembled in a generally accessible publication, or if a school of thought prefers to separate the core of the linguistic analysis from the philological or anthropological shell in which the selected forms were found embedded).

## 2. Classification by Scope

Historically the oldest and, until this day, the typical and most widely consulted etymological analysis is the entry found in a representative ETYMOLOGICAL DICTIONARY. Monolingual dictionaries emphasizing etymology (e.g., S. de Covarrubias' *Tesoro* for Spanish, 1611; G. Ménage's *Origines* for French, 1650 and 1694) precede by a wide margin multilingual, i.e., comparative, dictionaries, such as F. Bopp's, for Indo-European (1847), and F. Diez's, for Romance (1853).[1] Midway between these extremes is the dictionary essentially devoted to a single language, but conveying, apropos of congeners, stray bits of information on cognate languages, such as W. W. Skeat's work for English (1882, 1910), from which etymological data may be gleaned on German, Dutch, and Scandinavian, or the revised editions of W. Gesenius' *Hebräisches und aramäisches Handwörterbuch* (e.g., 16th ed. of 1915), with its profusion of collateral forms drawn from other Semitic languages.

The average entry in an etymological reference work may be couched in popular language and still represent the distillation of genuine scholarly research, as is true of F. Kluge's highly readable dictionary for German (including the editions revised by A. Götze), of O. Bloch's and A. Dauzat's, for French (1932 and 1938, respectively, with later revisions in both instances), and of B. Migliorini's, for Italian (1950, 1953). Or the phrasing, though erudite, may be unencumbered by BIBLIOGRAPHY, a level of specificity chosen by A. Ernout and A. Meillet for Latin, particularly in the first two editions of their *Dictionnaire étymologique* (1932, 1939; the 3d ed., of 1951, and the 4th, of 1959–60, refer the reader less sparingly to learned publications). There are other possibilities: Each entry may contain a plain selective bibliography, as in A. Prati's Italian dictionary (1951), or a bibliography reflecting the author's avowed bias, as in the *Indogermanisches etymologisches Wörterbuch* (1949– ) of J. Pokorny (who admits his prejudice against studies operating with laryngeals); or else it may be burdened by a practically exhaustive bibliography, a probably not inaccurate assessment of the apparatus in J. B. Hofmann's revision of A. Walde's Latin dictionary.

A comparable measure of freedom prevails with respect to the SELECTION OF WORDS subjected to scrutiny. The selection may range from very broad to quite narrow, except that the former possibility,

---

[1] Strictly speaking, no historical, let alone etymological, dictionary can be truly monolingual, since, by definition, several time levels are involved. For the sake of convenience, one may attach this imprecise label to such etymological dictionaries as illustrate the convergence of different lexical currents upon a single literary language (say, of Ibero-Basque, Latin, Gothic, Western Arabic, and Amerindian on Spanish).

on the whole, is typical of pioneer works (e.g., Diez's) and the alternative, of their modern counterparts. Further limitation of the stock is possible through explicit or implied concentration on certain ancestral layers (cf. A. de Cihac's segregation of Latin and non-Latin [Hungarian, Turkish, Albanian, etc.] strains in Rumanian, which S. Puşcariu, in 1905, strove to emulate in a dictionary left incomplete; or R. Dozy's and W. H. Engelmann's joint venture in the Hispano-Arabic field), through emphasis on arbitrarily chosen grammatical categories (thus, the torso of R. J. Cuervo's Spanish syntactic dictionary consistently favors verbs, pronouns, and prepositions, never failing to etymologize them), or through confinement to a single regional or social dialect (e.g., G. Rohlfs' Calabrian vocabulary and his dictionary of Modern Greek speech islets in southern Italy).[2]

Each word chosen for succinct etymological identification may be presented in a SEPARATE ENTRY. In languages favoring derivation and composition this procedure, entailing awkward repetition, is characteristic of reference works in which etymological information is distinctly subordinate to other services, e.g., Webster's *New International Dictionary* (2d ed., 1950), of the Spanish Academy Dictionary (18th ed., 1956), of A. Darmesteter, A. Hatzfeld, and A. Thomas' *Dictionnaire général* (1890–93), and of comparably planned standard works. The alternative for the straight etymologist is to group words by LEXICAL FAMILIES, of various degrees of inclusiveness, a course charted by the overwhelming majority of contemporary workers in the Indo-European field. Through use of cross-references some scholars go even one step farther and discuss under a master entry semantically related words of diverse provenience, e.g., names of the weekdays, of the cardinal points, certain mutually conditioned sets of pronouns, and the like. J. Corominas has probably advanced too far along this road of concentration (1954– ).

The entry may VARY IN SIZE, starting from an epigrammatic remark and swelling to monographic proportions, as in W. von Wartburg's monumental thesaurus (1928– ); and within the entry, the space reserved for the etymological discussion may be relatively

---

[2] Infrequently, selective etymologizing serves the opposite purpose of eliminating categories of words deemed irrelevant. This policy M. R. Haas has adopted on a minor scale in her *Tunica Dictionary*, especially as regards borrowings from American-French.

exiguous, as in the laconic comments of the *Thesaurus Linguae Latinae*, or excessive, as in Corominas' discursively phrased dictionary. It also happens that rather detailed and fairly sketchy entries (and the corresponding discussions) alternate, according to the objective intricacy of each problem or to the author's private preferences; E. Gamillscheg's and again J. Corominas' dictionaries are examples in point.

In a monolingual etymological dictionary the BASE may function as the entry, a rarely exploited possibility (W. von Wartburg's dictionary, which at first glance seems to illustrate this architecture, in fact subsumes a wealth of dialect forms under each entry, hence can hardly rank as monolingual); or the PRODUCT acts as the entry, a standard practice for several centuries. If a work is bipartite and bidirectional, both arrangements may be tried out consecutively, cf. the unique pattern which V. García de Diego adopted in 1954. In multilingual etymological dictionaries dealing with a single language family, one expects to find the material listed by inferred prototypes or by the recorded archetypes of an ancestral language. A combination of these two categories is also possible; cf. W. Meyer-Lübke's *Romanisches etymologisches Wörterbuch* (1911–20, 1930–35), whereas G. Gröber's earlier pilot project, a vehicle for Vulgar Latin reconstructions despite its miniature size, is reminiscent of, say, Pokorny's Indo-European dictionary. The pioneers sometimes proceeded differently: Bopp's *Glossarium Sanscritum* (in later editions, titled more graphically *Glossarium comparativum linguae Sanscritae*) consistently started out from Sanskrit words, subordinating to them in rank their IE cognates, a hierarchy no longer recognized. Diez, less understandably, followed suit by recording pan-Romanic words under the corresponding Italian entries. Whichever the sequence preferred, an appended alphabetical index, if competently executed, ordinarily enables the reader to visualize the connections in reverse order.

Given the chronological precedence of the dictionary over the lexical monograph, the ETYMOLOGICAL NOTE, as a genre of scholarly output, originally served the subsidiary purpose of either filling gaps in the latest authoritative dictionary or of proposing conjectures at variance with those advocated by recognized lexicographers. Thus, N. Caix, as a Romanicist, and R. Thurneysen, as a Celticist, were fundamentally content with enriching, elaborating, and critically sifting the information furnished by Diez's dictionary (1853, 1861, 1869–70), to which A. Scheler, an etymologist in his own right known

P

from his research in French, independently provided a formal comprehensive Supplement. C. Salvioni, intimately acquainted with North Italian and Raeto-Romance dialects, and O. Nobiling, at home in more than one sense with (Brazilian-)Portuguese, extended a similar treatment to G. Körting's less meritorious compilation (1891, 1901, 1907). On the Spanish side alone, A. Castro, V. García de Diego (1923), and R. Menéndez Pidal (1920) each went with a fine comb over the original edition (1911–20) of Meyer-Lübke's comparative dictionary. Even more assiduously, M. L. Wagner re-analyzed hundreds of entries pertaining to the Sardinian lexicon in the original as well as in the revised (3d) edition of that same dictionary.

In preference to supplementary notes some etymologists have poured out a great wealth of fresh or revived hypotheses (either impressionistically stated or supported by evidence) in extended BOOK REVIEWS of etymological dictionaries. Among Romance scholars, known for their sympathy with this practice, the technique reached its height some thirty to forty years ago. The crowning accomplishments were possibly the critiques of J. Jud, saturated with felicitous ideas and trenchant formulations. Conversely, the writings of J. Brüch and L. Spitzer slanted in this direction rate, at best, as controversial. A lone American counterpart was the pioneer M. A. Todd's review article.

Another manifestation of this vogue of small etymological gleanings correlated to a major dictionary project has been the PRE-PUBLICATION, as it were, of a discovery. The etymological note was launched as a trial balloon, frequently years ahead of the corresponding entry in a planned dictionary — if that dictionary came at all into existence. C. Michaëlis de Vasconcelos herself, by the colorful titles which she gave to some collections of her notes, characterized them as so many preliminaries to a future Luso-Hispanic dictionary, which she eventually no longer found the strength to write. E. Gamillscheg also had recourse to this preview technique, eliciting from his colleagues criticism from which, in his definitive dictionary (1926–28), he sometimes refused to benefit. Corominas' scattered notes, after the lapse of a few years, logically became the ingredients of his separately published dictionary.

Although crudely manufactured HISTORICAL GRAMMARS did exist long before 1800, the flowering of this particular projection of linguistic facts falls into the period 1850–1915. Since historical phonology (and, to a lesser extent, morphology) may be described as a skillfully arranged mosaic of etymological equations, a few of them upheld or impugned in extended comments, a manual of historical grammar so viewed contains a well-sampled collection of, by and large, irreducibly short etymological notes. (These notes occupy a lower level of abstraction than the respective schemes of sound shifts and of inflectional, derivational, compositional, and syntactic changes.) Some distinguished historical grammars have actually been used over the decades as mines of etymological information, formulaic and denuded of all frills. In a book structured like R. G. Kent's *Old Persian*, which wraps together, in a single handy package, grammar, inscriptional texts, and lexicon, it is even difficult to decide whether the section on phonology or the section on the lexicon contains the greater wealth of etymological nuggets.

What matters most in such context is the weighty etymological DECISION, i.e., the support of one out of two or several rival etymological hypotheses which an authoritative grammarian is willing to throw into the balance. A grammar may also contain a few original lexical solutions; yet, all told, it is unusual for an experienced and versatile scholar to avail himself of a grammatically slanted work as the ideal or the exclusive medium for propounding etymological conjectures. True, exceptions are on record, including É. Benveniste's *Origines* from which Indo-Europeanists, I understand, have culled numerous fresh explanations. Equally rare and, in the long view, uneconomical is the circumstantial treatment of grammatical points in an essentially etymological study, a procedure exemplified by the excursuses in J. Gilliéron's Genealogy of the Gallo-Romance names of the bee and by the very core of H. M. Flasdieck's more recent book-length report on the British street-name *Pall-Mall*. Here the announced project threatens to serve as a mere pretext or façade for an utterly different inquiry.

Given the early and operationally close ties between textual criticism, historical grammar, and etymology (all three occasionally subsumed, and not by laymen alone, under the vague label "philology"), the careful EDITION OF TEXTS has yielded, as a frequent by-product, a harvest of etymological observations. The optimal conditions prevail in the case of ancient languages known almost entirely from a single monument or from a severely limited number of texts.

One can envisage two typical situations. The first involves an etymological GLOSSARY attached to a text or to the collected writings of an author — an arrangement at present out of fashion, since it normally entails casual presentation of etymologies, as in W. Förster's book-length vocabulary to Chrétien de Troyes (an exception, as regards the degree of elaboration, is Menéndez Pidal's masterly vocabulary to the "Cantar de Mio Cid"). For a while, such etymological glossaries were commonly appended to chrestomathies and textbooks, as an aid to beginners, and enjoyed added prestige if the compiler had earned a reputation as an independent worker (C. Voretzsch, J. D. M. Ford). The more recent tendency, a wholesome innovation, has been to disregard etymology completely in such word lists and to concentrate instead on the exact synchronic delineation of meanings, constructions, and paradigms (L. Foulet, C. C. Marden) — a noteworthy parallel to other modern trends favoring minute description in preference to hasty reconstruction.

The second situation involves dubious INDIVIDUAL WORDS, on which the disputed dating, localization, and authorship of a text may hinge. Thus, generations of Slavic scholars (at present, especially R. Jakobson and, among his associates, K. H. Menges) have busied themselves with the etymologies of some intrinsically recalcitrant or insecurely transmitted words peculiar to the Old Russian "Igor' Epic". It is impossible to separate the etymological inquiry into OF *mun(t)joie* (war-cry or religious exclamation) from the painstaking textual interpretation of the "Chanson de Roland", as shown by the studies of L. H. Loomis and of her critics.

If exacting textual criticism demands again and again the etymologist's craft and equipment, neatly edited TEXTS, by way of compensation, provide him with effective tools for his own digging. The bridge between Gr. *makár(ios)* 'blessed, happy', on the one hand, and OPtg. *magar*, OSp. *maguer(a)* 'although', on the other, may appear impassable, but the ingenuous speech of a mountaineer girl, recorded (1034*d*) and stylized by that keen observer Juan Ruiz (ca. 1330), plus our collateral knowledge of conservative Italian usage (*magari*) provide the otherwise unavailable intermediate stages.

The AUTONOMOUS ETYMOLOGICAL NOTE, neither designed to supplement, correct, or announce a dictionary, nor forming part of, or preparatory to, a historical grammar or a glossary, but written for its own sake, arose ca. 1850 and reached its all-time peak a few decades later. Among Romanicists, K. A. F. Mahn may be the earliest devotee of this genre; A. Thomas in France, H. Schuchardt in Austria, and C. Salvioni in Italy were its unsurpassed masters, who created three distinctive styles, and J. M. Piel in Portugal (before his eventual transfer to Germany) beside J. Haust in Belgium have been its most seasoned rearguard strategists. The etymological note purports to solve the problem of a word origin with a minimum display of heavy erudition; its elegance is inherent in its terseness. No attempt is made to piece together the full history of the word; only characteristic glimpses are given (unfortunately, some less than accomplished scholars confuse "characteristic" with "selected at random, so as to favor a solution arrived at a priori"). Almost invariably, the note carries with it a margin of risk; if, at its best, it solves a problem with an admirable economy of means, it remains, at its weakest, a flashy rather than witty piece of writing which, once refuted, evaporates without leaving a trace, since the array of facts it boasted, in all likelihood, was chosen haphazardly, to fit a single whim. The ultimate decay of this genre, as the lexicon of each language becomes more open to historical inspection, is inevitable, in so far as only an insignificant part of the total of word histories may be compressed into a few sentences without loss of vital information. The not too numerous words that lend themselves to this approach are either those exhibiting no major change of meaning, no external influence of associative processes, scarcely any effect of linguistic diffusion (and their etymologies were established long ago in the better-known languages), or words of anecdotal background like *macadam* and *sandwich*.

The modern substitute for obsolete sequences of loosely strung etymological notes has been PLANNED RESEARCH in etymology. Such research, aside from the writing of a dictionary as a life-long project, may assume different forms. The simplest to describe is the full-sized etymological ARTICLE devoted to the origin and early development of a single word, in particular an article calling for plentiful documentation and likely, as a result, to swell to monographic proportions.[3] E. J. Dobson's attempt to place E. *boy* 'churl, servant, (after 1400) male child' in an appropriate social setting, to delimit its fluctuating semantic ambit, and to determine its overtones at successive time levels, with a view to tracing it cogently to A.-Norm. *(em)buié, -boié* 'slave, serf', from *buie* < L. *boia* 'fetter, chain' illustrates this isolative approach at its most conscientious.

---

[3] A separate article may also enter into a specific relation to a dictionary project; thus, W. von Wartburg's study of the Gallo-Romance progeny of L. *albus* 'white' was astutely timed so as to show its readers the advantage of the novel classificatory method which was to preside over the author's current spadework on a new-style dictionary.

Ordinarily it is the fragmentary or otherwise ABERRANT RECORD of a word that cautions the linguist to pause and grant it the benefit of microscopic examination, splitting his attention between the slightest oscillations of form, meaning, and area. Thus, the volume of material which N. Törnqvist amassed in an attempt to analyse G. *Ufer* 'shore', orig. 'slope', as a blurred Germanic compound ($<$ *ô-* + *fê²r*) rather than a unitary cognate of Gr. *'ēpeiros* 'continent', derives its justification from the disquieting absence of the word from Old High German. M. B. Emeneau's etymological curiosity about Proto-Drav. *\*va-* 'to come' and *\*ta-* 'to give, bring' is due to their singular morphological anomaly, attributable to the loss of the so-called transition suffixes *\*-a-* and *\*-ar-* (except in Kui) and to the ensuing mixture of variants according to a formula changing from language to language. The painstaking establishment of an etymology may serve an ulterior purpose, as when M. R. Haas undertakes her meticulous study of the Proto-Gulf word for 'water' preëminently in defense of her own classification of Gulf languages (Muskogean, plus Natchez, Tunica, Chitimacha, and Atakapa), a classification significantly divergent from J. R. Swanton's, M. Swadesh's, and E. Sapir's.

More widely accepted and far more economical in terms of the long-range investment of human resources is the publication of a CLUSTER OF CLOSELY RELATED NOTES, especially those based on first-hand knowledge of the same background, past or present, on the acquaintance with the same group (not necessarily family) of languages, and on the application of the same analysis to the chosen corpus of data (field notes, excerpts from texts preserved, gleanings from dialect maps, etc.). These characteristics apply, at two extremes of a spectrum of tastes, to H. Rheinfelder's inquiry into the Italo-French lay religious vocabulary and phraseology rooted in the Catholic liturgy and to B. E. Vidos' and H. and R. Kahane's researches in the spread of Mediterranean nautical terms (involving probings, aside from Southern Romance, also into Middle and Modern Greek, Anatolian Turkish, Vulgar Arabic, and the lingua franca of seaports). V. Bertoldi's bold studies in the archaic Mediterranean substratum, T. Frings' contributions (in response to Jud's programmatic article of 1914) to Latin-Germanic lexical contacts, and A. Steiger's explorations along the axis Middle and Near East–Western Europe signal the high-water mark of pertinent European specialization. Two of the leading American representatives of this approach have been D. S. Blondheim and W. A. Read, each endowed with an unusual combination of skills: The former, in A. Darmesteter's wake, brought to bear his knowledge of Latin, Old French, and Biblical beside Late Hebrew on the cryptic rabbinical glosses; the latter, without staking out any sweeping claims, in fact launched comparative Caribbean lexicology by setting in motion, from the colonial Mississippi Delta as his operational base, the disparate resources of Louisiana (and Canadian) French, Louisiana Spanish, West Indies Dutch, Haitian Creole, Cherokee, Island Carib, etc.

Refinement in a different direction may be achieved when such etymologically rebellious words as are suspected of interlocking or echoing one another are attacked in PAIRS OR TRIADS or when a whole lexical FAMILY is jointly subjected to stringent, yet imaginative analysis. Thus, Jud, in a brilliantly executed (if not wholly convincing) article, recognized the dual anomaly in the coinage of It. *menzogna*/F. *mensonge* vs. Sp. Ptg. *mentira* 'lie', two deviations from the norm which he was inclined to attribute to a single pattern, twice activated, of analogical interference. The unknowns here were not the root words, but the derivational schemes. Ernout, with an etymologist's flair for detecting and bringing into full view the hidden and the inconspicuous, restored the full semantic range, blurred at the surface, of L. *uenus* 'erotic desire, sexual intercourse', *Venus* 'goddess of love' by focusing not only on the nuclear formation, but on the satellites as well: *uenustus* 'gracious', *uenerius* 'pertaining to physical love', *uenārī* 'to strive for > to hunt', *uenēnum* 'poison', *uenia* 'favor, pardon', etc. Studies in lexical polarization, some of them etymologically motivated, fit quite smoothly into this context.

Apart from folk etymology, homonymy is presumably the most formidable natural enemy of the etymologist. One way of facing its inroads squarely is to select, as the avowed specific object of an etymological experiment, the unraveling of a HOMONYMIC KNOT or tangle. This has been done by many scholars on a variety of scales: tentatively by F. Lecoy and almost casually by J. Corominas with respect to Hisp. *cach-*, yet quite elaborately, long before them, by E. Richter in regard to Romance *bur(d)*.

Between the two World Wars, European continental scholars engaged successfully in the genetic analysis of SYNONYMS and near-synonyms as a focus of lexical research, with special reference to dialect geography. For a while this "onomasiologic" approach, of which B. Quadri has submitted a mid-way appraisal, was contrasted with semasiology, i.e., linguistic (as opposed to philosophical) semantics; conceivably synonymics would have been a less pretentious and more apposite designation. The typical starting point was the map of a linguistic atlas, which, under favorable conditions, offered up to twenty carefully localized and transcribed lexical types, some of them etymologically transparent, others opaque. These latter a trained worker etymologized with the aid of the complicated machinery available for each language; eventually a broad attempt was made to reconstruct the actual sequence of events, in terms of linguistic geology (or paleontology). In this kind of research project, etymology represented a vital link, but solving an equation was scarcely the ultimate goal of each venture. What mattered principally in the end was the emergence of a clear-cut, harmonious lexico-cultural pattern, with special attention paid to the coördinates of time and space. These studies, characteristically titled "The names (or designations) of . . .", were for the most part extended doctoral dissertations, often bearing the hallmark of a formal academic exercise. A few won wide recognition, including E. Eggenschwiler's in the Romance names of the 'bat'.[4] An isolated early counterpart in this country is H. R. Kahane's genetic inventory of the names of the 'cheek' (and, indirectly, of the 'jaw') in Italian dialects, with marginal inclusion of Greek and Germanic bases. The subtlest interpretation of etymologically challenging maps we owe to K. Jaberg, who also excelled in the combined study of lexicology and folk beliefs (witness his article on the 'birthmark'). Exploratory onomasiologic advances beyond the confines of a single language family (ordinarily Romance or Germanic) have been few by comparison; one such daring experiment is C. Tagliavini's inquiry, cutting across Indo-European, Semitic, and North African languages, into the names of the pupil of the eye.

In its most ambitious form, the ETYMOLOGICAL MONOGRAPH follows the trajectory of a single word and its satellites across formidable language barriers and over a period of centuries and even millennia.

---

[4] The rash of these monographs, coinciding with the crest of the vogue of linguistic atlases, seems to be almost over. In the Romance domain one of the latest that has come to my attention is H. Kröll's on the designations of 'drunkenness' in colloquial Portuguese (understandably, an investigation placing heavier stress on metaphors than on etymologies). Perhaps J. Renson's recent massive attack on the Romance (especially the French) designations of the 'face' marks the most luxuriously exhaustive treatment on record, illustrating the method carried to perfection in actual accomplishment, i.e. driven past its peak in promise, challenge, and latent possibilities.

The fortune of this genre is inevitably tied up with the etymologist's grasp of cultural and linguistic diffusion. If more than trivial lacunae remain to be filled in, the resultant itinerary may best be symbolized by a dotted line, as when É. Benveniste traces Class. Lat. *obrussa*, Low Lat. *obryza* 'cupellation of gold', lit. 'earthen container', through Greek to Hittite-Hurri *ḫubrušḫi*, from *ḫabur-*, *ḫubur-* 'earth', via a lost Semitic link; independently, the possibility of Hittite-Greek borrowings also aroused E. Sapir's keen curiosity, though he was even less explicit about the channel. B. Hasselrot's inquiry (a classic of its kind) into the migratory fruit name which ultimately yielded E. *apricot* leads the reader from Imperial Rome via Greece and the Near East (at first Hellenistic, later Arabicized) along the North African coastline and across the Straits of Gibraltar to Spain, and from there, through the Pyrenees, to Paris as a new focal point of pan-European expansion. The infiltration of indigenous New World words such as *Carib*, *cannibal*, and Shakespeare's *Caliban*, into the various European languages throughout the colonial period was the object of P. Henríquez Ureña's stimulating and sensitively phrased reports. Two book-length projects, A. S. C. Ross' intricate reconstruction of the Eurasiatic trajectory of 'ginger' and H. M. Flasdieck's simultaneous pan-European study of 'tin' and 'zinc' (which German pairs off more effectively: *Zinn* and *Zink*) represent an extreme degree of sophistication along this line. A more modest American equivalent would be E. W. Bulatkin's fairly recent scrutiny of the Romance words for 'nuance', a lexical study broadening out, despite its sharp focus, into the history of the Graeco-Romance manufacture of colors and dyes.

Like every genre, the etymological article carries with it certain drawbacks and advantages. Compared with the independent note, it tends to displease the linguistic analyst by the fact that the NUCLEAR PROBLEM of word origins dwindles to a disproportionately small size, becoming the terminal point of a long and sinuous preliminary inquiry: The straight quasi-mathematical analysis appears dangerously diluted. Yet the advantages outweigh this deficiency: While the intuitional conjecture, supported by scant (if any) evidence, is as easily deflated by adverse criticism as a punctured balloon, the profusely documented etymological monograph is resistant, if not entirely immune, to such attacks. Granted that the analysis of the foundation may be marred by an error, the superstructure need not crumble at the first stroke of a pickaxe wielded by a hostile hand (cf.

the unequal value of the chapters in A. Farinelli's account of Sp. *marrano* 'crypto-Jew'). The etymological article, like any other full-scale biography, rarely derives its only value from a definite solution of the problem of parentage.

The chief advantage of the article over the corresponding dictionary entry is the incomparably greater measure of freedom that the linguist enjoys in shaping it. Each case receives individual attention: The word is embedded in a cultural context uniquely its own, the volume of documentation is determined by the degree of regularity in the changes undergone, etc. Characteristically, most advances in etymological technique have lately been achieved in such medium-scale ventures inviting experimentation and tactical maneuvering rather than in the rigid framework of a dictionary, whose author is necessarily haunted by the restraining ideal of consistency.

### 3. Classification by Material

Another criterion for classifying etymologies is the quality and quantity of the MATERIAL utilized. In this respect, pioneer researchers were content with a scientifically valid, but somewhat rudimentary approach, subjecting forms extracted from ancient texts to increasingly rigorous historical and comparative analyses (along vertical and horizontal axes). The progress at that (one is inclined to say, philological) stage was measured: (a) by the expansion of the corpus of texts newly discovered or for the first time critically edited, with the concomitant revision of their vocabularies; (b) by the refinement of textual criticism, especially in dealing with infrequent or erratic forms apt to provide fresh clues to etymologies; (c) by a shift of emphasis in the selection of canvassed texts, away from standard genres favoring trite words and in the direction of technical treatises (bestiaries, lapidaries, recipes, etc.) which contain a store of words defying the most fastidious etymologist.

As Indo-Europeanists started ranging beyond the realm of extinct languages and as modern (especially, Romance) philology broke away from classical studies, DIALECT MATERIAL began to gain recognition in etymological debate, initially only at its fringes. A later generation of scholars contrived a state of equilibrium between philological and dialectological documentation, by setting out to fill the lacunae, unavoidable in lexical transmission, through systematic exploitation of present-day conservative dialects. This approach presupposes the elevation of dialect study, once (and, in part, until this day) the domain of well-meaning amateurs, to the rank of a respectable scholarly endeavor, a change by and large effected by G. I. Ascoli for south-western Europe and by his peers elsewhere. The new combined approach was championed, at the turn of the century, by a brilliant and cosmopolitan galaxy of Romanicists (R. J. Cuervo, R. Menéndez Pidal, J. Leite de Vasconcelos, A. Thomas, W. Meyer-Lübke, and many others, including their immediate associates and followers). H. Schuchardt, over a period of sixty feverish years, not only extracted every imaginable benefit from this pool of resources, juggling with a virtuoso's deftness his Romance, Slavic, Turkish, Hungarian, and Creole data, but boldly applied the method to the social and regional stratification of Latin. Contemporary front-line Latinists like Ernout, Hofmann, Niedermann, and the Swedes have studded their inquiries into the records of Antiquity with precise references to medieval Latin and vernacular formations and, as a second choice, to modern lexical material, ranging from Romance to Basque, Vulgar Arabic, and Berber, to the extent that Latin etymology (in particular, the study of submerged words) may profit from such data. In the Indo-Aryan field P. Tedesco practices a similarly balanced approach, striving to cast floods of light on Sanskrit words with the aid of New Indic regionalisms.

The EXPERIMENTAL AGE in etymology began when scholars, familiar with these two traditional methods and skilled in the use of their mutually corroborative evidence, deliberately set out to confine themselves to a single technique, either entirely new or novel in its isolation. The gamut of driving forces behind this voluntary abandonment of comfortably secure ground included the quest for fresh insights from which incalculably valuable results might be expected; the lingering fear that the most satisfactory technique, if employed beyond the point of saturation, may eventually become sterile; and, probably, some workers' special delight in ever renewed contact with slices of material particularly pleasing to them (archival data, accurately tagged specimens of material civilization, records of native speech elicited from informants, bibliographic apparatus of a well-stocked research library, etc.).

J. Gilliéron was less of a revolutionary than his shocked contemporaries were led to assume (much of his colorful phrasing he owed to É. Littré, homonymics before him had been cultivated by F. A. Coelho, and the cartographic presentation of linguistic facts is an invention usually credited to G. Wenker). However, the abrupt decision to dispense altogether with philological evidence (including dialect glossaries) in favor of UNRETOUCHED FIELD NOTES projected onto a series of maps as the sole guide to reconstruction was Gilliéron's private whim. He rarely attacked etymologically obscure formations, preferring to focus attention on the chronological sequence of words paired off as synonyms or homonyms, real or potential, exact or approximate. But the method intrinsically lent itself to extension toward purely etymological analysis.

Gilliéron's researches produced sharper repercussions among Romance linguists than in other quarters. Here the work of an entire team of dynamic and talented etymologists (K. Jaberg, M. L. Wagner, J. Jud, W. von Wartburg, E. Gamillscheg, G. Rohlfs) was aimed at the RECONCILIATION of cartographically streamlined dialect geography with the subtler and more complex methods of conventional etymology.

A different experiment consisted in the self-imposed LIMITATION TO SPECIAL TYPES OF HISTORICAL RECORDS, deemed more dependable than others. This applies to accurately dated and localized notarial documents, preserved in the original; these documents some younger etymologists, after 1920, began using to the strict exclusion of literary texts, which they held to be either too late for the chosen purpose or linguistically blurred by the uninhibited interference of successive copyists. Collections of charters had been compiled before by philologists sensitive to paleographic niceties (e.g., by P. Meyer in 1909, covering sections of southern France). E. Staaff, two years earlier, cogently drew grammatical conclusions from his meticulous edition of well-chosen Old Leonese texts. Menéndez Pidal succeeded in basing, by and large, on inconspicuous texts of this kind (some of which he himself had made accessible as early as 1919) a massive grammatical edifice of Proto-Spanish dialects (1926, 1929, 1951), with stray lexico-etymological appendages. At this point bold experiments with this selective method began all over Europe, not all of them, in retrospect, commanding an equal share of interest. G. Tilander wisely applied it to OPtg. *rousar* and relatives 'to rape', a verb coined in chanceries and apparently unknown in other environments. He was less well advised in relying on it when engrossed by the crux OSp. *es-, tres-, tras-quilar* 'to shear': Here the inclusion of texts other than municipal ordinances not only would have been legitimate, but might have considerably improved our perspective on a word etymologically elusive, but by no means limited to a single social sphere.

P. Aebischer and J. Hubschmid, both from Switzerland, operate almost invariably with this sampling of material. The former has made himself known preëminently, the latter exclusively, as an etymologist. These two scholars, instead of spreading their curiosity over the entire lexical stock of a given language, select small or middle-sized word groups, tracing with astonishing patience each formation through volume after volume of almost unreadably monotonous CARTULARIES and INVENTORIES. At the end, each interprets the emerging pattern diachronically, as a seasoned dialect geographer would do a linguistic map. Although their material is similar, their practices of selection and their territorial and chronological preferences happen to clash.

Aebischer concentrates on words of Latin ancestry, moves with ease through the maze of Low Latin records (favoring, as he should, those tinged by Romance speech habits), keeps within his purview texts written in the medieval vernaculars, and adds a mere sprinkle of modern dialect words. His tacitly assumed goal is EXTRA-PRECISE STRATIGRAPHY based on minute observation, not necessarily clarification of nebulous word origins, so that he only incidentally stoops to the discovery of new etyma. He seems to earmark words for investigation on the grounds of their repeated occurrence in his favorite medium (notarial texts) rather than of any inherent affinity of a higher order. His conclusions, though not invulnerable, appear on the whole sensible, conservative, discerning, and delicately shaded.

Hubschmid distills, from his vast readings, the small residue of those notoriously troublesome words that seem traceable to a pre-Latin, preferably even a pre-IE, SUBSTRATUM in western Europe and attempts to link them, somewhat recklessly, to geographically very distant cognates (or putative cognates). The aim almost looks like some kind of acrobatic performance; the result is etymological research with an unprecedented number of unknowns, and a minimum of controls; the punishment, a disturbingly high incidence of (in part, admitted, in part, not easily verifiable) errors; the atonement: an exceptionally rich collection of neatly extracted raw data, useful even to those fellow-workers who may disagree with the underlying scale of values, in general, and with the specific identifications announced, in particular.

Another experimental limitation has been attempted in regard to

ONOMASTIC, especially TOPONYMIC, data. Circumstances may impose this lopsided emphasis, as when a word of the ancestral language has survived only in proper names. One such very tentative tabulation of Latin petrifacts G. Sachs prepared years ago for the Iberian peninsula. In substratum studies this restriction occasionally yields gratifying results, cf. Menéndez Pidal's note on Proto-Basque *Javier-Chabarri*. In most instances, however, it is desirable and practicable to blend onomastic with dialectal shreds of evidence; witness Menéndez Pidal's and Hubschmid's independent analyses of Sp. *cueto* 'protuberance', divergent in all respects except in the only possible way of sampling the data. Toponyms, freely admitted into articles, have been slow in penetrating the barrier of etymological dictionaries; M. Vasmer's, for Russian, marks a promising departure from this inertia.

Etymological diagnosis based on the GEOGRAPHIC FACTOR alone has not, to my knowledge, yet been essayed. But geographic conditions may play the decisive rôle in assigning a debated word to a given lexical stratum, a classification which, in turn, may entail the definitive choice of a suitable base. Geographic proximity to another language, for instance, may tip the scales in favor of an assumption of borrowing: An obscure French dialect word generously represented in north-eastern patois but consistently absent from the west and the south is more than likely to be of Frankish descent. More problematic has been the attempt of the Italian neolinguists to infer patterns of relative chronology (conducive, in the last analysis, to etymological hypotheses) from the contrasting areal configuration of present-day rival words.

Patterns of MEANING AND IMAGERY as a clue to etymology have so strongly obsessed the minds of some scholars as to have allowed them to ride roughshod over other, not one whit less important, considerations. The ever-present conflict between semantic and phonic plausibility in assessing the merits of a conjecture was pointed up, half a century ago, by a memorable duel between A. Thomas, resolved to elude the temptation of semantic analogy, and H. Schuchardt, cheerfully prepared to yield to the lure. The skirmish ended in an impasse; meanwhile, scholars have begun to realize that the semantic tool, before being tried out again, needed a good deal of refurbishing. Not very long ago (1951) Benveniste reminded us of, among other hazards, the inadequacy, in etymological discussion, of such terms as "abstract" and "concrete"; of the dangerous discrepancies between lexical contours in the language explored and in the explorer's language used as a frame of "reference"; of the oft-neglected, indissoluble ties between meaning and construction.

If the linguistic logician instinctively shrinks from this path, the POETICALLY ENDOWED etymologist returns to it again and again. In his ability to solve etymologies or, at least, to suggest plausible rapprochements through the re-creation of faded imagery J. Trier probably has no living peer; witness his powerful treatment of the etymological motif 'mother — children' ~ 'root-stock' (or 'stem') — 'sprigs', with special reference to L. *māter, mātrīx, māteriēs*. This is visual linguistics at its most attractive. Unfortunately, Trier, despite his training, allows himself to be carried away by his fertile imagination. The inclusion of *matta* within the *māt-* complex is hazardous (as he himself senses), and even the bare mention of *matula* in this context seems preposterous. The poetic evocation of patterns of imagery simply lacks those controls that have helped make the acoustic branch of linguistics a possibly less pleasing, but, beyond doubt, more effectively organized science. The appeal of this method to the dormant graphic sensitivity in the linguist is healthy, and in conjunction with other, less intuitive approaches it acts as a precious stimulant; but when applied in isolation it has, one must admit, wrought havoc with not a few linguistic facts.

To solve an etymological problem in abeyance, a worker may, finally, decide on collecting, with equal zeal, linguistic and correlated, non-linguistic facts. The slogans *Wörter und Sachen, Wort- und Sachatlas* have centered attention about MATERIAL CIVILIZATION as a clue to etymology. Within the broad boundaries of this method one may substitute anatomical and even kinship terms for the names of tools and containers: What matters is not the fabric, shape, purpose, or palpability of the object, but the planned acquisition, on the part of the explorer, of technical knowledge beyond the confines of linguistics, and his ability to bring it to bear on lexical reconstruction. The worker's attention need not be focused on the terminal point of the inquiry, the actual etymological commitment: F. Krüger, in his Leonese and Pyrenean word studies, for the most part stops short of this final step, while Wagner, in cataloguing the Portuguese names (and corresponding varieties) of the mill-hopper, presses the etymological issues with genuine alacrity. Etymology so slanted easily becomes a semilinguistic discipline, the remaining half being claimed by a potentially unlimited number of complementary specializations. V. Bertoldi, to write convincingly on ancient and modern phytonyms, became an expert botanist, pharmacologist, and culture historian all in one; P. Barbier's protracted studies in European fish names prompted him to qualify as an amateur ichthyologist; É. Benveniste, in defining, with his usual precision, Upper Yukon animal names, showed respectable knowledge of Alaskan wildlife; O. J. Tallgren-Tuulio, before examining Hispano-Arabic names of stars and constellations (in whose study he became immersed for the sake of their transcription), deepened his understanding of ancient Graeco-Oriental astronomy. It is difficult to imagine the combination of some long-established science and of linguistics proper that an etymologist could not, under attractive conditions, be induced to straddle.

In one border-case the etymologist, aside from contributing to the identification of a specific word origin, finds himself delving into the HISTORY AND THEORY OF LINGUISTICS as a whole, the matrix of his own discipline. This happens when the critical digest of earlier scholarly pronouncements, normally a prefatory piece ancillary to the actual analysis of the chosen linguistic specimen, assumes, by way of exception, such proportions as to outweigh, in richness of results, the principal operation. Far and away the most rewarding section of Menéndez Pidal's inconclusive article on the topon. *Madrid* is his penetrating criticism of untenable Greek, Latin, Germanic, and Arabic conjectures; one can award a similar prize to Vincent's study of the equally controversial name *Gaul*. The literature on F. *aller* and congeners 'to go' became so prolific and scattered half a century ago (it has doubled in volume since then) that G. Stucke had to write an interim report for those in need of quick but thorough orientation. Primary linguistic material here almost yields in interest to secondary responses to etymology (if one may toy with an expansion of L. Bloomfield's dictum without injecting into it his animus).

## 4. Classification by Degree of Complexity

Possibly the boldest way of hierarchizing etymological problems is to arrange them in the ORDER OF DECREASING TRANSPARENCY. (The most challenging cases are indubitably those known as obscure, but the most rewarding, on the strength of the actual yield, are probably found at a respectable distance from either extreme.) Equations like

Rum. *deget* < L. DIGITU 'finger' and Rum. *piept* < L. PECTU(S) 'breast, chest' present no complications whatever, furnishing choice material for the establishment of sound correspondences along the time axis; but they fail to whet the very tools with which the etymologist must handle more resistant slices of material. At the opposite end of the scale are the notorious cruxes, i.e., problems still unsolved and, so far as foreseeable, often doomed to remain insoluble (cf. Ernout and Meillet's pessimistic comment on L. *adulārī* 'to fawn upon', *aestu-*, *aesti-māre* 'to appraise, value', *car-cer*, *-car* 'jail', *imitārī* 'to portray, act like', etc.). The intermediate categories are those most in need of careful analysis.

Alongside the truly simple solution one finds the DECEPTIVELY SIMPLE SOLUTION, usually because some unevenness which might have served as a clue has been smoothed out — through the agency of folk etymology or of another associative process. Thus, L. *aborigīnēs* 'original inhabitants', *āmanuēnsis* 'clerk', and *pedeplāna* 'rooms on the ground-floor' are no longer believed to reflect *ab orīgine*, *ā manū*, *pede plānō*, in this order; R. *samojéd*, on the surface meaning 'one who eats himself', is actually a disguise for something utterly different, etc. In this sector, sound correspondences lose most of their usefulness as guides to word origins, the historical record remaining the all-important clue.

Nothing teases an etymologist more than facing a PARTIALLY TRANSPARENT situation. The Latin fish-name *aci-pēnser*, *-pensis* has been plausibly explained as including a classifiable head and an unclassifiable tail. F. *louange* 'praise', *mélange* 'mixture', and *mensonge* 'lie, falsehood' are inseparable, by commonsense standards, from the corresponding verbs *louer*, *mêler*, *mentir* (genetically, all of them perfectly diaphanous), but their derivation has been a stumbling-block[5]. In Romance, minor disturbances of this kind are frequently caused by void non-final suffixes (interfixes), difficult of explanation, cf. F. *fort-er-esse* (orig. *-ece*), Sp. *fort-al-eza* 'strength, fortress'.

The hindrance to clear-cut analysis need not be an anomalous derivational or compositional pattern. In the case of F. *laisser*, It. *la-sciare*, *-ssare*, OPtg. *leixar*, OSp. *dexar*, Rum. *lăsa*, etc. 'to let, leave' < L. LAXĀRE 'to slacken' beside OSp. *dexar* ( > *dejar*), Ptg. Cat. *deixar*, Gasc. *decha*, Sard. *dassare*, Cal. Sic. *dassari* 'to let,

---

[5] Sp. Ptg. *mentira* 'lie', in its unique relation to the verb *mentir*, presents a parallel aberration. For an attempt to remove the obstacle to neat classification see *RPh.*, VI (1952–53), 121–172.

leave', the initial *d-* of the smaller second series has taxed the ingenuity of etymologists since 1600. It took scholars considerable time to pinpoint the difficulty: Leaving out the skeptics, agnostics, and spineless compromisers, one may distinguish between (a) those dissociating genetically *lexar* and *dexar*, tracing the former to LAXĀRE and the latter to DĒSERERE, DĒSINERE (Covarrubias), *DĒSITĀRE (Diez), *DĒ-IECTIĀRE, -IEXĀRE (Rice), or *DĒCESSĀRE (Nicholson), a school of thought now practically extinct; and (b) those who jointly link *lexar* and *dexar* to LAXĀRE, on five different, in part mutually exclusive, assumptions: (1) broad identification (Sarmiento, Schuchardt 1868, Coelho, Tailhan . . .); (2) sound change L- > *d-* (a. tendential pan-Romanic shift: Reinhardstoettner; b. consonant dissimilation: Cornu, Menéndez Pidal 1900; c. Sabinian idiosyncrasy: Silva Neto; d. consonant assimilation: Corominas); (3) DI-, *DĒ-LAXĀRE as the sole source of *dexar* (Ascoli, Guarnerio, Gorra . . .); (4) blend of LAXĀRE and *DĒLAXĀRE (Schuchardt 1891, Ford 1900, Menéndez Pidal 1908 . . . Wagner); (5) contamination of LAXĀRE by an unrelated word (a. DĒ: Ford 1911; b. DARE: Meyer-Lübke, Spitzer; c. Ar. mudaǧǧan: Schürr). This loose league of scholars, divided on many details of their platform, at least, has essentially agreed to hem in tightly the anomaly of L- > *d-* in this one word, a considerable methodological progress.

From here the number of difficulties in a given word may indefinitely increase. Thus, the consensus of most scholars is that F. *soin* 'care' and *be-soin* 'need' share a morpheme, but the origin of *soin* as well as of *be-*, viewed separately, and the compositional scheme of *besoin* remain dubious, a wide margin of three mutually independent unknowns left uneliminated.

## 5. Etymology and General Linguistics

This typological sketch, however modest, represents an attempt to bring about a rapprochement between etymology and general linguistics. Etymologists are frequently recruited from the ranks of scholars inherently wary of generalization and become imbued with such knowledge as does not lend itself smoothly to abstraction. In contrast, modern linguistics has been moving at a swift pace in the direction of increasingly abstract formulation. Hence two conflicting scales of values and not a few conflicts of personalities. But a complete break is undesirable, because etymology divorced from general linguistics degenerates easily into a genteel game or into a discipline ancillary to history, while linguistics deprived of its etymological roots tends to assume a degree of abstractness which the study of languages in its full richness hardly invites. There may thus be some point to our seeking to discover recurrent types, i.e., constants, in etymology, even if we agree to characterize it as the domain of individuality in language history.

## BIBLIOGRAPHY[6]

AEBISCHER, P., *Estudios de toponimia y lexicografía románica* (Barcelona, 1948).

BARBIER, P., "Noms de poissons. Notes étymologiques et lexicographiques", *RLR*, LI (1908), 385–406; LII (1909), 97–129; LIII (1910), 26–57; LIV (1911), 149–190; LVI (1913), 172–247; LVII (1914), 295–342; LVIII (1915), 270–329; LXIII (1925), 1–68; LXV (1927), 1–52; LXVII (1935), 275–372.

BENVENISTE, É., *Origine de la formation des noms en indo-européen*, 2 vols. (Paris, 1935–49).

—— "Problèmes sémantiques de la reconstruction", *Word*, X (1954), 251–264 (= *Linguistics Today*, eds. A. Martinet and U. Weinreich); included in É.B., *Problèmes de linguistique générale* (Paris, 1966), pp. 289–307.

—— "Le terme *obryza* et la métallurgie de l'or", *RePh.*, XXVII (1953), 122–126.

—— "Le vocabulaire de la vie animale chez les Indiens du Haut Yukon (Alaska)", *BSLP*, XLIX: 1 (1953), 79–106.

BERTOLDI, V., "Contatti e conflitti di lingue nell'antico Mediterraneo", *ZRPh.*, LVII (1937), 137–169.

BRÜCH, J., "Bemerkungen zum etymologischen Wörterbuch E. Gamillschegs", *ZFSL*, XLIX (1926), 209–318; L (1927), 299–355; LII (1929), 393–483.

BULATKIN, E. W., "The Spanish word *matiz*; its origin and semantic evolution in the technical vocabulary of medieval painters", *Traditio*, X (1954), 459–527.

CAIX, N., *Studi di etimologia italiana e romanza; osservazioni ed aggiunte al vocabolario etimologico delle lingue romanze di F. Diez* (Florence, 1878).

---

[6] All easily identifiable standard reference works have been omitted.

CASTRO, A., "Adiciones hispánicas al *Diccionario etimológico* di W. Meyer-Lübke", *RFE*, V (1918), 21–42; VI (1919), 337–345.

CIHAC, A., *Dictionnaire d'étymologie daco-romane*. Vol. I : Éléments latins; Vol. II : Éléments slaves, magyars, turcs, grecs-modernes et albanais (Frankfurt ª/M., 1870–79).

COROMINAS, J., "Indianoromanica", *RFH*, VI (1944), 1–35, 139–175, 209–254 [on *cach-*: pp. 33 f.].

—— "Problemas del diccionario etimológico", *RPh.*, I (1947–48), 23–38, 79–104.

CUERVO, R. J., *Disquisiciones sobre filología castellana*, ed. R. Torres Quintero (Bogotá, 1950).

—— *Obras*, eds. F. A. Martínez and R. Torres Quintero, 2 vols. (Bogotá, 1954).

DARMESTETER, A., and D. S. BLONDHEIM, *Les gloses françaises dans les commentaires talmudiques de Raschi*, 2 vols. (Paris, 1929–Baltimore, 1937); cf. R. Levy, *Trésor de la langue des juifs français au Moyen Age* (Austin, 1964).

DOBSON, E. J., "The Etymology and Meaning of *boy*", *MÆv.*, IX (1940), 121–154.

DOZY, R., and W. H. ENGELMANN, *Glossaire des mots espagnols et portugais dérivés de l'arabe*, rev. 2d ed. (Leyden, 1869) [1st ed. of 1861 by Engle-mann alone].

EGGENSCHWILER, E., *Die Namen der Fledermaus auf dem französischen und italienischen Sprachgebiet* (Bern, 1934) [Hispanic addenda by Y.M.: *HR*, XIX (1951), 238–263, 323–340; Catalan addenda by M. Sanchis Guarner: *RFE*, XL (1956), 91–125].

EMENEAU, M. B., "The Dravidian verbs 'come' and 'give' ", *Lg.*, XXI (1945), 184–213.

ERNOUT, A., "*Venus, venia, cupīdō*", *RePh.*, XXX (1956), 7–27.

FARINELLI, A., "*Marrano*", *Studi . . . Pio Rajna* (Florence, 1911), pp. 491–555; "*Marrano*": *storia di un vituperio* (Geneva, 1925). [For criticism see *JAOS*, LXVIII (1948), 175–184, and B. Migliorini, *LN*, X (1949), 50].

FLASDIECK, H. M., "*Pall Mall*: Beiträge zur Etymologie und Quantitäts-theorie", *Anglia*, LXXII (1954), 129–383.

—— *Zinn und Zink; Studien zur abendländischen Wortgeschichte* (Tübingen, 1952).

FOERSTER, W. *Kristian von Troyes; Wörterbuch zu seinen sämtlichen Werken* (Halle ª/S., 1914; rev. ed., by H. Breuer, 1933; reprinted, Tübingen, 1964).

FORD, J. D. M., ed., *Old Spanish Readings, Selected on the Basis of Critically Edited Texts* (Boston, 1911, 1939) [Etymological Vocabulary, pp. 177–312].

FOULET, L., in J. BÉDIER, *La Chanson de Roland*, Commentaires (Paris, 1927) [Glossary, pp. 321–501].

——, in W. J. ROACH, ed., *Continuations of the Old French "Perceval" of Chrétien de Troyes*, 3 vols. in 4 (Philadelphia, 1949–55) [Glossary: Vol. III : 2].

FRINGS, T., "Germania Romana", *Teuthonista*, Suppl. 4 (Halle ª/S., 1932).

GAMILLSCHEG, E., "Französische Etymologien" (I–II), *ZRPh.*, XL (1919–20), 129–190, 513–542; XLI (1921–22), 503–537, 631–647.

GARCÍA DE DIEGO, V., *Contribución al diccionario hispánico etimológico* (Madrid, 1923; reprinted in 1943).

—— "Etimologías españolas" (I–II), *RFE*, VI (1919), 113–131; VII (1920), 113–149.

GILLIÉRON, J. (with M. Roques), *Études de géographie linguistique d'après l'Atlas linguistique de la France* (Paris, 1912).

—— *Généalogie des mots qui désignent l'abeille d'après l'Atlas linguistique de la France* (*BÉHÉ*, CCXXV; Paris, 1918).

GRÖBER, G., "Vulgärlateinische Substrate romanischer Wörter", *ALLG*, I–VI (1884–89).

HAAS, M. R., "The Proto-Gulf word for 'water' (with notes on Siouan-Yuchi)", *IJAL*, XVII (1951), 71–79.

—— "Tunica dictionary", *UCPL*, VI:2 (1953), 175–332; cf. the companion piece, "Some French loan words in Tunica", *RPh.*, I (1947–48), 145–148.

HASSELROT, B., "L'abricot; essai de monographie onomasiologique et sémantique", *SN*, XIII (1940–41), 45–79, 226–252.

HAUST, J., *Étymologies wallonnes et françaises* (Liège, 1923).

HENRÍQUEZ UREÑA, P., "Palabras antillanas en el Diccionario de la Academia", *RFE*, XXII (1935), 175–186.

—— *Para la historia de los indigenismos* (Buenos Aires, 1938) [*Caribe*: pp. 95–102].

HUBSCHMID, J., "Studien zur iberoromanischen Wortgeschichte und Ortsnamenkunde", *BF*, XII (1951), 117–156 [on this author's background and techniques see the review article in *Lg.*, XXXVIII (1962), 149–186].

JABERG, K., *Aspects géographiques du langage* (Paris, 1936).

—— "The birthmark in folk belief, language, literature, and fashion", *RPh.*, X (1956–57), 307–342 [the German original was later included in the posthumous miscellany of K. J.'s writings, *Sprachwissenschaftliche Forschungen und Erlebnisse: Neue Folge*, ed. S. Heinimann (*RH*, LXXV; Berne, 1966), pp. 282–322].

JAKOBSON, R., "L'authenticité du *Slovo*", *Annuaire de l'Institut de philologie et d'histoire orientales et slaves*, VIII (1945–47), 235–360, esp. 240–262.

JUD, J., "It[alien] *menzogna*, fr[ançais] *mensonge*, esp[agnol] *mentira*", *VR*, XI (1950), 101–124.

—— "Probleme der altromanischen Sprachgeographie", *ZRPh.*, XXXVIII (1914–17), 1–75.

—— Review of W. Meyer-Lübke, *REW*[1], in *ASNS*, CXXVII (1911), 416–438.

KAHANE, H. R., "Designations of the cheek in the Italian dialects", *Lg.*, XVII (1941), 212–222 [cf. the same author's earlier *Die Bezeichnungen der Kinnbacke im Galloromanischen*, BBRPh., II:2 (1932)].

KAHANE, RENÉE, "Italienische Marinewörter im Neugriechischen", *AR*, XXII (1938), 510–582 [in criticism of D. C. Hesseling's 1903 monograph].

KAHANE, H. and R., "The Mediterranean term SURGERE 'to anchor'", *RPh.*, IV (1950–51), 195–215 [p. 195: brief list of earlier publications, superseded by Angelina R. Pietrangeli's analytical bibliography in *RPh.*, XV (1961–62), 207–220].

——, with A. TIETZE, *The Lingua Franca in the Levant: Turkish Nautical Terms of Italian and Greek Origin* (Urbana, 1958).

KENT, R. G., *Old Persian: Grammar, Texts, Lexicon* (New Haven, 1950).

KRÖLL, H., "Designações portuguesas para 'embriaguez'" (Coimbra, 1955) [reprinted from *RPF*, V, 27–85; VI, 74–134; VII, 17–120; cf. M. Alvar's appraisal in *RPh.*, XIV (1960–61), 77–81].

LECOY, F., "Étymologies espagnoles", *Rom.*, LXVIII (1944–45), 1–17 [on *cach-*: pp. 1–8].

LOOMIS, L. H., "The *oriflamme* of France and the war-cry *monjoie* in the twelfth century", *Studies . . . for Belle de Costa Greene* (Princeton, 1954), pp. 67–82; cf. ead., *RR*, XLI (1950), 241–260, and *Sp.*, XXV (1950), 437–456; W. A. Nitze, *RPh.*, IX (1955–56), 11–17, in criticism of H. Sperber's disagreement with E. Gamillscheg; J. Harris, ibid., X, 168–173; and, with special reference to *oriflamme*, H. and R. Kahane, "Contributions by Byzantinologists to Romance etymology", *RLiR*, XXVI (1962), 126–139, esp. 136 f.

MAHN, K. A. F., *Etymologische Untersuchungen auf dem Gebiete der romanischen Sprachen* (Berlin, 1855).

MARDEN, C. C., ed., "*Libro de Apolonio*", *an Old Spanish Poem.* Part II, Elliott Monographs, XI–XII (Princeton–Paris, 1922) [Vocabulary: pp. 67–185].

MENÉNDEZ PIDAL, R., "La etimología de *Madrid* y la antigua Carpetania", *RBAM*, XIV (1945), 3–23; reprinted, after some revision, in *Toponimia prerrománica hispana* (Madrid, 1952), pp. 189–220, cf. the reactions of J. Hubschmid in *RPh.*, VIII (1954–55), 221–225, and of Y.M. in *Sp.*, XXIX (1954), 588–594. The entire problem has been cast open for discussion anew by J. Oliver Asín, *Historia del nombre "Madrid"* (Madrid, 1959); cf. J. Hubschmid's appraisal in *RPh.*, XVII (1963–64), 175 f.

—— "Etimologías españolas", *Rom.*, XXIX (1900), 334–379.

—— "*Javier-Chabarri*, dos dialectos ibéricos", *Emerita*, XVI (1948), 1–13; reprinted in *Toponimia prerrománica hispana*, pp. 233–250.

—— "Notas para el léxico románico", *RFE*, VII (1920), 1–36.

MENGES, K. H., *The Oriental Elements in the Vocabulary of the Oldest Russian Epos, the "Igor' Tale".* Preface by R. Jakobson (New York, 1951).

NIEDERMANN, M., "Über einige Quellen unserer Kenntnis des späten Vulgärlateinischen", *NJKA*, XXIX (1912), 313–342.

NOBILING, O., "Berichtigungen und Zusätze zum portugiesischen Teil von [G.] Körtings *Lateinisch-romanischem Wörterbuch*",

*ASNS*, CXXIV (1910), 332–345; CXXV (1910), 154–157, 393–397; CXXVI (1911), 175–179, 424–432; CXXVI (1911–12), 181–188, 371–377.

PIEL, J. M., *Miscelânea de etimologia portuguesa e galega*, 1st series (Coimbra, 1953).

QUADRI, B., *Aufgaben und Methoden der onomasiologischen Forschung* (*RH*, XXXVI; Berne, 1952).

READ, W. A., *Louisiana-French* (Baton Rouge, 1931); posthumous rev. ed. (1963), reviewed by W. Bright in *RPh.*, XVIII (1964–65), 352–354; cf. the critic's afterthoughts, ibid., XIX, 490–495.

RENSON, J., *Les dénominations du visage en français et dans les autres langues romanes; étude sémantique et onomasiologique*. 2 vols. BFUL, CLXII (Paris, 1962). Cf. P. Guiraud's forthcoming review (*RPh.*, XXI).

RHEINFELDER, H., *Kultsprache und Profansprache in den romanischen Ländern* (Geneva, 1933).

RICHTER, E., "Die Bedeutungsgeschichte der romanischen Wortsippe *bur(d)*", *WAW*, CLVI:5 (1908), 1–138.

ROSS, A. S. C., *Etymology, with Especial Reference to English* (London [1958]); cf. the reviews by É. Benveniste in *BSLP*, LIV:2 (1959), 40 f., and, in a severe vein, by W. P. Lehmann in *Lg.*, XXXV (1959), 351–353.

—— *'Ginger', a Loan-Word Study* (Oxford, 1952).

SACHS, G., "Restos latinos en nombres de lugares españoles", *AR*, XIX (1935), 437–440.

SALVIONI, C., "Postille italiane al vocabolario latino-romanzo [di G. Körting]", *MIL*, XX (1899), 255–278.

SAPIR, E., "Greek *atýzomai*, a Hittite loan word, and its relatives", *Lg.*, XII (1936), 175–180.

SCHELER, A., Supplement to F. Diez, *Etymologisches Wörterbuch . . .*, 4th ed. (Bonn, 1878); 5th ed. (1887), pp. 703–818. Cf. the three successive editions of the author's own *Dictionnaire d'étymologie française, d'après les résultats de la science moderne* (Brussels, 1862, 1873, 1888).

SCHUCHARDT, H., "Romanische Etymologien", I–II, *WAW*, CXXXVIII:1 (1897), 1–82; CXLI:3 (1899), 1–222. For a full bibliography of the author's writings see the Forematter to *Hugo Schuchardt-brevier, ein Vademekum der allgemeinen Sprachwissenschaft*, ed. L. Spitzer (Halle a/S., 1922); expanded 2d ed. (1928).

SPITZER, L., "Aus Anlass von [E.] Gamillschegs 'Französischen Etymologien'", *ZRPh.*, XLII (1922), 5–34.

—— "A New Spanish Etymological Dictionary" [J. Corominas, *DCE*], *MLN*, LXXI (1956), 271–283, 373–386; LXXII (1957), 579–591; LXXIV (1959), 127–149.

—— Review, A. CASTRO, *Glosarios latino-españoles de la Edad Media*, in *MLN*, LIII (1938), 122–146, 554.

STEIGER, A., "Aufmarschstrassen des morgenländischen Sprachgutes", *VR*, X (1949), 1–62; for additional titles see the necrology in *RPh.*, XVIII (1964–65), 284–296.

STUCKE, G., *Französisch "aller" und seine romanischen Verwandten; eine kritisch-etymologische Untersuchung.* Diss. Heidelberg (Darmstadt, 1902).

TAGLIAVINI, C., "Di alcune denominazioni della 'pupilla'; studio onomasiologico, con speciale riguardo alle lingue camito-semitiche e negro-africane", *AION*, III (1949), 341–378.

TALLGREN[-TUULIO], O. J., "Los nombres árabes de las estrellas y la transcripción alfonsina", *HMP*, II, 633–718.

TEDESCO, P., "Sanskrit *munḍa* 'shaven'", *JAOS*, LXV (1945), 82–98.

THOMAS, A., *Essais de philologie française* (Paris, 1897).

—— *Mélanges d'étymologie française* (Paris, 1902); rev. 2d ed. (1927).

—— *Nouveaux essais de philologie française* (Paris, 1904).

THURNEYSEN, R., *Keltoromanisches; die keltischen Etymologien im EWRS von F. Diez* (Halle ᵃ/S., 1884).

TILANDER, G., "Origen y evolución del verbo *esquilar*", *SN*, IX (1936–37), 48–65.

—— "[Hisp.-Rom.] *Rausar, rousar, rouxar, roixar; rauso, rouso, rojo, roxo, roiso*", *BF*, VI (1939–40), 188–197.

TODD, H. A., "[William A.] Knapp's Spanish etymologies", *MLN*, I (1886), 117–120, 142–146.

TÖRNQVIST, N., "Zur Etymologie von n[eu]h[och]d[eutsch] *Ufer*", *SN*, XIII (1940–41), 253–290.

TRIER, J., *Holz: Etymologien aus dem Niederwald* (Münstersche Forschungen, VI; Münster, 1952) [pp. 136–143: *māter*].

—— *Lehm: Etymologien zum Fachwerk* (Marburg, 1951).

—— *Venus: Etymologien um das Futterlaub* (Münstersche Forschungen, XV; Cologne, 1963).

VASCONCELOS, C. MICHAËLIS DE, "Contribuïções para o futuro dicionário etimológico das línguas românicas", *RL*, XI (1908), 1–62.

——"Estudos etimológicos; contribuïções para o futuro dicionário etimológico das línguas românicas peninsulares", *RL*, XIII (1910), 222–432.

—— "Etimologias portuguesas", *RL*, I (1887–89), 117–132, 298–305.

—— "Fragmentos etimológicos", *RL*, III (1895), 129–190.

—— "Studien zur hispanischen Wortdeutung", *Miscellanea di filologia …* *Caix-Canello* (Florence, 1885), pp. 113–166.

VASCONCELOS, J. LEITE DE, "Notas filológicas", *RH*, IV (1897), 209–214; V (1898), 417–429.

VIANA, A. d. R. GONÇALVES, *Apostilas aos dicionários portugueses*, 2 vols. (Lisbon, 1906).

VIDOS, B. E., *Storia delle parole marinaresche italiane passate in francese* (Florence, 1939).

VINCENT, A., "*Gallia* et *Gaule*", *RBPhH*, XXVII (1949), 712–726.

VORETZSCH, C., *Einführung in das Studium der altfranzösischen Sprache*, 6th ed. (Halle ᵃ/S., 1932), Glossary: pp. 372–411 [1st ed., 1901; this textbook has now been replaced by G. Rohlfs, *Vom Vulgärlatein zum Altfranzösischen*].

WAGNER, M. L., "Rettifiche ed aggiunte alla terza edizione del *REW* …",

*AR*, XIX (1935), 1–30; XX (1936), 343–358; XXIV (1940), 11–67.
—— "Sobre os nomes da 'moega' nas línguas ibero-românicas", *Biblos*, XXIV (1948), 247–265.

WARTBURG, W. VON, "*Albus* und seine Familie in Frankreich", *ZRPh.*, XLI (1921–22), 182–192.

# 9

# The Uniqueness and Complexity of Etymological Solutions

## 1. A Modern Schism

IT would take an unprejudiced observer of our scholarly community not too long to discover a dividing line between the two groups of theoretical (or general) linguists and the devotees of etymology, some of whom are also students of proper names. The existence of this climate of estrangement has been widely acknowledged in recent years; but the causes of the aloofness, to the best of my knowledge, have never been carefully and impartially explored (opposing the older to the younger schools of thought solely in terms of scientific fashion seems to me begging the question of the essential difference). Indisputably, an ever smaller fraction of leading self-styled practitioners of modern linguistics cares to take active part in etymological research either as part of, or even as an adjunct to, their major endeavors. Conversely, a chosen few, at best, among professional etymologists seem to bother to present any close-knit theory of their own assumptions and operations, a corpus of postulates formally defined and binding on themselves, a strategy and a tactics for advancing from familiar into untrodden territory: All that one usually finds along this line is sporadic and incidental remarks, not infrequently written in a polemic vein.

This increasingly deepening mutual indifference if not distrust, in large part emotional rather than intellectual, between the two rival groups and the various, not always friendly, rationalizations that attach to it are, in a way, manifestations of the fundamentally different appeals of grammar or structure, which, by definition, views a language in austere and, mathematically speaking, elegant isolation from all other facets of the given culture, and of the lexicon, whose study, especially in the wake of dialect geography and *Wörter-und-Sachen* technique, encompasses wide stretches, in time and

Reprinted from *Lingua*, V:3 (1956), 225-252.

space, of the "realities" of the outside world. Also the rôle of a speaker (especially one endowed with imagination) in the shaping of lexicon and style is conspicuously greater than in the selection of such phonemes and grammatical morphemes as the members of a typical society are supposed to master. Consequently, humanists, as avowed students of individual accomplishment, quite properly tend to pay attention, of all linguistic disciplines, only to those that show the individual in action, while linguistically oriented social scientists, with equal justification, prefer to concentrate on such patterns of discourse, whether stable or changing, as directly affect large sectors of speakers.

## 2. The Margin of Chance and Intuition

There exist, however, subtler and more elusive lines that divide the two camps; one of these hardly visible frontiers deserves to be the subject of a separate communication. When a beginning, but already confirmed, linguistic scientist consults one of those slightly quaint etymological dictionaries that record and succinctly discuss all, or nearly all, conjectures that have accumulated, in extreme cases, over two millennia (one such compendium is Walde-Hofmann's meritorious *LEW*), a deep restlessness is likely to assail him from the start. Later this initial dizziness is bound to yield to two distinct, though not unrelated, feelings of discomfort.

First, having elected linguistics as the empirically straightforward approach to the analysis of language, the novice here faces a miscellany (rather than well-planned series) of operations in which sheer personal talent — call it horse-sense, ingenuity, or intuition — and, in the case of newly unearthed shreds of evidence, the whim of a chance discovery seem to preside in undue measure over the advance of knowledge. With some inconclusively debated issues in the domain of Latin and Romance it may look as if, from Paulus Festus and Isidore of Seville through Covarrubias, Ménage, and Muratori to sophisticated moderns, each scholar, when his turn arrives, were making a fling or shot at the enigmatic word, much as children, in old-time market places, used to win prizes by smashing, with a well-aimed ball, some steadily shifting bottle or pot. This first fleeting impression of a hit-or-miss method tolerated in etymology and of the generous allowance made for unforeseen findings and instantaneous flashes of thought (ordinarily pictorial associations) must bitterly disappoint and fatally repel the progressively numerous neophytes attracted to the linguistic fold by the magic promise of uncompromising stringency from the blueprint to the successful conclusion of a project.

Moreover, since numerous age-old controversies have ended in deadlocks, the most balanced reference books, in fairness to each respectable participant in a given dispute, often supply alternative solutions, intimating that, possibly for a long time to come, no clear-cut, unique answer to the question broached may be forthcoming. At this point an impatient reader coming from the ranks of linguistic disciplinarians is apt angrily to toss away the etymological dictionary as an unstimulating collection of mutually contradictory, non-committal, and unserious answers to an odd array of riddles, fit at best to provide entertainment for naïve antiquarians but surely no enlightenment worthy of exacting analysts.

### 3. Problems Widened, Narrowed Down, and Twisted out of Shape

If we agree to examine in microscopic detail typical sets of such tentative solutions, will this test bear out our strawman's suspicion that the successive explanations are not only at variance with each other, but mutually exclusive and, worst of all, that one hypothesis, in the long view, is almost as good (or, for that matter, as bad) as another? I think not, and my chief reason for sounding this note of optimism is that in etymology, as in some other scholarly pursuits, the object under study, up to a point, changes with the progress of research. For one thing, some objects from the outset recalcitrant to analysis opportunely vanish altogether in the course of minute inquiries: A well-informed investigator willing to go back to the primary sources occasionally succeeds in demonstrating that his predecessors were clashing over a non-existent formation (say, a spurious manuscript reading, a phrase extracted from an unauthentic book, or a ghost-word traceable to an oft-repeated misprint). For another, the size and delineation of a genuine etymological problem depend, in more than one way, on the judgment, élan, and industriousness of the scholar concerned: To limit oneself to a cursory discussion of Ptg. Sp. Cat. *cansar* 'to tire' is one thing, to contrast Hisp. *cansar* with its near-homophone It. (*s*)*cansare* 'to eschew' is quite another thing, and to build a many-tiered monograph around these two verbs plus their dissimilarly structured satellites is again a different proposition. This not only implies that the characteristic unit of diachronic inquiry at present is the lexical family rather than the isolated word; the boundaries of ambitious investigation may be pushed much farther, as a rule, at the discretion of the explorer. A case in point is lexical polarization: Sp. *piara*, originally a by-form of (dialectally preserved) *piada*, loses some of its strangeness when contrasted with its near-synonym *manada* 'herd' (*pie* 'foot, hindleg' ~ *mano* 'hand, foreleg'), Sp. Ptg. *mentira(s)* 'lies' becomes transparent once we have examined it alongside *vera(s)* 'truth', or *ju-, yura(s)* 'oath', etc. There exist other ways and means of effectively grouping erratic words, cutting across word-families. Take Juan Ruiz's unusual derivative *pecadezno* 'little devil', which some time ago one hasty worker interpreted as 'spotted' (from *peca* 'freckle') and another, almost simultaneously, mistook for an offshoot of *pez* 'pitch', simply because both were oblivious of the infrequent suffix *-ezno*, found in a few Castilian and Aragonese names of whelps. Placed beside Berceo's older *judezno* 'Jewish lad' and an unidentified Murcian scribe's *morezno* 'young Moor' (A.D. 1406), the formation appears less outlandish; against the background of Russ. *žid'ónok* (derog.) 'Jewish child', *čert'ónok* 'little devil', flanked by *jagn'ónok* 'lamb' and comparable names of cubs, it alerts us to the grim realization that in various parts of Europe, Jews, Moors (or other non-conformists treated as infidels), along with evil spirits, were popularly held in the same low esteem as animals.

The assemblage of scattered formations in pairs, triads, and longer linear sequences or interlocking clusters on each occasion involves not only a readjustment of focus, but also a fresh delimitation of the chosen object. Usually, this leads to the extension of the original scope through the belated discovery of hidden connections. By the same token, the researcher is free to tighten his study in mid-course, by eliminating such irrelevant or even obstructive ingredients as have infiltrated into the corpus of data through the inadvertence of pioneers and through secondary accretions (homonymy, folk etymology, figurative use): For illustration, every worker may draw on his own experience. Hence, if we wish to give point to our previous simile, let us modify the contention that in the etymological game each player flings the one available ball at the same bottle, trying his luck. Actually there are more variables to the whole situation: The size, weight, and shape of the object that we, as a team, seek to hit changes, or at least may change (indeed, if we are allowed to inject a wish, should change) with each partner, and so does the ultimate choice of the weapon. The climax comes, of course, when a fortunate player's strength and skill opportunely match the make and potential impact of a ball and the delineation and resistance of the object newly designed to be toppled.

It even happens (nothing shows more clearly that etymologists, whether they like it or not, all told are operating in a round) that one worker, deliberately or by sheer accident, twists the originally posed problem out of shape, without bothering to press the advantage if there is any to the new situation, while the next in line or one of the following may seize upon the fresh opportunity and deal the squarely hitting blow; or that a controversy sparked by a poor guess may lead through devious routes to an unforeseen solution or to the vigorous consolidation of a time-honored, tentatively abandoned hypothesis, as when B. Migliorini not long ago rehabilitated, with telling arguments, the traditional derivation of It. *ciarlatano, cerretano* 'mountebank' from the toponym *Cerreto*, after other scholars had suggested less plausible Asiatic or Byzantine sources.

#### 4. Breaking a Dilemma Through Outside Help

The more common and, in some respects, no less gratifying phenomenon is that one member of the team, at a crucial juncture, decides on his own to call in outside help. The rescue workers may come from different directions, including the domain of the ancestral language. As long as Hispanists were stubbornly focusing attention on OSp. *deçir*, Ptg. *descer* < OPtg. *dece(e)r* 'to come down', their various explanations of its origin failed to strike home. The list of suggested bases, aside from the Latin synonym DĒSCENDERE (an etymon intermittently favored, but in reality utterly improbable), includes:

(a) DĒSĪDERE 'to settle down' (F. Diez, 1853, 1870; F. A. Coelho, ca. 1890);[1]

(b) DĒCIDERE 'to fall down, drop', from CADERE (J. Cornu in 1878 — see *Rom.*, VII, 595 f. —, also in his grammar, ed. 1888 and 1906, and after him A. Scheler in 1887, G. Körting in 1891 and, with

---

[1] Bibliographic hints are purposely given with utmost brevity. In the case of well-known book titles, only the author's name and the publication date are listed. No mention is made in this schematic presentation of slight differences of opinion and sentiment. On appropriate occasions, I plan to discuss in considerably greater detail some of the examples here adduced.

reservations, in 1901 and 1907, Coelho in the Supplement to his dictionary, Meyer-Lübke in 1894, A. Gassner in 1897, O. J. Tallgren in 1907, R. Menéndez Pidal in 1908, J. J. Nunes — with reservations — in 1919, C. Michaëlis in 1922, and A. Nascentes in 1932);

(c) DĒICERE 'to cast to the ground' (E. Herzog in 1910, see *ZRPh.*, Suppl. XXVI, 139 n. 1, and Meyer-Lübke around 1911, in *REW*[1] 2530; endorsement withdrawn in the revised ed.);

(d) DISCĪDERE 'to fall down' (V. García de Diego in 1923);

(e) DISCĒDERE 'to walk off' (Menéndez Pidal in 1946).

The key to the problem lay in the hands of Latinists who, ironically, remained unaware of their ability to put it to good use. The Romance verb probably owes its genesis to the demonstrable confusion in Late Latin of DĒCĪDERE 'to cut off, hew off', from CAEDERE, and DĒSCINDERE 'to tear off', from SCINDERE (Ernout-Meillet), a knot in which DĒSCENDERE 'to come down', from SCANDERE 'to climb', must eventually have been caught in consequence of further contamination.[2]

More typical are cases involving a choice between two possibilities, with a cognate rather than the ancestral language supplying the missing link. The progressive stages of the breaking of an etymological dilemma may be illustrated with the record of inquiries into Sp. (indirectly also Ptg. and It.) *lindo* 'beautiful', originally 'of fine breed'. We may set off a preliminary phase, characterized by arbitrary, ephemerous solutions, which anciently drew little applause and appear utterly unacceptable from the present vantage point. These include Damião de Gois' *(des)lindado* 'delimited', conceivably more than a mere historical curiosity;[3] S. de Covarrubias' LĪNEA, proffered on the assumption that the word came into existence among painters

---

[2] See *Lg.*, XXXI (1955), 291; also Meyer-Lübke's pertinent analysis of the vowel quality of It. *scendere* (*REW*[3] 2588), an entry, incidentally, which fails to do justice to L. Spitzer's astute note in *ASNS*, CXXXVI (1917), 296–298, with further references to Löfstedt, Thielmann, and Engelbrecht.

[3] In the *Crónica de el-rei D. Manuel*, Pt. I, Chap. 21, *cristão lindo* (a clearcut Castilianism, in my view) is extravagantly associated with 'lindado deslindado e sem mistura'. For faint echoes of this rash assertion see Gonçálvez Viana, *Palestras*, pp. 68–71, who regards *deslindar* as leaning on the twin bases *linde* < LĪMITE and *lindo* < LĒGITIMU, and even J. M. Piel in *RPF*, IV (1951), 266 f. In addition to the ambigeneric n. *linde* and to the v. *lindar* < LĪMITĀRE Spanish not so long ago tolerated the n. *lindar* 'threshold' (C. Coloma's Tacitus tr., 1629, p. 226), traceable to a confusion of LĪMITĀRE, -ĀLE (Varro) with LĪMINĀRE; add *lindera* (Toledo Glossary, 318: 'margo'), adj. *lindero* (qualifying an old ox in Ruiz: GS, 1092a); also *lindaño* < Late L. LĪMITĀNEU (omitted from *REW*[3]) and *lindazo* ( < LĪMITĀTIŌ?) 'linde' and *lindón* 'caballete en que suelen poner los hortelanos las esparragueras y otras plantas' (Academy).

(not contradicted by the Academy in 1734; the same Academy's LINCTUS 'licked', hesitantly suggested in 1884 and echoed by a few derivative compilations; Meyer-Lübke's OHG *lindī* 'soft, gentle', a hypothesis launched at the beginning of his career (*ZRPh.*, VIII [1884], 216, 228);[4] and Goth. *\*linths* 'supple, pliant', with which G. Baist toyed for a moment only to withdraw it himself as phonetic-ally unfit (*KJb.* 1904 [1906], I, 202).

This takes us to the first conjecture that commands respect and still has supporters, to wit, Diez's equation Sp. It. *lindo* (beside Sp. *limpio*) < LĪMPIDU, arrived at through comparison with such doublets as It. *torbido* ∼ *torbo, nitido* ∼ *netto* (*EWRS*[1], p. 205; 3d ed., I, 250). This long-uncontested derivation was explicitly supported in 1876 by C. Michaëlis (*Roman. Wortsch.*, p. 291*b*), in 1878 by U. A. Canello with respect to Italian (*AGI*, III, 330) and by C. von Reinhard-stoettner in regard to Ptg. *lindo*, considered as native (*Grammatik*, p. 136), in 1880 by P. Förster (p. 89), in 1881 (posthumously) by P. F. Monlau, ca. 1890 by F. A. Coelho (see A. Nascentes — who remains undecided —, s.v.), in 1889, with reference to It. *lindo* alone, by F. Zambaldi (col. 672, s.v. *lampo*), in 1891 (also 1901, 1907) by G. Körting, in 1893 by A. Morel-Fatio (*Rom.*, XXII, 484),[5] in 1911 (*Estudio elemental de gramática*[3], p. 26), 1914 (Acad. Dict., 14th ed.), 1917 (*Dicc. de la lengua esp.*), and probably earlier by J. Alemany Bolufer, in 1913 by F. Hanssen (*Gramática*, § 62; the author was silent in his *Hist. Gramm.* of 1910), in 1921 by J. J. Nunes, with respect to Ptg. *lindo* and *limpo* (*Crestom. arc.*[2], p. lxxx), in 1929 by P. Fouché (*RH*, LXXVII [1929], 139: m. *limpio*, f. *linda*), in 1930 by H. B. Richardson à propos of Juan Ruiz's (in point of fact, un-related) *lyndero* — a rash statement rashly reiterated in 1946 by R. S. Boggs and his associates —, in 1945 by M. Alvar (*Estudios sobre el "Octavario"*, pp. 34, 64, 67: *lindo, llindo*). After a long silence Menéndez Pidal, as late as 1950, praised this as a model derivation, dubbing it impeccable (*RFE*, XXXIV, 4, where the pair *limpio* ∼ *lindo* is cited as a prize example of lexical bifurcation and plurilinear sound development, along with OSp. *rabdo* ∼ *rabio* < RAPIDU; also *Orígenes*[3], p. 535 n.).

[4] The Germanic base reappears in Alessio-Battisti's *DEI*, col. 2236*a*, as the tenta-tive etymon of dial. It. *lindo* 'liso, logoro' which the authors separate genetically from the Hispanism *lindo* 'pulito'.

[5] He adds evidence from ancient texts, identifies A. Moreto's play *El lindo don Diego* as the midway point in the semantic trajectory, infers Andalusian opposition to the term from its defense by F. de Herrera and Lope.

R

Over against this older, not yet completely discarded, derivation stands the younger hypothesis Sp. *lindo* < LĒGITIMU, first set forth, on the basis of a meticulous chronological classification of meanings, by R. J. Cuervo in 1902 (*RH*, IX, 5–11) and accepted, with strong reservations, by a critical G. Baist.[6] Supported by A. R. Gonçálvez Viana in 1906 (*Apostilas*, II, 73 f.; see also *Palestras filológicas*, 1931, pp. 68–71), later authoritatively endorsed by Meyer-Lübke (*REW*[1], *REW*[3] 4971) and, in his wake, by the two teams G. Alessio– C. Battisti (ca. 1951) and B. Migliorini–A. Duro (*Prontuario*[2], 1953), also by A. Prati (1951), for It. *lindo* (which is at present unanimously recognized as a Hispanism); and, among students of Spanish, by J. Corominas (*AILC*, I [1941–42], 175–180, with a detailed analysis of the cluster -*nd*-; II [1944], 180), A. Alonso (private communication, 1948), V. García de Diego (*Gramática*, 1951), J. M. Piel (*RPF*, IV [1951], 266 f., in conciliatory criticism of Menéndez Pidal), and, quite unequivocally, M. L. Wagner in 1953 (*ZRPh.*, LXIX, 383).

Undoubtedly, LĒGITIMU alone is the sought-for etymon. What obstructed the vision of Diez and his immediate followers was their inability to hierarchize the newly collected forms. Neither Zambaldi nor Morel-Fatio nor even Cuervo spelled out the Spanish provenience of It. *lindo* (this gap was filled by, of all workers, the amateur E. Zaccaria); and Portuguese scholars seem still unanimous in denying the Castilian extraction of *lindo*, despite the irrefutable evidence in favor of this derivation (late date of appearance, limitation to stereotyped phrases like *cristão lindo*, speedy withdrawal of native *lídemo*, *lídimo* before the cognate intruder, as in the parallel conflict of *tibo* vs. *tíbio* 'lukewarm'). Note that Diez's solution, accepted by many distinguished Romanists, starts from the erroneous premise that It. *lindo* is traceable to Latin in a straight line. Once OGal.-Ptg. *li(i)dimo*

---

[6] Baist, presumably mindful of DECIMU > *diezmo*, posited *leyezmo* as the ideal product of LĒGITIMU (note further MARITIMA > *marisma*, with the same aberrant *i*). Baist's argument is not free from serious flaws; for one thing, he seems to forget that LEGERE has yielded the triad Arag. *leyer*, Sp. *leer*, Ptg. *ler*; for another, one might be tempted to explain the *i* before *n* plus consonant as in *PENDICĀRE > Sp. *pingar*, were it not for OGal.-Ptg. *leídimo* > *liídimo* (*Crónica troyana*, II, 334*b*) > *lídimo* (*Visão de Tundalo; RL*, III, 114) beside *lídemo* (Fernão Lopes); see F. A. Coelho, *Rom.*, II (1873), 286; E. B. Williams, *From Latin to Portuguese*, §§ 35₃ and 53; V. García de Diego, *Manual de dialectología española*, p. 54. Has there been a contamination with *lidiar* < LĪTIGĀRE? H. Schuchardt, *Romanische Etymologien*, I (1897), 18 f., 22 f., 43, operates only with *limp(i)o* < LĪMPIDU, as does J. D. M. Ford, *Old Spanish Readings* (1911, 1934), p. xxxiv.

and OSp. *lindo* have been identified as a perfect pair of doublets (comparable to OPtg. *limpo* ~ OSp. *limpio*), Diez's edifice at once cracks and crumbles beyond easy repair. The outside help to break the magic spell of an impasse has in this instance been called in from neighboring Portuguese.

An equally challenging crux had long been OFr. *estuet* 'it is necessary' (infin. *estovoir*), until J. Jud, in a thoroughly documented and cogently reasoned article, sided with A. Tobler (1876 and, less resolutely, 1902) and E. Lerch (1941), against H. Suchier (1901) and E. Walberg (1911), in contending — and proving — that it was an outgrowth of mutilated EST OPUS rather than of impersonally used STUPET.[7] Jud's arguments, as often, revolve around both phonology and semantics, but what matters here is that it took the painstaking analysis of ancient forms from North Italy and Grisons to force a passage through the wall of resistance which the etymologically inconclusive Old French congeners had helped to erect.

## 5. Consequences of the Uniqueness of Etymological Solutions

Difficulties of this caliber we can hardly expect to resolve once we have set about processing our data mechanically in the alphabetical order of the words. Keen awareness of this situation may be one of the reasons why, at least in the Romance domain, the most inspired and adroit etymologists (H. Schuchardt, C. Michaëlis, A. Thomas, J. Jud, to name but a few) have consistently refused to produce more than fragments or torsos of etymological dictionaries and why others, who did publish fine samples of comprehensive reference works, sometimes started out, at the experimental stage, from a radically different organization of the assembled material (W. von Wartburg).

But if the etymologist enjoys a wide margin of liberty in matters of maneuvering, he is, beyond doubt, under the strictest obligation of ultimately supplying a single, unequivocal answer. If it is true that history deals inherently with unique situations involving mostly non-recurrent cause-and-effect relationships, the corollary is that etymology (the scientifically controlled art of piecing together word biographies), being a historical undertaking par excellence, invariably demands unique solutions. For two reasons, this is a point of major

---

[7] See *VR*, IX (1946–47), 29–56, with full bibliography (cf. E. Lerch, *RF*, LV [1941], 372–375), including references to the positions taken by G. I. Ascoli, G. Rohlfs, C. Salvioni, and J. E. Högberg. Add É. Bourciez's readiness, in 1910, to espouse the cause of EST OPUS (*Éléments*, § 276b).

significance both for the chronicler and the theorist of linguistic inquiries.

First, because the pioneer etymologists, unexposed to critical historicism, were wont to come up with multiple solutions, frequently without so much as signaling their personal preferences, let alone establishing any objective scale for gauging the various degrees of probability. In contrast, their present-day successors, I repeat, strive progressively toward the elimination of alternatives and, in exceptionally intricate cases, toward at least some kind of provisional rating of the available rival solutions in the order of decreasing probability.

Second, because structural (functional, descriptive) linguistics, toward the close of the third decade of its organized existence, seems to be veering in exactly the opposite direction. Initially, the new phonology was devised to help survey the objective sound structure of a language, as against the impressionistic, subjective records of fieldworkers taking note of entirely too many, yet never all, marginal oscillations. (One is reminded of the X-ray view of a bone structure, meant to capture all the essentials and nothing but the essentials, as contrasted with photographs or, better still, with interpretive paintings of glittering surfaces.) Yet such has been the dynamics of structuralism that in many quarters this initial goal of searching out invariables was before long abandoned in favor of balancing several competing theories of segmentation and distribution. A quarter of a century ago the non-uniqueness of phonological structures was explicitly affirmed and diagnosed by Y. R. Chao; in the recent past, even if one disregards the terminological differences between rival schools, the same novel pattern of multiple projections has tended to invade, with growing momentum, the province of morphology. If these two cross-currents continue flowing unchecked, we may, at some foreseeable future point, reach a stage of consistent uniqueness in etymological (identificational) and of equally pervasive non-uniqueness in structural (distributional) solutions, to use E. Haugen's memorable labels (*Lg.*, XXVII [1951], 211–222).

## 6. A True Dilemma

If it is correct that the gradual elimination of alternatives is one of the safest measuring rods of progress in etymology, it is doubly important to distinguish between true and false dilemmas. Ordinarily

a stronger etymological conjecture, one bolstered by a more powerful array of telling arguments, completely replaces its vulnerable
predecessor. The process may repeat itself several times; here, in
résumé, is the case history of a dual radical break in the discussion
of a single, narrowly circumscribed issue. The earliest serious
explanation of F. *haricot* (Brit.) 'kidney-bean' (recorded in 1640 by
A. Oudin) — a hypothesis advanced by F. Génin over a century ago,
backed up and reformulated by A. Scheler (1862, 1873), and echoed,
with striking delay, by the compilers of the *Dictionnaire général* —
was that it represented a mere offshoot of its distinctly older homo-
nym *haricot* 'mutton ragout' < OF *hericoq* (from *hari-*, *hali-goter* 'to
cut into slices'?). When G. Paris, taking the cue from J. M. de
Heredia's sparkling, if unprofessional, side remark, stated in 1880 that
the French word for 'kidney-bean' may well be a descendant of
Aztec *ayacotli* 'kind of bean', the new explanation, launched by an
imaginative writer and supported by an esteemed scholar, quickly
gained ground, almost entirely superseding the earlier equation:
K. Nyrop, in 1918, architectured an elaborate edifice of proofs
whose weight, by 1930, convinced even an initially skeptical Meyer-
Lübke. Before long, however, critics and dissenters, even though at
first unable to present a substitute derivation, began to point out the
weakness of the Heredia-Paris hypothesis (A. R. Nykl, in 1925, on
the Aztec and O. Bloch, in 1932, on the Romance side). Finally, in
1940 V. Bertoldi for the first time demonstrated that (*fève de*)
*callicot* initially referred to Calicut in the East Indies, an argument
which spelled the doom of the Mexican base. Of chief interest in this
context is the ebb and flow of endorsements and the inherent incompatibility of *ayacotli* in the New World with *Calicut* in India.
If M. L. Wagner, at first, applauded Nyrop's and later, with mounting enthusiasm, Bertoldi's diametrically opposite etymon, he implicitly disavowed his original decision; if W. von Wartburg, in the
'forties, was led, by the same current, to defend a position different
from his previous stand taken in an early fascicle of the *FEW*, he
did so at the cost of literally reversing himself. No compromise is
possible where the discrepancy reaches this latitude.

### 7. *A Dilemma Unresolved*

In regard to some alternatives, scholars, as a result of irremediable
gaps in the available information or of the ambiguity of the extant

evidence, have finally been driven into an impasse. The classic example of such a stalemate is F. *aveugle*; this case history lends itself all the better to a bird's-eye view as most of the pertinent data have been patiently assembled by O. Deutschmann (*RJb.*, I [1947–48], 87–153) in a monograph favorably judged by a critic of J. Jud's sterling impartiality.[8] To be sure, the effort of a major team of scholars has not been completely wasted; by dint of labor, they have acquired an enviable knowledge of the vicissitudes of *aveugle* from its earliest appearance in texts (*Alexis*) to its triumph, outside a few peripheral dialects, over *borgne* and the descendants of CAECUS and ORBUS; and their researches have yielded many other precious by-products. But the nuclear problem remains unsolved: Is *aveugle* traceable to AB OCULĪS as discovered in a 5th-century hagiographic text (*Actus Petri cum Simone*) shot through with ill-disguised Hellenism and solecisms, or may we link it to the Cassel Gloss 173: *albios oculos* '[OHG] staraplinter' (i.e. 'cataract') which, in turn, lends itself to a plurality of subtly shaded interpretations? The researcher's despair, after fifteen years of unflagging efforts, has been couched in eloquent words by Deutschmann (87, 153), an accredited spokesman for his guild:

> Es sieht so aus, als müßten sich für *aveugle* zwei Erklärungen (< *ab oculis* und *\*alboculus*) unverrückbar gegenüberstehen, ohne daß eine der beiden als sicherlich falsch und die andere als sicherlich richtig zu erweisen wäre. . . . Wir vermögen weder *ab oculis* noch *albus + oculus* umzustoßen; aber nur einer dieser beiden Ausdrücke kann ins Romanische übergegangen sein, um dort frz. *aveugle* zu ergeben.

The alignment of forces around the two dominant conjectures and the major variations may be broken down thus (the dilemma was explicitly stated by Diez as early as 1853):

(A) AB OCULĪS and variants.[9]

---

[8] *VR*, XI (1950), 252 f.; unfortunately, Jud refrained from publishing some doubtless noteworthy reservations at which he vaguely hints. G. Rohlfs, *ASNS*, CXC (1953–54), 70–73, prefers ABOCULĪS as a base and reasons that it may have spread strongest at the expense of ORBUS rather than of CAECUS. My intention is to add only a sprinkling of old and new bibliographic references to those marshalled by Deutschmann and to make in passing a very few minor corrections. To simplify matters, I abstain from re-analyzing the assumed movements of *aveugle* up and down the social scale, the channels of transmission posited (medical, legal, hagiographic jargon?), the radiation of the new word from its focal zone (Ile de France, Normandy, Picardy, possibly also Champagne) into circumjacent areas (and, presumably via Middle Latin, as far south as 13th-century Lombardy, Genoa, and Tuscany), and the controversial relation of adjective to corresponding verb (cf. Meyer-Lübke, *Grammatik der romanischen Sprachen*, IV, 27b).

[9] This tabulation is radically different from Deutschmann's tripartite system.

1. Med. Lat. ABOCELLUS (Du Cange): G. Ménage;
2. *ABOCULUS: F. Diez, *Gramm.*, II (1838), 345 f. and 3d ed., II (1871), 420; id., *Wtb.* (1853), p. 32, with a preamble in 3d ed., I (1869), 40, and *Altroman. Gloss.* (1865), p. 120; A. Scheler, *Dict. d'étym.* (1862, 1873, 1888); A. Brachet. *Dict.* (1868); U. A. Canello (1878); G. Gröber (1884); É. Littré (1885); G. Körting (1891); C. Nigra (1898); H. Berger (1899); G. Paris (1900); A. Darmesteter and A. Thomas (*Dict. gén.*). The connection with Late Gr. ἀπόμματος has been variously assessed by these scholars, of whom Canello and Paris, incidentally, analyzed *ABOCULUS as postverbal;
3. AB OCULĪS, sometimes spelled as one word ('deprived of eyes'): W. von Wartburg (hesitatingly in 1910, vigorously in 1922 [Fasc. 1 of Vol. I of *FEW*] and in 1950 [revision of O. Bloch's *Dict.*]; Meyer-Lübke (*REW*[1] ca. 1911 and *REW*[3] ca. 1930, with different exemplification); O. Bloch (1932); E. Löfstedt (1933); A. Dauzat, *Dict. étym.* (1938); L. Spitzer (1944; see *Lg.*, XX, 243); E. Lerch (1947). Representatives of this school usually bring in Late Greek under some pretext, except Lerch who starts from ABSQUE OCULĪS, a schema common in early Vulgar Latin;
4. AB OCULŌ: quoted from Petronius as a distant prototype or a significant parallel by Brachet (1868), B. Bianchi (1877), Meyer-Lübke (several editions of *Hist. frz. Gr.*, §§ 188, 196), and E. Richter (1934).

(B) ALB(U) OCULŌ and variants: extracted from the Cassel Gloss 173, which has been variously emended (first comment by J. G. von Eckhardt, *Comment.*, I, A.D. 1729); revived, despite Diez's demurrer, by E. Herzog (1902), K. Nyrop (1904), the ophthalmologist O. Gerloff (1906), and especially E. Gamillscheg (1928), on the grounds of M. Niedermann's discovery of ALBUM IN OCULŌ and ALBUM OCULĪ in Pelagonius and Marcellus Empiricus; for criticism see L. Spitzer, *ZRPh.*, XLVI (1926), 573, 580.

(C) Both bases indiscriminately accepted or rejected: G. Körting (1907); L. Clédat, *Dict.*; K. Voretzsch, *Einf.*; O. Bloch (1932); O. Deutschmann (1947); in a way, the young W. von Wartburg (1910).

Easily the most disquieting aspect of this situation is that Deutschmann has succeeded in removing a heavy layer of deep-rooted, oft-repeated errors;[10] has deftly separated primary from secondary

---

[10] Including Diez's misrepresentation of the actual relationship, within Byzantine Greek, of ἀπόμματος and ἐξόμματος; the widely shared unwarranted belief that not only the -gl- cluster, but also the stressed vowel of OF *avo-*, *avue-gle* denounced that word as semilearned; details, too numerous to be here identified, in G. Paris' reconstruction of the trajectory; Lerch's indiscriminate treatment of AB in relation to Late L. ABSQUE 'without'; the adjudication of *avuegle* to the medical, instead of to the hagiographic, strain of the lexicon, championed by Meyer-Lübke, Löfstedt, and

transformations in French dialects; has focused attention on such potentially decisive circumstances as the widespread use of ALBUS OCULUS and OCULUS ALBUS, beside ALBUM (OCULĪ) and ALB-ŪGŌ, -ĪGŌ, -ĀGŌ, -ĒDŌ, -ĀMENTUM in late Antiquity and the early Middle Ages; has demonstrated his acumen in segregating Latinized disguises of Romance forms (e.g. *avocul-us, -atus, -atio*) from the mainstream of the Latin vocabulary; has, with circumspection, dated and localized lost prototypes, available originals, their earliest extant copies and, by implication, noteworthy lexical innovations that occur in them, cf. the pertinent section of the *Actus Petri cum Simone* (from the Greek), our only direct testimony to the substandard use of AB OCULĪS [adj.] 'blind' (as against the trivial adverbial phrase 'on account of one's [sick or tired] eyes'); has further determined the exact semantic shade of OHG *staraplinter* by ingeniously exploiting the position of the gloss within the context. Yet, while the monograph has either solved the side issues that seemed to encumber the path or, at least, has sharply outlined their contour by silhouetting them against the established facts (as in the crucially important case of the relative chronology of Late Gr. ἀπὸ ὀμμάτων vs. Late L. AB OCULĪS), the central etymological problem is still being kept in abeyance. The nearest that Deutschmann comes to its solution (143) is to suggest that the German glossographer who redacted the Cassel Glosses may have been seduced into rendering 6th-century Gallo-Rom. *avuógle* (< AB OCULĪS) by *albios oculos* or some less distorted sequence if his assumed Romance informant happened to draw his attention to the widespread contemporary use of the medieval surgical term ALBUS OCULUS — and a tissue of conjectures hemmed in by so many qualifications is hardly apt to satisfy an exacting etymologist. Thus we seem doomed to moving on and on in a vicious circle.

## 8. A Specious Dilemma

It is less easy to trace the history of a specious etymological alternative. Yet a supposed dilemma, upon closer inspection, may fade away because the assumed basic contrast is lacking. Take Sp.

von Wartburg (A. Schiaffini, *Problemi del lessico italiano* [Rome, 1952], pp. 21, 176 f. an advocate of AB OCULĪS as the starting point, repeats this error); the classification as borrowings from French, rather than as reflexes of medieval Latin, of nonsyncopated forms recorded in ancient Lombardy, Genoa, and Tuscany; the faulty semantic analysis of VACUUS AB OCULĪS by von Wartburg, to say nothing of errors previously corrected by other critics.

OPtg. *preguntar* (Ptg. *perguntar*, variously pronounced, according to the region, [pr̥-], *pèr, per-*), OSard. *percontare* beside *pregontari*, Logud. Campid. [preɣont-āre, -āi] 'to ask (a question)'. Covarrubias, in the wake of Paulus Festus, left to his readers the awkward choice between PERCONTĀRĪ and PERCUNCTĀRĪ which, to his generation of humanists, were apparently, on the authority of the ancients, two distinct words. Present-day classicists realize that PERCONTĀRĪ (MS vars. PERCUNTĀRĪ, PERCONTĀRE) 'to ask particularly, question strictly' is an archaic Latin derivative from the Hellenism CONTUS -Ī 'pole used for pushing a boat along, long spear or pike' (Varro, Vergil, Tacitus), preserved in Spanish, if only as a relic: *cuento* 'regatón o extremidad de la pica, pie derecho o puntal', etc. It has been suggested that the anciently widespread graphy PERCUNCTĀRĪ may be due to the associative interference of either CUNCTOR -ĀRĪ 'to hesitate' or of CUNCTUS, pl. -Ī 'all' (plausible semantic bridges: 'to explore cautiously' or 'to search every corner'). Of no mean importance is the fact that CUNCTĀRĪ and CUNCTUS, already on their wane in Imperial Latin, were totally eclipsed during the transition of Late Latin into Romance.

The two rival assumptions have not fared equally well. PERCUNCTĀRĪ at the outset boasted some advocates (the 18th-century lexicographer J. Stevens; then, after a lapse, the 1884 ed. of the Academy Dictionary and derivative compilations and, after the turn of the century, A. Garcia Ribeiro de Vasconcelos, J. D. M. Ford; also, temporarily at least, R. Menéndez Pidal), but was flatly rejected by C. Michaëlis in a glossary drafted in 1906 and published in 1922. In contrast, the twin bases PERCONT-ĀRĪ, -ĀRE have drawn increasingly strong support from a galaxy of scholars, ranging from the redactors of the original Academy Dictionary and R. Cabrera through F. Diez (accompanied, as usual, by C. von Reinhardstoettner, P. Förster, F. A. Coelho, and G. Körting), J. Leite de Vasconcelos, E. Gorra, É. Bourciez, J. Alemany Bolufer, and W. Meyer-Lübke to a mature Menéndez Pidal (1920), M. Niedermann, V. García de Diego, A. Magne, and many moderns: Dialect geography, lexical stratigraphy, and manuscript filiation independently tend to bear out this derivation of a word preserved, of all provinces, only in Sardinia — where, we know through Wagner, it is autochthonous — and in the Iberian Peninsula, both territories colonized in close succession at an early phase of Roman history; all the more so as the base is amply attested in leading representatives of archaic Latin (Naevius, Plautus, Novius).

The question is more intricate than appears on the surface. If

CONTUS has yielded Sp. *cuento*, one misses in the paradigm of PERCON-TĀRĪ's successor the familiar alternation *o* ~ *ue*, depending on the stress. Cornu (1888, 1906), surely aware of this difficulty, started out from the authentic by-form PERCUNTĀRE. Simultaneously, Baist likened *preguntar* to *nunca*, *punto*, etc., observing the parallel effect on the preceding back vowel of L. -NCT- in Spanish and Florentine territory; add to the shreds of evidence that he cites Ptg. *besuntar* < BIS UNCTĀRE and Sp. *empeguntar*, from PICE and UNCTĀRE. Hanssen (1910, 1913) spoke of an arrested or thwarted sound law. Meyer-Lübke, in both versions of his dictionary, had recourse to the forced spelling PERCŌNTĀRE, without bothering to explain the abnormal vowel lengthening. All of these scholars have failed to take into account OGal. *pregontar* (*Crónica Troyana*), which may, but need not, owe its existence to false regression; and most of them have insufficiently stressed the fact that the divorce of PERCONTĀRĪ from CONTUS, inferred from two fundamental deviations of sound development — voicing of velar, generalization of monophthong —, must be traced (if it is to fall into any pattern) to a markedly early date.

Scholar after scholar has made it plain that somewhere between PERCONTĀRĪ and *preguntar* the intermediate form Hisp.-Rom. *PR(A)ECONTĀRE may safely be reconstructed; this variant, if accepted, accounts for the voicing of -C- (confusion of PER-, PRŌ-/POR-, and PRAE- has long been observed on Spanish soil). In ancient Portugal *preguntar* dominated over *perguntar* by a wide (initially, a very wide) margin; at the preliterary phase *preguntar* is therefore likely to have been the near-exclusive product of the Latin verb. PR(A)E-CONTĀRE, I repeat, is not a different etymon, but a separate adjacent segment of the same trajectory: It refers to a later period than PER-CONTĀRĪ, -CUNCTĀRĪ and is fittingly limited to the Peninsula, to the exclusion of ancient Sardinia, since the dwellers of the far-flung provinces by then were beginning to lose contact with one another.

*Preguntar*, followed by *por*, has at all times meant 'to search, ask for'; otherwise, 'to ask (a question)'. If, in the last analysis, PERCON-TĀRĪ is its base, the first meaning would seem to be traditional and the second, currently dominant, would historically represent a mere extension. On record is even a short-lived departure still farther away from the primitive meaning, in the direction of *pedir* 'to ask (a favor)'. Coincident with this semantic proliferation has been the growth, in terms of frequency, of *preguntar* at the expense of its rivals, the local descendants of INTERROGĀRE and DĒMANDĀRE. The earliest conflict was preliterary, as Meyer-Lübke rightly stresses (*Das Katalanische*, p. 147); ca. 950 we find, on one occasion, 'interrogat' used, in clerical environment, as a popular Hispano-Latin substitute for *consultat* (Glos. Sil. 228). At present *entrugar* has a precarious hold over some Asturian subdialects. Conversely, the competition between *demandar* and *preguntar* permeates numerous texts stretching over centuries.

The old suspicion that *preguntar*, at the dawn of history, may have intervened in the genesis of *barruntar* (OSp. *varruntar*), dial. *berruntar* 'to guess, conjecture' bears further probing. Corominas, in sizing up earlier opinions, has hardly come up with positive results, but then his analysis in some respects is faulty: On the chosen time level, he should have operated with the semantic range of PERCONTĀRĪ (center of gravity: 'searching out'), not of *preguntar* (center of gravity: 'asking'), and might have capitalized on the widespread by-forms based on *berr-* rather than *barr-*, which, occurring in backward dialects, bid fair to represent the earlier of the two variants (cf. VERRERE > *barrer*). Is it sheer coincidence that, in the lexically conservative West, OGal. *pregontar* matches OLeon. *barrontar* beside *varronta* 'news brought by a spy' (*Alexandre*, MS O) and Alent. *aberrontar* 'to notify, have knowledge of. . .'? Finally, starting from the old premise that the verb initially referred to the wild boar (Covarrubias), he could have built a bridge to the richly diversified progeny of VERRĒS: Sp. *berr-aco, -ón* 'male hog', *berr-enchín* 'foaming, grunting of a wild boar', *verr-aquear* 'to grunt like a boar', *verr-iondo* 'ruttish', Salm. *verr-ecer* 'to fecundate the female' (speaking of hogs), etc. Why not posit that *berruntar*, as the product of an early amalgam, originally signified 'to trace and hunt down a boar'?

In sum, we have no reason to doubt that, in this instance at least, the ancient manuscript readings (PER-CONTĀRĪ, -CUNTĀRĪ, -CUNCTĀRĪ) all represent snatches of actual speech and that diversified strata of Latin of which they are mere samples have persisted in the Peninsula. PERCONTĀRĪ, it may plausibly be argued, lives on in western *pregontar*, whose original area, judging from *verrontar*, may have been quite extensive. Although the raising of a once open vowel before *n* + cons. (*PENDICĀRE > *pingar*, cf. *ping-ajo* 'andrajo') is not in itself unusual, there is an excellent chance that *pre-, per-guntar* may, in a direct line, perpetuate the amply attested var. PERCUN(C)TĀRĪ. Latin words showered onto the soil of Hispania not as carefully sifted out units, but dissolving, as they were falling down (and often long before) into bundles of variants, each of which finally succeeded in taking root in a different corner of the Peninsula.

## 9. The Complexity of Etymological Solutions

A unique solution, then, is not tantamount to a simple solution: The situations with which an etymologist copes again and again have been recognized, over the years, as not just occasionally, but preponderantly, even typically, complex. A geographically far-flung, derivationally ramified word family entirely free from the impress of associative interference (blends, false regression, folk etymology, polarization, serialization, hypercharacterization, etc.), and, sometimes concomitantly, of diffusion must, at this writing, rate as the exception rather than the rule. True, in the vast majority of cases the ever-latent disturbance remains localized in a dual sense: first, because it makes itself felt as a strictly regional idiosyncrasy, often one confined to a specific social milieu; second, because it affects a formation of subordinate importance at the periphery of an otherwise normal family. Yet it is equally correct that, given favorable conditions of growth (taboo, a bothersome state of homonymy, the rarity of a sound sequence, the awkwardness of a morphological schema, the response to a general craving for the rejuvenation of a lexicon), the anomaly may spread from outlying zones to the heartland of a country, and, along a different axis, from the margin of a word family to its very core. A consequence of this complexity is that no apodictic argument is more specious at the early stage of an etymological debate (unless the supply of fresh data is known to have been exhausted) than that the seemingly simpler out of two or three rival solutions is necessarily the superior or the only correct one. In general, the only defensible procedure is to collect a growing multitude of data, directly or indirectly pertinent to the nucleus of the given problem, and only then to reëxamine the question as to which of the offered solutions fits with maximum smoothness into the greatest number of independent contexts (phonological, semantic, areal, etc.).

## 10. Compromise Solutions

The sharpened awareness of the preëminently complex character of etymological solutions not only represents a much-needed corrective to their earlier characterization as unique, but also entails a fresh perspective in which past etymological debates may dispassionately be sized up in retrospect. Although such discussions, to the lasting detriment of scholarship, often tend to assume an undesirable degree of violence, the bald truth is that, in more instances than one might suspect, two or more at first glance incompatible etyma turn out, upon reëxamination, to be each partially correct. Such a situation, which is a flexible compromise rather than a stalemate, crystallizes whenever scholars agree to label one base out of at least two under consideration as the actual rootword, the original progenitor, and each of the others as the focus of a secondary, tertiary, etc. contamination or, to vary the metaphor, as a cause of the ultimate deflection of the word at issue from its ideally normal course.

OSp. (d)espedir tr. 'to dismiss', refl. 'to take leave', much like OGal.-Ptg. (d)espir 'to shed', is traceable to L. EXPEDĪRE, as was cogently demonstrated by Diez and confidently reiterated by an expert of Cuervo's rank. But Cornu, in 1880, taking up a different thread at the very juncture where Covarrubias had left off, classed (d)espedir — implicitly severed from (d)espir — with L. EXPETERE and has since drawn the support of Michaëlis, Ford, Menéndez Pidal, and, surprisingly, only a few years ago, of Corominas. Minute examination of the total corpus of evidence shows that EXPEDĪRE, by all odds, was the correct primary base, but also that, barring secondary association with the strongly entrenched *pedir* family (based on PETERE), the word could never have evolved its paradigm and achieved its semantic ambit in the vernaculars. At the peak of the controversy, all participants felt that, as responsible scholars, they had to take sides, with either Diez or Cornu. From today's vantage point, Diez's insight appears astonishingly deep and Cornu's alternative shrewd, though less meritorious than would have been a nuanced modification of his predecessor's formula: In etymology, as in other directions of scholarly pursuit, radicalism, for all its flamboyance, carries with it the seeds of its own destruction.

## 11. Typical Blends

Illustrative examples of blends can be multiplied indefinitely. DĒSIDIA 'idleness', for semantic reasons, is quite unlikely to have furnished of itself the foundation for Sp. *desear*, Ptg. *desejar* 'to wish', whose sound structure it admirably fits; why hesitate to bring in the concomitant pressure of DĒSĪDERĀRE, well entrenched in colloquial

Latin on the testimony of cognate languages? (The assumption of such a conflation, incidentally, relieves us of the uncomfortable necessity of operating, in Meyer-Lübke's wake, with such improbable bases as *DĒSEDIUM, DISSIDIUM, see *REW*³ 2590). Ptg. *cotovelo* 'elbow' is traced by some lexicologists to the family of its Latin synonym CUBITUS (yet by Meyer-Lübke, on at least two occasions, to CUBITĀLIS transmitted by Arabic!), by others, in particular J. Hubschmid, to the substratal base *cotta* evocative of 'something sharp or protruding'. Neither hypothesis, taken in isolation, proves entirely satisfactory: CUBITUS is too plentifully represented in Romance, Old Portuguese included (*cóvedo*, *-ado*), to be completely brushed aside, the more so as Sp. *codillo*, although semantically remote (*REW*³ 2354), authorizes us to project the diminutive *CUBITELLUS, a perfect parallel to GEN-ICULUM, -UCULUM from GENŪ 'knee', into the local variety of colloquial Latin. On the other hand, such a base, granted that it existed, would have given rise to *covedelo* (later, if we heap hypothesis upon hypothesis, to metathesized *codevelo* and, with labialization of the intertonic vowel, *codovelo*), but, without outside interference, certainly not *cotovelo*: At this terminal point the agency of *cotta* must have made itself felt. — The kinship of Sp. *ronda* (OSp. *rolda*, *robda*, also *arrobda*) 'night patrol, beat' < Ar. *rubṭ* (pl.) and of Sp. (*ar*)*rebato* (anciently also *-e* and *-a*) 'sudden attack, fit' (whence *arrebatar*) < Ar. *ribāṭ* 'fortress' cannot be questioned after J. Oliver Asín's painstaking demonstration (1928), sanctioned by Steiger, Meyer-Lübke, and Neuvonen. But at some point the Oriental intruder seems to have impinged on the French descendant of L. ROTUNDA transmitted into Spanish (cf. *lonja* < LONGA); witness this sentence from Pérez Galdós: ". . . iba por *rondas*, travesías y calles como una flecha" (*Misericordia*, Chap. VII). — The family of It. *accordare*, Sp. *a-*, *re-cordar*, etc. has been moored alternately (a) to Gr.-L. CHORDA (Meyer-Lübke, *REW*¹ 83 [1911], *REW*³ 71*a* [fasc. I, 1930]; W. Förster, *Wörterbuch* [1914]; von Wartburg, *FEW*, I, 13 [1922], and at much earlier times, starting with Ménage, since this derivation is explicitly rebutted by Diez and by Cuervo) and (b) to L. COR, -DIS, pl. CORDA 'heart' (R. Cabrera, 1837; F. Diez, 1853, 1869; A. Brachet, 1869; P. F. Monlau, 1881; G. Gröber, "Substrate . . .", *ALLG*, I [1884], 234; É. Littré, 1885; R. J. Cuervo, 1886; J. Alemany Bolufer, repeatedly; E. Gamillscheg, *ZRPh.*, XLIII [1923–24], 516, and *EWFS*, fasc. 1 [1926]; F. de B. Moll, 1928–30; von Wartburg, revision of O. Bloch [1950; note contrast to his earlier view]; B. Migliorini [1953]; and J. Corominas [1954], who separates from the common stock the semantic strain 'to awaken', tracing it to *acordado* [= *cuerdo*], from the archaism CORDĀTUS [Ennius, Plautus]). Some of these scholars (Gamillscheg, Migliorini, the later von Wartburg) grant the possibility of contamination by CHORDA. The compromise hypothesis of two interlocking homophones, *ACCORDĀRE and *ACCHORDĀRE, has been championed — but not quite identically formulated — by O. Bloch (1932), A. Dauzat (1938), and the team G. Alessio–C. Battisti (1950). This time, the final clarification has issued from the laboratory of a great Latinist, A. Ernout, who demonstrated beyond any reasonable doubt that COR, -DIS is at the center of the Latin and Romance family, granting freely a liberal margin of secondary influence to CHORDA.[11] — I have stated elsewhere my reasons for supporting the derivation of OPtg. *lazerar*, OSp. *laz(d)rar* 'to suffer' from LACERĀRE 'to tear' and for granting, at the same time, to LAZARUS a small measure of late influence in Portuguese (*NRFH*, VI [1952], 209–276).

## 12. Merging Two Different Techniques of Analysis

The increasingly appreciated importance of crosses will almost inevitably lead to fresh attempts at refining our fairly crude techniques of analyzing lexical contamination. At this moment, one group of scholars is engaged in a quest for social (historical, cultural, that is, non-linguistic) contents in which each such process can most smoothly be embedded. Another group, with equal élan and, sometimes, superior rigor, tries, as accurately as possible, to determine the specific points of contact within the fabric of language: a particularly exposed derivative, a vulnerable section of the paradigm, a stem variant susceptible of misinterpretation, an ambiguous or unstable syntactic ("contextual") by-form. In the hands of a many-

---

[11] "*Cor* et *c(h)orda*", *RePh*, XXVI (1952), 157–161. Ernout's particular merit consists in having disclosed the incipient stage of the influence of imported CHORDA upon the vernacular COR, -DIS family, a stage perfectly observable within the confines of Latin. Cf. his philological analysis of characteristic overtones of CONCORS (Cyprianus Gallus), CONCORDIA (Quintilian), CONCORDĀRE (Boethius), also of DISCORDIA (Vergil, Lucan) and DISCORDĀRE (Statius, Avitus, Boethius). Ernout points to the near-synonyms CONSENTIŌ ~ ADSENTIŌ as the pair that may have provided the long-sought model for CONCORDŌ ~ *ACCORDŌ and, in the process, literally demolishes Meyer-Lübke's slipshod entry. Both Ernout and Corominas seem to be unaware of M. Singleton's judicious note on OSp. *acordar* (*Lg.*, XVII [1941], 119–126), which anticipates some of their findings.

sided and imaginative scholar, these two ordinarily disparate analyses, under favorable circumstances, lend themselves to stimulating combination. Thus, to account for the anomaly of PUBLICUS, an adjective consistently correlated in Roman literature to POPULUS, but genetically extracted from PUBES, É. Benveniste convincingly sets up the formula PUBLICUS = *PUBICUS × Arch.-L. POPLICUS, then goes on to identify military assemblies (CONTIŌNĒS) and religious rites as the locale or background of the merger, the earlier Greek dichotomy ἡβηδόν vs. πανδημεί as the probable source of a semantic loan translation into Latin, and the respective adverbs in -ICĒ, well ahead of the underlying adjectives in -ICUS, as the actual spearheads of the conflicting word families that must have clashed at the dawn of history.[12]

### 13. Erratic Patterns of Etymological Debates

From most of the examples so far adduced it seems to follow that, with surprising regularity, two rival etymological conjectures tend to crystallize and to rigidify at a certain stage of the discussion, while the remaining hypotheses, by the same token, evaporate for lack of cogent arguments, convincing evidence, appropriate background, etc. Such a gradual trend toward dichotomy or polarization has been, indeed, exceedingly common in the annals of etymological research: To quote two classic alternatives not yet mentioned, cf. OProv. *trobar*, F. *trouver* < TURBĀRE [AQUAM] vs. Gr.-L. CONTROPĀRE or OSp. *quexar*, Ptg. *queixar* < COAXĀRE 'to croak' vs. *QUESTIĀRE 'to complain' (or else *QUAESTIĀRE from QUAERERE) as analyzed and, in part, discarded *Lg.*, XXI (1945), 142–183. Yet it would be most hazardous to infer from these statistically unsifted examples any inherent necessity for a binary configuration of the final (or, preferably, next to the final) score in any etymological debate. Not only are there numerous triads on record, but we have to reckon with a hard core of overlapping, highly erratic, vaguely or bizarrely delineated, and even amorphous patterns of opinion. One extreme example may suffice to hammer home the point.

The history of OF *re(s)ver* 'to roam, rave' (> F. *rêver* 'to dream'), *desver, derver* 'to madden, be mad' is a proverbial crux. By the turn of the last century, at least two dozen tentative solutions of the intricate problem (some of them at that juncture definitely obso-

---

[12] "Pubes et publicus", *RePh.*, XXIX (1955), 7–10.

lescent or obsolete) had been proffered, emanating from scholars of a wide range of calibers. These include the following Latin or pseudo-Latin etyma (assembled in large part, at my request, by Mlle Geneviève M. Corréard[13]):

1. REVIDĒRE: P. Labbe (1607–67), cited by G. Ménage;
2. (RE)PUER-ĀSCERE, *-ĀRE: Ménage; rejected by Scheler (1862);
3. *RE-EX-UARIĀRE, with a reference to Sp. *desvariar*: J. L. Frisch (1666–1743), here quoted via E. J. Hauschild's key (1843) to Diez's Romance grammar;
4. (Late L.) DĒUIĀRE: Du Cange, II (1842), 827*b*, also III (1884), 89*a*, and, probably, earlier editions; mentioned s.v. *endéver* by Scheler (1862) who also quotes the base Low L. [*]DĒ-EX-UIĀRE, without identifying its advocate; found less than satisfactory by Diez (1870), but revived by E. Staaff, *Uppsatser. . . . P. A. Geijer* (1901), pp. 251–264, whose elaborated version was severely criticized by G. Paris, *Rom.*, XXXI (1902), 448 f., by P. Marchot, and by their successors;
5. *RE-EUĀRE 'to rejoice', presumably from Gr.-L. EU(H)ĀNS: Diez toyed with this possibility in 1853, Scheler mentioned it briefly in 1862;
6. DISSIPĀRE 'to scatter' > *des-*, *der-ver* beside RAB-IE, -IA > *rêve* (interpreted as a dialectal variant), cf. E. *rave*, Burg. *ravasser*: a dual hypothesis launched by Diez (1853), pp. 608, 717, adopted by G. F. Burguy (1869–70), and amplified by Scheler (1862) through the addition of Pic. *réder* < *RABIDĀRE and OF *revelé* 'proud'. Later Diez abandoned DISSIPĀRE, while clinging to RABIĒS (1870); Körting (1891) questioned RABIĒS, flatly rejected Scheler's extension; *REW*[1] 249 disapproved of RABIĀRE, leaving DISSIPĀRE unmentioned;
7. DIABOLUS and its derivatives, cf. E. *devil*, Prov. [Sp.] *endiablar*, Ptg. *endiabrar*, reminiscent of *resverie*: É. Cachet (1809–57); favored by Scheler in 1862 s.v. *endéver*, but no longer in 1873;
8. DĒ-SAEV-ĪRE, *-ĀRE 'to rave, rage': proposed by L. Diefenbach (1806–83), mentioned by Scheler in 1887 (Suppl. to *EWRS*[5]), s.v. *desver*, and by G. Gröber, *ZRPh.*, V (1881), 178; favored by F. Neumann, *ZRPh.*, XIV (1890), 563; rejected in *REW*[1] 249;
9. DĒROGĀRE 'to diminish', on the strength of OF *enterver* < INTER-ROGĀRE: Diez mentions it as not quite satisfactory in 1870, *REW*[1] 249 rejects it;
10. DĪRU-ERE, *-ĀRE 'to tear asunder' > *derver*: mentioned, without express endorsement, by Diez (1870), s.v. *desver*; championed by K. Bartsch, *ZRPh.*, II (1878), 307, whose note Scheler quotes in 1887, but Meyer-Lübke omits from *REW*[1] 249;

---

[13] Miss Corréard's own monograph, in which she appropriately credits two Berkeley teachers with having stimulated her curiosity, has meanwhile appeared: "Contributions à l'étymologie de *rêver* et *desver*", *Travaux de l'Institut de Linguistique* (Paris), III (1958 [–60]), 95–135.

S

11. DĒSIPERE 'to act foolishly', esp. 3d pers. DĒSIPIT: Diez (1870), s.v. *desver*, and Scheler (1873). Körting (1907) misses substitution of *a* for *i* through recomposition, and Meyer-Lübke, using unjustifiably \*DIS- for DĒ-, repudiates the whole idea (*REW*[1] 249);

12. \*D(Ē)-ĒBRIĀTUS 'intoxicated': briefly mentioned and at once abandoned by Scheler (1873), s.v. *endêver*;

13. \*ERRĀTĀRE from ERRĀRE 'to rove, stray about', on the strength of OF *embla(v)er*: S. Bugge, *Rom.*, IV (1875), 364 f.; quoted by Scheler in 1887, less favorably in 1888 (*Dict.*[3]), s.v. *rêve*; despite much praise, not wholly accepted by Körting in 1891, explicitly rejected as too bold in 1901 and 1907; left unmentioned in *REW*[1] 249;

14. \*DIS-VĀ(DE)RE (instead of Ē-): J. Ulrich, *Rom.*, VIII (1879), 264; seriously questioned by G. Paris in an editorial footnote; quoted non-committally by Scheler in 1887 (s.v. *desver*) and in 1888 (s.v. *endêver*); rejected by Körting in 1891 (except for \*REVĀDERE > *rever* [sic]), but rehabilitated in 1896 (*ZFSL*, XVIII: 1, 271 f.), 1901, and 1907, with *resver* newly attributed to \*RE-EX-VĀRE and *desver* analyzed as *de* plus *resver*;

15. \*DĒ-EX-RĪPĀRE, var. \*DIS-: Ulrich, *Rom.*, IX (1880), 579, a note in which G. Paris' new editorial criticism (assonances require ę, not ẹ) is incorporated and parried. Rejected by G. Gröber, *ZRPh.*, V (1881), 177 f., on account of prefix; quoted non-committally by Scheler (1887), s.v. *desver*, and (1888), s.v. *endêver*; omitted from *REW*[1] 249. Scheler (1862) and Diez (1870) also refer obliquely to Sp. *derribar*;

16. DĒRĪVĀRE > *derver*: E. Schwan, *Gramm.* (1888), § 153; criticized by F. Neumann, *ZRPh.*, XIV (1890), 563, withdrawn by Schwan in 1893 (see Cohn, *ZRPh.*, XVIII [1894], 202), left unmentioned in *REW*[1] 249;

17. \*DISVIDUĀTU (from VL. [gloss] DĪVIDUĀRE, based on DĪVIDUUS 'divisus') > OF. *desvé*: G. Cohn casually weighed, then eliminated, this possibility (*ZRPh.*, XVIII [1894], 204), left unrecorded in *REW*[1] 249;

18. \*DĒSUĀTUS 'dem eigenen normalen Sein entfremdet' > adj. (> ptc.) *desvé*: Cohn, *ZRPh.*, XVIII (1894), 202–212; termed monstrous by Körting (1896), who nevertheless made a separate entry (2924) in 1907, an attitude contrasting with Meyer-Lübke's silence (*REW*[1] 249);

19. REBELLĀRE > OF *reveler* > *rever* (through "dédiminutivisation", speaking with Gilliéron): suggested by the pioneers Chevallet and Scheler, formulated stringently by Cohn in 1895 (*Abhandlungen . . . Tobler*, pp. 269–288), accepted in the main by Tobler himself (*ASNS*, XCV [1895], 203 f.), rejected by Körting (1896, 1901) and by Meyer-Lübke (*REW*[1] 249);

20. \*REQU(I)ĀRE 'to rest', based on RE-QUIĒS: C. Nigra, *AGI*, XIV (1898), 297; rejected by Körting (1901) and by Meyer-Lübke (1911);

21. *DISAEQUĀRE 'to unsettle the balance' (cf. INĪQUĀRE in Laberius) >
*desver* ~ *dessiver*, thought of as parallel to *disner* ~ *desjeuner*:
Ulrich, *ZRPh.*, XXIII (1899), 418; called unlikely if not impossible
by G. Paris, *Rom.*, XXVIII (1899), 635; mentioned by Körting,
for the first time in Suppl. to 1901 ed. of *LRW* (2810), and rejected
in *REW*[1] 249.

To these Gallo-Roman equations must be added some even less
well substantiated, random attempts at derivation from Greek
(ῥέμβειν: H. Estienne; B. de Roquefort, *Dict.*, 1829; Noël and
Carpentier, quoted by Hauschild, 1843, a suggestion shrugged off
by Diez and Scheler), from Gaelic (*rabhd*; mentioned by Diez, 1853,
and by Scheler, 1862), and from Germanic (A. de Chevallet, 1812–
58; F. A. de Reiffenberg, 1795–1850; É. Littré, each coming up with
a different etymon — for details see Scheler, 1862 and 1873). Other
scholars showed an agnostic attitude: A. Brachet (1868), A. Thomas
(*Essais*, 1897, pp. 120 f., à propos of a Basque loan-word), later also
L. Clédat, the redactors of the *Dictionnaire général*, and O. Bloch,
*Dict.* (1932). Let us finally mention the mere reconstruction of links,
without any concomitant etymological commitment, (a) between
*desver* and *resver* (J. J. Ampère and F. Génin, in the wake of
P. Labbe) and (b) between *derver* and *desver* (Neumann, *LGRPh.*, VI
[1885], col. 241, and G. Paris, *Rom.*, XV [1886], 620, in parallel
reviews of W. Koeritz's dissertation; also W. Meyer-Lübke, *Rom.*
*Gramm.*, I, § 529, and Cohn, *ZRPh.*, XVIII [1894], 202; on Pic.
W.-F. -*rn*- ~ Franc. -*sn*- see later J. Brüch, *ZFSL*, LVI [1932], 72).

After 1900, at least three of the older conjectures were tentatively
revived or proposed anew, without reference to the findings of pioneers, and surrounded by a battery of new supporting or collateral
arguments. P. Marchot championed DĒRĪVĀRE > *der-*, *des-ver* (an
idea once cherished by Schwan), stressing syntax and phraseology
(*Rom.*, XLVII [1921], 221–226); R. Loriot reverted to Staaff's
-VIĀRE 'sortir de la bonne voie, s'en écarter', concentrating on Picard
toponymy and on the penetration of the word into Germanic (*Rom.*,
LXIX [1946–47], 463–495; 554); G. Alessio associated *desverie* with
Sp. *desvarío*, It. *svariato di mente*, granting that *desver* may involve
contamination with *\*dessevét* < DISSIPĀTU (*RLiR*, XVII [1950], 174 f.).

There has been no dearth of fresh hypotheses, of which, to my
knowledge, the latest and, to my taste, the most daring and brilliant
(though not necessarily correct) was offered in 1936. The newly
suggested etyma, predominantly Gallo-Roman, include:

(a) AESTUĀRE 'to be passionately moved': J. Vising, *Rom.*, XXXVII (1908), 157–160, who reaffirms the fundamental unity of *desver* and *resver*; accepted by Meyer-Lübke (*REW*[1] 249; approval withdrawn in *REW*[3], 1930–35) and Dauzat (*Dict. étym.*, 1938, 1946); defended by its proponent against Marchot, *Rom.*, XLIX (1923), 98–104, with an insistence on the preponderantly intransitive use, cf. mod. dial. (*en*)*dêver*;

(b) Frk. *\*reufan* 'to tear apart, break' as a loan translation of COR RUMPERE, on the assumption that *derver* is an emphatic variant of *rever* and that rhizotonic *\*(de)-rieve* became extinct at an early date: E. Gamillscheg, *ZRPh.*, XLI (1921), 518–520; criticized by Spitzer (1922) and Vising (1923) and withdrawn by its advocate (1926, 1935);

(c) a compromise between Marchot's DĒRĪVĀRE > *derver* and, concurrently, a Germanic base for *resver*, except that this time the Frankish counterpart of OHG *hriuwan* 'to sadden, annoy' was implicated: L. Spitzer, *ZRPh.*, XLII (1922), 25 f.; rejected by *REW*[3] 4210;

(d) VL (gloss) REFRAGIUM 'opponent', Ch.-L. REFRAGIUM 'resistance', Merov. REFRAGARE 'to oppose' connected with *rever* via *\*revrer* and with OF *enrievre* 'stubborn' (the last base as against Tobler's IRREVERĒNS and Thomas' *\*IRRÉPROBUS*, with *derver* < *\*DERE-FRAGARE* and *desver* = *dever* < *derver* (through consonant dissimilation) relegated to the periphery: E. Gamillscheg, *EWFS* (1928; fasc. 1926), p. 359*a*; reaffirmed *ZFSL*, LIX (1935), 73 f.; rejected by *REW*[3] 4210 and criticized by Jud (1936);

(e) REUEHĪ 'to be carried away' (on the basis of medical and mystic literature): E. G. Lindfors-Nordin, *ZFSL*, LIX (1935), 46–69; approved by Gamillscheg on semantic and syntactic, but rejected on phonic and stylistic grounds (ibid., pp. 70–74); termed unsatisfactory by Jud (1936);

(f) ÉXVAGUS > *\*esvo* taken as the starting point for a new revolutionary paradigm tending to replace traditional EXVAGĀRĪ > OF *esvaiier*; OF *enresde* 'violent, furious' is a cognate involving -IDUS: J. Jud, *Rom.*, LXII (1936), 145–157; endorsed by W. von Wartburg in his revision of O. Bloch's *Dict.* (1950).

A hostile critic may be tempted to quote inquiries into *rêver* as a perfect example of disunity and arbitrariness in the ranks of leading etymologists, with some scholars changing sides or injecting new ideas at an alarming rate. On the positive side of the ledger is the indisputable fact that approximately from 1895 (Cohn, Staaff) the brief, thin, nonchalantly drafted note has tended to yield to the elaborate, sophisticated, conscientiously documented article, called upon to cover more and more ground: textual criticism, dialectology, toponymy, derivational patterns, syntactic sequences, phraseological details, semantic spectrum, lexical diffusion beyond solid language frontiers, etc. What matters most in this context, however, is neither the distressing initial diversity of hypotheses, nor the heartening progressive refinement of method, but the pathetic (and, fortunately, exceptional) inability of seasoned scholars to reduce the multifarious conjectures still worth debating to a few characteristic archetypes. The fact that a triad of near-synonymous verbs is involved (*derver, desver, resver*) seems to point in the direction of a simple or compound lexical blend, whose study cannot make headway without a preliminary painstaking inventory of all the variants classed according to date, place, construction, and meaning.

## 14. A Future Typology of Etymological Solutions

This leads us to a new type of research, not yet essayed, it seems, at least not on a major scale and for its own sake, as it were: a typology of etymological solutions (or, at least, of the latest stages of etymological discussions). On an earlier occasion the suggestion was made to collect and re-analyze in retrospect, as so many deterrents, the more noteworthy errors made by distinguished etymologists, including gratuitously inferred hypothetical bases (*Word*, VI, 42–69). In a few chosen instances, there may be a point in substituting for this gallery of memorable aberrations a chronologically slanted account of oscillations, reverberations, and reversals of etymological opinion, whether eventually proven right or wrong. It has, after Schuchardt, become a truism to claim that each single word (or, for that matter, each lexical family) has a history of its own. Some of these biographies are so dramatic and have, in fact, been so effectively dramatized by scholars versed in the art of writing that it seems permissible, by gently stretching the metaphor, to speak of veritable plots and dénouements. If this is so, then the meandering path of each etymological discussion, not in the raw shape of dry minutes and summaries but in the organized and distilled form of what French scholarship so aptly calls "l'historique du problème", richly deserves to be set aside as A PLOT WITHIN A PLOT and, in its own right, to form part, to however modest a degree, of the history of ideas. If we care to remember that even semilearned and scholarly identification of word origins, under exceptional conditions, has succeeded in powerfully influencing the development of lexical units, then the larger and the smaller plot, the trajectory of a word and the trajectory of scholarly opinion observing its course, will figure justifiably in our descriptions as tangential.[14]

[14] It would have been unrealistic to attempt to make 1967 rather than 1955 the terminal point for the garnering of documentation in every single vignette. Suffice it to remark that the elusive relation of Sp. *pingar* to its hypothetical base is reëxamined in my forthcoming paper, "Le nivellement morphologique comme point de départ d'une 'loi phonétique': La monophtongaison occasionnelle de *ie* et *ue* en ancien espagnol", to appear this year in the *Mélanges Jean Frappier*.

# 10

# A Typological Classification of Dictionaries on the Basis of Distinctive Features

## 1. Background

THIS paper embodies a report on an experiment undertaken some two years ago.[1] The results of this specific experiment may or may not lend themselves to generalization. From the mid-'forties, I had engaged for fifteen years in various studies of Romance etymology and derivation, with a clearly discernible emphasis on Hispanic material. These researches were based in part on the perusal of original texts, but, inescapably, a wide range of dictionaries had been tapped for miscellaneous bits of information. There exists a tradition among lexicologists to offer to their fellow-workers, besides the genuine fruits of their researches, also an inventory of the tools employed. Thus, W. von Wartburg's monumental *Französisches Etymologisches Wörterbuch*, slanted in the direction of dialectology, was accompanied by a bibliography of patois vocabularies. Instead of preparing, along traditional lines, a similar Hispanic bibliography, containing items either arranged in a straight alphabetical sequence or subdivided into several regional groups — say, Asturian, Andalusian, Mexican —, I began asking myself whether a pervasive classification by lexicographic genres was at all feasible. A rough break-down of this kind was, of course, nothing new, since numerous research-library catalogues make it a point to distinguish between mono-, bi-, tri-

Reprinted from *International Journal of American Linguistics*, XXXVIII:2 (1962), Part IV (*Problems in Lexicography*), eds. F. W. Householder and S. Saporta, pp. 3–24.

[1] A condensation, with modifications, of my article "Distinctive features in lexicography: a typological approach to dictionaries exemplified with Spanish", *RPh.*, XII (1958–59), 366–399 and XIII (1959–60), 111–115. The longer article was searchingly appraised, along with several other writings of mine, by Karl D. Uitti, "Problems in Hispanic and Romance linguistics", *HR*, XXXIV (1966), 242–255.

257

lingual and polyglot dictionaries and likewise set apart encyclopedic, historical, comparative, and etymological reference works and surely many other sharply delineated varieties, especially those appealing to a specific kind of reader. As is frequently the case with classification, the core of the difficulty seemed to lie in the overlapping of the categories hastily established on the basis of first impressions. To adduce but one example: Aside from straight etymological dictionaries, geared to the one purpose of supplying information on word origins (on various levels of scholarly sophistication), there exist all-purpose monolingual dictionaries and, far less commonly, bilingual dictionaries which, in response to the layman's curiosity, also carry stray bits of etymological information, representing, in a way, mixed genres of lexicography. In simplified listing, should such transitional types be altogether disregarded and the pure types alone be placed in the focus of attention? Such an arbitrary decision would tend to curtail unduly the available material. The alternative would be to do justice to as many titles as possible, on condition that either the number of categories be radically increased or that each item, i.e., each lexicographic venture, instead of being treated as an inseparable unit, be decomposed into a number of salient features allowing of a large number of combinations. The obvious model that I had in mind was the separation of a speech sound into a number of distinctive features, an analysis originally practiced with particular skill by the school of European phonologists, but at present widely adopted on both sides of the Atlantic. Was it legitimate to regard a reference book as a bundle of characteristic features which could be reassembled in some kind of arrangement that might be expressed in a simple formula? The article in question stopped short of this last step of providing actual formulas, but was designed to lead the reader to the precise point from which a succinct formulaic labelling could be freely envisaged.

For this particular experiment, limited to a single language and involving, all told, not much more than five hundred items, the distinctive features were chosen so as to satisfy two fundamental requirements: range and neatness of contour. First, the greatest possible number of the vocabularies and glossaries collected at random were to lend themselves to this type of composite characterization. Second, any degree of redundancy in the delimitation of distinctive features was to be scrupulously avoided, each being selected on the basis of its discreteness, i.e., independence of the others. The existence of tendential convergences and affinities was, from the outset, taken for granted, but every feature, to qualify for inclusion, was to preserve under any circumstances its unmistakable identity.

## 2. A Set of Broad Classificatory Criteria

These aims, it seems, call for the establishment of the following three classificatory criteria, each subject to further subdivision:

1. Classification by RANGE;
2. Classification by PERSPECTIVE;
3. Classification by PRESENTATION.

**2.1. Range,** i.e. the volume and spread of the material assembled, represents, from the layman's and the specialist's viewpoint alike, the most obvious criterion; it is also the most objective, involving by definition tangibles alone. Further subdivision is possible, according to whether attention is focused on (a) density of entries, (b) number of languages covered or resorted to, (c) degree of concentration on strictly lexical data (at the expense of *realia*, proper names, and the like).

**2.2 Perspective:** Under this label it is advantageous to subsume several broad directions in which bundles of lexical facts are apt to be projected, irrespective of the scope of each vocabulary and of the favored style of presentation. Perspective essentially involves the collector's deliberate or semi-naïve attitude toward the chosen slice of material, i.e., the type of curiosity that drives him in the first place to delimit and launch his project. The specific attitude is best determined if one selects the proper components of the ensemble from a number of oppositions, binary or triadic: (a) with regard to the time axis, the outlook may be historical (dynamic) or synchronic (static); (b) with regard to the basic arrangement, the sequence may be conventional (alphabetic), semantic (ordering by "parts of speech" or provinces of life), or entirely arbitrary (chaotic); (c) with regard to avowed purpose, the prevalent tone may be objective, preceptive (also, viewed from the opposite pole, prohibitive), or jocular. In theory, any vocabulary may be scrutinized from all three angles, and the combination of the three separate analyses determines the composite perspective. On a higher plane of abstraction one may attempt to establish certain steady or tendential relationships between sub-classes within the three categories of temporal projection, sequence of items, and purpose of enterprise.

**2.3. Presentation:** If operating with "perspectives" helped us account for the broad policies, "presentation" serves as a convenient term for subsuming narrower preferences, such as typographic style, use of special symbols and abbreviations, inclusion of incidental grammatical remarks, latitude of definition, volume of verbal documentation and of graphic illustration (if any), and many similar externals. In other words, perspective concerns the lexicographer's logistics and strategy, while presentation involves his tactics. To achieve simplification, analysis may be reduced to the discussion of four salient points: (a) definition; (b) exemplification; (c) graphic illustrations (including maps); (d) special features (localization in territorial terms, on the social scale, or along the axis of "affectivity"; marking of pronunciation).

Ideally, a formal bibliography or a research-library catalogue may well be based on this (or any improved) set of classificatory principles. While conventional bibliographies and catalogues adequately describe the externals of a publication (format, number of pages, place and date of appearance, etc.), a typological repertory may effectively convey an analytical bird's-eye view of the inner configuration of each item (short of value judgments): its spatial and temporal range, its degree of selectivity, the interplay of its three basic perspectives (distance from the historical axis, schema of arrangement, and level of discourse), plus its editorial and typographic techniques of presentation.

### 3. Some Special Conditions

The lengthy original monograph underlying the present paper supplied only a few particularly representative instances of a given variety or subvariety, sometimes out of more than twenty available illustrations. As long as the classificatory schema is valid, expanding such a skeletal documentation to one of fuller size or of relative completeness remains a matter of space budgeting. Little more than a vague hint of the preliminary bibliographic spadework can be provided in the present epitome.

What marks an item for inclusion in a typological survey is less the intrinsic quality of craftsmanship than the novelty of the architectural design. In extreme cases, an elaborate work, structured along conventional lines, may fall short of acceptance, if it enriches the existing models by no truly original device or daring combination of familiar devices. Conversely, a departure from earlier practice — even if deemed by hindsight a failure or, at best, a controversial accomplishment — deserves consideration, as an attempt at innovation. At its most austere, a typological classification should steer clear of value judgments; in practice, succinct appraisals amounting to merely parenthetic remarks may be condoned, as long as they do not interfere with actual analytical operations.

Aside from its intrinsic significance and charm, the typological approach may produce a wholesome controlling effect: It is apt to disclose noteworthy gaps, identifying combinations of features not yet tried out, and may thus open up avenues of approach not only to all sorts of impracticable oddities, but also to rewarding possibilities so far overlooked. In chosen instances one can point out how similar lacunae have been successfully filled by fellow-workers concerned with other languages.

Typological sketches are not meant to replace the time-honored genre of formal bibliographies, which are, by and large, more circumstantial, and which silhouette with equal sharpness each work captured by the observer's lens, lending themselves smoothly to evaluative comments. Typology, being the more abstract mode of classification, simply acts as a corrective of straight bibliographic records, breaking loose of anecdotal detail and of the all too often obtrusive "human element". Jointly, bibliography and typology reflect the dual focus of linguistics on individual facts of language, viewed in their undistorted richness and uniqueness, and on the underlying broader patterns.

### 4. Classification by Range

This approach, we recall, allows of further subdivision, according to the variable emphasis on (1) density of entries, (2) number of languages, and (3) extent of concentration on purely lexical data.

**4.1. Measurement of density.** Though ideally a dictionary's relative density, being a quantitative feature, should be subject to precise measurement, there exist in practice almost insurmountable obstacles to a neat statistical tabulation. It is, of course, possible to compute the actual number of entries, and some publishers flaunt it in a subtitle or in commercial advertisement (others claim credit not for the total coverage, but for specific accretions, choosing some earlier authority as an appropriate frame of reference). The figures thus obtained, though accurate in isolation, lend themselves to no meaningful comparison, in the absence of generally accepted norms for the selection and grouping of entries. Thus, a few reputable lexicographers, for the sake of maximum compactness, consolidate homophones, subsuming under a single entry two or more words treated separately by such (more conservative) authors as prefer to heed semantic or etymological considerations.

In the case of a living and dynamically changing language, the primary hindrances to a valid comparison of coverage are: (a) the essential instability of its lexicon, a condition precluding the establishment of any definitive repository based on exhaustive excerpts from a finite corpus of texts; (b) the, strictly speaking, incompatible scopes of even the best lexicographic projects so far launched, as a result of sharply divergent objectives and techniques. Among the compilers of dictionaries few have bothered to lay down binding norms or to abide by any. Numerous dictionaries allow the inclusion of archaisms, whether or not marked as such; only a few workers resolutely attempt to weed out obsolete terms by starting from entirely fresh collections of raw data or settle on a compromise by making carefully pre-established concessions to the dominant preference (e.g., by respecting the usage of a few classics, explicitly identified). As regards coverage in breadth, it seems inadmissible, then, to maintain that a given dictionary contains, say, 80% of the total lexicon, as long as that total remains undefined, and it is hazardous to assert that one dictionary is more comprehensive than another, unless they are modeled on exactly the same pattern. To compound the difficulty, lexical range is concomitantly determined by coverage in depth, i.e., by the wealth of recorded meanings (including, rightly or wrongly, contextual connotations) and congealed sequences ("idioms"). Since an objective, absolute classification of meaning has so far remained an unattainable goal, much depends on the intended degree of elaborateness and, in a bilingual venture, also on the distance between the two languages at issue: For practical purposes, a Spanish–Portuguese dictionary need not be as detailed on the phraseological side as, say, its Spanish–Aztec counterpart. Under these circumstances, it may often be wiser to dispense altogether with statistics and to rely on rough impressionistic appraisals for their provisional usefulness. One paradoxical comment on monumentality in this field: Frequently, the most voluminous collections must receive a conspicuously low rating on grounds other than that of sheer size.

At the opposite extreme of the continuum, one encounters exceedingly brief and casual word-lists: collections of medieval glosses (some of them very meager and not even organized as miniature vocabularies), miscellaneous records of dialect forms, countless short arrays of words pertaining to ultramodern slang or to certain professional jargons of striking, sometimes perverse, appeal to readers at large. Most of these lists, scattered over obscure or ephemeral periodicals, are doomed to remain practically unavailable for ordinary research purposes. Other short word-lists difficult of access to the uninitiated include the vocabularies — some of them gems of neat workmanship — appended to collegiate editions of literary masterpieces in classical and modern foreign languages and, on the trade-book market, glossaries accompanying contemporary novels and short stories written in a national language, but, for the ordinary reader's comfort at least, excessively spiced with regional flavor. To these nuggets of knowledge one may add those extra-brief word-lists (sometimes reduced to a single page) that form part of the typical "academic" editions of classical and medieval texts. There exist trustworthy catalogues of such editions, both mono- and bi-lingual, but very few and, at that, fragmentary master-lists of the items actually contained in these minimum lists.

We have so far worked on the assumption that dictionaries represent variously scaled abridgments of an ideally complete lexicographic record. This premise requires a corrective: Not a few compilations include words that have never existed in the reality of living speech or of written usage. This excess baggage embraces, first of all, isolated GHOST WORDS — old misprints or spurious readings inadvertently carried over from one dictionary into another. Such blemishes modern workers, at the cost of hard labor, endeavor to ferret out one by one. Far more numerous and, worse, more insidious are the LATENT WORDS smuggled in deliberately. In languages possessing an arsenal of productive suffixes (such as Slavic or Romance) a lexicographer can quite unobtrusively manufacture, by the hundreds and thousands, derivatives of his own making. These formations are readily understandable and give the appearance of authenticity; the truth is that speakers, for some reason or other, have not bothered to activate on the same scale all these grammatical potentialities. It is difficult to detect such camouflaged illicit entries, especially in view of legitimate border-line cases (nonces); an unduly geometric design of representative word families, a dictionary's too heavy saturation with certain recurrent derivational schemes at once arouses the suspicion of an experienced reader.

The average dictionary not only tends to overlook differences in chronological levels, but, as a rule, represents a medley of diverse social and regional dialects. Full-scale lexical treatment of a strictly defined social dialect has so far been relatively infrequent; concomitantly, however, the social category of speakers may be implied in the researcher's choice of a regional sector (rural versus urban speech). In inquiries concerned with peculiar linguistic milieus (immigrants, "bohemians", and the like), the threads of regional and of social dialects are inextricably interwoven.[2]

The unadorned dialect vocabulary must be distinguished from monographs balancing lexicography with grammar and with specimens of texts, also from word indexes attached to or implied in grammatical analyses. The dialect area selected as a unit may vary from a hamlet to a continent, the controlling factors being the diversification of speech, the configuration of the terrain, the pattern of political allegiances, and the availability of field-workers and informants. As research grows more and more specialized, master dictionaries for dialect groups become an urgent desideratum. Not the least effective technique for gauging the scope of a regional vocabulary based on field-work is to determine the number of interviewers and interviewees. Most regional vocabularies, instead of affording a total view of the chosen lexicon, are satisfied with recording deviations from standard usage, like so many tidbits; a few subdivide them further into archaisms, broad and narrow localisms, foreignisms, etc. A special, neatly detachable strain in a given regional variety may be the object of a separate vocabulary. This is true in particular of those monographs which concern themselves with autochthonous Indian words absorbed by a national variety of American Spanish, e.g., the Araukan components of Chilean.

The range of a philological vocabulary may be delimited by the

---

[2] At this point, the original monograph examines in considerable detail the patterns of dialect vocabularies and those of philological glossaries.

distance between points selected along the time axis. The historical dictionary of the future may dissolve into a series of chronologically bounded vocabularies reflecting a roughly fixed number of super-imposed layers. One finds a variety of narrower scopes in exegetic vocabularies, assembled around the usages of individual authors, texts, or genres — some of them aiming at exhaustiveness (concord-ances), while others are overtly and explicitly, or tacitly and loosely, selective. The compiler's readiness to do full or partial justice to the manuscript tradition and the inclusion of supporting evidence, in varying dosages, from miscellaneous collateral sources, yield two further yardsticks for the measurement of lexicographic scope. Though dialectology stresses space, while philological analysis entails movements along the time axis, the two approaches are not mutually exclusive, since artistic works may display adequate and not infre-quently unique specimens of speech dialectally tinged — inviting glossaries straddling the two disciplines.

The density of a vocabulary may be determined by the degree of commonness (in statistical terms, frequency) of the words to be included — a distinctly modern criterion. In certain lines of practical work (preparation of graded elementary textbooks, dilution of fine literature for classroom use) the need has arisen for precisely cir-cumscribed core vocabularies. Some workers distinguish between the coördinates of "range" and "frequency", for which one may substitute breadth and depth of penetration. Aside from statistically slanted word lists there exist at present comparable tabulations of phrases (idioms) and syntactical constructions; from all such store-houses of data one may extract direct or, at least, indirect information on this particular aspect of the lexicon. Printed sources may be freely supplemented or even replaced by samples of spontaneous or con-trolled speech. One may subdivide the body of the vocabulary into several layers, on the basis of increasingly higher frequency; one worker (1941) discriminates between four such groups, recording them both separately and in a master-list in which raised numerals act as classifiers and noteworthy transparent derivatives not caught in the meshes of the statistical network are added as a bonus.

The various formats that have become the stock-in-trade of the publishing business specializing in dictionaries frequently offer excellent outlets for the varying patterns of amplitude selected by the lexicographers — or by the masterminds in charge of their projects.

**4.2. Number of languages involved.** A second way of classifying dictionaries by range is to rate them by the number of languages covered or resorted to. Does the use of a second language entail no more than a special type of definitions, namely translations, and does the contrast between mono- and bi-lingual works consequently involve a matter of presentation rather than of scope? The answer to this question is in the negative; not only is the argument hardly applicable to pluri-lingual dictionaries, which patently mark an increase in coverage, not a refinement in explanatory technique, but worse, it discounts the fact that numerous bilingual dictionaries are bipartite, hence geared to serving two separate needs measurable in terms of sheer volume.

The monolingual dictionary constitutes a fairly recent genre: Even the earliest editions of many tone-setting Academy dictionaries, which one inclines to regard as monolingual almost by definition, made it a point to translate all entries into Latin. In a conservative country like Spain, the unadulterated monolingual dictionary is a creation of the 19th century. By modern standards, the only admissible residue of Latin in any such reference work would be the identification of vernacular names of, say, plants and animals by the tags assigned to them in international scientific nomenclature.

The bilingual dictionary (or, if it happens to be short, glossary) is the vocabulary *par excellence*, associated from time immemorial with casual exposure to, or systematic training in, foreign languages, dead or living. In western civilization, which is not the sole inventor of this genre, rudimentary glossaries (Greek–Latin, Latin–Germanic, Latin–Romance) are traceable to late Antiquity and the early Middle Ages; throughout, the preponderance of Latin, either as the tool language providing the "glosses", or as the language requiring itself a measure of exegesis, is quite evident. It took the tremendous shifts of the 16th century to stimulate a large-scale demand for bilingual reference works involving either two modern western languages (say, Spanish and Italian, or Spanish and English), or one western and one "exotic" language, the latter typically one of special concern to colonizers and missionaries (e.g., Granadine Arabic, Aztec, Maya). The only recent additions to this stock of patterns are dictionaries prepared in the "western" style, but serving to contrast two "exotic" languages — of which one, for instance, may very well be Japanese; and a sprinkling of dictionaries pairing off a major "natural" with some "artificial" or "auxiliary" language, e.g., Esperanto, Ido (or Reformed Esperanto), and Volapük.

Many, if not most, bilingual dictionaries are bipartite, irrespective of size and quality. Occasionally (as in the case of Slabý-Grossmann's German–Spanish venture) the two parts were produced by different compilers, each starting with a clean slate, and, as a result, show unintentional discrepancies in bulk and craftsmanship. Then again, in some instances the two sections deliberately have not been planned on the same footing, the need for translations from the foreign into the native language being apparently deemed far more urgent than translation in the reverse direction. This consideration favors the coupling of a full-sized "dictionary" and a meager "vocabulary" typically one fourth or one fifth its size, which in reality is little more than the makeshift index. This asymmetric architectural design would be inappropriate where the two languages are equal partners, as regards social prestige and actual use (say, English and Russian); it is marginally acceptable if some kind of hierarchy has crystallized, the dead language normally surpassing in importance its living counterpart as an object of lexicographic curiosity, since few persons would care to translate modern texts INTO Latin or Old Norse, while dialect speech and cant, for similar reasons, carry greater weight as exhibits than the corresponding literary tongues, used preëminently as "tool languages".

At least two categories of bilingual dictionaries are seldom bipartite. Temporarily, this restriction applied to those compiled by proselytizing clergymen for overseas use. Then again, dialect vocabularies and glossaries of medieval words — if at all classifiable as bilingual — almost never contain so much as an index of meanings cast in the modern language chosen as the frame of reference, let alone a full counterview of lexical relationships, to the lasting detriment of advanced research.

A trilingual dictionary may be the outgrowth of a bilingual prototype, whether the author (or a reviser) himself arranges for the expansion or a plagiarist enlarges upon a chosen model. Frequently a preëxistent cultural or political climate favors such a necessarily high-aiming venture. Thus the dual foundation of classical learning accounts for such dictionaries as involve Greek, Latin, and a modern vernacular. Since the interest of Spaniards, Frenchmen, and the Dutch-speaking natives for a while converged on Flanders, it is small wonder that, in response to this demand, a trilingual dictionary

T

should have been engineered at the critical point (1640). Two import-ant French–Spanish–Basque dictionaries, M. de Larramendi's (1745) and R. M. de Azkue's (1905–06), have their roots in the geographic position of the Euskarian territory, astride the Pyrenees. In another context, one may find a trilingual dictionary at the intersection of two or three cultural traditions; cf. the obvious historical pattern under-lying F. Cañes' voluminous *Diccionario español–latino–arábigo* (1787). As a rule, trilingual dictionaries, chiefly for reasons of economy, are unidirectional, i.e., each offers maximum usefulness only to that segment of consulters which has mastered the privileged among the three languages (e.g., Spanish in the case of Cañes). Where differently architectured works of this type bear on the same subject, the expert is best served by combining imaginatively these sources of informa-tion.

Theoretically the quadrilingual dictionary leaves room for a vastly increased variety of sequences and combinations, but in practice few of these mathematical possibilities have been exploited on account of the comparative rarity of the genre. The kernel of Howell's genteel *Lexicon tetraglotton* (1660) is a unidirectional dictionary providing for the translation of each English entry into French, Italian, and Spanish. Terreros y Pando's life-work contains three volumes of consecutive Spanish entries translated into French, Spanish, and Italian, and, in a fourth volume, three alphabetic indexes in the reverse direction, each with separate paging.

In contrast to the polyglot Bible, a milestone in the growth of Humanism, the multilingual dictionary, as a scholarly institution, has failed to exert any lasting influence on European (still less on American) intellectual life. Compilations of this kind have usually been manufactured either as saving devices (to economize time, effort, production costs, shelving space) or as veritable *tours de force*, for the sake of the bizarre effects. Of late, the best-known among them have tended to involve from five to ten languages; the arrange-ment offers almost limitless possibilities of variation.

On the whole, dictionaries contrasting more than two languages have failed to maintain the position of eminence which the intel-lectual élite assigned to them in the 17th and 18th centuries, as works of scholarship and even of art. In the contemporary world, they have been relegated to the unattractive rôle of tools in strictly commercial and industrial relations, quite unexciting on the linguistic side. The need for these glossaries of technical terms may soon altogether recede as a result of the invention of electronic translating devices. In a way, the steady decline of the polyglot dictionary has been, paradoxically, a direct consequence of increased lexicographic sophistication: If the semantic, syntactic, and phraseological details which a fastidious reader nowadays demands of his mono- or bilingual dictionary were furnished on this grandiose scale, the resulting increase in bulk would at once defeat the chief purpose of lexical telescoping.

**4.3. Extent of concentration on lexical data.** Much as biographical dictionary and straight bibliography for centuries tended to represent a single undifferentiated genre, so dictionary and encyclopedia were not always recognized as guides to discrete provinces of knowledge. The infiltration of any encyclopedia-style data is recognizable (a) by the inclusion of proper names, sometimes accompanied by biographic vignettes and profuse geographic descriptions; (b) by a prodigality of comments on ordinary words that seems far in excess of the need for sober definition.

Encyclopedic entries may be relegated to a supplement or a string of supplements (gazetteer, etc.), as has become the dominant fashion in recent decades. Also, they may be intercalated, so as to form part of the same unique alphabetical succession of items as the ordinary words. Finally, the trained observer may be in a position to grasp them obliquely, through internal analysis of the definitions. In the first eventuality, there subsists a clear boundary between purely lexical and other bits of information; in the second, the frontier-line is less sharply perceptible; in the third, these extraneous, non-lexical ingredients are submerged beneath the unruffled surface of a deceptively balanced and unified dictionary.

Where the publisher furnishes supplements, by way of bonuses to prospective buyers, one finds a motley array filling needs at present preferably met by separate books (rosters of proper names, guides to pronunciation, grammar, and conversation, collections of proverbs, miniature rhyming dictionaries, lists of synonyms, corrections of misprints, and the like). It has likewise become increasingly customary to provide a separate list of toponyms and anthroponyms in glossaries to medieval texts.

The larding of dictionaries with non-lexical elements, presented as matters of sober fact or in a genial vein, became fashionable toward 1700. In some of its key points (Paris, Barcelona) the book trade, for two long centuries, continued stuffing dictionaries with shreds of information which no discriminating linguist would, but the less knowledgeable public at large frequently does, expect a lexicon to provide into the bargain, as it were — through interfiling, in the compiler's workshop, of authentic word cards and brief excerpts from encyclopedias. This hybrid genre has been mostly known under the name of "encyclopedic dictionary". The same publishing centers have tolerated multi-volume encyclopedias shot through, in defiance of common sense, with genuinely lexical entries.

The least easily detectable dilution of a bi- or tri-lingual dictionary is achieved by the inclusion of such parenthetic information as is linguistically immaterial. The ideally tight dictionary adds comments to translations only under three conditions: (a) where ambiguity might result from maximum concision, as in the case of glosses involving homonyms; (b) where circumlocution is inherently in order, on account of a physically, socially, or linguistically conditioned lack of nearly perfect lexical equivalents; (c) where grammatical complications may foreseeably arise. Any other remarks should be rated as redundant. At certain periods, this ideal of stringency was not yet — or no longer — appreciated. Thus, in the Renaissance dictionary, the two halves of each succinct correspondence were of approximately equal length, except where a lexicographer bothered to adduce "authorities" in support of the posited equations. Two centuries later, at the height of the "encyclopedic vogue", the entries, as a rule, remained brief, but the glosses tended to become more and more inflated.

### 5. *Classification by Perspective*

The three basic perspectives, as defined at the outset, involve (1) the fundamental dimension (diachronism versus synchronism), (2) the basic arrangement of entries (conventional, semantic, or arbitrary), (3) the level of tone. Accordingly, the typologist must arrange for three separate analyses.

**5.1. The fundamental dimension.** The ideal synchronic dictionary would be one least contaminated by acknowledged or, worse, unacknowledged archaisms (many of them — this is the root of the difficulty — firmly engraved, at the very least, in the passive memory of the average literate speaker). The logical avenue of approach to

the unadulterated diachronic view is the historical dictionary, provided its materials are so ordered as to bring out plastically the
dynamics of lexical development, with heightened attention to the
succession and mutual compatibility of meanings. For not a few
languages, even those subject to philological inspection, no dictionary aiming uncompromisingly at this particular goal exists or is
clearly in sight at present. In the existing historical dictionaries, all
too frequently the meaning listed first is not the oldest on record,
nor indeed the oldest by the standards of reconstruction, but the
one most familiar to moderns or held "fittest" to have acted as a
semantic fountain-head.

Over against the historical ordering of linguistic facts one may
place etymological studies, i.e., conjectural research in the PRE-
HISTORY of the lexicon. These inquiries fall into several categories,
the simplest criterion of classification being that of scope. Even the
full-sized etymological dictionaries are diversified, some being
ostensibly confined to a single language (Kluge, Skeat, Wartburg),
while others are avowedly comparative (Diez, Meyer-Lübke,
Pokorny). In practice one can hardly draw a sharp line of demarcation
between isolationists and comparatists; and titles are scarcely reliable
guides to treasuries of etymological hypotheses and material. Conceivably the clearest separation lies between those dictionaries which
start from the base, real or assumed, and lead the reader to the
product(s), and those that invite one to follow the opposite course.
At least one recent venture, V. García de Diego's (1954), is bipartite
and tries, between two covers, to afford both views in close succession
(unfortunately, with less than satisfactory results).

Aside from fully integrated etymological dictionaries one encounters loosely strung miscellanies of etymological notes, of varying
length; "gleanings", for the most part provided by gaps and deficiencies in recently published book-length reference works; and all
sorts of concomitant references to etymological clues, usually of
scant value to the expert — in glossaries attached to anthologies and
chrestomathies, in old-fashioned dialect word-lists, and the like.
There exist further etymological vocabularies devoted to specific
lexical strains — say, Arabisms, Gallicisms, Italianisms, and Lusisms
in Spanish; that is to say, closely coherent groups of borrowings.

**5.2. Three contrasting patterns of arrangement.** The basic
arrangement of dictionary items may be alphabetic, semantic, or

casual. Each of these categories lends itself to further subdivision; a loose combination of the first two patterns is likewise conceivable.

The alphabetic arrangement, though strictly conventional, is so overwhelmingly dominant that the ordinary person associates with this familiar sequence the very genre of the dictionary, on a par with a catalogue, a directory, or a mailing list. Even where an ancient text has been edited with every conceivable paleographic nicety, the accompanying glossary, as a rule, parades the words in normal script, following the alphabetic order. Such occasional deviations and complications as do come to mind represent frills; thus, as regards Old and even Classical Spanish, there exist conflicting traditions for placing words beginning with *c*, *ch*, *h*, *i*, *j*, *k*, *y*, *z*, to say nothing of *l*, *n*, *r* vis-à-vis *ll*, *nn* (*ñ*), *rr* (*R*). In dialect works the use of phonetic (less so of phonemic) transcription imposes an aberrant sequence of letters on account of special characters and unfamiliar diacritic marks. A few lexicographers assemble in alphabetic order not all words, but only the heads or reputed heads of families. A final formidable obstacle to quick, smooth consultation has been in some countries the inflationary spiral of supplements and even supplements to supplements, a veritable cancer-growth, especially where the accretion amounts to a mere handful of last-minute gleanings.

Remotely akin to the alphabetic dictionary is the rhyming dictionary which ideally absorbs the totality of a lexicon, distributing the items on the basis of form rather than of meaning. What sets it apart is not only the choice of the stressed vowel rather than of the initial letter as the classificatory norm, but also the departure from the straight linear sequence in favor of sundry groups of varying size. Students of suffixes have derived considerable benefit from rhyming dictionaries and from their close congeners, the "reverse" (*rückläufig*) dictionaries, of which there exist specimens, e.g., for classical Greek, Latin, French, and modern Russian.

The semantic (analogical, ideological) dictionary unites words by bonds of meaning. Its roots are old; thus, Isidore of Seville's *Etymologiae* subdivide the entire material into certain provinces of cosmic structure and human endeavor. Within each group and subgroup so circumscribed, one may, but need not, maintain the alphabetical order. The result of such a compromise is a mixed classification. Consistently semantic ramification is difficult to achieve, because only relatively few and isolated semantic "fields" (e.g., anatomical, color, and kinship terms) fall into a neatly delineated schema. Another prototype of the semantic dictionary is the book-length list of synonyms, actually near-synonyms. The project of such a book, typically — but not exclusively — monolingual, may materialize in different ways (clusters of synonyms supported by well-chosen quotations from authors; "ideological index" to a standard dictionary; array of regional or temporal counterparts of each basic entry — an arrangement sometimes called "onomasiologic" in the Central European tradition of modern-language scholarship.)

Concerning recent experiments with the fragmentation of the "world of words" into discrete semantic provinces, one may safely affirm that, where short texts are involved, such an approach has turned out to be unpromising. However, the method, duly refined, may some day yield satisfactory results when extended to distinctly bulkier objects — say, the complete works of a prolific writer noted for his abundant and delicately nuanced lexicon. The worthwhileness of semantic classification, in other words, seems to increase proportionately with the absolute size and the relative density of the network. Meanwhile, Roget's *Thesaurus*, Boissière's *Dictionnaire analogique*, and Casares' *Diccionario ideológico* remain interesting testing grounds.

If it is true that the time-honored "parts of speech" (as against the modern descriptivist's form classes) were semantically rather than behaviorally defined, then some older dictionaries resorting to them (e.g., P. de Alcalá's *Vocabulista arábigo*, which, under each letter, subdivides the entries into verbs, nouns — a category here comprehending adjectives and past participles as well — and adverbs, then reserves a concluding cross-alphabetic section for numerals) show close affinity to the semantic ordering.

It is unusual for any book-length dictionary to present its entries in completely haphazard fashion, yet a few books, not only by amateurs, illustrate just this bent for eccentricity, which, the sober-minded may argue, squarely defeats the very purpose of a reference work. A grammar, whether historical or descriptive, even though not primarily planned as a lexicographic guide, may incidentally be so used, in default of a more appropriate source, if equipped with a handy index. Without this device the lexically oriented scholar may find its consultation forbiddingly time-consuming — just how prohibitive depends not only on the neatness and transparency of organization, but also on the reader's skill, knack for hunches, and sheer luck. In the case of a loose collection of notes, with etymological, phraseological, or puristic overtones, the alphabetic order is common and desirable, but far from obligatory, especially in periodicals. One also comes across miscellanies displaying a fundamentally free sequence with intermittent stretches of alphabetic ordering.

**5.3. Three contrasting levels of tone.** The tone of a dictionary may be detached, preceptive, or facetious. Only the first possibility insures a rigorously erudite approach; what complicates matters is that some normative and jocose dictionaries, though plainly falling short of the minimum standard for scholarly performance, nevertheless may contain slivers of information which, after proper filtering, are apt to be of real help to the serene researcher.

The category of dictionaries designed to report facts objectively includes the great majority of mono- and bi-lingual reference works and practically all historically slanted glossaries. Among regional word-lists, however, the consensus of taste is less in evidence. Many of these vocabularies are intended to be descriptive, with a light undercurrent of innocuous pride in local traditions. Ordinarily enlightened amateurs are at their best when native dialect speech represents to them neither a matter of painful "guilt or inferiority complex", nor the pretext for some morbidly passionate commitment, still less a source of cheap entertainment, but a quietly treasured possession, a kind of revered family piece surrounded by affectionate curiosity.

Over against this gratifying attitude one finds all too frequently the purist's preceptive (normative, didactic) approach. Regionalisms are collected for the purpose of warning the group of speakers concerned AGAINST their use. Outside the domain of dialectology, there also exist all sorts of corrective and remedial dictionaries exposing impropriety of speech and writing — among the semiliterate, certain peculiar population groups (e.g., immigrants), snobs succumbing willingly to the influence of foreign usage, white-collar workers endangered by professional hazards (translators, journalists), and the like. Though the analyst may find himself in basic disagreement with the bulk of this output, he can, with a measure of skill, extract useful information from such lists of "dos" and "don'ts", provided they are not entirely arbitrary.

A playful, teasing attitude toward language may be part of a general cultural pattern and heritage. Inevitably, a sophisticated worker's initial reaction to the brochures and pamphlets, mostly by unknowns or incompetents, containing all sorts of lexical scraps and tidbits is violently unfavorable; but, after calming down, he may discover that these humorously tuned collections are not necessarily worthless, if seen and assessed in the proper perspective, after very careful sifting.

Can any sets of relationship be established between these three major patterns of arrangement? A historical dictionary may correspond to alphabetic, infrequently to semantic, seldom (if ever) to casual ordering, and its tone is likely to be matter-of-fact rather than admonitory or exhilarating; a synchronic dictionary, unless scientifically designed, need not be hemmed in by comparable restrictions. Alphabetic arrangement goes well with a descriptive, preceptive (curative), or entertaining purpose and matches equally the diachronic and the synchronic perspectives, while casual arrangement and amusement values are at all times easily reconcilable. These few examples show the tendential rather than obligatory character of all conjunctures.

## 6. Classification by Presentation

The four salient points to which we agreed to reduce the aggregate of narrower preferences were definition, verbal documentation, graphic illustration, and the presence of special features (e.g., localization or phonetic transcription).

The degree of specificity and of fullness in a lexical definition ("gloss") represents some kind of continuum, ranging from extreme parsimony to profusion of technical detail. However desirable the goal of maximum information, one is led to posit, in two directions, a saturation point, beyond which further accumulation of details threatens to detract from the architectonic vigor of a tightly built dictionary. One such menace is the infiltration of historical or naturalistic excursuses, in most instances, mere bric-à-brac; even those minute descriptions of household utensils and trade tools that so conspicuously benefit the *Wörter-und-Sachen* school of etymology belong, strictly speaking, in a portfolio or a manual of material civilization. The other kind of otiose super-abundance stems from the indiscriminate recording of contextual shades of meaning: The harmoniously structured dictionary must remain a compact depository of steady designations.

In appraising documentation, it is advantageous to separate the literary language (past and/or present) from, on the one hand, living dialect speech, unsupported by texts, and, on the other, such samples of regional speech as are reflected in locally colored literature.

Where literary usage alone is at issue, the specificity of documentation may oscillate between (a) a generously carved-out passage, (b) a shorter segment of that passage, (c) a bare reference to line, quatrain, folio, page, or chapter, and (d) a simple computation of frequency — range plus incidence — at best interspersed with occasional quotations of characteristic words in their immediate environments (e.g., qualifiers). A few dictionaries, gambling on the layman's indifference, identify the author cited, but neither the particular work nor the specific locus, thus obviating all possibility of effective control.

In the rare dialect glossaries displaying the chosen words in any kind of meaningful context, the compiler faces the dilemma between coining suitable model sentences of his own (if he happens to be an uninhibited speaker of that dialect) and citing such utterances of his informants as he has unobtrusively overheard or — a quicker but less felicitous alternative technique — deliberately elicited. Some such glossaries have a comparativistic superstructure.

If the tradition of a national literature has favored the production of texts entirely or partially dialectal (an example of the latter would be the dialogues, as against the narrative sections, of a novel or short story), it is possible to manufacture a regional vocabulary based in its entirety on excerpts from written and, as a rule, published sources, or to combine field-notes and aural impressions with the testimony of *belles-lettres*. At this juncture, the support of folklore plays a signal part: Proverbs, riddles, nursery rhymes, puns, and idiomatic sayings may be either appended as a separate exhibit or absorbed as an essential ingredient, sometimes specifically announced in title or subtitle.

Though stylized adornments embellished a few of the older vocabularies, the inclusion of functional pictorial material became standard practice only after 1800. For the purpose of a lexicographic, rather than typographic or bibliophilic, survey one may distinguish between drawings, sketches, and photographs, on the one hand, and charts and maps, on the other.

The drawing or sketch in a dictionary adds that dosage of concreteness which quickens the lay reader's grasp of a scientific definition or an abstract description. The photograph contributes the dual touch of authenticity and plastic suggestiveness. The option between drawing and photograph dwindles frequently to a matter of printing costs and available space; where the budget allows for separate plates, these may be inserted between pages, assembled at the end of the volume, or segregated in an accompanying portfolio. An independent volume containing drawings or photographs of objects rich in lexicographic implications or else an imaginative combination of both media is equally conceivable. Pictures pertinent to linguistic inquiries are normally in black and white, the chromatic scale being regarded more as a potential amenity than as an actual asset; nevertheless multicolored plates, the trademark of leading encyclopedias, might be useful, especially to the sensorially perceptive etymologist, as a frame of reference for the vernacular nomenclature of minerals, flowers, birds, and garments. A different use of photographic plates may be visualized in connection with painstaking editions of medieval glosses and glossaries.

While iconography, as a rule, plays a subordinate rôle in lexical undertakings, it may in exceptional cases assume a commanding position. The German "Duden" method embodies a miniature pictorial encyclopedia: In imitation of the "direct" approach, it bluntly juxtaposes label and image, rather than entry and gloss, in a preëminently semantic ordering of the lexicon, thus short-circuiting wearisome definitions. There exist well-established adaptations in numerous other countries. The affinity of the underlying principle and practice to recent trends of language instruction and to current auditive experiments centered around wire and tape recorders is unquestionable. What ties these endeavors together, harmonizing them with broader cultural trends the world over, is their strong sensory, anticonceptual proclivity.

Regional dictionaries and monographs accompanied by folding maps or smaller charts are no longer uncommon. The inclusion, in studies of this scope, of a small-scale linguistic atlas remains a desideratum, for the most part unfulfilled; and even where one has been provided, as in T. Navarro's monograph on Puerto Rican, complete integration of the lexical and the cartographic sections proves difficult of achievement.

Special features worthy of mention include: the use of abbreviations or peculiar ideogrammatic classifiers to mark for a given word its grammatical or semantic category, social plane or emotional slant, or else territorial limitation; the extra measure of attention accorded to pronunciation, conducive to the parenthetic use of phonetic transcription, or at least, to the consistent marking of stress (a side-line leads from here to the orthological dictionary as an autonomous genre); the narrow specification of locale, unless implied in the announced scope of the project: a message conveyed in a variety of ways, e.g., by substituting arbitrary numerical symbols for recurrent reference to townships and villages and, where generations are contrasted, even to informants.

## 7. Special Dictionaries

The classificatory schema here advocated is so flexible as to be readily adaptable to all but an inconsequential percentage of lexical compilations. Any vocabulary offering a fair cross-section of a lexical system, however selective or arbitrarily arranged that cross-section may be, should, at least in theory, be analyzable in terms of distinctive features. A few residual groups of vocabularies, however, which cannot be credited with presenting such a cross-section, must be segregated from the common flock.

The words "vocabulary" and, especially, "dictionary" upon occasion apply quite loosely to any reference work arranged by words or names (collection, index, check-list, catalogue, set of paradigmatic tables, gazetteer, etc.); in most instances, the confusion may initially have been caused by the alphabetic order as the common trait. As a result, the visitor to a library finds on dictionary shelves collections of idioms, literary clichés, proverbs, family and given names, toponyms, fictional personages, topics and topoi, and the like.

The second exceptional group comprises highly specialized vocabularies of trades, crafts, arts, and sciences unrepresentative of the core of the common lexicon. Among these, lists of navigational terms, including terms of shipbuilding, have been in special demand since the 16th century. Agriculture has been another longstanding purveyor of technical dictionaries. A matter of heightened concern to our own guild is the dictionary of linguistic or grammatical terms. The problem lies in drawing a cogent borderline between straight vocabularies of this kind and, among the older vintage of scientific treatises, a few so clearly patterned and, terminologically, so comprehensive as to provide, at a glance, the needed lexicographic information without, in the process, acquiring the status of a formal dictionary, not even one of the "semantic" variety.

## 8. *Interaction of Distinctive Features*

Systematic inquiry into the interaction of the features here iso-lated — aside from the three "perspectives" already viewed from this angle — would in itself require a study of monographic propor-tions, but a few random examples of seemingly admissible and in-admissible (or, at least, common and uncommon) constellations of such traits are easily supplied. Customarily, there prevails a definite relation between size and tone: Dictionaries written in an entertaining vein tend to be slender. Again, historical slant and profusion of pictorial illustrations do not go together: Maps, sketches, drawings, and photographs befit the synchronic dictionary, geographically oriented. Graphic documentation and a tone either morosely pre-ceptive or irrepressibly jocose are, for all practical purposes, mutually exclusive. Bi- and pluri-lingual dictionaries are very seldom dia-chronic, overwhelmingly favor alphabetic arrangement, increasingly shy away from pedantry and jokes; also, they display the barest minimum of graphic illustrations, since the cumulative effect of a gloss (i.e., definition) and a drawing would tend to be tautological.

# I I

# Words, Objects, Images*

*Shapes, Makes, and Names of the Flail in Portugal*

THE twin methods of "Wörter-und-Sachen" and "Sachen-und-Wörter", devised half a century ago by such imaginative scholars as Meringer and Schuchardt and associated subsequently with an autonomous journal and with several atlas ventures, require no formal introduction at this late date. These particular approaches are closely tied up with dialect geography (especially its cartographic projection and its stratigraphic analysis), with genetically slanted lexicology, and with ethnography, the last-mentioned as delimited in the heartlands of the European continent (*Volkskunde*). By the same token they are diametrically opposed to all shades and varieties of structural (or functional), probably less so of straight descriptive linguistics, inasmuch as, by definition, they consistently view a given language in its closest possible relation to the respective nonlinguistic environment. Those concerned with the history of our science have not failed to observe that the fashion (which initially spread from Germany proper and Austria) reached its all-time peak in German Switzerland, and at its present declining stage still commands positions of sustained strength in Italy and Belgium and in some active provincial centers of French scholarship such as Lyon, i.e. in territories where linguistic structuralism has failed to make noticeable headway. The propagation of the joint inquiry into languages and the correlated material civilizations has been prompted in no small measure by the voluntary or enforced migration of scholars from one country or continent to another. But the chief reason for its conspicuous success in some research centers and its apparently complete failure in others may well be the specific intellectual climate prevailing

Reprinted from *Language*, XXXIII (1957), 54–76.

* *Coisas e palavras: Alguns problemas etnográficos e linguísticos relacionados com os primitivos sistemas de debulha na Península Ibérica.* By JOSÉ GONÇALO C. HERCULANO DE CARVALHO. (Reprinted from *Biblos*, Vol. XIX.) Pp. xii, 413, with 13 maps. Coimbra, 1953.

in each instance of exposure to the new doctrine and techniques. Except for Catalonia, the fashion has come only at a fairly advanced hour to the far-flung Luso-Hispanic countries, including the bulk of Spain and, overseas, Argentina and Mexico. It has lately struck Portugal with particular force, presumably because that country, since the pioneers F. A. Coelho and J. Leite de Vasconcelos, has never witnessed any unduly sharp separation of anthropology and linguistics. The book under review, an impressive doctoral dissertation accepted by the University of Coimbra, is thus far the strongest proof of the eminently successful acclimatization of the two methods on Portuguese soil.

**1. Background of the research project.** Herculano de Carvalho's book embodies an inquiry carefully thought out to the last detail, and carried out unhurriedly and with perceptible zest. Some of this excellency the work owes to the author's methodological schooling in Romance linguistics in general (as this field is understood throughout Europe) and to his training in field work, with dual emphasis on anthropological and linguistic recording, in particular. He brings to his task a splendid knowledge of the older technical literature, which by now has become so exasperatingly scattered that only the most conscientious workers make it a point to consult it beyond an obligatory minimum. To this scope of reading in a variety of languages (including Swedish) he has added several years of intensive and diversified apprenticeship, first at Lisbon, where he came into contact with philology, then at Zurich (1946–49), where the tenancy of a university lectureship gave him the opportunity of fruitful co-operation with J. Jud, and finally, after a three-year interlude of concentrated field work (1949–52, chiefly in Viana, Braga, Vila Real, Guarda, and Faro), at Coimbra, where the newly appointed professor had the benefit of M. de Paiva Boléo's and, for a while, J. M. Piel's advice and constructive criticism. Independently, he established liaison with J. Dias and F. Galhano, both active at Oporto's Ethnological Research Center; each supplied him with valuable bits of information on the side of *Sachen*. To round out his experience, Herculano de Carvalho coöperated on at least one venture with Lisbon's quite differently oriented Centro de Estudos Filológicos. As a result of such a balanced acquisition of factual and methodological knowledge, the author shows no trace of parochialism. He is cosmopolitan through and through and, it would seem, a born syncretist, with an enviable flair for the best that every national tradition of European learning offers. His attitude toward the American output, which he knows at first hand only fragmentarily, is also friendly.

In his analyses, the author gives the impression of a mature and experienced scholar, whom the severest critic cannot accuse of frivolity or naïveté. For one thing, he is consistently willing to recognize the possibility of alternatives (87, 103 f., 109 n. 1, 111, 137, 141, 147 f., 155, 160, 186–189, 197, 206) or the interplay of several concurrent factors (92). For another, his phrasing betrays unusual caution, as shown by the avoidance of reckless generalizations or unnecessarily categorical statements and by liberal strewing of qualifiers such as "certain", "probable", "possible", "not unlikely", "at least partial", "seemingly" (116 f., 138, et passim). He is realistic enough to reckon with a margin of error due to careless reading of ancient records (138) or to the scarcity of available data (124, 196 n. 2), and he does not discount the possibility of an informant's plain ignorance (124). Not the least engaging of his talents is the ability to postpone decisions until further data may help scholars to force a break-through (96 f., 187, 189).

**2. Scope and structure of the project.** The attractive outward appearance of the book bespeaks its unhurried gestation and the care and craftsmanship that went into its actual writing, proofreading, and manufacture. Given the inherent difficulty of the copy, the number of misprints is negligible, and the few that one may ferret out are mostly self-explanatory and plainly attributable to the typesetter's slips.[1] The full range of available typographic devices

---

[1] Particularly commendable is the neat presentation, with rare exceptions (89, 113), of German names, titles, and passages. There is an understandable sprinkling of misprints in quotations from Spanish sources (83, 142 f.; 144, 208, etc.). What is the function of the grave accent-mark on the *u* of Ptg. *dubitativamente* (137, 418); confusion with *dùbiamente?* The Index seems to show that *maneca* (148 n. 2) is a misprint for *manecra* (144 n. 2); on this unusual suffix, inadvertently omitted from the list of formatives (372), see p. 183 (§ 90). In one passage the author writes "after the accent", where the context leads one to expect "before the accent" (134 l. 8). Those familiar only with COLLĪNA 'hill', which has a steady -LL-, may fail to grasp the proposed derivation (157) of topon. *Cunha* (vars. *Cuia, Cuya*). OGal. *manleira*, if truly an equivalent of Sp. *manlieva* (145), is a compound twisted out of shape and having no bearing on Miñ. ⌈*manle*⌉ 'flail'. On the whole the book has a satisfactory network of precise cross references; yet there remains a residue of vague promises of forthcoming (and of equally nebulous reminders of past) discussions, hardly admissible in an overloaded monograph of this size (30 f., 56, 66, 75, 95, 98, 102 f., 104, 106, 111, 117, 121 f., 148, 155, 160, 163, 182 f., etc.).

U

(including boldface and small capitals, and fonts of different sizes) has been put to use,[2] the spacing from cover to cover is pleasant to the eyes, abbreviations are employed within proper limits and are adequately explained; even an exacting reader encounters practically no traces of large-scale inconsistency, redundancy, fragmentariness, or abrupt transition. Additional features (which one has reluctantly learned no longer to take for granted in Hispanic linguistics) include a pervasive matter-of-fact style (in particular, the absence of rhetoric, poetization, personal innuendos, and, worse, politically tinged controversy), a sustained level of serene and dignified courtesy, and distinct readability, achieved through the cumulative effect of sharply delineated architecture, frequent midway summaries, and the relegation of details to footnotes and supplements. The usefulness and amenity of the book are further enhanced by sixty-one drawings of varying sizes scattered over its pages (for the most part, deft sketches of tools discussed in the introductory section; but Nos. 1 and 58–61 are miniature charts) and by the extremely elaborate, indeed slightly crowded, linguistic folding maps appended to the monograph (one wishes the publisher had provided a matching portfolio). These maps are similar in planning and execution to those previously devised by Paiva Boléo in his programmatic paper (for an appreciation see *Lg.*, XXVIII [1952], 124–129) and are based on his still unpublished collection of rural teachers' responses to a widely distributed questionnaire.

The orderly internal structure of the book confirms this visual impression of tidiness. In harmony with Herculano de Carvalho's avowed purpose, as announced in title and Preface, he devotes, after a succinct Introduction, the first, fairly autonomous section of his investigation (7–113) to ethnographic research in the shapes and makes of the flail, as used in rural districts of Portugal and the adjoining parts of Spain, and to the various correlated techniques of threshing. Descriptive classification, on the basis of leisurely personal observation and of extensive readings, again and again serves as a

---

[2] Let me at once make a qualification: The author uses square brackets, ordinarily reserved for phonetic transcription, to achieve an effect which J. Jud's school produces through a set of raised half-brackets. Thus, W.-Gal. [*manle*] and Ast.-Leon. [*manal*] (119), by which Herculano de Carvalho subsumes bundles of regional variants under sharply individuated lexical types, disregarding phonic variations as etymologically irrelevant, should by all means have been listed as ⌐*manle*¬ and ⌐*manal*¬, i.e. marked with a sign suggesting indifference toward, rather than emphasis on, phonetic accuracy.

stepping-stone to attempts at genetic reconstruction, in part with the aid of collateral materials and analyses furnished by fellow-workers. From here on the dialectologist and historical linguist in Herculano de Carvalho takes over until the conclusion of the monograph (115–313). Chap. I of the second section deals with the geographic pattern of the eight basic and of several less common names of the flail (115–121), with some attention paid to the speech of the Atlantic archipelagos, but not, except for one brief remark (148 n. 2), to Brazilian Portuguese, a source of serious disappointment to those readers who recall the beneficial effect of American-Spanish studies on the exploration of peninsular Spanish dialects. Chap. II, in similar fashion, deals descriptively with designations for the top of the flail, subordinating four sporadic to five dominant types (121–125). At this point the angle of observation changes sharply: The author temporarily abandons the synchronic survey and offers, in Chap. III, a historically slanted regional catalog of Luso-Hispanic descendants of MALLEUS, an important local prototype of the names of the flail, together with his report on the correlated verb for 'threshing' (125–131). Chap. IV, one of the highlights of the dissertation, comprises several major excursuses. To do justice to a series of special problems raised by MANUĀLE and MANUĀRIA, the author examines the divergent modern developments of L. [nw] in the pan-Romanic perspective (132–150). He then concentrates on another set of phonological problems (centering about the loss of L. -N- in the west of the Peninsula) apropos of Gal.-Ptg. ⌐manle¬, Gal. *malle*, and Ast. *mache* (150–153); and eventually shifts his attention to the dialectal rival forms ⌐moual¬ and ⌐moueira¬, whose discovery in the first place must be credited to himself (132, 153–166). Here the perspective changes again: Herculano de Carvalho turns now to an approach associated with onomasiology, a discipline favored by dialect geographers from Central Europe; it is roughly translatable by 'cross-dialectal synonymics'. He begins the new survey by focusing attention, in Chap. V, on the diversified names of the flail viewed as a whole (168–182). In Chaps. VI and VII he shifts the spotlight to the separate names of its two principal parts (182–190 and 191–221, with an exceedingly conscientious analysis not only of the richly nuanced progeny of PERTICA, but also of the products of the suffix -ICU, -ICA, in general). He concludes the operation with an equally detailed critical enumeration, in Chap. VIII, of the names of those protective pieces (made of leather, iron, or horn) that are attached, respectively, to the longer and to the shorter part of the standard flail (221–261), and in Chaps. IX and X, of those of some other accessories (261–271). The last two chapters lead the reader to distinctly higher levels of abstraction. Chap. XI reviews, in condensed form, the entire array of major findings, with special attention to the coördinates of time and space (272–297). Chap. XII, taking into account all data previously ascertained by Herculano de Carvalho himself and some equally weighty collateral facts brought to light by other workers, concerns itself with the configuration of the linguistic structure of the Portuguese territory (297–313), if one may, like the author, use "structure" here in the sense understood by European dialect geographers such as Menéndez Pidal, Frings, and the German-Swiss team, rather than by students of descriptive grammar during the last three decades.[3]

This recapitulation of the content suffices to measure the author's originality and versatility. He has selected a severely limited segment of his native vocabulary — one whose potential interest to the linguist was pointed out, long before him, though in part with respect to different geographic areas, by such masters of Romance scholarship as Schuchardt and Meyer-Lübke (both in 1909) and Jaberg (1937). Through hard work he has succeeded in sifting and vastly increasing the volume of raw data, and he has made it a point to examine each cluster of formations in several perspectives, situating it on a modern map and projecting it onto cartographic views of older evolutionary stages, tracing phonetic and semantic trajectories from Latin to Portuguese and from Portuguese back to Latin, relating the whole tool to its constituent parts and vice versa (in his dual capacity as a linguist and as a student of material civilization), and rising from the observation of minute facts to respectable heights of generalization. None of these approaches, in isolation, is exclusively his own, but the imaginative combination of methods here essayed has been rare.

---

[3] The author fails to take any position toward the latest currents of structuralist thought, but his misgivings about excessive schematization (133), understandable in a dialect geographer, semanticist, and culture historian, lead one to assume that, if squarely faced with a decision, he might have been less than friendly to these currents throughout the 'forties. Aside from being a seasoned phonetician (as shown by his enumeration and analysis of the vars. of *pírtigo*), he is undoubtedly familiar with the concept of phonemic contrast (206), but seems to eschew possibilities of exploiting the new tool to the full, even in European fashion. Thus, one misses any attempt to correlate the loss, in certain environments, of *g*, i.e. $[\gamma] < $ -K- in Portuguese dialects (205 n. 1: *fios* < *figos* < FĪCŌS; cf. C.-Ast. *tsueu* < LOCŌ) with the concurrent loss of $[\delta] < $ -T- and $[\beta] < $ -P- from peninsular dialect speech: Cast. *na* < *nada* < NĀTA; C.-Ast. *reu* < *rabo* < RĀPU.

The thoroughness of workmanship and the earnestness of the endeavor, added to the author's unobtrusive versatility, make for a truly excellent and, above all, readable dissertation, a model study in more than one respect.[4]

3. **Material civilization and the structural approach.** The ethnographic section falls into a descriptive chapter, devoted to the Portuguese and North Spanish varieties of the flail (7–64), with a few glimpses of evolutionary trends (11, 15–17, 33),[5] another chapter dealing in similar terms with rival devices for threshing (64–85), and a broad synthesis of the underlying historical growth (85–113). This section is as rich in detailed and precise information, especially in regard to geographic border lines, as the remainder of the book, but makes more difficult reading.

For one thing, the uninitiated will surely miss, at the outset, a

[4] For completeness, let me add that a string of supplements rounds out the corpus of the inquiry: separately assembled legends and comments to the thirteen appended maps (313–335, with hundreds of geographically pinpointed, broadly transcribed, and accurately defined forms and by-forms, conveniently arranged in alphabetical order); a list of such incidentally elicited formations, worthy of mention, as fall outside the semantic confines of the maps (335–338); a micro-toponymic list of the numerous localities alluded to in the text (total 1285), arranged from north to south, in the order of larger administrative units (districts and *concelhos*), with an additional, easily manageable apparatus of bibliographic references attached to a large proportion of these items — henceforth an indispensable tool for any research project in Portuguese dialectology (339–353); a parallel list, more rigorously selective, of Spanish localities covered (total 272), correspondingly arranged by provinces (353–355); a workable list of abbreviations other than those of book titles (357 f.); a master bibliography which unfortunately does not aim at exhaustiveness, as quite a few magazine articles cited in the text have been omitted here (359–369); an alphabetical subject index giving attention to phonological phenomena and to crucially important suffixes, i.e., to the less obvious features of the inquiry (371–375); separate indexes for Latin etyma (377–379), for Galician-Portuguese formations (379–396; in itself a helpful technical vocabulary), and for their Romance counterparts, again subdivided according to the specific languages involved (397–403); an index of graphic illustrations, with indication of place and present ownership of each model selected and with full credit to draftsmen (405–407); a short list of stray additions and corrections, the latter less complete than one might have expected (409); and a detailed, analytical table of contents (410–413).

[5] Methodologically noteworthy is the inference, drawn from the present-day diffusion of *corno*, *corna*, and *corn-elha*, *-exa* as designations of the standard leather sheath, concerning the use of horn for the manufacture of such sheaths, once conspicuously wider (16). Does this situation imply — since horn and iron obviously represent more durable, hence superior materials in relation to leather (17 f.) — that some sort of regression to a less advanced technique has taken place? This pessimistic conclusion would be perfectly compatible with other sporadic symptoms of deterioration and impoverishment discovered by the author himself (41).

288 WORDS, OBJECTS, IMAGES

brief definition (better still, a characterization) of the flail as used in almost all of Portugal and Galicia and vestigially in other sections of Northern Spain as far east as Catalonia. Such a statement, potentially of great usefulness for the study of the metaphoric extensions of the flail's names across language and dialect borders, would immediately set it apart from other tools displaying comparably sharp and suggestive contours, like the ax, the pickax, the shovel, the pitch fork, the saw, and the comb.[6] The typical features of a European flail, reduced to its bare essentials, include a long slender bar (E. *handle*, G. *Stiel*) at one end of which a stouter or shorter stick, occasionally curved or rounded (E. *swingle*, dial. *swiple*, G. *Schwengel* or *Klöppel*) is so attached as to swing freely. Normally it serves to beat the grain out of the ear, but it may also separate beans from their pods and qualify for the handling of flax and for other subsidiary functions (51 f.). There are many variables: The connection between the two sticks shows several degrees of elaborateness (fabrics: leather thong, rope, chain; techniques of fastening: hanging, hinging, tying), the material out of which the sticks are carved is almost always wood — but these are scarcely essential features; witness the medieval military weapon called *flail* (not a characteristic of the Iberian Peninsula: 168 f.), in which the swingle was a metal ball or a piece set with spikes and the short handle was in general of metal. The irreducible elements that make up the pattern, then, are three: (a) a difference in length between the two bars, ordinarily in favor of the handle (note some traces of the abnormal ratio in León: 56, and in Upper Aragon: 59); (b) the irreversible distribution of functions between them; (c) the provision for free swinging, yet solid attachment. This last-named condition explains such figurative uses in English as (obs.) *flail* 'swinging part, as a gate bar or the lever of a press'; (anat., surg.) *flail joint* 'joint showing abnormal mobility'; (coll.) *to flail about* (*one's arms*, etc.).

For another thing, the Portuguese literary language, known as exceptionally averse to lexical economy, hence tolerant of synonyms,[7]

[6] The introductory paragraph of Chap. 1 fails to do justice to the flail observed in a state of motion, the only state that is linguistically relevant (7).

[7] On the strikingly protracted coexistence of *morno*, *tib(i)o*, and *tépido* 'lukewarm', drawn from different sources or via diverse channels, see *Rom.*, LXXIV (1952), 145–176. Characteristically, in Asturo-Leonese, which is more economically structured, the two sheaths are subsumed under a single name: *capiešas* or, less specifically, *arreos del porro* (56: M. Menéndez García's private information). Similarly, German scholars do not distinguish between *Hauben* (Schuchardt) or *Lederkappen* (Ebeling), see 57, 55.

accepts, it would seem without adequate semantic differentiation, such parallel designations (7, 9) of 'flail' as *malho* and *mangual*, of 'handle' as *cabo* and *mangoeira* (but 'swingle' is invariably *pírtigo*, a word which, as if by compensation, shows numerous regional by-forms),[8] of 'leather, horn, or iron sheath attached to the top of the handle' as *casula* and *carapulo*, and of a frequently matching 'sheath attached to the top of the swingle' as *enced-ouro, -oiro* and *ces-, cir-oiro* — all in all four designations which the author does not hesitate to use interchangeably. Moreover, the upper loops of the sheaths are called either *argolas* or *aselhas*, and the connecting (preponderantly circular) link has the alternative labels *anel* and *meã*. Finally, in subtype Ab the narrow leather laces squeezed through special holes made in the *cisoiro* (13) are referred to indiscriminately as *cintas* or *ensacas*. However abundant the number of dialect formations at issue, Herculano de Carvalho, as a matter of policy, should have selected, for consistency's sake, just one standard word for the 'flail' and for any of its parts. Seduced no doubt by the lure of stylistic variation, he cultivates the interchange of rival words, often on the same page and within the same sentence, to the serious discomfort especially of the foreign reader.[9]

One can raise more serious objections pertaining to the core of the argument. The reader learns early enough (2) that the author's criterion for the subdivision of all peninsular flails into four basic types (A, B, C, D) is, in each instance, the adoption of a specific fashion for connecting the two bars,[10] and soon after (3), he is

---

[8] Add to the Index (394a) an interesting example of *pítago* from 11 n.

[9] Here are some examples, from the first sixty pages, of the author's inappropriate choice of synonyms for his exposition: *malho* (18, 20 f., 25, 27, 33, 35 f., 38, 41, 53, 57 f.) corresponds exactly to *mangual* (20 f., 24 f., 27, 29, 31, 33, 35 f., 38 f., 45, 47 f., 49, 51 f., 53, 58 f., 60); *cabo* (9, 10, 13, 19 f., 23, 25, 29, 31, 33 f., 36, 38 f., 41, 43, 45, 47 f., 49, 52 f., 56, 57 f., 59 f.) is indistinguishable from *mangoeira* (9, 13, 17 f., 19 f., 21, 23, 25, 27, 38 f., 40, 58), as is *casula* (10, 13, 16, 18, 23 f., 25 f., 27, 29, 35, 40, 47, 51, 53, 56 f., 58) from *carapulo* (16, 18, 27, 33). The confusion reaches its peak with *encedoiro* (13, 16, 23, 31, 33, 35, 53, 55 f.) and *encedouro* (10, 18, 32 f., 35 f., 36, 40, 53, 58) vying with *cisoiro* (9, 13) and *cesoiro* (23, 27, 31, 36 f., 47, 54 f.). Upon occasion, *anel* and *meã* are used differently (35), because the connecting link need not be circular, but here too one finds a good deal of overlapping (17, 27, 40 f., 51, 59). *Cinta* (23, 31 f., 38, 53) and *ensaca* (23, 31, 33, 53, 55) cover exactly the same ground and are introduced late in the discussion, though not quite so late as *presa* (38 f.). It is to be regretted that the author did not insert, at the very start of Chap. 1, a table of all standard technical terms, with their admissible synonyms in parentheses.

[10] As expected, in not a few areas two or more types coexist, through stabilization of an incomplete shift, or else with substitution of one for another. More note-

alerted to certain discrepancies between the author's (still undefined) own classificatory system and that of his principal foreign authority, the Swedish comparative ethnologist Dag Trotzig's *Slagen och andra tröskredskap* (published in 1943), a book not within easy reach of Hispanists and one of whose doctrine only stray elements are mentioned (8 f., 112). At this point one misses a provisional definition, however summary, of the controversial four archetypes. Instead, Herculano de Carvalho plunges immediately into a minute enumeration and localization of the three variants and subvariants of Type A (9–35), carefully recording the measurements of each constituent part as he roams from hamlet to hamlet and inspects museum collections, in his effort to delineate important zones on the basis of isomorphs (12, 18, 24, 36, etc.). All the while he keeps injecting into the discussion vague references to the more rudimentary Type B (18, 25, 27 f., 29, 31; centered around backward Bragança in the extreme northeast), to the even more primitive Type C (29, 31, 33, 35; entrenched along the central stretch of the coastline, and in the process of being dislodged by A and B), and to the marginal, frequently improvised Type D (33; distinctly southern, with prongs into the Azores), without bothering to provide a preliminary description before these types, at length, come up for circumstantial analysis. Only after a long delay does the reader learn that Type B is characterized by a single sheath, placed as a rule on the swingle (35), that Type C has no sheaths at all (40), and that in Type D the connecting ring is replaced by a straight strap or lace (of widely varying length), which may be wound repeatedly around or between the upper rims of the two sticks.

Again, the suggested subdivisions of Type A may make the skeptical reader pause. The distinguishing marks of the receding Subtype Aa, confined to the extreme northwest, one hears, are two leather sheaths nailed and sewn (by means of thin leather threads) to the adjoining ends of handle and swingle; these sheaths form two loops connected, in turn, by a circular thong (10). The currently dominant Subtype Ab, stretching (though not *en bloc*) from the north to Setúbal, Beja, and an isolated outpost in western Algarve, differs from Aa in that the leather sheath of the handle may be either sewn and nailed or

---

worthy is the allocation of different duties to rival types, as when the one deemed more old-fashioned becomes an auxiliary tool assigned to women or given away to children as a toy (40).

just nailed to its top, whereas the sheath of the swingle is so artfully attached as not quite to envelop its top, which exhibits a small set of protruding hooklets (in Galicia as many as six: 53). Subtype Ac, concentrated to the north of the Mondego and prevalent in Braga, Vila Real, and Viseu, is almost exactly identical, except that the leather here yields to iron.

Clearly, then, the subdivision of Type A involves combined consideration of fabric, shape, and mode of attachment. This interlocking of criteria is in itself not very satisfactory; phoneticians, for instance, have learned to keep apart the point and the mode of articulation. But the suggested hierarchy gives rise to yet other questions: If the fabric is all-important, why not establish a separate category for flails connected by means of an eel-hide thong (9, 51; similarly in León: 56) or for those in Viseu that have the handle sheath made of horn (6–8)? Again, if the design matters, what about the occasional addition of a wooden peg to the equipment of Subtype Ab (13)? The considerably varying shape of the swingle (13, 21, 25, 38) also deserves a greater share of attention, and so do the differently shaped knots used to reinforce the *meã* (9 f.). In short, the suggested pattern of classification lacks cogency.

These strictures are not meant to imply any grave doubt as to the exactness or validity of Herculano de Carvalho's findings. Least of all would I like to give the impression of suspecting that his laborious piecing-together of the mosaic might have been dispensed with or that it has failed to lead to significant results. Such a conclusion would be unfair. On the contrary, the chances are that the author's experience and flair have often led him to make the right classificatory decisions and that his material (in which he himself points out some residual gaps: 3, 25, 27, 31, etc.) offers a high guarantee of authenticity (note his elaboration on Krüger: 55, and his corrections of Schuchardt: 49 n. 2 and 57 n. 1). The one reproach that one may gently address to Herculano de Carvalho is that he has given too little attention to the organization of his facts. A few extra weeks devoted to this kind of final polishing, and some acquaintance with any method of hierarchizing data through structural analysis, would doubtless have cleared away the last remnant of arbitrariness and inconsistency that one detects in his classification.

**4. The range of linguistic sources.** The heterogeneous channels of information tapped by the author show an impressive degree of resourcefulness on his part, a wide range of curiosity, and an uncommon power of coördination. On the one hand, he proves himself a full-fledged Romanicist by deftly using linguistic atlases of Catalonia, Italy, and Corsica (127 f., 135), etymological dictionaries of French (138 f.; 185 n. 5: correction to *FEW*), and other material rarely referred to by the Portuguese; in this respect, the limit to his conscientiousness is the lack of important foreign books even in his country's best-equipped libraries (138 n. 1: unavailability of J. Ronjat's historical standard grammar of Occitanian; 162 n. 1). Also, he proves his discriminating judgment by having recourse to Krüger's *Hochpyrenäen* for raw data (2 et passim), yet by selecting Schuchardt rather than Krüger as his guide where interpretative finesse matters most (127; see also 90 n. 2).

On the other hand, he remains a versatile Portugalist, handling with equal delight and competence specimens of his native speech on any social plane and time level and in any corner of his small country, even those notoriously difficult of access. Particularly meritorious is his use of unpublished sources, such as those, valuable despite their acknowledged faults (3, 123 n. 1), collected by Paiva Boléo through correspondence as early as 1942 (responses to P. 437 of his question-naire; see *Lg.*, XXVIII [1952], 124–129) and those loaned by Oporto's Ethnological Research Center (4). Reactions to the author's own questionnaire on the techniques of threshing (4, 118) came from 159 Portuguese localities and from numerous insular and peninsular points (Canary Islands, Asturias, Santander, and especially Anda-lusia, where M. Alvar, with an enthusiastic staff of co-workers, gave assistance: 67, 71, 84), to say nothing of detailed epistolary explana-tions contributed by experts like P. Scheuermeier (110 f.). This plentiful collateral information stood the author in particularly good stead where he confronted threshing techniques alien to Portugal, or only vestigially represented there, such as those using appliances descended from the Roman TRĪBULUM (from TERERE 'to grind') and PLŌSTELLUM (from PLAU-, PLŌ-STRUM 'car'), or animal power, an essentially southern Mediterranean technique (64–85). Interesting is his reliance on older lexicographers, not only R. Bluteau (132) but also J. Cardoso, B. Pereira, and A. Barbosa (71, 128 f.), but these, however authoritative, should not have relieved him of the necessity of plowing, almost unaided by alphabetical glossaries, through piles of medieval vernacular material — an onerous task, but currently found to be more and more rewarding, far beyond the earlier expectations[11]. The impressive medieval record of *trilhar* might have induced him to assign a higher rating to this verb on Portuguese soil.[12]

5. **Delineation of zones and analysis of areal patterns.** The author is at his best in delimiting and interpreting lexical zones. After broadly distinguishing between heavily, lightly, and sporadically represented lexical types (115–117), he attempts to determine the extension of each, then proceeds to the closest possible reconstruction of the sequence of territorial shifts.

In his classification the author is distinctly less schematic than the Italian neolinguists, who are usually content with such inclusive and essentially relative categories as larger vs. smaller or central vs. peripheral (marginal) zones.[13] Like most dialect geographers, European and American, he separates at the outset metropolitan from overseas (in this instance, insular) territories, which were settled in

[11] For older Spanish exemplification the author falls back on the usage (as of 1513) of the well-known agriculturalist G. A. de Herrera rather than on the pioneer lexicographers Palencia and Nebrixa. For older Portuguese he invokes (74, 89) the testimony of Valentim Fernandes' *Reportório dos tempos* (eds. 1552, 1563). Here more conclusive medieval evidence could easily have been produced. Thus, *trillar* was a favorite with Juan Ruiz and acceptable to Sem Tob. The Escorial Glossary (ca. 1400) renders by 'trillo' *contri(c)torium* (No. 1039) and *tritura* (No. 2027), and by 'trillar' *tritillo* (No. 3062), a bizarre formation which presumably owes its *-ll-* to erratic association with its vernacular counterpart, its conjugation class to the pressure of TRĪTŪRĀRE beside *TRĪTĀRE 'to grind thoroughly' (*REW*[3] § 8922; cf. Du Cange), and the interfixed segment possibly to TRĪTILE (gloss) 'quod teri potest', cf. ŪTILE, VOLĀTILE (A. Castro, *Glosarios latino-españoles de la Edad Media* 303*b*–304*a* [Madrid, 1936]). Note the early instance of figurative use in *camino trillado* (*Cuento del Emperador Ottas*, ed. J. Amador de los Ríos, Chap. LIV). Interesting, not least on etymological grounds, is the translation of *despolio* and *spolio* by 'esbulhar' in a Latin–Old-Portuguese verb dictionary (ed. H. H. Carter; see *RPh.*, VI [1952–53], 80, 93, 101). V. García de Diego's divergent etymology 'trilhar' *RFE*, XII [1925], 5), questioned by Meyer-Lübke (*REW*[3] § 3422: FOLLIS), thus becomes even more problematic. (DĒ)SPOLIĀRE is a widely recorded dual base in Romance (cf. Sp. *despojar*, F. *dépouiller*, etc.); the source of the consonantal deflection -P- > -*b*- has not yet been determined (cross with *esboroar*, the western cognate of Sp. *desmoronar*? Cf. *PMLA*, LXIII [1948], 785–802). Here and there, in discussing side issues, Herculano de Carvalho does go to the medieval sources (184, 198).

[12] In the aforementioned 14th-century verb glossary 'trilhar' serves to gloss *calco, decalco, inculco* (*compremo, contero*), and *proculco* (Nos. 717, 795, 1425, 2220; see Carter's ed. in *RPh.*, VI, 79 f., 85, 91, 103). This exuberance of the glossographer hardly jibes with the author's timid assertions regarding area and chronology of the word (98 f.). See also Frei Joaquim de Santa Rosa de Viterbo, *Elucidário*[2], II, 260*b*, s.v. *trilhoada* (Lisbon, 1865).

[13] Yet he does operate, on a grand scale, with peripheral zones as a clue to archaism, in terms of the Age-and-Area Hypothesis (98, 101), apparently without managing to draw the same consequences from the facts as his chief model, D. Trotzig.

radically different fashion,[14] and parenthetically establishes among the former a number of neatly graded binary and triadic oppositions, e.g. connected vs. disconnected, compact vs. diffuse vs. completely scattered (121). Through the joint application of separate criteria he arrives at such complex characterizations as "small and isolated" and even "homogeneous, sharply silhouetted, but lacking continuity" (118). Also, he opposes genuine zones to mere clusters or successions of extrazonal points, among which borderline points and isolated outposts represent especially clear-cut cases (115–117). At intervals, he correctly admits the seldom acknowledged dependence of our visual cartographic impressions on the often accidental density of the available documentation (116, 123).

More original and inevitably more problematic than Herculano de Carvalho's static view is his dynamic grasp of areal configurations. In general, as an alert native observer and occasional participant of the shifts, he has a flair for recent accretions (88, 92, 96 f., 116 f.), which it might have taken a foreign explorer many years of residence and adjustment to acquire. In the discussion of older linguistic ebbs and floods, however, intuition must yield to analysis. Thus, the author argues that a profusion of dots outside a sharply profiled zone may point to "previous wider expansion" (118), especially if one discovers semantic support for this contention, such as the prevalence of the pars-pro-toto meaning in scattered islets (119). In this event the dots are lone vestiges of a submerged, formerly adjoining area. In other situations the author weighs the wisdom of rating dots as outposts (118). There seems to be no way of deciding, from the configuration of the territory alone, whether the presence

---

[14] There is a marked relationship between the material civilizations and the dialects of the Atlantic archipelagos and of southernmost Portugal (Algarve), which calls to mind the often claimed and often disputed *andalucismo* of New World Spanish, including the dialect of the Canary Islands (47, 72 f.). Algarve, in turn, despite its ties to neighboring Baixo Alentejo (109), is rather sharply separated from the remainder of the country (116, 123, apropos of *malho* and ⌐*moueira*⌐). In other instances one observes a near-coincidence between the usages of the islands and those of rugged, retarded northeastern Portugal, including, along the north-south axis, the districts of Bragança, Guarda, and Castelo Branco (68 f.). The likeliest explanation of the overlap is that the Algarve-Açores isoglosses have been caused by conditions of climate and settlement, whereas the second bundle of isoglosses points to a common degree of general lag behind more advanced centers. But the situation is complicated by other affinities of the extreme south to the northeast (97). For a cursory survey of the parallel problems surrounding the relations of metropolitan to insular and to overseas Spanish see my contribution ("Hispanic Philology") to Vol. IV (in press) of the series *Current Trends in Linguistics*, ed. T. A. Sebeok.

of dots (whatever their distributional pattern) indicates an advance or a retreat. What tips the scale in favor of one of these alternatives is either an independently clarified fact of material civilization (descriptive, e.g. the archaic shape of the tool designated by a given word: 121, or evolutionary, e.g. the presumably parallel spread of the millet culture: 116), or else separately established concatenations of human affairs, again assumed to have paralleled or preceded linguistic events, as in the case of the Galician settlement in Salamanca (117) or, conversely, the Leonese settlement in Miranda and Vimioso (95 f.).

On the whole, the author displays an admirable grasp of the dynamics of dialect history, as when he tentatively identifies starting points (102 f., 107 f.: Lugo, Oviedo, and Braga), neatly separates isoglosses, traces itineraries, and sharpens his stratigraphic perception to the point of recognizing fresh advances superimposed on earlier temporary retreats (117, speaking of *mangual*). The level of abstraction at which he prefers to operate is best defined by a reference to K. Jaberg's masterly *Aspects géographiques du langage* (1936). He could conceivably have reached a somewhat higher plane of generalization by contrasting more plastically the linguistic and nonlinguistic arguments that are apt to be injected into each typical analysis and by establishing some kind of operational scale, preferably not too rigid, by which the reader might have tested each inference drawn from a given areal configuration.

**6. Lexical contamination and pressure of derivational schemes.** The author takes delight in giving a meticulous account of all manifestations of cultural hybridism. Thus, in his research into material civilization (66, 76, 104 f., 107 f., 110) he excels in showing how, by way of compromise, two rival procedures, under exceptional circumstances, may be transformed into two consecutive phases of a single complex procedure (78, 85 f., 92). A different way of settling such clashes is to relegate the less profitable of two accepted techniques to peculiar, marginal uses (87, 91), sometimes depending on the actor's efficiency (women, children) or on the quantity of the produce on hand (80 n. 3). Here, he might have added, we can probably see characteristic, temporarily arrested stages of a gradual transition. On a higher level of analysis Herculano de Carvalho shows keen understanding of the interplay of conditioning factors, as when, brushing off Krüger's naïve naturalistic simplifications, he traces the conflict of threshing techniques to preferences imposed by peculiarities of climate and terrain and blended with another, entirely unrelated set of preferences of a historical and cultural order (90, 96).

The author operates freely with the assumption of lexical crosses, especially between cognates and near-synonyms of similar appearance. Thus, dial. (Leiria) *malhal* is analyzed as *malho* × ⌐*moual*⌐ (116), and NW-Sp. *may-al, -ar* as *mayo* (< *mallo*) × ⌐*manal*⌐ (117). The Ptg. vars. *ma-lha, -ya* (cast off by *malho* < MALLEU), at first left unexplained (126), are eventually attributed to the influence of *maça* < \*MATTEA (131; the reverse influence is made responsible for Ptg. *maço*). Langued. *mani-airal, -eiral* 'handle of a flail' is labeled as an outgrowth of MANUĀRIUS with the ending of the rival adj. MANUĀLIS (139).[15] After an initial silence (146 n. 2) the author freely admits the impact of the MANICA subfamily on *mangueira* (150). MANUĀRIA and MANUĀLIS reappear amalgamated on Portuguese soil (147). The probability of a contact between MANĀLE and MALLEU, ruled out (despite Krüger's advocacy) for Gal. *malle* (151 f.), is ultimately affirmed for Gal. *manllo* (153), although phonetically this assumption is far from indispensable, cf. *NRFH*, IX (1955), 240 f., 265-273. See further 166, 174, 183, 188 n. 1, 189, 208.

Each process, viewed in isolation, is presented as cogently as is feasible with lexical mergers, but one lingering doubt remains: Why is an individual word almost invariably held responsible for another word's deflection from the norm while the author, by implication, minimizes the powerful agency of lexical schemes, as opposed to units? Is one to accept at its face value the claimed unique influence of *malho* on *maça* to justify *maço*, and the equally unique influence of *maça* on *malho* to justify *malha*, when twin masculine and feminine formations in names of tools and containers permeate the Romance lexicon — a point recently pressed, with widely divergent results, by B. Hasselrot and by H. and R. Kahane? In other words, Herculano de Carvalho tends too strongly to dissolve the rich fabric of associative interference into a myriad of attractions and encounters on the

---

[15] The author's own material suggests further possibilities along this line; thus, Gal. *ma(n)da* 'herd' (cf. Sp. *manada*), which I might have mentioned in *BH*, LIII (1951), 41-80, may provide the long-sought clue to Sp. *desman(d)arse* 'to stray from the flock, go astray' beside OSp. *mal-, des-mandado* 'disobedient', from *mandar*, a tangle not quite satisfactorily explained in *UCPL*, I: 7 (1947), 274. For a more ambitious attempt to come to grips with this problem see my recent article: "Sobre el núcleo etimológico de esp. ant. *desman(d)ar, desma(n)o*: lat. DĒ-, DĪ-MĀNĀRE", *Fil.*, VIII (1962 [–64]), 185-211.

smallest conceivable scale, disregarding the powerful pressures which words consolidated into sharply divided groups (i.e. into inflectional and derivational patterns) exert on one another and, with even greater momentum, on relatively isolated words, incapable of much resistance to focused attraction.

**7. Luso-Hispanic relations.** A result of the author's cosmopolitan attitude is his excellent grasp, from the outset (x–xi), of the close interdependence of Western Spanish and Portuguese. The prerequisite for this state of affairs is the extreme fluidity of the linguistic frontier, attributable in large part to its periodic violation by seasonal workers (for some new evidence see 97). Every insider knows that the lack of any durable liaison between the Spanish and the Portuguese teams of linguists has created a chasm in pan-Hispanic studies, leaving to uncommitted foreigners like W. Bierhenke, W. Ebeling, O. Fink, W. Giese, and H. Messerschmidt the task of building bridges. From this fault Herculano de Carvalho's book is completely free. As a result of the wider perspective gained through readings and personal contacts, the new sense of proportion instilled in any earnest traveler far away from home, and the coöperation of some younger Spanish colleagues compensating for the apathy of bureaucrats (5), our author, possibly as the first Portuguese linguist since Leite de Vasconcelos and Gonçalves Viana, shows a solid knowledge of Spanish conditions, and has the will to appraise them impartially; here and there he credits his Spanish colleagues with superior skill (202, 207). The claim that Extr. (Alburquerque) *mangual* is a Lusism (106) is balanced by the admission that Ptg. *manganilho* has spread from (Spanish) Extremadura to Baixo Alentejo and to Central Algarve (120; cf. 171). There are numerous other Portuguese words in *-ilha* < -ELLA (the author himself mentions *manilha*: 143 n. 2) and in *-ilho* < -ELLU which must have been absorbed through similar channels;[16] incidentally, the suffix *-ez* attached to adjectival abstracts, as against ancient *-ece* and semilearned *-ice* < -ITIE, is also a feature imported from the East. Some statements, though subject to future probing, must be commended for their very attractive formulation: Thus, Ptg. *maneira* is declared a Castilianism only in certain connotations (142 n. 2). On the other hand, there are many glaring omissions,

---

[16] Here are a few examples from the author's own documentation: Alent. Alg. *manganilha* (62 f.), Ptg. *manganilho* (120), Miñ. Trasm. *manilha* (143 n. 2), (bot.) *negrilho* (25, 27), *serguilha* (125).

as in the case of *manada* 'herd' (148) which, on account of its -*n*- and its semantic category suggestive of migration, should at least have been suspected of foreign extraction. It is refreshing to read that Sp. *mallo* < MALLEU, of obviously non-Castilian transmission, stems in all probability from Leonese (126 n. 1). To those who remember the quasi-obligatory, high-pitched rejection of the slightest hint of Spanish cultural influence on Portuguese, emanating from scholars even of M. Rodrigues Lapa's caliber, and the simultaneous insistence on the Portuguese ancestry of any non-Castilian, "Western" trait in Spanish (a claim ruthlessly pressed, for instance, by R. de Sá Nogueira as late as 1948), Herculano de Carvalho's serene outlook seems to herald a long-awaited turning-point.[17]

**8. The balance between Latin and Romance.** Given Herculano de Carvalho's meticulousness, it is small wonder that he should correct minor errors in the existing etymological dictionaries. Thus, he deems the semantic ambit of the products of MALLEUS wider than Meyer-Lübke assumed (*REW*[3] § 5268); in particular, he shows that the original meanings have lingered on in a sizable territory (125). Also, Extr. *marco* (beside And. *márcola*) is ably traced to MARCUS 'hammer' (190). This demonstration is grist for those who argue that the gap between Latin and the conservative varieties of Romance has been vastly exaggerated. In sifting Meyer-Lübke's data, the author exposes formations of dubious authenticity (126: Sp. *majo*) and points to outright lapses and misprints (136: MANUĀLE > Gen. *manuá*, not *manvá*; 146 n. 1: Alent. *maroval*, not *manoval*; cf. 182 n. 1). Despite this sprinkling of corrections, one is forced to admit that in the tracing of vernacular forms to their bases, the supreme test of a Romanicist's skill, the author unfortunately falls short of our expectations.

At the root of this deficiency is the disproportion in the attention accorded to Latin and Romance, as if the two were totally different entities rather than slices of the same material. While each Romance

---

[17] This does not imply uniformly flawless analysis of Spanish material. Despite Moz. **yannair** and Gal.-Ptg. *janeiro* < IĀNUĀRIU, possibly pronounced [jan·áiru] in some varieties of provincial Late Latin, the -*n*- of Cast. *enero* cannot reflect -NN-; the difference in the pretonic vowel, in reverse ratio to Ptg. *jejum* ~ Sp. *ayuno* < IĒIŪNU beside IĀIŪNU in Plautus, confirms the suspected lack of any Common Vulgar Latin base. Forms like *junio* 'June', *julio* 'July' open up the possibility of learned or semilearned status. Several Arabisms like *añafil* < AN-NAFĪR 'kind of musical pipe' belie the validity of the suggested relative chronology (146 f.).

fact is presented with an almost excessive lavishness of data regarding the socio-economic, the chronological, and the territorial coördinates, most Latin facts are surrounded by an aura of abstractness, as if Latin had no dialectal cleavage (however dimly visible), no historical axis worth envisioning, no spectrum of semantic shades and phraseological idiosyncrasies for each word examined under sharp focus. In short, Herculano de Carvalho's Latin is the highly normalized and conventional medium of written communication found in any college dictionary or grammar. This simplified contour of a dead language conceivably would not have been out of place in a structural sketch, where the boldly drawn features of one system lend themselves to comparison with those of another. But there is little justification for the attempt to balance such a flat, schematic view of Latin against a richly nuanced, multidimensional, overelaborate projection of a derivative language. The two perspectives, whatever their separate merits, simply fail to invite any fruitful comparison.[18]

Because hypothetical bases represent heavy mortgages, their introduction ought to be kept to the barest minimum.[19] Take the positing of *MANU-ELL-US (beside -ELL-A), on the basis of OF *manel* 'handful', Burg. *menevel* 'sheaf', and Occ. *manello* (f.), *manèu* (m.) 'handful of tow' (138–140). Since MANUS in Gallo-Romance is feminine, it suffices to assume a single diminutive in -ELLA at the Latin stage, by analyzing *manel, meneval, manèu* as so many variants of a late and regionally restricted back-formation. Exacting readers may similarly

---

[18] Contrast also the author's painstaking transcription of Portuguese dialect forms with the fairly slipshod spelling of Latin, especially as regards vowel quantity: MANUALIS, JANUA (132, 134) for MANUĀLIS, IĀNUA, etc.

[19] The author might have inserted the asterisk more scrupulously. He omits it occasionally where it belongs (136: MANUELLA, elsewhere starred; 130 f.: MALLEĀRE is inferential and should have been so marked; only the p.ptc. in -ĀTUS is supported by written testimony), and places it where it is supererogatory (134: r. MANUĀRIA, an error carried over from Hanssen; 134 f., 142: r. IĒNUĀRIUS, an inscriptional variant, see Lindsay's and Niedermann's discussions quoted by Ernout and Meillet; conversely, IĒUNA remains undocumented). Also it seems safer to spell the base of Nuor. *mazzúkku*, Logud. *mattolu* [*]MATTEOLU (here the author may have relied too heavily on Wagner, *Das ländliche Leben Sardiniens* 32), since an offshoot of *MATTEA (*REW*³ § 5425; see also §§ 5425a, 5426), *MATTIA (*Dict. étym. l. lat.*³ 695) 'club' is involved, a late imported word, reconstructed from Vegetius' compound and suffixal derivative, respectively, MATTIOBARBULUS 'kind of javelin' and MAT(T)IĀRIUS 'soldier so armed' and unrelated to either MAT(T)IA, MAT(T)IOLA 'entrails' (the equivalent of Gr. *periphora* in glosses; see *REW*³ §5412) or Arnobius' MATTEOLA (7.231), the diminutive of the Hellenism MATTEA 'tidbit, delicacy', identified as such by Varro (assuming, in turn, that the pairs of words last mentioned were mere homonyms).

x

frown on *(AD)MANUĀRE, as long as it lacks support less fragile than It. *ammannare*.

The author's cavalier attitude toward Latin may have misled him into more hazardous statements. A sizable section (132–150) of Chap. IV, devoted to the rival types MANUĀLIS and MANUĀRIA, revolves around the unsettled question of medial Lat. [nw] in Romance. Herculano de Carvalho leads off (§ 33) with the formal presentation of a dilemma: Some Hispanists (Castro, Krüger, Bierhenke), in an effort to explain Ast.-Leon. *manal*, operate with *MANĀLIS (cf. OProv. *manal*, OF *manel*: 139); others, including Meyer-Lübke, are satisfied with MANUĀLIS. A similar dichotomy (§ 35) exists in regard to Sp. *manera*: A. Alonso's base *MANĀRIA contrasts with F. Hanssen's earlier etymon MANUĀRIA. The author, after canvassing hundreds of widely disseminated Romance reflexes, concludes that the second hypothesis alone (i.e. MANUĀLIS) is defensible. The truth, I believe, is that the dilemma itself is illusory. Positing MANUĀLIS or *MANĀLIS as the prototype of *mnaal* practically amounts to two ways of stating the same thing, with different degrees of explicitness.

An alternative argument, more cogent than Herculano de Carvalho's, might run as follows. In early Imperial Latin we already find isolated instances of wavering between [nw] and [n]. Witness, within the family of IĀNUA 'entrance, door' beside IĀN-US -ŪS and -Ī 'passageway', the coexistence of IĀNU-ĀLIS and IĀN-ĀLIS (Ovid), to say nothing of IĀN-ITOR, likened by Ernout and Meillet to (H)OL-ITOR 'gardener' (from HOLUS -ERIS 'vegetable') and to PORT-ITOR 'tollgatherer' (from PORTUS -ŪS 'harbor'); add the adj. IĀN-EUS and the compound IĀN-IGENA (Ovid).

Insecurity increased through the combined agency of lexical processes, morphological leveling, and sound shifts. From ANNUS -Ī 'year' the parallel adjectives ANN-ĀLIS and ANN-UUS branched off; their subsequent contamination produced ANN-UĀLIS in Low Latin (cf. the amalgamated suffixes -ĀNEUS, -ĪNEUS, -ĀTĪCEUS, -ĀRĬCEUS, etc.). At the Romance stage rhizotonic ANNUUS was doomed to sterility, but ANNĀLIS and ANNUĀLIS both survived (cf. *Lg.*, XXXI [1955], 279). In the light of these facts, the author's comment on Sp. *añal*, Ptg. *anal* (134 f. n. 4) invites revision; he is on more solid ground in discussing OProv. *anoal*, OF *anvel* (140 nn. 1 f.).

Midway between the domains of lexicon and morphology lies the case of MANUĀLIS and MANUĀRIUS. The collapse of the U declension in colloquial Low Latin (except possibly in retarded southern Italy), the concomitant reduction of the stem MANU- to MAN-, and the impact of the lexical polarization PED- ~ MAN- (favoring the stem pattern CVC and directly involving the descendants of PED-ĀLIS and PED-ĀRIUS)[20] all contributed to the replacement of morphologically and derivationally obsolescent MANUĀLIS and MANUĀRIUS by more advanced *MANĀLIS, *MANĀRIUS, a virtually predictable trend pointed up by losses of such lexical units as could not smoothly conform to it (e.g. MANUĀRE 'to steal', recorded in Gellius, would have collided, through the elimination of [w], with MĀNĀRE 'to flow' after the loss of phonemic contrast between the short and the long central vowel). This trend need not have spread from a single area, but may have arisen spontaneously at different places wherever associative interference and structural remodeling exerted pressure on the MANUS family. Herculano de Carvalho admits that Sp. *manilla*, at least in some dialectal acceptations, may be a secondary product (143 n. 2), but he separates this group with unwarranted sharpness from the other uses, whose aggregate he analyzes as primary (134 f., 142), overlooking the more attractive possibility of a gradual retreat of the petrifact *MANUELLA before its morphologically rejuvenated variant *MANELLA.[21] Again, from his Italian dialect material (where -*nn*- < [nw] and -*n*- < -N- are mostly distinguishable), the author infers that, within the same zone, *MANUĀTA is far less densely represented in proportion to (implied) *MANĀTA than is, say, *MANUELLA in proportion to (implied) *MANELLA, etc., but inexplicably chooses not to press the point.[22] To those who prefer to view Latin in motion rather than statically, two explanations of the discrepancy suggest themselves: Either the -ĀTA derivative originated after the -ELLA

[20] On this string of problems see *AGI*, XXXVI (1951), 49–74; *BH*, LIII (1951), 41–80; *BICC*, VII (1951), 201–244; *Lg.*, XXVII (1951), 485–518; and *UCPL*, XI (1954), 34–37, 142–150. In the last-mentioned monograph I might have stated more forcefully that the implied withdrawal of VL MANUA before *MANIA was just another consequence of the erosion of MANU- in favor of MAN-.

[21] The attempted separation of primary from secondary *mane(i)ra* (142) may also be too rigid for some readers' taste.

[22] Parenthetically the author makes what seems to me a misleading remark on the plausibility of direct descent of *MANUĀTA from (slangy) MANUĀRE. The various guesses which he later hazards in retrospect (137 f.) confirm one's initial impression of his admitted helplessness. He mentions, without endorsing or rejecting it, the explicit introduction of *MAN-ĀTA by J. M. Piel (145 n. 1). When he himself operates with *manata* (147), his use of italics rather than small capitals points in the direction of a hypothetical proto-Portuguese form: Should we not in this event expect him to posit *manada*?

diminutive (no data for an independent analysis of the assumed sequence happen to be available), in which case the more modern radical MAN- may, in the interval, have further crowded out, as the core of newly fashioned derivatives, its slowly receding predecessor MANU-; or, by a more radical solution, *MANUĀTA may altogether be declared a mirage, It. *man-ata*, OF *man-ee* (139), OProv. Cat. Sp. *man-ada* (142 f.), etc., being either independent parallel derivatives from *man-o* and its var. (if of late coinage), or (if of early coinage) descendants from Late L. *MAN-ĀTA. The minority group (OF *manvée*,[23] Tusc. *mannata*: note the geographic gap) could then be explained away as an assortment of sporadic contaminations of ⌜*manata*⌝ or *MANĀTA with locally preserved products of MANUĀLIS and MANUĀRIUS, products which, by virtue of the older status of the -ĀLIS and -ĀRIUS derivatives, would tend to show a measure of retardation in the maintenance of [nw] or of some such close equivalent as [nˑ].

As frequently in historical linguistics, it seems difficult to reduce the diverse processes to a common denominator. If IĀ-, IĒ-NUĀRIUS produced contrasting results (F. *janvier*, It. *gennaio* vs. Sp. *enero*, ONav. *ja-*, *je-nero*, with Ptg. *janeiro* posing a separate problem; H. Lüdtke, *BF*, XIV [1953], 167, regards the last-mentioned as semilearned), whereas FEBRUĀRIUS, despite the likelihood of a similar split through semantic affinity to 'January', shows consistent loss of [w] in Romance and, so far as I can judge, in Celtic (*REW*[3] § 3231), one reason for the discrepancy may be the more thorough rejection of the subjacent FEBRUŌ -ĀRE family than of IĀNUA, and another the incompatibility of medial [brw] with many early Romance phonemic systems. Different circumstances prevailed in the case of *MINUĀRE, the assumed substitute for MINUERE 'to decrease': At first the weight of widely used MINŪTU (Sp. *menudo*, Ptg. *miúdo* 'small', etc.), and later the threat of collision with MIN-ĀRĪ, -ĀRE 'to menace, goad, drive' (*REW*[3] § 5585) may well have tipped the scales in favor of [menwáre] (see *BH*, LVII [1955], 84–128, esp. 104–106).[24]

Thus *MANĀLE is conceivable not as a genuine alternative to

---

[23] In this connection one regrets all the more that the sorely deficient Index to *REW*[3], s.v. *manvele*, should refer the reader, through the compiler's inadvertence, to § 5280, an entry discarded in the course of the revision. A more serious inconsistency: The *REW*[3] admits the possibility of a split in the case of MAN(U)ĀRIUS (§ 5332), but not of MANUĀLIS (§ 5331); it lists ANNUĀLIS to the exclusion of ANNĀLIS.

[24] In other words, despite A. Alonso's precedent (134) one may doubt, on lexical grounds, that *MINUĀRE and MANUĀLE are analyzable as on a par.

MANUĀLE, but only as a more advanced by-form, which could have arisen, through polygenesis, at widely scattered points in Vulgar Latin. The simplification of [nw] to [n] is one of several solutions open to speakers of Romance from the time when a new pattern of stress and syllabification transformed UĪ-NE-A 'vine' into [ví-nja] (for the most part structurally acceptable) and, probably with a certain delay, MA-NU-Ā-LE into [man-wál], in the long run found to be structurally unacceptable except to some Italian dialect speakers, especially in Liguria, Emilia, Abruzzi, and Calabria (136).[25] Rival solutions included [nw] > [ngw], [nw] > [nv] or [mb], [nw] > [n˙], characteristic, in this order, of Hispano-Romance, Gallo-Romance, and Italo-Romance.[26] Gascon and Galician-Portuguese, inimical to -N-, occupy a position apart (141, 145).[27] A similar situation faced speakers with respect to unprecedented consonant clusters shaped as a result of violent syncope, as in the case of -zr-: LACERĀRE 'to tear, mangle' > OSp. lazrar, lazdrar, ladrar, lazar, etc. 'to suffer' (NRFH, VI [1952], 209–276). All told (and Å. W. Munthe seems to have sensed this state of affairs; see 147 n. 2), the equation manal < MANUĀLE simply spans a few more centuries than manal < *MANĀLE, in most instances implying the latter as an intermediate stage.

9. **Phonological problems.** From the author of a "Wörter-und-Sachen" monograph one need not customarily expect any detailed discussion of historical phonology. Herculano de Carvalho's conscientiousness forbids him to shirk this added responsibility;[28] the performance that he volunteers turns out to be creditable, but probably less than distinguished.

Take his statement on the difficulty of formulating diachronic correspondences in the case of rarely or uniquely represented sound

[25] There are scattered traces also in Old Provençal, extending to Old Franco-Provençal (140). Repeatedly a delayed solution of the undesirable situation is observable, e.g. in Italy through the introduction of an antihiatic consonant: N.-Cal. [jánua] ~ [jánuwə]. Rarely (as in OIt. continovo) the retardation was due, at least in part, to learned influence; cf. the author's reaction (136) to Meyer-Lübke's and Rohlfs' explanation of manovale and Genova respectively (add MANTUA > It. Mantova).

[26] Vestigially also in French? See p. 138 and FEW, V, 29.

[27] The reputed shift [nw] > [ng], involving a late secondary simplification of [ngw] in Ptg. mingar (145) and contact with MANICA in the remaining instances (146), should hardly have been accorded the same rank as other developments.

[28] Yet one misses mention of the loss of diphthongs through the epenthesis of nasals, apropos of Gal. monza ~ Miñ. mouça, moiça (151); see BF, XIV (1953), 37–40, and NRFH, IX (1955), 267.

sequences (149).[29] Despite very limited range, a sound change may appositely be labeled "regular" as long as it fits smoothly into a broader, independently established pattern, cf. OSp. fut. *yxtré* from *exir* 'to leave' (unique cluster -*xtr*- < -x'R), echoing *mintré*, *pondré*, etc. — a point repeatedly touched upon in this collection of essays (see esp. p. 190). Here some familiarity with tenets of structuralist thinking might have set the author straight.

In other instances the focus on the historical background seems not sharp enough. The modern toponyms *Mangualde*, *Moalde* (also spelled *Mualde*), and *Mualdo* may reflect (as claimed by J. da Silveira, denied by J. M. Piel) VĪLLA MANUALDĪ and MANUALDU, in this order (153 f.), provided one remembers the roughness of these equations: They cannot be used to reconstruct elusive transitional stages of dimly perceptible sound changes. After all, MANUALD-Ī, -U are not actual etymological bases, but clumsy adaptations of Germanic forms to medieval Latin usage, with scribal habits and the limitations of the only available alphabet erratically determining the choice of each character; this much the author belatedly admits (156). Vernacular toponyms, in turn, though rooted in oral transmission, occasionally show traits of retarded (semi-learned) development (cf. 164). Hence the risk of checking on a problematic sound shift by forms which, although they are obliquely interrelated, cannot easily be likened to successive points along a single unobstructed line of development.

In applying phonological principles the author displays a pervasive conservatism and a certain lack of assurance. The oft-claimed dependence of the outcome of [nw] on the quality of surrounding vowels and on the position of the segment vis-à-vis the stressed vowel (133 f.) remains, in the specific contexts where it is invoked, entirely unproved (148 f.).[30] Conversely, the bifurcation, presumably at the medieval stage, of *canle* and *cal* < CANĀLE, *manle* and *mal* < MAN(U)ĀLE, etc. (150 f.) involves partial loss vs. "consolidation" of nasal resonance, a complicated process which, among several factors, may hinge upon the preservation of the original stress pattern at the critical stage *$c\tilde{a}\tilde{a}l(e)$, *$m\tilde{a}\tilde{a}l(e)$. I find no reference in

---

[29] One is surprised, in this context, to see Ptg. *ilha* 'island' quoted as a native product of ĪNSULA (149 n. 1). The Old Portuguese form was *īsua*, neatly matching Sp. *isla*; *ilha*, a relative newcomer, is an unmistakable Catalanism.

[30] The author admits that the early dating of [nw] > [n·] before front vowel is invalidated by the dichotomy Ptg. *manoeira*, n., vs. *maneiro*, adj. (149). What, incidentally, is the justification for speaking of palatalized *a* in the case of It. -*aio* (ibid.)?

the pertinent chapter to this mutual dependence of nasal release and accentuation,[31] nor indeed to the rôle of the fluctuating apocope of final -e, including the possibility of false restoration.[32]

The discovery of the dialect forms ⌐moual⌐ and ⌐moueira⌐, cogently explained as archaic, rustic vars. of mangual and mangoeira, is one of the focuses of phonological debate, in which not all the arguments will enlist the reader's unqualified support. The shift [manwál] > [mangwál] is clearly a sequel to an upheaval in traditional syllabification; the author quotes A. Alonso's pronouncement to this effect, yet seems to withhold his approval (154 n. 2) and chooses to operate with a questionable hypothesis of the "natural instability" of *[ŋ] instead of simply explaining the epenthesis of [g] as a wholesale transfer of the cluster [gw] from words like LINGUA, facilitated by the sudden need, around 400, to render word-initial Gmc. [w] in Romance dialect speech. Despite the noteworthy parallelism of Trasm. calhota = canlota 'wooden conduit feeding a water-mill', the margin of risk in tracing topon. Calle to canle via *canlle (152 f.) remains disturbingly wide — certainly too wide for us to use this sequence in support of the dubious equation manlle > malle (which other scholars try to solve by introducing the attraction of the synonym mallo as an independent factor). Given the spread of Calle through all four Galician provinces and the local acceptability of -nll- or [∼λ], one wonders why *canlle, if it actually was the prototype, should have been consistently replaced on such a sweeping scale (unless, of course, by forcible Castilianization). Be that as it may, the late local shift manle > manlle can hardly be associated with the conspicuously early transformation of word-initial CL-, FL-, PL- into (c)ll- etc., a transformation quite uncharacteristic of Galician (152, 166). Why not start with the locally preëxistent group [nλ] as in SINGULŌS > OGal. senllos (beside Sp. se-ños, -ndos, the latter indirectly reminiscent of medrar 'to thrive' < *mellrar < MELIŌRĀRE)

---

[31] Some ramifications of this problem transcend the scope of this review, e.g. quinta < OPtg. quintãa, venta < OPtg. ventãa (cf. Sp. ventana).

[32] Lapesa's programmatic article of 1951 examines only the core of the problem. It seems hardly accurate to speak of "perfect parallelism" (150 f.), within the framework of northwestern dialect speech, between manle ∼ mal, canle ∼ cal, on the one hand, and ga(n)do, mo(n)llo, mo(n)ça, on the other: The maintenance of the final vowel controls the medial nasal, or is controlled by it, only in the first two pairs. Contrary to the author's claim (164 f.), manguaule is a typical cross of manguale and manguau (< -ual). As for aberrant mangualde (165), confusion with a nearby toponym may indeed have been operative; can the coexistence of arrabal and arrabalde, etc., have paved the way?

and agree that the later [nl], [ ˜ l] tended to be pressed into this mould? Again, if the rise of *mangueira* for *mangoeira* is ascribed, quite properly, to the pressure of *mang-a* < MANICA (150, 163), why not admit that Low L. FŪNIC(UL)U '(small) rope' may have influenced Gal. *fungueiro* (beside *fu-*, *fum-eiro*), *afungar*, (*a*)*fungadoiros*, and their distant outposts, Alent. *fangoêro* and Baixo Beir. *fingueiro*, all based on (PĀLUS) FŪNĀRIUS (155)?[33] Finally, the author wonders why *minguar* did not produce a by-form comparable to ⌐*moual*⌐, ⌐*moueira*⌐. Of his two tentative explanations (they seem alternative rather than cumulative), the one concerning the diverse social status of the words carries more conviction than the other, referring to the contrast in the preceding vowel.[34] But the decisive argument should have been the much closer cohesion of the MINUS than of the MANUS family: Witness the author's own plausible statement on the cross of [*]*mãueira* with *moer* 'to grind' (155, 161) and the parallel disintegration of the once close-knit lexical clan of PĒS, PEDIS (Sp. *despejar*, *pihuela*, *tropezar*, *piara*, etc.). The least excusable passage of the book is the jumble of stray observations on the reputed interchange of nasal vowels (164): *amparar* ~ *emparar* in reality reflects the rivalry of the prefixes ANTE- and IM-, *acalentar* ~ *acalantar* similarly involves two competing verbal suffixes, *avental* ~ *avantal* 'apron' presupposes lexical contamination, etc.

In supporting his phonological decisions, Herculano de Carvalho occasionally has recourse to a kind of crude statistical estimate which is less cogent than he seems to think. Thus, to explain the shift of Sp. *piért-ega*, *-iga* ( < PERTICA) to *pértiga*, except along the fringes of the Spanish-speaking domain, he envisages the possibility of pressure exerted by the satellites *pert-egal*, *-igal*, *-iguero*, but immediately discards his own conjecture on the grounds of the lower frequency of these derivatives, without supplying any actual figures (197). Even if available percentages were to confirm this claim (which seems very likely), the argument would carry little weight, since the pressure of what is, in terms of frequency, a minority group may perfectly well effect a change if this is supported by convergent

---

[33] FŪNĀRIUS, a recorded var. of FŪNĀLIS (Ernout and Meillet), should not have been starred.

[34] I find no valid indication, in the author's own laconic comment (159 n. 2), that the nonexistent syncopated products of *MINUĀRE, which he playfully suggests, would have been phonologically inadmissible, nor do I grasp the potentially distinctive influence which he seems to impute to a front vowel between the two nasals.

pressures or actualizes certain heretofore latent benefits. In this instance, the author advances a rival explanation (196 f.) which, if correct, should not be thought of as an alternative but as an additional reason for the monophthongization of -ie-. Personally, I am inclined to discount the effect of post-tonic i on the diphthong of piértiga and to propose instead the relative infrequency of diphthongs in Spanish proparoxytonic substantives as a possible concomitant. In Castilian, always more favorable to neat patterning than the peripheral dialects, a relationship between the syllabic-accentual and the diphthongal schema began to develop, and the first retreats from the diphthong in the antepenult, as in pértiga, were facilitated or prompted by the collateral pressure of such derivatives, however sparingly used, as had had from the start an immutable monophthong, e.g. pertig-al, -(u)ero. This counter-proposal illustrates the need for visualizing an ensemble of influences at work rather than alternatives between isolated pressures, and drives home the futility of superficial statistic reasoning.[35]

**10. Miscellaneous problems.** It is impossible to discuss in detail all the problems raised in a book of this size; here are some quick side glances. Surprisingly, this storehouse of information makes no mention of Sp. Ptg. triscar, which, with It. dial. tresca (n.), trescà (v.), goes back, as was already evident to Diez in 1853 (EWRS 354 f., s.v. It. trescare), to Goth. þriskan 'to thresh (by crushing under one's feet)'.[36] True, the Hispano-Romance off-shoots, as early as the medieval stage, show only figurative meanings (Duelo, quatr. 191a; Libro de buen amor, quatr. 1228c); but the semantic sphere of the Italian dialect words, collected in Piedmont, Lombardy,

[35] A more severe criticism must be brought against J. Corominas, DCE, I, 19b, who brushes off a fellow scholar's microscopic study of OSp. assechar > acechar 'to spy on, watch' with the facile comment: "No convence, en absoluto, su explicación de la c por influjo de acechança (donde se debería a dilación consonántica), pues precisamente acechança . . . es forma muy rara en comparación de asechança, acecho y acechar". Although relatively infrequent, asechança, judging from its record, may very well have triggered the transformation of ass- into aç- inasmuch as this transformation carried with it an important articulatory advantage: the anticipation of the affricate(s). — A side issue of the rebellious pi(é)rtiga problem is the fact that the monophthongization -ie- > -i- in a word containing p- and -r- would have caused no surprise in Spanish, c.f. pri(e)sco 'kind of peach' < PERSICU, pri(e)s(s)a 'haste' < PRESSA. Paradoxically, the expected forms pírtig-o, -a are peculiar to Portuguese, not to Spanish.

[36] The author makes passing mention of Gmc. þreskan (87 n. 2) without a hint of its Romance progeny.

Emilia, Lazio, and Abruzzi, is quite unequivocal. The only point still at issue is the choice between Meyer-Lübke's derivation of It. *trescare* 'to dance' directly from Ostrogothic (*REW*[1] and *REW*[3] § 8715) and Gamillscheg's suggestion of a link with Frk. *\*þreskan* via OF *treschier*, OProv. *trescar*.[37] Such an omission is the less understandable as this borrowing of the verb par excellence for 'threshing' would have fitted admirably into the general cultural framework which the author has built around the assumed adoption, in the Iberian Peninsula, of Germanic threshing techniques (104): The introduction of the pioneering Type C of the flail is said to have paralleled, in the 5th century, the acceptance of the Suebian quadrangular plough, as established independently by J. Dias.

Lexical and even grammatical coincidences, too numerous to be casual, between Western Hispanic and Southern Italian dialects happen to be in the very limelight of scholarly discussion today. Herculano de Carvalho not only contributes new data (MANGANELLU, familiar from Extr. *manganilho*, reappears in Apulia, see *AIS*, map *1473*, PP. 707, 716; the southern prong of Type D of the flail spread from South Italy to South Portugal in the 7th century), but tentatively associates this admixture of the Southern Italian dialect strain with the Byzantine occupation of Baetica and adjacent territories — if confirmed, a conjecture of unlimited potentialities (110–112, 144, 171–173).

The student of Gallo-Romance will find not a few stimulating suggestions. One of these involves the dating of the assibilation of initial [k] before [a] in Northern French, apropos of CAPPA (112). The French provenience of Ptg. *aste* 'handle', a Gallicism which in large part overlaid indigenous *asta* < HASTA (184–186), is definitively demonstrated. This situation is reminiscent of the overlap produced by the partial eviction of native *frade* 'friar', *mónago* 'monk', and *preç(i)o* 'price' by their counterparts *freire* (*fraile*), *monge*, and *prez*, imported from across the Pyrenees.

In a book studded with etymological equations it is obvious that any critic will find some unpalatable. The base *EXCUT-ITĀRE (178) strikes one reader as unfortunate in the extreme, in spite of the parallel *EXCUT-ICĀRE (*FEW*, III, 290) or rather on account of it;

[37] "Historia lingüística de los visigodos", *RFE*, XIX (1932), 237, and *Romania Germanica*, I (Berlin and Leipzig, 1934), 393. The Germanic provenience of *triscar* has become a commonplace; see R. Lapesa, *Historia de la lengua española*[3] (Madrid, 1955; also earlier editions), p. 83, and comparable textbooks.

in the light of Thomas' and Gamillscheg's findings it is unrealistic to assume that a group of speakers of provincial Latin, speakers known to have been bent on variation, should have selected, of all available verbal suffixes, the one with a dental surd for a verb stem ending in that same consonant. What is the excuse for projecting *MANUPARĀRE onto the level of Latin (178), if the earliest medieval texts in unison show either *amparar* or *emparar* (or else *anteparar*)? The addition of *m-*, demonstrably at the close of the Middle Ages, is due to secondary contamination with *man-tener*, favored by the presence of a syllable-final nasal in both words.

The linguistic semanticist will find food for thought also — for instance, illustrations of pars-pro-toto (118 f., 122, 167 f.) and of the introduction of a nonce substitute or Verlegenheitsausdruck (124), studied independently by W. von Wartburg some thirty years ago.[38] Very attractive and to the best of my knowledge not yet examined on a large scale is the possibility that verbs, subject to a more rapid sense development than the correlated nouns, may have precipitated modifications secondarily extended to the latter, as when Ptg. *malho*, orig. 'hammer', was transmuted into a 'flail' through the instrumentality of *malhar* (127 f., 131).

In conclusion, let me repeat that Herculano de Carvalho's is one of the most impressive dissertations in Romance linguistics that have lately come to my attention. In wealth of information, accuracy, and elaborateness, it represents an almost flawless labor of love. In his analysis, the author shows a high degree of originality, but occasionally lays himself open to more than trivial criticism. In the synchronic perspective, the rigor of the proposed classification does not quite match the abundance and neatness of stray observations. In the diachronic perspective, there remains a considerable disproportion between the graphic presentation of Portuguese dialect stratification and the awkward telescoping of events within the boundaries of provincial Latin. Also, medieval Portuguese evidence fails to come into full view, with the result that a verb of the pivotal importance of *triscar* is left out of the picture. Fortunately, Herculano de Carvalho is a young scholar of great flexibility, open-mindedness, and capacity for concentrated work in the field and in the library

[38] The problems centering around lexical vacuums (119) may have been too strongly dominated in the past by inquiry into homonymic clashes. It would be tempting to explore the possibility of correlating these problems with those raised by some European structuralists as regards the filling of empty pigeonholes in a changing sound system.

alike. He stands an excellent chance of rising to an even higher level of balanced performance.[39]

[39] [As is common knowledge, the author, four years after the publication of the book here examined, underwent a change of heart, becoming an out-and-out convert to European-style structuralism; see his *Fonologia mirandesa*, I (reprinted from *Biblos*, XXXVI [1958]), p.3 — also G. Hammarström's review of that monograph in *RPh.*, XV (1961–62), 350–356 — and the candid Post-script (pp. 217 f.) to his *Estudos linguísticos*, I (Lisbon, 1964). Less well known are the reasons for his disappointment with the earlier allegiance and for his eventual apostasy; a few shafts of light are shed on this situation by Herculano de Carvalho's incisive review — to appear in Vol. XXI of *RPh.* — of W. Giese, *Los pueblos románicos y su cultura popular; guía etnográfico-folklórica* (Bogotá, 1962)].

# 12
# Studies in Irreversible Binomials

## 1. Preliminaries

In the typical newspaper headline *Cold and snow grip the nation* it is proper to set off the segment *cold and snow* as a binomial, if one agrees so to label the sequence of two words pertaining to the same form-class, placed on an identical level of syntactic hierarchy, and ordinarily connected by some kind of lexical link. There is nothing unchangeable or formulaic about this particular binomial: Speakers are at liberty to invert the succession of its members (*snow and cold* . . .) and may with impunity replace either *snow* or *cold* by some semantically related word (say, *wind* or *ice*). However, in a binomial such as *odds and ends* the situation is different: The succession of its constituents has hardened to such an extent that an inversion of the two kernels — *\*ends and odds* — would be barely understandable to listeners caught by surprise. *Odds and ends*, then, represents the special case of an irreversible binomial.[1]

Reprinted from *Lingua*, VIII:2 (May 1959), 113–160.

[1] There would be little point in surveying here microscopically the terminological imbroglio. Most deplorable is not the fact that different labels have been used by linguists and folklorists for the same neatly delimited phenomenon, but that the delimitation itself has been rarely effected. Thus, one finds in *Lean's Collectanea: Collections by V. S. Lean* [1820–99], II (Bristol, 1903), 899–940, a fine annotated list of such groups as *bale and bless*, *bacon and beer*, *bag and baggage*, classed with *bear away the bell*, *bear the badge* (*the blame, the brunt*), etc. under "Alliteratives": The author, inattentive to the principle of concomitancy, focused his interest on one side of a complex situation to the extent of losing sight of the other. Logan P. Smith's less erudite book *Words and Idioms: Studies in the English Language* (Boston and New York, 1925), p. 184, takes cognizance both of words meaningless by themselves but combining into phrases familiar to everybody (*spick and span*, *tit for tat*, *jot or tittle*) and of archaic and poetic words normally avoided except when paired off (*use and wont*, *kith and kin*); not only is he at a loss for a suitable common denominator, but he blurs the picture by mixing the second group with differently patterned "idioms". More articulate parœmiologists and lexicographers operate with some such tab as "parallelism" of words and word groups (F. Seiler, *Deutsche Sprichwörterkunde* [Munich, 1922], pp. 209–211, presenting an elaborate morphological picture of phrase-initial and phrase-final repetition, simple and dual contrast, and phrase-initial repetition reinforced by phrase-final contrast) or "binary phrases"; J. Casares, *Introducción a la lexicografía moderna* (Madrid, 1950), § 37, even expressly mentions "combinaciones binarias de carácter estable", but applies

In dealing with binomials it is helpful to agree on a set of abbreviatory symbols. Let A stand for the first and B for the second member (with C, D, etc. reserved for any additional members in such multinomials as may come up for parenthetic mention) and *l* for the link which, we recall, is not under all circumstances equally essential and which, as will be demonstrated, need not occupy in the flow of speech the precise mid-point between A and B;[2] also, let F represent the entire formula.

The present paper has been conceived as strictly exploratory. Its purpose is to examine, with the aid of a severely limited material, the wisdom of saddling binomials, once defined, with the performance of important operations in linguistic analysis. No statement here must be construed as excluding or limiting further possibilities, apt to take shape in unforeseen contexts. The primary aim throughout has been to build, with a modicum of data, a strong case for more generous use of a category not yet fully established rather than describe exhaustively its range of applications.[3]

[2] In a trinomial one visualizes either a single link between B and C, as in G. *Weib, Wein und Gesang, (für) Gott, König und Vaterland* (not quite so readily one inserted solely between A and B, at least not in Standard Average European) or a pair of links ($l_1$, $l_2$), normally identical, each placed between two contiguous members, or else the absence of any link (G. *Kinder, Kirche, Küche*). The various potentialities of complex linkage increase in direct ratio to the growing number of members.

[3] I am indebted to several fellow-scholars for their provocative comments made after a partial reading of this paper, at the meeting of the Linguistic Society of America in New York on December 30, 1958; moreover, to Professor Archer Taylor, for spontaneously channelling to me a vast amount of pertinent English material, gathered at Bloomington, Ind., in July 1958 from informants and correspondents, especially Mr. Richard L. Castner of Portland, Maine, or culled from extensive readings, in particular G. L. Apperson, *English Proverbs and Proverbial Phrases* (London, etc., 1929) and *The Oxford Dictionary of English Proverbs*, 2d ed. (Oxford,

this ticket mainly to quasi-compounds such as *arco iris* and *piedra imán*. "Paired words" as a term of English philology evokes "the marriage of classical and native elements" for the sake of rhythmical and rhetorical effects, a stylistic device which W. Nash recently illustrated with *Othello* (*ES*, XXXIX [1958], 62–67). In his scattered notes, yet to be discussed, W. Th. Elwert favors the categories "Synonymendoppelung", "Synonymenbinom", "Koppelung", reconcilable with V. Bertolucci Pizzorusso's "iterazione sinonimica" traced to medieval Latin prose (*SMV*, V [1957], 7–29): This implies again a partial view of a problem best examined when envisaged in its totality, a view certainly not incorrect, but neither very rewarding. It is hoped that the term binomial, used here in a distinctly narrower sense than by B. L. Whorf (who applied it to sequences like *pane of glass, cup of coffee*), has acquired through this deliberate semantic shrinkage a sharpness of contour that will enable the explorer to extract from it, to use a phrase cherished by Sapir, a heuristic service.

## 2. *Binomials and " Idioms "*

In dealing with binomials, in general, and with the minority group resisting inversion, in particular, one does well to steer clear of any reference to the ill-defined category of "idioms" or phraseological formulas. These have been variously spoken of as sequences yielding imperfectly to routine grammatical analysis, as passages strikingly rebellious to literal translation (this phrasing manifests simultaneous concern with more than one language), as semi-autonomous pieces of congealed syntax (a view implying the supremacy of the historical perspective), as word-groups whose aggregate meaning cannot be fully predicted even from thorough knowledge of the separate meaning of each ingredient (a semantic approach), and, in stylistic or esthetic terms, as clichés, i.e., as combinations once suffused with fresh metaphoric vigor, but gradually worn thin by dint of use. Strictly speaking, none of these diverse or overlapping characterizations fits all irreversible binomials, as defined here at the outset in austerely formal terms. Thus, on the semantic level F may quite adequately represent the exact sum of its constituents, as in *husband and wife, knife and fork, hammer and tongs.* Syntactically, a binomial, in contrast to a typical "idiom", need not be contained within a clearly demarcated phrase: in this respect *back and forth,* R. *vverx i vniz* 'up and down' clash with *hard-and-fast (rule),* G. *an und für (sich).* Stylistically, the record of few binomials duplicates the meteoric rise and precipitate downfall of once successful metaphors.

## 3. *Delimitation of "Irreversible" and "Formulaic"*

"Formulaic" is not necessarily connotative of "irreversible", nor is the opposite always true. The two qualifiers must first be examined separately, each on its own merit.

Our possibly least vulnerable conjecture on progressive irreversibility, at least with respect to typical situations in Standard Average European, may run thus: Among the countless free binomials floating in the air — (*she was*) *happy and gay;* (*the*) *cold and obvious (fact is that*

1948), also from the file of *Notes and Queries;* to Professor Percival B. Fay, for miscellaneous bits of precious advice; to Professor D. W. Maurer, for information on the aberrant use of binomials in thieves' argots; to my late wife, María Rosa Lida de Malkiel, for a profusion of Spanish and a sampling of Greek illustrations; to Miss Barbara M. Yates and Miss Elizabeth H. Wierzbiańska, for helpful documentation from (Western) American English and Polish usage, respectively.

. . .) — not a few display a mild preference for a certain succession — and a concurrent avoidance of the inverse sequence — conceivably by margins as narrow and ordinarily imperceptible as 50 to 55%. Among such loosely attached binomials a fraction of preferred sequences may, with the passage of time, become increasingly current, at the expense of their opposites (as should be statistically demonstrable under ideally favorable conditions), until one particular arrangement of the two words once freely matched stiffens, tending to become obligatory. One must reckon, then, with a continuum of subtly graded possibilities of matching. On this scale definitive coalescence (entailing irreversibility) represents one extreme; unimpaired freedom of variation, the other. At the concluding stage of lexicalization there remains only an exiguous residue of unmistakably "frozen" sequences that are nevertheless reversible, e.g. *on and off* beside *off and on, then and there* alongside *there and then.*[4] Even so, on close inspection such dwindling phraseological doublets almost predictably reveal hidden differences of frequency, social acceptability, or semantic nuance. Thus, G. *Freud' und Leid*, in harmony with a powerful bias yet to be presented, seems considerably more widespread than *Leid und Freud'.*[5]

However, even very marked prevalence of, say, A + B over B + A, in purely relational terms, does not of itself suffice to insure the intrinsically formulaic character of F, unless its claim to this privileged status is independently vindicated by absolute frequency of incidence. For two discrete reasons *cat and mouse* amounts to a

[4] At this juncture the unavoidable question arises: How does one go about determining the formulaic "flavor" of a lexical group, if the sequential evidence for once is inconclusive, A + B (say) being approximately as common as B + A? I should think that in such an impasse (comparatively rare in the languages examined), the semantic argument, as an adjunct to the statistical criterion, would be apposite, whichever operational technique one cares to adopt. Those favoring substitution, for instance, may contend that — aside from the dimension of formality — *on and off* is in the closest vicinity of *intermittently*, while *on the spot* borders on *there and then*: This argument, if accepted on principle, indirectly presupposes considerably blurred contours of *on, off, then,* and *there.*

[5] It is theoretically conceivable that in some language an obligatory sequence may emerge as a pervasive grammatical pattern assigning to the longer member a place before or behind its shorter partner or converting the difference in stress into the controlling factor, with the result that the binomial becomes as rigid as the sequence *mon vieux* . . . or *ce grand* . . . in French. In such a language irreversibility would not depend on the occasional compression of a frequent, but fluid group into a hardened lexical formula. There is some point, then, in considering "irreversible" and formulaic as two distinct conditions on the theoretical plane, despite their frequent interlocking and even merger in practice.

virtually unalterable binomial formula: First, because *mouse and cat*, outside a distinctly atypical context, would sound offensively "unidiomatic" — for reasons yet to be explicated — and, second and no less important, because *cat* and *mouse*, as a result of their peculiar real-life "companionship" and the speakers' conditioned reaction to it, are not infrequently paired off, as are *boy* and *girl, brother* and *sister, sun* and *moon*, etc. *Girl-and-dog* (*murder case*) also yields an exciting headline or a suitable title and, under ordinary circumstances, sounds or reads distinctly smoother than *dog and girl*, entitling one to speak of latent irreversibility. What prevents it from becoming a ready-made formula is this, that our society fails to pair off habitually *girls* and *dogs*, making the absolute incidence of this binomial so low as to bar it from the status of a "formula". Any newspaper page supplies a list of such binomials, engaging to ear and eye, but failing of the promise of ultimate crystallization:

> *black and sooty, brash and loquacious, bright and rosy, choice and chance, cold and aloof, cuts and bruises, force and violence, gay and laughing, glory and grandeur, grim and weary,* (*a*) *long and beautiful* (*friendship*), *moody and despondent,* (*an*) *open and inviting* (*door*), (*a*) *strong and bitter* (*political factor*).*

Between the two extremes of this new scale, on the one hand, the studiedly bizarre, preferably unique word pairs so matched as to satisfy even a modernistic poet in his search for the unprecedented, and, on the other, the familiar, soothingly trite combinations, one discovers again a rich gamut of gradual transitions. The point at which one begins to speak of "frequent" combinations is, of course, selected with complete arbitrariness. Significantly, even in non-formulaic binomials, to the extent that they are tendentially irreversible, one dimly recognizes certain schemes in the recurrent preferences of ordering, e.g. in English, the excess, in sheer length, of B over A (contrast, measured by any yardstick, *grandeur* with *glory, despondent* with *moody*, etc.; and, in terms of syllabic wealth, *rosy* with *bright, sooty* with *black, weary* with *grim, bitter* with *strong*). These hazy proclivities suggest patterns which one expects to find more neatly delineated in corresponding full-grown formulas. Such patterns, in turn, need not (and in Romance and Germanic, as a rule, do not) coincide with those controlling similar word-sequences deprived of the characteristic link (*thin brown hands, hoarse young voice, great big burly kids*).[6]

[6] Irrespective of the intonational contrast (marked by a comma) between (a) *big*

This impressionistic pilot study dispenses with any binding statistical computation of frequency, freely mingling and lumping formulas and near-formulas. A more rigorous monographic inquiry moored to verifiable statistical data would have to start from the premise that all in all two distinct continua are involved: the (relative) irreversibility of binomials is determined on one scale and their currency on another, so that an irreversible binomial, to qualify for the rank of a "formula", must at once fulfill two conditions, of which one — the second — has of necessity been arbitrarily laid down.

### 4. Reversible Binomials

The countless reversible binomials offer problems of their own which, in most instances, are best attacked from a position other than that of linguistics. Thus, assuming there exist, in real life or in fiction, two playmates, Vánja and Mítja, the reasons for any mention of them, in conversation, report, oral story, or fine literature as R. *Vánja i Mítja* rather than *Mítja i Vánja* may be effectively explored in sociological, psychological, or esthetic terms (margin of age, order of appearance, closeness to narrator, importance of rôle, etc.). If there emerges a schema of definite preference, linguistic conditions are likely to have acted, at best, as a lubricant. In contrast, irreversible binomials, especially those used with high frequency ("formulas"), are primarily analyzable from the linguistic platform, though real-life conditions and the distorting social prism through which individuals view these conditions cannot be entirely excluded from consideration.

### 5. Degree of Reversibility

Rigidity of word order must be understood as allowing of several degrees. A foreign speaker of French saying *mer la* for *la mer* is unlikely to convey any assimilable message. If, through some lapse of memory or through inexperience, he inverts the prescribed sequence

---

black wolf, good old Joe and (b) long, low start. On these sequences there exists an impressive corpus of researches; cf. A. A. Hill, *Introduction to Linguistic Structure; from Sound to Sentence in English* (New York [1958]), pp. 175–190, with a reference to an unpublished dissertation by C. W. Barrett, and N. Garver, "The grammar of prenominal modifiers in English" (paper orally presented at the 1958 meeting of the LSA).

of members (while respecting their immediate environments) in *au fur et à mesure (que)* 'in proportion (as)', he stands a fair chance of being understood and even corrected by a few patient listeners.[7] Similarly, side by side with completely unelastic G. *ab und zu*, F. *d'ores et déjà* 'from now onwards', one stumbles upon binomials whose inadvertent dislocation would scarcely make them unintelligible to the sensitive interlocutor (e.g. L. *hīc et nunc, by leaps and bounds*) and comes across others that in fact seem marginally reversible even in the flawless speech of natives. This is true not only of groups firmly soldered ("lexicalized"), such as the twin formulas *on and off* alongside *off and on*, but also of instances in which a mild disruption of the customary order may serve a special end, by producing a spontaneously comic effect in unrehearsed speech or a calculated departure from the boresome norm in pretentious literary style. In a language, for instance, enforcing in ordinary context the schema ⌐*by day and by night*¬, a dramatic reversal of A and B may infuse into F a strongly suggestive (one suspects, exhilarating) quality.[8] *Male and female* is entirely too trivial to arouse much attention; in *female and male* the unexpected inversion generates just enough explosive power to make the reader or listener pause for a precious moment. Then again dialectal or idiolectal peculiarities may be at issue, gently pitting speakers addicted to the sequence *ball and bat* against others favoring *bat and ball*. A similar state of practically free variation obtains between *socks and shoes* and *shoes and socks* (while *shoes and stockings*, under the sway of a rhythmic pattern, is unalterable), also between *groove and tongue* and *tongue and groove*. American reporters covering the latest uprising in Cuba were linguistically split, insofar as some observed, at a very fluid stage of developments, *black-and-red*, and others, *red-and-black* (*bands*). A cleavage in real-life conditions may also spark differentiation, as when *gas and oil*, normally requested by motorists at service stations, is in semantic contradistinction to *oil and gas*, as used in the professional jargon of the oil industry.[9]

---

[7] *Au fur et à mesure* need not invariably precede *que* and function as a conjunction; for a semicolloquial example of its absolute (adverbial) use see *BSLP*, LIII: 2 (1958), 26.

[8] One instance of jocose inversion may be the title of Steinbeck's novel *Of Mice and Men*, pointless unless it calls up memories of the mocking alternative (*are you, is he*) *a man or a mouse?* (The title has also been inspired by a line from Robert Burns' poem "To a Mouse".)

[9] A point of semantics is here actually at issue: When preceding *oil*, *gas* refers to the fuel ('gasoline'); when following *oil*, it stands for 'natural gas'.

## 6. Multinomials

In many languages one encounters also traces of multinomials (particularly trinomials) congealed into obligatory sequences, e.g. *Tom, Dick, and Harry*; Sp. *fulano, mengano y zutano* (or *perengano*); or, in the language of mathematics, *X, Y, and Z*. An overtone of mathematical progression is further discernible in the musicologist's *pairs, triads,* (or *duets, trios,*) *and quartets.* Asymmetric patterns of elaborately courteous forms of address underlie Br.-E. *Ladies, Lords, and Gentlemen* and F. *Mesdames, Mesdemoiselles et Messieurs,* beside stylized, but slightly more "natural", hence less rigidly formal, binomials: *Ladies and Gentlemen, Mesdames et Messieurs,* mandatory in most European societies (Sp. *Señoras y Señores,* G. *meine Damen und Herren,* alongside the Nazi vulgarians' *deutsche Männer und Frauen*). The letters of the alphabet, whether Hebrew, Greek, or Latin, represent the classic case of a latent multinomial; ordinarily the recital of the first two (R. < Ch.-Sl. *ázbuka,*G. < Gr. *Alphabet*) or three (coll. E. *ABC*) suffices to evoke the name of the whole.[10] The linkage of trinomials tends to assume a high degree of intricacy: In *Protestant, Catholic, and Jewish,* one may interchange, but hardly ever disrupt, the order of A and B, while C, for obvious non-linguistic reasons, clamors for a fixed place apart; conversely, the sequence of *Christians, Jews, and Muslims* may be rearranged with greater freedom, in accord with the chosen perspective. In references to all three media of entertainment *movie(s)* either precedes or follows *radio* and *television,* but is not normally wedged in between them, again on account of the longer semantic distance of A from either B or C than of B from C. While the members of the Trinity appear in an immutable order, facetious or malicious variations upon it exhibit a higher degree of looseness: The historian reproaching Spanish colonizers with the triple pursuit of *Glory, Gold, and Gospel* (note capitalization) might have arrayed in different fashion the incisive terms of his indictment. Rhythmic and

---

[10] Only binomials are admissible in simultaneous references to the first and last letter, to suggest totality (*alpha and omega, from A to izzard,* etc.). On some linguistic implications of the alphabet see "Diachronic hypercharacterization in Romance", *ArL,* IX (1957), 109 n. 1; "Form versus meaning in etymological analysis: Old Spanish *auze* 'luck' ", *Estudios dedicados a James Homer Herriott* (Madison, Wis. and Madrid, 1966), pp. 167-183, esp. 175 f.; and "Secondary uses of letters in language", *RPh.,* XIX (1965-66), 1-27 — reprinted without change (except for the split into two instalments) in Vol. 1 (1967) of the *Journal of Typographic Research,* pp. 96-110 and 169-190, and included, after thorough revision and expansion, in the present miscellany, as its concluding essay (see pp. 357 ff.).

semantic progression harmonize in G. (*für*) *Gott, König und Vaterland.*

Changing conditions of life, normally in the direction of increasing complexity, may transform a binomial into a trinomial, as when the military's long-standing dualistic formula *on land and on sea* has yielded ground, within the lifespan of one generation, to less homogeneously structured *on land, on sea, and in the air*: Here linguistic streamlining seems to lag behind technological progress. Such expansions are frequently tampered with for the sake of a jocular effect, as when irreverent *soul, spirit, and spark plugs* flanks time-hallowed *soul and spirit*. The effect is heightened if the additional ingredient is nonchalantly injected before, rather than after, the consolidated binomial, as in *to (hiss,) kiss, and make up*, recently launched by a Californian humorist.

### 7. Orchestration by Rhyme and Alliteration

A binomial may without difficulty assert itself under its own power. Yet in numerous languages F acquires added strength and appeal if the matching is supported by an extra measure of suggestive outward resemblance between A and B, a token of partial identity which produces a potent welding effect on the whole. One such companion feature straddling many language frontiers is rhyme, e.g.

*heckle and jeckle, by hook or (by) crook, (a) rough-and-tough (speech), to toil and moil, town and gown,* G. *(mit) Ach und Krach, (mit) Rat und Tat,* F. *(n'avoir) ni feu ni lieu* 'to have neither hearth nor home', Sp. *corriente y moliente* 'regular, all right' (lit. 'running and grinding'), *a roso y vell-oso* (beside *-udo*) 'completely, without exception', *de tomo y lomo* 'bulky and heavy, of consequence' (lit. 'of some volume and [square-shaped] animal's back'), *sin ton ni son* 'without rhyme or reason' (lit. '. . . tone nor sound'), R. *ni dat' ni vzjat'* 'just so, exactly' (lit. 'neither give nor take away'), *šútki i pribaútki* 'jokes and playful sayings', *šívorot na vývorot* [*šý-*] 'topsy-turvy' (lit. 'collar inside out'), Pol. *tędy i owędy* 'this way and that'.[11]

---

[11] Much pertinent information was amassed and scrupulously winnowed by J. Morawski, "Les formules rimées de la langue espagnole", *RFE*, XIV (1927), 113–133. It is not devoid of interest that Sp. *sin . . . ni* 'without . . . or' should represent an approximation to rhyme and Ptg. *sem . . . nem* a perfect rhyme (reminiscent of *sim . . . não* 'yes . . . no' as regards the spread of nasalization). To be sure, scholars may in both instances attempt to account separately for the baffling phonological convergence of L. *sine* and *nec*. The degree of abnormality will dwindle once we analyze the characteristic mutual rapprochement of each pair as a partial result of semantic solidarity plus syntactic vicinity.

Examples of rich rhyme include *plundering and blundering*, G. (*auf*) *Schritt und Tritt*, Sp. (*tomar*) *las duras y las maduras* '(to face) both benefits and drawbacks' (lit. 'to take the hard ones and the ripe ones' [f.]), and R. *žit'ë-byt'ë* [*žy-*] 'day-to-day life' (lit. 'living-existing'). One encounters further stray instances of assonance (*hit or miss, rise and shine*, Sp. *de zoca en colodra* or *de zocos en colodros* 'from bad to worse', R. *plot' i krov'* 'flesh and blood') and of presumably significant coincidence between concluding segments smaller than required for a rhyme, e.g. single consonants and consonant clusters: *East and West* (as against G. *West und Ost*), *North and South, from first to last* (*first and last*), *good or bad*. Imperfect rhymes involving one accented and one unaccented vowel underlie *male and female* (the latter, deflected from OF *femele* through lexical polarization) and, initially at least, *man and woman*; cf. Pol. *ni w pięć ni w dziewięć* 'without rhyme or reason' (lit. 'neither in five nor in nine', a linguistically potent, if arithmetically quaint, assortment).

Reiteration of the initial vowel, except possibly in extra-short *on and off*, turns out to be a weak magnet. One is even led to wonder whether in Sp. *afuera y adentro, allí y allá* (beside Ptg. *cá e lá*, sporting the rival adjunct of a rhyme) it might not be advisable to operate with the repetition of a (fading) morpheme. Conversely, echoing of initial consonants (alliteration) is widespread and effective. In the Germanic languages it serves as, far and away, the dominant soldering device:

(a) *bed and board*, (*a type*) *big and black, birds and bees, bit and blow, bred and born, bruised and battered,* (*the ailment's*) *cause and cure, chalk and cheese,* (*without*) *chick or child,* (*to receive*) *cove* ('chamber, closet') *and key, cup and can, deaf and dumb,* (*to make*) *ducks and drakes, dust and dirt, fair or foul, fire and flood, fish or fowl, to forgive or forget, friend or foe, hale and hearty, to harp and harrow, to have and to hold, health and happiness, to help and/or hurt, to hem and haw, hide* (*n*)*or hair, horse and hounds, hot and heavy, house and home, Jack and Jill, judge and jury, kith and kin, life and limb,* (*by*) *line and level, to live and learn, loud and long, to make or mar, man and maid, a man or a mouse, to meddle or make,* (*with*) *might and main, now or never, part and parcel, penny-wise and pound-foolish, from pillar to post, to pitch and pay, poor and pert* (*— and proud, — but pious*), *popcorn and peanuts, pots and pans,* (*to go to*) *rack and ruin, to rant and rave, rhyme or reason, right*(*ly*) *or wrong*(*ly*), *rock and roll, rough and ready, safe and sane* (*— and sound*), *neither scrip* ('satchel') *nor screed* ('shred'), (*with*) *shot and shell, at sixes and sevens, start-and-stop* (*sign*), *from stem to stern,* (*to fight with*) *sticks and stones, stress and strain, sweet and sour* [in notable preference to *bitter*, more

relevant, but less effective], *tattered and torn, from top to toe, to toss and turn, to turn and twist, warm and winning, wild and woolly, wind and weather, to woo and win, zip and zest;*
(b) G. (*in*) *Bausch und Bogen,* (*durch*) *dick und dünn, gang und gäbe, im grossen und ganzen, hin und her,* (*mit*) *Kind und Kegel,* (*in die*) *Kreuz' und Quere, kurz und kernig, Land und Leute,* (*nach*) *Lust und Laune,* (*mit*) *Mann und Maus, mehr oder minder,* (*bei*) *Nacht und Nebel,* (*von*) *Ruf und Rang, Wind und Wetter,* (*ohne sein*) *Wissen und Wollen.*

Rich alliteration underlies *tried and true* and G. (*das*) *Drum und Dran, klipp und klar.*

Other language families have more sparing recourse to alliterative reinforcement: F. *bel et bien, ni peu ni prou, sain et sauf, tôt ou tard,* Sp. (*echar a*) *cara y cruz* 'to flip up a coin' (lit. 'heads or tails'), *en cruz y en cuadro,* lit. 'crosswise and square', *más o menos* 'approximately' (lit. 'more or less'), (*no temer*) *rey ni roque* 'to be afraid of nobody' (lit. 'neither king nor rook'), *de rompe y rasga* ( = coll. Am.-Sp. *a rompe y raja*) 'determined', lit. [to the point of] 'breaking and ripping', R. *styd i sram* 'shame' [on you], with a play on near-synonyms, *tut i tam* ( = Pol. *tu i tam*) 'here and there'.

Occasionally the segment shared includes, aside from the initial consonant or consonant cluster, also the following vowel: *cash and carry,* (*through*) *thick and thin,* Sp. *sano y salvo,* G. *ganz und gar,* but the languages examined hardly capitalize on this further possibility. One can, of course, speak only of gross identity between the short *a* of *ganz* and the long one of *gar.*

The third force available for amalgamating A and B is the repetition of a morpheme, whether grammatical (affix) or lexical (root morpheme). Its agency, in isolation, can be best observed with a final morpheme, frequently unstressed: *obverse and reverse* (*sides*), *sooner or later* = R. *ráno íli póz(d)no, upwards and downwards,* and, on the phrasal level, *on again, off again.*

These three forces form an intricate network of alliances. Alliteration and echoing of the word-final segment may work hand in hand, as in *tit for tat, to meddle and muddle,* and in R. (*razbít'*) *v pux i* (*v*) *prax* '(to beat) to shreds' (lit. 'to fluff and to dust'). This concomitancy is doubly efficacious if that segment is coterminous with a morpheme: *bigger and better,* (*to go*) *farther and faster,* G. (*auf*) *Biegen und Brechen.* The repetition of a final morpheme easily coincides with rhyme: *hither and thither, highways and byways,* F. *jambe de çà, de là* 'straddling'; note that the morpheme reiterated need not contain the rhyming vowel. The echoing of such word- and phrase-initial morphemes as begin with a consonant is implicitly alliterative (*day in and day out, betwixt and between*, F. *mi-oral, mi-écrit* beside *comme ci, comme ça*).

In non-poetic discourse, rhyme and alliteration (to which, for completeness' sake, one may add rarely isolable morphological parallelism) function as occasional, less than essential, ingredients endowing with an extra touch of cohesiveness certain particularly suggestive word sequences. They act as spices, giving, if adroitly sprinkled or shaken, an appetizing quality to the staple food of communication. Binomials represent a feature similar in its effects, but one more thoroughly grammaticized in its structure. Small wonder that, given their optional and peripheral status within the total economy, rhyme and alliteration, on the phonological level, and parallelism, on the morphological level, all three tend to support one another and separately or jointly serve to underpin binomials.

It would at first glance be tempting to discuss under this rubric of orchestration also such highly colloquial formations based on an interplay of initial consonants and stressed vowels as (a) *boogie-woogie* (*piano*), *namby-pamby* (*parents*), *willy-nilly*, *quakey-shakey* (*marriage*), *razzle-dazzle* (*news*), *roly-poly* (*character*) and (b) *shilly-shally, tip-top* (*form*), *a tisket a tasket* (a bouncy nursery rhyme), with interesting counterparts in other languages (F. *bric-à-brac* 'curios', a word exported on almost as wide a scale as the objects so collectively labeled, beside *de bric et de broc*, both preceded by *en bloc et en blic* [15th–16th centuries], *à bric et à brac* 'à tort et à travers' [1632]). As will be made plain, the resemblance is specious: This new group of words is characterized by fanciful elaboration on a single theme, not by a deft amalgam of two preëxistent formations.

### 8. *Mutual Relation of the Two Members*

One may set off several types of meaningful relationship between A and B (disregarding, at least provisionally, any influence that the link, in its own right, may exert as a part of the ensemble). Some of these relationships are purely formal, as when A and B are the same word, or B represents a morphological variation upon A, arrived at through inflection, derivation, or composition. Other, more numerous relationships are of a semantic order: Thus, A and B may be near-synonyms or mutually complementary, or else B may be the opposite, a part, or a consequence of A.

**1. Patterns of formal relation.** (1) A and B may be the same word. There is something primitive, archaic, cyclopean about this arrangement; cf. the chain in Cl.-Hebr. *'ayin l<sup>e</sup> 'ayin, šen l<sup>e</sup> šen*, imitated in all European languages (G. *Auge um Auge, Zahn um Zahn*; Sp. *ojo por ojo, diente por diente*; R. *óko za óko, zub za zub*; etc.). This scheme has maintained its undiminished vitality in modern languages:

> *class against class, dozens upon dozens, face to face (with), (to go) hand in hand, hand-to-hand fighting, (as) man to man, on and on, one-to-one correspondence, point-to-point equivalence, season by season, shoulder to shoulder, side by side, so-and-so, step by step, (at) such-and-such (an address), from time to time, wall-to-wall (carpets), years and years;* F. *côte à côte, tête-à-tête;* Sp. *hombro (contr)a hombro, paso a paso, (hablar) a tu por tú* 'to speak rudely', — *de tú por tú* 'to be on familiar terms'.

Not included in this category is straight repetition to the extent that it has come to represent an indefinitely extendible morphological device, as in *four by four (inches), more and more* (cf. *higher and higher*, etc.), and It. *pian piano*, a kind of subdued superlative absolute.[12]

(2) Not infrequently B embodies some variation upon A. In richly inflected languages a declensional or conjugational paradigm may have been at work: L. *diem ex diē* 'day after day', *pār prō parī* 'tit for tat', R. *málo po málu* 'little by little', *šag za šágom* 'step by step'. Comparable effects are produced by the intervention of an affix (primitive vs. derivative, or two derivatives in opposition) or by a play on composition: *bag and baggage, bear and forbear*, G. *(nach bestem) Wissen und Gewissen* 'to the best of (one's) knowledge'.

**2. Patterns of semantic relation.** (1) A and B are near-synonyms and the use of F adds color and emphasis to the bare statement:

> *beck and call, checks and balances, death and destruction, each and every, fair and square, fears and anxieties, first and foremost, graft and corruption, hard-and-fast (rules), heart and soul, (with) intent and deliberation, (defiance of) law and order, (by) leaps and bounds, nip and tuck, null and*

---

[12] On It. *pian piano, sola soletta*, and vars. see K. Jaberg, "Elation und Komparation", *Festschrift Édouard Tièche* (Berne, 1947), pp. 41–60. The situation in Spanish is complicated: *de cuando en cuando* and *de tanto en tanto* 'from time to time', *de trecho en trecho* 'at intervals', also *de casa en casa, de flor en flor, de rama en rama* are lexicalized units, but the pattern lends itself to unlimited extension in modern literary style (*de chimenea en chimenea, de tejado en tejado*, etc.). It is clearly marked by the special tag *de . . . en* (for A = B), contrasting with standard *de . . . a* (for A ≠ B, e.g. *de Viena a Madrid*; exception: *de vez en cuando*, patently a blend of *de cuando en cuando* with *una* or *alguna vez*, esp. *una y otra vez, una que otra vez*). For further discussion see Section 9, below, including n. 9.

*void, soft and easy, ways and means* (— *and traditions*); G. *an und für* (*sich*), *schliesslich und endlich*; F. *us et coutumes*; R. (*xodit'*) *vokrúg i ókolo* 'to walk around, avoid a straight approach'.

In certain styles, both conversational and literary, the pairing-off or massive accumulation of synonyms may become a pervasive feature: cf. OProv. *planh e sospir* 'deep sigh', lit. 'complaint and sigh', and its Old French counterparts.[13] Where Shakespeare has recourse to this artifice, "the familiar Saxon word acts as a kind of gloss to the rarer classical word"; also, "the second word may extend or modify the meaning of the first, or it may repeat the notion already contained in the first, and thus have a purely decorative function" (Nash).

(2) A and B are mutually complementary, forming a single team referring to a characteristic composite dish, to a pair of tools seldom used in isolation, to a notion bipartite, but lacking any definitive cleavage:

> *assault and robbery* (— *and battery*), *bar-and-restaurant* (*business*), *book-and-art store*, *brush and palette*, *cheek by jowl*, *cuts and bruises*, (*on one's*) *elbows* (*hands —*) *and knees*, *fame and riches*, *fang and claw*, *food and drink*, *from floor to roof*, *full and equal*, *gold and silver*, *ham and eggs*, *hammer and sickle* (— *and tongs*), (*to stand*) *head and shoulders* (*above*), *hat and coat*, *Letters and Science(s)*, *lock and key*, *meat and potatoes*, (*sound*) *mind and body*, *Mom and Dad*, *men and materials* (— *and matériel*), *pistol and ammunition*, *place* (*space —*) *and time*, *potatoes and gravy*, *salaries and wages*, *soul and spirit*, (*one's*) *stick and hat*, *words and pictures;* G. *Blut und Boden*, *Dichtung und Wahrheit*, *Hände und Füsse*, *Hören und Sehen*, *Reih' und Glied*, *Wollen und Können*; F. *mes yeux et mes oreilles;* Sp. *pan y agua* (— *y vino*), (*con*) *pelos y señales* 'with minutest details', *punto y coma* 'semicolon', *a sangre y fuego*, (*echar*) *sapos y culebras* 'to utter angry abuses', (*contra*) *viento y marea;* Pol. *deszcz ze śniegiem* 'sleet' (lit. 'rain with snow'), *głodno i chłodno* 'hardships' (lit. 'hunger and cold'), *jeść i pić* 'eating and drinking', *ogniem i mieczem* 'with fire and sword' (cf. L. *ferrō ignīque*).

[13] Taking his cue from S. Pellegrini, "Iterazioni sinonimiche nella *Canzone di Rolando*", *SMV*, I (1953), 155–165, W. Th. Elwert presented his ideas in "La dittologia sinonimica nella poesia romanza delle origini e nella scuola poetica siciliana", *Bollettino del Centro di studi . . . siciliani*, II (1954), 152–177, followed by the two consecutive postscripts "Zur Synonymendoppelung vom Typ *planh e sospir*, *chan e plor*", *ASNS*, CXCIII (1956–57), 40–42, and "Zur Synonymendoppelung als Interpretationshilfe", ibid., CXCV (1958), 24–26. He recognizes traces of such pairs as *plangō* and *plōrō* in early Church Latin (in the Itala more than in the Vulgate), but regards Old Provençal lyric as the principal channel through which the device of carefully matching synonyms penetrated into many western literatures and credits the primacy of *planh e plor* over *chan e plor* and *planh e sospir* to the concomitant agency of alliteration.

(3) B is the opposite of A. The contrast may be expressed either (a) syntactically or (b), on a much wider scale, lexically:[14]

(a) *to be or not to be, the eat-or-be-eaten battle;*
(b) *assets and liabilities, big (great —) and small, dead or alive, fast-and-loose, freedom or death, give-or-take, (to fall) heads or tails, love and hate, laughing and sobbing, married or widowed (— or divorced), near and remote, open and shut, to sink or swim, to stand or fall, talent and technique, (one's) triumph or defeat, true or false (the truth or falsehood of . . .),* up and down, war and peace, win or lose; G. *Dichtung und Wahrheit, hin und her, Wollen und Können;* L. *ultrō citrōque* and *ultrā citrāque* 'on this side and on that, to and fro'; F. *par monts et par vaux, à pile ou face, c'est à prendre ou à laisser;* Sp. *ni carne ni pescado* 'neither fish nor fowl' (lit. 'neither flesh nor fish'), *¿pares o nones?* 'odd or even?' (lit. 'even ones or odd ones?'), *(como) perros y gatos* 'on hostile terms' (lit. 'like dogs and cats'), *por sí o por no* 'in any case',[15] *vaivén* 'swing, seesaw, coming and going'; R. *dněm i nóč'ju* (= Pol. *dniem i nocą*) 'by day and by night', *stároje i nóvoje* 'old and new (happenings)', *ni voobščé, ni v částnosti* 'neither in general, nor in particular'; Pol. *lądy i morza* 'land and sea' (pl.), *mniej lub więcej* 'more or less' (lit. 'less or more'), *orzeł i reszka* 'heads and tails' (lit. 'eagle and tails'), *prośbą i groźbą* 'with pleas and threats' (sg.), *śmiech i łzy* 'laughter and tears', *od stóp do głów* 'from head to foot' (lit. 'from feet to heads'), *tam i zpowrotem* 'back and forth' (lit. 'there and back'), *wojna i pokój* 'war and peace'.

(4) At rare intervals, B is a subdivision of A or viceversa; where numbers are involved, one may state the relations in fractions or multiples. In scientific discourse *genus and species* serves as an example; sequences of wider currency include, on the one hand, *dollars and cents;* on the other, *months and years, (every) nickel and dime.* The precedence granted to *dollars* over *cents* and to *months* over *years* may reflect our habit of marking prices (bills, etc.) and dates.[16] Folk-speech tolerates illogical coördination, in either direc-

---

[14] If the opposition is brought out derivationally (as in: *the advantage or disadvantage of . . .*), the pattern 1:2 rather than 2:3 is involved.

[15] Cf. *un sí o un no* 'yes or no', *no decir un sí ni un no* 'to be evasive or secretive, *sin faltar un sí ni un no* 'accurately, punctually, circumstantially, exhaustively', *entre ellos no hay (ellos no tienen) un sí ni un no* 'they are in complete agreement', *sí por sí, no por no* 'truthfully, candidly'. The colloquial adverbial phrase *un si es no es (turbado)* 'somewhat (confused)' patently forms part of this cluster; the disguise of *sí* 'yes' as *si* 'if' is a misspelling presumably rationalized as a consequence of the monosyllable's pretonic position.

[16] In English and cognate languages the mathematically smaller element of a numerical binomial obligatorily precedes the larger: *five-and-ten-cent-store, thirty or forty customers, the third or fourth, twice or thrice as many, to double or triple.* German has stretched this principle to the extent of applying it even to compound numerals: *fünfundzwanzig,* cf. *four-and-twenty* in archaic English nursery rhymes.

tion, of a whole and of a part entering into that whole, as in Sp. *aves y gallinas* 'poultry', lit. 'birds and hens', as against *rosas y flores*.

(5) Quite exceptionally, B functions as the consequence, inevitable or possible, of A. This is especially true of binomials involving verbs or verbals (deverbal abstracts, participles): L. *dīuide et imperā*, imitated by some modern languages ('divide and rule'); *to shoot and kill* (as against *to shoot to kill*), *spit and polish; the rise and fall* (— *decay, decline*); possibly also *married or widowed* (cf. 2:3); and, on a high level of abstract thinking, *if and when* 'if at all, and, in the affirmative case, when . . .' (the less logical *when and if* has also left traces).

Given the fluidity of any semantic classification, one expects cases of overlapping. According to one's stand, *checks and balances, goods and services, wages and salaries* may all involve opposition or complementation; *heart and soul* may rate as near-synonyms, mutual complements, or, unlikely as this eventuality appears at first glance, irreconcilable opposites ("poles"), cf. the semantic equivalent F. *corps et âme*.

## 9. The Link

The connective between the two members is typically a preposition or a conjunction: *side by side, black and white*, R. *s mésta v karjér* 'abruptly, immediately' (lit. 'from [the horse's] stand or post into the race'), *styd i sram*, Gr. *Héllenēs kaì bárbaroi*. There exists a loose connection between the sevenfold relation of A to B, the form-class favored, and the choice of the link. If A equals B, the form-classes preferred in a typical IE language are nouns and adjectives and the link (prevailing by a narrower margin) is a preposition: *bit by bit, little by little, season by season, time after time* beside, it would seem, less common *again and again, by and by, (to run) neck and neck (with)*. If B is the near-synonym, complement, or antonym of A, the predominant type of link is a conjunction tying together primarily nouns and adjectives, e.g. (a) *part and parcel* beside less typical *cease-and-desist* (*order*), G. *Sturm und Drang, Wind und Wetter*, Sp. *liso y llano* 'simple, easy' (lit. 'smooth and even'), *sano y salvo* 'safe and sound'; (b) *cloak and dagger, coat and vest, fire and smoke, needle and thread, pen and pencil, text and tune, tooth and nail*, Sp. *carne y huesos* 'flesh and bones', R. *grom i mólnija* 'thunder and lightning'; (c) *ebb and flow*, G. *Alt und Jung*. Prepositions are here less common: G. *schwarz auf weiss*.

Can one categorize the prepositions and conjunctions according to the services they render in cementing binomials? The situation in each language family (indeed, in every language at each stage of its growth) invites separate examination, at least provisionally. In English and its congeners the size and the meaning of *l* seem to be important factors, though atypicality lacks prohibitive force.

As regards size, the monosyllabic link numbering up to three phonemes leads by a wide margin of range and particularly of incidence: *and* (folksy *'n'*), *by, on, or, to* beside rare *after* and *against* (also *but*); cf. G. *auf, und,* quite infrequently disyllabic *oder*; R. *da, i, na, po, v, za,* rarely *íli,* very rarely *skvoz'* (*smex skvoz' slëzy,* lit. 'laughter through tears', is not indigenous).

With respect to the meaning of conjunctions, three sets of relationship: (a) conjunction proper, (b) alternative, and (c) disjunction, are all adequately represented, roughly in this order of frequency:

(a) *rats and mice, this and that, town and gown,* G. *Hände und Füsse,* Sp. *invierno y verano, pan y queso,* R. *den' i noč'* 'day and night', Hebr. *ba-y·ōm uβal·aylā* 'by day and by night', *le 'ōlām wā'æδ* 'for all eternity' (lit. 'for future and duration');

(b) *all or nothing, heads or tails, sooner or later,*[17] F. *près ou loin, tôt ou tard,* Sp. *más o menos, tarde o temprano, o todo o nada;*

(c) *neither chick nor child, neither kith nor kin, neither fish nor fowl,* F. (*ne savoir*) *ni A ni B,* Sp. *ni rey ni roque,* and, in their closest vicinity, Sp. *sin ton ni son* beside *without rhyme or reason,* G. (*ohne sein*) *Wissen und Wollen.*

The semantic classification of prepositions is more intricate. Certain spatial relations which tend to appear in symmetric distribution are quite sparingly represented: 'above', 'beneath', 'before' and 'behind', 'this side of' and 'beyond'. (*To fall*) *head over heels* is a fairly isolated sequence. Conversely, one may copiously exemplify relations indicative of iteration, reciprocity, opposition, or compensation where A = B (*time after time, friend against friend, bit by bit, side by side, dollar for dollar, one to one;* Sp. *año tras año*). Equally abundant are

---

[17] In modern English *and* and *or* act like close rivals. In some instances, the use of one or the other opportunely leads to semantic differentiation, cf. *give and take,* symbolic of a bidirectional process (with a moral overtone of parity or equity) as against *give or take* (*two hours*) suggestive of an equal margin of error on either side of a point chosen along a scale. Colloquially *and,* probably as a result of its distinctly greater currency, tends to trespass on the domain of *or*: One hears and even reads (*a question of*) *life and death;* cf. *life-and-death* (*struggle*) = Sp. (*lucha a*) *vida o muerte.* Logicians or jurists rather than untutored speakers have recently launched the artificial compromise formula *and/or.*

relations suggestive of direction or delimitation, often expressed —
by virtue of a familiar metaphor — through spatial imagery even
where temporal distances are involved; A and B are then preponderantly non-identical and even lend themselves to polarization: *from
cellar to garret, from dawn to dusk, from first to last,* (a) *floor-to-ceiling*
(*window*), *from head to toe*; It. *d'alto in basso,* Sp. *de pies a cabeza*
( = F. *de pied en cap,* R. *s nog do golový,* Pol. *od stóp do głów*). Where
the relation A = B is squeezed into the same frame, the resultant
type suggests intermittency, except that Spanish then substitutes
*de . . . en* for *de . . . a* and Italian, similarly, *di . . . in* for *da . . . a:
from time to time,* R. *ot vrémeni do vrémeni* alongside erratic Sp. *de
cuando en cuando, de tarde en tarde* (with intensification: *de mal en
peor*), and It. *di tempo in tempo.*[18]

Russian tolerates zero links on a generous scale, particularly in
folk speech: *žit'ë-byt'ë* 'day-to-day life', *kotóryj den', kotóryj god*
'year in, year out' (lit. 'which day, which year?'), *učít' umú rázumu*
'to teach one worldly wisdom' (lit. 'intelligence / reason'); also in a
negative vein: *ne mnógo ne málo* (*pjat' let*) 'approximately five years'
(lit. 'not much, not little'), and with characteristic repetition of a
preposition which, on its second appearance, functions vicariously as
a link: *po dobrú po zdoróvu* 'safely, without harm' (lit. 'in a friendly
fashion / in a sound way'), *do porý do vrémeni* 'provisionally' (lit.
'until the time / until the term', with synonymic variation).[19] Side by
side with this schema one finds in Russian also less racy types
reminiscent of Romance and Germanic: (*izjézdit'*) *iz koncá v konéc*
'to travel all over' (lit. 'from end to end'), *rvët i méčet* 'is furious' (lit.
'tears and flings'), (*služít'*) *véroj i právdoj* 'to serve loyally' (lit. 'with
faith and truth' [or 'justice']), *te íli inýje* (indef.) 'some' (lit. 'those or
others'). Other language families tolerate this construction on a
more modest scale: *day in, day out,* G. (playful) *soso lala* 'fairly,
reasonably well' (the latter a reduplicative nonsense word; for tone

[18] Similarly German imposes the use of *von . . . zu* (*von Stunde zu Stunde, von
Zeit zu Zeit*) instead of *von . . . nach* to signal intermittency rather than distance.
This pattern of matching *von* and *zu* must be distinguished from their junction in
certain titles of nobility: (*Herr*) *von und zu* (*Stein*). F. *de jour en jour* has acquired a
progressive meaning: 'as the days pass'. Cf. n. 12, above.
[19] Similarly in Polish: *na łeb na szyję* 'headlong' (lit. 'on the head, on the neck')
beside such more numerous full-bodied binomials as *o chlebie i wodzie* 'on bread and
water', *chuchać i dmuchać* 'to take excessive care [in dealing with living beings]' (lit.,
'to blow [against the cold] and puff [against the heat]'), *do bitki i do wypitki* '(he) is
a jolly good fellow' (lit. 'for fighting and for drinking'), *do tańca i do różańca* '(she)
is good for everything' (lit. 'for dancing and for reciting the rosary').

and meaning cf. F. *comme ci, comme ça*). F. (*sens*) *dessus dessous, au jour le jour*, Sp. *un si es no es*, Gr. *ándres gynaîkes*. The pattern abuts on compounds of the type It. *chiaroscuro*.[20] Derivational and syntactic conditions may favor the zero link, compressing the binomial, as it were, to its barest minimum: *East and West*, but *East-West territory*; G. *West und Ost*, but *Westöstlicher* (*Divan*); *wear and tear*, but *hit-run* (*car*), *lend-lease* (*bill*); R. *Pëtr i Pavel*, but *Petropávlovskij*; Am.-E. *down 'n' outer* 'underdog' is emphatically colloquial in its deviation from this trend.

Where an overt link exists, it is commonly placed between A and B: L. *sūrsum ac deorsum* 'up and down'. However, it may also be retroactively attached at the tail end, as in L. *terrā marīque, longē lātēque* 'far and wide', or may consist of two non-contiguous elements, of which one ($= l_1$) precedes the core of F, while the other ($= l_2$) finds a niche between A and B, expanding the skeleton of the binomial to $l_1 + A + l_2 + B$. Homeric *patēr andrôn te deón te* illustrates yet another possibility. Among the ideally suitable composite links (*either . . . or*, G. *entweder . . . oder, sowohl . . . als auch*, L. *aut . . . aut*, etc.) some turn out too cumbersome to qualify for this particular service; easily the most satisfactory results are achieved with the aid of negative correlatives: *neither . . . nor*; G. *weder . . . noch*, L. *nec . . . nec*, It. *nè . . . nè*, F. *ni . . . ni:* (*ne savoir*) *ni A ni B* 'not to know A from B', Sp. *ni fu ni fa* 'neither one thing nor the other', (*no tener*) *ni pie ni cabeza* 'to be absurd', OF *ne . . . ne: ne cuers ne cors* 'neither heart nor body', R. *ni . . . ni: ni dat' ni vzjat'* ($=$ *toč' v toč'*), *ni k selú ni k górodu* 'irrelevant' (lit. '[is a road leading] neither to village nor to town').

The pattern of composite link reconciling prepositional and conjunctional ingredients, in this order of distribution, is exemplified by *without . . . and* (G. *ohne* or *sonder . . . und*, Sp. *sin . . . ni*) and *between . . . and* (and its foreign counterparts). That the latter group stands halfway between conjunctions and full-fledged prepositions follows from Sp. *entre yo y tú* 'between me and you', 'both I and you', with the nom. *yo, tú* substituted for the obj. *mí, ti* which any authentic preposition would have governed.[21]

---

[20] Note the loan translations of this once highly fashionable term of painting: pre-Cl. Sp. *claro escuro* as early as in Juan de Mena, mod. *claroscuro*, F. *clair obscur*, G. *Hell-* beside *Halb-dunkel*, etc.

[21] What has become in Spanish the accepted norm, frequently rendered in translations by 'both X and Y', exists in other languages as an unacknowledged conversational variant (cf. coll. Am.-E. *between Frank and I*). The hybrid status

Another sequence showing *l* yanked out of its expected position is *by fair means and foul,* with *fair* and *foul* torn asunder rather than jointly preceding or following *means.* It is arguable that historically the "illogical" ordering, apparently confined to English, arose through contamination of these latter possibilities of adjectival position (the former primarily in the Anglo-Saxon, the latter preëminently in the Latin tradition), in a climate of intense Germanic-Romance symbiosis uniquely characteristic of the English language. However that may be, the titillation of the unexpected plus the concomitant pressure of sequences like *in town and out* have helped transform a mere infelicity into a stylistic adornment valued for providing a break in the monotony of frozen patterns; cf. *sweet notes and sour, The Cold Wind and the Warm* (title of a modern play).

The number of links available for use in trinomials is typically quite reduced, *and* beside less frequent *or* providing the best services:

> (a) *bell, book, and candle; calm, cool, and collected; man, woman, and child; rag, tag,* (also *tag, rag,* —) *and bobtail;* R. (*èto vsegdá*) *býlo, jest' i búdet* 'this has always been, is, and will be so';
> (b) (*in any*) *way, shape, or manner.*[22]

## 10. Expanded Binomials

The formula $A + l + B$ and its closest variations mark the bare frame of a binomial, a frame self-sufficient in many instances (and even occasionally reducible to AB, a plain juxtaposition), while in others one finds it draped in miscellaneous fashions.

If the grammatical equipment of a language includes one or two sets of articles, their (a) absence, (b) unique presence in initial position, or (c) repeated presence before nominal members (including words nominalized) makes for considerable diversification:

> (a) *brain and brawn, facts and figures, by fits and starts, friend(s) and*

[22] The lapidary style of tripartite statements architéctured on the model of Caesar's laconic message *uēnī, uīdī, uīcī* and favored by political programmatic sloganeering (G. *ein Volk, ein Reich, ein Führer!*) and by modern eye-catching advertisement (*one week, one line, one dollar*) gains in "punch" by dispensing altogether with links. Such complete paratactic sentences, however, are very rarely coterminous with trinomials. Metric considerations may favor the introduction of a link, as in Hernando de Acuña's famous sonnet: "Un monarca, un imperio y una espada".

of 'between' may be attributed to the fact that it is the only preposition fundamentally governing two nouns (loosely used, even more than two: coll. *between Bill and Bob and their mother*).

*foe(s), from hand to mouth;* F. *pieds et poings (liés);* Sp. *con alma y vida, con pelos y señales, a sangre y fuego, de tomo y lomo, a tuerto o a derecho, contra viento y marea;*

    (b) *the ifs and ands;* G. *das Drum und Dran, im grossen und ganzen, in die Kreuz' und Quere;* F. *les hoirs et ayants cause;* Sp. *la flor y nata, las vueltas y revueltas;*

    (c) *the birds and the bees, the quick and the dead;* F. *les causes et les effets;* Sp. *(a) las duras y (a) las maduras.*

Aside from each language's general budgetary provisions for articles, several complicating factors enter into the picture: to mention but a few, the unequal affinities of singular and plural to articles, the rôle of prepositions as temporary barriers to their spread, the dissimilar need for attaching them to intrinsic nouns and to words contextually nominalized.[23]

In some English binomials the articles rival possessives or demonstratives, with varying degrees of freedom of alternation; others are obligatorily preceded by a possessive, a demonstrative, or some such quantifier or qualifier as *all* and *every*, if they are nouns, and by *too* — ordinarily repeated —, if they are adjectives: *one's (own) flesh and blood, (to follow) their ins and outs, in this day and age, to all intents and purposes, in every nook and cranny, (every) now and then, too little and too late* (the last word is most plausibly analyzed as an adverb).

A and B may be root morphemes susceptible of no further synchronic analysis, as in *day and night, a sangre y fuego,* or each member may muster an equal number of morphemes, typically two, which in turn are either bound or free: *a/live and kick/ing, foot/loose and fancy/ free, up hill and down dale, from the crown of the head to the sole of the foot.* Bi- and pluri-morphemic clusters may have one constituent in common; by dint of repetition this segment that they share, whether grammatical or lexical, welds them the more indissolubly together

---

[23] The use of the article may be imposed by external conditions having little or no direct bearing on the inner structure of F, but rather flowing from the grand strategy of the entire sentence. In highly colloquial, not to say journalistic, English, an indefinite article has thus become the commonest way for speakers to usher in any nominal or verbal binomial pressed into service as a qualifier: *a bows-and-arrows project, a cat-and-dog life, a file-and-forget work.* Contrariwise, a nominal or adjectival binomial followed, immediately or at short distance, by *of* is ordinarily heralded by a definite article: *(the) bread-and-butter (of the festival), (the) life and soul (of the book), (the) how and (the) why (of it), (the) hot and healthy (blood of both).* Binomials relatively protected from such influences, hence most amenable to sharply focused observation, are those found in adverbial phrases in which either they or their immediate constituents occupy the terminal segment of the whole: *(to a) greater or lesser (degree or extent).*

Z

(as do rhyme and alliteration through a similar hammering effect): *bigger and better, hither and thither, sooner or later, upwards and downwards, for better or for worse, highways and byways, day in and day out, on again and off again*, and, in the penumbra of grotesquely facetious formations, *tweedledum and tweedledee* 'trivial difference'. Unusual concatenations of circumstances: In *betwixt and between* the common prefix and the two distinctive radicals happen all three to have faded; in R. *ni voobšče ni v částnosti* symmetry is jeopardized because the contour of the first trimorphemic half is less sharply outlined than that of the second; *upside down, inside (and) out, indoors or out, in town and out* are so many illustrations of a noteworthy compression achieved through unique mention of the common ingredient within the confines of A (cf. also *believe it or not*, Sp. *quieras que no* 'whether you like it or not').

Speakers sporadically pair off a mono- and a bi-morphemic member, especially in a language replete with binomials such as English:

> *beans and brownbread, bought and paid for, broom and dustpan, coffee and doughnuts, few and far between, fire and brimstone!, to fish or cut bait, hail and farewell, (come, despite) hell and high water!, skull and cross bones* (emblem).[24]

*Rockets and guided missiles* seems on its way to join this majority group.[25] Witnesses to minority usage include *corned beef and cabbage, by railroad and/or bus (— plane)*. Examples of subtler disparity in volume or design between the two halves: *between the devil and the deep (blue) sea, over the hills and far away*. Two facts stand out, so far as English is affected: First, for the most part it is B rather than A that contains the larger number of morphemes (the margin almost never exceeds one); second, the semantic attrition of *brim-* pushes the respective compound to the very edge of the category, placing it in the neighborhood of semianalyzable words (Bloomfield's *cranberry*).

Repeating a preposition may fulfill a variety of purposes,[26] e.g. serve to restore clarity by counteracting the disruptive influence of

---

[24] Cf. Pol. *placz i zgrzytanie zębów* 'weeping and the gnashing of teeth'. The Russian equivalents (*plač* and *skrežetánie zubóv*) are less habitually joined.

[25] *To live and let live* stands apart, reminding one by its configuration of G. (*nach bestem*) *Wissen und Gewissen*.

[26] The initially legalistic term *au fur* (obs. var. *à fur*) *et à mesure* described an aberrant trajectory, representing, on O. Bloch's authority, an elaboration on *au fur et mesure* (17th century), which in turn was an amplification of OF *au fuer* provoked by the obsolescence of *f(e)ur*.

*not* in English (*matters of fact and not of fancy*) or add a touch of emphasis and plasticity. At this juncture oscillation is not uncommon, given the dispensability of this ancillary feature: *by hook or* (*by*) *crook*.

## 11. The Position of the Binomial in the Sentence

In Standard Average European a binomial self-contained may be transferred from one context to another with a fair measure of freedom: *all and sundry, fire and water, odds and ends.* This is especially true when it represents an adverbial group, from whichever form-class its members, solidly glued together, have been recruited: *first and foremost, now and then, still and all, win or lose*; G. *ab und zu,* R. *vverx i vniz* 'up and down', Gr. *nûn kaì aeí, nun te kaì pálai.* Certain pairs of semantically self-sufficient verbs also enjoy relative syntactic autonomy: *to hire and fire, to hem and haw.*

Other binomials, particularly those hinging on adjectives and the majority of such as contain transitive verbs, lack that degree of independence and maneuverability. However, speakers enjoy limited freedom in attaching them to varying numbers of words that qualify for rounding out their meaning:

(*cars, jobs, salaries*) *bigger and better,* (*fish, pups*) *fresh and frisky,* (*books, friends, ideas*) *old and new,* (*to be able, know, learn to*) *read and/or write, a rough-and-ready* (*analysis, frontier-life, manner*); *give or take* (*a dollar, a mile, a year*) *in either direction.*

A third group of binomials is confined to a strictly limited number of successions, sometimes to unique sequences, permeated with the unmistakable flavor of "idioms", sayings, proverbial phrases, i.e., essentially lexicalized or nearing the point of lexical congelation. The limiting factor may be a preposition:

(*for*) *better or worse,* (*to*) *bits and pieces,* (*in*) *this day and age,* (*with*) *hammer and tongs,* (*by*) *leaps and bounds,* (*by*) *line and level,* (*under*) *lock and key,* (*with*) *might and main,* (*without*) *rhyme or reason,* (*through*) *thick and thin,* (*without*) *welt or guard;* G. (*auf*) *Biegen und Brechen,* (*ohne*) *Furcht und Tadel,* (*im*) *grossen und ganzen,* (*in*) *die Kreuz' und Quere,* (*über*) *kurz und lang,* (*nach*) *Lust und Laune,* (*bei, durch*) *Nacht und Nebel,* (*mit*) *Rat und Tat,* (. . . *von*) *Ruf und Rang,* (*ohne*) *sein Wissen und Wollen;* Sp. (*a*) *sangre y fuego,* (*de*) *tomo y lomo,* (*contra*) *viento y marea.*

Very frequently this controlling function devolves upon a verb:

(*to give one*) *cards and spades,* (*to play it*) *cool and coy,* (*to receive*) *cove and key,* (*to want one*) *dead or alive,* (*to play*) *fast and loose,* (*to blow*) *hot and cold, (to know) the ins and outs, (to live as) man and wife, (to mind one's) p's and q's, (to be or sit) on pins and needles;* G. *(ihm vergeh-t* or *-en) Hören und Sehen, Kopf oder Schrift (lesen)* 'to toss up', *Mord und Brand (schreien);* F. *(c'est) à prendre ou à laisser;* Sp. *(ir, tomar) las duras con* (or *por) las maduras.*

Verb and preposition may jointly exercise the controls: G. *(mit) Mann und Maus (untergehen).* One can obviously point out transitional cases between the three groups here examined.

### 12. Mutual Adjustment of the Two Members

Whenever a language happens to preserve two or more variants of a given word, the one normally less or even least favored — as the older, rarer, or socially unattractive — may, by way of exception, receive preferential treatment if such a choice consolidates the balance of a binomial. In German, for instance, where, much as in English, the trend is toward either equality of length as between A and B or greater length of B, one finds *Freud' und Leid, Hab' und Gut, Reih' und Glied* in preference to standard *Freude, Habe, Reihe.* At intervals such an arrangement may yield a fringe benefit, such as a rhyme, perfect or imperfect (*Freud': Leid*). The effectiveness, in this respect, of *to and fro*, presumably at the stage corresponding to the pronunciation [to] and [fro], gave an additional lease on life to *fro*, more advantageous — in this context alone — than *from.* In the United States the trinomial *reading, (w)riting, 'rithmetic* won out over its competitor *read, (w)rite, and cipher* on account of the splendid orchestral support (alliteration) received from the proverbial three R's. Frenchmen went to the length of transforming half-understood *feur* < OF *fuer* (L. FORUM) into *fur* for the sake of a tempting approximation to (and, colloquially, a rhyme with) *mesure*, in whose company *fur* is uniquely allowed to occur. A similar latitude of tolerance is familiar from proverbs, riddles, and songs (G. *wie die Alten sungen, so zwitschern die Jungen*).

### 13. Relation of A and B to F

Semantic relations of different orders obtain between the two members, taken separately and jointly, and the binomial, as a whole. If, to tap the reservoir of English examples, the link is *and*, the binomial may literally represent the exact sum of A plus B, as in *brother and sister, husband and wife, heroes and heroines, shoes and socks, shirt and tie, cup and saucer, knife and fork, ham and cheese, lamb and salad, salt and pepper, joy and sorrow, right and left, Greek and Latin.* Elsewhere the two items evoke so many conspicuous features of an unnamed multifaceted whole — as if speakers were bent on identifying that whole by a few strokes, bold but hardly random, rather than on describing it by means of a tedious bill of particulars. The rich imagery suggested by *blood and thunder!, flesh and blood,* (Biblical) *milk and honey, soap and water, song and dance, sugar and spice, tooth and nail* transgresses, if one may judge from introspection, the precise contours of the twin objects expressly mentioned. Between these two extremes of literalness and symbolism there stretches a continuum of finely graded possibilities. Literalness prevails in matter-of-fact statements in prose; symbolism, loaded with magic power, reigns supreme in blessings and curses, in emblems and circumlocutions, in poetry.

The same potency of figurative use explains why A and B, viewed in isolation, may be highly technical words which, except in this privileged context, are hardly ever on the average speaker's lips. Usually the meaning of just one member, either A or B, has begun to lose some of its transparency (cf. n. 1, above). Examples in point are *warp and woof* (beside rarer *warp and weft*) and *to hem and haw.* G. *in Bausch und Bogen*, at present almost exclusively associated with verbs of (sweeping) condemnation and rejection, pertained originally to the realm of commerce, if it is true that *Bausch* stands for 'pad, bolster' and *Bogen* for 'sheet'. The domain of law is represented not only by oft-mentioned F. *au fur et à mesure*, but also by G. *mit Kind und Kegel* 'with the whole family', beside antiquated *er hat nicht Kind noch Kegel, für Kind und Kegel sorgen*, in which *Kegel*, totally opaque to the uninitiated, signifies 'child born out of wedlock', cf. the family names *Kögel* and *Kegelmann*. Lexical archaisms of other than technical background are embedded in *spic(k)-and-span* 'new and fresh'; *spick* seems identical with obs. *spick* 'spike or nail', cf. G. *funkelnagelneu*, likewise suggestive of the shiny metal surface of an unused nail. Morphological erosion obscures the meaning of A and B in G. (*das ist*) *gang und gäbe* 'this is the usual thing'.

Can a pattern be established for this process of partial or almost total blurring? Do languages tend to dispense with the translucency of A rather than of B, or vice versa? The scant evidence on hand allows of no such categorical assertion. What has prolonged the lifespan of

*Kind und Kegel* and *au fur et à mesure* beyond normal expectancy is the pleasing interplay of alliteration and rhyme, respectively, with a desirable distribution of syllabic weight (ratio 1 : 2). As for *spick-and-span*, it probably owes its survival, continued momentum, and progressive liberation from the adjunct *new* to the coexistence of the playful type *chitchat, riffraff, splish-splash*, characterized by a neatly prescribed alternation of short stressed vowels, by a preference for noisy consonants effectively spread over each syllable, and by a discernible measure of semantic imprecision.

### 14. Binomials Versus Compounds

Binomials as here narrowly defined, especially if devoid of a link, may come into contact with those compounds whose constituents pertain to the same form-class and are conjoined rather than subordinated: *composer-critic, editor-novelist, gentleman-farmer, teacher-scholar*, and an occasional adjective like *bittersweet*.[27]

The techniques for drawing a dividing line between the two categories will vary from language to language. With many living languages a contrast in prosodic conditions may yield a clue to the descriptivist. An inflectional feature may likewise serve as a classificatory criterion; thus, even if the absence of a link in *teacher-scholar* were not a distinctive trait, the pl. *teacher-scholars* would set this compound apart from

> *birds and bees* (*— and beasts*), *boots and saddles, bumps and grinds,* (*raining*) *cats and dogs, cocks and hens,* (*these*) *comings and goings, cups and saucers,* (*not . . .*) *deeds nor words,* (*on*) *elbows and knees,* (*all*) *eyes and ears,* (*to all*) *intents and purposes,* (*by*) *leaps and bounds, pots and pans, rats and mice, at sixes and sevens, sticks and stones, ups and downs,*

which en bloc exhibit the comportment of true binomials.[28] Where,

---

[27] G. *bittersüss* is a pertinent counterpart, less so *bitterböse, bitterernst* (in these *bitter-* tends to acquire a limiting effect: 'angry, serious to the extent of bitterness'). Note the same contrast between, on the one hand, G. *vollschlank* 'slightly buxom' lit. 'buxom/slender', and, on the other, *vollwertig. Butterbrod*, in contrast to *bread and butter*, involves no coördination, inasmuch as *Butter-* limits the way of serving or consuming bread. On ⌐*bittersweet*⌐ see A. G. Hatcher, *Modern English Word-Formation and Neo-Latin; a Study of the Origins of English* (*French, Italian, German*) *Copulative Compounds* (Baltimore, 1951), and É. Benveniste's substantial review in *BSLP*, XLVII: 2 (1951), 182–185.

[28] The situation is different when a singular and a plural are paired off, e.g. (a) *bacon and eggs, beer and skittles, cat and kittens, cheese and crackers, coffee and rolls, fame and riches, fish and chips, fox and hounds, fuss and feathers, head and shoulders, meat and potatoes, neck and heels, skin and bones, skull and cross bones, from soup to*

as in Spanish, formal adjustment of A to B or vice versa is infrequent, an erratic by-form, all circumstances considered, points in the direction of composition: cf. *agri/dulce* with its characteristic connective *-i-* (as in *verdi/negro, verdi/seco* beside *verde, altibajos* 'uneven ground' beside *alto*) versus *agrio*, OSp. *agro* 'sour' < ACRU and the relic *agre* < ACRE in *vin/agre*, lit. 'sour wine' (unless one interprets *vinagre*, alternatively, as a borrowing from Gallo-Romance).

A historical boundary can be drawn most effectively between binomials and the playful ("expressive") variety of reduplicative compounds exemplified by *crisscross, splish-splash*, F. *pêle-mêle*.[29] The starting-points are radically different. The history of an authentic binomial begins with the gradual rapprochement of two independent words, one of which, in the course of their joint travel across the ages, may influence the other or merge with it into a new unit not easily divisible (which some linguists label "hypermorpheme"). Conversely, formations structured like *crisscross* and *splish-splash* (here distinguished from congeries of nonsense words, such as G. *dideldumdei, lirumlarum*, Sp. *patatín, patatán*, copiously represented in nursery rhymes) have a single starting point: *cross, splash*; the desired measure of jocose variation is achieved by the prefixing (*dilly-dally*) or suffixing (*whimsey-whamsey*) of fanciful by-forms, in harmony with a pre-existent vocalic schema. Not a few of these formations may have been spontaneous; others were arrived at through gradual elaboration, and in chosen instances (including that of F. *pêle-mêle*) several transitional stages along the main line as well as some abortive experiments staged along side-lines are open to inspection.[30] The penetration of *pêle-*

---

[29] See M. R. Haas, "Types of reduplication in Thai (with some comparisons and contrasts taken from English)", *SIL*, I: 4 (May 1942), 6 pp. (separate paging).

[30] Conceivably OF. *mesle, mesle* 'mix, mix!' or 'confuse, confuse!' was a command akin to Sp. (narrative) *pinta que pinta* 'painting like mad', *dale que dale* 'doing something obstinately' and remotely similar to F. (concessive) *coûte que coûte* except for an amusing extra touch of irony or sarcasm. Medieval texts, including MSS of Chrétien's romances, reveal a good deal of imaginative toying and tampering: *melle pelle, pelle melle, brelle mesle, melle et brelle* (the 19th-century straggler *méli-mélo* stands apart). The speakers' eventual choice displays a thoroughly satisfactory balance between qualitative variety (oral vs. nasal release), economy (both initial consonants are labials), and clarity (the strategic second place has been assigned to semantically transparent *mêle*). Cf. the earlier statement on *bric-à-brac*.

---

*nuts* (obligatory plural in *coat and pants*) or, in inverse order, (b) *beans and brown-bread, cookies and cake, peaches and cream, potatoes and gravy* alongside semantically isolated *Letters and Science* (originally *Sciences*). The marked numerical superiority of (a) over (b) is in consonance with the oft-observed tendency of English to shorten A, while lengthening B.

*mêle* and *bric-à-brac* into English might have run afoul of serious hindrances, had not these formations satisfied the demands of both languages, the lender and the borrower, for a certain type of acoustically appealing compounds. Diachronically, Am.-E. *mumbo-jumbo* 'fetish, bugaboo', whatever the status of its prototype in western Sudanese, also seems more of a jocular compound than of a binomial.

A cross between compound and binomial — in highly colloquial discourse — is exemplified by *pribbles and prabbles* and Sp. *mondo y lirondo* 'pure, without admixture'. Of the five critical features involved the link (*and*, *y*) ascends to the binomial, so does the (optional) rhyme in the Spanish, and the (equally optional) alliteration in the English phrase; the legacy of the compounds includes vocalic variation (*i–a*) and, above all, the coinage of such nonce-words, the etymologist's despair,[31] as *prabble* and *lirondo*.

As is to be expected, even languages genetically and typologically very much akin may clash in their preferences for binomials versus compounds, unless they altogether dodge the issue by having recourse to a third solution. Take the names of color patterns: Where iridescent, opalescent, or merging hues are to be suggested (not necessarily contiguous on the chromatic scale), German favors straight composition: *Grünblau*, *Schwarzrot*, *Graubraun*; English, the use of a limiting qualifier: *greenish blue*, *reddish black*, *greyish brown* (speaking of hair, also *graying brown*). For sharply contrasting colors in adjacent surfaces (emblems, escutcheons, flags, neckties, etc.), German again champions composition: *Schwarzweiss* (distinct from *Schwarz auf Weiss*), *Blauweiss*, also triadic *Schwarzrotgold*, whereas English here resorts to *Blue and Gold*, *in black and white*, *a gold-and-white theater*, *a red and white stocking*, *a red and yellow river of flame*, beside *Black, Red, and Gold*.[32]

## 15. Sequence of Members

Inevitably any study in irreversible binomials culminates in an attempt to answer the primordial question: Can any specific reason be adduced for the precedence of A over B? One may distinguish

[31] L. Spitzer's and J. Corominas' approaches to the ancestry of *lirondo* (see the latter's *DCE*, s.v.) are infelicitous, inasmuch as both are under the delusion that the process essentially involved a blend of two or three isolated words. Actually one witnesses here the conflation of two patterns of juxtaposition.

[32] Characteristic of English is again the spread of *and* at the expense of other connectives; contrast *in black and white* (and, similarly, Sp. *blanco y negro*) with G. *schwarz auf weiss*, R. (instr.) *čërnym po bélomu*.

between two orders of possible answers: those that aim to explain
the crystallization of individual sequences, a string of problems comparable, as regards their severely limited breadth and their historical
slant, to pinpointed etymological riddles; and those broad enough to
aid the analyst in the recognition of certain patterns. Only the latter
category need concern us here.

By way of preliminaries, remember not only the slight margin of
vacillation among speakers of the same language, not infrequently
within the same family (*Dad and Mom* ~ *Mom and Dad, broom and
dustpan* ~ *dustpan and broom*), but especially the predictable discrepancies, as regards hardened sequences, between individual languages. *By land and by sea* matches Gr. *katà gên kaì katà thálattan*
and F. *sur terre et sur mer*, but clashes with G. *zu Wasser und zu
Lande* and with Sp. *por mar y tierra. Public and private* echoes Sp.
*público y privado*, disagreeing with Gr. *ídios kaì dēmósios*. English
distinctly favors *cat and dog*, especially in stereotyped expressions:
*cat-and-dog* (*life*), (*to rain*) *cats and dogs*; Spanish insists on (*como*)
*perros y gatos*, and French on (*comme*) *chien et chat. Odd or even* is at
variance with Sp. *pares o nones*, as is *black and white* with Sp. *blanco
y negro. From head* (or *top*) *to toe* is diametrically opposed to Sp.
*de pies a cabeza*, R. *s nog do golový*, and Pol. *od stóp do głow*, all four
sequences inescapably rigid.[33] Such divergencies are encouraging,
since they prompt one to reckon, to an appreciable extent, with the
agency of purely linguistic forces.

Researches so far conducted have led to the isolation of six discrete
forces frequently operating in unison. Nothing in the resultant
pattern indicates that further additions are impossible or unlikely,
and the discovery of a much richer interplay is to be expected.

**1. Chronological priority of A.** By this force we mean not the
precedence of the referent of A over the referent of B in real-life

---

[33] A few additional examples may dispel any residual doubts. *From north to
south* and Sp. *del sur al norte* are antipodes, while *east and west* contradicts G.
*West*(*en*) *und Ost*(*en*). *More or less*, G. *mehr oder minder* (or *weniger*), F. *plus ou moins*,
Sp. *más o menos*, Ptg. *mais ou menos*, It. *più o meno*, R. *bóleje íli méneje* form an overwhelmingly powerful league — but one whose pressure has fallen short of dislodging
Pol. *mniej lub więcej*. Even in the case of a modern political emblem propagandized
as transcending national boundaries a trace of non-conformism is detectable:
*hammer and sickle*, which may have suggested itself through its appealing vowel
sequence *a . . . i* (*i . . . a* would have evoked frivolity or futility) and, more important, through such preëxistent groups as *hammer and tongs*, displays a suspicious
deviation from orthodox R. *serp i mólot*.

situations (*divide and conquer, spit and polish, hit and run*), but the expansion, with the passage of time, of a monomial (A) into a binomial (A + *l* + B). To describe its action, let us examine, by way of digression, the more neatly observable transformation of some binomials into corresponding trinomials. *Here and there* has been occasionally converted into *here, there, and everywhere; eat and drink,* into *eat, drink, and be merry; lock and stock,* into *lock, stock, and barrel; vim and vigor* (apparently on a less wide scale) into *vim, vigor, and vitality; snakes and snails,* into highly comic *snakes and snails and puppy-dog tails.*[34] Sometimes the central rather than the concluding member of a trinomial seems to represent an accretion: (*to live*) *high and handsome* beside less trivial *high, wide, and handsome;* for still other variations see Section 6, above. Once this principle of gradual elaboration, by way of afterthought or deliberate anticlimax, has been accepted, at least as an ever-present strong possibility, it is arguable that some monomials may have undergone a comparable extension to binomials through a process of refinement and self-correction (humorous effects are less likely in this transition). In our own time, *man power* has begun to yield to *man-and-woman power,* still fairly infrequent as of this writing. Older examples can be unearthed only through detailed paleontological probings. An inconspicuous *drum corps* — if lexicographic records corroborate this conjecture — may have been metamorphosed into more specific and, let us admit, more impressive *drum-and-bugle corps* or *fife-and-drum corps.*[35]

[34] One suspects a similar line of development — pending confirmation by historical records — in the cases of *apples, peaches, and cherries — fair, fat, and forty — hook, line, and sinker — (an easy) hop, skip, and jump — round, firm, and fully packed — screwed, blued, and tattooed.* Students of primitive Christianity reckon with the extension of a pristine binity into a trinity and even a quinity. On the other hand, some trinomials may conceivably owe their very existence to an intrinsically triadic configuration, e.g. those based on Caesar's laconic *uēnī, uīdī, uīcī* (including Lope de Vega's *vine, miré y fui vencido*), traffic signs of the type *stop, look, listen* (which the late A. Stevenson wittily applied to his exploratory tour behind the Iron Curtain almost ten years ago), or facetious Sp. *correve(i)dile* 'gossip, mischief-maker', lit. 'run, see [= look], and tell him'.

[35] The implication is obvious: Had the original tag been *bugle corps,* the "padding", applied in the reverse direction, might have produced *\*bugle-and-drum corps* — all other conditions being equal. The point is that they were not exactly equal, *bugle* [bjugl] being, by the discernible margin of one phoneme, the longer form with a distinctly stronger claim to the position of Member B. In other words, *drum and bugle* "sounds better" than its opposite which, on account of this handicap, may not have been quite so readily adopted, even if some speakers had attempted to launch it. The pièce de résistance in this chain of speculative arguments is the

**2. Priorities inherent in societal structure.** Pairs of words may next be ordered in accordance with a hierarchy of values inherent in the structure of a given society, or alliance of societies.[36] The originally patriarchal character of those most intimately associated with IE and Semitic languages is echoed to this day by such sequences as:

*Adam and Eve, boys and girls* (also, in the maternity ward: *a boy or a girl?*), *brother(s) and sister(s)* (R. *brat i sestrá*, Pol. *brat i siostra*), Br.-E. *butler and cook* (as a household team), *father and mother* (R. *otéc i mat'*), Am.-E. *guys and dolls, heroes and heroines, husband and wife* (R. *muž i žená*, Pol. *mąż i żona*), *Jack and Jill, King and Queen, man and maid* (*— and wife*), *Mr. and Mrs.* . . . (G. *Herr und Frau* . . ., etc., Sp. *Señor* . . . *y Señora*), *Romeo and Juliet* (*Paul et Virginie*, etc.), *son and daughter*.[37]

An equally powerful social prism elevated parents above children, the old above the young (provided they were assigned to the same level of prestige by virtue of family background or occupation); this particular scale extended to the realm of animals: *cow and calf, hen and chicks, father and son* (in firms: *Dombey and Son*), *man and boy, mother and child*, G. *Mutter und Tochter, Onkel und Neffe, Tante und Nichte*, R. *ocý i déti* 'parents (lit. fathers) and children'.[38] The supremacy of ruling classes shines through in stereotyped *master and servant, merchant and farmer, poet and peasant, prince and pauper, rich and poor*; Sp. *nobles y pecheros* (*— y villanos*). The same rigid subordination prevails in reference to the figures of the chessboard (Sp. *ni rey ni roque*) and to two sharply discrepant professions that the same individual, paradoxically enough, may have exercised, as when Hans Sachs was called anticlimactically *ein Schuhmacher und ein Poet dazu* (invariably in this order). Within the same setting it is

---

[36] This hierarchy applies also to divine and supernatural powers and allegorized abstractions, cf. the device *Dieu et mon droit*; Sp. (*sin encomendarse*) *a Dios ni al diablo* 'recklessly' (lit. 'commending oneself neither to God nor to the devil'), Pol. *Bog i ojczýzna* 'God and fatherland'.

[37] Courtly society tended to rank the sexes differently; therefore the conflict between *men and women* and *ladies and gentlemen* resolves itself into a clash of currents of nonverbal culture. Cf. R. L. Stevenson's essays entitled *Virginibus puerisque*.

[38] The reason for this illogical pairing, familiar from the title of Turgenev's trailblazing novel, seems to be primarily rhythmical: *\*roditeli* ('parents') *i déti* would have placed an excessively long A ahead of B; *\*ocý i synov'já* (or poet. *syný*) would have made B inopportunely oxytonic, quite apart from the disadvantage of an obtrusive rhyme. Concomitantly, *ocý* suggested itself on account of its mildly poetic overtone.

---

fact that *drum*, if relegated to the position of B, is preceded by a word of equal syllabic and phonemic weight: *fife-and-drum corps*. Yet this entire embroidery is in urgent need of historical corroboration.

customary to assign different rungs of the ladder to humans versus animals; to stronger or more highly prized versus weaker or less valued animals; to animate beings versus contraptions, and so on:

> (*food for*) *man and beast*; *horse and cow*, *cat and mouse*; *horse and buggy* (— *and cart*), *man or machine*; *the sun and the moon*.

If it is true that the dictates of society impose a more or less arbitrary time perspective on a language,[39] then the acceptance by historically-minded Western societies of a straight line stretching from the past through the present to the future not only has predetermined expressly temporal formulas, such as *before and after*, *yesterday and today*, and the fuller trinomial *past, present, and future* (cf. R. *èto vsegdá býlo, jest' i búdet*), but, less obviously, has also prearranged untold pairs in which relative timing — with or without a suggestion of cause-and-effect connection — is subtly implied:

> *cash-and-wrap* (*counter*), *clean-and-wax* (*job*), *heat 'n' eat*, *kiss-and-tell* (*beau*), *live and learn*, *seize and hold*, *shoot and kill*, *sit 'n' snack*, *spit and polish*, *stop and shop*, *wait and see*, *wear and tear*, *woo and win*; *birth and death*, *challenge and response*, *marriage and divorce*, *question and answer*, *rise and fall*, *wedding and reception*; *from rags to riches*, *from start to finish*.

Cultural ranking controls the exact labeling of meals: *fish and chips*, *meat and potatoes*, *pork and beans*, *scotch and soda*;[40] the arrangement,

---

[39] This hypothesis is traceable to B. L. Whorf's challenging speculations whose validity was later examined in two symposia; the proceedings (or epitomized results) of these have become available in two separate miscellanies: (a) *Language in Culture*, ed. H. Hoijer (Chicago, 1954); (b) *Language, Thought, and Culture*, ed. P. Henle (Ann Arbor, 1958).

[40] Binomials pervade the English menus on both sides of the Atlantic (*cake and ice cream* or, in reverse order, *corned beef and cabbage*, *fish and chips*, *ham and eggs*, etc.). The construction is overtly coördinative, except that the position of the members implies a minimum of subordination (A stands for the main dish, B for the vegetable or any other accompanying feature). In most languages subordination is made more explicit by the use of some characteristic preposition upgrading one item and downgrading the other. In the jargon of French cuisine *à* indicates three things — (a) a national or social style (. . . *à l'anglaise*, *à la turque*, . . . *à la boulangère*, *à la ménagère*, *à la meunière*); (b) a sauce or gravy (. . . *au beurre noir*, *au jus*); (c) the accompanying item: *oie farcie aux pommes, foie gras d'oie aux truffes, rognons sautés aux champignons, dinde farcie aux marrons, jambon frais aux fèves de marais*. The emphasis is clearly on qualifiers and characterizers conveying a soupçon of the manner of cooking and seasoning. Slavic languages use different devices; e.g., Russian suggests the three meanings signaled by F. *à* (a) by *po* (*čšúka po židóvski*), (b) frequently by *pod* (. . . *pod bélym i krásnym sóusom*), (c) by *s* (*baránina s kartófelem i smorčkámi, piláv s rísom i černoslívom, kotléty s pečěnym lúkom, vepr' s xrénom, barán'ja grudínka s répoju, govjádina s sardél'kami*). Polish similarly links the satellite by means of *z*: *figa z*

however casual, of furniture, crockery, and household tools: *table and chair, cup(s) and saucer(s)*; the distribution of rôles and significant ingredients in ritualistic ceremony, artistic performance, light entertainment, sports, and daily living: *words and music, piano and orchestra, theme and variations, prelude and fugue, fox and hounds, dine and dance*; the procession of metaphysical entities: *body and soul* (also F. *corps et âme*, Sp. *cuerpo y alma*). To a speaker immured within a single culture and less than highly sophisticated each of these fairly arbitrary successions is bound to appear "natural" or "logical".

**3. Precedence of the stronger of two polarized traits.** The third force is operative only in those binomials in which antonyms are pitted against each other. Their relative order may be dictated by the same leanings, on the part of the speakers, that preside over the selection of an active and a passive partner in lexical polarization.[41] In many speech communities pairing off habitually such opposites as 'right' and 'left', 'black' and 'white', 'true' and 'false', 'light' and 'heavy', 'day' and 'night', 'mountain' and 'valley', there develops a tendency for one of the two contrasted features to assume the status of a basic or positive trait and for its opposite to signal the lack of that trait, i.e., a reversal of the normal situation.[42] The ranking, at least as a relativist is tempted to view it, is again intrinsically social, but this time, unlike under (2), it manifests itself exclusively in the verbal layer of a culture. Whereas lexical polarization betrays the stronger partner diachronically through the measurable influence it

[41] On this phenomenon see my articles "Lexical polarization in Romance", *Lg.*, XXVII (1951), 485–518, and, from a higher vantage point, "Diachronic hypercharacterization in Romance", *ArL*, IX (1957), 79–113, esp. 103–106, and X (1958), 1–36.

[42] C. F. Hockett remarks in his contribution to the miscellany *Language in Culture*, ed. H. Hoijer, p. 120: "The pairing is not just semantic; it is also shown structurally. In each pair, one member is the 'major' member; this is shown by the selection of that member, rather than the other, in asking a colorless question about the degree of the particular quality".

---

*makiem* 'fig with poppy-seed' (fig. 'absolutely nothing'), *flaki z olejem* 'tripe with oil' (fig. 'utterly boring'), *groch z kapustą* 'peas and cabbage' (fig. 'confusion, pell-mell'). Correspondingly the traditional Spanish construction is with *con: huevos con jamón, pichones con naranja, pollo con arroz, tortilla con jamón* (or else *en*, to suggest enclosure: *trucha en pan, perdices en escabeche*). This holds true even of sauces: *lengua con salsa de almendra, merluz con salsa verde*, also *arroz con leche*, although here the Gallic fashion has made some inroads via loan translations: *merluza a la vinagreta, perdices a la crema, pollo al vino blanco*. English gastronomy, then, is fairly isolated in falling back on binomials.

exerts on the weaker, diverting it from its normal orbit, the stronger partner in an average IE bi- or multi-nomial asserts its superiority synchronically by rushing to occupy the first place. In English the link is, for the most part, *and*, not infrequently *or*, in exceptional cases zero (e.g. *upside down*):

> *all or nothing, black and white, to buy and sell, credit and debit, (to play)*
> *fast-and-loose, feast and famine, friend and foe (— and enemy), full or*
> *empty, give and take (— or take), good or bad, hand and foot, heaven or*
> *hell, hit or miss, hot and cold, laughter and tears, life and/or death, light*
> *and dark, love and hate, more or less, old and new, rights and wrongs*
> *beside right(ly) or wrong(ly), (through) thick and thin, ups and downs,*
> *upper and lower, victory (triumph —) or defeat, war and peace, win or*
> *lose, work and play, yes or no.*

Differences between languages are acutely perceptible here. *The quick and the dead* jibes with Sp. *vivo o muerto*, R. *živój íli mërtvyj*, but clashes with *dead or alive*, the ordering of which obeys a rhythmic rather than semantic principle. English is tolerant of *left and right* beside *right and left*, while German resolutely supports *rechts und links*, echoing F. *à droite et à gauche*, OSp. *a diestro y a siniestro*. Many, but not all, languages oppose 'mountain' to 'valley': *(over) hill and dale*, G. *Berg und Tal*, F. (obs.) *à mont et à val*. *Back and forth* strikes an outsider accustomed to G. *vor- und rückwärts* as a baffling sequence, possibly rooted in a motion characteristic of a widely practised trade (cf. naut. *to back and fill*); in sheer phonetic bulk *forth* perceptibly exceeds *back* (even where *r* has been muted), cf. R. *vzad i vperëd*. *Ebb and flow* for once matches G. *Ebbe und Flut*, while the very derivation of F. *re-flux* 'ebb' leads one to expect its subordination, in sequential terms, to *flux*; literary usage has actually sanctioned, since Corneille and Fénélon, the formula *le flux et le reflux*, cf. R. *prilív i otlív*.

**4. Patterns of formal preferences.** A force of exclusive concern to the linguist and apt to elude the vigilance of a sociologist is the purely formal preference of numerous speech communities for a certain configuration of the binomial, describable by the qualitative and quantitative distribution of sounds, accentual and tonal schemas, total lengths of segments (with separate attention to the number of syllables, to the number of phonemes, and to their phonetic duration), and the like. The power of this agency is best testable where inter-ference by its rivals is at a minimum, e.g., in stereotyped pairs of synonyms and in designations of matching objects where the pressure of social hierarchization seems weak or altogether inoperative.

Thus, Modern English displays a very marked partiality to SHORT PLUS LONG: either monosyllable plus (normally paroxytonic) disyllable, or two monosyllables of unequal size; rarely a mono- or di-syllable plus a polysyllable. Microscopic examination of each case history would have to take into account not only contemporary pronunciation, including the latitude of its major territorial and social varieties, but also such phonic conditions as prevailed at the presumable locale and time of the actual coinage and initial acceptance:

*aches and pains, aid and abet (— and succor), all and any, at or near . . ., beam and rafter, bed and board, beer and wine, big and little, bow(s) and arrow(s), buckle and (bare) thong, bumps and grinds, by and large, cap and gown, (to give one) cards and spades, cheap and nasty, (without) chick or child, to chop ('to barter' > 'to alter') and change, cops and robbers, death and destruction, (to make) ducks or drakes (of or with) 'to throw away carelessly', eating and drinking (— and scratching), neither my eye nor my elbow, facts and figures, fair and foolish (— and sluttish, — and softly), (to win) fame and fortune, far and away (— and wide), fast and furious, fat and fulsome (Am.-E. — and sassy 'saucy'), fine and dandy (— and fancy), (to go through) fire and water, (a dress) fits and flatters, (by, to cry in) fits and starts, fun and games, (creatures) furred and feathered, fuss and bother, ghosts and goblins, glow and glitter, gold and silver, guts and glory, hale and hearty, hares and hounds, (to agree like) harp and harrow, health and happiness, high and dry (— and mighty), (over) hill and dale, horse and rider, (to run) hot and heavy, hue and cry, in and out, joy and sorrow, Am.-E. kit and caboodle 'crowd, pack', lamb and salad, law and order, lean and lanky, (by) leaps and bounds, (without) let or hindrance, long and lazy, for love or money, low and lonely, meek and mild, neat and clean, neck and crop 'bodily, completely', (in every) nook and cranny, now and again (— or never), null and void, odds and ends, oil and vinegar, part and parcel, peace and quiet (— and prosperity), to pick and choose, (to sit on) pins and needles, poor but honest, pot and kettle ('equally black'), pure and simple, (to live or lie at) rack and manger 'in reckless abundance', (to go to) rack and ruin, rags and tatters, root and branch, rough and tumble (— and ready), safe and sound, salt and pepper, sex and slaughter (— and drinking), shoes and stockings, sin and shame (— and corruption), slick and slimy, to slip and slide, slow and steady, snips and snails 'odd ends', soap and water, sound and fury, a spit and a stride, (to walk the) straight and narrow, strong and stormy, stuff and nonsense, tea and coffee, to and fro, tried and tested (— and true), true and trusty, up and down, (exchange of) views and volleys, vim and vinegar, waifs and strays, (the) whys and wherefores, wind and weather, (by one's) wits and fists.*

An accurate statistical tabulation would no doubt bring out even more graphically the preponderance of this pattern. Exceptions do exist (*chapter and verse, classes and masses, a gentleman and a scholar, hither and yon, mended or ended, pepper and salt, salaries and wages, tattered and torn*, the last-mentioned echoed by *forlorn* in a famous nursery rhyme), but fail by a wide margin to exceed 10% and can almost invariably be accounted for by powerful constellations of special circumstances inimical to this deep-rooted predilection.[43]

Various other languages exhibit the same tendency in more sporadic fashion:

G. (*mit*) *Ach und Krach, Furcht und Schrecken, kurz und bündig (und kernig), Land und Leute, Lug und Trug, (nach) Lust und Laune, (bei) Nacht und Nebel, Pech und Schwefel, voll und ganz, Wind und Wetter, wirklich und wahrhaftig;* F. *au fur et à mesure, mes yeux et mes oreilles;* Sp. *ni carne ni pescado, dares y tomares, ir y venir, (hablar) largo y tendido, mondo y lirondo, con pelos y señales, de pies a cabeza, a roso y velloso, sal y pimienta, sano y salvo, (echar) sapos y culebras, tira y afloja;* Ptg. (*não confundir*) *alhos com bugalhos;*[44] R. *bez védoma i soglásija* 'without knowledge and consent', *sploš' da rjádom* 'oftentimes' (lit. 'throughout and side by side'), *šútki i pribaútki* 'jokes and sayings', *v dol' i poperëk* 'lengthwise and athwart', *vstréčnym i poperéčnym* 'to everybody' (lit. 'to those walking in the opposite direction and across');

---

[43] This picture represents a gross simplification of reality, inasmuch as it has been drawn without any previous agreement on the yardsticks of measurement. Here are, succinctly outlined, just a few of the complications all too easily overlooked in a bird's-eye view. *Bright* and *shiny* each number five phonemes; does the fact that the latter alone spreads them over two syllables recommend it for the position of B? *Life* contains four phonemes, one more than *limb*; did this ratio prevail at the time when the sequence *life and limb* crystallized? How does one go about counting the (partially preserved) *r* in *hair, hearth, short*? In cases like *pots and pans, cats and dogs* (beside older *dogs and cats*), *time and tide* (*tide and time* recorded as late as 1592), where the number of phonemes and syllables is equal, does the phonetic duration of contrastable sounds merit separate consideration? Add to the multiplicity of verifiable facts the latitude of interpretation in the analysis of an utterance into its constituent phonemes: *key* allows of the segmentations [*ki:*] and [*kij*]. As a result of this overgrowth of intricacies, utmost care must be exercised if one analyzes along the suggested line such binomials as include members of approximately equal size, e.g. *beck and call, blood and iron, boot and sole, brush and comb, bull(s) and bear(s)* (in the jargon of Stock Exchange brokers), *chalk and cheese, come and go, cross and/or pile, great cry and little wool, deeds nor words, a feast or a fast, free and easy, hearth and home, here and there, hide nor hair, hip and thigh, knife and fork, (by) line and level, (under) lock and key, the long and short (of it), merry and wise, once and again (— and away), from pillar to post, pots and pans, rain or shine, to rant and rave, safe and sane, (when all is) said and done, short and sweet, (with) shot and shell, sink or swim, (nothing but) skin and bone, slow but/and sure, snow and ice, song and dance, ways and means, wild and woolly, young and old.*

[44] Private communication of Professor F. G. Lounsbury, who overheard the phrase in Brazil.

Pol. (*szkóda*) *czásu i atłásu* 'waste of time and money' (lit. 'and satin'), (*rozmawiać jak*) *gęś z prosięciem* 'to talk like a goose to a young pig' (= 'conversation de sourds').

## 5. Precedence of A due to internal diffusion.

As the fifth force one may set down internal diffusion, i.e., the imitation of a characteristic segment (either A . . . or . . . B) within the tradition of a single language. The first timid modulations may involve mere variants; once a pair or a cluster has sprung into existence and the sequence falls into an attractive pattern on rhythmic and semantic grounds, the new model stands a more than even chance of provoking imitation of some sort through its appeal to imaginative minds. This inner proliferation is not uniquely peculiar to any language but it seems more strongly pronounced in Germanic than in Romance (and in English than in German).

In a few chosen instances one dimly recognizes the semantic background of a given prepossession, as when the upper parts of the human body (*head, neck, hand*) are granted a privileged position:

> (*over*) *head and ear, from head to foot, head over heels, head and shoulders* (*above*), (*not to make*) *head or tail* (*of*); *neck and crop* (*— and heels, — or nothing*), *hand and foot* (*— and glove*), *hand over head* (*— over fist*), (*on one's*) *hands and knees, from hand to mouth.*

A staple food like *bread* indisputably qualifies for leadership: *bread and butter* (*— cheese, milk, water*).

Elsewhere it is the sheer frequency of certain binomials, in unison with their particularly stimulating contours, that has provoked flurries of imitation among speakers pre-conditioned to this genre or figure. *Hot and cold* served as the common starting-point for such relative newcomers (some of them doubtless ephemeral) as *hot-and-bothered, hot-and-healthy, hot-and-heavy, hot-and-spicy,* with *hot-and-* gradually congealing into a favorite prefix-like segment and B acquiring the desirable proportions of a disyllable stressed on the penult. Antonymous (*to search, in places*) *high and low* blazed the trail for less transparent (nearly synonymous?) *high and dry, high and handsome, high and mighty.* We recall the development of *fair-and-* as being equally dynamic. The molecule *good and* . . . may have cut loose from polarized *good and evil* and from the vigorous phrase (*to shake*) *good and hard,* propagating to *good and ready,* (*for*) *good and all,* and climaxing in *good and made* (*— and sick, — and dead*), (*to be*) *good and finished* (*with*), (*he gave him his*) *good and proper,* in which *good and* is practically tantamount to an adverb ('completely'). *Cut-and-* has failed to advance quite so far, being paired off alternately with past participles *(cut and dried)* and imperatives (obs. *cut and come again*, of meat that cries: "Come cut me!"; and slangy *cut and run*). *Try and . . .* is noteworthy as the colloquial equivalent of standard *try to . . . . (To be) up and walking (climbing,* or any other suitable verb of motion) genetically represents a telescoping of two disparate constructions: *to be up* plus *to be walking;* so potent is the tendency to recruit A and B from the same form-class as to prompt speakers to use *up* participially: *(an) up-and-coming writer,* and even as a fully inflected verb: (coll.) *she ups and gets engaged, they up and shoot themselves* (Rupert Brooke), with *up and* providing a suggestion of 'suddenness, unexpectedness'.[45] An eloquent example of the proliferation of B is: *double, (little —, neck —) or nothing,* with overtones of gambling. Finally, a binomial may be stationed at the intersection of two currents of diffusion; thus, *once and for all* connects, on the one hand, with *once and again (— and away);* on the other, with *(for) one and all (to hear), still and all.* The exact itinerary cannot, of course, be traced without painstaking attention to minute historical detail.[46]

The power of this force is sufficient to overcome adverse rhythmic conditions: *hands and knees* called into being *elbows and knees,* much as *life or death* paved the way for *freedom or death,* though *elbows* and *freedom,* being distinctly longer than their partners, would normally tend to occupy the position of B. In other instances this force overrides considerations of social hierarchy, usually after some struggle: *cat and mouse,* obviously uninvertible, after some oscillation tipped the scales in favor of *cat and dog,* while *cock(s) and hen(s)* prepared the listener for *cock-and-bull (stories):* Without this counterforce one would expect a dog to outrank a cat and a bull to eclipse a cock. Sometimes the connection is oblique: The matching of *hunger and*

---

[45] Otherwise a preposition very rarely matches an adjective; *by and large,* as against trivial *by the by, by and by,* Am.-E. *by and then,* actually involves two adverbs in nautical use: '[alternately] close-hauled and free'.

[46] Similarly the geneticist may feel inclined to examine jointly *back and forth (— and edge), before and after (— and behind), black and blue (— and white), cold and damp (— and wet), (to play) fast-and-easy (— and furious), (the) long-and-short (of it)* beside *(to confer) long and hard, odds and ends* (rare var.: *— and events), over and above (— and beyond).* The cluster *life and soul, life or death, (threat to) life or limb, (the) lives and loves (of . . .), to live and learn, to live and let live* shows a more intricate convolution. *Pen and pencil* and *pen-and-ink (drawing)* may have originated independently, yet buttress each other. Examples from other languages: G. *kurz und gut (— und bündig, — und kernig)* and, in a broader sense, Pol. *to i owo, tędy (i) owędy, tam i zpowrotem;* Sp. *sano y salvo (— y bueno).*

*thirst* (= G. *Hunger und Durst*), rhythmically awkward, derives its justification from *eat and drink*, smooth in every respect and demonstrably influential, since it was expanded into *eat, drink, and be merry*, left its impress on *eat and run*, and exerted lateral pressure on obs. *meat and drink*.

**6. Transmission of sequences through loan translation.** The sixth isolable force engaged in the shaping of sequences is external diffusion, i.e., borrowing via loan translation. Literalism has at all times held sway in organized religion; so a dogma carries with it, across language borders, not only the elements of which it is composed, but, to the very limit to which syntax can be stretched, the design by which these constituents are soldered, cf. the various renditions of *Father, Son, and Holy Ghost*, frequently overruling rhythmic and other considerations. The poetic passages of the Old Testament, saturated with imagery, and the happenings and parables narrated in the Gospel abound in binomials with which many other languages have ever since been resounding: Thus *cherubim* customarily precedes *seraphim*, *milk and honey* sounds so homemade as to remind few speakers of Ex. 3: 8 (Hebr. 'æræṣ zᵉbat ḥālāb ūdᵉbāš), *loaves and fishes* 'material benefits' calls to mind John 6: 9, 26. Lexical clusters and complete proverbial sayings traceable to pagan antiquity, such as *Scylla and Charybdis*, *bread and circuses* (L. *pānem et circēnsēs*), *divide and rule* (L. *dīuide et imperā*), (*the question*) *here and now* (L. *hīc et nunc*) also tend to assume the rôle of fixed binomials, even at the cost of breaking — as does the last-mentioned — a deeply ingrained native preference for a rhythmic model. Captain Bayard (1473–1524), long regarded as the embodiment of chivalric virtues, has gone down in history not only as *le chevalier sans peur et sans reproche*, but also, in German annals, as *der Ritter ohne Furcht und Tadel*, in Spanish, as *el caballero sin miedo y sin tacha*, and in Russian, as *rýcar' bez stráxa i uprëka*, whereas English only partially follows the prototype: *fearless and faultless knight*.[47]

**7. Interplay of the six forces.** The next step after isolating these six forces as best one can is to observe their subtle interplay. It is

---

[47] Playful reduplicative words here excluded from further inquiry are also liable to migration: cf. *mishmash* ~ G. *Mischmasch*, *zigzag* ~ G. *Zickzack*, F. *zigzag*, the international *pingpong*, etc. In the process, their evocative power may be materially reduced. On *zigzag* see my essay "Secondary uses of letters in language", included in this volume (pp. 357 ff.).

not uncommon to recognize two forces pressing jointly in the same direction, as in (*to play*) *cops and robbers, crown and country, drawn and quartered* (2, 4); *to do or die, to make or break* (*a man, one's future*) (3, 4); *black and chartreuse, blue and silver* (4, 5). On the other hand, forces counterbalancing or partially blocking one another are less often and less directly observed in action: Since binomials in many instances are something of a dispensable frill or adornment rather than a strict necessity for the conveyance of messages, they simply may not come into existence unless produced by an ensemble of favorable conditions. At rare intervals the relative magnitude of potentially opposing forces can be indirectly gauged. Thus, the contrast between mandatory *life and/or death* (3) and prevalent *dead or alive* (4) suggests that the quantitative superiority of *alive* over *dead* (in numbers of phonemes, syllables, and morphemes), an excess tending to predetermine its place as Member B, outweighs the latent claim of *dead* to the same position, on semantic or socio-cultural grounds.[48] However, the scanty evidence at hand does not encourage the establishment of any hierarchy — even remotely comparable to Bartoli's areal norms — by virtue of which any of the six forces here isolated would be shown conclusively, i.e. to the point of predictability, to take precedence over the others.

## 16. Areas of Application

A dynamic speech community cheerfully accepting binomials as a welcome embellishment or a nourishing ingredient of oral and written expression may give tremendous impetus to their spread. Just as certain cultures delight in jokes, especially puns, or spice small talk and day-to-day messages with proverbs, riddles, or songs, so others seem to revel in interlarding with binomials actual utterances or the storehouse of available labels. Characteristic of the present-day American scene is the mushrooming use of binomials in all kinds of tags, titles, and names other than those — protected by tradition — of

[48] Attention has been drawn in earlier sections of this chapter to the resolution of some other conflicts, as visible in *elbows and knees, freedom or death, hunger and thirst* (5 suspending 4), and *divide and rule* (6 suspending 4). If subordination of the smaller to the larger unit and of the remote to the near-by be regarded as social conventions, then *chapter and verse* and *hither and yon* (cf. *here and there*) may rank as illustrations of 2 suspending 4; in the case of the latter one may likewise invoke 3 as the driving force. The most elusive of the six forces is 1, whose impact must be laboriously pieced together from fragmentary or lacunary historical evidence. One suspects its share of influence in the case of antirrhythmic *Auto-and-Truck Rentals.*

persons and geographic entities. Business is fully aware of this trend and alive to its challenge, and aggressive advertisement techniques have intensified a hundredfold the resultant "divertimento".

Examples can be picked out at random, if one bothers to scan lists of book titles (especially, but not exclusively, fiction and drama): *Of Men and Marshes, The Old Man and the Sea, Pride and Prejudice*;[49] motion pictures: *Chills and Frills, The Barbarian and the Geisha*; film series: *People and Places*; ballets: *Beauty and the Beast* < F. *La Belle et la Bête*; musicals: *Plain and Fancy*; radio shows: *Bid 'n' Buy*; popular magazines: *Sight and Sound*; trade journals: *Tailor and Cutter* (British); lectures of popular appeal: *Ranch and Range*; non-professional societies: *Pets and Pals*; funds: *Saints and Sinners*; clubs: *Town and Country*; contests: *Love and Life*; firms: *Cut 'n' Curl* (Oakland hairdresser), *Stop* (*Park —*) *and Shop* Market; restaurants: *Owl and Turtle* (San Francisco); coffee-houses: *Cup 'n' Saucer, Sit 'n' Snack* (both in New York); services: *Wash-and-Wear* garments ("we clean 'em, you wear 'em"); miscellaneous catch words used by advertisers: *Nice 'n' Strong* (promoting facial tissues), *Ship and Travel, Shop and Save*.[50] All these labels patently cater to popular taste (note the fashionable substitution of studiedly informal 'n' for academic *and*), and the whole trend ties in with mnemonically effective fancy names of bars and restaurants (*Hotsy-Totsy*), newspaper columns (*Flickety-Flack*; cf. *flic-flac*, the equivalent of G. *klipp, klapp*, and laughter-provoking *rickety*), also of brands and

---

[49] Binomials in book titles are an old convention, especially where they announce the names of the chief protagonists: *Erec et Enide, Calisto y Melibea, Persiles y Sigismunda, Hermann und Dorothea, Ruslán i Ljudmíla, Tristan und Isolde.* Closer to modern taste is the coördination of abstracts (*The Decline and Fall . . . , Dichtung und Wahrheit, Grandeur et servitude . . . , Pride and Prejudice, Sense and Sensibility, Prestuplénije i nakazánije, Vojná i mir*), of emblems (*Le rouge et le noir*), and of categories of persons, suggested by a plural, primarily among Russian novelists (Turgénev's *Ocý i déti* matches Dostojévskij's *Unižennyje i oskorblénnyje*; cf. D. H. Lawrence's *Sons and Lovers* and the contemporary bestseller *The Naked and the Dead*), or by a singular (Moratín's *El viejo y la niña*). What sets off modernism at its least restrained is, first, the infiltration of "flashy" binomials into such fields, ordinarily averse to playfulness and flamboyance, as historically oriented humanities (M. I. Rostóvcev, *Élinstvo i iránstvo . . .* ; Ju. Tynjánov, *Arxaísty i novátory*) and pure science (H. George's *Progress and Poverty* and Herdan's recent *Languages as Choice and Chance*); second, the ever quickening increase in frequency, which cannot be demonstrated without statistic tabulations; and third, the surprise element created by the juxtaposition of words rarely matched in unpretentious discourse (Maugham's *The Moon and Sixpence* and Hemingway's *The Old Man and the Sea*).

[50] The current fashion in American advertising is to avoid the use of a capital in spelling Member B — for the sake of greater intimacy?

manufacturing techniques (*Hi-Fi* [hàjfáj] for *High fidelity records*). A further ramification of no mean importance is the order, especially if it is not alphabetical, in which the names of business partners appear, with B more often than not surpassing A in length: *Funk and Wagnalls*, *Mills and Malan* (co-owners of a Seattle shop), *Rodgers and Hammerstein*.

## 17. Special Stylistic Effects

Aside from their general spicing effect binomials may from time to time be called upon to perform specific duties of no slight concern to the stylistician.

In bilingual environment or among sophisticated users of a language discernibly composed of variegated lexical strains, some held esthetically in higher esteem than others, B may function as the gloss of an A too cryptic to be promptly apprehended or, conversely, as the disguise, the sublimation of an A too plain to satisfy by itself. Such situations, we recall, arose more than once throughout the long birth pangs of literary English.

In a different climate there may develop the fashion — conceivably restricted to certain styles or levels of discourse — of splitting, for emphasis' sake, any fissionable whole. Instead of lumping together (as the situation objectively demanded) all denizens of Burgos refusing hospitality to the Cid, the composer of the oldest extant Spanish epic visibly enjoyed segregating men from women ("mugieres e varones, burgeses e burgesas"); also, on more than one occasion he zestfully substituted for colorless 'nobody' (*nadi*, *ninguno*) the gaudy binomial *moros nin cristianos*.[51] Less than a century later Gonzalo de Berceo perfected this technique of ornamental fission.[52]

The very cohesiveness of an irreversible binomial lends it a cachet of racy folk speech resisting artful elaboration by the literate. And yet masters of elegant English style have succeeded in denting this line of resistance at its most vulnerable point, namely where the identity of A and B neutralizes the issue of reversibility. An ornamental adjective inserted before B, supererogatory by colloquial standards, may embellish such a sequence at the discretion of a writer rhetorically

[51] See *Cantar de Mio Cid*, ed. R. Menéndez Pidal (Madrid, 1908–11; 2d ed., 1944–46), pp. 338, 374, 573, 766.
[52] *Milagros de Nuestra Señora*, ed. Solalinde, quatr. 24 *a–c*: "Quantos que son en mundo justos e peccadores, / coronados e legos, reys e enperadores, / allí corremos todos, vassallos e sennores".

inclined: *day after endless day (went by)*, *(they trudged) mile after weary mile*.[53] I know of no counterparts in other European languages of such gently extendible binomials.

As regards nonliterary style, suffice it to point out the numerous binomials used as effective circumlocutions in the "Australian" rhyming argot which has of late struck roots in the prisons of North America's West Coast.[54] The fundamental code of this argot consists in replacing a given word ("meaning") by two or more words of which the last ordinarily rhymes with it, thus providing the clue. Not all substitute groups are binomials, as here defined, but quite a few are:

> *apple and banana* 'piano', *bacon and eggs* 'legs', *ball and bat* 'hat', *bing and biff* 'siff', i.e. 'syphilis', *bees and honey* 'money', *block and tackle* 'shackle', i.e., 'legiron' or 'handcuff', *boat and oar* 'whore', *bottle and glass* 'arse, buttocks', *bottle and stopper* 'copper', i.e., 'policeman', *brace and bits* 'tits', i.e., 'teats', *bread and jam* 'tram', *brothers and sisters* 'whiskers', *bubble and squeak* 'speak', *bugs and fleas* 'knees', *bull and cow* 'row', *cats and kitties* 'titties', i.e., 'breasts', *chair and cross* 'horse', *cheese and kisses* 'the Mrs.', i.e., 'one's wife', *cheese and spices* 'prices', i.e., 'morning line on horses', *chews and molasses* 'glasses', i.e., 'spectacles', *chip and chase* 'face', etc.

The enormous social range of the deliberately moulded or modified binomial is one of its most salient features, placing it in one class with protean and ubiquitous rhyme and alliteration.[55]

---

[53] This procedure is not without parallel; cf. concise *once in a while* beside more graphic *once in a long while*.

[54] My information is based in its entirety on D. W. Maurer's stimulating and carefully documented article " 'Australian' rhyming argot in the American underworld", *AS*, XIX (1944), 183–195.

[55] Despite its restriction to a small number of better-known languages this paper affords hardly more than a fleeting glimpse of the total problem thus narrowed down. Within this self-imposed limitation numerous side-issues such as the obvious link between *boy and girl*, *East and West* and *boy meets girl*, *East greets West* have been disregarded. Also, only the surface of the available bibliography has been skimmed. In retrospect, attention should particularly be drawn to R. D. Abraham's article "Fixed order of coördinates — a study in comparative lexicography", *MLJ*, XXXIV (1950), 276–287. The value of that study resides in a freshly collected pile of material (five hundred English and four hundred Spanish "coördinates", i.e., binomials, plus a handful of examples from German, French, and Italian thrown in for good measure); in the survey and judicious appraisal of earlier opinions voiced by O. Jespersen (1905), O. Behaghel (1909), F. N. Scott (1913), J. Morawski (1927), and the latter's predecessor C. Salvioni — all of them staunch supporters of rhythmic hypotheses and Morawski also a keen student of characteristic successions of sounds; and in his broad counter-proposal to the effect that an interplay of rhythmic and semantic forces determines the configuration of each formula. Less cogent, as the author himself admits in a series of candid disclaimers and retractions (285 f.),

## 18. Concluding Remarks

In recent years, linguistic science has been experimenting on a generous scale with new delimitations and fresh groupings of facts. Essentially each proponent has had to show cause why his suggestion deserved attention, first, by arguing the inner logic of the segmentation advocated, its freedom from circularity and inconsistency (this point needs no restatement); and second, by defending its wisdom, the direct benefit scholarship may reap from its acceptance, and the

---

is his proposed array of nine categories of semantic preference: "The desirable usually precedes the undesirable, the more important the less important, the light the dark, the masculine the feminine, the positive the negative, the principal the subsidiary, the greater the smaller, the near the far, the top the bottom, the present the future" (284). Abraham cites many noteworthy examples here omitted, e.g. *bride and groom, dot and dash, flint and steel, Pat and Mike, push and pull, tall and thin,* and documents a few colorful "quadruplets" and even one "quint": *peanuts, popcorn, crackerjack, and candy*; Sp. *amar, honrar, cuidar y obedecer*; (Cub.) *Fulano, Zutano, Mengano y Esperancejo*; *(vinieron) Pedro, Pablo, Chucho, Jacinto y José* 'everybody came'.

Here are some additional bibliographic clues. L. Spitzer, "Estudios etimológicos", *AILC*, II (1942–44), 14, adduces some Latin "fórmulas bimembres... usuales en donaciones y testamentos". For Spanish W. Beinhauer, "Beiträge zu einer spanischen Metaphorik", *RF*, LV (1941), 1–56, 184–206, offers a storehouse of information (esp. 8, 17, 28, 30, 34, 39 f., 46 f., 191); on *corriente y moliente,* originally applied to smoothly running millstones, see M. Herrero, *RFE*, XXVII (1943), 93 f. E. Lommatzsch's Introduction (dated 1915) to Tobler-Lommatzsch, *Altfranzösisches Wörterbuch,* I (Berlin, 1925), pp. xiii-xiv, lists groups such as *bec a bec, bien et bel, ne tite ne mite, tost et isnelement,* etc.; many pertinent passages have been examined in other contexts, cf. M. Roques, *Rom.,* LXXIII (1952), 194 (*Erec*); E. R. Curtius, *ZRPh.,* LXVIII (1952), 187 (*Girart de Viene*), and M. Dubois' review, in *RPh.,* XIV, 336ff., of A. Burger's Villon vocabulary. The Italian scene was surveyed in C. Salvioni's masterly review (*GSLI*, XXXIX [1902], 366–391) of R. L. Taylor, *Alliteration in Italian* (New Haven, 1900); for new bits of information see S. Heinimann, "Einige affektische Verstärkungen der Negation im Italienischen", *VR,* XI (1950), 189–201(esp. 190, 194, 200), and F. Ageno, "Premessa a un repertorio di frasi proverbiali", *RPh.* XIII (1959–60), 242–264. Spitzer's stylistic approach, in terms of affectivity (hysteron proteron; see *Aufsätze zur romanischen Syntax und Stilistik* [Halle, 1918], pp. 274–280), was sharply rejected by K. Ringenson ("*Dies et diurnum*", *SN,* X [1937–38], 33 f. and 46). A purely literary opposition, such as Med. L. (12th-century) *nani et gigantes* (J. de Ghellinck, *ALMA,* XVIII [1945], 25–29), need not have left any linguistic reflex. Interesting side-issues include the use of onomatopoeia: "nec *mu* nec *ma* argutas" (Petronius, 57.8; A. Ernout: 'Tu ne sais dire ni *a* ni *b*'), cf. OProv. *ni bat ni but,* etc. (I. Frank, "*Babariol — babarian* dans Guillaume IX", *Rom.,* LXXIII [1952], 229); the loss of meaning suffered by a loan translation, as when G. *das A und das O* lamely imitates *alpha and omega*; the suggestive shape of certain fictional names, such as Gogol's *Ljápkin-Tjápkin*; the slightly archaic overtone — a potential source of elegance — attaching to *peu ou prou, sans feu ni lieu* in modern French (cf. M. Bataillon, *BH,* LIV [1952], 290, 323).

amount of concessions and adjustments that this acceptance may entail.

To begin with the latter, irreversible binomials, not unlike the tonesetting varieties of hypercharacterization,[56] represent one of several features transcending the minimum bounds of linguistic economy and therefore serving the needs of expression much more than those of bare communication. In a cross-section of a language model they may claim a not inconspicuous place at or near the border-line between tightly structured grammar and loosely connected lexicon. Denude a language of its share of uninvertible binomials, and its "mechanism" can still be manipulated with reasonable efficiency; but it will have lost much of its rich orchestration. This is doubly true because binomials happen to be so closely inter-twined with other supporting devices through a system of alliances ("concomitancies") that any attempt to strip a language of them would unfailingly produce a far-reaching chain reaction.

The operational advantage of pressing into service binomials as here defined consists in that numerous loose ends disappear and that facts long deemed too elusive or accidental to warrant serious atten-tion suddenly fall into tidy patterns, complex and partially over-lapping, to be sure, but nonetheless confirmed by each new finding.

Binomials can be satisfactorily examined within the framework of grammar at its austerest. But the results of the analysis become incomparably richer and scarcely less precise if one takes into account not only the morphological skeleton, but also the semantic, stylistic, and broadly cultural pulp and teguments.[57]

---

[56] See *ArL*, IX (1957), 79–113; X (1958), 1–36.

[57] [Aside from eliciting a few standard reviews, notably those by G. Gougenheim (*BSLP*, LVIII: 2 [1963], 154) and N. P. Sacks (*HR*, XXX [1962], 342 f.), this paper has received sustained attention on the part of two scholars: D. L. Bolinger, "Binomials and pitch accent", *Lingua*, XI (1962), 33-44, and the late U. Weinreich, in the second of his three lectures — jointly titled "Problems in the analysis of idioms" — which were delivered at the 1966 Linguistic Institute hosted by the University of California, Los Angeles, and which are to be included, after due revision, in the volume now in press (ed. J. Puhvel) embodying most forum lectures of that vintage.]

# 13
# Secondary Uses of Letters in Language

## 1. Preliminaries

THE primary use of the letters of the alphabet requires no comment. The history of script in general, and of the alphabet in particular, has of late produced a spate of valuable books, varying in scope, emphasis, and level of presentation;[1] in these monographs and in earlier treatises alphabetic writing has been quite properly contrasted with alternative preferences for hieroglyphics (and other pictographs), cuneiform characters, syllabaries, ideo- or logographs, and other media of written communication. The common denominator of all these vehicles for recording ordinary speech and other forms of discourse is the strict limitation of writing to the task of perpetuating preëxistent modes of actual language. As a result, it

Originally published, in much shorter form, in *Romance Philology*, XIX (1965–66), 1–27; reprinted — unrevised and spread over two installments — in Vol. I (1967) of *The Journal of Typographic Research.* © 1965 by The Regents of the University of California.

[1]D. Diringer, *L'alfabeto nella storia della civiltà* (Florence, 1937); id., *The Alphabet, a Key to the History of Mankind* (New York, 1948; rev. ed., 1951), and *Collier's Encyclopedia*, ed. 1964, I, s.v. *Alphabet*; J. Février, *Histoire de l'écriture* (Paris, 1948, see É. Benveniste, *BSLP*, XLV:2 (1949), 29–31; rev. ed., 1957); I. J. Gelb, *A Study of Writing; the Foundation of Grammatology* (Chicago, 1952; rev. ed., 1963); G. R. Driver, *Semitic Writing from Pictograph to Alphabet* (London, 1948; rev. ed., 1954); J. Friedrich, *Entzifferung verschollener Schriften und Sprachen* (Berlin-Göttingen-Heidelberg, 1954) — with special reference to the ancient East (for criticism see É. Benveniste, *BSLP*, LIII:2 [1957–58], 52 f.); M. Cohen, *La grande invention de l'écriture et son évolution* (2 vols.; Paris, 1958) beside *L'écriture* (Paris [1953]) and the same scholar's severely negative review (in *BSLP*, XLV:2 [1949], 31 f.) of J. Bonnaert, *Petite histoire de l'alphabet* (Brussels, 1949); H. Jensen, *Die Schrift in Vergangenheit und Gegenwart* (Berlin, 1958; orig. *Geschichte der Schrift* [Glückstadt, 1925]). For a popular presentation of certain angles see also P. E. Cleator, *Lost Languages* (London, 1959; paperback, New York, 1962); cf. the review by W. Winter in *RPh.*, XVIII (1964–65), 124 f. Aggressively popular in tone and chiefly concerned with non-verbal messages is L. Hogben's *From Cave Painting to Comic Strip; a Kaleidoscope of Human Communication* (London, 1949). On one variety of "pre-script" (ritualistic pictography) see M. Griaule and G. Dieterlen, *Signes graphiques soudanais* (Paris, 1951): "Mais à aucun moment il ne s'agit proprement d'une écriture, d'un procédé de communication" (Benveniste, *BSLP*, XLVII:2 [1951], 261).

has been axiomatic with many linguists that script and print serve to reflect and to preserve the given stage of a language, without ever seriously interfering with its growth.

There exist, however, several additional, increasingly important functions of the letters which fail to meet these qualifications. Though some of these functions are limited to specific languages, most cut across speech communities, literary traditions, graphemic systems, and — broadly speaking — cultures. Of these concomitant uses the present paper, panchronic in its general orientation, aims to provide a bird's-eye view, stressing those functions which — counter to assertions so frequently repeated — do tend to influence languages, increasing or otherwise modifying their actual store of resources. It would be an exaggeration to affirm that writing systems are glottogonic, that they are apt to give rise to wholly new varieties of speech. But it is defensible to contend that under favorable circumstances ingredients of a graphemic apparatus may percolate into the spoken language, which that apparatus was initially called upon to merely represent.

Not all the derivative functions of letters will be included in our survey, because some transcend the matrix of language proper. The names of the letters — not infrequently in keen rivalry with numerals — have been put to excellent use in certain highly technical notations and elaborate systems of labels. In particular, musical nomenclature as favored throughout the English- and German-speaking countries (with noteworthy antecedents in classical Greek: A, B Γ, Δ, . . . 2d c. B.C.; Byz. π A, B ου . . .) and international scientific terminology (especially its logico-mathematical and chemical branches) both make ample, neatly defined use of conventional letters. In fact, there have emerged traditions for distinguishing between Latin and Greek fonts (the latter ordinarily reserved for angles, in geometry, and for rays, in exact sciences) and, within each font, for contrasting capitals with lower-case characters (e.g., points vs. lines). In symbolic logic imaginative scholars have lately drawn on a wide selection of traditional as well as newly devised characters. Only at rare intervals do we expect to cross the path of mathematicians in the course of this paper, however.[2]

[2] One special aspect — inviting separate study — of the relation of letter to cipher is the widespread use of the former for numerals. In most instances one observes the substitution of one set or progression (alphabetic order) for another (succession of numbers), e.g. in Hebrew, in Arabic — to the extent that a modified version of Indic numerals has not been adopted instead, along the eastern fringe

Even closer to home the humanist must narrow his choice. As is well known, letters and numbers played a signal rôle in magic formulas and in medieval mysticism, both Christian and Jewish. One cannot appreciate the recondite meaning of some Dante

of the domain —, and in Old Church Slavic, including its adaptation to the needs of Old Rumanian. The Romans, on the other hand, tolerated a mixed system, using certain capital letters as downright abbreviations, e.g. C = *centum*, M = *mille*, while allowing I = 1, V = 5, L = 50, and D = 500 to stand apart.

Similarly, where the current system of foliation or pagination forces us to intermingle letters and numerals, the former category may involve abbreviations (fol. 12r° = 12 *recto*) or may, on a more abstract plateau, symbolize mere succession (p. 128c = p. 128, 3rd column from left). In references to poetry, a combination such as 57 *f* means: 'strophe 57, line 6'.

Letters and numerals compete strongly in modern city planning and environmental design, with Washington D.C. emerging as a classic grid of radial streets alphabetical AND numerical. Further incidental points of contact between letters and numerals: composite identifications in automobile plates, in a cumbersome system of telephone numbers now rapidly becoming obsolete (e.g.: LA[ndscape]5-0839), etc.; oblique, euphemistic references to obscene, i.e. socially controversial or restricted, words through exclusive mention of the number of letters contained (Am.-E. "four-letter words"), cf. n. 49, below; allusive, circumlocutional substitution of 'number of letters contained in the alphabet' for the specific figure, as in the following passage from the Florentine historiographer Giovanni Villani's *Nuova Cronica* (1st half of 14th c.): "Fe' edificare tante badie quante lettere ha nell'a,b,c" (see R. Accademia d'Italia, *Vocabolario* . . ., A-C [Milan, 1941], p. 10a).

Grading of accomplishment may be by letter (American system: A through F) or by number; in the latter eventuality, the top quality may be marked by the lowest number (German system: 1) or by the highest number (Russian system: 5 = *pjatërka*) within the range set aside for this purpose. There exist combinations of the two competing systems, e.g. A1 'supreme quality'; conceivably this particular prefixation of A has spilled over into the parlance of astronauts: A-o.k. In American collegiate slang grades are given names: A→Ace, B→Bomb, C→Cook (var. *Hook*, in deference to that letter's stark curve); these nouns, in turn, give rise to verbs: *I bombed that exam, he cooked that course.* The usage is very fluid.

Concerning cabalistic numerology and its linguistic echoes in Hebrew-Yiddish, let me quote verbatim from a memorandum by the late U. Weinreich, my principal authority in this domain: "First, it was extremely common from the beginning of printing until recently to give the printing date of a book (on its title page) by means of a Biblical phrase the numerical values of whose letters added up to the number of the year. With maximum ingenuity and luck, the calculation was exact and the phrase suitable in spirit to the content of the book. A cruder variation of this device was to take a suitable phrase and print selected letters of it in larger type, the sum of the selected letters adding up to the year. Calculation by means of letters, whether for purposes of divination or others, is known in Hebrew and Yiddish as *gimátriye*, an (Aramaic?) adaptation of Gr. *geometria* with a strange shift in meaning. The system is, I think, quite well known to lay Yiddish speakers and forms a background for a peculiar genre of numerological punning. Thus, because the words *gelt* and *blote* yield the same numerical values (112), the independently developed proverb, *Gelt iz blote* 'money is nothing' can be underpinned by a numerological motivation: «Gelt» *iz begimátriye* ['numerologically'] «*blote*»." Could it be that geometry and geomancy have been here confused?

passages without reference to this material, and one will be hard put to savor fully the short story *El Aleph* by the contemporary Argentine writer Jorge Luis Borges without a measure of familiarity with the cabalistic tradition.[3] Again, in the realm of literary whims and experiments one discovers several that have indirect bearing on our problem, as when a few figures of the Renaissance, equating (as was then the custom) letters and sounds, arbitrarily declared one or two such symbols unbearably ugly and proceeded to expel them from their writings;[4] a policy adopted (this time, to be sure, in a facetious key) by the American humorist James Thurber in *The Wonderful "O"* (1957).[5] The reason for these voluntary retrenchments is that letters as carriers of sound form part of literary topic and stylistic ornamentation, but hardly of language proper.

One additional deduction: It is of course true that designations of the letters of the alphabet — though no longer so heavily fraught with meaning in the modern languages as they were in, say, Hebrew and Phoenician, where *bet* meant 'house', *gimmel* 'camel', and *dalet*

[3] On Dante one of the latest treatments is by R. Dragonetti, *Aux frontières du langage poétique: études sur Dante, Mallarmé, Valéry* (Rom. Gand., IX; Ghent, 1961), pp. 81–92; cf. K. D. Uitti's perceptive analysis in *R.Ph.*, XVIII (1964–65), 117–124, esp. 119 and n. 5. The mystical and symbolic meanings ascribed to letters by cabalists are examined by J. Abelson, *Jewish Mysticism* (London, 1913), pp. 98–106. On one mid-20th-century echo see L. A. Murillo, "The Labyrinths of Jorge Luis Borges, an Introduction to the Stories of the Aleph", *MLQ*, XX (1959), 259–266.

Major bibliographical items in the broad field of magic: F. Dornseiff, *Das Alphabet in Mystik und Magie* (Leipzig and Berlin, 1922); K. Preisendanz, *Papyri graecae magicae* (Leipzig and Berlin, 1928–31); P. Kraus, *Jābir ibn Ḥayyān: Contribution à l'histoire des idées scientifiques dans l'Islam*, 2 vols., Mémoires de l'Institut d'Égypte (Caire), XLIV (1943) and XLV (1942); F. Cabrol, *Dictionnaire d'archéologie chrétienne et de liturgie*, s.vv. *abécédaire, alphabet*, etc.

[4] This attitude was abetted by the desire of many literati to identify their vernacular as closely as possible with Latin, viewed as the supreme model of elegance. See E. Buceta, "La tendencia a identificar el español con el latín", *HMP*, I (1925), 85–108, and "Composiciones hispano-latinas en el siglo XVII", *RFE*, XIX (1932), 388–414; cf. R. Lapesa, *Historia de la lengua española*, 4th ed. (Madrid, 1959), pp. 202–205. A useful florilegium of such encomia was prepared by a student of A. Castro and P. Sáinz Rodríguez: J. F. Pastor, *Las apologías de la lengua castellana en el Siglo de Oro* (Madrid, 1929).

[5] As a pure "jeu d'esprit" or literary exercise, without any recourse to heavy-handed justifications either esthetic or "genealogical" (purity of descent, etc.), such experiments of commission or omission have been carried on in Romance countries at distinctly later dates. Thus Rubén Darío, while still a resident of Nicaragua, wrote a short story ("Amar hasta fracasar") in which he shunned all vowels except *a* (some experts question the authenticity of this attribution); as late as May 1950, H. F. Miri published in the Argentine journal *El Hogar* the story "Querer es perecer", from which he mock-pedantically banned all vowels save *e*.

'gate'[6] — in other respects constitute members of the total lexicon and, grammatically, of a certain form-class and are thus subject to given rules of comportment. Speakers have to decide on their gender (this has long been a controversial issue in France no less than in modern Greece, and standard Italian preferences, based on an artificial norm, fail to match those of Tuscan proper) and on the formation of their plural in speech and script ("two *t*'s", alternatively spelled: "two T's"). In terms of affixation, the names of letters may act as the heads of small word-families referring to idiosyncratic defects and provincialisms of speech, e.g. Cl.-Gr. *rōtakízō* 'to make excessive or improper use of /r/' and Byz. *rōtakismós* 'pronunciation of [r] as [γ]', Sp. *cecear* 'to lisp' (hence *ceceo* 'lisping' [n.], *ceceante* 'id.' [adj.]), R. *a-kat'* vs. *o-kat'* 'to pronounce as *a* or *o* an unstressed sound marked by *o* in standard spelling' (flanked by the abstracts *akanje* and *okanje*), etc.[7] Grammatically similar, if semantically different, are *chiasmus*, a term of rhetoric, and *lambdoeidés* 'suture of the human skull'. One may entertain legitimate doubts as to the propriety of calling this use "secondary".

To the extent that folklore and literature utilize and even maximize certain latent or weakly developed possibilities of linguistic exploitation of the letters, their eloquent testimony will be welcomed. Yet where verbal artists determinedly cut off their links with common

[6] The Western world has of late unexpectedly witnessed a partial return to the paleo-Semitic system since, for reasons of enhanced clarity or as a mnemonic device, letters have again — optionally or mandatorily — become associated with certain key words. This elaboration occurs in the spelling-out of unfamiliar names (particularly over the telephone in long-distance calls), in all kinds of signalling messages, in labelling outposts (as when the U.S. Army favors the tags *Abel*, *Baker*, *Charlie*, *Dog* . . . , while the Alabama National Guard prefers *Alpha*, *Bravo*, *Charlie*, *Delta* . . . ,), etc. See *The New Yorker* of April 10, 1965, p. 128*b*. Granted that the association of a letter and a word which it ushers in is most familiar from a primer (cf. *The Infant's Alphabet* [Philadelphia, c. 1824]): "Was an *Angler*, and a Fish he caught,/Was a *Bird* that for *Betsey* was bought,/Was a *Cutter*, that sailed on the main", etc.), the same device — in our age of search for artistic immediacy, for hard-hitting abstractness, and, sometimes, for infantilism— may invade adult poetry, as in this poem by Claribel Alegría: "Sale rugiendo/el camión/de la bodega./Bramando cuesta arriba/sofoca la lección:/*A* de *alcoholismo*,/ *B* de *bohío*,/*C* de *cárcel*,/ *D* de *dictadura*,/*E* de *ejército*,/*F* de *feudo* de catorce familias/ . . ." ("Documental", *Casa de las Américas*, N° 32, Sept.–Oct. 1965, p. 81).

[7] On *ceceo*, *ciceo*, *siseo*, and many related terms, either traceable to Renaissance grammarians and orthoepists or coined by modern analysts of their teachings, see A. Alonso, *De la pronunciación medieval a la moderna en español*, ed. R. Lapesa, I (Madrid, 1955), 91–450, passim; cf. my review in *RPh.*, IX (1955–56), 237–252, and several elaborative papers by D. Catalán Menéndez-Pidal.

experience and its correlates in spoken and written language, in-
dulging flights of unfettered imagination, the privacy of their individual worlds will be here respected through discreet silence. The
celebrated sonnet "Vowels" by that daring visionary Arthur Rimbaud
is a case in point:[8] Undeniably it involves the use of certain letters
(or sounds? — The margin of doubt is significant . . .) in polished,
highly personal art, but the thread connecting the poet's synesthetic
hallucinations with patterns of accepted usage, or even with any
conceivable sublimation of these patterns, is so tenuous that the
most esoterically minded among his peers will not henceforth be
called to the witness stand:

> A noir, E blanc, I rouge, U vert, O bleu: voyelles / je dirai quelque
> jour vos naissances latentes. / A, noir corset velu des mouches éclatantes
> / Qui bombinent autour des puanteurs cruelles, // Golfes d'ombre;
> E, candeurs des vapeurs et des tentes, / lances des glaciers fiers, rois
> blancs, frissons d'ombelles; / I, pourpres, sang craché, rire des lèvres
> belles / dans la colère ou les ivresses pénitentes. //

What then remains under consideration after such drastic
curtailment?[9]

---

[8] For this piece no accurate date is available; it is usually included with the
precocious poet's "Poésies" (1869–71) and thus antecedes by a margin of forty
years the pictorial use of letters and near-words in still lifes by the generation of
Picasso. To the bulging literature on this celebrated poem add V. E. Graham,
"Rimbaud's *Voyelles*", *Kentucky For. Lg. Quart.*, XI (1964), 192–199. Less
widely known is the fact that Mallarmé, in private life if not in his writings, also
associated vowels with color impressions, an idiosyncrasy shared by his disciple
P. Valéry. Cf. this entry in Valéry's diary (10.X.1891), recording a confession of
Mallarmé's presumably made at their first meeting: "*A* vermillon, *u* bleu-vert
[P.V.: moi aussi], *o* noir, etc.". The diary was opened at this page on the occasion
of the "Paul Valéry pre-Teste" Exhibit. (Univ. of Paris, Dec. 1966), Specimen 120.
    As was to be expected, Rimbaud has found a host of followers, including
J. Weinheber (1892–1945), "Ode an die Buchstaben"; for one incisive comment
on Valle-Inclán's fanciful embroidery on the "luminous" and "morally wholesome" quality of *A*, etc., see P. G. Earle's critique of a collection of essays by
R. J. Sender in *NRFH*, X (1958), 447–449, esp. n. 1. Undeservedly forgotten,
on the other hand, is Goethe's facetious short piece "Séance" (ca. 1797), in which
a riotous assembly of three orders of letter-sounds which have achieved varying
degrees of autonomy (vowels, consonants, certain consonantal digraphs) is
depicted in an effort to ridicule the unproductive session of a contemporary
German academy.
    [9] I also deliberately leave out of reckoning the many-pronged issue of spelling
pronunciations. The initial step is ordinarily the enforcement of an etymological
spelling, which may involve an etymology judged by hindsight as correct (OF
*doit* 'finger' > mod. *doigt*, in forgivable deference to DIGITUS) or false (OF *pois*
'weight' > mod. *poids*, in unwarranted deference to PONDUS, the actual base
being PĒNSUM, cf. Sp. *peso*); see G. Gougenheim, "La fausse étymologie savante",

## 2. Identification of Relevant Secondary Uses

One derivative use, sharply contrasted with all the others, relates to the CONVENTIONAL ARRANGEMENT of letters in standard alphabetic order. Two kinds of sequences come to mind. On the one hand, the brusque juxtaposition of the initial and final links in an extended chain serves to evoke 'totality' in phraseological or paroemiological context (It. *dall' «a» alla zeta*). On the other, a deftly chosen segment of the chain, pronounced as a single lexical unit, may convey a special message, as when *alphabet*, *ABC*, and their counterparts have come to designate the very institution of the alphabet (or the primer from which it is taught or else, figuratively, the content of that primer: the rudiments of any discipline, the basic facts; cf. the Madrid daily *ABC* and, ironically, Denmark's fairly recent musical review *A.B.C.*). Not all such latent possibilities have reached fruition: While $x$, $y$, and $z$ are individually used in mathematical equations for carefully hierarchized unknowns,[10] laymen have apparently felt no need for amalgamating them into a single word (*$XYZ$*) conveying some such message as 'triad of unknowns'.

The second use, most trivial of all, involves ABBREVIATIONS. Under favorable circumstances, these may lead to the crystallization of linguistically autonomous units where two or more letters, carved out from one word or, more frequently, from several successive

[10] Historically, the tentative choice of $x$ as a symbol for the prime unknown is due not to the position of the given letter within the alphabet, but to the fact that in Hispano-Arabic rendition $x$- /š/ happened to be the initial letter of the Oriental key-word for '(some)thing' (*šajš*). But the lasting success of the abbreviation may independently be attributed to the smooth expansibility of the pattern within the terminal segment of the standard European alphabet. Conversely, the abbreviation $N$ for 'any, unidentified'←NESCIŌ, eminently successful in mathematics, turned out to be conspicuously less so in language, though Russian classics would use $N$ as an equivalent of Western $X$, e.g. (*gospodin*) $N$. 'Mr. X', *v gorode N*. 'in a town to be left unnamed'. The serializing power of $X$ is not without parallel: Sp. *fulano* 'so-and-so, Mr. X', of transparently Arabic parentage (cf. Hebr. *pᵉlōnī*), generated a close-knit sequence: *çutano* 'Mr. Y' and either *mengano* or *perengano* 'Mr. Z'; all adventitious members of this series are etymologically opaque. Further elaborations may lead to quadripartite structures, e.g. Cub. *Fulano, Zutano, Mengano y Esperancejo*. Cf. p. 397, below.

*RPh.*, I (1947–48), 277–286. The actual pronunciation need not be affected by a pretentious or would-be-erudite spelling; Br.-E. /nevju/ perpetuates OF *nev-out*, *-eut* < NEPŌTE, but Am.-E. /nefju/ goes further in adjusting itself to the arbitrary spelling *ph*. The whole problem has been carefully surveyed for Modern French (V. Buben, *Influence de l'orthographe sur la prononciation du français moderne* [Bratislava, 1935]). In postclassical Spanish such Latinizing graphies as *digno, columna* (for older *dino, coluna*) are likely to have functioned as wedges for the actual re-introduction into spoken Spanish of the clusters *-gn-* and *-mn-*.

words, come alive as a new, easily pronounceable unit, such as
G. *BZ*/*Bɛcɛt*/←*B*(*erliner*) *Z*(*eitung*) *am Mittag* (a famous inter bella
venture), Fr. *URSS* /ürs/ vs. R. *SSSR* /èsèsèsèr/, Am.-E. (1964)
*SNCC* /snɪk/ and older /keo/ '(to) knock out'. These examples
clearly constitute a mixed bag, according to whether the full name
of the letter is involved, its phonetic value alone is at issue, or appeal
is made in actual pronunciation to sounds not at all represented in
the written form; the second possibility is known as an acronym.
This acronymic variety is ancient, boasting precedents in the
medieval Hebrew tradition (*tenak* 'Bible', RAMBAM 'Maimonides'),
but has of late gained tremendously in momentum.[11]

In the third use, which is spreading even more rapidly at this
moment under the combined pressure of science, industry, commerce, and modernity cultivated as a style, the SHAPE of a letter
(typically, the printed capital) furnishes a handy frame of reference:
*A-beam*, *S-curve*, *T-shirt*. The SIZE rather than the configuration
is at issue in the phrase *not an iota* (or, on a more vernacular level,
*not a jot or tittle*, the latter a cognate of Sp. *tilde*; the ultimate source
is Matth. 5:18; in papyri, *iota* designates the stroke on a sun dial).
What sets off this function from the two preceding ones is the
characteristic limitation to a single letter — a feature likewise peculiar
to the remainder of the functions here surveyed.

The fourth use — latent rather than real or, at best, vestigially
documented — refers, strictly speaking, to sounds rather than to
their graphic representations. But given the widespread equation
of sound and letter, even among highly literate and tone-setting
members of western societies, and given the further fact that the

---

[11] Such abbreviations as involve the first and the last letter of a word (*Dr.* =
*Doctor*, *Mr.* = *Mister*, *Mt.* = *Mount*, *Sr.* = *Señor*, *vs.* = *versus*), or the first
letter and the concluding segment (*Mlle* = *Mademoiselle*, *Mme* = *Madame*),
or else the first and the last letter plus some central pillar for additional support
(*Bldg.* = *Building*, *Mgr.* = *Manager*, *Msgr.* = *Monsignor*, *Mrs.* = *Mistress*) tend
to remain strictly graphic and seldom come alive as elements of speech in their
own right. British spelling favors setting them apart through the omission of a
period, thus: *Dr* = *Doctor*, as against *Dr.* = *Drive*. There also exists a Western
tradition for abbreviating in written form the Latin word, but actually reciting
its local vernacular equivalents, for writing, that is (in a German-speaking country,
say), *p.* and reading it *Seite*, or for interpreting (in the British sphere of influence)
*viz.* as *namely*. All these uses are at the opposite pole of those here examined.
The highly abstract character of abbreviations is eloquently demonstrated by the
frequent marking of the plural through reduplication — purely graphic, never
phonic (E. *pp.*←*pages*; Sp. *EE. UU.*←*Estados Unidos*; internationally: §§←
*paragraphs*).

near-phonemic script favored in certain influential communities makes this deeply rooted confusion venial, it seems marginally permissible to invoke, by way of short-cut, the acoustic value attached to a letter, or simply the ACOUSTIC IMAGE of that letter. Since metaphoric qualifiers have from Antiquity surrounded the discussion of sounds (*gracilis* lit. 'thin', *pinguis* lit. 'fat', etc.), one might expect to discover, in phraseological inventories, at least a few traces of "letter-sounds" used as congealed frames of reference;[12] free-wheeling poets striving to escape from the boredom of stereotypes may have advanced much farther.

The fifth use involves neither the delineation of the written character, nor the impact on the ear-drum and nerve system of the actual speech sound which that character symbolizes, but the highly conventional LABEL given to both in spelling-out aloud, reciting the alphabet, and other verbal identifications of "letter-sounds". These labels show varying cross-linguistic diversity (the discrepant designations of *h*, *j*, *q*, *x*, *y*, and *z* are notoriously difficult to keep apart for the polyglot). Under favorable conditions they acquire a certain vitality of their own, which may be vindicated in facetious or intimate context: puns, rebus-like puzzles, veiled statements (*IOU* = *I owe you*), and so forth.

The various categories here isolated are not rigidly delimited in real life; there exist all kinds of transitions and overlaps, some of them on an international scale. Thus, in a phrase like *Mind your p's and q's!* 'be meticulously careful!' the prime reference is to the (perilously similar) shapes of the two letters at issue — a resemblance entailing the need for extra tidiness (cf. *dot every i*) —, i.e., to the "third use"; but the effectiveness of the saying is enhanced by the fact that *p* and *q* occur consecutively in alphabetical order ("first use"). In contrast, note the relative colorlessness of the Ptg. idiom *fazer q.c. com todos os "ff" e "rr"* 'fazê-la com a maior perfeição'.

---

[12] The power of the metaphor in phonetic nomenclature has recently been explored by Iván Fónagy, *A metafora a fonetikai münyelvben* (Budapest, 1963). The book is also available in German translation: *Die Metaphern in der Phonetik; ein Beitrag zur Entwicklungsgeschichte des wissenschaftlichen Denkens* (The Hague, 1963); appended to it is an important bibliography transcending the bounds of phonetics. See M. Mayrhofer's review in *Die Sprache*, X (1964), 117 f., with a reference to late medieval ballads on the *ABC*, as studied by E. Lommatzsch, *Miscellanea Academica Berolinensia*, II:1 (1950), 172. In the mid-'fifties the late Harvard scholar R. Poggioli, interestingly, toyed with the parallel idea of devoting a book-length monograph to the impact of the metaphor on the habitual phrasing of literary analysis ("flowering", "current", "influence", "vogue", "peak", etc.).

Again abbreviations can be very artfully devised, as when the University of California's Committee for Art and Lectures at Berkeley calls itself *CAL* (a name generations of students have used as the affectionate designation of the campus itself), echoing in this respect the nationally known *AID* ( = *Agency for International Development*), *CARE*, and *SPUR*. A pioneering example of this use (1919) is the title of the ephemeral French avant-garde journal *SIC — Sons-idées-couleurs*.[13] As abbreviations (acronyms) these forms basically illustrate the second use; concomitantly they display the stylistic value of the fifth use, however. Another sophisticated arrangement, which selects the letters in the order of their appearance in the alphabet, simplifies memorization; when this mnemonic aim is achieved, the first and the second use are simultaneously pressed into service.

### 3. Segments of the Alphabetic Array

The succession of the letters in those conventional alphabets (Greek, Latin and Standard European, Church Slavic, etc.) which ultimately hark back to the Hebrew-Phoenician tradition has left characteristic reflexes: lexical, phraseological, and paroemiological.

Lexically most noteworthy are the designations of the alphabet itself, based either on the first two letters of such scripts as Hebrew-Yiddish (*alefbeys*), Greek (*alphabet*), and Cyrillic (Ch.-Sl. and R. *azbuka*), or as many as three: G. *ABC* /abece/, E. *ABC* /ebisi/, OF *abeçoi* 'primer', F. *abécé* (since 13th cent.), Sp. *abecé* (one of the earliest attestations: *Cancionero de Baena*). There is a strong presumption that OSp. *abze* (vars. *abce, auze, alze*) 'fate, luck', invariably feminine, and OGal.-Ptg. *avezi, avizi*, which in conjunction with *boõ* and *mau* meant '(un)lucky', reflect L. *ABC* stressed ábecè and interpreted in the semantic context of ancient magic (cf. E. to *spell* alongside to *cast an evil spell*).[14] The use of the four

---

[13] It was edited by P. A. Birot; see *TLS*, 18.11.1965, p. 121. The year 1921 witnessed the foundation of the *P.E.N. Club*, with dual allusion (a) to *p(oets)*, *e(ssayists)*, *n(ovelists)* and (b) to the *pen* as a writing tool.

[14] *Auze* occurs in *Mio Cid*, vv. 1523, 2366, 2369, — also in *Santo Domingo*, 420c (*por su auze mala*); *abçe* in *Signos*, 26b (*por su abçe mala*); *auçe* in *Milagros*, 778a; the *Alexandre* wavers between *alze* (*mala*) (O, 545a) and *abze* (P, 557). The only derivative on record is traceable to Berceo: "Por end(e) te diçen todas las gentes bien *auzada*" (*Loores*, 137d). The Old Galician *Cantigas* contain such sequences as "um home (o demo) *avezimau*", "um mouro *avizimau*". The Old Portuguese version of the Arthurian *Demanda* enriches the inventory by *aveziboo* 'venturoso, feliz, próspero'; the lifespan of *avezimao* extended to the period of Gil Vicente.

SECONDARY USES OF LETTERS IN LANGUAGE 367

initial letters has also left vestiges: F. *abécédé*, Sp. *abecedario* (1578), Fr. *abécédaire* (16th cent.: G. Tory, adj. and n.) from Late L.

In ancient Spain, then, *auze*, restricted to a few formulaic combinations, was still dimly recognizable as a noun; along the Atlantic Coast it merged with its stereo-typed qualifiers 'good' and 'bad' to form a sharply polarized pair of compound adjectives.

One finds a plethora of etymological conjectures, starting with T. A. Sánchez' AUCILLA 'little bird', extracted from Apuleius. In his comparative dictionary, F. Diez avoided the downright rejection of that hypothesis, but voiced a preference for AUSPICIUM 'divination by means of birds', deflected from its original gender — so he argued — through the pressure of its synonym *suerte* 'fate'. In his earliest gropings, G. Baist favored APICE 'top, summit' (*ZRPh.*, VI [1882], 167; cf. VIII, 224), while J. Cornu — abandoning, on G. Paris' advice, his first trial ballon, *ALICE (from ĀL-ES, *-EX 'winged [adj.], bird [n.]' — concentrated on *AUICE 'little bird' ("Études sur le *Poème du Cid*", *Rom.*, X [1881], 76 f.) and G. Körting, *LRW*, was content to elaborate on Diez (AUISPICIUM). The general fatigue after so many conflicting fireworks showed for the first time in a lame statement by E. Gorra (*Lingua e letteratura spagnuola delle origini* [Milan, 1898], pp. 58, 79n.), whose own leanings were split between AUITIA (pl. of AUITIUM 'winged race, swarm of birds') and AUSPICE 'one who observes the habits of birds', though he also made it a point to adduce AUCILLA and [*]AUICE; AUITIUM later haunted the imagi-nation of J. da Silva Correia (*RL*, XXX [1932], 103 f.). Meanwhile, C. Michaëlis de Vasconcelos, in a free variation on Cornu's hunch, endorsed *AVICE, starting from an unsupported reconstruction *AU-IX, -ICIS 'bird' (for class. AUIS, in *Appendix Probi* style, as it were); see her critical ed. of the *Cancioneiro da Ajuda* (Halle, 1904), II, 84 ("que um pássaro de mau agouro significou acontecimentos desastro-sos"). At this juncture Baist returned to the fray, proposing in a brilliant reversal of his earlier guess ABC as a base defensible on cultural grounds ("Etymologien", *ZRPh.*, XXXII [1908], 423 f.), but failed to convince Menéndez Pidal who, in the Glossary accompanying his monumental edition of *Mio Cid*, II (Madrid, 1911), 489 ff., classed *AUICE in lieu of AUICELLA 'little bird' as an instance of false regression, likening it to *peonza* 'top' (toy) from *peoncilla* and to children's *gabanzo* 'overcoat' from *gabancito*. This view drew the applause of J. Cejador y Frauca, *Vocabulario medieval castellano* (Madrid, 1929), s.v., and, more surprisingly, of J. Corominas, *DCE*, I (Bern, 1954), 63*b* (s.v. *aguzanieve*) and 337*a* (s.v. *ave*); but Meyer-Lübke, in 1911 and then again in 1930, authoritatively supported Baist's etymon A.B.C. (*REW*[1] and *REW*[3] § 16: "ausgehend von der vielfach bezeugten zauberisch-mystischen Verwendung des A.B.C.") and, on the second occasion, pointed out, in explicit refutation of Menéndez Pidal's alternative, that any regression would have led to a formation in *-a* rather than in *-e*. Of all verdicts returned A. Magne's (ed. of *A Demanda do Santo Graal*, III [Rio, 1944], 96 f.) is probably the least tenable: The Brazilian scholar was willing to separate geneti-cally the Old Spanish from the patently related Old Galician-Portuguese word, tracing the former to *A.B.C.* and the latter to *AUICE. One minor argument against Baist's conjecture might be the consistently feminine gender of OSp. *auze*, observ-able through the prism of its qualifiers; but note that OIt. *abbicci* was epicene and that the general preference for the feminine in descendants of Latin words ending in *-e* or a consonant is demonstrably a salient feature of Spanish (cf. *frente* 'forehead', *liebre* 'hare', *col* 'cabbage', *miel* 'honey', *sal* 'salt', etc.). For a more searching dissection see my article "Form Versus Meaning in Etymological Analy-sis: Old Spanish *auze* 'luck' ," in *Estudios dedicados a James Homer Herriott* (Madison, Wis., 1966), pp. 167–183.

*abecedarius* (St. Augustine);[15] even if at the incipient stage the
-*d*-, as is not implausible, had a different origin,[16] it was surely
reinterpreted ex post facto as the fourth link in a tightly organized
chain. (The manifold poetic, liturgic, and didactic uses of abecedaria,
old and modern, do not concern us here.) On the dialect level, there
has been observed, at widely scattered points of ROMANIA, a conceivably very old reduction — in the mouth of children? — of *ABC*
to ⌐*be-a-ba*⌐.[17]

[15] The alphabet viewed as a social institution and the web of magic and mystic
beliefs attached to it, with their time-honored esthetic offshoots (*acrostic*, orig.
'poem in which the first and the last letter of each line, if they be taken in order,
will spell a word — sometimes the author's name — or a sentence — e.g., the kernel
of a message or a hidden meaning') and present-day trivial gastronomic ramifications
(European *alphabet crackers*, American *alphabet soup*), exceed the limits of this
paper. For one set of archeological data see A. Diederich, "ABC-Denkmäler",
*Rhein. Mus. f. Philol.*, LVI (1901), 77–105; cf. further E. Schröder, "Über das
*spell*", *ZDA*, XXXVII (1893), 241–268, esp. 263. The discussion of these problems
has spilled over into Germanic and Romance etymology; see n. 14, above, and cf.
the following memorandum (1965) from Renée T. Kahane: "As we will show in
a forthcoming study, *abece* is used in Wolfram's *Parzifal* (453,15) with reference
to geomancy (correspondences between geomantic figures, letters, and numbers).
In the Alfonsine *Lapidario* (Montaña, p. 63*a*), «*abecé de Saturno*» refers to stars
and constellations of the Zodiac". On the former point see H. and R. Kahane,
*Krater and Grail* (Urbana, 1966), pp. 145 f.; on the latter, H. Ritter and
M. Plessner, *Picatrix* (London, 1962), pp. 111 and 127.

[16] Epistolary comment by Dr. Renée T. Kahane: "Would it not be simpler
to consider the -*d*- as the reflection of the dental in the Greek model *alphabetárion?*
This suggestion is supported by such Latin vars. of *abecedarius* as *abecetaria*,
*abicitale*, *abicitarium* (*ThLL*), where the *t* as a rendering of *d* would be meaningless.
Gr. *alphabetárion*, on the other hand, is a regular formation on *alpha* and *beta*,
recorded since the 10th century, but doubtless earlier".

[17] A still very young Leo Spitzer, in his brilliant comment on an earlier note
(1911) by O. J. Tallgren[-Tuulio], established the initial bridge between Ptg.
*b-á-bá* (Queirós), Cat. *be-a-ba*, and S.-It. *bi-a-ba* ("Etymologisches aus dem
Catalanischen", *NM*, XV [1913], 158). In the 1st fasc. (1922) of his *FEW*, W. von
Wartburg then added Loth. *bé-a-ba* from Uriménil (Vosges), as recorded in
N. Haillant's *Essai* (Épinal, 1882), and Langued. *beaba*, uniquely attested in Abbé
P. A. Boissier de Sauvages' *Dictionnaire languedocien-français* (Nîmes, 1756).
Eight years later Meyer-Lübke rounded out the slowly emerging picture by adduc-
ing Sw. *beaba* (*REW*³ § 16); is his dubious Ptg. *baba* a hasty misrepresentation of
Spitzer's datum?

Wartburg, s.v., visibly puzzled by the distortion itself and by its geographic
diffusion, called this form bizarre ("seltsam") and termed its dispersal "merk-
würdig"; and Meyer-Lübke, influenced by this phrasing, spoke of "eigenartige
Umstellung und Doppelung". The echoing of the bilabial *b* loses some of its
oddity once *be-a-ba* is analyzed as a nursery or grammar school word; as a bilabial,
/b/ is, of course, a favorite with children, and the learning of the alphabet has
figured prominently in didactically slanted children's songs (examples from
Catalonia: Vich, Llufriu de l'Empordá, Pollensa, in Alcover, *DCVB*, I, 30;
in modern Greek songs from Cephalonia, the chain of the names of the letters

Interestingly, in several languages the Greek and the Latin designations are allowed to coexist with a subtle semantic differentiation: The former provides the learned label, the latter evokes the unsophisticated environment of the elementary school where the first knowledge of the letters is inculcated. Contrast G. *Alphabet*, adj. *alphabetisch* 'alphabetic', *Analphabet* 'illiterate person'[18] and *ABC-buch* 'primer', *ABC-schütz(e)* 'beginner, tyro'. The same opposition obtains in Albanian (*alfabet* vs. *abece*), while in Russian — mutatis mutandis — *alfávit* (also *alfavít*) and *ázbuka* are comparably paired off.

Like the words for 'grammar' (which may be a book of rules applying to the chess game or to ballroom dancing) and those for 'dictionary' (which may parade, say, biographic vignettes of sculptors), those for 'alphabet' lend themselves to all kinds of familiar, jocular, and artistic extensions (Lope, *Peribáñez y el Comendador de Ocaña* [1614], Act I, Sc. 9: "El *abecé* de los recién casados", involving two alphabetically arranged sets of character traits desirable in a spouse; but the *X*, erratically, symbolizes in one instance "buena cristiana", in the other two arms crossed, i.e. clasped around

---

[18] Italian temporarily even used the verb (18th cent.) *alfabetare* (cf. E. *alphabetize*), before that the noun (16th cent.) *alfabetato* 'repertorio tenuto in ordine alfabetico'; to this day it tolerates the facetious regression *alfabeta* (m.) 'literate person'.

---

may be interrupted for the sake of rhyme). In a primer, a child is, at first, acquainted with a *B*, then with an *A*; in the end, he is trained to pronounce them jointly, in a single syllable. There exist, particularly on Italian soil, reductions of tripartite *ABC* to a bipartite skeleton; cf., on the one hand, OIt. *abbi* (its direct offspring can be heard in rural Toscana to this day) and, on the other hand, apheresized Sic. *bizzé* and Apul. (Maglia) *mizzé* beside fuller Cal. *ammeccé, ambeccé* (*REW*[3]§ 16, and G. Rohlfs, *Dizionario dialettale delle tre Calabrie*, 3 vols. [Milan, 1932–39], I, 89*a*, with careful localization of two field-notes). Italian, incidentally, still wavers between the standard labels *abbiccì*, endorsed by Dante, and *abbeccé*, favored by Leopardi, who found support for his preference in Marchegiano usage; the word is masculine at present, but its use as a feminine was once condoned (cf. OSp. *auze*, n. 14, above).

Understandably, the progeny of vernacular *ABC* shows much livelier growth, as regards derivation and "accidenti generali", than do the descendants of austerely erudite ALPHABĒTUM. Apheresis, antihiatic interfixation (-*r*-), and addition of diminutive suffixes have all three affected Cat. Val. (*a*)*beceroles* 'primer' (Alcover, *DCVB*, I, 31*a*; II, 367*b*); cf. doc. A.D. 1439: "Unes *beceroles* capletrades d'aur"; *Spill*, v. 13,594: "*Baceroletes* fluxes liçons", while apheresis in conjunction with suffix change have moulded Cat. *becedària* 'small piece of canvas displaying embroidered letters' (*DCVB*, II, 367*ab*). Nevertheless, a few minor accidents did befall the Graeco-Latin counterpart; thus *FEW*, I, 76*a* cites metathesized Havr. *aflabet* and, through the influence of *croisette*, Ard. *alfabęt*, as recorded in C. Bruneau's *Étude* (1913).

the bride's neck). Illustrations from America's present-day book market, for the most part "low-brow", can be effortlessly garnered. One current best-seller of self-explanatory appeal is entitled *The ABC of Gourmet Cooking*; a Dallas insurance company has lately distributed a pamphlet: *The ABC's of Good Posture*; passengers riding East Bay buses are warned against dangers of smoking in forests through posters marked *Smokey's ABC*. (For a combined suggestion of 'apprenticeship, noviciate' and 'refinement, sophistication' one expects some such more exacting title as 'primer'; cf. Stefan George's *Die Fibel, Auswahl erster Verse* [1901].)

More interesting are the alignments of the first and the last letter to suggest the totality of a scale, spectrum, or series, the pan-European model being *from alpha to omega* (R. *ot alfy do omegi*); cf. the symbol AΩ used as a graphic reminder of the beginning and the end of earthly life on ancient Christian tombs. In *The Golden Aphroditis — a Planned Discourse* (London, 1577) by the minor Elizabethan writer John Granger, the female protagonist is called AΩ as a reminder that she is the first and last daughter of Diana and Endymion. Adaptations include E. *from A to Z*, G. *von A bis Z*, F. *depuis A jusqu'à Z*, Pol. *od A do Z*. The Modern Greek counterpart means '[to tell] with full details'; in this context *omega* may alternate with *beta* (Cephalonia), or substitutes appear for both consonants, e.g. 'with the *nu* and the *sigma*'. A spelling reform entailing the elimination of some letter at the head or at the tail of the series may require a corresponding change in phraseology. Precisely the latter modification has taken place in contemporary Russian through the loss of Θ and *v*; hence the refreshing title of a well-known children's book of verse by S. Ja. Maršak: *Vesëloje putešestvije ot A do Ja* 'A merry trip from "А" to "Я".' Perhaps one may call it Russia's answer to William M. Thackerey's *An Alphabet — Alphabetarium for Children*. Quite unusual, on the other hand, is the bidirectional approach of Isidore of Seville (I, III, 9): "*A* et *O* . . . *O* et *A* . . . ut ostenderet et initii decursum ad finem et finis decursum ad initium"; see G. R. Sarolli, "Dante — scriba Dei (II)", *Convivium*, N.S., VI (1963), 538.

Then again the names of consecutive letters, preferably of the first two, can be put to effective use in suggesting the string of events, the succession of steps in planning an enterprise, the need for consistency, the mutual complementarity itself. Thus G. *Wer "A" sagt muß auch "B" sagen* is echoed by Pol. *Jeżeli sie powie*

"*A*", *trzeba powiedzieć* "*B*".[19] Conversely, the inability to attach *B* to *A* or to discriminate between them will serve as a token of ignorance and boorishness, cf. *He does not know A from B*, F. *ne savoir ni A ni B*.[20]

There are on record all sorts of sobriquets and facetious variations through capricious segmentation of words critically important or acting as irritants in a unique historical context. Thus, among Jews subjected to severe tribulations under Hitler, there circulated the harmless joke on the prevailing racism: *Sind Sie a-risch? — Nein, ich bin be-risch* (Berlin, mid-'thirties). It is perhaps not inaccurate to surmise that certain alert, literate, and (hyper)sensitive individuals, in handling geographic and personal names beginning with one of the two "extreme" letters of the total alphabetic spread, remain critically aware of the special position allotted to these prime classifiers in membership lists, directories, gazetteers, etc. Living in *Aachen* or *Aarhus* (before it became *Århus*) or else in *Zurich*, and bearing some such conspicuous name as *Abel* or *Zygmunt*, might make even the average person more "alphabet-conscious" than would spending one's sheltered life in *London* or *Madrid*, close to the midriff of the alphabet, and feeling protected from alphabetic exposure by comparatively neutral names like *López* or *Miller*.

Other phraseological groupings of labels for letters are less

---

[19] From Grisons, the citadel of Western Raeto-Romance, W. Gottschalk, *Die bildhaften Sprichwörter der Romanen*, 3 vols. (Heidelberg, 1935–38), III, 207, reports: "Tgi ca ha getg *A*, quel gi era buger *B*" = "On n'a pas plutôt dit *A* qu'il faut dire *B*" (obviously an adaptation). Cf. Yid. *Ver es zogt beyz muz sogn giml*, involving the second and the third letter of the Hebrew alphabet, plus the allusion to *beyz* 'evil', while *giml* may concomitantly serve as an abbreviation for *gut*.

[20] In the metaphoric expansion of the ambit of the single word *alphabet* it is the reference to the rudimental and elementary which prevails (much as the letter *A* stands for 'first step'; cf. the Spanish proverb: "Aunque el burro estudió, de la *A* no pasó" and the Russian sayings *ni aza* (*ne znat'*, *ne ponimat'*, *ne smyslit'*), while Modern Greek uses equivalents of 'He is still at the alphabet' and 'He cannot even say *alpha*'; thus, Sir Flinders Petrie, the British dean of Biblical archeologists, is reported to have appealed to pottery as "the essential alphabet (= 'basic tool') of archeology". But in conventional graphic representations the letters of the alphabet, artfully arranged in four or five rows — first widening, then tapering off — provide a compelling emblem evocative of all-embracing totality. The Italian publisher Riccardo Ricciardi deftly uses this emblem for his *Documenti di Filologia*, circling it by the tasteful motto: "Quantumquis circumi numquam me complecteris". The same implication of global grasp or spread justifies E. Noulet's choice of the title *Alphabet Critique 1924–64* for his four-volume collection of reprinted critical essays arrayed in the alphabetic order of the author's names (Vol. I: A–C, etc.).

diaphanous and, like any other etymological puzzle, invite minute historical investigation. Here are, at random, some examples from colloquial Spanish, both standard and regional: *entrar con haches y erres* 'tener malas cartas el que va jugar la puesta'; *no decir uno ni haches ni erres* 'no hablar cuando parece que conviene' (Acad.). The starting point for this particular use seems to be a card game. On the other hand, *C* and *B*, in this erratic order, are paired off in Sp. *por ce o por be* or, more laconically, *ce por be* 'detenidamente, punto por punto'. Colloquial usage, observable particularly in Platense, seems to favor a lame compromise between these two no longer transparent binary groups: *por hache o por be* 'por una u otra razón, por causa desconocida'.

A point of special interest is the occasional use of peculiar names (preservation of archaisms or *ad hoc* coinage?) for letters included in such idiomatic formulas. Thus, the Russian tag for 'M' is normally *èm*, but in the binomial, not infrequently lengthened into a fanciful trinomial, *ni bè ni mè* or *ni be ni me* (*ni kukaréku*) 'neither fish nor fowl' ( = *ni to ni së*), *mè* or *me* is substituted for the standard label to match more closely, for the sake of smooth integration ("Einreihung") or forceful polarization, its counterpart *bè* (*be*).[21]

Typical of our own century's candid admission of "crazes" are stray hints of non-existent letters and numbers. The Continental market recently witnessed the success of a book (translated from English) whose title was conceivably more provocative than its content: *La lettre après "Z"*. There has existed for a long period of time the German saying *Da schlägt's dreizehn*, lit. 'the clock strikes thirteen', i.e. 'something absurd is happening', but it took the folly and turmoil of the Second World War to induce the young Roumanian novelist C. V. Gheorghiu (1916–   ) to produce a sensational book titled *The Twenty-Fifth Hour*.

[21] The Russian Academy dictionary, Vol. I (1948), s.v., equates the more easily recognizable *bè* (*be*) ingredient of the congealed sequence with the name of the letter. As sounds, /b/ and /m/ share, of course, the distinctive feature of articulatory locus (bilabiality). The striking use of *mè* for *èm* calls to mind the cross-linguistic occurrence, in proverbs and other playful arrangements, of archaic or provincial verb forms tolerated for the sake of perfect rhymes which might otherwise be endangered, e.g. G. *Wie die Alten sungen* [= standard *sangen*,/ *so zwitschern die Jungen*; for further exemplification see my "Studies in Irreversible Binomials", *Lingua*, VIII:2 (1959), 113–160, esp. 137 f., included in the present volume, p. 334. Note that within ultramodern Russian, according to B. F. Korickij's dictionary (1963), CIIIA 'USA' may be pronounced not only [š:á], [essá], [esšea], but also [sešá] or [sešeá] through substitution of *se* for *ès* as the label of the first letter.

## 4. Abbreviations

Though the use of abbreviations is very old, their current vogue is unprecedented. Also, while the motivation was once consistently utilitarian (scarcity of costly writing material, lack of precious time, etc.), it has in this century become smart and stylish to use them in certain contexts. The modern world's two leading countries are most commonly referred to in this manner: *US(A)* and *USSR* ( = R. *SSSR*), as are also the major international organization (*UN*), influential political, military, economic, and cultural alliances (*NATO, SEATO*) and agencies (*UNESCO*), and countless entities of the body politic. The old, thoroughly outmoded acrostic has now been replaced by the acronym and its variants;[22] in fact, the officious book market already offers dictionaries of the constantly mushrooming acronyms.[23]

[22] This is not the place to review the history of the acrostic, which left such important traces in Guillaume de Machaut, Froissart, Gervais du Bus, Villon ("Ballade de bon conseil", "Ballade des contre-verités"), also in medieval Latin and even in medieval Hebrew poetry. The device reached its climactic point in the 14th and 15th centuries.

Emblems, heraldry, and religious iconography might be singled out as important sources of abbreviations in the Western tradition; *I.N.R.I.*, almost obligatory in pictorial representations of the Crucifixion scene, is a case in point. The emblematic reduction of the phrase *Ad maiorem Dei gloriam* to the initials of the four constituent words is vividly evoked by the very title of R. Pérez de Ayala's novel (1911) *A.M.D.G.; La vida en un colegio de jesuitas.* Not entirely unrelated is the cabalistic method of *nutrikun* which, in curious reversal of the standard procedure, entails the interpretation of a plain word as an acronym.

[23] One such venture is H. Baudry's *Nouveau dictionnaire d'abréviations*, «*D.A.*» *françaises et étrangères, techniques et usuelles, anciennes et nouvelles*, rev. ed. (La Chapelle Montligron [Orne], 1956), cf. M. Cohen's ironic assessment in *BSLP*, LII:2 17 f. The American counterpart appeared later: M. Goldstein, *Dictionary of Modern Acronyms & Abbreviations* (Indianapolis, 1963). The Gale Research Co. (Detroit, Mich.) advertises (a) its 212-page *Acronyms Dictionary*, the 2d ed. of which (c. 1966) has been renamed *Acronyms and Initialisms Dictionary*; (b) an 8,500-word *Code Names Dictionary*, including cover words, slang terms, nicknames, and sobriquets, the whole introduced by Eric Partridge, the well-known author of *Dictionary of Slang and Unconventional English.* This "far-out" cultural matrix might merit special interest on the part of the sociolinguist. The Russian equivalent, M. Shapiro reminds me, is B. F. Korickij's *Slovar' sokraščenij russkogo jazyka* (Moskva, 1963). The standard treatise on abbreviations in modern French is H. Kjellman, "*Mots abrégés et tendances d'abréviation en français*", UUÅ, Year 1920, No. 2; cf. L. Spitzer's favorable and stimulating appraisal in *LGRPh.*, XLIII (1922), cols. 27 f., with a heavy stress on the intrinsic intimacy of many shortened forms and on the reckless exploitation of this mood by hard-boiled advertisers. Kjellman himself isolates and examines several abbreviatory schemata of little concern to us here, e.g. those involving (a) reduplications: *bobosse* = *bossu* 'hunchback', (b) apocope: *sous-off(icier)*, esp. *auto, métro, photo, stylo, vélo*, which

**Truncation.** The psycho-social matrix of the craving for abbreviations (on the one hand, a connubium of science and advertising; on the other, an urge for privacy, seclusion, humor, imagination) is not at issue here;[24] what matters is less the root of the fad than the specific linguistic conditions under which it materializes and thrives. Even within the frame of this general limitation one further retrenchment is necessary: Such abbreviations as involve chunks or torsos of words — the classic example is *do, re, mi, fa, sol, la, si —*, as against plain letters (typically, initial letters), do not qualify for inclusion. Thus, such instances of plain "truncation" as G. *Sozis* 'Socialists' and, later, *Nazis* 'National Socialists', *Gestapo* ←*Geheime Staatspolizei* or E. *commies* 'Communists', Am.-E. — typically, in the jargon of college students — *Caltech* 'California Institute of Technology', also *Comp(arative) Lit(erature)*, *Home Ec(onomics)*, *dorm(itory)*, *prof(essor)*, or — in the plural — coll. *fed(eral)s*, *seg-(regationist)s*, or again R. *Smerš* 'counterespionage agency' ( ←*smert' špionam!* 'death to the spies!'), *Čeka* 'state police', lit. 'emergency commission' ( ←*Črezvyčajnaja Komissija*), *Gensek* 'executive secretary' ←*General'nyj sekretar'* do not answer the description of the

---

[24] The connotations are very numerous and sometimes elusive; they may involve secrecy, mock-secrecy, encoding, as in *(V)IP*←*(Very) Important Person*, with overtones of top-level diplomacy; evocation of an intimate circle of workers, of a coterie, etc. (*SLOM*←*Selective List of Materials*, readily understood only at the MLA Headquarters); folk-etymological, sometimes pious reinterpretations, as is conceivably true of *SOS*←*Save Our Souls*; malicious distortions — reading into *SPQR*, as did Rabelais, *si peu que rien*, or into the Spanish epistolary formula *s(u) s(eguro) s(ervidor)*, as have done college students, some nonsensical remark (*siempre serás salvaje*), or else decoding, as with Berkeley's *FSM* (1964–65)←*Free* (later: *Filthy*) *Speech Movement*; veiling, if not total avoidance, of taboo words, of downright profanity, etc., or squeamish reference to "intimate" body functions (*S.O.B.*, *T.B.*←*tuberculosis* [once a scare word], *V.D.*←*venereal disease, B.O.*← (*offensive*) *body odor, W.C.*←*water closet* 'toilet'); rescue of inordinately long and foreign-sounding words for familiar objects from the sphere of pedantically academic discourse (*T.V.* beside *telly*←*television*, cf. F. *télé*). The original formula may be almost universally forgotten, as in Am.-E. *G.I.* 'enlisted soldier' (← *Government Issue*, stamped on certain supplies; a derivation not universally recognized).

---

call to mind coll. E. *homo(sexual)*, *memo(randum)*, *mono(nucleosis)*, *polio(myelitis)*, *psycho(path)*, with a link to *hobo* and *wino* 'chronic wine-drinker', and (c) apheresis: (*mar)chand*. Interesting is his discovery that the French "letter-words" (which bear squarely on our problem) reflect, in the last analysis, an English fashion. On the current state of affairs, in Spanish see R. Lapesa, "La lengua desde hace cuarenta años", *Rev. de Occid.* (Nov.–Dec. 1963), pp. 193–208, esp. 201 f., and D. Alonso, *Del Siglo de Oro a este siglo de las siglas* (Madrid, 1962), pp. 7 f.

problems directly relevant in this context;[25] conversely, *AEG*←
*Allgemeine Elektrizitätsgesellschaft*, *GMBH*←*Gesellschaft mit be-
schränkter Haftung*, *SA*←*Sturmabteilung* and *SS* (written with two
stylized S's: angular and elongated)←*Schutzstaffel*, or *GPU*
(a later name for *Čeka*) decidedly do. Compounds involving an abbre-

[25] This type of abbreviation — involving juxtaposed slices of key-words — reached
its peak during and after the Russian Revolution, though the genesis of the model
precedes the political events. Early examples include *ispolkom*←*ispolnitel'nyj
komitet* 'Executive Committee' and *linkor*←*linejnyj korabl'* 'battleship'; cf.
*agit*(*acionnaja*)-*prop*(*aganda*), *pol-* and *torg-pred*←*politiceskij* and *torgovyj pred-
stavitel'*, respectively, *kol-* and *sov-xoz*, *glavkom*←*glavnokomandujuščij*, *kombrig*←
*komandir brigady*, *univermag*←*universal'nyj magazin* 'department store', *polit-otdel*,
and *raj-kom*, *diamat*←*dialektičeskij materialism* (as a school subject), *filfak*←
*filologičeskij fakul'tet*, even *medsestra* 'medical nurse' and *medsanbat* 'medico-
sanitary batallion'. These expressions are not facetious (unless a humorist sinks
his teeth into them), nor are they restricted to any milieu, hence hardly endowed
with intimacy — certainly no more than straight acronyms such as *GUM* 'department store'; note the stylistic contrast to E. *Mag*(*azine*), *mod*(*ern*) *hairdo*, (*P*)*op
Art* (*optical* as a variation on *popular*), etc., with rare exceptions, such as *ASPAC*←
*Asian and Pacific Council*. Similarly, *Gestapo*, under another totalitarian régime,
was preceded by *Sipo*←*Sicherheitspolizei* and later followed by *Vopo*←*Volkspolizei*,
while *Politische Polizei* was, for obvious reasons, left alone. Progressive pre-
revolutionary Russia favored literation (*èser*←*social-revoljucioner*), occasionally
with additional consonantal support from other segments — medial or final —
of the words concerned, e.g. *kadet*←*konstitucionnyj demokrat*, *èsdek*←*social-
demokrat*. (In these abbreviations *-ek* and *-er* are actually to be pronounced with an
/è/.)
    The attachment of case-endings in contemporary Russian abbreviations is
controlled not by morphosyntactic but by phonic considerations: Contrast *kom*
(*andir*) *brig*(*ady*) [gen. sg.] 'commander of a brigade' with *zav*(*edujuščij*) *otdelom*
[instr. sg.] 'section head', a cumbersome solution necessitated by the speakers'
built-in resistance to pronouncing *\*zavotd* with a -*td* discernibly different from
the -*d* [t] of *zavod* 'plant, factory'. Where no such recalcitrance is involved, a
shortcut will invariably be welcome, regardless of the grammatical case at issue;
cf. *zavuč*←*zav*(*edujuščij*) *uč*(*ilišcem*) 'school administrator' (instr. sg.). On the
grammatical side, this leads to an entirely new situation: *kombrig*, *zavuč* behave
like any ordinary primary noun, while *zavotdelom* is indeclinable, as is *načštaba*←
*nač*(*al'nik*) *štaba* 'chief of staff' (gen. sg.), where an excessive accumulation of
consonants was perhaps to be avoided.
    The reason for the higher status of the *linkor* type in Russian is that its closest
rival, the *Emcee* type (= *Master of Ceremonies*) — eminently successful in intimate
and semi-formal English — has been rejected or reduced in scope after some
experimenting, because it created difficulties in a language whose grammatical
scaffold was neatly geared to certain word-final vowels, and to the lack of others.
Thus, *K.D.* for *konstitucionnyj demokrat* 'member of the Liberal Party' could
be orally interpreted neither as *kᵎade*, which would have given a neuter appearance
to a word inherently masculine, still less as *kadᵎe*, *kadᵎè*, which would have imparted
to that word an utterly unwelcome exotic tinge. The coexistence of non-abbre-
viatory *kadet₁* 'student at a military academy' (from F. *cadet*, cf. G. *Kadett*) and
of the politically colored *-ist* series, plus *demokrat*, produced the abbreviation
*kadet₂* 'member of the Liberal Party'.

viation and a full word, in this order (type ⌐U-boat⌐), are of peripheral
relevance and invite, after incidental mention, a brief separate
discussion (under "Mixed types", below).

This mid-20th-century cyclopean technique of compounding
words by piling up the initial segments of components is also en-
countered in certain toponyms: Am.-E. *Reston*←*R*(*obert*) *E. S*(*imons*)
+ suff. -*ton*<*town* (LIFE, 24.XII.65, p. 145), *Calneva Drive* (in
West Los Angeles)←*California, Nevada*, the self-explanatory
toponym *Texarkana*, S.-Am. *Bolpebra*←*Bol*(*ivia*), *Pe*(*rú*), *Bra*(*zil*)
— a dot on the map marking the point of abutment of these three
countries (see F. Jensen, *RPh.*, XIX [1965–66], 528, who cites
further examples). Occasionally, it is found in geographically
flavored names of firms, witness the oil company *Caltex*. This
method of "a new, humanly managed form of word development"
(F. M. Chambers) contrasts with the juxtapositional welding of
one word's head segment to the next word's tail segment, a technique
equally fashionable, but prevailing in other provinces of the lexicon
matching different real-life contexts (cf. the end of n. 37, below).

**Deceptive abbreviations.** Certain very special situations must, at
the outset, be deducted from the reservoir of an increasingly abundant material. There exist deceptive cases, as when an *L-train*,
known to Chicagoans and formerly to New Yorkers, stands for
*El*(*evated*), in sharp contrast to Berlin's *U-Bahn* (*Untergrundbahn*
'subway') and *S-Bahn* (*Schnellbahn* 'rapid transit'), or when *X*
before a telephone number functions as a substitute for *Ex*(*tension*).
The abbreviation proper, though clearly isolable, is here subordinated to a kind of rebus-like puzzle (see Section 7, below). *K.O.*
'knock-out punch in boxing' is a genuine abbreviation (favored by
sensational headlines) which, with the world-wide prestige of this
American sport, has spread even to countries where its compositional
design is not fully understood, cf. G. *K.O.* /kao/, and *T.K.O.*←
*technical knock-out* is following suit; but *O.K.* may well be a pseudo-
abbreviation for the following visibly related words (of controversial
ancestry[26]): a verb enjoying considerable acceptance on the scale

[26] The older literature on the subject is unfathomable. Even the critical digest
of earlier conjectures has swollen to inordinate proportions; see, in *AS*, W. A.
Heflin, "*O.K.* and its Incorrect Etymology", XXXVII (1962), 243–248, and A. W.
Read's successive elaborations: "The First Stage in the History of *O.K.*", XXXVIII
(1963), 5–27; "The Second Stage in the History of *O.K.*", XXXIX (1964), 5–25;
"Later Stages in the History of *O.K.*", XXXIX, 83–101; "Successive Revisions
in the Explanation of *O.K.*", XXXIX, 243–267.

of formality ('to confirm, endorse') and a far commoner, distinctly more familiar adverb or interjection (some educated speakers willingly use *to okay*, but are reluctant to substitute *O.K.* for 'all right'). Trenchant It. *W* for *Evviva!* is unique in its use of a single foreign letter, or graphic approximation thereto, as near-equivalent in shape of two identical native letters; placed upside down, the sign conveys the opposite message: 'abbasso!'. Arbitrarily disguised as an abbreviation of two words is *I.D. Card←IDentification card.* Where written abbreviations involve foreign-language formulas, their reading-aloud, I repeat, may involve the substitution of vernacular equivalents: *e.g.←exempli gratia* (commonly pronounced "for instance"); *i.e.←id est* ("that is"). A Greek letter, endowed with its original value, has infiltrated Latin script in *Xmas← Christmas*, popular in the English-speaking countries; cf. also *X Science←Christian Science* and recall the above-cited passage from Lope's *Peribáñez*.[27]

**Literation versus acronym.** The two basic varieties of the acronym are conditioned by the readers' desire either to pronounce each letter with its full label, a procedure known as "literation", F. "épellation" (Am.-E. *GOP←Grand Old Party*, R. *RSFSR* /èrèsèfèsèr/ 'Great Russian Soviet Republic', G. *KPD* /kapede/←*Kommunistische Partei Deutschlands*, Braz.-Ptg. *UDN* /udene/←*União Democrática Nacional*, similarly *PTB←Partido Trabalhista Brasileiro* and *PSD← Partido Social Democrático*), or to credit each letter strictly with its phonetic value, as in *WAC←W(omen's) A(rmy) C(orps), radar← ra(dio) d(etecting) a(nd) r(anging)*, R. *TASS←T(elegrafnoje) A(genstvo) S(ovetskogo) S(ojuza)*, and coll. F. *URSS* /ürs/. The latter device (the acronym *stricto sensu*) is the more remarkable of the two, both linguistically (because it tends to create entirely new words, not

---

[27] In his memorandum W. E. Geiger observes the disturbing polysemy of the symbol *X*, which stands for 'Christ, Christian' through dual reference to the Greek letter X (in *Christ*) and to the cross as associated with the crucifixion. In addition *X* acts as a traffic symbol: *X-walk* 'cross-walk', *X-road* 'cross-road', *RXR* (or *RR-X*) 'railroad crossing', accompanying *cross* in its semantic expansion through — to use B. Migliorini's apposite term — "synonymic radiation". Within the modern context of congested highway traffic, but with a hint of the older religious use, the cross, as a deterrent, may mark the spot of a fatal automobile accident. As if this measure of ambiguity were insufficient, the *X* is used as an elementary mathematical symbol ('multiplied by'), functions informally as a rebus for *EX(tension)* in telephone numbers, and plays a rôle impervious to the uninitiated in the all-important *X-ray* = F. *rayon X*, Sp. *rayo X*, It. *raggio X* (as against G. *Röntgenstrahl* and its Russian derivative).

just strings of familiar labels for letters which, in the last analysis, represent mere compounds) and stylistically (inasmuch as the boldness of certain uncommon sound sequences may have some kind of shock effect, sounding a clarion call to action, provoking laughter, etc.). Preferences as between the two procedures vary widely from language to language and from abbreviation to abbreviation, depending, broadly, on national attitudes toward humor, improvisation, originality, and, narrowly, on degrees of sheer pronounceability; for G. *KZ*←*Konzentrationslager* 'concentration camp' (pronounced /kacɛt/) speakers seemed to have little choice a generation ago, though in present-day America the comparable difficulty of pronouncing *SNCC* monosyllabically has been successfully circumvented by the introduction of an auxiliary vowel: /snɪk/ (obviously preferred to *snack*, inopportunely reminiscent of a light meal, and to *snuck*, offensively suggestive of 'sneaking'[28]). For *AMTCL* one actually hears both /æmtæ̀kl/ and /æmtɪkl/. Emphatically informal /snɪk/, appropriate to the language of students, clashes with mildly informal *U.C.* /jusi/ 'University of California' —

[28] In colloquial American English, *snuck* rivals *sneaked* as the simple past. The vocalization of *SNCC* reminds many observers of Lewis Carroll's "jabberwocky" in *Through the Looking-Glass and What Alice Found There* (1871–72), specifically of the line: "The vorpal blade went *snicker-snack*". There exist fanciful variations on this theme. Thus, the title of the journal *PMLA* (= *Publications of the Modern Language Assn.*) was pronounced *Paméla* by some South American philologists, who, exercising their imagination along a different line, also took delight in equating *JAOS* (= *Journal of the American Oriental Society*) with CHAOS, χάος, and in poking fun at their own pseudo-Canaanite BAAL←*Boletín de la Academia Argentina de Letras*.

In general, the matter of pronounceability requires cautious handling. While it is true that phonetic conditions have made literation the "logical solution" in the cases of *GHQ*=*General Headquarters*, *ICBM*←*Intercontinental Ballistic Missile*, and *FLN*←*Front de la libération nationale*, say, it is arguable that the marginal phonic admissibility of certain acronyms has been more a help than a hindrance, instilling into them a by no means unwelcome dosage of uniqueness, exoticism, modernity, and, above all, memorability. Cf. R. NÈP (= Lenin's *Novaja Èkonomičeskaja Politika*), Sp. *ALPI* (= *Atlas lingüístico de la Península Ibérica*), G. *UFA* (the name of the leading motion-picture company). Word-initial *mx-* is extremely rare in Russian, but the preëxistence of *mox*, gen. *mxa* 'moss' sufficed to sanction *MXAT* for *Moskovskij Xudožestvennyj Teatr* and even *mxatovcy* for its celebrated players. While the adoption of an acronym hinges, to a certain point, on its pronounceability, it is also true that the acceptance of a near-utterable acronym by an enterprising speech community and the predisposed speakers' efforts to articulate with increasing tidiness a given residually troublesome consonant cluster included in the favored neologism may transform the acronym into a powerful wedge for the rejuvenation of a rigidified sound system. Processes of this kind have recently been reported from Spanish American quarters by A. Rabanales O.

never /ək/ or /juk/ —, *UCLA*, *USC*, etc., and with neutral *FBI* ←
*Federal Bureau of Investigation*, *CIA* ← *Central Intelligence Agency*.
Italian goes very far in liberalizing the actual pronunciation of
acronyms through all sorts of assimilations and metatheses: If *Usa*,
*Urs(s)*, and *Onu* ← *Organizzazione delle Nazioni Unite* create no
difficulty, *M.S.I.* ← *Movimento Sociale Italiano* would, were it not
for its jocular resolution into *miss*. Epenthesis and metathesis are
not, incidentally, the only remedies available; under certain circumstances a deft excision (in particular, apheresis) will help, cf. *CIS* ←
[*Peace Corps*] *Career Information Service*. In sum, the great novelty
of these "Buchstabenwörter", as Leo Spitzer dubbed them, consists
in the fact that script here, for once, serves not to capture and
perpetuate the fleeting facts of live speech, but to provide the
materials from which certain, increasingly numerous, ingredients of
that speech are fashioned in the first place.

Nowhere is the explosive novelty of this reversed hierarchy of
relations more dramatically exemplified than in the (normal) derivatives from (abnormal) primitives, as in facetious F. *râleur* 'ordnance
officer', from *R.A.L.* ← *Régiments d'artillerie lourde*, involving, for
good measure, a morbid pun on *râler* 'to have a death-rattle', also
It. *missino* 'Neofascist' from *M.S.I.*, or *le udine* 'members of the
*U.D.I.*' ← *U(nione) D(onne) I(talia)ne*; cf., on the other hand,
*erpéiste* from *R.P.* ← *Représentation proportionnelle*, *técéfiste* from
*T.S.F.* ← *télégraphie sans fil*, and *cégétiste* from *C.G.T.* ← *Confédé-
ration générale du travail*, also Braz.-Ptg. *udinista*, *petebista*, *pessedista*,
all six involving literation. In exceptional cases, where primitives
invite literation, semijocose derivatives may lend themselves to
acronymy; contrast (in academic jargon) *MIT* ← *Massachusetts
Institute of Technology* /emaiti/ with *mitnik* 'transformational
linguist' [trained at *MIT*], echoing *beatnik*, and note the mod. It.
nickname *piselli* 'members of the Social Democrat party *P.S.D.I.*',
with a transparent pun on *piselli* 'peas'.[29]

---

[29] In modern Russian, on the other hand, literation is perfectly compatible
with suffixal derivation, cf. the successive designations of a 'security policeman':
*ček-ist*, *ènkaved-ist* (from *Narodnyj Komissariat Vnutrennix Del*), *èmvedist* (from
*Ministerstvo Vnutrennix Del*), *kageb-ist* (from *Komissariat Gosudarstvennoj Bezo-
pasnosti*), cf. Am.-E. *ADA-er* 'follower of "Americans for Democratic Action" ',
Berkeley's *FSM-er* beside *FSM-ist* (1964); so is truncation, e.g. *pol-* and *torg-
predstvo*, cf. Am.-E. *Aggies* 'students of a college of agriculture'. One acronym
newly surrounded by a circle of derivatives is *VUZ* 'college' ← *Vysšeje učebnoje
zavedenije*; cf. *vuzovec* '(male) college student', *vuzovka* 'coed', *vuzovskij* 'collegiate'.

CC

Viewing matters in the evolutionary perspective one notices a tendential shift from truncation to literation, cf. the substitution of *MIT* for older *Tech*, and from literation to the acronym proper, cf. Am.-E. *AWOL* and *SNAFU* and esp. F. *Jeunesse Ouvrière Chrétienne* →*J.O.C.* /žiose/→*JOC* /žok/.[30] Contrast further the ultramodern *SAM*←*Surface-to-Air Missile* with such older formulas from both sides of the Atlantic as *C.O.D.*←*Collect on Delivery* and *R.A.F.* To use a subtle typographic distinction rapidly spreading among North America's fine printers, the neologism *N.A.S.A.*←*National Air Space Administration* is rapidly being transformed into NASA.[31] Whatever one may think of the underlying political programs, linguistically the liberal slogan *CA-PR-EW*←*Catholics, Protestants, Jews*, exemplifying truncation at its most vacuous, is vastly inferior to the narrowly segregationist watchword *WASP*←*White Anglo-Saxon Protestant*, an acronym which, by stigmatizing non-members of the alleged élite group, really stings (see a Spring 1966 installment of the syndicated column "At the Movies with Pauline Kael").

**Mixed types.** Until recently, the "mixed" type ⌜*U-boat*⌝ presented no major complication: Barring those instances of "Urschöpfung", to be discussed at a later juncture (see Section 5), where the letter-segment evoked a sharply profiled shape without suggesting any specific word (as in *A-frame, T-shirt*, etc.), the compound's first element was a letter standing for a full-blown word. Thus, one accounts for *A-bomb* ( = *atomic*), *G-man* ( = *Government*, i.e. 'federal police agent'), *H-bomb* ( = *hydrogen*), G. *D-Zug* ( = *Durchgangs-*), *E-Boot* ( = *Eil-*), *S-Bahn* ( = *Schnell-*), *U-Bahn*

---

[30] I owe this datum and a few others to Mr. Michael K. Toconita, who generously allowed me to read in manuscript a paper of his entitled "Abbreviations, Words Formed by Literation and Acronyms in Three French Dictionaries". Cf. *Linguistics*, No. XV (June 1965), 66–77.

[31] The elegant use of small capitals without interjacent dots, for genuine acronyms, against large capitals, each followed by a dot, for literations, has lately been spearheaded in North America by *The New Yorker*.

---

In a derivationally uninhibited language like English, which encourages formations such as *to zero in*, it is small wonder that colloquially — and, at this initial stage, still semihumorously — the verb *to T.A.* 'to perform the duties of a T[eaching] A[ssistant]' should be inching forward; cf. the boxing term *to K.O.*←*knock out*, also *to X* 'to cross out' (see *Time*, 17.III.67, p. 10). Bolder is the following statement, recently overheard from the lips of a *C* student: "If I *A* ['earn an A-grade in'] the final, can I *B* the course?" G. *KZ*←*Konzentrationslager* and Am.-E. *DMZ*←*Demilitarized Zone* illustrate the detachability of prefixes; derivational suffixes seem not to enjoy any comparable prerogative.

( = *Untergrund-*), *U-Boot* ( = *Untersee-*). English and German seem to enjoy a position of leadership along this line.

Another modernistic short-cut, fostered, it would seem, in military circles, prefixes to the noun at issue, typically a time unit, its own initial letter, thus marking it cryptically as the unit that really matters in a context clear to the initiated: *D-day* is the critical day for the start of an eagerly awaited operation; *H-hour*, the decisive hour, etc. One finds traces of this use in ultra-modern French: *L'heure H*, and elsewhere.[32] The starting-point is patently the well-known preference of logicians and mathematicians for "Point *P*", "Sentence *S*", etc. (*Zero hour* — which involves a numeral, not a letter — has its root in a different military tradition, but not — counter to a widespread belief — in the kind of count-down practiced at missile sites.)

The abbreviation reaches its maximum of effectiveness where a blunt gesture conjures up the convolution of a letter readily associated, in turn, with a slogan or catchword. Churchill's famous rallying formula "V for Victory" and the accompanying aggressive movement of two adjoining fingers immediately come to mind.[33] (These were often reinforced by the first four notes of Beethoven's Symphony No. 5 in C Minor, which symbolize the International Morse Code for the letter "V" — dot, dot, dot, dash.)

**Interplays of analogy.** The world of abbreviations, a separate microcosm though hardly one hermetically sealed off from other avenues of communication, has its own rules for interplays of analogy. The extreme rarity of word-final *-rs* in modern French makes one wonder whether the formal and semantic proximity of *URSS* /ürs/ and *ours* /urs/ 'bear' (the name of the animal traditionally emblematic of that country) could be plausibly attributed to coincidence; here

---

[32] I know of one facetious variation on *D-Day*. On July 15, 1964, at the height of the Republican Party's San Francisco Convention, one local newspaper came out with this flashy headline: "*B-Day for Barry Goldwater*". One is tempted to place in this area of connotation the title of the motion picture, *Dial "M" for Murder*.

[33] The element of humor is very potent in all categories of abbreviations; coll. G. (Berlin) *j.w.d.* /jotvede/←*ganz weit drauszen* derives its impact from the jocular symbolization of the initial consonant in *ganz* by *j*, in tribute to the local substandard pronunciation. Intimacy, restriction to a closed social circle (G. *Uni*←*Universität* among students), even to the sphere of a single family or a couple, and prudishness have been additional factors in truncation, literation, and acronymics alike; cf. n. 24, above.

the thread of a common noun of long standing and that of an ultra-modern abbreviation for the name of a country appear inextricably interwoven. Conversely, a perceptive observer not so long ago reported from Alabama that the highly erratic, if amusing, abbreviation SLIC for *S.C.L.C.* ← *Southern Christian Leadership Conference* was launched by some experimentally minded speakers involved in an event all participants of which freely used SNIC for *S.N.C.C.*[34] Here, strictly within the realm of nascent acronyms, one minor irregularity is seen gradually spawning another, of far greater magnitude.

**Proper names.** The use of abbreviations in proper names is a multi-dimensional problem transcending the narrow frame of this essay. Let me simply enumerate its most conspicuous dimensions: the affectionate truncation of first names in hypocoristic variant forms (cf. E. *Abe, Dan, Dave, Sam, Sol* for men; *Pam, Pat* for women, though in the ranks of the latter the addition of *-ie, -y* is widely practiced, regardless of age: *Jackie* from *Jacqueline, Abby* from *Abigail*[35]); the acceptance in certain social contexts of literation in familiar address and in deliberately informal signatures — a fad that has frequently led to the coinage of nicknames;[36] the use of

---

[34] See Renata Adler, "Letter from Selma", *The New Yorker* (10.IV.1965), pp. 121 ff., esp. 121c and 122b.

[35] Other languages achieve roughly the same effect through reduplication of the core syllable: *Pepe* from OSp. *Jose-pe*, or through suffixation (often in conjunction with truncation), cf. It. *Giacom-ino*, G. *Hein-i* (from *Heinrich*), *Rud-i* (from *Rudolf*), and *Ton-i* (from *Anton*), R. (a) *Alë-ša* (from *Aleksej*), *Anto-ša* (from *Anton*), *Ja-ša* (from *Jakov*), *Ma-ša* (from *Mar'ja*), (m., f.) *Saša* (from *Aleksan-dr* or *-dra*), or (b) *Kolja* (from *Nikolaj*), *Kostja* (from *Konstantin*), *Nastja* (from *Anastas'ja*), *Petja* (from *Pëtr*), *Polja* (from *Paulina*), *Sonja* (from *Sof'ja*), *Tolja* (from *Anatolij*), *Vanja* (from *Ivan*), *Volodja* (from *Vladimir*), or else (c) *Pavlik* (from *Pavel*). Truncation in this context involves apheresis as often as it does apocope; and a teasing effect can be produced by the addition of a masculine suffix to a feminine name, as in French (*Marie*~*Marion*), under conditions investigated by Gilliéron and, later, by Spitzer and Hasselrot. On the Spanish material see P. M. Boyd-Bowman, "Cómo obra la fonética infantil en la formación de los hipocorísticos", *NRFH*, IX (1955), 337–366; the Russian side is highlighted by E. Stankiewicz, "The Expression of Affection in Russian Proper Names", *Slavic and East European Journal*, XV (1957), 196–210.

[36] In current American English practice, addressing a person (often an older partner or one particularly respected) by his initials — say *X.M.* for *Xavier Miller* — marks the selection of a level of social contact approximately intermediate between those characterized by "first name" and "formal" address. In academic circles nicknames have frequently sprouted from such literations; thus, the late medievalist Ernest H. Kantorowicz (cf. *RPh.*, XVIII, 1–15) was known to his

initials alone (or of an initial plus a favored segment of the family name) in the identification of authorship and, at a later stage, the creation of an acronymic *nom de plume*.[37]

**Sequences of identical letter-sounds.** One cluster of minor problems concerns the succession of identical letter-sounds, entirely by themselves or as parts of longer formulas, as the -*AA*- in *NAACP*←*National Association for the Advancement of Colored People*, the -*LL*- in *FILLM*←*Fédération Internationale des Langues et Littératures Modernes*, the -*RR*- in *UNRRA*, the -*SS* in *OSS*← *Office of Strategic Services* and, at the opposite end of the political spectrum, in *TASS*. Here the acronym, as a written formula, is unimpeachably explicit; but in oral delivery it falls short of yielding

[37] Such *noms de plume* have, to be sure, a slightly journalistic ring. Thus, the contemporary Argentine writer Héctor F. Miri signs his pieces *Hefeme*, an odd composite in which one discerns *efe* for the middle initial and *eme* for *M-*, but no *hache* for *H-*. At the beginning of this century, one of two Russian writers bearing the same name *Vasilevskij* added to that name *bukva* 'letter', and the other *ne-bukva* 'non-letter'. One protagonist in Vladimir Tendrjakov's novel *Svidanije s Nefertiti* (Moscow, 1964) is nicknamed by his classmates "*Myš* without a soft sign', to distinguish rather coarsely, or even derisively, the spelling of his name from that of the common noun *myš'* 'mouse'. Teams of writers and artists may devise semi-jocose names to mark their joint authorship; such artificial names, as a rule, are composite, containing torsos or fragments of each member's original name. Frequently, the initial syllables are conjoined; thus, the exiled Russian poets *Mixail Gorlin* and *Raisa Blox*, romantically linked and later married, signed some of their poems *Mirajev*, while three Russian painters working on their home-ground, *M. Kuprinov*, *P. Krylov*, and *Nik. Sokolov*, exhibit under the joint name *Kukryniksy* (1965). The first name *Vladen*←*Vlad(imir I. L)e(ni)n* or *L)en(in)* has been officially admitted in the Soviet Union. If the first syllable from one man's name and the last from his partner's name were to be amalgamated, the result — in terms of linguistic architecture — would be the same as in E. *liger* 'cross-breed of lion and tiger', Am.-E. *brunch* (*breakfast* × *lunch*), *smog*, and *hottle* 'hot bottle' (for tea or coffee), a pattern of blending which J. Vendryes examines in *BSLP*, XLIV:2 (1947–48), 33 f.; in February 1967 it was enriched with *dawk* 'mediator between *doves* and *hawks*'. In experimental poetry this technique has been carried to unusual lengths; thus, Blas de Otero compressed the title of his collection "Án[gel fieramente humano]" plus "[Redoble de concien]cia" to *Ancia* (1958), possibly with an additional pun on *ansia* 'anxiety'. Cf. also *Tanzania*, the name of a new African country (*Tanganyika* × *Zanzibar*); *Frisco*, in highly informal reference to *San Francisco*, with a playful hint at *frisk(y)*; F. *franglais* 'Anglicized French' and Am.-E. *Spanglish*; also the series *Mari-bel*, *Clari-bel*, *Flori-* (beside *Flora-)bel* (from *María Isabel*, etc.), which currently enjoys wide acceptance in the Spanish-speaking countries.

---

intimates as *EKa* (pronounced in German fashion), because he signed his memos "E.Ka.". Extra-economical newspaper headlines, on the other hand, have propagated the use of initials for the names of American presidents (*FDR*, *JFK*, *LBJ*).

an accurate clue to the full name, especially where consonants are at issue, and the language involved is, like French, unprepared for gemination; as a result, one nugget of the information to be conveyed tends to go astray. Where no segment precedes, or follows upon, the bare repetition of a consonant, speakers must have recourse to literation. A certain shrillness of the message — perhaps in unavoidable recoil from the threat of monotony — is, typically, the consequence. This overtone may be welcome as a purveyor of emphasis or even as a tool of intimidation; not for nothing did Himmler's *SS* almost match, in its graphemic pattern, the American South's older *KKK ← Ku-Klux-Klan* (initially organized: 1867–77; revived in 1915), a name which has, rather characteristically, outlasted such early regional competitors as "Knights of the White Camellia", "White League", and "Invisible Circle". By the same token, any gentler message will be clad in a less strident phonic garb; witness the semi-formal *Three-D Policy* ("Determination, Deliberation, Discussion") not so long ago proclaimed by the President of the United States, a slogan which, on the linguistic side if not in substantive value, calls to mind the *Tridelts* (members of the *Tridelta* — ΔΔΔ Sorority). Hollywood fans to this day remember *3-D movies* 'three-dimensional motion pictures'.

**Transmission from language to language.** Where latter-day contacts between languages of roughly comparable structure are involved, abbreviations are apt to spread in different fashions. One possibility is, first, to translate the full name of the agency, bureau, organization, etc., then to produce, from the resources of the target language, a new abbreviation, entirely independent of the old. *U.S.A.* thus becomes *EE. UU.* in Spanish and СШA in Russian (while F. *États-Unis* and G. *Vereinigte Staaten* seem compatible with unassimilated, capsulized, *U.S.A.*); *U.N.* emerges as *ONU* in French and Italian (cf. F. *onu-s-ien* 'employee of the United Nations), OH in Russian, etc. The formidable *CIA ← Central Intelligence Agency* is presented to diffident Russians as ЦРУ ←*Central'-noje Razvedyvatel'noje Upravlenije*. The alternative is to carry over, into the target language, the phonic content of the literation from the source language, as when Russian newspapers in New York transcribe NATO by НЭЙТО and SEATO by СИТО, blurring in the process the identity of some vital constituents of the original formulas. A rival transliteration, not quite so reckless, renders *A.F.L.* by

ЭйЭфЭл and *C.I.O.* by СиАйО, using the interplay of capitals and lower-case letters as a means of helpful audio-visual guidance and hierarchization.[38]

## 5. The Shape of the Letters

If the conventional sequence of the letters in the alphabet is something inherently abstract, the individual configuration of each link in that chain involves an immediate appeal to the readers' and writers' visual impressionability. Especially if the printed capital letters are slightly stylized, in the directions of straightening, rounding, or tightening, their basic geometric design may stand out very sharply, as when the O in Latin script, reduced to its bare essentials, signals a complete circle; the T suggests three quarters of a cross and the C, three quarters of a circle; the A marks a triangle on two feet (in contrast to Greek delta = Δ, a plain equilateral triangle) and the B, two semi-circles springing from a perpendicular line, etc. Some of the distinctive Cyrillic characters (the Ш and the Ж, say) display a beautiful symmetric contour. Within the realm of anatomy, two salient malformations of human legs are crisply described by the German tags *X-Beine* 'knock-knees' vs. *O-Beine* 'bandy legs, bow legs' (a pattern imitated by Estonian; cf. mod. Gr. λαβδός [adj.] 'knock-kneed', from the characteristic outline of λάβδα). In modern American industry and merchandising, in the symbolization of traffic rules (made international of late on European highways), and in many other domains of contemporary living, the angle or curve of the capital letter conveys a brief message, instantaneously assimilable and extremely graphic. What could be more plain than a *Y* for: 'Watch out for the bifurcation of the cause-way!'

[38] I cannot here expatiate on all manner of abbreviations currently employed in technology, but shall quote from W. E. Geiger's helpful memorandum on the use of Radio and TV international call-letters, "an easily datable category which may reveal trends and fancies in letter usage, e.g. (a) esoteric: *WBBM* and *WGN*, both Chicago; (b) partially transparent: *WCOP*, Boston (*W-C-O-P* or *W-COP*), and *KBEE*, Modesto (*K-B-E-E* or *K-BEE*); (c) network affiliation: *WCBC*, New York, and *KCBC*, San Francisco (Columbia Broadcasting System); (d) place or origin: *KPHO*, *Pho*enix, Ariz., and *KCMO*, *K*ansas *C*ity, *Mo.*; (e) metaphorical or humorous (designating some local trait or its desired opposite): *KOOL*, Phoenix, and *KOLD*, Tucson (a pleasant relief from Arizona's desert climate?), or *KABL*, Oakland–San Francisco (evoking S.F.'s historic *Cable*-Cars)". A preference for metaphor over literation seems to characterize the names of those stations established after 1945. Add Radio *KAL* — a student-operated and -managed radio station in Berkeley—suggestive of *Cal(ifornia)*.

or, viewed in the opposite direction, for 'Merging traffic'? Grammatically the pattern, at least in English, involves a compound, in which the first ingredient (the name of the letter) serves as the prime qualifier of the second; cf. the dressmaker's *A-skirt* and *V-neck-*(*sweat*)*shirt* (or *-blouse*, or *-sweater*); the architect's *A-frame*; the butcher's *T-bone-steak*; the driver's and traffic-policeman's *U-turn* (as against clumsier *hairpin-curve*), etc. Adoptions of this striking pattern in the Romance languages have necessitated certain adjustments to different syntactic conditions, cf. F. *décolleté en V*.

One visualizes two different classificatory approaches to this copious stock. The analyst may take as his point of departure the "designatum" and ask himself what material features of mid-20th-century civilization best lend themselves to this category of labelling. Up-to-date reference works like the *Webster-Merriam New Intern. Dict.*[3], supplemented by first-hand experience and reports of witnesses, show *T-* as an accepted qualifier of *abutment, bandage, bar, beam, bob, bolt, bulb, cart, cloth, connection, crank, cross, hinge, iron, pipe, plate, rail, rest, slot, square*; *T-straps* in women's shoes were a fad ca. 1960. On balance, not all these bits of evidence fall under our rubric: Since *T-cloth* is described as 'cotton-cloth stamped with a T, made in Great Britain and sold in Asia', the convolution of the subject is not at issue and the item must be discarded from our list (just as *U-boat* and *U-turn* belong to mutually clashing categories). An amusing side-line, in the direction of parlor games (rebus), is the use of the tag *T-spoon* — in reference to a tool not at all shaped like a *t* — for 'tea spoon' in the dining rooms of Sproul Hall and Rieber Hall, UCLA (personal observation, Nov. 1965 and July 1966); Berkeley's alternative answer to the problem is the gradual switch to the de-Briticized label *coffee-spoon*. The remaining cases, however, seem homogeneous (a *T-cart*, e.g., has a "body shaped like a T") and prove that handicraft and industry have been the main contributors and that deft mechanics, inventive construction engineers, and imaginative manufacturers, jobbers, and retailers of tools must all have had a heavy share in this nomenclatural vogue. From strictly technical and technological use (*I-beam*), the pattern spread to laconic captions in newspapers and mass-circulation weeklies; cf. *Life* (24.XII.65, p. 144): "The *T-shaped* grouping at lower left".

Far more exciting for the graphemicist is the classification by letter, i.e. by the "designans". Capital letters in modern Latin

... is also noted for its angularity, which has been highlighted by the title of a widely acclaimed British motion-picture: *The L-Shaped Room*. The *S*, characterized by litheness and sinuosity, is familiar not only from road signs (*S-curve*), but also from a compound like Pol. *esyfloresy* (pl.) 'arabesque design based on the letter S'. Noteworthy is the fact that the association of a characteristic curve with the configuration of capital *S* is equally germane to the naïve, the artistic, and the scientific mind; thus, Virginia Woolf's evocation ("The Letter *S*, she [Orlando] reflected, is the serpent in the Poet's Eden": Signet, p. 113; *Orlando, a Biography*, appeared in 1928) is reconcilable with the austere social scientist's preference for the graphic key-term *S-curve*. The sharp changes in direction marking the outline of the *Z* — noted for its acute angles — have added to the cross-linguistic appeal of G. *Zickzack*, F. *zigzag* (older spelling: *zigue-zague*), etc.; [40] on the moral level ('shiftiness, fickleness'), they account for coll. F. *être fait comme un z* 'to be a fraud'. From the Yiddish matrix of jokes one can adduce *kómets-berdl* 'Van Dyck beard' (*ḳameṣ*-shaped).

---

[39] Amusingly, some cultured and refined speakers of English associate *queue* (in reality, an obsolescent word for 'tail', of transparent French ancestry) with the queerly shaped letter *Q*.

[40] E. *zigzag*, Sp. *zigzag*, Ptg. *ziguezague*, Pol. *zygzag*, R. *zigzag*, etc., in some instances with further derivational offshoots (e.g., F. *zigzaguer* and Sp. *zigzagueo*); but It. *zigzag* seems unicuspidal (*una strada a zigzag; andare, cominciare a zigzag*). The starting point is apparently G. *Zickzack*, characterized by its neat vowel alteration *i–a* within a rigid consonantal frame. Such lexical items are, as a rule, facetious in tone and onomatopoeic either in actual origin or, more frequently, in secondarily acquired overtones; cf. W. Busch's slightly discrepant "*Ricke-racke, ricke-racke*/geht die Mühle mit Geknacke" in the most celebrated episode of *Max und Moritz*; also Sp. *tictac* beside E. *tick-tock*, *ping-pong*, and many other increasingly current words, some of them truly international, others definitely confined to a single language — particularly the verbs: to *flip-flop*, *tittle-tattle* (to a few such items a suffix is firmly welded: *wishy-washy*, *shilly-shally*). The *z*,

who experimented, until recently, with rival dialects, differently spelled, as literary media used to taunt each other with such reproaches as "blinding the *e*'s" (in reference to *e*) and "clashing vowels". The Yiddish stereotyped phrase *mit dogesh* 'with emphasis, with heavy insistence' involves a dot-like diacritic mark (placed inside, seldom alongside, the character) which denotes the gemination (lengthening) or the obstruent pronunciation of certain consonants in Hebrew. A freewheeling writer, taking his cue from phraseology so slanted, is at liberty to go much farther in his similes and metaphors, as did in fact a French romantic poet in musing: "Sur le clocher jauni, /La lune,/ *Comme un point sur un i*", or as did Christian Morgenstern in his "Fisches Nachtgesang", suggesting by the marks ordinarily reserved among classicists for vowel length vs. brevity (–◡) the closed or open mouths of a school of fish.

Imaginative, artistically inclined persons go very far along this line. An exiled Albanian may grimly recognize in *K* (evocative of *Kommunizëm*) the dim silhouette of a man dangling from a gallows. (For an empty gallows capital Cyrillic "g", namely Г, would provide a matchless sketch.) In his *Greguerías* R. Gómez de la Serna muses repeatedly on the profile of letters, both capital (*S, X, T, H, F, W, D*, in this order) and lower-case (*ñ, ü*); usually the object will suggest the letter: "El cisne es la *S* capitular del poema del estanque" (p. 49); sometimes the shape and the specific place of the letter within the alphabet jointly stir the writer's imagination: "La *H* es la escalera del alfabeto" (p. 78); or one letter will evoke another (p. 92); or else a letter will suggest an action devoid of relationship

then, was initially — on the articulatory or the acoustic-auditory level — an incidental element of *zigzag* and by no means a prime determinant of its meaning. But with the gradual rise of literacy, the secondary, visual association of the shape of *z* with the word's semantic content turned out to be so opportune and spellbinding as partially to overlay (or to reduce to subordinate rank) the original set of relationships. A separate etymological cameo on this pan-European word is a pressing desideratum.

to other letters (p. 99). But these artistic rêveries and idiosyncratic reactions, which take us back to Rimbaud, transcend the precinct of language proper, viewed as the backbone of speech-communities.[41] The shape of numerals has likewise ceased to be taken for granted; for one example of the fascination it exerts on a sensitive cartoonist see Saul Steinberg's phantasmagoria (*Life*, 10.XII.65, pp. 59–70).

[41] I cannot enlarge here on the artistic potentialities of the letters. The elaborate ornamental uses of letters in Oriental, esp. Arabic, script are well known; so is the fact that the intricacy of Chinese characters tends to blur the frontier between painting and exquisite writing. Modern Western taste rejects the pretentious ornamentation that encumbered certain styles of late-19th-century lettering through flourishes, distentions, elongations, crosshatching; in particular it frowns on the capitals of "la belle époque", clumsily loaded with nudes, etc. On the other hand, the 20th century has discovered a concealed affinity between calligraphy and the visual arts, a kinship for which ultramodern "precisionism" provides the clinching argument. Isolated letters and word fragments have figured in avant-garde paintings since shortly before the First World War. Georges Braque's "Soda" (1911) and "Oval Still Life" = "Le violon", Gino Severini's "Dynamic Hieroglyphic of the Bar Tabarin" (1912), Pablo Picasso's "Card Players" (1913–14) and "Green Still Life" beside "Pipe, Glass, Bottle of Rum" (1914), and Juan Gris' "Breakfast (1914) beside "Grapes and Wine" — all eight displayed in New York's Museum of Modern Art — are cases in point, illustrating (to quote a recent comment on Leningrad's Hermitage Collection) the "interplay of geometric planes and commercial lettering"; and in "Private of the First Division" (1914) by Kazimir Malevič isolated Cyrillic letters and whole words in Cyrillic script are allowed to act as analogous ingredients. As early as 1916–18 Paul Klee composed picture-poems, the almost illegible text of which merged with the colored squares; toward 1930 he was inspired by Arabic script. In his "W-geweihtes Kind" (1935) the W-shaped frown on the child's contorted face invites a dual or triple inter-pretation: (a) letter *W* /ve/, (b) *Weh* /ve/ 'grief', perhaps (c) *W-eihe* 'consecration'. Characteristically, in Joan Miró's piece "Woman With Undone Hair Greeting the Crescent Moon" (1939) the Chinese character for 'woman' flanks her symbolic delineation. A semi-abstract painting by the young experimentalist Günther Kraus (b. 1930) — on display in Vienna's Museum of Contemporary Art — is catalogued as "Großes *I;* Begegnungen, Überschreitungen". Into Saul Steinberg's "Design" both stylized (embellished) and non-stylized letters enter on a par, as important components. In Mark Tobey's "Calligraphic Structure" (1958) one sees stylized, dimly recognizable letters and light-colored "litteroid" signs projected against a background of red. See R. Étiemble, *The Written Word* (London, 1962), pp. 88 (Fernand Léger, "Still Life" [1925]), 90 (Henri Michaux, "Signs" [1951]), 91 (Marinetti, "Words" [1919]), 94 f. On words, fragments of words, near-words, often typographically interrupted, elided, bisected, see "Text into Texture", *TLS* (25.III.1965), p. 230 (mostly on "poem-prints") and two illustrations repro-duced on p. 225; for a good short essay on the area where the visual and the literal overlap turn to Ferdinand Kriwet, *Leserattenfänge; Sehtextkommentare* (Köln, 1965).

I am, on the whole, not concerned here with such uses as involve modified shapes of the letters. But let me quote, for the sake of its typographic piquancy, this excerpt from G. A. Shipley's memorandum: "In the South-west and West of the United States, the alphabet is put to distinctive use in branding horses and cattle (also, less generally, sheep). The simplest brands are ordinary letters, usually paired off (*CB, RL*). Quite frequently the shapes of the letters are altered. The

## 6. The Acoustic Image of the Underlying Sound

Given the widespread equation of sound and letter in certain cultures, it is theoretically conceivable that in a few set phrases (e.g., in acoustically slanted similes) names of letters evocative of sounds might occur as welcome frames of reference. One can imagine, savored in isolation or arranged in sets, stereotyped comparisons of the type: ⌐shriller than an *I*¬, or ⌐dull as an *O*¬, or ⌐hissing like a [š]¬, or again ⌐no less flat than a [. . .]¬, etc.

In the introductory section of his recent monograph (see n. 12, above) I. Fónagy has arrayed numerous cross-cultural testimonies on the use, from time immemorial, of impressionistic qualifiers in the classification of sounds: thin or sharp vs. thick, light or brittle, fragile vs. heavy, weak or empty vs. strong, clear vs. dark (or murky), straight vs. skewed, high vs. low, narrow vs. broad or flat, acute vs. obtuse, white vs. black, cold vs. hot or steaming, delicate vs. rough, quick or nimble vs. slow, and even male vs. female. Understandably, his authorities have, for the most part, been grammarians and teachers of diction (in some corroborative tests his own children have acted as "subjects");[42] Dante appears briefly as a witness (p. 23) for the existence of soft, woolly, gliding, smooth, and hairy sounds — but it is Dante the theorist rather than the practicing poet that has here been appealed to. If the inquiry were to spill over into the adjoining domains of *belles-lettres*, folklore, and untutored laymen's reactions (where pertinent material, precariously dispersed, can be assembled only through chance discoveries), there is a high probability that the slot here posited through logical extrapolation might effectively be filled.

## 7. Puns on the Label of a Letter

In some instances, we recall, the conventional name of a letter

---

[42] Few went as far in embroidering as F. Cascales who, in his *Tablas poéticas* (1617), called *p* "soberbia e hinchada" and *u* "sutil y lánguida".

most common deformations are achieved by combining two letters into one character (ß←*JB*, И←*NL*) [these ligatures are reminiscent of Arabic script]; a common var. involves the reversal of one member of a set (⅃B←*BL*, ꓭB←*KB*). Occasionally one letter will absorb another: ₭←*DK*; but 𝗣 would be interpreted 'Circle P' (see below). Many brands are formed by letters accompanied by qualifying or distinguishing signs, e.g. A̱, ⟨A⟩; these qualifiers have conventional names, and such brands are «read»: A̱ 'Rocking A', ⟨A⟩ 'Diamond A'. Further variation is achieved by «resting» a letter on its side (Ɐ), whereupon it ranks as 'Lazy'. Some combinations are quite intricate".

(as used in spelling-out a word, say; also in reciting the alphabet), or at least its "peak", approximately coincides with the acoustic value of the phoneme so designated; cf. the tags of the vowel sounds in such languages as German, Russian (except for ы), Spanish, and Italian. In other situations the label attached to the letter is discernibly different from any correlated sound effect; note especially the discrepant designations of the *H* in the major European languages (It. *acca*, F. *ache*, Sp. *hache*, Ptg. *agá*, etc.). In characteristic Semitic alphabets, particularly in the Hebrew, the name for each consonant pillar and each diacritic sign or vowel symbol is a full-bodied word which, more often than not, is endowed with some primary meaning, hierarchically far weightier than its derivative orthographic meaning; e.g. H. *'ajin* 'eye' (and sign for a pharyngeal consonant), *jad* 'hand' (and sign for a prepalatal semiconsonant). The situation obtaining in the Greek and the Old Cyrillic alphabet (as used for Church Slavic) is partially reminiscent of Semitic (Phoenician) so far as the length of the labels — as distinct from their partially voided semantic (in particular imagerial) content — is concerned. Both kinds of label, the natural or sound-imitative and the conventionally autonomous, enter occasionally into word-plays, in rebus fashion. In cultures exploiting humorous situations — to produce the impression of informality, light touch, extemporaneousness, originality, gaiety, banter, irrepressible naughtiness, persiflage aimed at all that seems stale and stuffy — this flashy device is effectively harnessed in ticketing fancy food items, unconventional ("exotic") types of entertainment, all such services as appeal to the customer's unashamed hankering after modernity and escape from normalcy: *Bar-B-Q ← barbeque*, *The hungry i* (name of a San Francisco night club famous for its comedians and vocalists, with *i* standing — one guesses — for [ogling, staring] "eye" or — so legend has it — for "intellectual", with a possible side-glance at "I" 'ego', while the lower-case letters are impudently thrown in for additional shock), *U-drive* and *U-haul* (two recent manifestations of the "do-it-yourself" fad) beside less sharply silhouetted *U-save* (supermarket), etc. Particularly amusing, on account of the built-in chain reaction of surprises, is *U-Smile* (name of a motel outside Kansas City, Mo.) which, on further thought, resolves itself into *U.S. Mile.*[43] Semi-

---

[43] In this twilight zone one may also place the spelling "eye" for the letter "i", which, as a result of its intrinsic palsy, suffers from poor visibility. In many cities with "alphabet streets" (e.g. Washington, D.C., and Sacramento, Calif.), the

humorous in background, perhaps, and reminiscent of $X$ for 'extension' is the salesman's abbreviation $XL \leftarrow extra\text{-}large$, in reference to men's shirts; this particular symbolization of size by letter clashes with (a) the entering of a given letter into a reduplicative set: $AA$, $A$ (for eggs), $AA$ through $EE$ (for shoes) and (b) one series of consecutive letters: $A$, $B$, $C$, $D$ (for men's pajamas).

Whatever one may think of the latter-day commercialization of these jocular elements, their primary use in comic rhymes, riddles, parlor games, anecdotes, etc. is unassailable. Of the many examples that come to mind let me adduce just two. In the 'forties the following comic rhyme swept all of U.S.A.: *ABCD goldfish?* ('Abie, see de [ = the] goldfish?') — *LMNO goldfish!* ('[H]ell, [th]em ain' [n]o goldfish!') — *OSAR goldfish* ('Oh, [y]es, [th]ey are goldfish').[44] The other illustration immerses us in a multilingual milieu. Yiddish, in its basic layer an alloy of German dialects, but one imposing on its users — all of them literate — familiarity with the Hebrew alphabet, represents a patch of unsurpassably fertile ground for all kinds of cross-cultural puns. To appreciate the joke one must remember that G. *Heu* /hoj/ 'hay' corresponds to Yid. /he/, while the letter $H$ happens to be also known as /he/, in Semitic tradition, as against standard G. /ha/. The story itself is short enough: An avaricious

---

[44] The supply of rebus-like jokes and riddles is, of course, inexhaustible. The former category may be further illustrated with *YYUR/YYUB/ICUR/YY4me* ("Too wise you are,/ too wise you be,/I see you are/too wise for me"); the latter is aptly exemplified with the question: "Which five letters may form a sentence expressive of forgiveness?", prompting the answer: *IXQSU* ("I excuse you"). Half a century ago, Latin American adolescents drew much inspiration of this kind from H. Pipiritaña, *Media tonelada de chistes*; the German-speaking countries have their own supply of *Witzkisten*, and a veritable subliterature has sprouted the world over. While games of chance and strategy, viewed as a topic of sober scientific analysis, are rapidly becoming an accepted part of the collegiate mathematical curriculum, a study of the playful ingredients of language has of late crystallized in lay quarters under the name of LOGOLOGY. Witness Dmitri A. Borgmann's spearheading venture *Language on Vacation*, sponsored by a publishing house as respectable as Scribner's. According to reviewers, the book deals with palindromes, reversals, transposals, word squares, ciphers, anagrams, crytograms, polygraphs, and the like, to the delight of all "doodlers with numbers and letters". At proof I can report the publication of Borgmann's latest book: *Beyond Language; Adventures in Word and Thought*.

---

*I Street* appears as *Eye Street* on maps and some streetsigns; similarly, *Jay* stands for *J* in such contexts. Through further, less justified extension of this principle, a bifurcation in a California road or highway may be referred to as a *wye*; thus, the Y-shaped junction of a well-travelled East–West "cut-off" with the north–south highway a few miles to the south of Napa is known to motorists as the *Napa Wye*. But aviators still record *V-* and *Y-formations* (of planes).

Jew is reported to have fed his donkey a gradually diminishing daily ration of hay until, at the bitter end, he offered him, instead of any food, a complimentary glimpse of *H* in a Hebrew primer.

Within the Biblical tradition of Christianity, *aleph* was occasionally used in medieval Europe as an interjection, in token of self-commiseration ( = F. *hélas!*, G. *wehe mir!*, It. *ohimè!*, R. *gore [mne]!*), the frame of reference being Lamentations 1:1. As an exclamation, *aleph!*, a pure Hebraism, functions in a Latin poem by the late-15th-century Florentine Arrigo da Settimello; Dantesque *aleppe* (in Pluto's inarticulately violent invective, see *Inf.* VII:1: "Pape Satàn Pape Satàn *aleppe*") is likely to represent Tuscanized *aleph* (cf. the treatment of Gr.-L. PH in *Giuseppe*), while *pape* may echo Terentian *papae* παπαί 'indeed'.

## 8. Interactions of the Separate Functions

After categorizing as neatly as possible the secondary uses of alphabetic letters in actual language, one is led to revert to the question: Is it possible to identify combinations of these functions or overlaps between them? The answer is in the affirmative. (Because there have been incidental hints to this effect all along, a measure of repetition is unavoidable; but a concluding restatement has its justification.)

Several rather different situations come to mind. Hypersensitive persons (such as poets), who have been cultivating experiences in synesthesia, are apt, I suppose, to establish connections between the graphic thinness of an *I* and a certain phonetic thinness (or shrillness) of the corresponding sound [i], or, for that matter, between the roundness of an *O* as a letter and the rounding of the mouth in the pronunciation of [o], if not of [ɔ].

Such sensory cross-connections involving the interplay of the third and the fourth use retain their validity in art and have exerted a modicum of tolerable influence on learned nomenclature, but are unlikely to affect the humbler forms of speech.

A speaker's leaning toward acronymic abbreviation, on the other hand, may very well be paired off with his preference for granting autonomy to short segments of the alphabetic array. Characteristic of ultramodern trends, particularly in the English-speaking world (ironically, also in the Soviet sphere and in Israel), is in fact the selection of such abbreviatory slogans, titles, and names, especially for aggressively marketed brands and for dynamically fostered movements, as lend themselves either to conspicuously easy memorization or to strikingly effective enunciation (best of all, to both). Whereas previously an infectious sequence of catchwords was first launched on its own merits and only then was the wisdom of some kind of space-saving abbreviation separately tested, the stage reached at the mid-century point demands that in preliminary deliberations about catchwords, at the very moment of their "incubation", the optimal advantage to be derived from the impact of their prospective compression be allowed to intervene as a prime determinant of the final choice. The three most fitting mnemonic devices available in the Western World are (a) either to arrange the acronym in such manner that it may convey, in capsulized form, an appropriate message of its own; cf. the appeal of such richly suggestive neologisms as R. *MIG* (name of a military jetplane) 'eye's wink, moment', *CARE* and *CORE*←*Congress of Racial Equality*,[45] as against the colorless, linguistically indifferent *AFL*, *CIO, HUAC*, etc. of earlier vintage (to say nothing of *RENFE*, the uninspiring name of Spain's national railway company, and of downright cacophonous *SSSR*); (b) or, by way of alternative, to array the letters in sequential order, as in California's (and other

---

[45] Additional examples: Am.-E. *CATS*←*Children's Amateur Theater Service*; *FLIC*←*Film Lovers' Independent Cinema* (*Society*), with a hint of coll. *flick* 'motion picture', both organizations with headquarters in San Francisco (1965); *SCOPE*← *Southern Community Organization for Political Education*; *VISTA*←*Volunteer in Service to America*; *VOW*←*Villagers Opposed to the War* (Berkeley, Oct. 1965); *YANK*←*Youth of America Needs to Know* (a group allegedly close to the John Birch Society); G. *ODESSA*←*Organization der ehemaligen SS Angehörigen*, with the name of a Russian seaport beckoning — as a haven of safety, a dream-like avenue of escape, or a nightmare of remorse? It is rumored that *SIR*←*Society for Individual Rights* (San Francisco) seeks to attract homosexuals. From Italy I can report *FIAT* (with Biblical reverberations)←*Fabbr. Ital. Aut. Tor.* and *UNICA*← *Unione Nazionale Italiana Caramelle* (*e*) *Affini*. A rebellious student movement might have gathered more than ephemeral strength had the surging defiance been first expressed by the organization's threatening full name, then epitomized and driven home, in punch-line style, by a hard-hitting acronym (say, *FIST*←*Free, Independent Students for Turmoil*). The alert layman has by now become thoroughly sensitized to the presence of acronyms, real or latent. Thus, the celebrated San Francisco wit and columnist Herb Caen wondered (*Chronicle*, 14.v.65) why *Trans American Trust* "comes right out with *TAT*", while its rival *Title Insurance & Trust* holds back with *\*TIT*, the upshot of the joke being the subtle suggestion of the long consecrated humorous binomial *tit for tat*. That same columnist, known for his indulgence in lexical acrobatics, was quick to oblige his readers with the facetious acronym (17.VIII.65) *STET*←*Society for Typographic Errors that Titillate* (= typos). Particularly witty (and informative of its scope) is the name of the Californian travel agency *AMIGO*←*HondurAs, GuateMala, Costa Rica, NicaraGua, El Salvador*.

states') *ABC* Agent, vividly calling to mind the "Alcoholic Beverage Control Act"; (c) or else to achieve a striking monochromatic effect through repetition: *BBB←Better Business Bureau*. Where meaningful authentic words fail to crystallize, there remains the residual possibility of the emergence of such acronyms — bordering on works of art — as suggest names hauntingly beautiful and at the same time not implausible, e.g. *EUDEBA←E(ditorial) U(niversitaria) de B(uenos) A(ires)*.[46] Of these various techniques it is clearly *ABC* alone that illustrates an overlap between the first and the second function.

Of the exceedingly rare interlocking of the first and the third use no other example is on hand but *Mind your p's and q's!* (see Section 2, above). If the anecdote tracing the formula to *Mind your pints and quarts!* is based on ascertainable historical fact,[47] the dual motivation, pictorial and sequential, of the contrast $p:q$ would explain the immense appeal and rapid spread of an initial tavern joke.

The following combination of uses may be unprecedented. Dartmouth College sponsors a summer educational program for underprivileged children called *ABC←A Better Chance*. The abbreviation conjoins two varieties of the first use—the vivifying sequential effect and the topical suggestion of the program's actual goal: imparting the "ABC" (and its implications) to children. This message is more exciting in its polyphony than such combinations of the first and of the second use as *AB←Assembly Bill*, *ABC← American Broadcasting Company*, and *ABCD←Accelerated Business Collection Delivery* (a new U.S. mail service, launched in 1965). What is hidden behind the alluring title of Victor Rozov's celebrated movie script (1961): АБВГД?

[46] Ever new such deceptively euphonious, "romantically" sounding names seem to be crystallizing. The latest that have come to my attention are *ARAPA← American Research and Professional Association* (Berkeley, Spring 1965) and *ERIC← Educational Research Information Center* (Washington, D.C., 1966–67). Linguistically relevant is the fact that, to increase the percentage of vowels and thus to enhance the audio-oral attractiveness of their brain-children, the engineers of formulas currently pepper them with *o*'s (from *of*) and *a*'s (from *and*), cf. *CORE*. The *t* of the prep. *to* was used to full advantage in one short-lived *ad hoc* coinage: *METEI←Medical Expedition to Easter Island*, a formula manufactured in 1965. Contrast this practice with the older strict confinement to the nuclear words, as in *AFL←American Federation (of) Labor* and *CIO←Congress (of) Industrial Organizations*, where *of* is left unrepresented.

[47] Derived from the manner of serving beer in English pubs (16th and 17th centuries). One had to "mind" the *p*'s and the *q*'s, because they were marked on a board, and the customer paid later by the number of marks.

DD

In the past, some linguistic scientists have gone out of their way to stress the derivative character of script as against speech.[48] It was probably wholesome or even necessary to drive home relentlessly the distinction in rank; but once the point has been made, it is equally wholesome to remind ourselves that, tape, phonograph record, radio, and television screen notwithstanding, one can observe a present-day global trend toward increased "old-fashioned" literacy. To this rational curve has been superadded, as a discrete feature of style, the fascination for the abstract and distilled. The chances are that, riding the combined crest of these two vogues, the names, sounds, shapes, and successions of letters (the last-mentioned in small segments of the alphabet and in either crude or sophisticated abbreviatory successions) will play a progressively influential part in the phraseological contour and in the lexical deposit of all languages whose speakers resort to alphabets.[49]

[48] No expert has taken a more uncompromisingly vigorous, indeed, rigid stance on this matter than the late L. Bloomfield; see my review, in *RPh.*, XVI (1962–63), 83–91, of his posthumous book *Let's Read; a Linguistic Approach* (1961), ed. C. L. Barnhart, with special reference to the Introduction — the review is included in the present volume. My own stand on this score coincides, by and large, with D. L. Bolinger's ("Visual Morphemes", *Lg.*, XXII [1946], 333–340), who spoke up courageously at a moment when it was almost hazardous to do so; see especially his remarks on "Visual paronomasia": visual puns, intentional misspellings, and other non-phonemic signs, such as dashes, quotes, spacing-out (pp. 337–339).

[49] I owe certain data and ideas to my late wife, María Rosa Lida de Malkiel, and to a number of friends: R. D. Abrahams, A. L. Askins, Rina Benmayor, W. Bright, D. Catalán, F. M. Chambers, O. Elizabeth Closs, Louise G. Clubb, P. B. Fay, W. E. Geiger, V. Golla, J. L. Grigsby, R. A. Hall, Jr., Henry R. and Renée T. Kahane, Raimundo and Denah Lida, M. Mayrhofer, B. Migliorini, Josephine Miles, Arshi Pipa, M. R. Rohr, M. J. Ruggerio, M. Shapiro, G. A. Shipley, R. Stefanini, A. Taylor, Eero and Marilyn M. Vihman, U. Weinreich, Alina and Elizabeth H. Wierzbiańska, B. M. Woodbridge, Jr. See also n. 30 above for a special acknowledgment to Mr. Michael J. Toconita.

There are several side-issues which limitations on space have prevented me from going into. One rewarding direction might have been the study of commercial brand-names; Leo Spitzer's Smith College lecture of February 19, 1948 ("American Advertising Explained as Popular Art"), included one year later in his book *A Method of Interpreting Literature* (pp. 102–149), is quite unenlightening on this major facet of the chosen "Gebrauchskunst". I have been unable to consult the Illinois dissertation by Jean Praninskas, *The Processes and Patterns of Trade Name Creation.* — The jocular expansion of abbreviations, briefly hinted at in n. 24, actually represents an autonomous "secondary use", because it interposes between two full-blown word groups a mediating literation of implicitly equal rank; cf., in the parlance of American military advisers stationed in Vietnam, *Viet Cong*→ *V.C.*→*Victor Charlie* and, on the home front, *Vietnam Day Committee*→*VDC*→ *Very Damn Clean* (advertisement of a Berkeley launderette, Nov. 1965). *ACT* can be read alternatively *Always Collecting Trash* and *Active Conservation Tactics*, depending on the user's stylistic preference. The motivation is not necessarily jocose; superstition, pooh-poohing, and still grimmer attitudes may be behind this "verblümter Ausdruck". In fact, purposefully distortive decoding has become a fashionable pastime or parlor game in our own generation. In American society, *TV* has become such an inveterate abbreviation for *television* that its occasional use for *transvestites* (*Time*, 21.1.66, p. 40*b*) exudes special pungency. — Regarding the use of Latin *N*, in Cyrillic environment, for 'X' by Russian classics, note that Gogol, in veiling the locale of his narratives, wavered between *NN* (*Dead Souls*, opening line) and raised triple star, thus: *po ulicam sela* \*\*\*, to which he even dared attach an adjectival suffix: \*\*\* *skoj cerkvi* (*Evenings* . . .); cf. p. 363, above.

At proof I can briefly expatiate on a few minor matters. To the bibliography cited add E. S. Sheldon, "The Origin of the English Names of the Letters of the Alphabet", [*Harvard*] *Studies and Notes in Philology*, I : 2; id., "Further Notes . . .", ibid., II : 4. The Soviet-style abbreviations do indeed go back to a technique introduced by the First World War staffs, e.g. *naštakor←načal'nik štaba korpusa* 'chief of staff of an army corps'. On the modernistic poet Xlebnikov's attempt to distinguish between "active" and "inactive" vowels and on N. Gumilëv's reaction see S. Karlinsky, *Marina Cvetaeva: Her Art and Life* (Berkeley, 1966), p. 145. Racy Russian idioms involving (obsolescent) names of letters include: *propisat' ižicu* 'to make a reprimand' and *znat' na jat'* 'to know exactly' beside *sdelat' na jat'* 'to do properly'. The latest blend that has come to my attention (and one very bizarrely compounded ) is Am.-E. *slurb* 'suburban slum'. An apocopated acronym is Central California's *BART←Bay Area Rapid Transit* (*System*). Alongside a multitude of effective latter-day abbreviations, either endowed with meaning, such as *ACT←American Conservatory Theater*, *ACCESS←Action Coördinating Committee to End Segregation in Suburbs*, or just euphonious, like *NaBisCo← National Biscuit Company*, *MIRV←Multiple Independent Reëntry Vehicle*, one observes, alas, such infelicities as the structurally hybrid and, on top, cacophonous *CINCPAC←Commander-in-chief*, *Pacific*. To the roster of facetious reinterpretations add *DZ*, ordinarily *Demilitarized Zone*, but among academicians *Dogmatic Zealot* (S. J. Hayakawa); J. Horwitz expands racist *WASP* into *Wholesale, Angry, Sensational Paranoia* (*Time*, 8.IX.67). The fact that *ABC←Audit Bureau of Circulation* (headquarters: Chicago) has just celebrated its fiftieth anniversary may yield a valuable chronological clue to the rise of a fad. A rare example of the spread of American-style humor to the Soviet Union is *UKSUS* (lit. 'vinegar')← *Upravlenije Koordinacii Snabženija i Uregulirovanija Sbyta*, a fancy economic agency ridiculed in a satirical short story by B. Jegorov (1964). An acronym within an acronym is *PAR←Perimeter Acquisition Radar* (*Life*, 29.IX.67).

A separate chapter could have been devoted to certain implications of taboo. The counting of letters entering into a controversial word, and the circumlocutory substitution of that number of letters for the lexical item discriminated against are familiar from colloquial English; specifically, from latter-day obscenity issues in this country (books, stage, campus demonstrations), which have revolved around notorious *four-letter words*. This mode of evading offensiveness is not new; cf. Plautus' *trium litterarum homo = fur* 'thief', F. *cinq lettres* as a "verblümter Ausdruck" for the item denoting 'excrements', Ptg. (sporad.) *onze letras* (or *dez-e-um*) = *alcoviteira* 'bawd, procuress'; see J. da Silva Correia, "O eufemismo e o difemismo na língua e na literatura portuguesa", *Arquivos da Univ. de Lisboa*, XII (1927), 445–788, esp. 529 f., and "Ecos vocabulares e fraseológicos", *RL*, XXX (1932), 103; cf. p. 359, above. Alternatives include:

(a) Retrenchment through the use of the word-initial letter followed by ellipsis, a procedure familiar to readers of nineteenth-century editions of Puškin's frivolous verse (thus: *ž*. . . . 'buttocks') and involving a very thin veiling, particularly where the incriminated word happened to rhyme with one innocent enough to have been left unabridged;

(b) Conspicuous, hence self-correcting, replacement by a word of very similar shape and preferably quite unrelated meaning, to provoke all the stronger guffaws of laughter;

(c) Oblique evocation of the word through hint of an anecdote or episode associated with its uninhibited pronunciation, as in F. *mot de Cambronne* (which the general in question, incidentally, disputed having ever uttered under strain);

(d) Substitution of a modern foreign equivalent (*derrière* among coy, prissy, or demure speakers of English) or of an unimpeachably learned Latin term.

"For writing that is full of spelling errors, e.g. by a semiliterate, the Yiddish expression is *Noyekh mit zibn grayzn* 'Noah with seven mistakes'. The conundrum is based on the fact that the Hebrew name of this Biblical personage has only two letters all told, so that considerable ingenuity is required to make seven errors in it" (U. Weinreich).

# Topical Index

THIS Index is geared to serving as a guide to notions, technical terms, occasional metaphors, and a very few schools of thought discussed in the essays. Words cited and other slivers of linguistic materials adduced, names of authors, and titles of publications have been, by the same token, rigorously excluded; and the languages drawn upon have not been inventoried. Since the book is monolithic neither in design nor in execution, a small residue of redundancy and overlap has turned out to be ineradicable; a few cross-references have been provided to palliate any resulting inconvenience. The relatively few entries that appear in quotation marks are either foreign terms retained for the sake of their unique flavor, or tentative labels, or else highly colloquial designations which, within certain limits, are apt to serve a good purpose. In the matter of alphabetic sequence I have been guided by practical considerations. Thus, "evolutionary advance" and "geographic advance" are listed under the head-word rather than under the qualifiers because most readers are likely to be concerned more with the book's specific and conceivably original statements on advances and retreats in linguistic growth than with its meager offerings on such inexhaustible subjects as evolution and geography.

cycle of emphasis, 62
cyclopean arrangement, 323, 376

dating, 182
daughter language, 11, 73, 124f.
deceptive solutions, 219
declension, 97, 127, 142, 300
decoding, 374
"dédiminutivisation", 252
definitions, 260, 275
deflection, 9, 247, 264, 293, 296f.,
    301f., 307, 317, 367
deformation of letters, 390
delineation of problems, 231f.
demography, 23f., 28, 60, 145
derivation, affixal, 3, 17, 84, 97,
    176, 178, 187, 193, 205, 219,
    323, 369
"dérivation impropre", 99
"design" of a language, 15
"détaillisme", 59, 64f.
determinant of evolution, 17, 22, 27,
    394
diacritic mark, 272, 388
dialect (regional, social), 15, 57,
    77f., 110, 121, 123, 196, 202,
    264, 276
  differentiation (cleavage), 20f., 82,
    299
  geography, 18, 43, 55, 71, 101,
    136, 147, 209, 215, 229, 243,
    281, 285, 295
  group, 78
  mixture, 35, 174, 191
dialectal preference, 317
dialectology, 67f., 212f., 216, 254,
    257, 265, 285
  historical, 138
dictionaries, 257–279
  perspective, 259f., 270–275
  presentation, 260, 275–278
  range, 259, 261–270
didactic purposes, 126, 130, 132,
    139f., 165–174, 195, 265
diffusion, 19, 55, 61, 79, 101, 110,
    113, 139, 195, 211, 246, 255
digraph, 362
dilation, 38

dilemma
  broken, 233–246
  false, 300
  irreducible, 185
diminutives, 91 (cf. "dédiminutivisa-
    tion")
"diptology" (synonymic), 324
"direct" approach (in language
    learning), 277
direction of shift, 22f.
directional signs, 3
discrete forces, 339
disguised forms, 242
disjunction, 327
dislocation of sequences, 317
displacement (territorial), 20
dissimilation, 11, 14, 24, 36f., 38,
    105f., 107, 110
dissimilatory loss, 42, 110
distinctive feature, 71f., 258, 278
distortion, 374
disturbance, 9
documentation, volume of, 7, 29,
    128f., 212, 275f., 294
doublet, 38, 142, 235, 314
"drift", 24, 61, 110, 120
dynamic categories or characteristics,
    115f., 125, 148, 301

ecclesiastic impact, 57, 111
echoing of nasal, 37f.
economy
  of effort, 4, 13f., 22, 61, 101, 122,
    337, 355
  of research, 190
"Einreihung" (= "inquadramento")
    372
elaboration, morphological, 322f.,
    332, 337, 340
élite, 170, 173
ellipsis, 397
emblem, 351, 373, 381
emphasis, 333, 384
empirical approach, 230
"empty case", 120
encoding, 374
encyclopedia, 93, 269f.
ensemble of causes, 45

morphophonemics, 98
morphosyntax, 3, 17, 94, 98, 375
Morse Code, 381
mosaic, restoration of, 103, 291
mouth-to-mouth transmission, 8, 304
multidisciplinary, 83
multilingual dictionary, 268
multinomial, 318
multiple
 causation, 307
 solution, 278
multipronged movement, 26
mysticism, 359f., 367

nasal infix, 39f.
nascent form, 382
natural language, 266
"natural" sequence, 343
nautical terms, 208, 278
near-grammar, 134
near-pronounceable, 378
near-synonymy, 255
near-word, 362, 389
neogrammarians, 39, 62, 71, 84,
 109, 194
neolinguists, 18, 216, 293
neologism, 378
network (of entries), 261
nickname, 373, 382
"nom de plume", 383
nominalization, 331
nonce, 264, 309, 338
nonexistent
 language, 30
 letter, 372
 word, 306
nonindigenous word, 33
nonsense word, 166, 311, 337, 374
normalized language, 299
normative grammar, 62
notarial documents, 214
nuclear
 formation, 209
 problem, 185, 211, 246
numeral, 15, 109, 170, 358, 389
numerology, 359, 367
nursery word (or rhyme), 14, 39,
 337, 346, 368

object of study (variable), 232f.
"objective" dictionary, 259, 274
oblique evocation, 397
obscenity, 397
obsolescence, 17
obsolete word, 262
onomasiology, 87, 184, 209f., 273,
 285
onomastics, 144, 184, 216
onomatopoeia, 101, 183, 197f., 354,
 387
operational
 advantage, 36, 355
 arrangement, 169, 176, 196
opposites, semantic, 325f., 327
ornamental fission, 352
ornamentation, 58, 324, 330, 350,
 360, 387, 389
orthoepy, 361
orthography, 90
orthology, 278
"outposts" (in dialect geography),
 294
overcorrection, 9
overlap (esp. syllabic), 38f., 365
 of categories, 258
 of disciplines, 95f., 190
overseas language, 294

"padding", 35, 340
pairing, 343
paleography, 95, 214, 272
paleontology, linguistic, 52, 210
panchronic change (development),
 11, 39, 87
pantopic development, 11
paradigmatic
 intricacy, 17
 leveling 110
 perspective, 13
paragoge, 37, 111
parallelism, 311, 322
parastratum, 101
parasynthetic verb, 45
parataxis, 330
parent language, 1, 48, 80, 125, 132
parlor games, 392
parochial habit, 56

EE